Routledge Revivals

Folk Law

Folk Law

Essays in the Theory and Practice
of Lex Non Scripta

Edited by
Alison Dundes Renteln
and Alan Dundes

Volume II

Routledge
Taylor & Francis Group
Revivals

First published in 1994 by The University of Wisconsin Press

This edition first published in 2018 by Routledge
2 Park Square, Milton Park, Abingdon, Oxon, OX14 4RN
and by Routledge
52 Vanderbilt Avenue, New York, NY 10017, USA

Routledge is an imprint of the Taylor & Francis Group, an informa business

A Library of Congress record exists under ISBN:

ISBN 13: 978-0-367-11053-6 (hbk)
ISBN 13: 978-0-367-11068-0 (pbk)
ISBN 13: 978-0-429-02463-4 (ebk)

Folk Law

Edited by Alison Dundes Renteln and Alan Dundes

Folk Law

Essays in the Theory and Practice of
Lex Non Scripta

Volume II

The University of Wisconsin Press

The University of Wisconsin Press
114 North Murray Street
Madison, Wisconsin 53715

Published in paperback by the University
of Wisconsin Press in 1995

First published in hardcover by Garland Publishing, Inc.,
in 1994, as Volume 7 of Garland Folklore Casebooks

2 4 5 3 1

Printed in the United States of America

Library of Congress Cataloging-in-Publication Data

Folk law : essays in the theory and practice of Lex non scripta /
edited by Alison Dundes Renteln and Alan Dundes.
p. cm.
Includes bibliographical references.
ISBN 0-299-14344-9 (pbk.)
1. Customary law. I. Dundes Renteln, Alison. II. Dundes, Alan.
[K282.F65 1995]
340.5—dc20 94-812

To Carolyn Dundes,
Mother and Wife

Contents

Volume II

Cases of Folk Law

The goal of field investigators of folk law has shifted from a search for rules to an understanding of legal process. This is paralleled in folklore theory by a move away from text to a study of text in context, or the performance of a text. To be sure, there has always been a certain fascination with cases involving folk law, but the early reporting of them tended to be more anecdotal than analytic. The attempt to document actual cases of legal disputes has yielded valuable insights into the nuances of folk law and confirming that there is much more to the study of folk law than enumerating abstract "laws." On the other hand, many case reports fail to generalize, preferring instead to limit any conclusions drawn to the case at hand. What is presumably needed is a kind of dialectic between rules and cases. To understand a given rule, one should have at one's disposal a gamut of cases involving that rule. And there should be analyses of different cases pertaining to similar circumstances so that general folk laws can be extrapolated.

J.F. HOLLEMAN

Trouble-Cases and Trouble-less Cases in the Study of Customary Law and Legal Reform

Among those scholars who prefer to study cases involving folk law, there is a debate about what kinds of cases are the most useful for such study. One group argues that "trouble-cases," that is, cases involving dispute of some kind bring folk law into focus best. But an alternative view, championed by J.F. Holleman in the present essay is that routine or "trouble-less" cases provide the optimum data for analysis. The argument is analogous to that found in psychology. Some say that from the study of abnormal *psychology, we can better understand psychology in general. Others claim that it is normal psychology which should be stressed. No doubt there is right on both sides of this argument, and the ideal study should include both kinds of cases. In the words of a proverb, it is the exception that proves the rule.*

The following essay provides the historical background of the argument favoring the use of cases in folk law research and pleads for the greater use of trouble-less cases in particular.

For other considerations of cases by J.F. Holleman, see his Issues in African Law *(The Hague: Mouton, 1974). For further discussion of the trouble-case method of investigation, see John G. Hund, "The Roles of Theory and Method in Investigating Primitive Law,"* The Comparative and International Law Journal of Southern Africa, 7 *(1974), 208–214.*

I

I first went, as a student, into the field (Zululand, 1938) without the benefit of a clear theory of investigation of customary law.* Llewellyn

Reprinted from Keebet von Benda-Beckmann and Fons Strijbosch, eds., *Anthropology of Law in the Netherlands: Essays on Legal Pluralism* (Dordrecht: Foris Publications, 1986), pp. 110–131.

*This paper was published earlier in *Law and Society Review* 7 (1973): 585–605. We thank the editors of the journal for their kind permission to publish it in this volume, in a slightly revised version.

and Hoebel's *Cheyenne Way* (1941) had not yet appeared; and years later[1], when I ended my fieldwork among some Rhodesian Shona tribes (1952), Hoebel's classic *The Law of Primitive Man*, which further elaborated the theoretical angle of this kind of inquiry (1954: Ch. 1–4) had yet to be published. I did not, however, course entirely haphazardly through this field. I was trained in (mainly African) ethnography and (Roman Dutch) law, had learnt to read the decisions and interpretations of (South African) European courts on 'native law and custom' with some critical reservation, and had found in works like Schapera's *Handbook of Tswana Law and Custom* (1938)—probably still the best of its kind as regards Africa—a suitable, systematic frame for the pursuit of my inquiries and the exposition of my findings. Moreover, my home background had acquainted me with some of the work and aims of Dutch scholars on Indonesian *adat* law who, inspired by the great jurist Van Vollenhoven,[2] then seemed to be leading the field with their efforts to arrange the rich variety of Indonesian folk law and practice into a coherent system with a distinctly *indigenous* imprint. Van Vollenhoven's early and repeated insistence upon the need "*het oostersche oostersch te zien*" (to perceive that which is oriental through oriental eyes),[3] instead of seeking to fit Indonesian concepts into the familiar categories and analytical schemas of Western jurisprudence, had obvious application also to the African field.

In retrospect I find that, without consciously theorizing about my method of research (or, for that matter, about a working definition of 'law' itself), I did employ a combination of the descriptive, ideological (rule-seeking) and case-focused approaches advocated by these senior American fellow-workers. My conscious indebtedness to them, and especially to Hoebel, came very much later when, facing students and preparing some of them for juridical anthropological fieldwork, I had to find a methodological baseline from which to proceed upon the paths of field enquiry. Chapter 3 of Hoebel's *Law of Primitive Man* proved to be a simple and stimulating introduction, and it provided a suitable frame for relating the first object-lesson which I myself received in Zululand while visiting the hamlet of the headman of a tribal ward. Here it is.

> Sitting with our backs against the rough poles of the circular cattle corral, we were sharing, together with five or six other homestead heads, a large pot of beer which he had ordered one of his wives to place before me as a token of welcome. A few yards away, a couple of youngsters were struggling to force a reluctant she-goat into the goat's pen and joining the cattle corral, kicking up a lot of dust. The headman shouted to a young woman that her goat was spoiling our beer. She hastened to help put the animal inside. He explained that she was his younger brother's wife, mother of

one small son, hard-working, and good at making clay-pots, too. In fact, that was how she got this goat. I asked a few questions. It appeared that she sold or bartered her pots in the neighbourhood. She raised some chickens, too, which she sold at the small district centre of Nongoma. When she had earned eight shillings, she bought a young she-goat, now grown and about to have kids. . . . It was not an uncommon form of enterprise, for several other women in the neighbourhood were doing likewise. Here was an obvious opportunity for discussing property rights of married women with a panel of knowledgeable men. The following are some extracts from my field notes:

Q: "That goat therefore belongs to her?"
A: "It belongs to her, for she made the pots and found the money".
Q: "Her husband approves?"
A: "He approves; he loves her for she is a good wife." . . .
Q: "She can sell the goat if she wants to?"
A: "She can sell the goat."
Q: "Without telling her husband?"
A: "She will first ask her husband."
Q: "And if he says 'No'?"
A: "Then she cannot sell."
Q: "But why not? You said it is her goat because she earned it herself."
A: "It *is* her goat, but she is [like] the child of her husband. That is why she cannot sell without asking him."
Q: "Does this mean that the goat really belongs to the husband?"
A: "So it is. The husband is the *umnini* (owner) of the woman, the woman is the *umnini* of the goat, therefore it is really the husband who is the *umnini* of the goat. . . . It is because he agrees to her making pots that she found the money to buy the goat. So it is really through his *amandla* (power, authority) that she has this goat."
Q: If he is the real owner, could he sell the goat?"
A: "He could sell it if he wants to."
Q: "Without asking his wife?"
A: "She is his child, he need not ask her."
Q: "So this the true law of the Zulu, that a husband is the owner of property (*impahla*) like a goat which his wife has earned with her own labour, and that he can sell this property without asking her?"
A: (with some solemnity, all men present nodding in agreement) "*Impela! Umthetho wesiZulu!*" (Indeed, the law of the Zulu!)

Methodologically, I had now travelled some way along the "descriptive" road to what appeared to be practice, and followed the "ideological" line which produced a "legal rule"—Hoebel 1954 (1968 edition: 29). Now the test of case-oriented inquiry.

Q: "Could you tell me about any examples of this having happened?"

A: "Of a man selling his wife's property without consulting her? *Ngeke* (never)! He would be like a rogue[4] stealing from his wife."

Q: "But you all agreed that he could do so under Zulu law *ngomthetho wesiZulu* . . .)."

The headman thoughtfully took a pinch of snuff before he replied. "You do not understand," he explained patiently. "You asked about the law of the Zulu and we told you the truth. But it is also like this, that a man who likes to live peacefully with his wife knows that he should always discuss such matters with her. *U zau khuluma nendlu* (lit. one should talk with one's 'house')."

Some time afterwards, however, I did strike a trouble-case in which this issue cropped up and was tested in the "crucible of conflict" (Llewellyn and Hoebel 1941: 29). At first sight, it looked a simple matter.

The woman (complainant, assisted by her elder brother) demanded back the money which her husband had received by selling 'her' fowls without her knowledge or consent, and which he had used to buy himself a new shirt. But in the hands of the little *ibandla* (gathering) presided over by the local headman[5] the matter proved to be considerably more complicated. The husband had, in fact, first "talked with his wife", but she had refused, accusing him of loitering, "chasing after beer and other women", and of neglecting her. He, having as long a list of complaints about her, "had stayed quiet for a long time", nursing his grievances and even complaining to her family about her casual behaviour as a housewife and her habit of "not listening" to him. One day she left to visit her family ("leaving me like a dog that has to find its own food"). The coast being clear he had collected some of her chickens ("I did not take all"), which he sold at Nongoma for six shillings and ninepence. He had bought a khaki shirt for six shillings, and "intended to buy something nice" for his wife with the remaining ninepence. But when he came home she had flown into a temper, attacked him with a large wooden ladle, kicked over a cooking pot ("so I went hungry again"), and then left to sleep with neighbouring friends.

It was a howler of an *indaba* (affair), which produced as much merriment among some as indignation among others. After a lengthy and often acrid public discussion, the headman delivered his judgment. It was clear (he said) that this "was not merely a matter of selling chickens", but of a long-standing trouble between husband and wife who had both failed the law[6] of *ubulanda obuhle* (maintaining amicable social relations, especially between in-laws). Both were guilty (*necala*): the woman because she had not "listened well enough" to her husband; the husband because he had neglected *(ukuyeka)* his wife—"the one who bears your children and who looks after you when you are ill." Both were severely scolded, and sent home with the warning that further trouble between them would have serious consequences. There was neither an explicit affirmation nor a denial of the husband's right to sell his wife's chickens. Yet, by implication, the 'rule' had been tested, or

> rather the way it should have been observed in a spirit of reasonableness between parties. This lesson did not go unheeded, because two months later I heard that the husband had gone to work in the mines of Johannesburg, and had sent money home to his elder brother with a message for his wife. When the brother-in-law showed her the money (thirty shillings), he said that his brother had asked him to look after it, but to give her some if she needed it. She took five shillings to buy soap and a piece of cloth for her child, and another five shillings because she wanted a little she-goat for herself. The brother-in-law said: "*Kulungile* (it is alright), for it is not forgotten how he was helped by the money of your chickens to buy a shirt."

What I myself learned from this one interview and trouble-case went far beyond the province of proprietary rights. Most important was the early warning that I, as a Westerner, would find it difficult to formulate specific rules of law in a way that would adequately reflect the indigenous norms actually governing the resolution of disputes in which they might be considered relevant. Hence, when years later I wrote a largely case-based book on some fields of tribal (Shona) substantive law, I did not set out to present a tribal *corpus juris* of "strictly defined rules", but rather a coherent arrangement of "broad concepts and guiding principles, the practical application of which (amply illustrated by case material) varied with virtually every case in which they were reflected" (J.F. Holleman 1952a: X).

The difficulty of presenting the substantive law of a pre-literate people in a collection of carefully formulated rules is illustrated, for instance, in Pospisil's highly readable and thought-provoking *Kapauku Papuans and their Law* (1958). He presents his law material in some 120 systematically arranged abstract rules, formulated with the help of his informants, each rule being followed by a brief (too brief) report of actual disputes and the outcome of these, in order to see whether or not the stated rule had been adhered to. In this way, by a simple process of quantification, he could determine the incidence of rule deviation. The results are interesting. Though in more than half the number of cases the outcome was *not* in conformity with the formulated rule, yet in the overwhelming majority of cases these easily excitable and highly individualistic Kapaukus accepted the headman's decision as a just one. One of Pospisil's conclusions therefore is that "it is not the abstract rule that affects the Kapauku people, but the actual decision of the headman . . . although in the majority of decisions the people assume that he complies with the rules" (1958: 255). Fortified by these results, Pospisil (1958: 256 f) restricted the field of law to the rock-bed of legal decisions and such principles as could be abstracted from them, thus excluding stated rules not confirmed by such decisions ("dead rules").

The trouble with this method is that, however carefully such abstract rules are formulated without the heat of actual conflict with its concomitant incidents, real-life disputes so often present a much more complex set of issues than can be covered by a single rule. This means that, even when the main focus of dispute does involve the subject matter of such a rule, circumstantial factors (not covered by the rule) play a role in the decision-making process and may lead to an outcome which is not strictly "in accordance with the rules". The incidence of this kind of deviation is likely to be higher still if—as Pospisil usually did—such rules also include quite specific forms of redress or punishment. For in this respect even the most developed law systems permit the decision-making authority a considerable latitude. Pospisil's test, though interesting as an experiment, is therefore not, I believe, altogether valid, because the values he compares (abstract rules focused upon single interests or actions, and conflict situations likely to involve a plurality of these) are often not really comparable.

Few, if any, workers in the field of research will deny that, especially in societies without a strong authority structure, conflict resolution very often (like politics) is the art of seeking feasible compromise rather than the enforcement of more or less clearly stated rules of conduct, and that to the outside observer the incidence of rule deviation may indeed appear to be high. Having repeatedly observed the same phenomenon myself, I would, however, be inclined to distrust not so much the existence of cohering concepts and "ideal" norms as a society's legal frame of reference, but rather the efforts of formulating individual rules without relating them to a wider context in which also other interacting needs and values influence the course of social peace and conflict.

II

Since Llewellyn and Hoebel's Cheyenne study, several other anthropologists, some with legal training as well, have concentrated on the detailed description and analysis of trouble-cases for the study of unwritten law. The case method, focused upon 'law-in-action', the *process* of 'dispute settlement' or 'conflict resolution', became their favourite tool in research and comparative theory-stimulating study. This may well, as Gulliver (1969: 12) believes, at least partly have been the result of "a weariness with past endeavors to achieve acceptable definitions (of the key-concept 'law') and . . . increasingly fruitless controversy". But partly also it must be because organized responses to situations of social stress caused by impermissible deviations from ideal norms and precepts offered fresh scope for a better understanding of the actual regulation of human conduct. For this reason both Gulliver (1969: 13) and A.L. Epstein (1967: 208), theoretical exponents and skillful practitioners of this method, re-emphasized Hoebel's early dictum (1942: 966) that the study of "primitive law, like common law, must draw its generalizations from particulars which are cases, cases and more cases". This emphatic statement not only proclaims the absolute priority of the case method in the study of unwritten law, but leaves no doubt that its focus should be the *trouble*-case and no other case material. Trouble-cases are, in Epstein's words, the fruitful "units of analysis" in which the presented "material is used not so much by way of illustration but as providing the raw data for analysis, the various strands in the skein of facts being teased out and dissected to reveal underlying principles and regularities".

In this way field scholars like Gluckman, Bohannan, Gulliver and Epstein himself (to mention only a few who, like myself, worked in Africa) have indeed immensely enriched our understanding of a number of major principles and of ideas, and the way these are actually applied in the judicial processes of differently organized types of society.

Yet, in order not only to reveal underlying principles and regularities, but also to present a reasonably comprehensive and coherent picture of the substantive and living law of such societies, this method would necessarily require an adequate number of trouble-cases in all significant fields of social activity governed by the rule of law. Unfortunately, this is rarely possible. Hoebel himself has admitted that: "It is a rare ethnologist who can stay around long enough to sit on a bag of cases full enough to round out the law picture" (1954: 20). But the inadequacy of such material need not be due solely to the inevitable limits of an investigator's local tenure and opportunities for observation, or of his informant's experience and powers of recollection. For there are, in probably every society, certain avenues of social and economic activity in which the passage of legal traffic and transactions takes place regularly but with very few known cases of litigious collision.

In my own fieldwork in Mashonaland I struck a few of these. In the field of marriage law, for instance, I could reap a rich crop of matrimonial trouble-cases and litigation arising from obligations (such as bridewealth payments) under the marriage contract. Yet, in spite of a kinship system which prohibited, in principle at least, the marriage between all cognates no matter how far removed[7], as well as between classes of affines, there were very few known contraventions of marriage regulations. Those that I did discover (all dealt with by family moots whose proceedings were merely reported to me) would have been totally inadequate for a valid deduction of general principles.[8] Another field concerned contracts (apart from betrothal and marriage); and a third, perhaps more surprisingly, land rights. With regard to the latter, in the more remote parts of Mashonaland no agrarian reform had yet been introduced by the Government at that time (1946–48), and land still appeared to be fairly plentiful. The customary system of shifting cultivation was practised in a rather easy-going manner. This resulted in a considerable mobility of rights to residential and arable holdings, but led to very few overt disputes about individual land use. In fact, I struck only a few that had required formal adjudication, and my informants were hard-pressed to recollect more. Yet there was little or no confusion about the recognized principles which governed the control, occupation and use of land,[9] and as to who should give way to whom in the event of conflicting claims under various circumstances. I was therefore compelled to test my findings based on the normal and *trouble-less* practices I had observed by lengthy discussions of hypothetical disputes.

Now Epstein (1967: 210) found that his informants "were much less at home in the discussion of hypothetical issues" than in expounding points involved in (trouble-) cases they had actually dealt with, because their "mode of legal thinking was particular . . . (being) embedded in the matrix of social relationships", rather than abstract in the sense of conceiving rules of law as "logical entities". I agree with him, up to a point, Obviously, trouble-cases not only present a rich and compact source of concrete facts which invite further clarification by knowledgeable informants; they often also provide the observer-inquirer with cues for questions which he may be less likely to think up himself when posing hypothetical cases. But once an investigator has lived long enough in a community to have a reasonably clear impression of its everyday life and normal range of activities, he does not always need trouble-cases (however much he will welcome them as dramatized set-pieces for observation and analysis of contending views and interests) to get a fair idea of the normative principles of lawful actual behaviour.

In the first place, in the overwhelming majority of such activities people do, as a matter of course, pursue their interests and behave in a manner so as to *avoid* legal disputes. In Vinogradoff's words, they have acquired "the mental habit of recognizing rules imposed by social authority".[10] This voluntary observance of the law is therefore its most common form of maintenance. At the same time the knowledge so gained of actual practice, and of local conditions and relationships which affect such practice, also indicates the scope within which the inquirer can still fruitfully pose questions without inviting his informants to start guessing about hypothetical circumstances beyond their practical experience. (When, in the Sabi valley in 1946, I ventured to ask about water rights of people cultivating along a hypothetical irrigation furrow, my informants could only hazard guesses, because no one had any experience yet of artifical waterworks. This inquiry, though not entirely useless, remained inconclusive.)

Secondly and more specifically, many of the more important legal transactions, such as marriage, the allocation and transfer of land or valuable movable property, the undertaking of (reciprocal) services such as cattle agistment, often take place in the presence of the local authority, family heads or interested others who are in a position, if necessary, to challenge their execution (though the absence of such persons need not invalidate all of these transactions). Dutch scholars of Indonesian adat law have long since recognized that this practice is not so much a matter of 'witnessing' such transactions in order to provide reliable 'evidence' in the event of future dispute, but rather as authoritatively 'attested' or 'supported' forms of law observance (*gesteunde naleving*),[11] and of 'preventive law care' (*preventieve rechtszorg*),[12] aimed at removing legal uncertainty and avoiding, as far as possible, the prospect of future dispute. In this way the particular contents and validity of (new) legal relations are actually tested by people of juridical knowledge and judicial authority. Their affirmative cooperation (or intervention) or mere acquiescence may lack the explicitness and drama of a judgment invoked by conflict and argument; it nevertheless falls within the sphere of legitimate control and authoritative legal sanction. Why then should these incidents not be given the same analytical attention as the trouble-case with which the case method has become so closely identified?

Surely this wide and varied field of observable common practices—of specific instances of voluntary and attested law observance—offers an abundance of concrete cases, though of the trouble-less kind. If properly recorded, they likewise constitute invaluable 'units of analysis', which by their very nature reveal the relevant principles and regularities, *as well as much of the permissible leeway*, of lawful conduct. They are nodal points in the development of socio-legal relations. They, too, present the particulars (less rich perhaps in their individual content than trouble-cases but far more numerous and accessible in many fields of law) from which the generalities are drawn (cf. Hoebel 1942: 966). In fact, it is the common trouble-less cases of normal practice that usually constitute the normative frame of reference by which trouble-cases themselves are being judged. Adequate attention to them would, moreover, provide guidelines and specific clues for the probe into the illuminating prehistory of many a trouble-case itself, and thus facilitate the difficult execution of what has become known as the 'extended case method'.[13] For the latter refinement, especially if it aims at covering also the aftermath of trouble-cases in order to present them as links in chains of continuous social interaction makes even heavier demands upon the fieldworker's time and opportunities for a wider investigation of the field of law. The 'bag of cases' to which Hoebel referred may well contain specimens of rare value, but they will be fewer in number and even less likely to 'round out the law picture'. In her overview of studies in legal anthropology, Sally F. Moore rightly observes, with reference to the work of some major exponents of the case method approach: "In fact, none of these writers... has presented substantive law as a system. Instead, each has taken what he considers to be the most important consistent theme in culture and society, and has traced signs of that theme through some substantive rules" (1970: 270).

III

I must stress that I do not wish to detract from the value of the case method, which I myself certainly found the most stimulating part of my fieldwork. But I do consider that its commonly accepted province (that is, institutionalized dispute settlement or conflict resolution) is unduly restricted, and that its application should be widened to include at least the kind of trouble-less cases I have indicated above. (In the last part of this paper I shall refer to other situations in which these are indispensable.) Some of the reasons for my belief I have mentioned: a broad insight into the guiding normative principles and values covering the full range of socio-legal traffic tends to be sacrificed to a preoccupation with (thematically oriented) intensive probes into the causes and remedial treatment of collision cases. However important these may be, they still constitute only a minority phenomenon. Moreover, since the 'incidence of collision' may vary considerably from one area of the law to another, the *over*-emphasis on conflict—and this represents the bulk of what ultimately appears in print in this type of study—is bound to lead to an uneven coverage of the total field of law. It may, in fact, even lead to a distorted presentation of widely accepted and commonly observed legal principles in comparatively trouble-free areas. In the space allotted to me, I can unfortunately give only one example of this in some detail, but it should suffice to substantiate this point.

In 1946, in the Sabi Valley, Hera tribal area, land was still considered to be plentiful, and the people enjoyed a considerable freedom of movement within the boundaries of their tribal wards (*dunhu*) in the pursuit of their traditional system of shifting cultivation. Land disputes were, as I have stated, rare in this area.

Having exhausted his fields, M had in July—dry winter season—staked a claim to a piece of cultivable land in the traditional manner of *Kumpeta gombo*, by lopping off branches from a number of trees and stacking them around the trunks to be burnt later in preparation to clearing a field for

> cultivation with the onset of the rainy season (early November). As his proposed field was some two miles from the place he intended to leave (though still in the same ward), he had made cursory inquiries at neighbouring hamlets. He had learnt that this site had, some eight or ten years before, been left by N, who had taken up residence and arable land about four miles away (same ward), and that N had given no indication of his wanting to return to his old site. Strictly "according to rule", M ought to have "told the *sadunhu* (ward headman) beforehand", but had not done so. This omission was not uncommon, for I had found that, in contrast with the practice in more densely populated areas, the majority of these ward members, when taking up new land, had merely notified the headman at a convenient opportunity after the event. It would also have been a matter of common prudence and practice for M to notify N of his intention to occupy the latter's abandoned fields, something which he had also failed to do.
>
> Early in September, when M was about to set fire to his dried stacks (*mavivi*), N turned up and excitedly claimed that this was *his* fallow land, (*makura*) which he and his father (buried at some stone outcrops nearby) had "ploughed for many years", and that he intended to return to it "soon". M promised to "stay away from the grave", but otherwise refused to budge. After a heated argument N "climbed the court" (*kukwira pa chivara*) of the ward headman.

Elsewhere[14] I have described the judicial procedure among the Hera, and it will suffice here to give the outcome of the case, the principal arguments advanced during the process in which, as usual, public opinion was freely expressed, and compare this judgement with the generally accepted legal principles involved.

> M's right to proceed with his cultivation was confirmed, but he was told to "plough away from the grave"—which he would have done anyway. N's claim to the disputed area was not denied, but the headman asked him, "What can I do, for you never told me that you wanted to return to your *makura* again".
>
> Now I had, several months earlier, on three or four occasions discussed this very issue as a hypothetical problem with different panels of informants, and the 'rules' had been beyond dispute. Here was a question of two preferential rights; the one derived from prior possession and use;[15] the other based on the customary manner of *kupeta gombo*, staking a claim to virgin land or land once used but apparently abandoned by a previous cultivator. When I had posed them as concurrent claims, all had without hesitation agreed that the former claim would "always" prevail.[16] "For the people cannot deny (*kuramba*) that he was the first who cleared the land, causing it through his labour (*basa*) to grow food for his children and for brewing beer to propitiate his ancestral spirits (*kupira midzimu*)". Even the

presence of a family grave had been mentioned as a particularly strong argument in favour of the former occupier.

At the trial, what appeared to tip the balance in favour of newcomer M was the assumption, in spite of N's denial, that because N "lived not so far away, he knew" (must have known) about M's preparation, and that "by explaining things nicely" at a much earlier stage, he could easily have persuaded M "to look elsewhere" for land. One neighbour even suggested that N had deliberately delayed his intervention until M's preparations were well advanced (M. had started to move part of his homestead in order to be close to his new fields), in order to "cause trouble (*kutambudzika*) for M". N hotly denied this allegation and stuck to his opening statement: "One day I knew that someone was taking my *makura*, because I saw *mavivi* that I had not seen before and there was a person wanting to put fire to them". M's omission to notify N was glossed over after another neighbour's comment: "Why? Even we who live close by never heard that you wanted to return".

Not expressed at the headman's *chivara* (courtyard) was a piece of information which, though presumably common knowledge to insiders, I picked up incidentally only much later: N had not been a pleasant co-operative fellow when he was living in that locality, and his neighbours had been rather pleased when he left. Neither they nor the headman (whose hamlet was in the same neighbourhood), liked to see him coming back. Social (or if you like, 'political') considerations had clearly prevailed over legal principles in the court's judgment.

If there had been a fair number of adjudicated disputes in this particular field of law in that locality, I would have had comparable judicially tested material from which to draw legal regularities. In that event this deviating judgment would probably have evoked my immediate suspicion that an element of social antagonism as regards N might have been the mainspring of the decision in favour of M (in itself, of course, a not uncommon occurrence in a community of interdependent members who value social harmony and peaceful mutual co-operation). A search in this direction would then have been a likely first exercise. But this was the only trouble-case in which this particular issue had been tested before a recognized judicial forum, and no such social antagonism was expressed. Nor did the headman appear to behave unduly arbitrarily (something which normally provokes critical public response). So I concentrated on the legal issues and arguments in this trouble-case. According to the theory as regards case-tested law, I should have attached great value to its legal authority. This I found difficult, for the verdict was a reversal of what I had learnt from observed trouble-free practice and repeated discussions on the relative weights of these competitive preferential claims. I was prepared to grant merit to the seemingly plausible and reasonable arguments that N's longtime silence had somehow stopped him from exercising his right (though this, too, was contrary to some of my experiences), and that a decision in his favour would have caused undue hardship to competitor M. Even so, with the knowledge then at my disposal, I had expected the court to stipulate that M, after having had the benefit of one or two years' cultivation, should vacate the field if N himself really wanted to resume the active use of it. But no such injunction had been part of this judgment.

So this trouble-case stood oddly at variance with several trouble-less cases in which a newcomer had, under apparently similar circumstances, as a matter of course given way when a former occupier had intimated that he intended to "return to his *makura* some time" in the future. Yet the "rightness" (*mururamiro*) of its decision was affirmed during subsequent discussions with some of the same informants who had previously stressed the weight of a former occupier's right to return to his old holdings. It was only several months later, when my African assistant came back from a beer party at which N had caused trouble, that I was able to evaluate this 'test-case' of N versus M. He remarked: "That fellow N is said to be often causing trouble". And he added casually, "It was also said that this is the real reason why C (ward headman) preferred to give those *makura* to M".

I think the lesson is clear. Whatever the merits of this trouble-case (and it taught me a good deal about non-legal values influencing the process of law), it was not the most reliable guide for the discovery of certain norms of substantive and living Hera law. The issue is not, perhaps, the theoretical potentials of the trouble-case technique so much as the practical limitations upon its full employment imposed by circumstantial factors, including the fallibility of the fieldworker himself. As a fieldworker I was not without experience, but in that locality I had not (yet) been sufficiently posted on some of the existing social tensions. This is a situation in which all fieldworkers find themselves at some time or other, and it is doubtful if they can ever fully overcome this difficulty. Even extrovert folk like these Hera retain some reticence in airing the hidden reasons for some of their behaviour in a fieldworker's presence. For he remains an outsider, however cordially he may have become accepted in the community; and however purposeful and skilled his search, he will owe some of his best insights to the chance remark or 'lucky break' that comes his way without his conscious bidding.

Therefore, in the study of the substantive law and its practice, and in an area of the law in which litigation is rare, a fieldworker relying mainly on a case-method focused upon actual trouble-cases may get a skewed idea of the accepted principles and regularities in that area. Under such circumstances it is the case-studies of normal, trouble-free practice that are more likely, if I may here borrow Llewellyn and Hoebel's words, to be "the safest main road into the discovery of law. Their data are most certain". (1941:29). Or to put it quite bluntly: (1941:29) the trouble-less case then becomes a necessary check on the trouble-case, rather than the other way around.

IV

My arguments thus far clearly referred to fieldwork in situations in which the norms, institutions and processes of folk law, though neither static nor unaffected by foreign legal and administrative importations, are still the main determinants of social conduct and legal order in ethnically more or less homogeneous communities. These have been our principal and richest hunting grounds in the search for customary law; and this law (itself often ethnically or locally varied) was looked upon by colonial administrations as well as legal anthropologists as a separate entity or distinct sub-stratum within a territorial frame of legal pluralism. But the advent of independent statehood in most of the ex-colonial world has changed these premises, thereby creating new dimensions, problems and priorities for legal anthropological research.

The demands for legal reform have assumed a new urgency, and inspired a search for unification of large areas of substantive law in order to resolve the plurality of both indigenous and imported legal systems. Moreover, the reorganization of the judicial system, likewise aimed at greater unification and centralization, has affected (sometimes radically) the legal status and operation of the traditional courts and moots, the very sources of customary case law upon which fieldworkers have so heavily relied in the past for authoritative data. Indeed, the new statehood has rendered even more acute the very question of what the law actually is (or ought to be) in any given situation, locality, population group or social stratum in the new national realm. This means that law may have become an even more elusive quarry than before, and we shall have to review this changed law-scape in order to consider how our methodological approaches may lead into the discovery of a positive *and effective* law. The problem is a vast one, and obviously reaches far beyond the scope of this paper. Yet a few aspects should be briefly touched upon because they have a bearing on points I raised in the earlier sections of my paper.

There is a felt need in the new states of Africa and elsewhere for the development of new systems of 'national' law. If only for reasons of political stability and economic development they aim at 'modernization' and a considerably greater unity than the legal pluralism of (pre-)colonial times. At the same time, in Anglophone countries probably more than in Francophone countries, there appears to be a growing desire that, as far as possible, the new national law should also reflect the traditional cultural image of its peoples, as presented by the viable principles and concepts of their customary laws. Scanning the African scene in the mid-sixties, Schiller (1965: 176 ff) found that, of the various possible legal policies open to them, "the fusion of indigenous and non-indigenous law . . . is the guiding policy, expressed or unexpressed, for most of the emerging states of Africa", and that such a policy would involve "the directed evolution of the indigenous law".

Even without the fusion with whatever non-indigenous law that may be retained, modified, newly imported or purposely created, the direction of the evolution of such *indigenous* law as may effectively be retained will pose immense problems. Most of these countries have ethnically and culturally heterogeneous populations, and regional and local differences may be great. Moreover, social and economic development (mainsprings of legal change) may vary considerably from one region to another and, especially, from rural environments to urban. Whether legal reform is directed mainly by specific legislation (a tempting device for governments understandably impatient to find short-cuts to modernization), or through the hierarchy of the officially recognized courts, the main problem remains essentially the same: how to prevent the law from slipping out of its social context; or in Ehrlich's terms, how to prevent the divergence between the evolved positive law and living law. For the success of any legal reform depends not least upon its acceptance at grass-roots level, where the main volume of legal traffic takes place. But it is at this level, too, that local or regional differences are most marked, and at which ill-advised or premature changes, imposed from above to bring about greater uniformity, are most likely to disrupt the social fabric and to impede rather than speed up economic enterprise and development by the people themselves. Besides, the substantive customary law of many ethnic groups has not yet, or insufficiently, been recorded.

A project like Allott's (London School of Oriental and African Studies) *Restatement of African Law*,[17] is a major effort to abstract and systematize the unwritten rules of customary substantive law. It may well become a useful guide, both to officers of the new government courts which (officially at least) have replaced the traditional and 'home-grown' tribal authorities, and to law reformers seeking generalities in the variety of customary law which might serve as building material for a more unified national system. But its very method of gathering information (making use of existing written material, much of it inevitably rule-oriented responses to hypothetically posed cases from acknowledged indigenous experts) is almost bound to produce systems of 'ideal' rules and principles.

Even if these do reflect the present situation rather than an idealized past, they will still have to be applied with a flexibility which takes full account of their social context in order to be more than a lifeless skeleton without living flesh and blood.

But whatever reformed and more uniform law is being applied by the new and gradually more professionally trained judicial officers of these young states, there is a real danger that the gap between the positive and the living law—a not uncommon feature in colonial times when professional and semi-professional (European) courts dispensed justice in African cases—may actually widen. In this event the greater certainty of the law (one of the principal aims of progressive unification by means of legislative and/or judicial action) may actually result in greater uncertainty among common folk, and in their estrangement from an administration of justice which, only too often, they fail to understand. Or perhaps worse still as for instance R.E.S. Tanner (1970) and Hoebel (1954:45f) have illustrated in respect to East Africa and Pakistan respectively, the legal and judicial systems may be abused by litigants as well as law enforcers to further aims other than justice.

The problem of estrangement is aggravated by the fact that, in many cases, the traditional local adjudicators (chiefs, headmen, village or family elders) are no longer officially recognized as part of the existing judicial structure. (In most of the relatively recently developed *urban* communities, of course, they never effectively struck root.) This does not mean that they no longer operate. On the contrary, both Tanner and Hoebel confirm my own observations and inquiries in post-colonial Africa and information (both oral and written[18] from Indonesia) that at grass-roots level the means of dispute settlement continue to operate according to locally accepted norms and practices. Depending on the kind of wrong committed or redress sought, they are often preferred to the officially appointed courts of justice and other government agents. But how much legal authority is to be attached to their pronouncements in trouble-cases depends largely upon whether they are viewed folk-wise or through official eyes. While their formal recognition may run counter to political aims and sensitivities regarding the often still vulnerable images of national unity and centrally directed development, their *non*-recognition tends to screen off this world of living folk law, obscuring its internal growth and misgrowth in regional and local diversity, and thus inhibits the very chances of law reformers to direct its successful evolution towards a more uniform and integrated part of an emerging national legal system.

If, as I firmly believe, the most effective way of legal reform is by (suitably statutorily empowered) judicial rather than direct legislative action,[19] and by building upwards from carefully examined ground-level structures rather than by projecting lofty plans and premises downwards through the hierarchy of state authority, every effort should be made to open up the communicating passages between the officially recognized upper storeys and the non-recognized but crowded basement of the existing legal structure. To ignore what actually goes on below, and to discount the pace and trends of development there, is almost bound to perpetuate and aggravate a situation summed up bluntly by a Pakistani student quoted by Hoebel (1965: 45): "The law of the police and courts is not the law of the people". This is the kind of legal dichotomy worse than the pluralism of pre-national past, for it means that the national body of law is bisected head from trunk. In such a situation to uphold a view that law proper is that which statutes prescribe or courts apply, would be juristic arrogance and sociological nonsense.

One way of helping to counteract this danger, and to contribute to a wisely directed evolution of customary law and the creation and effective reception of more unified modern law, is constant and vigilant research into the different ways of law observance and its enforcement on all levels. This is a task for which probably few government courts are equipped. Yet, if they (and their governments) are genuinely concerned about the efficacy and effect of their judicial labours, they should welcome and facilitate such studies by others trained to do so.

Here lies an immense and barely explored field of problem-oriented and theory-stimulating research, which should be of major concern to their own law schools and social sciences departments, if necessary aided by non-national others. Its study should include, on the one hand, a scrutiny of the role of government courts and other legal agencies, and of the actual effect of their activities in all fields of law enforcement, as well as a thorough probe into other existing avenues (traditional or non-traditional) of dispute settlement and the kinds of legal issue (social problem) that tend to elude the official channels of redress. R.E.S. Tanner's paper, referred to above, points up some of the problems to be encountered here.

On the other hand, and especially in the urban areas and in non-traditional social and economic situations, there should be a complementary search for new regularities and nascent norms of popularly approved conduct aimed at avoiding trouble. These may well be at variance with the precepts and formal application of hitherto recognized rules of positive law (customary or received), but they do reflect the way common folk, without direction from above, are seeking to meet and accommodate the challenges of a changed social context and the uncertainties of an ill-adjusted (or absent, or inaccessible) law. All this needs, of course, to be related to the particular social stratum or sector in which they move.

This kind of research is not merely a desirable check on the efficacy of the judicial system in which government and people must put their faith. It should, as I intimated, provide concrete building material meriting the careful consideration of those responsible for the direction of legal reform. That is why it should be a continuous effort, aimed at evaluating legal innovation, whether internally evolved or imposed from above, and the likely reasons for its acceptance or non-acceptance by the population. Hilda and Leo Kuper, distinguishing approaches to unification of different laws in terms of emphasis either on "law shaping society, or society shaping laws", note the primacy given to law in such unification programmes. They rightly state: "There may be an element of false deduction in this approach. Since the unity of a society is often expressed in a unified system of law, the unity of law becomes associated with the unity of society, and from being an index or consequence of that unity is transposed into a cause. One of the results of a hasty unification of law may be to stimulate the growth of a diversity of deviating customs" (1965: 23).

I now return to the method of such research, and in doing so I hope to summarize my main arguments. For obvious reasons a good deal of this research will have to be case-oriented, and trouble-cases, as far as possible with their pre-histories and aftermaths, will be vital units of analysis. Broadly speaking they fall into two categories: those dealt with by government courts; and those whose resolution is sought through other, (folk) channels of adjudication. The latter category will as a matter of disciplinary orientation attract the special attention of (legal) anthropologists interested in social control, although its decisions have little authority in the national frame of law. But it is the first category to which lawyers are likely to attach more importance (positive law!). Yet it should be clear from what I have noted above, that in the pluralistic situation still existing in most new states, and with evidence of a threatening dichotomy between positive and living law, the chances are that many a trouble-case tried by government courts will present a picture of law divorced from its social context. A careful inquiry into the effect of their judgments is therefore necessary to give some idea of their divergence from social reality. Nor is it unlikely that, at the lower and often still insufficiently trained levels of the formal judicial hierarchy, case law may present a less than reliable interpretation of even the prescribed rules of positive law. So also in this respect the value of these judgments as authoritative legal statements may be doubtful, and needs to be tested against the very sources of law on which their authority is claimed to be based. Valuable such cases nevertheless remain, perhaps not so much as discrete legal entities but as bits of socio-legal tissue, the loose strands of which invite further search and effort in the hope that, fitted to other pieces of comparable material they may reveal distinct designs in the complex fabric of law.

Yet, in order to discover current and newly emerging regularities of popularly accepted conduct as evidence of the internal growth of law through changes in social relations and economic traffic, also a fair sample of what I have called the trouble-less cases of prevalent and trouble-avoiding practice should be included in the focus of attention. With regard to marriage, family and property, for instance, the validity of marital unions, rights and obligations of conjugal partners, the legitimacy of children, proprietary rights and liabilities of wider kindred, are but a few aspects in which popular practice is seeking to accommodate problems of changed values by socially acceptable (if as yet ill-defined and formally untested) ways of conduct. These may still be insufficiently developed and not widely enough accepted to be considered truly normative, but they deserve close attention as possible indicators of the direction and future shape to which the internal growth of the living law may lead. There remains, of course, also a great deal of *troublous* practice for which *no* suitable remedy has as yet been found. Many women and children, drifted apart from husbands and providers in the tidal cross-currents of outgoing custom and new, still uncontrollable usage in changing (especially urban) societies, could testify to this.[20]

Add to all this the analytical description of the social and cultural context as the necessary frame of reference for the existing and developing law, and we are back to the three main methodological approaches of legal anthropological inquiry (ideological and rule-oriented; descriptive and practice-oriented; disputes, motivation- and result-oriented) which Llewellyn and Hoebel distinguished in 1941. They then stated: "The three approaches are related; indeed they flow each into the other" (1941:21). Yet their own skillful treatment of trouble-cases in particular, and their infectious belief that these, "sought out and examined with care, are thus the safest main road into the discovery of law", have inspired many others to pursue and refine a case method focused almost exclusively on conflict and its resolution. This has paid great dividends in our deeper understanding of the intricate process of law actively engaged in mending or re-aligning its breached fences with the cultural and social means at its disposal.

But I have posed the question whether this preoccupation with what goes on in the 'crucibles of conflict' has not in fact detracted attention from the rest of the premises, inventories and less obtrusive activities of the workshops of law in society; and whether such gains in depth may not inhibit comparably successful efforts to widen our knowledge and understanding of the growing bodies of substantive law. I believe the answer is yes.

Students of law in culturally pluralistic situations (and these exist virtually everywhere in the third world) are faced with insufficient time and opportunity to cover a very broad canvass. Each will be inclined to select the way most likely to reveal those aspects of the total picture in which he is particularly interested, leaving the rest barely sketched or not at all. This is, of course, their good academic right. Nevertheless their active interest in society raises expectations also in circles other than academic. Governments, law reformers and common folk have a moral right to expect practical benefits from such research efforts,[21] especially during the growing pains of new statehood and nation building. One of the central problems facing them is the evolvement of a system of *effective* law. This would require at least the critical and systematic examination of the whole living body of substantive and procedural law (customary, received, newly created) and of ways to promote its essential "principle of growth" (Cardozo) towards greater maturity and social integrity.

It is a Herculean task, and if one hand is unequal to it, more hands closely joined in its pursuit will be necessary. Legal anthropology has the skills and tools to make a vital contribution. But the gist of my argument has been that for a successful application, whether by workers operating singly or as a team, there should be a much closer integration of, and equal emphasis on, all components of the methodological triad of legal anthropological approach.

Notes

1. A hectic, intervening six-year period as a civil servant in an exclusively non-African part of the country put a premature stop to my Zulu research, which yielded no more than a couple of (Afrikaans) contributions to the journal *Bantu Studies* (1940, 1941).

2. Professor in the University of Leiden from 1900 until his untimely death, at age 59, in 1933. Hardly anything of the great volume of his own penetrating writings on adat law and legal policy (he was a leading authority in other fields of law as well) was known outside Dutch-reading circles. His standard work, published in instalments between 1906 and 1931 (Brill, Leiden), is *Het Adatrecht van Nederlandsch Indië*, two hefty volumes, to which a companion volume of his collected essays (excluding his smaller books) was added posthumously (1933). It was not until late 1981, that an English translation of selections from vols. I and II, *Van Vollenhoven on Indonesian Adat Law*, was published (see J.F. Holleman, 1981). To non-Dutch scholars it is mainly the English translation of his disciple Ter Haar's concise *Beginselen en Stelsel van het Adatrecht*, 1939 (*Adat Law in Indonesia*, edited and with an introduction by E.A. Hoebel and A.A. Schiller, New York 1948), that has given a glimpse of the activities of the pre-1940

'Leiden School'. (For a brief evaluation of its methodological approaches see Hoebel 1954:33f; more fully, in Sonius 1981:XXIXH.)

3. But he also saw the limitations of Western scholars, however sensitive their approach, in interpreting indigenous concepts and arranging indigenous legal categories. He hoped for a 'Javanese Blackstone' or 'Balinese Grotius', that is, only "a son of the land writing in his own language", could produce the most convincing and inspiring work in this respect (1931:879); J.F. Holleman, 1981: 261.

4. The term used was *isikelemu*, derived from the Afrikaans-Dutch *skelm*.

5. He was also the senior man of the defendant's local lineage segment.

6. The term was *isiko* (custom, principle, characteristic), often used instead of *umthetho*, which tends to have a more specific connotation as an explicitly laid-down rule or command.

7. In practice the genealogical range of prohibition, though still considerable, may be narrowed (J. F. Holleman 1952a:50–59).

8. Cf. Allott et al., 1969:8–9).

9. The conceptual schema among the Shona very largely conforms to the hierarchical one outlined by Gluckman (1943;1965: ch. 3).

10. 1913 (1961 reprint of 3rd edition): 39.

11. Holleman 1920:375ff,1927: 48ff; Logemann 1923:114–134; Van Vollenhoven 1931:247–256.

12. The term is Logemann's. For a recent illustration see Jaspan (1971:47–49).

13. Gluckmann 1967:xvff;1955 (2nd edition 1967):372ff; Gulliver 1969:14 ff. Van Velsen (1967:129ff) prefers to call it 'situational analysis'.

14. Holleman 1952b.

15. N would have lost this right if he had moved (*kutama*) to *another* ward or chiefdom. Moves within the same ward are indicated by the verb *kusuduruka*, which has a connotation of (relative) proximity. The distinction is crucial, for the ward is, with regard to arable land, the vital unit of "estate of administration" (to use Gluckman's term).

16. But even an unlawful occupier, if he had actually sown his seed, would normally be permitted to reap his crop before he had to give up the field.

17. For a brief but balanced evaluation of this project, see Moore 1970:288–289.

18. E.g. Van den Steenhoven 1970; Sugijono 1971:493–496; Jaspan 1971.

19. For a succinct discussion of various opinions on preferred choices of action, see Schiller 1965:180–185; Alliot (1967:87) reported that, so far, the independent states of Africa had already produced over a hundred 'codes' covering various fields of law, including both criminal and civil.

20. In the geographically widely oriented *Survey of African Marriage and Family Life* (ed. A. Phillips) of 1953, major problems of social change and legal maladjustment receive a good deal of critical attention. Having been out of print for many years, this work was re-issued in two separate volumes—by different publishers, see references below. Unfortunately its material content has not been updated, except for the inclusion of some post-1950 literature and, more thoroughly, changes in marriage laws. Yet it remains an invaluable guide in a

vital field of socio-legal problems and law reform. Nothing quite comparable has yet been achieved in other fields of law in changing society.

21. But what use the authorities concerned will actually make of such research findings is an altogether different matter. For as Allott observes in a thoughtful study on the future of African law, "A government tends to assign the goals first, and then call for the means of attaining them; it does not first conduct a survey to see the limit of practical possibilities" (1965:225).

References

Alliot, M.
1967 'Problèmes de l'unification des droits africains', *Journal of African Law* 11:86–98.

Allot, A.N.
1965 'The Future of African Law', in: H. and L. Kuper (eds.), *African Law: Adaptation and Development*, pp. 216–243, Berkeley and Los Angeles: University of California Press.

Allot, A.N., A.L. Epstein and M. Gluckman
1969 'Introduction', in: M. Gluckman (ed.), *Ideas and Procedures in African Customary Law*, pp. 1–21, Oxford University Press for International African Institute.

Epstein, A.L.
1967 'The Case Method in the Field of Law', in: A.L. Epstein (ed.), *The Craft of Social Anthropology*, pp. 205–231, London: Tavistock Publications.

Gluckman, M.
1943 'Essays on Lozi Land and Royal Property', *Rhodes-Livingstone Papers* 10, Livingstone: Rhodes-Livingstone Institute.
1965 *The Ideas in Barotse Jurisprudence*, New Haven: Yale University Press.
1967 *The Judicial Process among the Barotse of Northern Rhodesia*, Manchester: Manchester University Press (first ed. 1955).
1967 'Introduction', in: A.L. Epstein (ed.), *The Craft of Social Anthropology*, pp. XI–XX, London: Tavistock Publications.

Gulliver, P.H.
1969 'Introduction' in: L. Nader (ed.), *Law in Culture and Society*, pp. 11–23, Chicago: Aldine Publishing Company.

Haar B. ter
1939 *Beginselen en Stelsel van het Adatrecht*, Groningen/Batavia: Wolters.
1948 *Adat Law in Indonesia*, English translation of Ter Haar 1939 and with an introduction by E.A. Hoebel and A.A. Schiller, New York: Institute of Pacific Relations.

Hoebel, E.A.
1942 'Fundamental legal concepts as applied to the study of primitive law', *Yale Law Journal* 51:951.

1954 *The Law of Primitive Man*, (1968 ed.), New York: Atheneum.
1965 'Fundamental Cultural Postulates and Judicial Law-making in Pakistan', *American Anthropologist 67 (December)*:43.

Holleman, F.D.
1920 'Adatrecht van de Afdeeling Toeloengagoeng', *Indisch Tijdschrift van het Recht* 112: 375–408.
1927 *Het Adatrecht van de Afdeeling Toeloengagoeng (Gewest Kediri); een onvoltooide studie*, Buitenzorg/Java: Archipel Drukkerij voor de Adatrecht Stichting, Leiden.

Holleman, J.F.
1952a *Shona Customary Law*, Cape Town: Oxford University Press (1969 reprint by Manchester University Press for University of Zambia Institute for Social Research).
1952b 'Hera Court Procedure', *Native Affairs Department Annual* (NADA) 29: 26.
1960 'African Marriage at the Cross-Roads', *Race Relations Journal* 27/28: 153.
1974 *Issues in African Law*. The Hague: Mouton for the Afrika-Studiecentrum, Leiden.
1981 ed. *Van Vollenhoven on Indonesian Adat Law*. The Hague: Nijhoff for Koninklijk Instituut voor Taal-, Land- en Volkenkunde (Translation Series 20).

Jaspan M.A.
1971 *The Redjang Village Tribunal*, Nijmegen: Publicaties over Adatrecht, no. 4, Nijmegen: Katholieke Universiteit.

Kuper, H. and L.
1965 'Introduction', in: H. and L. Kuper (eds.), *African Law: Adaptation and Development*, pp. 3–23, Berkeley and Los Angeles: University of California Press.

Llewellyn, K.N. and E.A. Hoebel
1941 *The Cheyenne Way*, Norman: University of Oklahoma Press.

Logemann, J.H.A.
1924 'De beteekenis der Indonesische getuigen', in: *Adatrechtbundel* XXIII: 114–133.

Mair L. (ed.)
1969 *African Marriage and Social Change*, London: Cass. (Reprint of A. Phillips (ed.) 1953, Part I, with new Preface, and original Introductory Essay by A. Phillips.)

Moore, S.F.
1970 'Law and Anthropology', in: B.J. Siegel (ed.), *Biennial Review of Anthropology*, pp. 259–293, Stanford: Stanford University Press.

Morris, H.F.
1971 'Review of Developments in African Marriage Law since 1950', in: A. Phillips and F. Morris (eds.), *Marriage Laws in Africa*, Reprinted Part II, with original Introductory Essay and new Foreword of A. Phillips

(ed.) 1953, London: Oxford University Press for International African Institute.

Phillips, A. (ed.)
1953 *Survey of African Marriage and Family Life*, London: Oxford University Press for International African Institute.

Pospisil, L.
1958 *Kapauku Papuans and Their Law*, New Haven: Yale University Press; Reprint 1964 by Human Relations Area Files Press.

Schapera, I.
1938 *Handbook of Tswana Law and Custom*, London: Oxford University Press for International African Institute.

Schiller, A.A.
1965 'Law', in: R.A. Lystad (ed.), *The African World; A Survey of Social Research*, New York: Praeger for African Institute Columbia University.

Sonius, H.W.J.
1981 'Introduction' in J.F. Holleman (ed.) *Van Vollenhoven on Indonesian Adat Law*, pp. XXIX–LXV.

Steenhoven, G. van den
1970 *Het Land van Kerenda*, Nijmegen: Publicaties over Adatrecht, no. 5, Nijmegen, Katholieke Universiteit.

Sugijono
1971 'Het belang van de adviezen van het dorpshoofd en de dorpsjustitie', *Bijdragen tot de Taal–, Land– en Volkenkunde* 127: 493–496.

Tanner, R.E.S.
1970 'The Selective Use of Legal Systems in East Africa', in: R.E.S. Tanner, *Three Studies in East African Criminology*, Uppsala: Scandinavian Institute of African Studies.

Velsen, J. van
1967 'The Extended–Case Method and Situational Analysis', in: A.L. Epstein (ed.), *The Craft of Social Anthropology*, pp. 129–151, London: Tavistock Publications.

Vinogradoff, P.
1913 *Common Sense in Law*, (1961 reprint 3rd edition revised by H.G. Hanbury), London: Oxford University Press.

Vollenhoven, C. van
1918, 1931, 1933
Het Adatrecht van Nederlandsch–Indië, (3 vols.) Leiden: Brill.

A.L. EPSTEIN

Injury and Liability in African Customary Law in Zambia

As an illustration of how cases may be utilized to seek general legal notions in a culture, we have selected the following essay by A.L. Epstein, who carried out fieldwork in Zambia in 1950. Epstein is very much an advocate of the use of cases. See his Juridical Techniques and the Judicial Process: A Study in African Customary Law, *The Rhodes-Livingstone Papers, Number Twenty-Three (Manchester, 1954) and "The Case Method in the Field of Law," in A.L. Epstein, ed.,* The Craft of Social Anthropology *(London, 1967), pp. 205–231.*

For other discussions of the advantages and disadvantages of the case method approach to folk law, see Richard L. Abel, "Case Method Research in the Customary Law of Wrongs in Kenya," East African Law Journal, *5 (1969), 247–291; 6 (1970), 20–60; and Max Gluckman, "Limitations of the Case-Method in the Study of Tribal Law,"* Law & Society Review, *7 (1973), 611–641.*

There has been little systematic discussion of the nature of liability for wrongs in African customary law though this is crucial for an understanding of any legal system and its underlying principles. Anthropologists have skirted this problem with descriptions of specific offences.[1] Colonial administrators, acting as magistrates, have seen the importance of the issues, but have sometimes generalized too hastily on insufficient evidence. Elias, a distinguished African lawyer trained in English law, has in his *The Nature of African Customary Law* (1956) criticized misconceptions that African law takes little account of the mental element and is marked by 'absolute liability', and insisted that on the contrary 'motive, accident, intention, etc., largely enter into every considered judgment'. But when he concludes that because English law looks at these elements in some instances and not in others, and that

---

Reprinted from Max Gluckman, ed., *Ideas and Procedures in African Customary Law* (London: Oxford University Press for the International African Institute, 1969), pp. 292–303, with permission.

the position is more or less the same in African law, and links this with an earlier discussion of whether there is a law of contract or tort in African law, or 'just an undifferentiated and confused mass of obligations without any underlying assumptions in both of legal principles', I believe that the initial taking over of English categories evades problems for investigation and confuses analytical issues.

Loss or damage may be variously sustained (e.g. through physical violence, through unintended consequences of another's act; through failure to fulfill prescribed or voluntarily undertaken obligations; etc.). But not all loss or damage is recognized as an 'injury' founding suit in a particular society; and the basis of liability for ostensibly similar injuries may vary between societies. On the face of it, the action which a Bemba father has against the man who seduces and 'eats the *cisungu*'[2] of his unmarried daughter has some similarity to the action for seduction in English law. But there are also important differences: the requirement of English law that in order to succeed the father has to show 'loss of services' would mystify the Bemba.

To establish categories of wrongs and to elucidate principles of liability we have to examine all forms of injury, and the extent to which liability (which should not be confused with responsibility) is affected not only by culpability but also by such factors as the circumstances in which an offending act occurred, the status and relationship of the parties, and so forth. This can only be done by sifting extensive and varied case-materials, and I shall outline how this may be done with data I collected in the African Urban Courts of Northern Rhodesia (Zambia) in 1950. There are no doubt important differences between these urban courts and those in tribal areas;[3] but urban court members had no training save experience in the tribal courts. Therefore in administering justice in the towns they operated with, and were guided by, the legal conceptions of their respective tribal laws.

Though I cite cases, I do not do so as if they were precedents in the sense of authoritative statements of customary law binding on the judges. There is not a complete consistency between cases, which vary with the circumstances; and there are good and bad judges, as well as good and bad decisions. But hearings and rulings are not haphazard: they are guided by expectations of both judges and litigants. Consistency is to be sought in the underlying structure of legal ideas and other assumptions of the judges, though they very rarely formulate these explicitly.

The most obvious and elementary instance of injury is the direct application of physical violence by one person to the body of another. Let us examine first an example of this type heard by the African urban court at Ndola. The matter involved a husband and wife, both Bemba, and had been referred to the court by the municipal location authorities.

The gist of the wife's complaint was that she had been assaulted by her husband, once on a public path when returning from a beer drink, and a second time when he had seized her violently and bitten off a piece of her ear and swallowed it. The husband's reply to these charges took the form of a statement made in the usual way. The trouble was, he said, that his wife had an excessive love of fornication. In Livingstone she had committed adultery twice, and in Ndola twice again. Once when he had gone on a visit to Livingstone he had left her at the Farms (a short distance out of Ndola), but she had decided to move back to the location. On his return he found his wife naked in the path, fighting with a man. They exchanged words and then, being drunk, they all started fighting. On the second occasion they were again drunk, and he had bitten her ear because she refused to listen to what he said: she behaved like a goat, and couldn't resist adultery when he was away for a short time. The statement of the parties concluded, they were questioned at length by the court. Part of the examination ran as follows:

Per curiam (to complainant): On the occasion when you were fighting and he 'broke your ear' were you drunk?
Comp: No, not in the slightest.
Per cur: And the other time, where were you coming from?
Comp: We were coming from the Farms.
Per cur: And you were all drunk?
Comp: Yes, we were all completely drunk.
Per cur: Was there any man to whom you had given beer?
Comp: No, none at all.
Per cur: How long have you been together with your husband?
Comp: It is seven years.
Per cur (to defendant): Where were you married?
Def: Here on the line of rail.
Per cur: And how many times has your wife committed adultery?
Def: On four occasions [i.e. with four different men].
Per cur: Is your wife then a cross-cousin?
Def: No, there is no relationship.
Per cur: How is it then that you did not divorce her and marry another?
Def: I hoped perhaps that one day she would give up her ways.
Per cur: Well, since it appears that you like your wife, what have you to say about this case?
Def: She herself knows the answer to that.
Per cur: Right. Now when you want to 'instruct' your wife, is it your custom to bite her ears?
Def: Well, I bite her ears because I get so angry.
Per cur: And you say that you want your wife?
Def: Yes, that is so and no lie.
Per cur: When you committed the assault were you drunk?

Def: Yes, we were all very drunk indeed.
Per cur: Well, what is the reason for all this?
Def: It's that she went and slept with other men when she ran away from her brother's house at the Farms.
Per cur: How many times have you assaulted her?
Def: Twice.
Per cur: Did you do wrong in 'breaking' her ear?
Def: Yes, as for that I was completely in the wrong indeed.

The defendant had earlier agreed that there were no witnesses who could speak on his behalf. His wife, however, was accompanied by her brother, who was invited to make a statement before the court. He confirmed the husband's testimony, saying that his sister seemed to think only of drinking and running after other men. He had nothing to say about his brother-in-law at all. The fact that his sister had had her ear bitten off was her own affair entirely since she always refused to listen to what he told her. At last the court passed judgment:

> As to all this, you, Frazer, we find that you have a case for [are guilty of] 'breaking' your wife's ear and swallowing it. Therefore the court finds that you should pay £5. You will take £3 and give it to your wife, the remainder will be paid to the court. Furthermore, we feel that you ought to divorce her otherwise you will kill her one day with your beatings. As for you, girl, we see that you have no child. This is because you love only fornication. So that the fact that you had your ear bitten off is your own fault (*mulandu*) entirely. You must cease this habit of committing adultery as though you were a dog which knows nothing of respect (*mucinshi*).

The facts in issue in this case were never really in dispute. The husband admitted the main charges against him, and he agreed in the end that what he had done was wrong. Yet the court devoted a good deal of time to the hearing, and it is clear from the whole line of questioning, as well as from the judgment, that it considered the husband had suffered considerable aggravation. In a sense the woman got what she deserved. But if this is so, why should she have been made an award of a fairly substantial sum of money? In many matrimonial disputes the court will often award a small sum—10*s*. or a chicken—to the aggrieved party. Such awards are best regarded not as compensation, but as an earnest of goodwill opening the way to full reconciliation. In the present case, however, far from seeking to reconcile the parties, the court actually advised a divorce. The award to the woman has to be seen therefore as compensation for damages received. Does it follow, then, that assaulting one's wife is an offence for which the husband is always liable irrespective of the blame that may attach to the wife's prior conduct?

Clearly not, for a husband's beating of his wife is recognized as an appropriate way of asserting his authority in the household, and I have recorded cases where an outsider who has attempted to intervene in a marital squabble has himself been found at fault. If, on the other hand, liability derives from the gravity of the damage sustained, why did the court not simply treat the matter as a penal offence and just impose a fine? I want to suggest that the court members here were not being inconsistent in their thinking, but that their finding flowed from certain assumptions about the nature of the human person which derive from tribal culture and philosophy.

A clue to the nature of these assumptions is contained in the court's reprimand to the woman that she should cease behaving like a dog that knows nothing of *mucinshi* (respect). The phrasing, of course, is designed to emphasize the repugnance of her behaviour in the eyes of the court, but the contradistinction of humans and animals recurs so frequently in judgment as to suggest that something more fundamental is involved than mere rhetoric. Thus in another case at Mufulira we find the court admonishing a man who sought a divorce because his wife complained of his frequent adulteries: 'You, fellow, you are a lunatic, you have no sense. It is time you came to learn that a man of sense ought not to roam about as though he were a wild animal of the bush.' That is to say, one is entitled to expect of one's fellow-men that their behaviour will conform to certain standards: man enjoys the gift of intelligence (*amano*), and knows therefore that in his behaviour he must display proper manners and respect (*mucinshi*); in so far as one does not measure up to these expectations one's humanity (*ubuntu*) is diminished. But there is also a further attribute of the person which is involved here. This is conveyed in the Bemba word, *-tuntulu*. *-Tuntulu* is an adjective meaning whole, complete, in good health, etc., but it also has overtones of wider import. Thus one may ask 'Is the animal dead (*Bushe nama naifwa*)?', and receive the answer, 'No, it is still alive (*iyo, ituntulu*),' This association of wholeness with life was brought home to me on one occasion when I was discussing with Bemba hereditary councillors the connection in Bemba thought between the east and life on the one hand, and the west and death on the other. One of the councillors (*Bakabilo*) present had especially important ritual duties to perform on the death of the Paramount Chief, and whenever he came to visit the capital he was required to stay in a section to the west of the village. He was being playfully chided by the other *Bakabilo* who always stay to the east, one of whom finally remarked: 'You are a prince of the dead, but we are of the living (*ifwe tuli batuntulu*).' The life-principle is a sacred value which finds its highest embodiment in the whole human person, which ought not therefore to be diminished, save in special circumstances. It is this basic postulate, I believe, which accounts for the overriding concern that the courts display in regard to physical violence to the person, and leads to the principle that one is liable in damages for any act which has as a direct consequence the diminishing of another's person, even though the act itself may have been prompted by that other's prior wrong.

In order to substantiate what might seem to be a somewhat fanciful line of analysis, and before seeking to develop the argument further, let me cite another and perhaps stronger case. This concerned a man who assaulted another for attempting to rape his daughter. He was ordered to pay £5 compensation for knocking out two of the other's teeth. He appealed to the African Court of Appeal on the grounds that the compensation awarded was excessive. I record below a few extracts from this hearing.

Per curiam (to appellant): Did you not beat John?

Appellant: I did.

Per cur: And is beating another person a good thing?

App: No, it is very bad indeed.

Per cur: Listen. If this seemed to you a case of rape why did you not report the matter at the [Police] Charge Office? We do not want to have people beaten here in Ndola. We want people to stay in peace here, and not be engaged in fighting. This person John was made by God but you want to destroy him. . . . What do you want the court to do for you?

App: I have appealed because the money was too much. In my opinion for the two teeth that he lost I should have been made to pay only £2. If three had come out I should have paid £3.

Per cur: Can you beat a person because you know just how much you will have to pay him?

App: No, that is not it.

Per cur: One thing you should remember is that John did not commit rape on your daughter. Did you find that he had done so?

App: No, but when I asked my daughter she hold me that John had attempted to rape her.

Per cur: You should know that rape is a 'civil' case; murder is a 'criminal' case, and so is assault.[4] Suppose that you had killed John, which would be the more serious case—that or 'rape'?

App: Murder would be the bigger one.

Per cur: Suppose you remove the frame from a bicycle do you think you can ride it?

App: No.

Per cur: Well, it is the same here with John's teeth. Since you knocked out two of his teeth he is unable to chew meat and other hard foods. You have spoilt the 'wealth' which was given to him by God. If a pot breaks, can it be mended?

The court then proceeded to point out how seriously such offences were regarded in former times. Some court members even thought the compensation awarded was inadequate, but they finally agreed that they ought not to interfere with the finding of the court of first instance, and the appeal was dismissed.

It will be observed that in this case, as in the previous one, the defendant did not seek to dispute liability for the injuries he had caused; his objection was merely to the amount he was required to pay as compensation. Again there is the concern with actual physical damage, a concern seen here in two ways. First, there is the stress placed by the court on the fact that the girl had not been raped, although the evidence seemed fairly clear that this would have occurred if the father had not intervened. Second, the gravity of the offence is reiterated as though it were tantamount to homicide. But what also seems important is that in both cases the offending acts, like the act of homicide itself, lead to consequences which are irreversible.[5] Under tribal conditions, at least, a person who has lost his ear or his teeth can never be made whole again. In the second case, indeed, wholeness as an attribute of the person was given quite explicit expression: like life itself it is a gift of God. The clear lesson of both cases, then, is that he who resorts to violence, even in defence of his legitimate interests, does so at his peril, since the consequence of his act may well be the maiming, or most heinous of all, the complete physical destruction of another person.

The tribes with which we are concerned are of the type characterized as 'states':[6] there was usually some degree of central administration, and the exercise of power and authority was controlled institutionally, often through an elaborate system of political offices. In such systems the application of physical violence becomes a monopoly of the state: not only does the state deny to the individual the right to take the law into his own hands, but it also arrogates to itself the right to inflict physical punishment for certain classes of offence. It is clear, therefore, why men who resort to violence should do so at their peril. But this still leaves unanswered certain questions posed by the case-material I have cited. Why, for example, was compensation awarded in both cases where the imposition of a fine or some other penalty would seem sufficient for the court to make its point? Africans in Zambia, however, do not see the matter in quite this way. For them the award of compensation for damages suffered to the person is one of the most basic and distinctive principles of their customary law. Indeed, among the most educated and Westernized Africans to whom I talked, the fact that compensation was so rarely awarded in a Magistrate's court was one of the major differences between the African and the European legal systems; it was this aspect of the latter which most puzzled them and aroused their criticism. In other words, the aims of an African court are seen as being as much redressive as penal. The judges should be as much concerned with the nature of the damage sustained as with wrongful acts as such, and this I suggest has its roots in assumptions about the human person as a whole being. I suggest further that this view of the problem also helps to account for a number of other features of legal doctrine and practice among the Bemba and certain other tribes of the region. Thus where a man has sustained physical injuries there is a reluctance to hear his case until the wounds have fully healed: once a case has been settled it cannot be reopened if the injury turns out to be more serious than was at first suspected; and here again the question of reversibility is relevant. Secondly, it may help to explain the widely differing responses of Africans and Europeans towards certain kinds of offence. A good instance of this is rape which, as mentioned earlier, was referred to by an African court as a 'civil' case. Such cases were indeed a source of much misunderstanding between urban court members and White magistrates. For the latter the essence of the offence is the forceful seizure of a woman and having intercourse with her without consent, and it commands a severe penalty. By contrast, African judges tend to treat such matters relatively lightly; the offence is classified as *bucende*, adultery or illicit fornication, and it is the infringement of the husband's marital rights rather than the affront to the woman herself which is the basis of the action.[7] The assumption here is that women in general are complaisant in sexual matters: if the offence occurs within earshot of a place of habitation and she does not cry out or make report immediately afterwards it is presumed that she consented to the act which carries no threat to her integrity as a person. On the other hand, if the offence took place in the bush it was viewed quite differently. The woman was no longer a person in a position to give or withhold her consent freely, since she had no protection against the threats of a man who, it was said, might kill her if she refused him. Such an offence was indeed a thing of mystical ill omen (*mupamba*) which defiled the country (*kushikule calo*); if it were not reported but was subsequently discovered, both parties were severely punished.

This reference to mystical notions also serves as a reminder that in traditional African thought the gravest threat to life and limb was not always provided by physical violence alone. There was—and is—a whole range of acts which Africans would immediately recognize as serious offences, actionable in customary law, but which the modern European would ordinarily react to with scepticism or dismiss as trifling or eccentric. In many of these cases the cause of action rests in a particular tribal belief which postulates a direct (though as we see it unverifiable) causal nexus between an act and its consequences, as for example in the notion that a woman who serves her husband with food while she is in an impure state may cause him to develop a serious bronchial ailment. In yet others the injury arises not from the physical damage as such that flows from the trespass but because the act itself appears as so unnatural that it at once indicates witchcraft. I want to suggest that the inference of witchcraft in these cases, which is the basis of legal liability, becomes less puzzling if seen in relation to those assumptions about the human person to which I have referred. Take the following example: among ourselves a man who preferred to have sexual intercourse with his wife while she was asleep might simply be regarded as having curious tastes in such matters. I was told that European District Officers to whom such complaints by African women were occasionally referred would dismiss them as a matter for the individual parties concerned. But to the African court members who have to judge such cases the practice has quite a different connotation. It is an abhorrent and unwholesome act which no 'reasonable man' would contemplate because it is tantamount to using a woman as a corpse. By his act the husband violates the integrity of his wife as a person: he has deprived her of part of her life-substance which he can then put to use magically in order to grow wealthy and powerful. The whole thing smacks of witchcraft and is believed to carry a serious threat to the woman's life.

In his work on *The Judicial Process among the Barotse* (1955), Gluckman has shown how the concept of the 'reasonable and customary man' lies at the heart of their jurisprudence, and I myself have analyzed the juridical thinking of urban court members in broadly similar terms.[8] If my present argument is valid that the concept of injury is bound up with assumptions about the nature of the human person, then I think we can see why 'the reasonable man' should assume such importance in African legal thought since, as I pointed out earlier, reason is seen as one of the defining characteristics of the human being. On the other hand, as an analytical concept 'the reasonable man' presents some difficulties, and Lord Devlin is not alone in seeking a word that would free us from some of its ambiguities.[9] In one of its aspects the stress is on rationality, the ability to see, for example, that certain consequences are likely to flow from a certain course of action. Yet the character of 'the reasonable man' in African law does not derive from the faculty of ratiocination alone, any more than does that of his English counterpart. He is a creature of custom and morality as much as of reason; in African thought he is above all a 'whole' man. Hence a man who has intercourse with his wife while she is asleep, or commits an act of sodomy with a boy, forfeits his claim to be a full human being. His behaviour is by definition 'unreasonable' because it confounds and confuses the basic dichotomies of African thought, here for example, of life and death, of male and female. His offence is much more serious than that of a physical assault: it is in the Biblical sense an abomination[10] and carries the most heinous threat of all to the integrity of the person—death by witchcraft.

This essay indicates that the notion of injury in some Zambian tribes is rooted in a concern to protect the integrity of the person. The cross-examinations cited inquire into motive, but in no case did drunkenness, provocation, or legitimate grievance affect liability. The irrelevance of motive emerges even more clearly in those cases which turn on the presence of witchcraft. In short, the data suggest that the courts concentrated on the acts and their consequences rather than on the motives from which they sprang. Nevertheless, it would be unwise on this basis to proceed to erect a general theory of 'absolute' liability in tribal law. The judicial process, I have said, is dominated by the presence of 'the reasonable man', and in the cases quoted the consequences which flowed from the defendants' acts were all of a kind that could reasonably have been foreseen and anticipated, even if they were unintended. In working towards a general theory of liability it would be necessary to carry the analysis further than I have been able to do here by examining cases where damage sustained was an unforeseen consequence or the result of negligence, the failure to take due care.

Notes

1. A notable exception is the recent study by Gluckman of *The Ideas in Barotse Jurisprudence* (1965), published after I had completed the draft of this paper.

2. A Bemba girl on reaching puberty traditionally went through a series of ceremonies known as *cisungu*. The first man to have sexual intercourse with her after she has reached this stage is said to 'eat the *cisungu*'. This should be the man to whom she has been properly married. For anyone else to do so is a serious offence.

3 See Epstein, 1953, *passim*.

4. Here the court was referring to the classification of English law which appears in the court warrant and sets out its constitution and legal powers. That the distinction is not always understood or followed in practice is seen in the reference to rape as a civil case. See also p. 632.

5.' I am grateful to Dr. R. Frankenberg for drawing this point to my attention and for other comments on the original draft.

6. Fortes and Evans-Pritchard (eds.), 1940, Introduction,

7. The rape of a nubile girl (*uwa cisungu*) would be regarded in quite a different light. 'Eating the *cisungu*' is, of course, yet another type of act whose consequences are irreversible.

8. Epstein, 1954.

9. Devlin, 1965, p. viii.

10. Dr. Frankenberg reminds me that the data presented throughout this paper suggest many parallels with ancient Jewish law. The topic is one that might repay further examination.

Bibliography

Devlin, P.
(1965) *The Enforcement of Morals*. London: Oxford University Press.

Elias, T. O.
(1956) *The Nature of African Customary Law*. Manchester: Manchester University Press.

Epstein, A. L.
(1953) *The Administration of Justice and the Urban African*, Colonial Research Series No. 7. London: H.M.S.O.
(1954) *Juridicial Techniques and the Judicial Process*, Rhodes-Livingstone Paper No. 23. Manchester: Manchester University Press.

Fortes, M. and Evans-Pritchard, E. E. (eds.)
(1940) *African Political Systems*. London and New York: Oxford University Press for the International African Institute.

Gluckman, M.
(1955) *The Judicial Process among the Barotse of Northern Rhodesia*. Manchester: Manchester University Press for the Rhodes—Livingstone Institute.
(1965) *The Ideas in Barotse Jurisprudence*. New Haven and London: Yale University Press.

ROGER HOWMAN

Witchcraft and the Law

It is a commonplace to say that every legal case is inextricably bound up in the culture in which it arises. It is not so commonplace to demonstrate all the nuances and implications of a particular cultural setting of a particular case. Moving southeast from Zambia to Zimbabwe, we consider a case involving an accusation of witchcraft in some detail.

Even the basic facts of the case were not easily determined. The individuals involved included Puna, a midwife, and a married couple, Runesu and Mazinyana. Mazinyana's husband, Runesu, engaged Puna to act as midwife, but he evidently erred by asking her not sufficiently in advance of the prospective birth and also by failing to pay her a proper fee. Later when Puna was struck with an eye ailment, she blamed Mazinyana, accusing her of causing the disease through witchcraft. Under the terms of a Witchcraft Suppression Act, anyone accusing someone of being a witch is guilty of an offence and so Puna is brought to trial.

For those readers whose belief system does not include witchcraft, we should like to recall the words of Exodus 22:18: "You shall not permit a sorceress to live." Such a biblical command surely implies the existence of witches. There is also the celebrated incident where Saul asks the witch of Endor to summon Samuel from the land of the dead (1 Samuel 28:7–15). The point is that many peoples did or do believe in witchcraft and therefore it is no surprise that there are legal cases involving this belief.

For representative discussions of witchcraft, see Lucy Mair, Witchcraft *(New York: McGraw-Hill, 1969) and Max Marwick, ed.,* Witchcraft and Sorcery, *2nd ed. (Harmondsworth: Penguin, 1982). For a valuable consideration of the legal ramifications with special emphasis on Africa, see R.B. Seidman, "Witch Murder and* Mens Rea*: A Problem of Society under Radical Social Change,"* Modern Law Review, *28 (1965), 46–61. See also Glanville L. Williams, "Homicide and the Supernatural,"* Law Quarterly Review *65 (1949), 491–503; Krishna Vasdev, "Ghosts, Evil Spirits, Witches and the Law of Homicide in the Sudan,"* Sudan Law & Reports *(1961), 238–244; A . Klingshirm, "The Trial of a Witch: A Document from Ghana,"* Africana Marburgensia, *4 (1971), 19–26; Onesmus K. Mutungi, "The Legal Aspects of Witchcraft in East Africa,"*

Reprinted from *NADA*: The Southern Rhodesia Native Affairs Department Annual (1948), 7–18, with permission.

Valparaiso University Law Review, *5 (1971), 524–555; Paul H. Brietzke, "Witchcraft and Law in Malawi,"* East African Law Journal, *8 (1972), 1–24; Onesmus K. Mutungi,* The Legal Aspects of Witchcraft in East Africa With Particular Reference to Kenya. *(Nairobi: East African Literature Bureau, Kenya 1977), L. O. Aremu, "Criminal Responsibility for Homicide in Nigeria and Supernatural Beliefs,"* International and Comparative Law Quarterly *29 (1980), 112–131; J.D. Ojo, "Supernatural Powers and Criminal Law: A Study with Particular Reference to Nigeria,"* Journal of Black Studies *11 (1981), 327–348; and Kharisu Sufiyan Chukkol, "Supernatural Beliefs and Criminal Law in Nigeria,"* Journal of the Indian Law Institute *25 (1983), 444–474.*

"I have nothing to say. I deny it." The old woman's words, winged with tones of resignation, sped from the dock across the listening Courtroom and out into the veld of Rhodesia.

The Assistant Magistrate watched her uneasily, hoping she would say something more in reply to the charge against her, something that would throw a little light on the case which the Prosecutor had just presented. But no further words came from the dock. The evidence was before him. To gain a little more time to still the uncertainty within him, the Magistrate ran through the papers, picking out the salient details:—

> "Rex versus Puna.
>
> "Puna did impute to Mazinyana the use of non-natural means in causing a disease in the said Puna, that is to say did name or indicate Mazinyana as a witch."

Then followed the women called as witnesses for the Crown—

> "Mazinyana stated: Last year the accused had eye-sickness. She consulted a diviner A, who visited our kraal. I was not present. Next day she said I was a witch (*Muroyi*) as the diviner had said I was the cause of her eye-sickness. She said if I did not believe her I could go to another diviner and that I was to leave the kraal. I went with others to diviner B for whom we threw the bones and all of us were cleared. Until diviner A came to our kraal there was no trouble between us. I had to leave the kraal.
>
> Tizirayi stated: Accused is my mother-in-law. A diviner A spent a night with us at tax time. Accused asked him to divine the cause of her illness. He said it was witchcraft (*Uroyi*) and caused by Mazinyana, who was not present. Next day accused told Mazinyana she was a witch (*Muroyi*) so she went to diviner B, who cleared her. She left the kraal.
>
> "Cross-examined by Court: Accused said she was a witch. The bones could not hold her as she was not present with diviner A. I believed diviner B, who cleared her."

The case was clear. The word *Muroyi* had been used, sickness attributed and a woman driven out of the kraal. Section 3 of the Witchcraft Suppression Act was contravened at every point—"Whoever imputes to any other person the use of non-natural means in causing any disease in any other person . . . that is to say, whoever names or indicates any other person as being a witch, shall be guilty of an offence and liable to a fine not exceeding £100 or to imprisonment . . . not exceeding 3 years."

The Prosecutor sat back awaiting the inevitable sentence. Why should the Magistrate waver over a case so legally unassailable!

But the man on the bench was not only a Magistrate. He was also a Native Commissioner. His mind was the scene of a conflict, a confusion, a striving to fit the sharp-edged, narrow and relevant instrument of a legal mind to the intangible, vast and impenetrable maze of African life. Where was Justice to be found? In the statute books and rules of procedure and evidence, or in something African he could not define?

He had been hoping for some guidance from the old woman, some explanation that would have brought a little certainty into his feelings about the case, but the legal segment of his mind remained unimpaired while the rest was a sphere of shadows, half-known native customs, terribly intricate, never final, always changing—yet clamouring to be considered in the name of Justice versus the Law.

Still the accused had nothing to say. The claims of Justice surged more strongly in his mind. Why should the Law forbid the bench to ask questions at such a crucial point? Criminal procedure in an English mental climate had evolved such a rule for good reasons no doubt, for above all an English Court is a judicial, not an inquisitorial body, and must not be drawn into an unfair contest with the accused, but how could it be justified when confronted with the African mind? It was so clear that the Prosecutor's case had been built up by long and tedious enquiry, innumerable questions, but it was a European mind that was directing the enquiry, asking leading questions, striving to mould the misty world of African magic and belief about which he knew little or nothing into something solid and legally presentable in court. Where else then was the Native Commissioner to seek, if the accused was to be given Justice, except in his own mind for Native custom is so far as he glimmered it, and in the explanations of the old woman herself?

Why not end the strain by sentencing her? Only an old woman. No one could query the case . . . no trouble. Too easy. The representative of the Law would break the Law. Metaphorically he came off the bench and turning to the old woman asked:—

"Why were you sick in the eyes?"

"I had been Mazinyana's midwife." The accused seemed quite certain she had given a complete and unanswerable explanation of the whole affair. Who was the Judge in South Africa who had referred to the "vague and irrelevant mind" of the raw native! So easy to say when it is European logic and experience which decide what is relevant. Her reply brought fragments of native custom petitioning his mind. Was he to let them influence his judgment? Was not a Judge drawing consciously and unconsciously on the whole range of British life and custom as his experience touched it when he considered a case? A Judge's mind was a British instrument of thought, it gave life, it gave meaning, it gave cohesion to the facts in the evidence. Surely then, the facts in this case, if they were to have any meaning, must be interpreted in terms of the culture of Africa!

"Did you consult 'diviner' A?"

"Yes, because my daughter-in-law was sick. I did not have sore eyes then."

"Did you consult 'diviner' B?"

"No. I heard that Mazinyana was calling people to go and divine. I thought it was for me she was going as I had been her midwife."

"Who is your daughter-in-law? "Sukai."

Sukai was found sitting under the trees at the edge of the office clearing with other relatives and was called as a witness. She said:

> "Diviner A, my cousin, visited us a few months ago. I was sick at the time. Accused had no illness in the eyes then. We asked him to divine the cause of my illness and he said my aunt's spirit was causing it as she wanted to be remembered by us. We asked him to sacrifice to her spirit, and since we had no beast we gave him £1 to get meat for a sacrifice, and off he went. I got better. Mazinyana left our kraal as she said the accused had said she was a witch (*muroyi*). We did not believe this as no one knew that any bones had been thrown and she had not thrown any. We went with her to diviner B to see if she was a witch, but all of us were cleared."

The mind of the Bench felt less dark. Many odd bits of native belief and custom were fitting into the case—if only he knew more about them! The legal mind was less dominant. The social mind felt a mist lifting and needed time to sort out the details, and to prepare a line of argument. The case would be remanded till Monday. And the week-end given to reading up notes on customs.

The Native Commissioner sat at his desk. A Sunday quiet hushed the bush around the Office. He was reading a Law Report. Glancing up, a row of empty Martini Henry cartridges caught his eye from the edge of the desk. They jolted him back from a world of Law to the multifarious duties of the Native Department. A gleam from a pair of burdizzos on the shelf pointed the lesson further. His was no job to be walled in by a legal mind. Out, out, his ideas must go, leaving no thread in the pattern of African life untraced, no impulse for change unheeded, no sentiment ignored—and if there be no end but confusion, no finality, at least there was the satisfaction of knowing that Administration was African life itself and not a flawless legal edifice, lifeless, incomprehensible, alien. He recalled an "old hand's" dictum: "Where there is Law there is no Justice." An exaggeration of course but a useful battle-slogan to oppose the equally distorted claim—"Where there is Law there is Justice"—made at a time when it was proposed to legalise the Native Department and turn its officials into Magistrates with higher legal attainments.

He went back to his Law Report. In the Rhodesian High Court case of Rex versus Mujuchwa in 1928 it was held that "though the word *muroyi* may include the sense of poisoning, it was in this case intended to include the use of non-natural means and that the accused was therefore guilty of contravening Section 2 (now 3) of the Ordinance," and was sentenced to six months' imprisonment. Here, for the first time, a doubt was aroused in judicial circles as to whether the word *muroyi* contained within itself the implication of "non-natural means," in other words did the use of the word *muroyi* automatically imply the use of non-natural means, thus relieving the prosecution of any need to prove the presence of non-natural means, and the Law of any obligation to define it?

Clearly the Judge had found himself in some confusion. He had pointed out that "the position raises a question of no little difficulty," and he had found a refuge from doubt on two grounds—one, that the Court Interpreter "has so consistently interpreted the word *muroyi* as a witch all through my experience" and two, that one Assessor who supported the interpreter was Native Commissioner of a district nearer to the scene of the case than the other. The Judge therefore held "that when the accused used the word *muroyi* and when these other people heard it they certainly intended to include the idea of non-natural means."

The old woman awaiting next day's verdict would find little comfort in hearing of that case!

The Native Commissioner went over to the cupboard where his notes on native customs were filed, his mind turning over and over the ideas implicit in the word *muroyi*. What could that assessor have been thinking of? Why, the word *muroyi* has a dozen meanings, sometimes natural, sometimes not. He would gather his notes into the various meanings to be found in actual Native life. Just notes, just accidental glimpses that had come his way like the prospector's specimens that betray the presence of the vast unknown beneath the surface.

The Meanings in Muroyi

1. *Muroyi in ordinary use.* A common man's name is Muroyi and a chief bears the title of Muroyi. A hill named Muroyi.

2. *Muroyi in Swearing.* The word is quite a common swear-word to use when incensed at someone's behaviour, and who has not heard *Kamwana aka karoyi*, as an elderly woman scolds some child who had refused to share his food with another—"that little child is a little witch."

3. *Synonym for Muroyi.* Chishukukuwire is a small snake which if found in a hut would necessitate purifying the place and would mean *uroyi* (witchcraft). The word is often used instead of Muroyi and is applied to those who spread scandal.

4. *Non-natural influence in Disease.* A certain Mudzwiti had been to the clinic four times, each time he returned home he fell sick again. His nephew said to him, "You know, Uncle, Madondo told me last week 'Your uncle is always ill. Because he took our beast a long time ago. If he returned it he would get well, if he won't he may die. Better he stay at the clinic. It is my mother (her spirit, she being dead) who is troubling him.'" Mudzwiti was so alarmed he took the matter to the chief, who brought it to the Office as *uroyi* (witchcraft). In the enquiry it emerged that Madondo's mother had paid damages of a beast many years ago because, having refused to be inherited, she had misbehaved sexually and as a result her daughter's babe had become ill and lost an eye. Her spirit was now raising the issue of this beast by afflicting Mudzwiti with illness. The gathering of elders agreed that the beast had rightly been paid, that the spirit was not justified in disputing this. Their general attitude was one of concern over the illness as *uroyi* and with Madondo's allegation which they felt deserved judgment for damages—but where is the borderline between this kind of spiritualism and witchcraft? The fact that a woman's misbehaviour affected even her grandchild is to be noted—non-natural means? A woman's misbehaviour is a primary influence for ill-health in her children, the malignant influence she passes to them being called *nuna*, and the closest approach to that word in English seems to be "a guilty conscience."

5. *Ku Dira Mvuri*—"to pour the shade or spirit." A man who interferes with another man's wife has a most dangerous influence over her husband should the latter fall ill and must on no account go near him. An uncle was ill. The whole kraal noted that his nephew would not enter his hut. He had been courting his uncle's wife. The illness is not due to the

nephew, but death will ensue if the nephew "poured his shade" over his uncle and he would be responsible. Non-natural means, but not witchcraft as we understand it, yet akin to *uroyi*. Another species of the power of a guilty conscience. As usual there is a counter-medicine called *azwiere* which hung round the neck of the sick man will ward off *dira mvuri*.

6. *The Witch by Inheritance and by Acquisition*. By strictly limiting the word *muroyi* to "witch" we find two kinds of witches. The acquired power, *uroyi bgwo ku temerwa*, and the inherited power, *uroyi bgwa mabvuti*.

There is a medicine known to witches which changes the heart and makes a person a witch. It may be deliberately acquired by cutting a vein and putting the medicine into the blood so that a person will say *wa ka ndi temera uroyi* (she cut for me *uroyi*), so I will go out with her naked at night. *Uroyi* might also be acquired by eating it so it was necessary to be most careful what you ate or drank from an uncertain stranger.

This kind of black magic was therefore deliberately acquired from another witch; there was no cure or preventative. It was such *varoyi* who had their ears, legs and arms cut off, who were banished, who were blotted out. They are well-known characters nowadays, feared by Native Messengers, Native Police and Chiefs—but who would dare mention them to Europeans!

One might well think that the Witchcraft Suppression Act was designed for these people, for those who practice the craft of the witch, or at least represent themselves to have the power of witchcraft. But instead confusion reigns. The witch is left free. The witchfinder is made to practice witchcraft or black magic, the very opposite of his own white magic, and the dominant conception of the "witchdoctor" bring illogically into one word the two extreme and contrasting philosophies of the "witch" and the "doctor," the bad and the good, witchcraft and anti-witchcraft. Little wonder the very word is shunned by those who know!

The second kind of *muroyi* inherits her power through a family spirit (*mudzimu* or *Shave* spirit). A woman finds herself, or someone else may find her, outside at night, she acts strangely, abnormally, she will be taken to a "diviner," who will diagnose the spirit. She will be called *mwana wa mabvuti* (child of the spirit). She has become a *muroyi wa mabvuti*. Such *waroyi* were often unconscious of their evil powers, quite unaware of doing any harm. Others were well-known characters. They were not necessarily harmful. People feared them for their possibilities of evil, but husbands continued to live with them and even the law distinguished them, for while a husband is responsible for his wife's actions any harm she causes as a witch is the responsibility of her own family in damages.

7. *The Emotional Witch.* A person is ill and either a professional or private throwing of the bones has revealed *uroyi* (witchcraft). No one knows who is the witch, although there may be suspicions. In the evening it is announced by the Kraalhead—only he can issue the summons—that all women will *bembera* next morning. *Ku danidzira bembera pa musha kuti tose ti gara kwazo no moyo wa ka chena* (to call to *bembera* in the kraal that we all may live nicely with white hearts). The next morning every woman brings a small pot of meal gruel (*ususu*) she has prepared, and having first tasted it herself, gives the patient a sip. In this manner the patient tastes the food of every woman in the kraal and the witch is thus offered an opportunity to include medicine in her *ususu* to cure or de-witch *(ku royanura or rowonora)* the patient without being revealed. If the patient does not recover then proceedings are taken to reveal the witch. All the women, and only women, are called to *bembera*. To single out one woman only would be tantamount to accusing her of being a witch.

There is more to this custom than an administration of de-witching medicine. Sharing food is symbolic of friendship, of atonement, of reconciliation—the cleansing property of eating together. Natives refer to the *bembera* as a means of cleansing the heart and acknowledge that a person generally knows who is bewitching him because the "heart is bad or ugly," and this communion purifies the heart.

It was in discussing the *bembera* custom that it became clear that the translation of the word *muroyi* is not always to be rendered as a "witch." Such words as *mbengo* (hatred), *godo* (jealousy), *ku tawura makuwu* (evil speaking, scandal) were constantly used to describe the characteristics of the *muroyi*. People living together in such intimate, daily, association must have the greatest difficulty in dealing with and controlling the deep, powerful and irrational emotions of envy, greed, malice, rivalry, hatred and frustration. There is no way out for these emotions, no escape mechanisms, and therefore they tend to be projected outwards, externalised into some malign or evil spiritual influence called *uroyi*. Anyone who gives way unduly to these emotions, is ill-willed, a bad mixer, is a *muroyi*. Anyone who falls ill or suffers misfortune is likely to interpret his distress in terms of the venting on him of those feelings of enmity which he knows someone else feels for him.

Rarely does one hear of a male *muroyi* or wizard, always they are women, old married women. When asked why, Natives have replied that it is women who have "very ugly hearts." Is it that women are more emotional, more temperamental, more confined to hard manual work over long periods and at the end of it confined once again to the kraal, prisoners within themselves? And does not polygamy put a premium on such emotions? *Godo* (jealousy) is only applied to women, and then as between co-wives. Such a situation between men is called *mbengo* (hatred), though *mbengo* may subsist between women who are not co-wives.

Muroyi in this context must imply some such translation as "anti-social." The social sanctions enforced against such a *muroyi* define strong moral sentiments and insist on a standard of conduct which few dared defy. Now the Witchcraft Act protects such *waroyi*. If anyone challenges them they have but to complain to the Police.

8. *The Social Misfit.* A very unpopular person, one who made kraal life unpleasant for everyone, *a no muzonda* as the Natives say, was always likely to find when she opened her door in the morning a heap of ashes of the *chinarara* or *muzeze* tree laid across her doorway. This is *ku dzinga muroyi* (to drive away the witch) and the person so blackballed would return to her father's kraal saying *wa ka isa chinarara ne dota pa musuwo wangu* (they put Chinarara ashes on my doorway). She would not dare cross her doorway, but would break a way out through her hut and never return.

There is nothing non-natural here, she is a witch, a person who is unendurable in the kraal.

9. *Collective Responsibility.* A certain Tapanya was accused, and convicted, of calling Madoro, the wife of his younger son, a *muroyi*. After the case it was found that Tapanya was head of his kraal, his elder son had died and his remaining son was the heir who would inherit the deceased's wife. At the inheritance ceremony the wife or wives to be inherited are required to jump over the bow of their deceased husband as it leans against the sacrificial beast (the *sendeka huta* or *darika huta* custom), and if any one of them has been unfaithful to him since his death the string of the bow will snap and she will have "burnt the grave" (*ku pisa guwa*). The *ku pisa guwa* is a most serious offence, it is even committed by anyone who has sex relations in the deceased's hut—and heavy damages are payable—before the dead man's spirit has been laid to rest.

In this case it was common gossip that Madoro was encouraging her husband to take his dead brother's wife long before it was proper to do so and eventually the Kraalhead himself, Tapanya, had to take notice and told Madoro that the widow was not to go to his son, "a widow should not be taken to wife by an heir till her husband's grave has been settled. Do not take the widow, if we burn the grave we will be *waroyi*, others will call us *waroyi*." Such was the collective significance of the use of the word *muroyi* in the eyes of the members of the kraal, although in Court of course witnesses were produced who testified to its individual application to Madoro who had promptly complained to the Police—protection again for the ill-disposed witch! The kraal version was checked. The dead husband's death had been registered six months previously.

Said one old man. "The time of *darika buta* is decided upon by the Kraalhead. If he sees that a widow mourns deeply, goes nowhere, remains dirty, he may postpone the time for a year, but if he sees she is flighty, forgetful of her dead husband and likely to burn the grave, he will hasten the ceremony. But a period of six months would be too soon to be proper."

Here we have a kind of collective responsibility for an act so abhorred by public opinion as to be called *uroyi.* Whatever may have been the original words used, "you are a witch" or "we will be witches," it is clear there was no non-natural influence about, but merely most objectionable behaviour. It is to be noted that the husband was not blamed. The Police, in their quest for the elements of a prosecution, obtained what they sought—the use of the word *muroyi* in association with a death—and a Court, either ignorant or powerless to get at the truth, condemned an innocent man to gaol for his efforts to maintain a moral standard in his kraal.

10. *Trumped-up Charge.* Ningi was charged with employing a "witchdoctor to indicate by the use of so-called witchcraft, to whit, the throwing of bones, the person who had caused the lameness of a certain ox." The complainant stated that he had been called a *muroyi* and accused of bewitching the ox.

In cross-examination by the Court the witnesses admitted that the accused had not instructed the witchdoctor to ascertain "who had caused the lameness," but to find out the cause of the lameness, and they agreed that the witchdoctor had said "the lameness was due to a departed spirit who wanted a sacrifice of a goat." Because of this the Attorney-General refused to prosecute. This time there was no injustice done, and the complainant's action in going to the Police was found to have arisen out of a dispute he had with the accused over some land, and he had tried to get rid of him with the help of the Witchraft Act.

11. *The Ritual Witch.* It is the person disclosed by ritual means as a *muroyi* who, in Native eyes, is the personification of evil, an influence to be eradicated; while it is the ritual agent who discloses her presence who is the primary object of eradication by the European Court, the *Nganga*, the so-called witchdoctor, the witchfinder or diviner. Could there be a more startling contrast in ideas of good and evil? If European law is then so utterly opposed to the ideas of the Native, so drastic in its penalties, so vague and confused in its definitions, it becomes imperative to distinguish the ritual witch from the other meanings in the word *muroyi* and to describe the process by which the word *muroyi* is ritualised and invested with real harmfulness for society.

Out of some situation of affliction and distress arises the driving need to consult the spiritual world. All the adult members of a kraal should be called together, to form a *gumbgwa*, a divination party, to visit a *nganga* (diviner). The essence of the *gumbgwa* is surprise, a sudden gathering to ensure that no-one may find an opportunity to go back to a hut or absent themselves in order to get *mugaranganda* the medicine which gives immunity from detection by the *nganga*.

Every member of the *gumbgwa* must take an "offering" called *museve*, which the Law calls "reward or payment" but which is really an essential contact point or link between the personality or spirit of the owner and the spirit of the *nganga*. A favourite *museve* is a a worn-out hoe (*chisarima*), a pot of grain, any bit of personal property which in the old days the *nganga* hung on the tree under which he divined for all the world to see, the tree becoming festooned with oddments as his fame and practice grew. But nowadays he is driven to secrecy and the modern *museve* of handkerchiefs, safety pins, old belts, tobacco and six-pennies or shillings are vulgarly termed "payments" and he is prosecuted for fraud.

That the *museve* stands for or symbolizes the personality of the owner is revealed by the fact that anyone unable to attend the *gumbgwa* through old age, illness, etc., will send a *museve* with some relation and that *museve* will be him or her, so much so that witnesses have given eyewitness evidence through both Lower and High Court as to what happened at a divination, and never been there at all. No one would contradict their assertion that they were present, for was not their *museve* there! Anyone failing to join a *gumbgwa* by *museve* would be acknowledging she would not dare the verdict of the bones.

On arrival the *gumbgwa* exchanges polite formalities with the diviner and the *miseve* are handed over. The *nganga* takes snuff, chews medicine and spits on the bones (*hakata*) as all the members of the *gumbgwa* settle round him in a semi-circle.

No reference is made to the purpose of the *gumbgwa*, there is no "soliciting," no "employing" or haggling over "reward or payment." The bones (*hakata*) are made by spiritual processes, they reveal the spirit world, what need then to explain the reason for the visit? And if a European in uniform demands to be satisfied as to "why we visited the witchdoctor, what we said to him, and what he said to us"—why, answer his secular mind as best you can and hope he is satisfied! I went to see a very renowned *nganga* one day, only to find he had died. His son demonstrated the technique of the *hakata* and then added, "My father taught me all he knew but I cannot divine (*shopera*) because his spirit (*shave*) has not come out in me." He explained, "When you spit on the *hakata* (*ku furisa*) at the new moon with *rukata* or *mumururu* (medicine) you pray (*pira*) to the *shave* spirit to help you, and the *miseve* you offer to the *shave*."

A *nganga* may use any number up to eight sets of *hakata*. A common number is four (*mishaku mina*) comprising sixteen bones. Spitting on them twice, top and bottom, he throws them on the ground and studies their meaning (*ku wuka*)[1]. The *hakata* will reveal the reason for the visit—death, disease, any misfortune in the kraal. Further throws will slowly become more specific, the various possible causes of the trouble being eliminated—an ancestral (*mudzimu*) spirit angered at neglect or some infringement of tribal law, the vengeance of an *ngozi* spirit seeking atonement for some old wrong, retribution for breaking some moral rule like adultery, a *shave* spirit seeking to express itself and so on. No, it is witchcraft (*uroyi*). Illness or misfortune may be due to any of these agencies, it is for the *nganga* to diagnose which one, so that the legal argument raised in Rex vs. Mashabele (S.R. 119/18) as to "Who" or "What" caused the illness should never arise, except when the Police have elicited the answers they want, or it is a quack-doctor.

Having diagnosed the presence of witchcraft that is as far as the *nganga* can go throwing the *hakata* himself. For the step from the general to the particular, from *uroyi* to *muroyi*, it is essential that the witch handle the *hakata* herself, or through her *museve*, and so reveal her identity. The leader or the *gumbgwa* then has to offer *mamburo* (from *ku pambura*, to divide) in order to have them all tested and the witch sorted out. Each one in turn throws. Anyone may be required to throw two or three times in order to make certain. The details vary but, "The bones refuse, you are cleared" (*dzi no ramba, wa pembedzwa*) the diviner may say and waits for the next one to throw. "The bones refuse to you, you are caught" (*dzi no rambira kwa u ri, wa batwa!*) comes at last. After everyone has thrown the diviner will dip his finger into meal and mark everyone except the witch with meal on the forehead, he will also hand her back her *museve*.

It is the return of the *museve* that is the public affirmation of a witch, whether she leave the "diviner" with it for everyone to see or whether it be returned to her in the kraal as proof of what the verdict was.

Such is the process of divination, only one of many versions, a succession of rites with a spiritual current running through them. But it must never be forgotten that the great diviners have been stamped out or reduced to secrecy by European Law, their traditional rites have been broken, the new generation of Natives knows little of proper procedure and divination methods. We have a situation where knowledge has died or faded but emotional fears persist and on this ignorance and fear a host of pseudo-diviners, quacks and irresponsible or illegitimate processes of divination thrive. No Court can now be certain it is dealing with a genuine divination which impresses the community with the conviction that one of its members is a witch, or with a false version of it that is merely ridiculous to the old people and half-true for the credulous modern generation.

Natives are emphatic that a person cannot be revealed as a witch in her absence, yet over and over again criminal action has been taken against someone for calling someone else a witch without any ritual authority whatever. Such people often clothe themselves in some degree of partial ritual authority and it is the weighing of "the degree of authority" which is the most perplexing question for a European Court, for it has no means of gauging the response of public opinion to the accusation. Natives agree that often a person in trouble goes secretly to a diviner and throws the bones for all whom he cares to name, everyone in the kraal as a rule, and one of them may be caught by the bones. But that is only suspicion. Normally the enquirer should go back, collect a *gumbgwa* and visit a different and distant diviner to have suspicions put to the test. However, it often happens that he is so upset at the very idea that X may be killing his child, or whatever the trouble is, that he rushes off to X and accuses her of witchcraft, taking revenge into his own hands with torture and serious assault in an effort to save his child.

What should be preliminary investigation leading up to authoritative public divination is here made the basis of an accusation, a distraught person acting too hastily, and what would be the position in Court if a private diviner in the dock should reply, "I only read the bones as thrown by my client. Everyone knows a *muroyi* cannot be revealed except she throw the bones herself, and this I took no part in."? Natives explain that in cases of private consultation there must have been bad feeling between the parties and that is why a *gumbgwa* was not formed.

Again it has to be noted that almost every Native can throw the bones and certainly every family-head has his family set which he consults on minor matters as we consult popular knowledge involving Aspro or Iodine, but on more serious matters, or when popular remedies fail, then recourse is had, as we do, to more skilled authority, and the diviner is appealed to. Before this happens the private bones may have shown witchcraft and an accusation based on ill-will and spite follows which will be obvious to the whole kraal as a case of emnity but which, in the eyes of the Law, is "non-natural influence."

Of course, when confronted with these cases in which no verdict has been given by a diviner, a Court finds itself in the strange and paradoxical position of having to insist upon something the existence of which is denied. "Did you go to a proper diviner and did the person you called a witch throw the bones? If not, what authority had you got for calling her a witch?" Some old hands of the Native Department have held that witchcraft being non-existent, imaginary superstition, it must never be discussed with Natives for fear of giving an impression that it exists. What would they say to such questions in Court?

Veil upon veil is drawn over divination by the Native. Everyone who attended fears the Police and will lie to save himself and his relations, and the whole community will ally itself with the diviner not only because he is their line of communication with the unseen but also because he is feared and respected for his power as the following case will show.

Takadayi returned from Johannesburg after four years absence and asked for a new Registration Certificate. His card showed he had served two months' imprisonment seven years ago for designating a witch so with no fear to induce him to distort the truth he was asked to say what happened.

> "My father fell ill. The local diviner said his *shave* wanted a blanket. But the blanket made no difference. We went to another and he said the *mudzimu* wants some cloth. My father died. It was then I formed a *gumbgwa* to go to a big diviner in another district. It was a small *gumbgwa*, nowadays we make small *gumbgwa's* for fear of the Police but we took *miseve* for our wives."

Then followed a description of what happened which ended with the mother of his nephew being held by the bones and she had complained to the Police. In the case which followed the big diviner was sentenced to two years' imprisonment and Takadayi to two months.

The original record was compared with Takadayi's version and other members of the kraal invited to say what happened. So the blatantly untrue statement of one witness that, "Takadayi said to the accused, 'are the witches X and Z?" The accused threw the bones and said, 'Yes, I find that X and Z killed your father'," was thrown into relief. In the course of this bit of research it was found that Takadayi had paid a small bull to the husband of the woman he had called a witch as damages and an accidental reference to five head of cattle drew out the surprising fact that Takadayi had, two years after the big diviner's release from gaol, paid him five head of cattle as compensation for having caused his imprisonment. It was impossible to let this pass and as a result the big diviner went into gaol again for extortion.

12. *Poison.* The Police investigated an assault case and found the word *muroyi* had been used. Chitindi was prosecuted for "imputing the use of non-natural means in causing the death of Chizuwa, that is to say he did call Runesu a wizard." The facts were that Chitindi returned from Johannesburg to find his relative Chizuwa had died and rumour had it that Runesu had put poison in his food so Chitindi picked a fight and came out the worse. There had been no divination, no suggestion

of non-natural means, no witchcraft. The action of poison is perfectly natural in Native eyes, everyone knows the effect of dip, but the word for poison is *uroyi* and the poisoner is *muroyi*, that is, apart from the word *chepfu*, a corruption from Afrikaans. Again there is the meaning of evilness, antisocial nature, in the word *muroyi*, for who else would administer poison! But it is quite distinct from any ritual process. And again a Court has to assume the existence of diviners and ask what ritual authority Chitindi had for calling Runesu a *muroyi* before it can find out in such a case that the correct translation of the word is "poisoner."

. . .

The Native Commissioner's mind felt cleared. The magisterial segment had shrunk, was dwarfed, by an all-embracing vision of both the Law and the Life of the people among whom he lived. The little black mouths of the Martini Henry cartridges seemed open in mute appeal for things African. He would draw up his reasons for judgment, to explain if he could to the prosecutor next day just why the old woman must go free.

> "Section 3 of the Act refers to non-natural means without defining it, but identifies it with calling a person a witch. In Rex vs. Mujuchwa this line of reasoning was queried, and in my opinion quite rightly. I cannot concede that the word *muroyi* implies non-natural influence. This being so, the prosecution has got to prove that non-natural influence has been associated in some way with the actual use of the word on every occasion, for the word in itself is harmless.
>
> The question then arises, what is this non-natural influence which is not legally defined? It is difficult, but in the absence of an answer many an innocent person has gone to gaol. The European, of course, answers, "Nonsense, there is no such thing." We must approach it from the native point of view; for them it is a tremendous reality, though it lives in their minds only.
>
> Without going into details of the many Native customs and beliefs concerning this non-natural influence it may be said that until a definite series of rites have been observed which concentrate or inject this non-natural influence into the word *muroyi* it remains a mere word. The existence of non-natural influence depends on whether or not the people believe it is there, and their belief in turn depends on whether or not the machinery or rites for mobilizing that influence have been set in action. In other words, has the proper person in touch with the spiritual or magical world thrown the bones in the proper manner and so produced in the minds of the community a conviction that a certain person is a witch?
>
> This line of argument seems to me to fit in with the ultimate intention of the Act, the intention to protect persons whom we Europeans hold to be innocent from what we may call the delusions of their fellows. If those

delusions have not been aroused by the proper rites then the person we seek to protect by the Law is in no need of protection and to apply the Law in such cases is to commit injustice.

In this particular case the evidence reveals that the proper rites have not been complied with, that the accused had not got non-natural backing, and that therefore the members of the kraal were under no delusions that Mazinyana was a witch. To a certain extent they did comply with proper procedure. Mazinyana formed a divination party—a *gumbgwa*—to consult diviner B and she and everyone else was cleared. In the face of this no-one could be under the delusion that she was a witch. The allegation of the use of non-natural means is therefore not proved.

There is another important aspect to be considered. The evidence on it is contradictory but the Crown has sought to prove that the accused consulted diviner A who threw the bones and as a result she accused Mazinyana of being a witch. It may be that in the eyes of the community this aroused suspicions; certainly Mazinyana felt obliged to put them to the test by throwing the bones herself before another diviner and then complaining to the Police. The accused's alleged use of the word *muroyi* has there caused a certain degree of trouble but whether this degree of trouble is sufficient to justify a wider interpretation of the meaning of non-natural means to cover this kind of trouble is indeed a most difficult matter. One is tempted to think that the fact of complaining to the Police is sufficient evidence of the seriousness of Mazinyana's position but it is only too true that Natives have discovered that to complain to the Police is a most effective means of retaliation, even when the circumstances are most trivial.

In this case the Court is not convinced that Mazinyana has suffered anything more than the personal ill-will of an old woman who, being the mother of the head of the kraal, has ample power and prestige to make life uncomfortable for her. Why this ill-will should be present is not disclosed. The accused is found not guilty and is discharged."

Sequel

Over a period of several months after the case the Native Commissioner probed into the life of the kraal, seeking here and there as chance offered to fit the parts of a jig-saw into a picture, trying to see if his judgment had been right or wrong, and slowly a background to the whole strange and complex affair emerged.

At the time of tax last year, diviner A, a headman on his way home from the Office, called in at the kraal of his cousin Sukai whom he found was ill. He was asked to divine with the bones for her and found that the spirit (*mudzimu*) of her dead aunt, his own mother, was feeling neglected and required the recognition of a sacrifice. No beast was available so Sukai gave him £1 with which to buy an animal to offer to the spirit. Sukai got well. At that time Puna was perfectly well.

Quite recently Puna suffered badly from illness in the eyes, in fact when the Police came to find her she was then in the clinic under treatment and the case was delayed till she was released.

Now Puna was a well-known midwife (*muchingi*) and the skill of midwifery is derived from a *shave* spirit. The gifts or payments made to a midwife are really an offering or tribute to the *shave* and it is believed that if the child is weaned before she receives these the midwife is liable to be afflicted with illness in the back or the eyes. These offerings are called *uchingi* and they must include meat which the midwife mixes with medicine and eats to prevent back or eye trouble.

Further, a prospective father should engage a midwife about seven months before the child is due, giving her as *uchingi* a fowl or 1s., and later, after the delivery, a goat or about 5s. to 10s. If, as many husbands do, he delays and has to rush about at the last moment to ask a midwife to attend his wife she will reply, "*Wa ka ndi ridzira mere*" (you called me in distress) and her *uchingi* will be a beast or about £1. Some tribes call this payment *mburamere.*

Runesu, the husband of Mazinyana, was such a husband. He delayed and only asked Puna at the last moment. After the birth he gave her *mubayiro muduku wo uchingi* (the small offering) and Puna, being a stately old lady, would not haggle—he might have thought she was asking too much (*ruchochoro*)—so she said simply, "If you do not know the proper thing to do go to your mother and ask her." Runesu never did this.

When Puna got eye sickness there was obviously only one explanation. She pointed out her affliction to Runesu saying, "You can see I'm sick, won't you help me, I was your midwife? You have never given me my *uchingi*." Runesu was somewhat worried by this but being of a mean disposition he decided to make sure the old lady was right so he told his wife to collect a *gumbgwa* and go to diviner B to find out if she or anyone else was responsible for Puna's illness. This they did and all of them were cleared, that is, of any personal influence—but the bones revealed that a *shave re songano* spirit was annoyed and causing trouble. On their return with the news Puna, who had not attended, commented, "I told you so. My *shave* gave me skill to help you. Give me my *uchingi* and my *shave* will make me well."

So those were the circumstances out of which that discomforting case had come! It was not so plain how Mazinyana and the whole kraal had drawn their conclusions. How the huts must have buzzed with comment and confused hearsay that had blurred the slender distinction between *uroyi* (witchcraft) and *uroyi* (responsibility for illness) and the upshot was that Mazinyana was pointed to as being responsible. Did she not deserve it, or at least her husband? She left the kraal and complained to the

Police who gathered statements in the approved style with no time-wasting irrelevances.

Runesu was most indignant about what his wife had done—"Complain to the Police!! That she should never have done."

Soon after the case Runesu had not only made the proper offerings to Puna's *shave* spirit but he had brewed beer for her to soothe her ruffled pride and he, his wife and the old woman who had been in Court were all living happily together once more.

In that kraal had Justice, in whose name so much is said and shouted to her discomfort, given a clue to her quiet presence!

(Native custom is drawn predominantly from the Ndanga and Chibi areas.)

Note

1. "To talk" is "*ku taura*." When a *shave* spirit talks through its medium it is said to *ku wuka*.

R.F. BARTON

White Man's Law Among Filipino Tribesmen

The Philippines consist of an archipelago of more than seven thousand islands, upon which live more than sixty different linguistic-ethnic groups. One of these groups is the Ifugao. The group was studied by Roy Franklin Barton (1883–1947), who was not trained initially as an anthropologist or folklorist. Barton had prepared for a teaching career and in 1906, he arrived in Manila. Eventually he made his way to the Cordillera Mountains of Central Northern Luzon Island where the Ifugao lived. Here from 1908 to 1915 he spent eight and a half years. He learned the language and studied the culture. As a government supervising teacher, he made the rounds of district schools, and because of his exceptional knowledge of folk law, he was sometimes called upon to adjudicate local disputes or to represent parties in disputes. This was surely an attestation of the people's respect for his efforts to understand the subtleties of their culture.

In 1916, Barton left the Philippines to return to the United States. At the University of California, where he decided to begin a career in dentistry, he met anthropologist A.L. Kroeber who urged him to complete his manuscript on Ifugao law. This was published as Ifugao Law, University of California Publications in American Archaeology and Ethnology *15, no. 1 (1919), reprinted by the University of California Press in 1969.*

In the following essay written for a popular periodical in 1930, we gain a glimpse of Barton's unique expertise in Ifugao folk law. At the same time, we cannot help but remark the somewhat amateurish aspects of his reportage. The very title of the essay reveals a patronizing, even condescending attitude. The approach is strictly anecdotal, and there are passages which border on racism. In an ogling description of "the most beautiful girl I ever saw in the Philippines," Barton tells us "Her features and bodily proportions were almost Caucasian."

Why then reprint Barton's cases? The cases do demonstrate the nature of Ifugao folk law and Barton's familiarity with the subject was unquestionably great. Few anthropologists or folklorists spend eight and a half years consecutively in the field. For more details of Barton's life, see A.L. Kroeber, "Roy Franklin Barton, 1883–1947)," American Anthropologist, *51 (1949), 91–95, Nancy Oestreich Lurie's*

Reprinted from *Asia*, 30 (1930), 410–416, 445–448.

"Introduction" to Barton's Autobiographies of Three Pagans in the Philippines *(New Hyde Park: University Books, 1963), pp. xxvii–xxxv, or Barton's own autobiographical account,* The Half-Way Sun *(New York: Brewer and Warren, 1930). For more of his writing on folk law, see his autobiography, specifically the chapter entitled "The Exaltation of Custom," (pp. 60–119), or* The Kalingas, Their Institutions and Custom Law *(Chicago: University of Chicago Press, 1949).*

For more on folk law in the Philippines, see Perfecto V. Fernandez, Custom Law in the Pre-Conquest Philippines *(Quezon City: U.P. Law Center, 1976); and Owen J. Lynch, Jr., "The Philippine Indigenous Law Collection: An Introduction and Preliminary Bibliography,"* Philippine Law Journal, *58 (1983), 457–534.*

For more recent discussions of Ifugao folk law, see Francis Lambrecht, "Ifugao Customs and the Moral Law," Philippine Studies, *10 (1962), 275–303; K. Hutterer, "Reciprocity and Revenge among the Ifugao,"* Philippine Quarterly of Culture and Society, *1 (1) (1973), 33–38; and Kyoko Kikuchi, "Acculturation among the Kiangan Ifugao—as revealed through several civil cases,"* SHA: *A Quarterly Record of Social Anthropology, 8 (4) (1976), 66–74. For further references on the Ifugao, see Harold C. Conklin,* Ifugao Bibliography *(New Haven: Yale University, 1968).*

"Wild Raspberry, this Apo will assist you when you come before the Apo Juez." So it was that Sergeant Juan Candelario, of the Philippine Constabulary, introduced us. *Apo,* literally "grandfather," is a term of respect in nearly all the Philippine languages. *Juez* is the local approximation of "judge."

I looked at my client who bore the ridiculous name of the bitterish little red berry that I had often stopped to pick on the tops of high mountains. Tomorrow morning he would be tried for killing a woman. He was an ordinary-looking Ifugao, though prematurely oldish. He returned my gaze passively, quite certain that this white man would not, could not, be of any assistance to him; strange people, these white men! It needed no keen perception to see that Wild Raspberry would never again feel any major emotion.

Twice a year, a judge, a prosecuting attorney—called a fiscal—a clerk of the court and an interpreter were in the habit of traveling by horse through the Mountain Province in northern Luzon and holding court in the capital of each subprovince. Murder and head-hunting comprised nearly all the cases—at least in the more remote subprovinces with which I was familiar. As a teacher, I was usually the only American about not somehow connected with the arrest and preliminary hearing of persons brought before the court. Slender and only qualification though this was, a judge would frequently, since no attorneys were available, appoint me to defend men accused of murder. In this present instance, the Judge had stopped at my house in Kiangan en route to Banaue and had asked me to come with him to defend the cases in that particular term of court.

"Tell me how it happened, Wild Raspberry."

"I came home and saw my children, the boy and the girl, lying in their own blood. The boy was still in the baby-carrying blanket," he said and stopped.

By questioning I drew out the facts. He was from Banao region. For a long time after his marriage, his wife had borne him no children, but he stayed with the woman because he liked her. Then a girl had come. Not until four or five more harvests had passed was the boy born—and it was two harvests ago that he began to talk. Notwithstanding that he was now too big to carry, the girl would always carry him slung in a blanket on her back.

"About two moons ago, as I was working in the fields," Wild Raspberry said, "a woman came running toward me. 'Our neighbor, Centipede, has gone crazy and killed both your children!' she screamed. I thought she was crazy herself, but still I ran home. There they were. The girl had fled from the man, the baby on her back. She was climbing up the ladder into the house. He killed the boy there—right on her back; I know, because there was blood on the ladder. And then he—"

I interposed hastily, "And what did you do?"

"I got my war-knife. I didn't take my shield. I wanted one hand for the knife and the other for a spear. They told me, 'He ran toward Ligaue.' I followed, I came to a clearing. There *he* was, killed already. He had attacked two women, working in their garden, and they had killed him. He had no brothers—only two sisters. I went back to the village and killed one of them."

"Why did you kill her? She had no guilt."

"There were no brothers."

"You don't understand me. Why kill anybody?"

He thought I was hard of hearing and raised his voice. "I should rather have killed a man, but there was no man to kill—only women. Yes, I was very angry. 'Why did you kill him?' I screamed at those women in the garden. 'We had to; he was going to kill us,' they said."

"He was insane; he was dead. Why kill anybody else?"

"They killed *two* of mine, the boy and the girl. Before I could kill the other sister, the police held me. How can an American know the feelings of men?" Unconsciously he arrogated to his own kind the name "men," as primitive folk are likely to do all over the world. "The girl was so high"—indicating—"and the boy, so high. He was in the baby-carrying blanket in which we always carried him!"

Wild Raspberry would have to go to prison—otherwise he would go back and kill the other sister: I knew that. But I wanted the Judge to hear him say, "The boy was in the baby-carrying blanket." In court next morning, after the witnesses had testified and after the confession had been read, I put Wild Raspberry on the stand. He was lifeless, unconcerned; he mumbled, barely answering the questions put to him; he was like a man nearly frozen to death. Before I had more than begun a little speech in his behalf, the Judge started looking up the *penalty* in the Code.

"Your Honor," I said, "I have not handled this case right. If I had, Wild Raspberry would have told you his story as he told it to me. In that case, possibly Your Honor would give him a sentence short enough for him to return to his own hills once more and even hope to beget children to replace the two he saw lying in their own blood."

"Nothing can influence the court once the guilt has been established. It is a singularly clear case, a unique case: not a lie has been told in it. But the defendant is entitled to the benefit of alleviating circumstances."

The Judge sentenced him to twelve years, four months and twenty days—a penalty correct to the day. But Death had already sentenced Wild Raspberry to only six months more of this strange imprisonment we call life.

A subsequent term of court brought me in touch with a case of peculiar sociological significance. Limitit, a youth of Ayangan, stood at the bar, charged with killing his father. "Are you guilty or not guilty"—translated into Ifugao—has the sense of "Are you at fault or not at fault." Limitit entered his own plea and said "Not at fault." Yet he had confessed all the facts and spoke of them with a candor almost pitiable. "He was my father," he remarked sadly; "I had a right to kill him. I gave him a good funeral—I sepulchered him quite decently."

His bearing and demeanor indicated that he had no consciousness of guilt, that he had performed only a very disagreeable duty. The testimony showed that Shining Torch, the father, was a wastrel and a gambler. He had raised money by mortgaging rice-fields that would be allotted to Limitit, who would stand toward his brothers and sisters as head of the family—almost a patriarch. Shining Torch had not made any effort to redeem the fields, though given plenty of time, and had persisted in a course likely to ruin his family irretrievably. Therefore Limitit, seeing no other way out of the situation, had killed him.

During the whole course of the trial, Limitit never seemed to realize why he was being tried. He kept insisting: "I sepulchered him properly.

I killed many chickens and three fat hogs." He seemed to think it was for not funeraling his father correctly that he was about to be punished.

I investigated the attitude of the neighbors. They said the old man was worthless and deserved killing for squandering the family property. Though warned, he had continued in his bad course. Besides, he was Limitit's father, and if Limitit wanted to kill him he had the right. At any rate, it was the concern of nobody else.

We who regard parricide as worse, circumstances being equivalent, than ordinary murder, may understand the attitude of the Ifugaos only if we take into consideration that the family is much more to them than to us: it is the Ifugao's only social group, his little nation. In the case cited, the father was a traitor to his group, wasting the inheritance that had come to his family from its forebears. In a land where a living must be eked from a tough, stony mountainside with wooden tools, the fields which represent the means of life handed down through the sweat of former generations are as sacred as the soil of a father land. The family merely exercised an attribute of sovereignty that nations recognize—the right to punish a traitor—and neighboring families accepted Limitit's act without criticism. But he was guilty according to white man's law, and he received a sentence of twenty years.

About six months before I left the Philippines Bureau of Education I was transferred to the subprovince of Kalinga. Strangely enough, it was there that I was to have, in a single term of court, the most interesting cases of my whole experience.

Not long after I had arrived at Lubuagan, capital of Kalinga, a middle-aged, aristocratic Kalinga named Star God came to me.

"Apo," he said, "I want you to be *abogado*—advocate—for my son when the Apo Juez comes."

"What is he charged with?"

"With killing a man. Do you think, Apo, that the Americans will kill him by machinery?"

"Well, I've heard talk about some such thing. You hill-folk are doing almost as much head-hunting now as before order was established. Why?"

"But, Apo, it was not a case of head-hunting. It was his cousin, who was spoiling my son's wife. Apo, I'm a rich man. Save my boy; I don't care what it costs!"

When the Americans took possession of the Philippines, they found in force a remarkably suitable system of law, codified, terse and equitable. It was the Code promulgated by Napoleon on the Continent and incidentally in Louisiana, where it is still in force. In the Philippines the so-called "unwritten law" is embodied in the Code to this extent: that, if a man legally married surprises his wife and her paramour *in flagrante delicto* and then and there kills either or both, the only penalty imposed is exile of twenty-five kilometers—about fifteen miles—from the site of the crime for two years. The exile is for the peace of the community and the safety of the husband. Our administrators made few changes in the Code and left the provision intact. They also left the Philippines judicial system unencumbered by juries.

The reason why Star God was alarmed lest the Americans kill his son "by machinery" was that recently there had occurred a political upheaval in the United States that had induced one in the Philippines. The Big Apo of the province had been replaced by a tenderfoot lawyer who knew nothing of the hill-folk and made no effort to learn. Not much is required to start the incompletely tamed Malay back to head-hunting; administrative changes of less importance than those made would have been quite sufficient. Head-hunting was revived, and as a preventive measure the delegate appointed to look after the pagan tribes of the Mountain Province had threatened to make head-hunting and murder punishable by death with executions public at the site of the crime.

I had a special interest in taking up the case in question. A man, to be eligible to receive the light penalty for killing his wife's paramour, must be legally married. During the Spanish régime in the Philippines, Church and State had been so united that a marriage ceremony, to be legal, had to be a Roman Catholic one. Persons united in wedlock by Protestant chaplains or missionaries in the days of our military occupation presently discovered that they were not married in a legal sense at all. A commission sent out by President McKinley dealt promptly with the situation, through the enactment of a statute governing marriages. In essence it stipulated that no special form of ceremony was prescribed, but the contracting parties, in the presence of a priest or minister of any religion or of the governor of a province or a judge of the court of first instance (there follows a list of the civil authorities who are authorized to officiate), must have declared their intention to take each other as husband and wife.

Perhaps the Philippines Supreme Court believed that pagan marriages were casual matings such as are fairly frequent among the poorer lowlanders, or perhaps it followed court decisions on American Indian marriages: at any rate it ruled that pagan marriages were not legal within the statute. I felt this decision to be erroneous and unjust. Are not they priests of a religion who pray: "Ancestral spirits and deities of the Sky-world, of the Under-world, of the Down-stream Region and of the Up-stream Region! You are exhorted to increase the soul-stuff of the 'children'—the bride and groom. Increase their rice-supply. Multiply their pigs and chickens. Give them many children, of whom let some be male and some be female." At least these men pray and ceremonialize a whole day at weddings. And, though bride and groom do not make a declaration of intention in words, is not their presence at their own wedding a declaration?

My sense of the wrong done the pagans had been sharpened by having read in the *Official Gazette*, shortly before Star God came to me, a decision of the Supreme Court denying the law's clemency to a pagan convicted of the same crime committed under the same provocation for which Star God's son was being held, on the ground that he was not legally married to his wife. I took the case, expecting to lose but intending to get into evidence the facts in regard to the pagan marriage ceremony, then to appeal and get a lawyer in Manila to handle the case before the Supreme Court.

We went to see the boy, Of-a-Soundness. He was a clean, handsome youth of about eighteen, completely mystified concerning the calamity that had befallen him. I interviewed witnesses and prepared the case as best I could, but ran into obstructions. Tied-Up, the slain, a second or third cousin, was also a first cousin of the *Presidente*, the American-appointed mayor of the region, a wealthy, aggressive man of whom our witnesses were afraid. Star God had a great deal of trouble to get them to come and tell me their story. Of-a-Soundness' wife, Tanggo, had no pity for him, and for her own reputation, if for no other reason, was telling a story quite at variance with his. Her family, of course, took precisely the stand that she did.

This Tanggo was the most beautiful girl I ever saw in the Philippines. Her complexion was like old ivory. Her features and bodily proportions were almost Caucasian, but her eyes had just a trace of slant, and she retained the lovely sloping shoulders and firm rounded breasts of the Malay woman. She would have no words with me, regarding me as an enemy. Self-willed and flirtatious, she was quite capable of causing a great deal more trouble in the world than she had already brought about.

The Judge was a Filipino of mixed blood, a man who would be a credit to any race. At this time there were three white men in the subprovince of Kalinga, the Lieutenant-Governor, a lieutenant of constabulary and I. We joined with the Filipino merchants, clerks and teachers in giving the Judge and his *entourage* a ball. But a book had come in the day's mail (we had three mails a week), and so, leaving the ball at a reasonable hour, I went home. While I was reading in bed, there came a timid rap at the door. In answer to may "Come in," a strange delegation of about ten men entered, most of them with the bearing and strong faces that indicated "centers"—heads of families.

"Apo, we wish you to be our advocate," they said.

They were insistent, but I, feeling that I had enough cases to handle, as persistently refused, and they went away. In a half-hour there came another tap at the door, and the same men entered. The foremost carried grandiosely in front of him a bag made by tying a section of a trousers-leg at one end. He advanced without a word and extended the sack. Looking in, I saw about a quart of silver money of all denominations. Ordinarily I was not paid for defending a case, but these centers, believing I had refused their case because I was not satisfied that I should be paid, had taken up a collection. The curious money-bag and proud bearing of its carrier aroused my interest.

"Well, put the sack over there in the corner," I said, as if such sacks were brought in every day. "What kind of case is this?"

"Cutting off the head of a man."

"Where are you from?"

"Sumadel folk are we."

Theirs was a large town a good half-day's hike away, set in exceedingly steep mountains. Although this town was situated in the subprovince of Kalinga, its people were predominantly Bontocs.

"All right. Tell me about it."

"Apo, it happened thus," said Head-Taker's Wreath, one of the centers, a man of magnificent physique, whose coarse, soot-encrusted features and long black hair falling on begrimed shoulders I have never forgotten. "The Dananao people kept stealing our irrigation-water and killing us besides. They killed one of my grandmothers. Of course we killed them too. The enmity continued after you *Melikanos* came, though there was not so much cutting off of heads. Two years ago, Gofinyachol Haree"—Governor Hale, who had performed the hard work of pacifying the Kalingas and bringing them to a semblance of order—"got us to make peace with Dananao. And we have kept the peace, Apo. It was not our fault we took the head!"

"Not your fault! Do you mean that you took it accidentally?"

"Yes, Apo, by accident. It occurred about two moons ago. A party of Dananao hunters followed a deer into our territory. Galanto, one of our men, was down in a gulch. He was bent over, looking at the tracks of the deer, when one of the Dananao hunters came to the bank above and threw a spear, into him. Balauwag, a boy, who saw Galanto fall, ran to a mountain spur, whence he shouted down to our town: 'The people of Dananao are killing us; they have killed Galanto!' But Galanto only fell—his soul did not leave him. The Dananao man, whose name was Angayon, thought he was dead and ran down to cut off his head. Galanto arose unexpectedly and slashed him in the shoulder. Angayon ran away.

"When the boy shouted to the town that Galanto was dead, there was an outcry of all the people. Those working in the fields rushed in. The men hurried for their shields; their eagerness was great. But we centers told the people: 'There is order now; we must obey the Melikanos. We must not fight Dananao. We must make a report to the Gofinyachol.'" The Center looked to me for approbation of this virtuous command.

Up to this point, the story had seemed to be holding up well to the truth, but I suspected it was now going to sag fearfully. Head-Taker's Wreath probably surmised that his last statement was being questioned. At any rate he bolstered his veracity by adducing evidence to confirm the part of his story I had never doubted.

"Galanto," he said, "come and show the Apo where the spear hit you."

A man came in from the hall, turned his back to me and bent to a right angle, displaying across his rump a great scar as yet hardly healed.

"You see, Apo," said "Head-Taker's Wreath triumphantly, "how the people of Dananao kept the peace!" Then he went on: "The centers told the people that the right thing to do would be to send a delegation to report the matter to the Gofinyachol. So we chose four men. Stand up, Serves-as-a-Hand and Lover's Harp!" Two men out in the hall stood up. "These two men were in the delegation. The other two, Father-of-Landslides and Too-Little, are in the calaboose awaiting the Apo Juez."

I glanced at the two men. They were ordinary poor folk and very young. "About as likely to be appointed delegates as for me to be sent to the Court of St. James!" I said to myself. "Wait," I went on. "What kind of spears did they carry?"

"None," said Head-Taker's Wreath.

Inasmuch as a pagan in those days was almost never without his spear and would certainly not dream of going fifty yards from his village unarmed, this was a daring statement. It took originality to invent it, and the other centers looked at Head-Taker's Wreath, astounded.

"Why should they carry spears on a peaceful mission to the Apo Gofinyachol? Somebody, seeing them, might not understand their peaceful purpose." The unction with which Head-Taker's Wreath said this made me laugh uncontrollably. The Center was pained, but laughter is contagious in all climes; the others caught it, and finally Head-Taker's Wreath laughed too.

"Since the Sumadel folk obey their centers so well, it is clear who will be to blame if any further head-hunting occurs." I said, to restore solemnity. "Go on."

"The men started off, single file. They expected no peril because they were going to make a report to the Apo. But a spear was thrust out of the grass along the trail, wounding Lover's Harp, the foremost. Lover's Harp, show where you were wounded." Lover's Harp advanced, raised his right arm and showed a faint white scar in the armpit, less than two inches long. The wound could have been of skin depth only, and I estimated the scar to be not less than two years old.

"Lover's Harp fell into the arms of his brother, Serves-as-a-Hand. Father-of-Landslides, the third in the line, leaped forward and slashed the man in grass with his ax. Too-Little, the rearmost, cut off the head. They brought it to Sumadel and buried it."

"Did you then perform the head-feast ceremonials?"

"We had to, Apo," Head-Taker's Wreath answered apologetically. "Could we enrage the Great Gods? Of course the young men danced and the old men prayed. But the head was not to be seen. It was buried. We didn't like to leave it to be eaten by wild hogs!"

"And the body out there in the tall grass—was it eaten by wild hogs?"

"We have heard that it was so, Apo; it must have been, because the Dananao people and the police did not find it till the next day."

"Of course, in that case, no spear-wound could have been recognized—in fact, no one could say for sure whose body it was!" I mused, thinking of the *corpus delicti* the fiscal would have to prove in order to convict.

"We have heard that the flesh was eaten from the bones, Apo."

"What about the man who started it all, the man who speared Galanto?"

"We complained against him. On the second day, the constabulary came to Sumadel and took Too-Little and Father-of-Landslides. We centers all came with them to Lubuagan and told the Gofinyachol how the Dananao man had speared Galanto. So the constabulary went and arrested him. He will also come before the Apo Juez—and I hope they kill by machinery!"

"That Dananao man whose head was taken—he must have been crazy to attack a party of four," I remarked, to see what he would say in explanation of a very weak part of his story.

"The ferocity of those Dananao folk! Who can understand why they hate us so? But perhaps he saw only one man when he thrust with his spear. The others were a little behind, and the trail was very crooked. Do you think, Apo, that the government will kill Too-Little and Father-of-Landslides by machinery?"

"That's hard to say. You had better go now, and let me think the case over."

Next morning, with Head-Taker's Wreath, I went to interview my clients in the calaboose. They told the same story I had already heard.

"Which of you really killed him?" I asked. "Did you, Father-of-Landslides, kill him with your head-ax, or did you, Too-Little, kill him when you cut off the head?"

Each began to put the blame on the other. As a matter of fact, I doubt if either knew. When an enemy is down, decapitation follows so quickly that no one has time to note whether the victim is dead or not. I told them the great question was not so much who killed him as whether the killing was done in self-defense.

"Did you tell the Apo Lieutenant anything about the case or put your finger on his pen while he made a mark on paper?" I asked.

"We did not," replied one. "Our father, Head-Taker's Wreath, told us not to tell him one word." It then came out that they were distant poor kin and that Head-Taker's Wreath was center for their family.

When this case was subsequently called in court, the fiscal moved to dismiss, saying he could find no witnesses able to give first-hand evidence. (As a matter of fact, with all but the bones eaten by wild pigs, he probably could not have proved who was killed). The Lieutenant-Governor objected that it would never do to "let those men get away with taking that head," and suggested that they should be punished for cutting the head off, if they could not be for killing the man. "Look up the law, Mr. Fiscal, and see what kind of complaint you might be able to bring against them," ordered the Judge.

The fiscal looked through the Penal Code and reported that it hardly provided for such an emergency—that the best he could do would be to bring a charge of mutilating a corpse, the penalty, for which would be a fine of one hundred *pesetas*—twenty dollars—and a short imprisonment. I suggested that such a punishment might give spectators in the court-room a wrong idea of the penalty for taking a head. The Judge delivered himself of a severe lecture and turned the prisoners loose. The Dananao man who had started the trouble, however, received a rather heavy penalty.

My sincerest sympathy was with Of-a-Soundness, the boy in the other case. He had told all when first arrested and had signed a confession that I was sure was truthful. But the law placed on us the burden of proving that he had slain the main *in delicto*.

"*Oyes! Oyes!* The Court of First Instance in and for the subprovince of Kalinga . . ."

Americans and Filipinos stood up, and the bailiff motioned imperiously for the Kalinga centers who packed the court-room to arise also. The Judge walked in. A ceremony hardly worth the name, yet one that always absorbs the attention of Ifugaos, Kalingas and Bontocs. It is of a sort their own cultures lack utterly.

These Americans, they have noted, pay no attention to magic or to the gods and but little to family ties, but they utilize and obey ceremonies that bind them together and make them act as one man, even though they have individual hatreds and grudges. Some of them manufacture guns and others bring these guns across the ocean, sailing great ships past the perilous "navel of the seas," put the guns in the hands of picked warriors in every tribe and drill these warriors through a ritual of march, countermarch, extending and closing ranks, with all the snap and precision of the locks of the guns themselves. And then they pay these folk, whom they use to extend their power, with money of whose manufacture they have also discovered the secret. Thus their group has become mighty, and surely there must be great virtue in their ceremonies. Whether civilized or uncivilized, the Philippine Malay has long been ready for, or at least desirous of, a social progress that he never, of himself, has attained. Perhaps the torpor of the tropics and his own intense personal pride have hindered.

"The United States versus Of-a-Soundness," called the clerk. The indictment was read, and I entered a plea of "Not guilty."

The confession, admitted into evidence, was in substance that for some time before the crime Of-a-Soundness had been aware of improper relations between his wife and Tied-Up; that ten days before the crime he had asked his father to remonstrate with Tied-Up regarding this most uncousinly behavior and to threaten him with death if he kept it up; that Star God had spoken to Tied-Up and Tied-Up had promised not to offend again. About sunset of the day of the crime, some Kalinga constabulary soldiers encamped at the river about a mile down the mountainside from the village. Tanggo, the wife, told Of-a-Soundness she had been informed that a kinsman of hers and a kinsman of his were in the detachment, and suggested that he go down and invite them to the house for a visit. He went, but found no kinsmen. His suspicions were aroused. Returning by a roundabout path and not finding his wife at home, he left his spear and took his head-ax. When he came upon the couple together, he set upon Tied-Up, who ran away. He followed, slashing whenever he could and finally inflicting a mortal wound.

Three or four prosecution witnesses testified that Tied-Up and Tanggo had not been together that night. Ongay and Bayinay, two girls of about seventeen, testified that Tied-Up, a cousin of theirs, had been sitting on a stone wall all the evening blackening his teeth after the fashion of Kalingas, and that Of-a-Soundness had set upon Tied-Up while he was thus beautifying himself.

"Were Of-a-Soundness and Tanggo legally married?" I asked two or three witnesses. One interpreter put the question into the Ilokano dialect, another into Kalinga. "Of course they were properly married," the witnesses answered. Since the fiscal made no effort to show that the marriage was a tribal one, it seemed best to let a sleeping dog lie, and I did not use the evidence I had prepared on the Kalinga marriage.

At last, in the stifling hot court-room, the evidence was in, and the court was asked what counsel had to say. The fiscal argued that whatever the past relations between Tanggo and Tied-Up might have been, the evidence showed that the two were merely sitting on the wall the evening of the attack. He held that inflicting sixteen wounds was a cruel manner of slaying, comparable to the Chinese execution by slicing; it looked as if there had been pre-meditation, too, but he would not press the point, since there were already enough aggravating circumstances to get the savage hanged. In the Philippines nocturnity, treachery, premeditation, cruelty or the use of poison in committing a homicide are circumstances that add to the severity of the punishment.

The evidence in regard to whether or not the defendant had found his wife and the deceased *in delicto* was highly conflicting, and no amount of argument could make it anything else. The burden of proof rested with the defense, but the court did not feel that I had proved the point. The Judge reached for his copy of the Penal Code and turned to the tabulation of *penalties.* I felt he was about to give a sentence of twelve to fifteen years. As a last resort, I asked to be allowed to call Tanggo to the stand, or, if this was not permitted, Ongay, one of the prosecution witnesses. An American court would never have tolerated such an irregularity of program—I could have recalled witnesses before the arguments, but not after. But the Judge wanted to decide the case aright, and Ongay was recalled.

"When was Of-a-Soundness arrested?"

"Three months ago."

"Who arrested him?"

"The *Presidente.*"

"What is your relationship to the *Presidente?*"

"He is my uncle."

"Is he the center of your family group?"

"Yes."

"Did he ever talk to you about this case?"

"Never."

"Your Honor, it is incredible that the *Presidente* did not talk to her both as a member of his family and as a witness of the killing—if she is a witness."

"Probably so, but the court cannot feel that the essential part of her testimony has been impeached."

Now came two or three minutes that seemed an hour. There can be no more agonizing situation than having the fate of another in your hands and not knowing the technique of saving him. By chance I asked, "What were you doing when you first saw Of-a-Soundness attack Tied-Up?"

"I was on the wall, blackening my teeth."

There came into my head a note I had made some time before: "Blackening the teeth is done by groups of mixed sexes who mutually assist each other, and is somehow correlated with sex and with exogamy.

Kin of the other sex may not be present." I felt on safe ground now, and the world grew brighter.

"You say that Tied-Up was your cousin?"

"Yes."

"You were blackening your teeth with your cousin?"

The witness showed some embarrassment as she replied. "He was not blackening his teeth."

"Where was he?"

"Sitting on the wall apart from us."

"How far away?"

She took a long time to consider how far away she could put him for decency's sake and still cling to her testimony that she had been in sight of him all evening. Finally she replied, "About twelve arm-spans."

"And now, Your Honor, I request that that portion of the witness' testimony in which she tells about the beginning of the attack be read from the record."

The clerk read out the following passage:

"Q. Where was Tied-Up? A. Sitting on the wall. Q. What was he doing? A. Just sitting there blackening his teeth. Q. State what happened. A. Of-a-Soundness came running out of the coffee-bushes behind. He didn't say anything, but I screamed to Tied-Up to run."

"Your Honor, I submit that the witness has lied, one time or the other."

"Yes," said the Judge, "she has."

I looked at Of-a-Soundness and felt irritated that he sat impassive, not knowing what a crucial moment it was in his life.

"Cause the defendant to stand," ordered the Judge. Then he pronounced sentence: "Of-a-Soundness, the Court finds you guilty of the crime of homicide, but with the extenuating circumstances mentioned in section so-and-so of the Penal Code, and sentences you to exile for two years at a distance at twenty-five kilometers from the site of the crime." He paused for a moment and then continued; "But some provision ought to be made for this boy during the two years he will be away from home. He ought to have something to keep him busy, whereby he can earn his living."

"If Your Honor will dictate a letter to the Provincial Board explaining the circumstances, it is probable they will find employment for him."

The Judge dictated the letter. Meantime, Of-a-Soundness—pending his transfer to Bontoc—was being put in shackles and led back to the calaboose between two *soldiers* with fixed bayonets. His father had heard the sentence but probably did not understand it. "Apo," he said, "is it good or bad?"

"Good. Go and tell him so."

He shook his head, incredulous.

Five days later I telephoned the warden at Bontoc Prison and asked him to call Of-a-Soundness to the phone. Star God was waiting outside the door. He had never talked on the telephone before. He recognized his son's voice, but his ears were pounding so with excitement that he could hardly understand and had to ask continually for repetitions. Finally he turned from the telephone. Never have I seen the stolid Malay countenance so lighted up.

"Apo, he says that he eats and sleeps at the prison, but he is not locked up nor made to work, and the food is very good and he comes and goes as he pleases. He says two great Apos are very kind to him. One is the Apo at the hospital. That Apo is said to kill the sick ones sometimes, cut out the sickness with knives and then make them live again. Is that true, Apo? I cannot tell you all he says, but he says, but he says the Apo of the sick is going to teach him how to take care of the sick ones—and give him a salary!" That salary it was, no doubt, that made the cup overflow. For, though not especially fond of wages, any Malay prizes a salary almost as his right arm.

"How much do I owe you, Apo?" asked Star God with a touch of trepidation. remembering, probably, his rash offers when fearing his son would be killed by machinery.

"I worked hard on that case. Bring me the head-ax that belonged to Of-a-Soundness and whatever else you want to."

Star God hurried to his village, a half-day's journey away. Late that night he rapped at the door. Entering, he delivered the head-ax and ninety dollars. He then sat on the floor, silent for a time. I asked him what he was thinking about.

"Apo, I shame to tell you. It is against the custom."

"But I am an American. Probably it is not against my custom."

"Do the kin of the girl ever arrange marriages in America, Apo?"

"Yes, the girl's mother always tries to."

"My daughters are all married, but my brother has one who is a widow. You would have to wait for her to grow up—she has many fields—I myself would pay the kin of the dead husband the indemnity for her remarriage," he offered. "And, Apo"—the conservative old man found it hard to say this—"the girl is pretty—large for her age—whitish of skin."

I felt very uncomfortable that the old fellow should break his custom on my account, at a cost of such agony. The fee and his gratitude I felt I deserved, but hardly this. So I never saw the proffered bride.

"No doubt you advise me well," I said. "But I have to return to America. My parents have ordered it, and I have to obey. I shall be gone in a month or two."

R.S. FREED

The Legal Process in a Village in North India: The Case of Maya

The complexity of folk law cases in India where there exist competing folk law systems: national, village, family, is well illustrated by the following case reported by anthropologist Ruth. S. Freed of New York University. Just as Barton recounted a case from the Philippines in which a son felt legally justified in killing his father, so in north India we have a case in which a father felt obliged or compelled to kill his own daughter. Once again such cases remind us of the relativity of individual folk law systems and their underlying codes of ethics and morality.

For further information about the case of Maya the reader may wish to consult the monograph Ghosts: Life and Death in North India *(New York: American Museum of Natural History, 1993) in which Ruth S. Freed and Stanley A. Freed discuss the influence of Maya's ghost (see chapters 15 & 21; Maya is referred to under the pseudonym, Illusion). See also Upendra Baxi,* The Crisis of the Indian Legal System: Alternatives in Development Law *(Delhi: Vikas Publishing House Pvt. Ltd.*, 1982, Chapter 11).

A young girl died in the village of Kurukshetra† in North India. She was immediately cremated. Her name was Maya: she was the daughter of Dharma, a Brahman. At first, she was reported to have died of cholera during the night, but, within hours of the first reports, relatives and neighbors were telling tales to the effect that the girl was pregnant, that the pregnancy was not caused by her husband but rather was due to adultery in her natal village, and that, therefore, her father killed and cremated her. The village watchman, whose duties include reporting births and deaths, informed the police that Maya had died of cholera. The police never investigated her death, for no villagers went to the

Reprinted from *Transactions of the New York Academy of Sciences*, Series II, 33(4) (1971), 423–435, with permission of the Annals of the New York Academy of Sciences and the author.

† Because of the nature of this case. I have masked the identity of the village, the individuals involved, and the years. The case of Maya took place in North India in a relatively recent decade.

police with a different version even though for almost a year thereafter they discussed the case. Although villagers gave varying reports of how she died, most accounts centered around the themes of illicit pregnancy, adultery, and killing and cremation by her father.

The analysis of the case of Maya reveals the nature of the legal process in the North village of Kurukshetra. The concepts of levels of law is important in understanding this case and the legal process, for not only are there two parallel sets of laws, those of the nation and those of the village, but within the village there are levels of law that are specific to caste, lineage, and family.[1,2] Each of these takes over where the other leaves off. At first it seems as though the death of Maya occasions no case in law, but analysis of subsequent events delineates what the law is and how it is handled at village, lineage, and family level rather than by police and through the courts. Beyond this, the law in the case of Maya provides an encapsulated representation of the culture of the village community in terms of its structure and values.

What the villagers conceive of as just might not be so deemed in the courts under the modern criminal code of India. Although it may seem that village and national law are in conflict, this proves not to be the case. At no time were the police informed of what happened. Had they been, they might have investigated the death of Maya as either homicide or murder. There were, however, two young men in the village who were policemen; they were in the same lineage as Maya and yet took no action. They were cognizant of the events leading up to her death. This suggests that policemen in this part of India investigate deaths and enforce the criminal code of law at the village level only if compelled to do so by complaints of villagers, especially when the policeman is himself a villager. The understanding of these levels of unwritten law at the village level is basic to understanding the case of Maya, for family, lineage, and caste laws take precedence over village law, and village law takes precedence over Federal law, providing that the individuals are within the circle or level of law involved.

Law in India still has its roots in Hinduism. Many principles that prevail today derive from the Laws of Manu, which in turn derive from the earlier *dharmasutras*. The primary basis of these principles is the concept of dharma, right conduct or ethical behavior, which in early times was laid down for castes, families, and individuals. Within this tradition, the state or kind interfered as little as possible with the individual. An individual was guided by neighbors, caste brotherhood, or village council. The villagers observed their own rules. Only when an infraction of rules occurred beyond the authority of the village did the individual resort to a higher power than that in the immediate community. The shifting rulers and kingdoms down through the centuries, including the British, fostered this tradition, which has persisted in Kurukshetra.[3,4]

Family or private law even today in Kurukshetra is consistent with Maine's theory that each family is like a corporation, with the male as the head or authority figure who enforces the law within the family and negotiates with other family heads in matters between families. A corollary of this is that all members of the family are in a position of status to the head. He has duties and obligations to them, but also the power of life and death over them. Family, or private, law operates separately from public law.[5] Under such a system of law, cases are settled, so to speak, out of court, with no formal procedures, and the head of the family may be both judge and executioner.[1]

A female is similar to a chattel or personal property in this system of family law because she is transferred through the marriage alliance, which consists of a series of transactions symbolized by ceremonies during which the girl passes to the family of the bridegroom.[2] The girl in these transactions has no say in the arrangements. These are undertaken by the male heads of the two families concerned in the same way that an officer might act for a corporation or for a club. In the series of transactions, exclusive sexual rights to the girl are vested in the groom, and rights to her offspring are vested in the family of the in-laws.[6] Obligations to the girl and her offspring are perpetuated for an indefinite period of time in her natal family. The transference of the rights in the girl is accomplished through a marriage system that enforces village and clan incest taboos and caste endogamy. The case of Maya pivots on this marriage system.

The investigation and analysis of this case proceeds along a sequence of events. Since the anthropology of law is the study of processes by which a case comes into being and by which it is settled, the sequence of events are those which lead to the death of Maya, the death itself, and the subsequent events and consequences following the death. The history of the case follows the development of interpersonal relations, family conflicts and problems, and the legal means by which they are settled.[1] The nucleus of these events starts with Maya's marriage and ends with her death. The questions asked are: (1) Who was Maya? (2) How did she die? (3) Why did she die? (4) What events led to her death, and how are they related to values, marriage, kinship, and land inheritance in Kurukshetra? (5) What evidence is there from subsequent events and reports to indicate how the case was settled? (6) What crime was committed, and how was it punished? The concluding question is (7) What is the law in this case?

Who Was Maya?

In this area of North India, village, caste, clan, and family are four identity symbols immediately communicated in encountering strangers. These symbols place the individual in a reference system of social status and expected role behavior. They provide the bases of Maya's identity. Sex and age are relatively apparent and require no additional identity symbols, but they are pertinent.

Maya died in her natal village. Her identity starts there. She was a Brahman girl of the Gōr caste and the Bhardwaj clan. Just before her death, her age was given by her mother as 15. About a year prior to her death, Maya had married and visited her in-laws and husband, but the marriage had not been consummated. She still lived in the household of her father, Dharma. The house is situated is a cul-de-sac in what is called Brahman Lane. This lane is the oldest section of the village settled by members of the Bhardwaj clan, and all of the families with property sites on the lane trace their descent from a Bhardwaj ancestor and constitute a lineage. The lineage consists of eight households. Each of the families in these households has property in Brahman Lane, and all but two of them have their main building there. Two exceptions reside on the peripheries of the village but maintain and use the ancestral sites.

At the dead end of Brahman Lane are the buildings and cattle sheds of Maya's father and Harischandra, her father's cousin. These two families are directly involved in the case of Maya. Dharma and Harischandra are cousins by descent from the same great grandfather in the patrilineage. Some background information on both families is essential to understanding the case. When both men were children, they lived under the authority of Dharma's father, Pandu, because Harischandra's father had died before he was born. He was his widowed mother's only child. The two boys grew up together. At the time of Maya's death, Harischandra was 41; Dharma, 34. Both men had gone to school. Harischandra finished higher secondary school; Dharma did not. When Dharma was 18. Harischandra got him a job in the factory in which he worked. However, Dharma did not stay there but returned to the village to farm the family land.

Dharma later separated from his father and his brother, and he and Harischandra arranged to share living quarters, cattle sheds, and other space. Dharma worked the land while Harischandra commuted to work for the railway. Harischandra had 2.1 acres of land, which he inherited from his father; Dharma had 0.4 of an acre, which he received on separating from his father and brother. The postindependence legislation of the 1950s provided occupancy tenants with rights to claim ownership of the land they cultivated as tenants.[7] As a result of this legislation, Harischandra and Dharma separated. Harischandra built himself a brick house; Dharma continued living in the old mud house. But, of more consequence, Harischandra thereafter farmed his own land in even years and hired a different person every odd year to plow it. Thus, Dharma was deprived of a partial share in a crop on which he had come to depend and no longer farmed land he may have considered almost his own. It should be pointed out that Harischandra and Dharma did not hold their land jointly, although they lived together. Because Harischandra and Dharma's fathers had the same patrilineal grandfather and there were no more immediate heirs, had Harischandra died as a child or without issue, his land would have reverted to Pandu and his sons.

Dharma represented the traditional villager in that he farmed, wore the dhoti, and interacted primarily with his lineage, caste, and villagers. He was taciturn and gave the impression of strength and dominance. His family consisted of a wife and five children. None of the females, including Maya, had gone to school. The workload of the family was heavy when the age and sex of the individuals are taken into consideration. Only his wife and Maya helped him with the work; his two sons, 10 and 12, attended school. The other girls were too small to work. In addition to cultivating his 0.4 of an acre in vegetables, Dharma farmed 13.1 acres of land on shares for a Jat (farmer caste) who was in military service. (Military personnel are exempt from occupancy tenancy claims). This contractual tenancy arrangement, however, was subject to yearly investigation by government officials, so that Dharma was always anxious about his main source of income. To work this and his own land, he owned two bullocks and his own plow and hired laborers at peak periods in the agricultural season.

Harischandra, in contrast, was urbanized in appearance and experience. He is best described as an anxiety-ridden man who, in attempting to please everyone, pleased no one. Because he commuted to work daily, he had little time for the affairs of his lineage, caste, and village. He seemed uninvolved in village life. His family consisted of a son, Arjuna, 17 years of age, who during the week lived in the town where his school was located and on weekends came home to help with the farming. As a result, he knew little of village life. He was an earnest young man, with high ideals, taking his schooling quite literally, devoted to his mother, and often disappointed and frustrated by his father, to whom he looked for support but who was indecisive and weak. The other children in the family were much younger: a boy 3 years of age; two girls of 1 and 6. Harischandra earned 135 rupees a month (at the time one rupee was equivalent to 21 cents), and he received other benefits from his job; he was considered well off by village standards, though by no means as well off as the large landholders in the village.

The teen-age youngsters in these two families, Maya and Arjuna, were reported to be close, like real brother and sister. Though cousins in the patrilineage, the relationship and living arrangements reenforced the ideal pattern of behavior expected between real brothers and sisters and also patrilateral parallel cousins.

The wives of Dharma and Harischandra, respectively, were Aditi and Devi, real sisters, a further link between these two families. However while Aditi was illiterate, quiet, and subdued, and looked old and worn, Devi, though some years older, was the opposite. She could read a little, was fun-loving, always dressed attractively, and moved around the village more freely than any other woman of childbearing age in the village. This was her main trouble. Some months prior to Maya's death, Devi had been caught in a liaison with a member of the Jat caste. This conduct had occurred on other occasions also, for the year previously it was said that she had been beaten by the village Brahmans. Her actions were to have repercussions on her family, to contribute to the deterioration of the relationship between the families of Dharma and Harischandra, and to affect village opinion in the case of Maya.

Although the personalities of Dharma, Harischandra, Devi, Aditi, and Arjuna are fairly clear, Maya never comes into focus with a personality of her own. It is as though no one paid attention to her while she lived; and after she died, the acts leading to her death seem to be all that remained. She was an illusory figure in the whole sad story. For a year after her death, no one spoke of her as having any distinguishing or endearing characteristics, as being loved or hated, stupid or intelligent, pretty, or ugly. Other than her mother, who said she missed her, all that anyone said was that she died, that her father killed and cremated her, and that she had had an illicit pregnancy. This last fact put her beyond the pale of further comment, for in the value system of Brahmans and the marriage system of the village, the chastity of the female is important. On it depends the honor and prestige of family and kin. What little was known of her indicated that she followed the usual pattern of young females, effacing herself before elders, that she lived in a family that was so hard-pressed economically that they had little or no time for a show of affection or appreciation, and that at the time of her death, she may not have known what was going to happen to her, although she probably feared the worst.

How Did She Die?

On the evening of June 23, an old Brahman woman, Satti Urmila, reported that Maya was ill, probably from cholera; she had eaten melon and drunk cold water afterward, and her stomach was swollen. Later that evening, her son, Satya Narayan, a close friend of Harischandra, said that the village had not had a case of cholera in many years and that Maya did not have cholera. The following morning, these two informants said that Maya had died at 4 a.m. and that her father cremated her immediately. Then both Satya Narayan and his mother said that Maya was five months pregnant, that the conception was the result of Maya's relations with a male in Kurukshetra, that when Maya went to visit her in-laws and they found out she was pregnant, they sent her back to her father, and that Dharma then hanged and cremated her. The stories of how Maya died were to veer and shift depending on the person telling the story, intervening events, and the degree to which the informants were involved with, or members of, the families of Dharma and Harischandra and their lineage. In general, however, all concerned the same elements: adultery, illicit pregnancy, sometimes incest, and death at the hands of the father.

Why Did She Die?

In American systems of law, the killing of young girls because they are pregnant, through either fornication or adultery, is seldom countenanced by courts. There are reservations with regard to adultery, for the "unwritten law" with respect to murder motivated by adultery may still be invoked, especially in a jury trial. Adultery, however, has some basis for being considered a universal crime. Hoebel notes that it is universal on the primitive level and general on the civilized level for the law to allow a husband to kill his wife caught in the act of adultery. For the law to allow the wife to kill her husband is rare.[8] Maya was not caught *in flagrante delicto*, but her death was attributed to an illicit pregnancy caused by adultery. To understand why her father killed her, if indeed he did, it is necessary to know why Maya's pregnancy was illicit and why she was adulterous.

What Events Led to Her Death, and How Are They Related to Marriage, Kinship, and Land Inheritance in Kurukshetra?

Descent is patrilineal. Residence after marriage is patrilocal. The male Brahmans in the village and their offspring are Gōr Brahmans of the Bhardwaj clan. The wives and mothers of these men are members of different clans but the same caste. The daughters of Bhardwaj Brahmans marry men from other than the Bhardwaj clan but of the same caste. Thus, there is both clan and village exogamy and caste endogamy. Within the village of Kurukshetra, all of the male Brahmans claim descent from one founding male ancestor, although they recognize that some of the families in the three Bhardwaj lineages in the village have perpetuated their lines through sanctioned adoption of a male heir, and also that other of the Bhardwaj families derive from ancestors who settled in the village after the original founding ancestor.

The land that the Brahman families own was supposedly granted to the founding ancestor and has descended through many generations and been divided through separation of joint households from time to time. The land is conceived of as going hand in hand with the genealogy or descent from the founding ancestor. It is always in the back of a man's mind that if he dies and has no sons, the land will revert to the next male in the line of succession. It is also in the mind of the male next in succession that he will inherit the land if his relative has no offspring, i.e., if he or his children die without male issue. Any clouding of the line of succession could cause serious conflict about land rights. This pattern regarding heirs is similar for all landowners in the area. Thus, when Dharma arranged for the marriage of Maya to a youth in another village, he knew that having a clear line of male heirs would be important to the family of the in-laws.

Parents arrange marriages for their children. The initiative for a marriage starts with her father of the girl. Acting upon information supplied by friends and relatives, the father visits many villages seeking a suitable husband for his daughter. In so doing, he looks for families who are not of his own clan, his mother's clan, or his mother's mother's clan. The bridegroom's side must likewise be sure that the girl's side is not of the groom's clan, his mother's clan, or his mother's mother's clan. This is the general rule regarding marriage that the Bhardwaj-Gōr Brahmans follow. There are a few men in the village who speak of further degrees of kin relationships on the father's and mother's sides, but they are not exactly sure what they are.[9]

The main thrust of these prohibited marriages is to avoid marriage with members of the Bhardwaj clan, secondly, with those who may be related through males or females on the boy's and girl's sides. The rule these Brahmans follow falls short of the classical injunctions of the Mitakshara.[9] In fact, the Brahmans of Kurukshetra have reduced and subsumed relationships through close kin for seven degrees on the father's side and four degrees on the mother's by combining them under a clan prohibition for father, mother, and mother's mother.

When a boy is found who meets these marriage rules, negotiations start that, if successful, result in a series of ceremonial transactions. The most important of these are the engagement, the boy's initiation rite just before marriage, and the marriage feasts and ceremonies. Immediately thereafter comes the first visit of the bride to her in-laws, a visit of one day and night, followed by her return to her natal village. Finally, at the request of the groom's family, the bride comes on her second visit and the marriage is consummated.

These transactions may take from one year to many years, depending on the ages of the bride and groom at the time of marriage. Beginning, however, with the engagement party, the families have a contractual arrangement that is considered binding. This promises that the parents of the girl will give her to the boy when she comes of age sexually, usually around fifteen, and that the boy will have exclusive sexual rights in the girl from the time of engagement and thereafter. He and his family will also have exclusive rights to her labor and her offspring. A series of gifts are exchanged by both sides, including an arranged dowry from the girl's side, during the many ceremonial transactions to make the engagement and marriage binding on both families. The marriage takes place any time after the engagement party but should take place by the time the girl attains physical maturity. The arrangement is between the families. Once the central rite of marriage, the circumambulation of the sacred fire and the tying together of the garments of the bride and groom, has been completed, the jural rights to the girl and to her offspring pass irrevocably to the family of the groom. Thereafter, the husband is recognized as both the jural and biological father of her children. This assures him and his descendants of a clear claim of descent in the patrilineage and land inheritance rights.[6]

At the time of Maya's death, she was in a transitional position, i.e., in the last stages of a series of transactions that would transfer her permanently from her natal village to her husband's village. All of the proper observances prior to this stage had been carried out. She had been engaged by her parents some years previously, went through the marriage ceremony a year before her death, supposedly around 14–15 years of age, and then visited her husband's village chaperoned by her brother. She spent one night there in the company of her mother-in-law and sisters-in-law, as is customary. Then Maya returned to her parents' village and stayed with them for one year before visiting her husband for the second time. Thus, up to the time of the second visit, the bride and groom had had no opportunity to be alone together and there had been no sexual union.

Before the second visit, there is a public display in the girl's village of the gifts she takes as the second part of her dowry. This announces publicly the final step in the marriage transactions—the second visit of the girl to her husband. Maya's gift display occurred on May 28. The gifts consisted of five cots loaded with clothes and bedding; a line on which were hung clothing, a quilt, and toys. When one woman commented on the "charming" toys, Maya's mother said, "They are for the groom's little sister. She can keep them to play with or give them away—whatever she wants." This remark may have been an index of Aditi's anxiety about the way in which Maya would be received by her in-laws, or it may have been the customary village reaction to compliments.

Just prior to the second visit, Aditi had indicated that Maya was 15. Later, a number of informants questioned her age; and Devi indicated that she was older than Arjuna and, therefore, could have been 19 or 20 years old. Often, after a marriage has been consummated, a girl may be found to be from one to five years older than her parents warranted. It is the ideal pattern for a girl to be married and to have gone to her husband for the second visit shortly after she reaches menarche; for it is considered risky to have a young female of physical maturity without a husband. Parents, however, put off marrying their daughters and sending them to their in-laws for a variety of reasons: They may need the girl to help with the work; they may not have the money to pay for the wedding and dowry; and they may be reluctant to part with their daughter. In the case of Maya's parents, all three reasons would have been valid if in fact Maya was closer to 20 years of age than to 15.

On May 31, Maya went to her husband's village. On June 9, Harischandra's mother's brother came to Kurukshetra to work out the details for the engagement party of Arjuna, which took place June 20. At this party, all of the members of the two families of Dharma and Harischandra were present. Also, there were senior representatives from each house in the lineage in Brahman Lane and representatives from leading houses in other lineages of Brahmans and Jats. There was a scattered representation of other castes, including the Nai (barber) who served the family of Harischandra. The gathering of men at Arjuna's engagement constituted a panchayat, witnesses to the engagement.

When the formal transactions and arrangements for the future marriage had been concluded, the young women and girls present sang a series of songs to celebrate the engagement. Maya was among those singing.

She had apparently returned to the village unannounced some weeks previously. Three nights later she was to die.

What Evidence Was There From Subsequent Events and Reports to Indicate How the Case Was Settled?

A timetable of events indicates:

Maya went to her in-laws on May 30.

She probably was returned to her parents immediately on the discovery of her pregnancy, say between May 31 and June 2.

The formal arrangement for Arjuna's engagement began on June 9.

The formal engagement party occurred June 20, at which time Maya was present.

Early in the morning of June 23, Maya died and was cremated.

On June 30, the mother-in-law of Maya together with women from her village walked through Kurukshetra weeping—a mourning party for Maya. One person said that the practice of public mourning in the village streets had been abandoned some 15 to 20 years previously. Since on this occasion the village elders allowed this display, was it perhaps a face-saving camouflage for both families and, possibly, a protective device? If so, it would indicate that the family of the in-laws was in accord with Dharma's actions.

From June 24 through May 30 of the following year, the versions of Maya's death varied around a norm. Most of them confirmed the earliest report, but from time to time there were slight variations. The main facts were that she was from three to six months pregnant and that she died because her father hanged her. A few alternative versions were that her father might have poisoned her or that she died from an abortion or from illness. Some informants named a specific man as being the partner in Maya's adultery, but more often three to five males were named as possibilities. These were members of her lineage, men closely involved with Maya's or Harischandra's family, including her own father and Arjuna, or men who had a reputation for having affairs with women. The most often mentioned were adult males who had no wives. The men accused were members of the Brahman, Jat, and Nai castes, so that the mating might have been in violation of familial, lineage, and village incest taboos and/or caste endogamy. Where a wide network of suspects was given, Arjuna was never included. Whether this list of names served as camouflage or was simply a speculative list of the most likely possibilities could not be ascertained.

On July 10, Aditi talked about Maya's death. She mentioned that her daughter was a great help to her and recalled that the family had spent more money for the second visit than they could afford. In describing the last day of Maya's life, she said, "Maya did not have a fever when she died. A swami gave her an enema because Maya's stomach was swollen. She was sick an afternoon and an evening. She fell on her cot and never said anything again. Once she got up and ran out of the house, but I held her arms down and put her back on the cot. Then she never talked or did anything again." Over and over, Aditi repeated that Maya's stomach was swollen. None of the other versions paralleled Aditi's. Her description does not gibe with the symptoms for cholera: fever, vomiting, diarrhea, dehydration, and a course of three days' illness.[10] It sounded more like the grief-stricken attempt of a guilt-ridden woman to cover up for her husband. The constant emphasis in some of the versions of Maya's death of her stomach's being swollen, even in the few versions attempting to cover up the pregnancy and hanging, seem to indicate an inability to get away from the fact of Maya's pregnancy.

For example, two days after Maya's death, one of the women in Bhima's household (one of the families in the Brahman Lane lineage) said, "Maya was all right in the morning; then at 1 P.M. she started to vomit. She had just returned from the reception of a Jat marriage party. When her mother returned from the fields, she found Maya's stomach swollen and very big, but there was no diarrhea. God wanted it like this." Here the blacksmith's wife intervened with the information that Maya had just returned from the second visit to her husband and noted that this was the time of first sexual union. Then she said, "If a girl is not sent to her husband for the second visit when she reaches maturity, she might become pregnant. But there has never been a case like this in the village. If this should happen, the husband's family might desert the girl. Or the husband or the girl's family might kill her, but this has never happened in this village." Thus, the blacksmith's wife gave a clear account of the situation, but with considerable tact and indirection because, perhaps, of the proximity of the Brahman woman.

Some months later, when Maya's death was again discussed, Satti Urmila clearly stated that she was pregnant. Her granddaughter then suggested that she shouldn't talk about the matter because of the prestige of Brahmans. Satti Urmila then veered to the subject of the evil eye and how Saibya, Harischandra's mother, was the only person in the village known to have it.

Again, on another occasion, the women from Bhima's and the blacksmith's household were discussing the members of Harischandra's house, and the blacksmith's wife said "Devi has a bad character; she doesn't look to her future or to the past" (meaning that she does not take care of her own or her family's reputation). "Harischandra is nice and very gentle, Arjuna just a child living away from home and going to school." Then she noted that Saibya, Harischandra's widowed mother, had always behaved properly in raising Harischandra but that "she gives the evil eye. No one says anything to her about it because she might start fighting."

A report from Devi shortly after Maya's death was that Dharma had started to hang Maya, when Harischandra intervened and begged Dharma not to kill her. Harischandra promised that he would get the girl an abortion, but Dharma refused and hanged her. A month later, Devi again referred to the hanging and said that Dharma had threatened Harischandra and made him put his arms around his son, Arjuna, swearing on his life that he would not report the matter to the police.

For a year after the death of Maya, the family of Harischandra was weighed down with worry. Harischandra was reported unable to sleep or eat. A month after Maya's death, he fell from a train because "he thought the police were coming for him" and he was taken to a hospital. Conversations with Devi indicated that he was anxiety stricken because of Maya's death but was mainly afraid that Dharma was going to kill him. Dharma was said to have threatened to do so if he went to the police.

As a result, there were a series of fights and disputes between the two families. On two occasions the police were called by Arjuna and Devi. Each fight had a specific cause: the first about the property rights of Harischandra and Dharma; the second about threats to Devi from the lineage because of her behavior. When the police arrived, the village elders immediately formed a panchayat to show the police they could handle the matter. Then the police and the panchayat discussed the nature of each complaint. At no time was Maya's death brought to the attention of the police. The way in which these police visits were handled indicated that the lineage and village stood behind Dharma. Complaining to the police, however, protected the lives of Harischandra, Arjuna, and Devi. Who would attempt to kill them after the complaints were on the police record?

The position of the lineage became obvious when Bhoj Lal, its nominal leader, did not invite Harischandra's family to the wedding of his son the following February. More to the point, at the time of Arjuna's wedding in April, none of the Brahmans in the village helped with the ceremonies, nor did they attend. The Jats, the dominant political group, sent representatives and helped secure Brahmans from a nearby village in order that the marriage might take place. The actions of the village Brahmans amounted to an outcasting in the immediate community.

In May, almost a year after Maya's death, Bhagwan, a close friend of Arjuna and the son of Satya Narayan, discussed the case in confidence. He said Arjuna was the male in question and that Devi, his mother, had fostered the affair. He based this opinion on an occurrence one day in Harischandra's house when he and Arjuna were studying together on the second floor. Devi called Arjuna downstairs, where Maya was bathing. Somehow Bhagwan caught a glimpse of her "naked in her bath" and from this implied that Devi encouraged Arjuna to see her thus. Bhagwan said that Arjuna immediately ran upstairs because he knew Bhagwan "had seen everything."

Bhagwan explained the death of Maya thus: When Dharma found the girl to be pregnant, he had two choices: he could send her to her in-laws or he could kill her. If he killed her immediately, the in-laws might make trouble and even file a complaint. (There had been a case of this sort a few years back in the village.) Also, he would not be sure of 100% village support. If he sent her to the in-laws, there were two possibilities: they might keep her even though pregnant, for they were gentle people; or they might send her back. If they sent her back, they were tacitly telling Dharma that it was all right to kill the girl. The village would then know that Dharma had exhausted all possibilities and had no other choice. Maya was sent to her in-laws even though she was pregnant, and shortly thereafter she was returned to her father, leaving him no alternative but to kill the girl. The village was clearly with Dharma on this. Feeling had shifted away from Harischandra mainly because he was unstable and afraid—i.e., they could not tell which way he would turn, and they did not want the police called into the village.

What Crime Was Committed? How Was It Punished?

Because the police were never called and because Dharma was in no way punished, he was not guilty of any crime at the village level. He killed his daughter, but he did not murder her. Instead of being a murderer, he was the judge and executioner of Maya. She committed the crimes. The first crime of which she was guilty was adultery. The evidence for the adultery is based on her marriage a year prior to her death, at which time there had been no consummation of the union, the fact that she became pregnant during a time when she was living in her natal and not her husband's village, and that she went to her husband for the second visit—the occasion for consummation—only when she was already three to six months pregnant. This evidence also substantiates the second crime of which she was guilty: incest.

Since Maya conceived in her natal village, the male partner was either a member of her lineage or clan or a member of another caste. If he was a member of her lineage or clan, she committed clan incest; if of her lineage, Arjuna, for example, then she committed an even more serious kind of incest, i.e., with one's patrilateral parallel cousin, similar to a sibling. If the relationship was with a member of another caste in the village, she violated the rule of village incest, i.e., this rule maintains that everyone in the village is fictively related[11] and perpetuates a system of marrying out of one's village. If of an other caste, she also violated the rule of caste endogamy. The most likely conclusion based on village opinion is that she committed incest with Arjuna, her patrilateral parallel cousin.

The weight of the evidence indicated that Dharma had hanged his daughter. Abortion although mentioned by a few witnesses, seems unlikely in the light of Devi's, Satya Narayan's, and Bhagwan's evidence, especially since Maya was at least three months pregnant and possibly as much as six. It would be too risky for a village midwife to undertake, and there was no evidence that Maya was taken to the city for an abortion. Cholera is more easily ruled out because the symptoms given by Aditi did not indicate cholera. The evidence of Satya Narayan and Satti Urmila immediately following the death was much too convincing for anyone to believe that she had died of cholera. Further, the symptoms described for Maya—especially the constant reference to a swollen stomach—indicate a knowledge of the fact that she was pregnant and an attempt to camouflage it.

The Concluding Question: What Is the Village Law for This Case?

Of first importance, the law of the village is that where the individuals concerned are members of one family or lineage, the family and/or lineage heads must be allowed to handle the matter themselves. This should be done within the village.

The second point is related to marriage, kinship, inheritance, and values. In Kurukshetra, the groom acquires exclusive sexual rights to the bride in order to establish a clear line of patrilineal descent for the inheritance of land. A married woman who is adulterous constitutes a serious threat to inheritance rights of the husband and the members of his lineage. The family of the in-laws also has proprietary rights in the wife and her offspring, who are in a position of status to the head of the family. The rights to the wife pass from her father to her father-in-law at the time of marriage; the transfer is symbolized by a series of ceremonial transactions. Thus, the father-in-law has the right of life and death over the daughter-in-law. In this case, he exercised it by returning Maya to her father, virtually saying "Do with her as you see fit." The demonstration of public mourning indicated that the family of in-laws was in accord with Dharma.

In acting as judge of his daughter. Dharma had first to consider how the pregnancy would affect his daughter's life. By sending her to the in-laws, he provided her only chance for life. Had they kept her, she might have gone on living as a married woman in her husband's village. When they returned her to her father, there was no further place for her to go. She could not remain in her own village; she and her natal family would be outcaste or nonacceptable. She could not earn a living in a city by herself, as she was illiterate, had no skills, and would have ended as the lowest form of outcast beggar or prostitute. The merciful recourse was to kill her.

Here the Hindu beliefs with regard to life and death are significant. A person's status in life is the result of actions in past lives and in the present; future lives depend on these actions as does the eventual release from the round of rebirths. What happened to Maya in her present life was related to her past. Since she had committed bad actions in this life also, the reasoning of her father and the villagers might be that the sooner she was reborn, the sooner her chance to perform better actions. Where a series of rebirths are involved in the eventual outcome of the soul, and the present life has a future worse than death, killing one's own daughter may be merciful. This is not to say the Dharma and Aditi may not have suffered remorse and guilt from Maya's death. However, they also thought that Devi had been to blame and had been the influence in Maya's life that caused their problems, that Arjuna had been Maya's partner, and that Harischandra had been weak. They could righteously point to them as the cause of their daughter's downfall. Dharma, in fact, expressed this in threats. The bad fortunes of Harischandra's and Dharma's families could also indirectly be attributed to Saibya's evil eye. This power of hers was related to the inauspiciousness of widowhood—the result of actions in past lives.

From the village point of view, the actions of Dharma as judge and executioner were expected of him in his role as head of the family. Harischandra fell short of his expected role in allowing his wife to act as she did. This influenced the villagers in the case of Maya, for they viewed the adultery of a married woman as a direct threat to their inheritance of land, their marriage system, and their values. Therefore, killing such a woman was punishment for the adultery. The outcasting of Harischandra's family on the occasion of Arjuna's wedding showed the village disapproval of the whole family's behavior, but in particular of Devi. As one man said, "Harischandra's wife could easily have been killed by this time. If a man can kill his own daughter, killing a woman in the village is an easy thing. The whole village will cover it up." The only reason Devi was not killed was because she complained to the police when the lineage threatened her. This was an index of the lineage's concerted action laying the blame for the whole sad affair on Devi.

There was no formal complaint of a crime, no court trial, no written code of law. Yet the crimes were judged and punished by Dharma and upheld by the members of his lineage and, later, by village opinion. The consensus with which the villagers interpreted these events indicates that village-level law, primarily that of the family and the lineage, was upheld. No one reported to the police that Maya had been killed. The police twice visited the village but investigated no further, nor did anyone mention the facts of the case to them. Two members of Dharma's lineage were policemen and knew of Maya's death. Yet they did nothing. The negative actions of the police reveal that they are sufficiently cognizant of village law to avoid investigation and prosecution unless absolutely compelled to do so.

References

1. Gulliver, P.H. 1969. Case studies in law in non-western societies. In *Law in Culture and Society*. L. Nader, Ed.: 11–68. Aldine Publishing Co. Chicago, Ill.
2. Moore, S. F. 1969. Comparative studies. In *Law in Culture and Society*. L. Nader, Ed.: 337–348. Aldine Publishing Co. Chicago, Ill.
3. Ingalls, D. H. H. 1954. Authority and law in ancient India. In *Authority and Law in the Ancient Orient*. H. M. Hoenigswald, J. de Francis & G. E. Mendenhall, Eds. *Supplement to the Journal of the American Oriental Society* (17) July–September: 34–45.
4. Sternbach, L. 1950. Law. In *India, Pakistan, Ceylon*. W. Norman Brown, Ed. : 116–117. Cornell University Press. Ithaca, N.Y.
5. Maine, H. S. 1963. *Ancient Law, its Connection with the Early History of Society and its Relation to Modern Ideas*. 147–149. Beacon Press. Boston, Mass.
6. Goodenough, W.H. 1970. *Description and comparison in cultural anthropology*: 12–13, 21–23. Aldine Publishing Company. Chicago, Ill.
7. Aggarwala, O. P. 1956. *The Punjab Tenancy Act, XVI of 1887 and Post Independence Tenancy Legislation in Punjab (India), Punjab (Pakistan), Pepsu, Himachal Pradesh and N. W. F. P. (Pakistan)* : 3–4, 20. Metropolitan Book Co., Ltd. Delhi, India.
8. Hoebel, E. A. 1968. *The Law of Primitive Man*: 286. Atheneum Publishers. New York, N.Y.
9. Madan, T. N. 1962. Is the Brahmanic gotra a grouping of kin? *Southwestern J. Anthropology*, 18(1): 59–77. Spring.
10. Lyght, C. E., W. P. Boger, G. A. Carden, A. Gibson, D. W. Richards, Eds. 1956. *The Merck Manual of Diagnosis and Therapy*: 919–922 Merck & Co., Inc. Rahway, N.J.

11. Freed, S. A. 1963. Fictive Kinship in North India. *Ethnology* 2(1): 86–103. January.

BEATRICE FARNSWORTH

The Litigious Daughter-in-Law: Family Relations in Rural Russia in the Second Half of the Nineteenth Century

The role of women is a difficult one in many societies. One of the factors that often contributes to the plight of women is the type of post-nuptial residence pattern. In those societies where the new bride is required to move into the home of the groom and thus falling under the nominal power of her in-laws, marriage involves a most demanding adjustment. Typically, the bride becomes a virtual slave to her mother-in-law and sometimes her status does not change from that of a household drudge until she bears a child, preferably a son. The question arises as to whether or not women forced into a new role as daughter-in-law had any access to legal redress of their grievances. In the following essay by Beatrice Farnsworth, a careful examination of local court records in nineteenth-century Russia tries to determine whether the stereotypic delineation of a passive daughter who meekly submits to the tyranny of in-law domination is accurate. In this study, it is not just one case that is reviewed but rather a whole series of cases is considered in order to illuminate the issue in question.

For additional discussion of nineteenth-century Russian folk law, see the references cited in the headnote to the essay by Samuel Kucherov above.

Russian folk wisdom regarded the daughter-in-law, the *snokha* (a word that also meant sister-in-law), as a source of family friction. Unable to coexist in the cramped quarters of the peasant hut, or *izba*, where a mother-in-law ruled over the stove and a father-in-law kept watch on the family purse, the daughter-in-law supposedly made evident her discontent. A host of proverbs and folk sayings attest to the idea of the *snokha* as troublemaker: the saying that the daughter-in-law "likes the family hands but resents the family pot" summed up this resentment.[1] According to this view, the daughter-in-law took but did not give.

Reprinted from the *Slavic Review*, 45 (1986), 49–64, with permission.

Twentieth-century historians, influenced perhaps by Soviet interpretations as well as by literary impressions, see the peasant daughter-in-law in the pre-revolutionary era not as a source of friction but rather as a helpless victim of family hostility: a husband's beatings, a mother-in-law's tyranny, father-in-law's sexual harassment.[2] Neither of these images of the *snokha*—dissatisfied troublemaker or invariable victim—has been subjected to investigation.

In fact, we know very little about the dynamics of the large peasant family in the nineteenth century or about the lives of its women. We have hints in estate correspondence before emancipation, according to Peter Czap, that many peasants found conditions within the patriarchal family "nearly impossible to bear."[3] An inquiry that takes us into the peasant household should provide not only a picture of peasant women's lives but also information about the individual and social tensions within the multiple family system. What was the actual situation of Russian peasant women? What were some of the problems between parents-in-law and daughters-in-law, brothers-in-law and sisters-in-law, husbands and wives? While much of the picture of family oppression is undoubtedly true, it is much less certain that peasant women after emancipation lacked recourse and passively accepted their fate. This essay will focus on the family position of the daughter-in-law and the possibility of redress of grievance in the peasant courts established after emancipation.

Insight into family acrimony may be gained from the potentially revealing record books of the township or peasant courts, institutions set up after the Emancipation of 1861 to adjudicate the civil disputes of peasants. The mission of these township courts, each presided over by some four to twelve elected peasant judges, was to administer justice in conflicts between peasants based on the "traditional peasant way of life," on so-called "customary" rather than imperial law.[4] The basic means to study the records of the township court is the *Trudy Komissii po preobrazovaniiu volostnykh sudov*, a massive work, providing reports of court cases.[5] Although of enormous value to the student of peasant society, the seven-volume study is not without its limitations. The work of a special government commission carried out between 1871 and 1874 under the direction of Senator M. N. Liuboshchinskii, the commission proposed "to collect such materials and information as would make it possible to obtain an accurate conception of the contemporary state of the peasant court."[6] Investigators for the commission, unable to examine each of the 11,786 townships into which European Russia was divided, selected townships that reflected the widest possible diversity of geographic, economic, and ethnic factors.

The nature of the court system and the inconsistencies of its record-keeping present the greatest problem to the student wishing to quantify rural social relations. Peasants did not bring all their legal disputes to court. Family quarrels, especially problems of division and inheritance, were sometimes handled locally by the village elder or assembly (*skhod*). Indeed in some locales all problems went first to the elder of the village commune, going to the township court only if there were an impasse.[7] The record is further blurred by the practice in some townships of not recording cases—especially family disputes—that the court resolved amicably. It is impossible, therefore, to know how many peasants actually appealed to the courts and with what kinds of cases. Obscuring matters further, the record varies in detail, not always indicating the relationship of the plaintiff to the head of household or making clear the structure of the family (nuclear, multiple, and so on).

Because the investigators for the commission chiefly wanted to obtain representative answers rather than to investigate the most active courts, they sometimes questioned elders and judges about their communities and court procedures in townships that recorded no cases at all.[8] Nor was there any balance in the total number of townships covered in each province: for Kostroma province the *Trudy* reported cases from sixteen townships, about half the total; for Tambov province from eighty-two, all of the townships in the province.

We have then a fascinating mosaic, huge (volume 1 alone runs to more than 800 pages), frustratingly incomplete, and based on the vagaries of local record keeping but providing a rich, if random, picture of peasant life.

This unwieldy panorama cannot tell us in how many instances in central Russia daughters-in-law were, in fact, involved in law suits, but it does indicate in its range of cases the variety of experiences of daughters-in-law in the township courts. If we assume that the cases recorded represent the most intractable conflicts, those that resisted solution at the local level, and if we pay close attention to disputes with a daughter-in-law as a party, either as plaintiff or defendant, we may arrive at a sense of her position within the family.

With this purpose in mind, I have focused on court cases in four provinces of central Russia: three in the Central Industrial Region—Moscow, Kostroma, and Iaroslavl′—and one in the Central Agricultural Region—Tambov. I selected provinces that represented different regions (hence both Iaroslavl′ and Tambov), but I was guided also by the practical need to choose provinces with an abundant number of recorded cases. Since for Kostroma province cases were reported for sixteen townships, the fewest among the four, from each of the other three provinces I selected at random sixteen to nineteen townships. From each of these four groups, I next selected eleven townships, each made up of several peasant *mirs* or communes (see table 1). In order to examine as wide a spectrum as possible of family cases involving women, I chose townships that had the largest number of cases featuring women. These townships tended, with a few exceptions, to be the same townships within the sample groups that had the largest number of recorded cases.

The resulting figures are not statistically rigorous; rigor is not possible given the incomplete nature of the *Trudy*. As we will see, however, they are suggestive in a comparative sense. For the years 1866 to 1872 the courts in these forty-four townships recorded 2,108 cases.[9] Of these, women were involved in roughly 685 (or 32 percent) of the cases. The majority of these disputes involved small-scale financial transactions usually centering on failure to pay wages for work completed, to fulfill contracts for which monetary advances had been given, or to make payments in the sale of livestock, firewood, or, sometimes, a hut. Other leading areas of litigation involved petty theft, perhaps of a goose, a load of hay, or clothing, and cases of physical assault or verbal insult. A man charged a woman with biting him, a woman charged a man with hitting her, another woman was accused of calling a villager a thief. Women also figured in cases of property damage: One woman charged that a man's horse had trampled her sown field. Another woman demanded compensation for her pig run over by a horse. Disputes over use of land, broken engagements, even dog bites brought women to court.

Family litigation was at issue in 51 percent of the 685 cases (347 cases), a figure which, we can assume, represents only a portion of the actual number. Despite the patriarchal organization of the family, in a significant number of recorded family disputes, 28 percent (97 cases), the daughter-in-law brought charges against her in-laws (including her brothers-in-law as well as her presents-in-law). Let us look at her grievances.

Perhaps because peasant life was closely monitored by the *mir* and, thus, eroded the concept of privacy, perhaps because privacy could mean little to people crowded together in a small hut, or perhaps simply because they felt terribly threatened, women did not appear reluctant to reveal details of their personal lives in these courts. The daughter-in-law described beatings by her mother-in-law, father-in-law, and brother-in-law or requested the right to live separately or with her own parents while her husband was away at wage work.

If she was widowed, a daughter-in-law frequently appealed to the court for part of her husband's share of the communal property. If her in-laws banished her, she might demand to be taken back into their home.

What help could a woman expect from the court? Much depended on the subjective opinion of the judges. Peasant justice was not blind. Ad hominem, or, in Russian, *po cheloveku*, was a guiding principle. What were the reputations of the plaintiff and the defendants? Was the father-in-law or brother-in-law known to be drunkard? Was the daughter-in-law a hard worker with a reputation as a good woman? Did she have children? How long had she lived in the family? Could she be expected to support herself? Balancing such considerations with the principles that parents and elders deserved respect and homesteads needed to be preserved at full working strength, the judges, often illiterate, tried to render equity. They could be inconsistent.

A daughter-in-law in Ziuzinskii township in Moscow province charged her in-laws with beating her but was informed that sons and daughters did not have the right to complain against parents. The court advised her to live in obedience to her elders.[10] Yet in Vysotskii township, in the same province, a father-in-law accused by his daughter-in-law of abuse was arrested.[11] Similarly, in Bol'shesel'skii township, in Iaroslavl' province, when a father-in-law contended that he beat his daughter-in-law because she was insubordinate, the court fined him 2 rubles and warned him that if it happened again the penalty would be greater.[12] The differing decisions may be explained not only by the subjective reactions of the judges to the litigants but by the makeup of the three communities. All three townships appeared to be relatively prosperous—this assumption is based on the facts that each paid its judges 40 rubles or more a year and that in each people derived a living from sources other than subsistence agriculture.[13] The townships in which the fathers-in-law were punished for abusing their daugthers-in-law, however, were more economically diversified and therefore, perhaps, more open communities. In Vysotskii township men worked primarily in factories rather than in agriculture. In Bol'shesel'skii industry and trade predominated and two-thirds of the males were at *otkhod.* In Vysotskii and Bol'shesel'skii townships, moreover, girls attended school along with boys, a phenomenon not frequently found in rural Russia in the 1870s.[14]

The majority of cases brought by a daughter-in-law against her in-laws involved property. A woman customarily arrived in her husband's home with her dowry (*pridanoe*), clothing, and such household items as towels and bedding. A daughter, if she had brothers, did not inherit within her own family. Her dowry, then, which might include money and some livestock, was in a sense her share of her family's property.[15] A daughter-in-law's personal property, over which she had exclusive control, might need to be protected from the avarice of her new relatives. We find seven such cases. In each the courts cooperated. Thus, a woman in Mokrinskii township in Tambov province charged her brother-in-law with breaking into her dowry trunk. He was given twenty blows. In a similar case in Khatunskii township in Moscow province a brother-in-law was ordered to provide compensation. A daughter-in-law in

Table 1. Court Cases Involving Women, by Township

Township	Years	Primary activity	Total Cases	Cases involving women (percentage of total)
		Moscow province		
Nagatinskii	1871–1872	vegetable marketing	9	4(44)
Pekhorskii	1870, 1872	factory work	5	2(40)
Shalovskii	1863, 1868, 1869, 1871	factory work	14	4(28)
Bun'kovskii†	1867, 1868, 1869, 1870–1871	factory work	18	11(61)
Iamkinskii†	1868–1872	factory work	15	9(60)
Kiiasovskii†	1869–1872	not indicated	44	21(47)
Khatunskii†	1869–1871	primarily trade	127	37(29)
Vysotskii†	1867–1872	factory work	47	19(40)
Pushchinskii†	1867,1869, 1871–1872	factory work	39	10(25)
Glazovskii†	1871	agriculture	136	34(25)
Bogoslovskii†	1871	seasonal work away from village (*otkhod*)	31	11(35)
Ziuzinskii†	1866, 1868, 1870–1872	vegetable marketing	80	25(31)
Vokhrinskii†	1869–1871	mostly agriculture;peasants hired out in winter	14	2(14)
Spasskii†	1871	mostly weavers	82	16(19)
Chaplyzhenskii	1866–1871	trades	29	8(27)
Dovydkovskii†	1868, 1871–1872	partly *otkhod*	58	36(62)
			748	249(33)

Iaroslavl´ province

Pleschcheevskii	1868–1871	partly factory work and *otkhod*	36	8(22)
Norskii†	1861–1872		68	19(28)
Krestobogorodskii†	1870–1872	agriculture, carrier's trade	80	23(28)
Koz´modem´ianskii†	1867–1869, 1870–1872	*otkhod*, joiners weavers	29	14(48)
Kurbskii†	1871–1872	*otkhod*	46	13(28)
Shopshinskii	1868,1871–1872	agriculture	29	7(24)
Serenovskii	1871	*otkhod*	17	3(17)
Tolgobol´skii†	1871	*otkhod*	24	9(37)
Putiatinskii†	1863–1865, 1868–1872	*otkhod* local trades	44	20(45)
Dievo-gorodishchenskii†	1869–1872	*otkhod*	50	16(32)
Velikosel´skii†	1869–1872	*otkhod*	40	12(30)
Boronishinskii	1871	*otkhod*	44	8(18)
Mar´inskii†	1869, 1871–1872	*otkhod*	111	40(36)
Kriukovskii	1871–1872	partly *otkhod*	33	10(30)
Povodnevskii†	1868–1871	*otkhod*	30	14(46)
Pokrovskii†	1870–1872	*otkhod*	54	12(22)
Bol´shesel´skii	1869–1871	partly *otkhod*	30	7(23)
Khopylevskii	1871	*otkhod*	16	8(50)
Ivanovskii	1871	*otkhod*	30	8 (26)
			811	251(31)

Township	Years	Primary activity	Total Cases	Cases involving women (percentage of total)
		Kostroma province		
Zarvazhnii†	1870–1872	*otkhod*	52	9(17)
Sobolevskii†	1869–1872	agriculture	15	9(60)
Noginskii	1867–1869	agriculture	8	1(12)
Krasnosel´skii	1867, 1871–1872	small scale manufacture	13	3(23)
Bashutinskii†	1868, 1870–1871	agriculture, some factory work	18	12(66)
Odelevskii	1869	agriculture, some factory work	9	4(44)
Ostrotovskii	1870	weaving and some factory work	13	2(15)
Mordvinovskii†	1870–1872	agriculture, work on Volga	95	35(36)
Gor´kovskii†	1861, 1863, 1865, 1866, 1871, 1872	weaving trades	46	9(19)
Diupinskii†	1868, 1869, 1871–1872	agriculture, textile production	33	10(30)
Vozdvizhenskii†	1864, 1868, 1869–1872	partly *otkhod*	29	14(48)
Esiplevskii	1861–1864, 1866,1867, 1871	primarily agriculture	38	22(57)
Molvitinskii†	1871–1872	otkhod	31	4(12)
Borovskii†	1869–1872	partly *otkhod*	20	4(20)
Troitskii†	1871–1872	*otkhod*	27	12(44)
Gorkinskii	1870	factory work	6	0(0)††
			453	150(33)
		Tambov province		
Chernianovskii	1870–1871	agriculture	17	4(23)
Gorel´skii†	1871–1872	agriculture	24	11(46)
Kulevatovskii†	1871–1872	agriculture	29	5(17)
Perkinskii†	1870–1872	agriculture	62	16(25)

Ot´iasovskii	1870–1872	agriculture	22	4(18)
Piterskii	1871	agriculture, *otkhod in w*inter	32	4(12)
Cherkinskii†	1871	agriculture, shoe-making in winter	23	10(43)
Kazachinskii†	1871	agriculture	47	19(40)
Taradevskii†	1871–1872	agriculture, in winter work on Don	44	20(45)
Algasovskii†	1870–1871	agriculture	62	14(22)
Rybinskii	1869–1872	agriculture	13	3(23)
Nesterskii†	1862,1871, 1872	agriculture	25	5(20)
Kargashinskii	1871–1872	agriculture	11	1(9)
Mokrinskii†	1870–1871	agriculture	31	6(19)
Barkovskii†	1871		36	4(11)
Bol´shekhomutetskii	1871	agriculture	22	4(18)
Vanovskii†	1870–1871	little agriculture, wheel and carpenter trades	62	14(22)
			562	144(25)

* Numbers are low because courts did not record reconciled cases.

\+ Township used in compiling statistics.

++ This township's incomplete records make it impossible to determine if women were involved.

Khatunskii township, presumably preparing to return to her parents, charged that her in-laws refused to surrender her property and they were ordered to do so.[16]

The more complex cases involved the demands of the widowed daughter-in-law against the jointly held property of the husband's family. In dealing with the peasant household it is important to distinguish between two kinds of property: land and household. A peasant family did not actually own the land it farmed. Before and after the emancipation of the serfs in 1861 the commune guaranteed each member household the right to farm an allotment comprising scattered strips of land. Allotments were periodically redistributed among members of the commune according to family size, that is by available mouths—*po edokam*—or by available labor. Tools, livestock, and the hut were, however, the common property of the family. The elder who headed the household, usually the father, was only its representative not its owner (although he may have acted as if he were). He had no right to dispose of the family possessions without the unanimous consent of all the adult members of the family, women as well as men.[17]

Although a son shared ownership in the household, if he were to die, his widow, if she were childless, might be left destitute, receiving nothing of her husband's share of the communal property in accord with peasant tradition that widows did not inherit.[18] Yet, if she were known to be industrious, and especially if she had lived with her husband's family many years and if she appealed to the court, its judges might award a childless widow one-fourth or one-seventh of her husband's share.[19] If she had sons the daughter-in-law generally received for them that portion of the communal property that would have gone to her husband had there been a family division.[20] A widow with daughters was less secure and more dependent on the generosity of her male in-laws than a widow with sons. In some localities, if she had daughters, a widow might receive at the discretion of her relatives a portion of the moveable property, for example, some grain and cattle.[21]

Among daughters-in-law the plight of the soldier's wife, the *soldatka*, resembled that of the widow. In twenty-three instances an in-law banished the *soldatka* or withheld property from her after her husband left for service. In one such case in Khatunskii township a *soldatka* charged her brother-in-law with ejecting her after refusing to permit her to use a horse that he and her husband owned in common.[22] The court gave her the right to use the horse and to remain in the house. In a similar case, in the same township, the court ordered a brother-in-law to permit a *soldatka* to remain at home and to share the use of the cow.[23] Another court in Krestobogorodskii township defended a *soldatka* against a father-in-law who denied her her husband's share of grain.[24] In other cases the *soldatka* charged her in-laws with petty theft—perhaps of a dress or a coat—and the court ordered that the items be returned.[25]

The plight of the *soldatka* must have reminded many a daughter-in-law that security did not necessarily lie within her husband's family. The problem was not new. Before emancipation, widows with minor children sought the protection of the *mir* governments when threatened with expulsion from their husbands' households. The *mir* obliged a father-in-law to provide for his son's family.[26] After emancipation, the widow could appeal to the township court. Evidently, a significant number of daughters-in-law felt the need thus to protect themselves. In fifty of the ninety-seven cases in which a *snokha* brought charges against her in-laws, she protested "unlawful" withholding by her husband's family of property due her or she appealed against banishment. Unfortunately, it is not always clear whether a daughter-in-law seeking property could have remained in her in-law's house had she wished to do so or whether she was, indeed, banished. In all but five instances, the widow or *soldatka* received a court-ordered settlement from her in-laws. If the sums involved exceeded the court's jurisdiction of 100 rubles or if, in the court's view, the plaintiff did not have a valid claim her suit was denied.

The daughter-in-law's plight was due in part to the implicit assumption that she deserved nothing because she was an outsider. This conclusion is reinforced when we look at the tenuous position of a son-in-law (called a *primak*) taken into his wife's household because her family lacked sons of its own. Reportedly treated with little respect by his wife's family, in popular parlance referred to as a henpecked wimp, he is said to have been "cruelly exploited."[27] Even after the death of his father-in-law, when he could formally become head of household, the *primak* might find that the real power in the family simply shifted to his wife and mother-in-law: one *primak* recalled that his opinion was never sought when household problems were discussed.[28] Like the *snokha*, the *primak* could be in a particularly weak position if his spouse died—even ejected without any property from the household in which he had worked. A resourceful *primak* protected himself, when he could, by a written agreement guaranteeing him property rights in the event of his wife's death.[29] Quarrels with in-laws brought the *primak* to court as they did the *snokha*.

Although in the patriarchal peasant family a father-in-law customarily wielded control, sometimes he did not succeed in enforcing his will and he too resorted to the courts. In 5 percent of the recorded family litigations involving women, fathers-in-law and mothers-in-law initiated cases against their daughters-in-law. (This percentage increased to 6 percent when cases brought by brothers-in-law against sisters-in-law are included). If most of the cases brought by the daughter-in-law involved violation of what she perceived to be her property rights, a father-in-law (in court as plaintiff more frequently than a mother-in-law) was most likely to charge his daughter-in-law with disrespect, going home to her own parents, or simply wanting to work away from his home while her husband was in the city at seasonal labor.

The father-in-law did not always win. If his daughter-in-law could convince the court that oppression from her husband's family was extreme, she might be permitted to live separately while her spouse was gone.[30] If a father-in-law, on the other hand, could demonstrate that his daughter-in-law's absence hurt his household economy, his case was strengthened. Consider the peasant in Moscow province who, four days after his daughter-in-law left his home to return to her parents, charged in court that because of her absence he had to hire a working woman at 15 kopeks a day to take her place. Demanding that her parents compensate him the 60 kopeks since she was working for them rather than for him, he insisted she return. The court arrested the daughter-in-law for two days, ordering her back to her husband's family.[31]

Friction between families was exacerbated by the efforts of a daughter-in-law's parents to protect her. In a young woman's relationship with her own family we find a familial closeness that continued after marriage. A father charges a son-in-law with beating his daughter.[32] A mother tries to ease the burden on her daughter by taking in her laundry.[33] The image of the peasant woman giving birth in the fields is familiar, but, in fact, a woman might return to her mother two or three weeks before delivery.[34]

Parental interference in behalf of a married daughter might bring punishment. In one case a mother was arrested for five days for encouraging her daughter to oppose her husband's family. A father was ordered not to invite his daughter home without her husband's permission.[35] In another instance a father was arrested for taking his daughter home.[36]

Given the situation with which a young wife had to cope, her parents' attempts to protect her seem reasonable. A father-in-law or mother-in-law, bringing a complaint against a daughter-in-law for insult, disobedience, or arbitrarily leaving home, inadvertently provided glimpses of sexual tensions created by the close proximity of unrelated men and women in the small peasant household. A mother-in-law asks that her daughter-in-law be punished for constant insult and disobedience. The daughter-in-law, denying the charges, argued that her mother-in-law and husband continually called her insulting names and beat her and that it all started when her brother-in-law raped her. Since then her husband and her mother-in-law had hated her, claiming that she had a sexual relationship with her brother-in-law. The court decided that the family discord did in fact stem from the rape but, declaring that rape belonged in a criminal court, rejected the mother-in-law's case.[37]

Fathers-in-law were particularly susceptible to the sexual pressure resulting from the presence of the young daughter-in-law. A father-in-law charged his daughter-in-law with abandoning his home. The daughter-in-law countercharged that she left because her father-in-law made sexual advances to her and then beat her for refusing him. The family denied the sexual advances and the daughter-in-law, unable to provide evidence, was arrested for seven days for slander. That the elder was charged by the court to watch the family suggests that the judges suspected the young woman was probably telling the truth.[38]

Although in these cases the court seemed reluctant to grapple with sexual conflicts, in other townships, courts reacted differently.[39] One of the most unpleasant features of life in the complex family was, as we have seen, the unwanted sexual approaches of a father-in-law, a practice known as *snokhachestvo*. Once this transgression was brought to its attention, the courts did not take it lightly. A court might consider *snokhachestvo* sufficient cause to justify a family division.[40] In a few recorded instances, a husband successfully intervened and received court permission to move out of his parents' house.[41] According to custom, *snokhachestvo* was punished by fifteen to twenty blows.[42]

A daughter-in-law, unless widowed, was also a wife. It is impossible to appreciate a woman's position as *snokha* fully without considering also her situation as spouse. The catalogue of grievances not only against in-laws but also against husbands was extensive. Over half (66 percent) of fifty-three cases brought by wives against husbands arose from beating. In others she charged nonsupport, failure to send money when working away from the village, or banishment from her home. In twelve instances a woman was motivated by a desire to obtain her passport and go away to work for wages or to recover her dowry and separate from her husband.

Most often (in thirty-five cases) a wife came to court to protest being beaten. In eight of these cases, a daughter-in-law charged her husband and his family with collaboration in her ill-treatment. One woman, accusing her husband of beating her, charged his mother with encouraging him. His mother claimed that her daughter-in-law had been rude to her. The court punished the husband with twenty blows for beating his wife and jailed his mother for three days for joining with him.[43] Another woman, charging her husband with oppressing and beating her, accused her father-in-law of instigating his son's actions. Her husband was flogged twenty times for beating his wife, and his father was jailed for three days for permitting his son's bad behavior.

The problem of wife-beating, endemic in Russian villages, defies easy explanation. We have seen that a man's family might abet him in beating his wife, but was such behavior sanctioned by the community and court? The popular assumption, endorsed by some historians, holds that Russian peasants had the right to beat their wives, that such behavior was sanctioned by customary law, which, looking back to the sixteenth-century *Domostroi*, asserted its beneficial effect.[44] Indeed, in certain localities, for example in the township of Dymer in Kiev, peasants claimed that disputes between husbands and wives never came to the court, that township courts would not hear a wife's complaints against her husband. If he beat her, she deserved it.[45] According to a leading student of the township courts, Semen V. Pakhman, the localities in which such attitudes prevailed were few.[46] In fact, it was not unusual for neighbors to report peasants guilty of physical cruelty to their wives. In Kriukovsksii township in Iaroslavl′ province an elder called such interference essential, since wives of abusive husbands might be too fearful themselves to go to court.[47] The assumption implicit in the elder's observation is borne out by court records. Customary law in the 1870s evidently did not assume a man's absolute power over his wife. (Whether it ever unequivocally did is an open question. Nina A. Minenko gives examples of eighteenth-century women in western Siberia going to local authorities for protection from cruel husbands.)[48] The township court was made up, after all, of ordinary male peasants who would not have defended the interests of women if there existed an unambiguous belief in the rights of husbands to exercise their physical will. The positive influence of the scribe was also a factor in undermining wife-beating. Sometimes the only literate member of the court, he read and explained the law to the judges. Although peasants did not come under the uniform code of law, in court decisions written by scribes we find occasional references to volume 10 in the code of civil law and to a law forbidding the arbitrary beating of one's wife.[49] Thus, one guilty husband told the court that he had not known "the law" that he could not beat his wife.[50] In fact, rural judges legally had no right to draw on the uniform code of law. That they occasionally did so demonstrated the essentially local and ad hoc character of so-called customary law, which makes it difficult to generalize about its properties. Nevertheless, we may conclude that in both the Central Industrial Region to the north and the Central Agricultural Region to the south, from Iaroslavl′ to Tambov, the courts, while reminding a woman of her obligation to obey her husband or even chastising her for disobedience, might punish a perpetual wife-beater, on his wife's complaint, with a three-day or five-day sentence or, more commonly, with a criminal penalty of flogging.[51] In seventeen of the thirty-five cases in which wives charged husbands with beating them, husbands were punished; ten were flogged ten to twenty blows. If the court reconciled the couple or if the wife was unbruised and could not produce witnesses, the husband was not penalized.

Wife-beating was punishable, then, throughout rural Russia but in certain areas it may have been more common for abused women to turn to the courts. Indeed, in areas of economic change where men seeking outside wages were less involved in agriculture and where women played a greater role in the community, the number of women involved in court disputes of any sort—wife-beating or otherwise—may have tended to be higher.[52] To make the point negatively, in the township of Dymer in Kiev province the courts did not accept complaints from wives against husbands. Dymer was an agricultural area marked by extreme poverty, backwardness, and the persistence of tradition.[53] By contrast, in Taganchevskii, a more economically diversified township in Kiev, where people worked in factories and both boys and girls studied together in school, women received the court's protection.[54]

It may be superfluous, in light of the above examples, to consider another popular assumption: that peasant women themselves accepted their husband's beating not as an abuse of power but as natural and legal. This is an appropriate point, however, at which finally to lay that notion to rest. Romantics have long explained that to women beating was a sign of love, an indication of masculine strength. If a husband could be brutal, so the argument went, he could also show mercy; his display of power was proof that he could defend his wife from harm.[55] While here and there one can find reports of Russian women who supposedly held this view, the many court cases recording women's angry protests against beating effectively discredit such a myth.[56]

Along with protests against beating, wives went to court in nine instances to charge their husbands with banishing them or refusing to provide support. In such cases, parents-in-law might have been the instigators of the husband's action. Unfortunately, since court records do not always indicate family structure, it is impossible to determine how many wives who appeared in court against their husbands in banishment cases lived in multiple families. According to one authority, however, banishment usually occurred at the initiative of the in-laws and within a multiple family.[57] Women were rarely banished from the small nuclear family if only because a husband living alone with his wife could not afford to lose the labor of his adult partner.[58]

Although a husband and wife were legally obliged to live together and courts were not supposed to approve acts tending toward separation,[59] in practice township courts varied in the way they handled cases of husbands banishing wives. A husband might be ordered to take his wife back.[60] Thus when a husband and his parents banished a wife, charging her with "ignorance and laziness," the court ordered the in-laws to compensate their *snokha* for her summer's work, to buy back her clothing they had pawned, and to take her again into their home.[61]

If a husband refused to live with his wife, he was obliged at least to support her. When a pregnant wife appealed to the court because her husband and his parents had banished her, the court ordered the husband to take his wife back or pay her 3 rubles a month in support.[62] Invariably, if a wife charged nonsupport, the court ordered the husband to provide support. Whether he was required also to live with his wife was not clear.

Just as the daughter-in-law tended to be the initiator in bringing charges against her in-laws, so too in recorded marital disputes, the wife was usually the plaintiff: fifty-three cases were brought by wives; twenty-eight cases were initiated by husbands. Husbands appealed to the court most often (sixteen recorded cases) charging desertion (see table 2).[63] In cases of desertion a husband's family might be a contributing cause. In one instance, a peasant appeared in court complaining that his wife refused to live with him. His wife contended that he and his family oppressed her. The court, calling in the mother-in-law and brother-in-law, ordered them to treat the daughter-in-law decently, and told the young woman to return.[64] In other instances, the wife might be punished—usually by a brief jail sentence—for leaving. Or her husband might be punished with flogging or arrest if the court determined that she left because he beat her or was a drunkard or failed to support his wife and children adequately.

A woman might appeal to the court for release from an intolerable family situation. If she and her husband could agree on a separation through mutual consent, she generally won her freedom. Of twelve requests by wives for separations, eight were granted. One means for a woman to escape from her husband and his family—particularly if she had no children—was to agree in court that in return for her passport she would pay her husband a sum of money that would enable him to engage someone in her place.[65] In one case, in Kostroma, the wife paid her husband 5 rubles a year so that he could hire a worker in the summer.[66] Another woman in Moscow province paid 20 rubles for a replacement.[67] Here is a separation agreement concluded in Moscow province in 1871:[68]

1. I, "I," willingly, in aversion to our family discord, permit my wife to receive from the township government a yearly passport to live where she wishes with the proviso that she pay me in the course of a year 12 rubles in the following way: June 6, 3 rubles, July 20, 3 rubles, October 1, 3 rubles and at Easter, 1872, 3 rubles.

2. And I, "H," will pay my husband 12 rubles at the aforesaid times with the understanding that my husband ask nothing more of me.

Table 2. Nature of Disputes by Family Relationship

Relationship	Inheritance or property division	Desertion by wife or daughter-in-law	Dowry	Beating, banishment, or oppression	Insubordination of wife or daughter-in-law	Dissolute life of wife	Sexual advance by male family member
daughter-in-law and mother-in-law	20			5	2		
daughter-in-law and father-in-law	33	4	1	7	3		3
daughter-in-law and both parents-in-law	2			6			
wife and husband	2	16	7	51	6	5	
daughter-in-law and brother-in-law	28		3	12	1		1
sisters-in-law	4						

Note: The predominant disputes are property disagreements between the daughter-in-law and her in-laws (87) and suits involving oppressive treatment of the wife by the husband (51). Since the purpose of this table is to show the varieties of family litigation, a case in which, for example, a daughter-in-law appealed against her father-in-law and brother-in-law will appear twice, once under the category of father-in-law and again under the category of brother-in-law.

Source: St. Samueli, "Rabotu proizvodstvennykh kommun i kollektivov—na novye rel´sy," *Partiinoe stroitel´stvo*, no. 15–16 (1931): 15.

As the above contract suggests, de facto separations were legally countenanced, although both in law and in popular opinion spouses had an obligation to live together.[69] Divorces were rare, but peasant courts, not bound by a rigid civil law, sometimes dealt more mildly with women than even customary law required.[70] Despite the law that spouses must live together, peasant courts appeared rather accepting of separation by mutual consent.[71] In seven of the eight separations countenanced by the court, husbands appeared to acquiesce. The historian Maksim Kovalevsky attributes this laxity on the part of the courts "in direct contradiction to the law" to the influence of rural tradition. Up to the mid-eighteenth century Russian clergy dissolved marriage bonds often for no other reason than incompatibility.[72]

In this article I have examined the place of the daughter-in-law in the peasant family through the records of township courts and have shown that the daughter-in-law appealed nearly five times more frequently against her in-laws than they did against her. Similarly, wives brought nearly twice as many cases against husbands as husbands did against wives. These statistics are significant, even though they do not necessarily mean that peasant women brought more suits than other members of the family. A father-in-law, mother-in-law, brother-in-law, or husband may have obtained satisfaction in one of the village's unofficial courts, or their disputes, if reconciled in the township court, may have gone unrecorded. Statistics suggesting that the daughter-in-law was the most litigious member of the family tell us only that the cases she brought against family members defied easy solutions, that women who used the courts were determined to resist family despotism, and their suits, not amicably resolved, were more often entered into the record.

We may conclude that peasant women in general, *snokhi* in particular, enjoyed status, asserted and exercised rights, and instigated family and community change to a degree not hitherto recognized. Yet a problem remains. Is it valid to conclude also that *snokhi* were generally discontented within the large family? Given the modest numbers with which I have dealt, the question is whether the cases in the *Trudy Komissii* represent the tip of an iceberg of dissatisfaction or simply the exceptional incidents in a society relying heavily on the extended family. Was there, in fact, a "silent majority" of satisfied or obedient daughters-in-law treated decently by their in-laws?[73] The question needs to be raised but, unfortunately, cannot be definitively answered. We can point only to the absence of evidence. If a contented population of daughters-in-law existed, it eluded folk wisdom, ethnographic investigators, and nineteenth-century historians. In the absence of documentation for the existence of this silent majority of satisfied daughters-in-law and in the presence of ethnographic and historical studies that suggest the contrary,[74] I tentatively conclude that the family conflicts of the forty-four townships in four provinces of European Russia represent the tip of the iceberg of discontent.

Notes

1. For proverbs, M. I. Zarudnyi, *Zakony i zhizn'. Itogi izsledovaniia krest'ianskikh sudov* (St. Petersburg, 1874), p. 157. Aleksandra Efimenko, "Krest'ianskaia zhenshchina," *Delo* (1873): 65–66.

2. A major contributor to the literary image of peasant women was Nikolai A. Nekrasov. See "Frost, the Red Nose" in N. A. Nekrasov, *Polnoe sobranie stikhotvorenii v trekh tomakh*, ed., K. I. Chukovskii (3 vols.; Leningrad, 1967), 2:109. For historians on peasant women, see Barbara Engel, *Mothers and Daughters* (Cambridge: Cambridge University Press, 1983), p. 8; Dorothy Atkinson et al., *Women in Russia* (Stanford, Calif.; Stanford University Press, 1977), p. 33; L. A. Anokhina and M. N. Shmeleva, *Kul'tura i byt kolkhoznikov Kalininskoi Oblasti* (Moscow, 1964), p. 174.

3. Peter Czap, "The Perennial Multiple Family Household, Mishino, Russia 1782–1858," *Journal of Family History* (Spring 1982): 25.

4. For the courts, see Peter Czap, "Peasant-Class and Peasant Customary Justice in Russia, 1861–1912," *Journal of Social History* 1 (Winter 1967): 149–79. Jurisdiction was limited to cases not involving property worth more than 100 rubles, arson, or murder. A township (*volost'*) was made up of several village communities.

5. *Trudy Komissii po preobrazovaniiu volostnykh sudov* (7 vols.; St. Petersburg, 1874).

6. Ibid., 1:ii.

7. Ibid., 3:57–58, 102; in Iaroslavl' province.

8. See Shungunskii township in Kostroma in ibid., 3:306–308 and Arapovskii township in Tambov, also in ibid., 1:10.

9. There are a few entries for 1861–1863; see table 1.

10. *Trudy Komissii*, 2:106.

11. Ibid., 2:206–207.

12. Ibid., 3:179.

13. For this standard of judgment, see Peter Czap, "The Influence of Slavophile Ideology on the Formation of the Volost Court of 1861 and the Practice of Peasant Self-Justice between 1861 and 1889," Ph.D. diss., Cornell University, 1959, pp. 79–82.

14. In Bol'shesel'skii township, Iaroslavl' province, up to thirty girls attended school and all four judges were literate with salaries of 40 rubles a year. *Trudy Komissii*, 3:176. For Vysotskii township, see ibid., 2:203. Two of the judges were literate; judges were paid 40 rubles a year.

15. Money and cattle were called *nadelok*. The money might go to her husband and the cattle might become part of the general property. Efimenko, "Krest'ianskaia zhenshchina," p. 93.

16. *Trudy Komissii*, 2:185, 190 (Moscow); 1:136 (Tambov).

17. Maksim M. Kovalevsky, *Modern Customs and Ancient Laws of Russia* (London: D. Nutt, 1891), p. 55. Only males were, in fact, consulted. Donald M. Wallace, *Russia* (1905 ed.; reprint, New York: Praeger, 1970), p. 89.

18. S. V. Pakhman, *Obychnoe grazhdanskoe pravo v Rossii* (2 vols., St. Petersburg, 1877–1879), 2:261; V. F. Mukhin, *Obychnyi poriadok nasledovaniia u krest′ian* (St. Petersburg, 1888), pp. 252–53, 261; *Trudy Komissii*, 1:15 (Tambov).

19. *Trudy Komissii*, 3:75, 85 (Iaroslavl′), and 3:388 (Kostroma); Pakhman, *Obychnoe grazhdanskoe pravo*, 2:270; Czap, "Peasant-Class Courts," p. 165.

20. Mukhin, *Obychnyi poriadok*, pp. 263–64. She could demand in court the right to run her husband's portion of the land allotment if she paid the taxes; ibid. She could also insist that her father-in-law not sell his farmstead since it was the future inheritance of her son. Ibid., p. 65; Pakhman, *Obychnoe grazhdanskoe pravo*, 2:273; *Trudy Komissii*, 1:686, 688 (Tambov); 5:78 (Kiev).

21. *Trudy Komissii*, 2:324, 363, 370 (Moscow); 3:394 (Kostroma); Mukhin, *Obychnyi poriadok*, p.266.

22. *Trudy Komissii*, 2:182 (Moscow).

23. Ibid., 2:195 (Moscow).

24. Ibid., 3:43 (Iaroslavl′).

25. Ibid., 2:212 (Moscow); F. Pokrovskii, "O semeinom polozhenii krest′ianskoi zhenshchiny v Kostromskoi gubernii po dannym volostnogo suda," *Zhivaia starina* 3–4 (1896): 464.

26. See V. A. Aleksandrov, "Semeino-imushchestvennye otnosheniia po obychnomu pravu v russkoi krepostnoi derevne XVIII-nachala XIX veka," *Istoriia SSSR*, no. 6 (1979): 48.

27. *Opyt istoriko-sotsiologicheskogo izucheniia sela "Moldino"* (Moscow, 1968), p. 108 (hereafter cited as *"Moldino"*); Anokhina and Shmeleva, *Kul′tura i byt kolkhoznikov Kalininskoi Oblasti*, p. 173.

28. *"Moldino,"* p. 109; Anokhina and Shmeleva, *Kul′tura i byt kolkhoznikov Kalininskoi Oblasti*, p. 174.

29. Mukhin, *Obychnyi poriadok*, p. 299.

30. Pakhman, *Obychnoe grazhdanskoe pravo*, 2:185; *Trudy Komissii*, 3:289 (Iaroslavl′); 3:393 (Kostroma).

31. *Trudy Komissii*, 2:170 (Moscow).

32. Ibid., 3:165 (Iaroslavl′); 5:132 (Kiev); 1:137 (Tambov).

33. *"Moldino,"* p. 108.

34. A. O. Afinogenova, *Zhizn′ zhenskago naseleniia Riazanskago uezda* (St. Petersburg, 1903), p. 76.

35. Pakhman, *Obychnoe grazhdanskoe pravo*, 2:89.

36. Ibid., 2:88; *Trudy Komissii*, 3:16 (Iaroslavl′); 5:91 (Kiev); 3:354 (Kostroma); 3:407 (Kostroma).

37. Ibid., 2:569 (Moscow).

38. Ibid., p. 577.

39. For cases in which both parties were flogged for fornication, see *Trudy Komissii*, 3:377, 379; a woman charged a man with rape; he countered that they had lived together lovingly. The court sentenced her to socially useful work and him to twenty floggings. Ibid., p. 142 (Iaroslavl′). A widow who charged

a man with fathering her child was awarded support; ibid., 1:138 (Tambov). See ibid., 3:379 (Kostroma), for a man fined 5 rubles for beating a woman who refused sexual intercourse. For other fornication cases, P. P. Chubinskii, *Trudy etnograficheskoi statisticheskoi ekspeditsii v Zapadno-Russkii Kraii* (St. Petersburg, 1872), pp. 18–19; 186–88.

40. I. Tiutriumov, "Krest'ianskaia sem'ia," *Russkaia rech* (St. Petersburg, 1879), vol. 4, part 1:292.

41. *Trudy Komissii,* 3:394 (Kostroma); also ibid., 158 (Iaroslavl'); A. Smirnov, *Ocherki semeinykh otnoshenii po obychnomu pravu russkago naroda* (Moscow, 1877), pp. 46–47.

42. A. A. Leont'ev, *Volostnoi sud i iuridicheskie obychai krest'ian* (St. Petersburg, 1895), p. 15; see *Trudy Komissii,* 6:100–101 for three-day jail sentence.

43. *Trudy Komissii,* 2:208 (Moscow).

44. Atkinson et al., *Women in Russia,* p. 33; Anokhina and Shmeleva, *Kul'tura i byt kolkhoznikov Kalininskoi Oblasti,* p. 174; Kovalevsky, *Modern Customs and Ancient Laws of Russia,* p. 45.

45. *Trudy Komissii,* 5:3, 33, 141 (Kiev).

46. Pakhman, *Obychnoe grazhdanskoe pravo,* 2:112.

47. *Trudy Komissii,* 3:144 (Iaroslavl'); for neighbor's report, see ibid., p. 354.

48. N. A. Minenko, *Russkaia krest'ianskaia sem'ia v zapadnoi Sibiri* (Novosibirsk, 1979), pp. 127–30, 135. Also see N. A. Kostrov, *Iuridicheskie obychai krest'ian starozhilov tomskoi gubernii* (Tomsk, 1876), pp. 20, 26, for relations between husband and wife.

49. Pakhman, *Obychnoe grazhdanskoe pravo,* 2:112–13; *Trudy Komissii,* 2:10 (Moscow). Judge refers to articles 106, 107, vol. 10, chap. 1 in *Svod zakonov grazhdanskikh.* See *Trudy Komissii,* 3:20 for judges guiding themselves by vol. 10 and by *Sel'skii ustav.* In the first half of the nineteenth century, husbands were forbidden in imperial law to beat their wives. Atkinson et al., *Women in Russia,* p. 33.

50. Pakhman, *Obychnoe grazhdanskoe pravo,* 2: 105–06; *Trudy Komissii,* 6:279–80 (Samara).

51. For punishment of wife-beaters, see *Trudy Komissii,* 1:32, 39, 295, 440, 443 (Tambov); 2:10, 66, 72, 100, 108, 140, 239, 274, 275, 360, 418, 425, 545 (Moscow); 3:72, 101, 183, 185, 208, 225, 236, 237, 263, 264, 272 (Iaroslavl'); 3:354, 383, 389, 413–15 (Kostroma); 3:444 (Nizhog); 4:109 (Kharkov); 4:260 (Poltava); 5:91, 132, 191 (Kiev); N. Astyrev, *V volostnykh pisariakh* (Moscow, 1896), p. 266; Tiutriumov, "Krest'ianskaia sem'ia," pp. 142–43. In one case, a wife was dealt fifteen blows for deserting her husband, but he received twenty blows for beating her.

52. See table 1; also wife-beating cases recorded in forty-four townships: Moscow, seventeen; Iaroslavl', eight; Kostroma, seven; Tambov (agricultural) three; and see F. Pokrovskii, "O semeinom polozhenii krest'ianskoi zhenshchiny v kostromskoi gubernii po dannym volostnogo suda," p. 459.

53. In Dymer with its 1,800 souls the elder received 40 rubles a year; the judges were unpaid. By comparison, in Ivanovskii township in Iaroslavl' with 1,479 souls the elder received 450 rubles a year; the judges 30 rubles.

54. *Trudy Komissii*, 5:161 (Kiev). Taganchevskii township had 2,505 souls; the elder received 210 rubles a year.

55. Efimenko, "Krest'ianskaia zhenshchina," p. 57; Kovalevsky, *Modern Customs and Ancient Laws of Russia*,p. 45.

56. For transcripts in which women protest beatings, see Astyrev, *V volostnykh pisariakh*, pp. 270–71; *Trudy Komissii*, 1:443 (Tambov).

57. Efimenko, "Krest'ianskaia zhenshchina," pp. 86, 88–89.

58. Ibid., pp. 86–87.

59. Ibid., pp. 83, 87.

60. *Trudy Komissii*, 2:168 (Moscow); Pakhman, *Obychnoe grazhdanskoe pravo*, 2:95–97.

61. Efimenko, "Krest'ianskaia zhenshchina," p. 89.

62. Ibid.

63. Four husbands also charged debauchery, one disobedience, two theft, one physical abuse, and one demanded (successfully) the wages his wife earned working away from home because he had to hire her replacement. *Trudy Komissii*, 3:139 (Iaroslavl'). A judge noted that husbands frequently charged wives with insubordination and wives charged ill-treatment, ibid., 2:93 (Moscow).

64. Ibid., 3:378 (Kostroma).

65. Pakhman, *Obychnoe grazhdanskoe pravo* 2:91.

66. *Trudy Komissii*, 3:384 (Kostroma).

67. Ibid., 2:555 (Moscow).

68. Ibid., p. 563. See pp. 555, 557, for other such agreements. Also Astyrev, *V volostnykh pisariakh*, pp. 224–25. Peasants expected wives to pay compensation for the loss of labor their desertion involved. Wallace, *Russia*, p. 545.

69. Pakhman, *Obychnoe grazhdanskoe pravo*, 2:86–87. See *Svod sakonov grazhdanskikh*, vol. 10, chap. 1, art. 103 for spouses' obligation to live together.

70. Efimenko, "Krest'ianskaia zhenshchina," p. 92, claims that township courts treated women with more sympathy than civil courts that were obliged to obey written law rigidly.

71. *Trudy Komissii*, 3:62 (Iaroslavl').

72. Kovalevsky, *Modern Customs and Ancient Laws of Russia*, p. 43.

73. I am indebted to Neil Weissman of Dickinson College for the contrasting image.

74. [V. U. Krupianskaia], *The Village of Viriatino*, trans. Sula Benet (New York: Anchor, 1970), p. 102; Pakhman, *Obychnoe grazhdanskoe pravo*, 2:23–24, 161–62, 185–86; M. I. Zarudnyi, *Zakony i zhizn'* (St. Petersburg, 1874), p. 118; Tiutriumov, "Krest'ianskaia sem'ia," 4, part 1:291–93; Mukhin, *Obychnyi poriadok*, pp. 223–77; Efimenko, "Krest'ianskaia zhenshchina," pp. 65, 72–73, 86.

HENDRIK HARTOG

Pigs and Positivism

For the last essay on specific cases, we have selected a rather extended discussion, a case involving the practice of pig-keeping in early nineteenth-century New York city. This should remind readers that cases of folk law are to be found in Europe and the United States as well as in Africa and Asia. The author, a Professor of the History of Law at Princeton Unversity, tries to view the case from two different perspectives. From a lawyer's point of view, the case is an example of formal legal doctrine; from a social historian's or social anthropologist's point of view, the case stems from dispute between different segments of society. The perspectives are not necessarily mutually exclusive, but they do represent alternative attitudes towards the importance of folk law or custom.

For other considerations of folk law in the United States, see Rupert B. Vance and Waller Wynne, Jr., "Folk Rationalizations in the 'Unwritten Law,'" American Journal of Sociology, *39 (1934), 483–492; for an interesting analysis of the possible influence of folk law (which the Stamp Act of 1765 attempted to abrogate) upon the outbreak of the American Revolution against England, see John Phillip Reid, "In Accordance with Usage: The Authority of Custom, The Stamp Act Debate, and the Coming of the American Revolution,"* Fordham Law Review, *45 (1976–1977), 335–368.*

I. Introduction

Did 19th century residents have a right to keep pigs in the streets of New York City? In 1819, a court said no. But in what ways, if any, did that decision conclude the inquiry? Did it mean there no longer was such a right, implying that there once was? Did it mean that the law could never recognize such a right? What was the legal significance of the judicial denial of the right to keep pigs in the streets?

Reprinted from the *Wisconsin Law Review* (1985), 899–935, with permission.

In this Article I will attempt to answer those questions using two rather different—and competing—interpretive strategies. The first, which I think of as the ordinary practice of American legal history writing, regards the case—and cases generally—as a text expounding and developing legal doctrine. The second, which I think of as characteristic of the practice of some social anthropology and some social history, visualizes the case as an instance or episode of conflict between contending normative orders.[1]

My goal is not to prove one or the other the better strategy.[2] Indeed, I think that each of these strategies reflects a distinctive legal vision, true in part to the ways Americans have experienced and argued about law for the past two centuries. We cannot choose between them without denying important features of our legal culture.

My goals are substantive. I want to use these contrasting strategies to make sense of the claimed and denied legal right of some 19th century New Yorkers to keep pigs in the streets of the city. I hope this study will help provide a starting point for a larger and more general study of the legal significance of American social customs. The relative silence of American legal doctrine on questions of customary law, a silence trumpeted by the legal language that enveloped efforts to rid New York City of its pigs, strikes me as pointing to the need to explore the problematic relationship between our social pluralism—the multiplicity of our social practices and normative identities—and the values we impute to legal order. But such a grandiose project will necessarily rest on numbers of smaller studies of the legal regulation of particular social practices, of which the essay that follows is an example. And whether such a larger project can ever be carried to completion, I can begin by trying to set out the complex relations between legal argument and social and political practice as they were revealed by the 1819 pig case and its aftermath. If I can succeed at that, the rest can wait, or perhaps, will follow.[3]

II. The Presence of the Pig

It is 1808. Next to the office of New York City's Board of Health on Broadway a man carrying a shovel is engaged in conversation with a woman. Near them, a Black (?) woman—a servant, surely—is hanging out the wash on a line tied between trees while she talks to a little boy. Meanwhile a huge pig walks by, attracting no one's attention.

Pigs were an ordinary part of the American urban landscape. How many residents kept them and how they were distributed around the different wards of New York City awaits some future student.[4] That they were present is incontestable. One would like to say that their place in the urban ecology is confirmed by the general silence about them.[5] Until the early 19th century, when swine were noticed, they were as natural a part of urban life as mud, manure, and the odors that once automatically accompanied increased human and animal density.[6]

Indeed, in a world without professional streetcleaners, a world in which private citizens were expected to provide the manpower (the term is in this context a misnomer) to remove the excrement and the wastes of urban street life, pigs assumed a necessary public role, particularly in wards whose residents lacked available servants. The result was, we might imagine, a peculiar urban ecological cycle, one which connected residents with their physical environment in a way that is difficult for us to imagine today. In brief, people ate pigs, and pigs ate the human and animal wastes and garbage which lined the streets of the city.[7]

Pigs wandered the streets of early New York City, just as they have wandered the streets of many pre-industrial cities, "prowling in grunting ferocity."[8] We ought not to imagine that this more organic image of urban life had a sweetness and gentility that is lost to us. To the contrary, all accounts of early urban pigs confirm that they were mean, dangerous, and uncontrollable beasts, hardly an urban amenity. They systematically destroyed pavements, occasionally killed children, and behaved in public in ways that were inconsistent with even the relaxed standards of cleanliness and propriety of early modern urban street life.[9]

Yet their presence in the streets was a given. Letting one's pigs run and fatten on the streets was an urban custom, just as letting pigs run in the woods and live on acorns was a rural custom, and it may be, although knowing whether it was is the problem of this essay, that city residents who kept pigs thought of themselves as owning a legal right to run their pigs in the streets of the city. They would have held, to use legal lingo, an easement over the streets, held by prescription or by customary right.

In a recent article on early 19th century New York City politics, Howard Rock describes some of the ways that the keeping of pigs in the streets became the focus of class conflict.[10] I shall have more to say on this theme further on, but for the moment it is important to note that the identification of swine with the lower classes was not an innovation of the early republic. Cronon suggests in *Changes in the Land* that 17th century disputes over the keeping of pigs often expressed a disguised class hostility.[11] And in New York City too there had been a long history of attempts by more elite city leaders to restrain and limit (even if they could not eliminate) the claims of less elite residents to keep their pigs.[12]

Early nineteenth century governmental debate first focused on draft ordinances that proposed to require all unpenned pigs to wear rings in their noses. Unringed hogs rooted with their snouts for scraps and excrement between the planks of footwalks. The land developers and elite homeowners who were working to improve the streets in front of their properties no doubt saw the destruction the pigs produced as undercutting their efforts and investments. In late 1809, therefore, the city passed a law fining the owner of any unringed pigs found in the streets,[13] a regulation which may have been seen as implicitly recognizing artisans' rights to keep (ringed) pigs on city streets.[14]

I am not certain what explains the more sustained effort to criminalize New York City's pig keepers that began around 1816. In part, the petitions and newspaper editorials that preceded and accompanied the campaign may have been motivated by a relatively new intolerance of urban nuisances. It may be that the coherence and the inclusiveness of the vision of pigs as a "bad thing," a public nuisance, was a new achievement of the city's developing governmental culture. We might read the petitions as asking, "Why should we expose ourselves and our properties to danger and harm, when we have a city government which should be capable of securing the public safety for our benefit?" Or, to put the matter slightly differently, "Why should the longstanding existence of the urban custom of keeping pigs in the streets prevent government from abating this nuisance, given the fact that city government has changed so many urban customs and practices in the previous quarter century?"[15]

Still, as Rock notes in his article, the new campaign initially came to naught. A law forbidding swine to run at large was first proposed to the city council in 1816, justified primarily as a way of preventing injuries to street pavements.[16] As drafted, the ordinance declared that any hog running in the streets could be taken by any person to a public pound. If the pig's owner wanted it returned, he or she would have to pay ten dollars to the person who "captured" the pig plus charges of twelve cents per day to the pound. After much delay, the law was finally called up for a vote in June 1817, at which time it was voted down. Then in October the same ordinance was passed into law.[17]

Petitions for repeal, protests, and remonstrances inevitably followed. Not only was the pig "our best scavenger," a street cleaner for parts of the city which badly needed cleaning but which were ignored by municipal employees, but it also provided cheap food for the poor in winter. All that the new law would produce would be increased street cleaning expenses and a "swarm of informers" to prey "on the defenceless poor."[18] And in early 1818 the city repealed the ordinance.[19] In June the council's committee on laws used a petition for relief by two men injured when their carriage was overturned by hogs as an excuse to reintroduce a law against swine in the streets. But the whole council postponed consideration of their draft. And at the council's next meeting the law committee's motion to have its report considered was voted down.[20]

Then in late 1818, Mayor Cadwallader Colden, sitting in his traditional role as judge of the quarter sessions court, impanelled a grand jury to hear evidence on the keeping of pigs in the city.[21] Soon the jury returned an indictment charging two individuals with the common law misdemeanor of "keeping and permitting to run hogs at large in the city of New York."[22] One of the two accused, Louis Lashine, came to trial on December 11. After proof was introduced that his place on Duane was "a receptacle for about forty hogs he offered no defense, and a jury convicted him and imposed a nominal fine.[23] The other defendant, a butcher named Christian Harriot or Harriet who lived in the northern part of the city on Spring Street, apparently did not concede the charge so willingly . He hired attorneys to defend him, and thus on January 5, 1819 a full trial was held in the sessions court on the question whether he could be convicted of maintaining a public nuisance because he owned pigs that were sometimes found on city streets.[24]

Van Wyck, the district attorney, began the case by examining a Mr. Ames, Harriet's neighbor and evidently another pig keeper, who reluctantly admitted that Harriet's hogs had been seen in the streets.[25] The district attorney then moved on to show "that hogs running in the streets are a nuisance, that they attack children even, and do various other [forms of] mischief."[26] A series of horror stories was produced to show the evil of pigs in the streets, for example: (1) hogs attacked children, (2) boys got into trouble by riding hogs, (3) ladies had been compelled to view swine copulating in open view, and (4) hogs defecated on people.[27] The defense called no witnesses.

III. *People v. Harriet* as a Legal Text

A. Who Decides Who Decides?

With the factual preliminaries out of the way the lawyers in the case next turned to the foundations of the legal case against Mr. Harriet. Granted that Harriet owned pigs which might have been found on city streets,[28] and granted that pigs had been known to engage in conduct of the kind detailed by the prosecutor, but did that mean that Harriet could be convicted of maintaining a public nuisance?

Both prosecutor and mayor-judge answered that question in the affirmative. Evidently the jury agreed, since Harriet would be convicted. But needless to say, the defendant's lawyers answered the question in the negative. They challenged the indictment on two grounds. The first was that a common law misdemeanor action was the wrong means to abate this nuisance, if nuisance it were. The second was that in any event keeping pigs in the streets of the city did not constitute a public nuisance.

Implicit in the first ground of Harriet's defense was a Jeffersonian distrust of common law or judge-made nuisance law.[29] What institutions should make laws that took away the right to keep pigs in the city? Not this sessions court surely, which enforced statutory misdemeanors as defined by common council and state legislature, but which should not arrogate to itself power that properly belonged to popular institutions. Indeed, the lawyers insisted that the sessions court was explicitly denied the power to act on this indictment by the state legislature, which in authorizing pounds for the confinement of hogs in particular specified circumstances, had recognized the right of citizens to keep hogs and allow them to run at large in all others.[30]

Further, English law declaring that hogs were not permitted to run in the streets of London could not serve as precedent for judicial action in this case because there never had been a right to run pigs in London. The problem here was whether a mayor's sessions court had the power to use nuisance law to change an existing right, not its power to restate rules already known.[31]

Finally, Harriet's lawyers pointed to the repeal of the 1817 ordinance which made it illegal to keep pigs in city streets. Repeal demonstrated that citizens had a right to keep pigs, "by the existing state of our corporation laws."

> If our corporation have seen fit to repeal the law which they themselves once passed of that description; and if they have not independence and stability enough to renew the act and free our citizens from doubt; is it to be endured, that severe and antiquated doctrines should be brought up from the English books to inflict a stigma and a penalty upon an honest and industrious fellow citizen . . .

And if this practice really was "a nuisance of the intolerable description alleged," then let the city government go about removing it in the right way. Let it draft a statute which could be sent to Albany for passage.[32]

The prosecutor's response rested, as did the mayor's charge to the jury, on his sense of the great need for immediate legal action and, correspondingly, on a lesser regard for the properties of institutional choice.[33] Who should decide was less important than that someone should. The "long indulgence this practice has received from successive grand juries; and even [from] the corporation," rather than legitimating pig keeping as a vested right, revealed instead the need to correct the evil now.[34]

At the same time, both prosecutor and mayor-judge insisted that the sessions court was the right institution to make this decision. Even "if the corporation had in fact expressly authorized swine to run at large in the streets," it would not, said the prosecutor, limit the authority of the grand jury to issue this indictment, for "the corporation cannot abrogate the common law." To which the mayor added that the corporation (meaning the common council) had no right to pass any law contrary either to state statute or to "the common, or unwritten law of the land."[35] The only question was whether the acts charged and proved constituted a nuisance as defined by legal authority and precedent. Where a remedy existed at common law, even a statute which gave a further or different remedy could not take away the common law remedy, unless the statute explicitly stated its intent to do so.

B. The Dream of a Pig-free City

Were the pigs Harriet kept in the streets a nuisance? His lawyers rested their defense on the claim that labeling pigs in the streets a nuisance was nothing less than a direct attack by elites on the way of life of the poor. "[A] great convenience, and almost an essential source on the score of provisions would be taken from the poor or less opulent of the citizens by a conviction." If this practice were indictable as a nuisance:

> the dandies, who are too delicate to endure the sight, or even the idea of so odious a creature, might exult; but many poor families might experience far different sensations, and be driven to beggary or the Alms House for a portion of that subsistence of which a conviction in this case would deprive them.[36]

Harriet's lawyers conceded that keeping pigs in the city might produce some "few and slight inconveniences." Yet, they insisted, those inconveniences were hardly sufficient to constitute an indictable nuisance. Whatever problems pigs caused could not be distinguished from the problems caused by urban dogs, cats, and horses, none of which were seen as indictable nuisances. In any event, a social practice could become a public nuisance only if it violated standards held in common by the entire population of a community.[37]

To the prosecutor, the fact that hogs "would attack children in the streets, and mangle them and commit all sorts of indecencies," was all that needed to be proved to reveal them as public nuisances.[38] The mayor, on the other hand, used his charge to the jury to develop a short essay on the law of nuisance and the significance of labeling pigs in the streets as a nuisance, an essay he probably thought responsive to the charges of defendant's lawyers.

What is a public nuisance? It is, said the mayor, "an offence against the public order and economical regimen of the state, and an annoyance to the public, such as produces disturbance in the reasonable enjoyment of life, property, or common comforts of life, and that, though no man's health be affected."[39] As such, the standard against which to judge the presence of pigs in the streets was made objective and distanced from the wishes of particular communities. The public which might be annoyed by the condition was not the populace directly involved, but rather the partially abstracted "public" characteristics of American federalism.[40]

Local conditions, of course, could not be entirely ignored. To use the apposite language of Mr. Justice Sutherland 110 years after *People v. Harriet* (explaining why it is constitutionally legitimate to keep apartments out of areas zoned for single family residences only), "A nuisance may be merely a right thing in the wrong place,—like a pig in the parlor instead of the barnyard."[41] The pig that is a nuisance on Broadway, in the built up part of Manhattan Island, might not be one on the northern outskirts of the city.

The mayor, however, refused to concede to the residents of particular neighborhoods any power to determine the presence of a public nuisance. The tolerance of particular communities, their acceptance of a particular social practice, could not control the legal issue. "A nuisance at Corlaer's Hook may not, of necessity, be a nuisance to the people at the Battery; but it must be such as that people at large would be offended if they happen to come to the place."[42] Using the inverted egalitarianism characteristic of American federalism,[43] the mayor made the equal citizenship of all in the city a justification for an attack by wealthier citizens on practices identified with poorer ones. The streets, we might paraphrase the mayor as saying, belonged to the people, not the pigs, and, as a corollary, neighborhood sensibilities had no particular right to consideration against the wishes of the sovereign "people" in control of the institutions of government.

But what made pigs a legally proscribable nuisance? The mayor restated the evidence the prosecutor had earlier raised about the dangers and harms produced by pigs. He could have left it there, but he did not, perhaps because in the last analysis it is difficult to see how these urban dangers and harms were distinguishable from many others left unproscribed. Instead, his charge to the jury shifted attention to the "great and proud city" he was charged with governing and the significance for its future of removing the pigs.

What was the pigless city he imagined? His jury charge suggested three features: First, a city whose cleanliness and health—the public good—would be produced by a paid bureaucracy, rather than through the more or less compulsory involvement of a citizenry in corporate governance. Traditionally, public services and goods had been a by-product of the commercial life of the community. Public docks and streets, for example, were often produced as conditions for grants of wharf space.[44] In poorer wards, streetcleaning resulted from the presence of pigs, which offered artisans some protection from total dependence on a market economy. Now, however, public goods—the products of instrumental state action—would be created, if at all, by specialized public means using public employees paid for by public tax dollars. "So, it is . . . said," the mayor noted, "that they [swine] are a useful sort of scavengers; but I think our corporation will not employ brutal agency for that object when men can be got to do it."[45]

Second, a city whose workers will be entirely dependent on a cash economy for their subsistence. "It is said, that if we restrain swine form running in the street, we shall injure the poor. Why, gentlemen! must we feed the poor at the expense of human flesh?"[46] Putting aside the hyperbole, one might still ask: how did he expect to feed the poor if they were denied their pigs? What did he expect them to live on? The obvious answer is that he expected a growing economy to provide jobs and a rising standard of living for the working classes, so that all could purchase food sufficient for a healthy diet. But one could as easily pose his vision in more Machiavellian terms: a working class without its pigs would be that much more dependent on the market and employers, that much more controllable in situations of labor conflict.[47] Most likely, he had not thought about the question at all, seeing the city as his, to be molded to suit his vision of urbanity.

Third, a city radically separated from the countryside. Maitland once wrote that those who wished to study the legal history of urban government would necessarily have fields and farms on their hands.[48] Throughout most of human history that has been sound advice. To the mayor, though, that history was one from which he wanted escape. A pig in the city, like Sutherland's pig in the parlor, was matter out of place.[49] And implicit in his dream of piglessness was a vision of a place where "our wives and daughters" can "walk abroad through the streets of the city without encountering the most disgusting spectacles of those animals indulging the propensities of nature."[50] That kind of nature had no place in urban life.[51]

What may be most striking about all this is the mayor's prescience. Just as the modern exclusionary suburb can be derived imaginatively from Justice Sutherland's 1926 language in *Euclid v. Ambler*, so the modern—that is to say, 19th century—city springs from the text of Mayor Colden's charge to the jury in *People v. Harriet*. The creation of a modern bureaucracy, the transformation of relatively self-sufficient artisans and mechanics into a working class, and the growth of a commercial rural agriculture dedicated to feeding urban residents are all commonly viewed as central features of urban modernity.

In what ways, we might wonder, did Colden's language help make that vision come to life?

C. The Silence of Custom

There is nothing surprising about the fact that neither the mayor nor the prosecutor ever suggested that pig keepers possessed any customary rights to run their pigs in the streets. Indeed, a corollary of the legal instrumentalism and social engineering that characterized their arguments would certainly be a general rejection of claims that an "inveterate practice"[52] might by its very existence constrain public policy and implementation.

Still, a generation of distinguished works of social history have demonstrated the extent to which claims of custom formed both the property and the political practice of poor and laboring classes in early modern England and America. Custom was "one of the normative weapons of the weak against the strong, one of the ways in which power was disciplined and concessions enjoyed."[53] We might therefore expect that Harriet's lawyers would have construed the practice of keeping pigs in the streets as a custom held by its practitioners as a legal right.

Did Harriet's attorneys ever raise such a claim? They began their summation stating that the practice of allowing pigs to run in the streets was of "immemorial duration,"[54] thereby invoking the standard common law vocabulary for claims to customary rights. But from then on their defense was shaped by an implicit concession that the pig keeper held no right that the state was obliged to recognize. In part their argument for governmental restraint was prudential: that the social evils produced by pigs running in the streets were (over)matched by social goods, thereby making the practice an inappropriate object of regulation and delegalization. In part it was framed by what my colleague Neil Komesar calls the problem of "comparative institutional choice:" not whether government per se could make the decision to forbid the running of pigs in the streets, but whether the sessions court was the right institution to make such a decision.[55] Harriet's lawyers never suggested that pig keepers should be thought of as owning a customary right (or easement) in the streets of the city or, alternatively, that the city was bound by its past conduct in accepting as legal the pigs in its streets to continue accepting that practice.

I elsewhere have argued that a custom-restrained way of conceptualizing municipal governance had become impossible by the end of the second decade of the 19th century.[56] Lawyers like those who argued Harriet's case could no longer think in terms of customary rights, at least not in making a formal legal argument for their client, certainly not if their adversary was the corporation of the city of New York. I am today, for reasons which will become apparent, far less certain than I was then that the silence of Harriet's lawyers can stand as strong evidence for my earlier claim, but I remain convinced of the significance of that silence.

Why not raise the claim of a customary right held by artisans and other relatively poor residents of the city? We can imagine that at the most basic level such a claim would conflict with the republican political commitments of American artisans. In the common law, customary rights always have been intimately bound up with status ascriptions. One reason that English "peasants" could plausibly claim particular manorial rights—such as grazing animals or gathering firewood—was precisely because they were publicly identified as peasants. Would American artisans have allowed their lawyers to label them similarly? Republican-egalitarianism might in this case have posed a direct challenge to the defense of traditional rights and usages which Sean Wilentz and Howard Rock have demonstrated also lay at the heart of so much of artisans' political practice.[57]

But let us lay aside the contradictions of American political identity and political theory. Hypothetically, could Harriet's lawyers have found in 18th century English common law principles a basis for arguing that their client had a customary right to run pigs in the streets?[58] I think the answer is no, but answering the question requires a short detour through the bramble bush of English customary law.

From Coke through Blackstone and beyond, custom was a (perhaps the) central category in English jurisprudence. It was a protean term, irreducible to clear or coherent categories. At times the whole of the common law was seen as an expression of the customs of the English people. At times the common law was itself characterized as a custom.[59] Analytic categories were easily overwhelmed by the descriptive uses to which the term "custom" might be put in legal practice.[60] Still, eighteenth century jurisprudence devoted much energy to the project of rationalizing and ordering the varieties of customs, and typically, legal theorists distinguished custom as a source of law from custom as a particular type of law.[61] It is the latter category which concerns us here.

As a particular type of law within the larger regime of the common law, custom was identified with "local" bodies of rules or rights which could be differentiated from those of the nation as a whole.[62] For some purposes these local or "particular" normative orders would be seen as exemptions from general law. For other purposes they would be regarded as property rights (usually) held by particular communities in their group of corporate capacity. Particular customs included distinctive forms of land tenure or distinctive use-rights: rights to gather twigs from royal or aristocratic forests, rights to collect tolls, rights to play cricket on specified lands, distinctive decision-making bodies, rights to collect dues, to hold banquets, to be exempted from general rules, obligations, or procedures. The varieties of particular customs existent in early modern England beggars the imagination and seems at times to swamp any notion of the common law as a coherent body of positive legal doctrine.

Using the examples above, it would seem a relatively easy task to characterize the long-standing social practice of letting pigs run on New York City's streets as a particular custom which the sessions court should have recognized. By "immemorial usage," it might have been said, residents of the city and/or artisans and/or the city's poor held the right to depasture their beasts in the corporation's close (the streets) or, alternatively, in the municipal commons (the streets).[63]

Characterization, however, is not everything, and before concluding that the silence of Harriet's counsel was an error, it is necessary to consider the ways eighteenth century courts and treatise writers treated claims to particular customs.[64] Many scholars have used the universe of particular legal customs as a symbol of the limited authority and reach of the state in the early modern world.[65] But the history of English customs is also a part of the history of the growth of state power, one important exercise of which was the "legalization" of customs by the courts.[66] At the same time that particular customs constrained and limited the exercise of national legal authority, legal authority set out a series of standards by which to recognize and control the existence and value of a legally enforceable custom. Blackstone summarized those standards as requisites that a custom be ancient, continuous, peaceable, certain, compulsive, and reasonable. In almost all cases the existence of the social practice had to be specifically proved. And insofar as the practice of the custom was in derogation of common law rules, it would be interpreted strictly.[67]

Applying two of these standards, certainty and reasonableness, to the claimed right to keep pigs in New York City's streets could only have been disastrous to Harriet's case. Keeping pigs may look like a custom not unlike (for example) the right to play cricket on specific lands. But the actual local practice of keeping pigs in the streets was unmistakably "uncertain," and therefore unenforceable as a custom, for there was no way of specifying in advance who owned the right. "Certainty" usually flowed from tenure: from a landed estate or some secure foundation in property. Manorial tenants could hold a customary right to let their pigs run on manor property. The residents of a village or town could not use their residency as a way of making similar claims on municipal property.[68] A particular custom might become the property of a particular trade, but again, that was so because a traditional apprenticeship process provided a structure of inheritance and of vested property rights which made certain who was entitled to the custom. By 1819 such a conceptualization of apprenticeship would have been almost inconceivable in New York City, and in any event nothing in the history of the social practice identified it unambiguously with a particular trade. It may well be that the greater number of pigs found in the streets belonged to butchers fattening the imported pigs before slaughter. But Harriet, as a butcher, could not lay claim to a right distinctively held by the members of his trade (and, of course, his lawyers never tried.)[69]

Similarly, the legal requirement that a practice be "reasonable" meant that its legitimacy could always be challenged. No practice, no matter how settled, could be maintained if a court determined that its exercise was unreasonable. And one might read both the prosecution's case and the mayor's charge as demonstrations of the unreasonableness of the practice of keeping pigs in the streets.

What made the practice unreasonable? Was it enough for the mayor to declare that unpenned hogs were a nuisance under New York common law? Eighteenth century English legal lore would have said, by contrast, that the inconsistency of the practice with central policy could not determine its unreasonableness. There was no necessity that a custom be justified by public policy or general legal reasoning. It was sufficient "if no good legal reason [could] be assigned against it."[70]

Did that mean that a committed application of legal precedent should have led to a determination that pig keeping was not an unreasonable practice? Probably not. In spite of the seeming clarity of the black letter rule, English legal practice during the 18th and 19th centuries was deeply divided on the proper relationship between central policy and inconsistent local practice. English courts often held void a usage or custom opposing an established rule of law.[71] A custom which benefited the individual to the detriment of the commonwealth was per se bad.[72]

What little American doctrine there was on the question was less ambivalent and posed a republican critique of any attempt to insist on the legitimacy of customs in the face of contrary legal rules.[73] The author of the only American legal treatise on customs concluded his unhappy examination of the case law language with the following restatement of the meaning of unreasonableness:[74]

> A usage or custom, as we have already shown, is not invalid simply because it is different in its effect from the general principles of law applicable to the particular circumstances in its absence. But if it conflicts with an established rule of public policy which it is not to the general interest to disturb; if its effect is injurious to the parties themselves in their relations to each other; if, in short, it is an unjust, oppressive, or impolitic usage, then it will not be recognized in courts of justice, for it will lack one of the requisites of a valid custom, viz., reasonableness.[75]

In the face of the burden raised by such a standard of reasonableness, not to mention the monumental difficulty of making the practice of urban pig keeping appear a certain custom, we can imagine that the swine's legal defenders reasonably concluded that they had nothing to gain by framing their claims in the form of customary right. And thus no one ever raised the kinds of arguments sketched out in the last few pages.

D. *The Law of Pigs*

Both prosecutor and mayor took pains to assure the jury that "this prosecution was not instituted from vindictive motives." Indeed, the mayor went on to admit that the defendant had been given an implicit license to keep pigs in the streets, "and that exonerates him from any immoral intent." Punishment would thus be nominal. (In fact, after the jury arrived at a guilty verdict, Harriet was fined only one dollar and costs.)[76]

The point was to establish a legal principle: that there was no legal right to keep swine in the streets of the city or, alternatively, that doing so constituted a public nuisance which left the perpetrator subject to criminal prosecution. From the mayor's perspective—indeed, from the perspective of what most of us think of as law—it may well be that the case succeeded in establishing that principle. No appeal was taken.[77] I can find no published cases anywhere in America after 1819 in which the issue was reargued.[78] While many cases discussed the power of cities to impound pigs and other animals found in city streets, all of them presume that a city may regulate to abate what is by definition a public nuisance.[79]

A distinctively bourgeois vision of a pig-free city had thus become a legal reality in New York City. A traditional social practice of municipal artisans had been publicly and formally declared unsafe, immoral, and, therefore, illegal.[80] To keep pigs on municipal streets was to commit a crime. The rights Mr. Harriet and his fellow pig keepers once thought they had in the streets of their city no longer were theirs to claim.

IV. *People v Harriet* as Episode

A. The Persistence of Pigs

> I cannot refrain from saying a few kind words on behalf of the favored pet of the Americans, the swine. I have not yet found any city, county, or town where I have not seen these lovable animals wandering about peacefully in huge herds. Everywhere their domestic tendencies are much in evidence; no respectable sow appears in public unless she is surrounded by a countless number of beloved offspring. These family groups are a pleasing sight to the Americans, not only because they mean increasing prosperity but also because a young porker is a particularly delicious morsel. Besides, the swine have shown certain good traits which are of real practical value; in the country they greedily devour all kinds of snakes and the like, and in the towns they are very helpful in keeping the streets "cleaner than man can do" by eating up all kinds of refuse. And then, when these walking sewers are properly filled up they are butchered and provide a real treat for the dinner-table.[81]

This passage, taken from the travel descriptions of Norwegian lawyer Ole Raeder, was written in 1847, nearly thirty years after *People v. Harriet*. It will, of course, surprise no one that the delegalization of keeping pigs in the streets did not eliminate pigs immediately from American city streets. But thirty years?

Throughout that time, pigs remained important as "local color" for foreign travellers. In *Martin Chuzzlewit*, based on Charles Dickens' 1842 trip to America, Dickens has Martin arrive in New York and go to a house distinguished by "jalousie blinds to every window, a flight of steps before the green street-door, a shining white ornament on the rails on either side like a petrified pineapple, polished, a little oblong plate of the same material over the knocker, . . . and four accidental pigs looking down the area." And while Martin waits to be let in, "the pigs were joined by two or three friends from the next street, in company with whom they lay down sociably in the gutter."[82]

Foreign travellers ascribed the pigs' continuing presence on the urban scene to two familiar intertwined causes, both of which can be drawn from Raeder's account. First, they presumed the centrality of pork in the American diet.[83] Second, they regarded urban swine as an odd solution to the problem of urban sanitation. Hogs fattening on wastes found on city streets were monuments to the inability or unwillingness of city government to provide effective street cleaning. They were, as Charles Rosenberg has written in his study of cholera in New York City, "the city's shame, but, nevertheless, its only efficient scavengers."[84] And the result was that the whole city could be characterized as a "pigstye."[85]

That New York City (like other American cities) semi-officially tolerated swine is suggested by an 1848 case involving a father's attempt to collect damages from the city after his son was killed by a pig loose on Chatham Street. The father based his suit on an 1839 ordinance imposing penalties on owners for any swine at large on city streets.[86] The result of the enactment of that ordinance was, according to the father, a municipal assumption of liability.

The New York Superior Court, on the other hand, characterized the injury as one "which no legislation can prevent, and which no system of laws can adequately redress." No government, wrote Judge Sandford for the court, "ever assumed, or was subjected to a general liability of this description." And the court refused to recognize any municipal duty to keep swine off the streets.[87]

The court had good reason not to hold the city liable for the death of the child. If the city were liable here, why not every time a vehicle injured some passerby while breaking the municipal ordinance "against racing and furious driving in the public streets?"[88] But note the analogy's implicit tolerance of pigs in the streets. Keeping them in the streets was a wrong, just as a speeding cart was a wrong, but also something close to an inevitable fact of municipal life.[89]

There were campaigns at various times over the thirty year period that followed *People v. Harriet* to rid New York City of its pigs. For example, Raeder told his Norwegian readers that the city had recently declared "war . . . against these animals; it was decreed that any pig found walking the streets of New York after the first of July of this year [1847] should be outlawed and become the property of anyone who could catch it." But in this case, as in others, the campaign failed. Raeder was uncertain "if the law was dropped or if a common feeling of sympathy prevented its execution, but at any rate I have seen pigs wandering about just as freely as ever, even after that ominous day, on Broadway itself, and evidently with perfect peace of mind, just as though no one had ever thought of depriving them of life, liberty, and the pursuit of happiness."[90] And as far as I can tell, pigs were kept openly and unashamedly in many parts of New York City throughout the first half of the 19th century.

THE POLICE, UNDER THE DIRECTION OF INSPECTOR DOWNING, CLEARING THE PIGGERIES OF BERNARD BILLY

Engraving by L.H.S. in *Frank Leslie's Illustrated*, Aug. 13, 1859.
Collection of the New-York Historical Society, with permission.

Rosenberg suggests that the end of New York street pig keeping came during the infamous cholera epidemic of 1849.[91] Public health officials had learned the intimate connection between fifth and the spread of disease, and though swine had a traditional status as fifth removers, a new campaign was initiated under color of municipal emergency which identified them as filth producers. City officials vowed to obliterate pigs from the face of the city. Owners resisted, sometimes violently, and many hid their pigs in basements and cellars, but by June, 1849 the police had taken five to six thousand pigs into custody. Thereafter, if numbers of pigs remained in the city, their presence in the streets had become surreptitious and unambiguously "criminal."[92]

B. The Persistence of Custom

How to explain the public presence of a criminalized pig through the 1840s? Since the 1930s, American socio-legal writing has provided a standard explanation for such situations in terms of the gap between "law-in-the-books" (*People v. Harriet*) and "law-in-action" (or here, "in-the-streets"). Gap analysis takes a variety of competing forms. Some focus on the intentions of the makers of the law, asking whether they really cared about enforcement. Some focus on the structure of implementation and enforcement. Some ask questions about the role(s) of legal norms in the social structure and wonder whether the gap is not a systemic feature of the social order. All of these analytic forms assume a separation between the legal norm as articulated—in this case that pigs are not permitted in the streets of New York City—and the social fact of human (and animal) behavior—in this case the persistence of pigs in the streets.

There are many problems with gap analysis, and I do not intend here to rehearse a theoretical critique which has been made many times before.[93] My dissatisfaction with this form of explanation is less subtle. Gap analysis rests on the presumed existence of a norm which in one way or another could have been enforced. Up to now I have proceeded by showing the ways that *People v. Harriet* revealed such a norm. And I am quite sure that for some New Yorkers—notably for the mayor, the prosecutor, perhaps even the defense attorneys in the case, and for other middle and upper class residents of the city—*Harriet* embodied the law. But it is equally clear from even the most cursory look at the records of the common council, that for many, and perhaps even the majority, of the active citizens of the city, *Harriet* meant little, if anything. The idea of a gap only makes sense where there is some shared consciousness (some accepted structure of legitimation, a hegemonic order) that the law was the law, and therefore, "ought" to be obeyed (since in gap analysis, law is a sphere of "oughts").[94] But as we shall see, there was no such shared consciousness on the question of the legitimacy of labeling pigs as nuisances throughout the first half of the 19th century.

Consider the following narrative of municipal law-making and law enforcement during the fourteen years following *People v. Harriet*. In November, 1819, ten months after the case, the common council asked its counsel to prepare an ordinance to make it illegal for pigs to run at large in the more settled parts of the city, implicitly assuming that in the absence of such a law pigs in the street were legal. A new law, similar to the one approved and rejected in 1818, was quickly drafted, and was quickly voted down.[95] Six months later the council passed a resolution "directing" that hogs not be allowed to run at large in the southern wards, which was referred to the police committee to consider how best to proceed.[96]

In November, 1820 the police committee made its report. The only way a law could be passed, wrote the committee, would be if animals found at large in the settled portions of the city were given directly to the almshouse for the use of the poor. Why was that the only way? We can assume one reason was that an explicit charitable intent would blunt the arguments of those who regularly marshalled support to defeat anti-pig legislation. The claims of the "poor" pig keeper would be trumped by the needs of the still-poorer resident of the almshouse. But the committee also argued that traditional forms of regulation, which rewarded "pignappers" and which put found animals into a pound where they remained until the owner paid a fine, "have proved entirely inadequate for the correction of the evil." Neighborhood solidarity almost certainly made the risks of pignapping far higher than the rewards provided by any municipal legislation. It was, moreover, usually impossible to identify the owners of pigs found in the streets, so that a pig keeper who chose to abandon his or her captured swine could avoid all punishment.[97] Conversely, if an owner chose to come forward and pay the fine, the pig would in short order be back on the street, defeating the purpose of the ordinance.

While the proposal to make pigs found in the streets the property of the almshouse could not solve the problem of the anonymity of pig keepers, it would, on the other hand, transfer responsibility for capturing pigs from private enterprise to the public hands of the almshouse commissioners.[98] Most important of all, it meant that a captured pig was permanently removed from city streets.

According to the police committee, the sole problem with passing such an ordinance was that it violated the city's charter, which only authorized the use of fines. Enabling legislation from the state would be needed, and so an application to the legislature and a draft statute were sent to Albany, which quickly did as the common council desired. And in late April, 1821 an ordinance reflecting the police committee's plan was read and passed.[99]

This law remained the model for municipal regulation of swine for the next decade.[100] The minutes of the common council provide conflicting evidence on how well this new law was enforced. In July the almshouse commissioners reported that their first attempt to carry it into effect "had been resisted and opposed . . . by a collection of Persons who exercised great violence towards them."[101] There is little in the records to indicate that many pigs were ever captured by the commissioners' agents. Yet the council minutes do suggest that the traditional practice of keeping pigs in the streets was threatened by the new regime. A petition from inhabitants of Greenwich Village, which was not included in the area affected by the ordinance, indicated that some pig keepers were moving to that northern clime.[102] And by July, 1821 the council began to receive a steady stream of petitions by pig keepers—a suspiciously large number of whom were "poor widows"—for the return of their hogs or for a monetary equivalent.[103]

In June, 1822, the council heard a petition to exclude the seventh and tenth wards from the operation of the new law. The request was referred to the alderman from those wards, who soon reported:

> [I]nhabitants in those two wards are nearly unanimous in the opinion that the law should be so amended as to admit swine running at large in those wards, and as the Laws are passed for the benefit of the Citizens their opinions Should be consulted [.] [T]hey also would state that the Bell carts [the carts of municipal garbage and refuse collectors] do not often come into those wards which makes it more necessary that the swine Should run at large to eat the garbage thrown into the Streets [.] [T]hey would also state that a considerable part of those two wards are but thinly inhabited.[104]

By July a law to exempt the area east of Market and Forsythe Streets had been presented to the full board and passed.[105]

Similar exemptions were considered (and often approved) by the council over the next decade. One of the responsibilities of the council over municipal life was to determine the applicability of seemingly general municipal regulations to different parts of the city. Some parts properly were subject to the municipal law which turned pigs found in the streets into food for the almshouse. Some were not.[106] Only in some wards would a pig in the street be considered a nuisance equivalent to a pig in the parlor.

Defenders of the pigs were, needless to say, not the only ones who petitioned the common council for relief. In March, 1825, for example, taxpayers from the Lamp and Watch District, which evidently had been exempted from the ordinance, successfully petitioned to amend the law to keep hogs from running at large in their ward. Four months later Moses Jaques complained that a butcher in his neighborhood kept "a large drove" of swine in the streets, "who being fed on the blood and offiles becom extreemly ferocious and dangerous to children." In March 1826, a petition asking that hogs be prohibited from running at large in the eleventh ward was referred to the police committee, which agreed and drafted an amendment to the existing law.[107]

The council minutes suggest that a more sustained campaign to eradicate the swine began towards the end of 1829. A petition for relief from hogs by inhabitants of the twelfth ward was followed by a report of the police committee recommending that the council extend the ordinance to the whole city, including the area north of Fourteenth Street. In February, 1830, a petition was read urging the council to ensure that the law was being carried into effect. Then, in June, the council itself resolved that the almshouse commissioners be directed to enforce the law.[108]

But then, evidently, the pig keepers regrouped, and the campaign came to a halt. In July, the superintendent of the almshouse reported that after he had taken several swine from the streets as directed by law, one of the owners of the pigs had brought an action in trover, and a jury had just returned a verdict in favor of the plaintiff? What should he do? And who would pay the damages awarded by the court?[109]

The council referred those questions to the police committee. But before it could report an answer, New York City's swine eradication program suffered a still more serious blow. In February, 1831, the superior court decided that the municipal law taking pigs off the streets and donating them to the poor house was unconstitutional, presumably because it took property without compensation.[110] And so, in 1832 the council reinstituted the public pound system of regulation which it earlier had declared to be an ineffectual response to the problem.[111]

How should this narrative be understood? A persistent gap analyst might insist that all that has been revealed is a failure by city government to implement the legal norm articulated in *People v. Harriet*. Yet it would be hard to overemphasize the wrongheadedness of that insistence. Whatever the common council was, it certainly was not an implementer—successful or not—of the "law" of *Harriet*. The minutes of the council reveal a studied ignorance not just of that case but of the significance of nuisance law as applied to urban pigs.[112] The behavior of all participants seems premised on the assumption that in the absence of explicit municipal regulation pig keeping was legal. The ongoing debate in the council was fundamentally about lawmaking, not problems of enforcement.[113]

In this context, *Harriet* itself may best be understood as an attempted usurpation of the ordinary lawmaking authority of the common council. As of 1819 the mayor of New York was still appointed by a state council and thus was not beholden to the artisans who worked to prevent municipal legislation and who helped elect the common council. The grand jury and the prosecutor indicted Harriet immediately after the defeat in the council of an attempt to outlaw the keeping of pigs. And at the heart of the mayor's arguments and those of the prosecutor was the claim that the council had no right to authorize a practice which was (or rather, which the mayor declared to be) illegal. The mayor may have thought that his charge to the jury satisfactorily resolved the questions of comparative institutional choice and jurisdictional authority raised by the case. There is no reason to think that members of the common council, let alone citizen pig keepers, shared in that opinion. While the case has all the markings of an authoritative text, and may be read as such (as I have in the first half of this Article), it likely struck some contemporary readers as about as authoritative as the council's implicit legalization of pig keeping no doubt struck Mayor Colden.

What then was the law of keeping pigs in the streets in the years after *People v. Harriet*? As should be apparent, the question does not admit a neutral, objective, singular answer, once we begin to think of pig keeping law as an arena of conflict, rather than as an unfolding text. How one characterized the law was an act of aggression, a way of claiming rights or of asserting authority. And any attempt by us to answer the question retrospectively inevitably will end with numbers of competing answers.

The point is not that participants could make the law into anything they chose. Of course that was not the case. Parts of the law belonged to one's antagonist. Parts (perhaps the most important parts) were constituted out of the conflict between competing groups, and belonged to no group in particular. We can, for example, imagine that nobody particularly liked the revised ordinance of 1832, which recreated a public pound system of regulation. To those who wanted no pigs at all, it was a recipe for disaster. It gave the ideological high ground to those who would allow the poor pig keeper to keep food on his or her table, since captured pigs no longer went to the almshouse. It seemed to authorize a structure of implicit, and implicitly corrupt, toleration of the pigs in the streets (much like the modern "revolving door" of prostitute regulation). Pig keepers, we might hypothesize, preferred this new law to its immediate predecessor. But for them, likewise, the law was far from ideal, and it certainly was not "their" kind of law. It gave new incentives to "pignappers." It meant that the city council had again labeled pigs as a "bad" to be regulated, and if possible, eliminated.

Still, what the law was depended on who was asking. Within the terms of the situation sketched out, there were three significant perspectives on the question. One, the mayor's, we know well enough already. A second, that of some model pig keeper. I will come to shortly. But first I should briefly turn to the perspective of the pig keeper's lawyers or, what is the same thing, that of the pig keeper seen as a rational maximizer, as a "bad man" (or bad woman) of the law.[114]

Let us imagine a pig keeper sitting in her lawyer's office in, say, 1831. She is, to use Holmes' language, someone who fears "the command of the public force" and who wants "to know under what circumstances and how far" she "will run the risk of coming against what is so much stronger than" she is. She has no ideological commitment to keeping pigs. It is simply what she does right now. It matters not a whit to her "whether the act [of keeping pigs in the streets] . . . is described [in the law] in terms of praise or in terms of blame, or whether the law purports to prohibit it or to allow it." All she cares about are the "material consequences" that the law may subject her to if she continues in her occupation. From her lawyer she needs information about what the courts and other public decision-makers "will do in fact" if they discover her pigs in the streets. That is what she means by "the law."[115]

What will she learn from her lawyer? On the one hand, he will tell her that her occupation may subject her to a criminal prosecution for maintaining a public nuisance, although he would certainly mention that in the only published prosecution the defendant was fined just one dollar and costs. There remains, as of 1831, a municipal ordinance which gives the almshouse commissioners authority to grab her pigs off the streets. But the common council has on several occasions reimbursed pig keepers for the loss of their property under the ordinance. And, the lawyer would note, a pig keeper whose pigs were snatched has recently successfully sued and been awarded damages for the loss of the swine. Whether or not that damage award could be sustained, the risk of governmental action would be highly dependent on where she lives. Some areas of the city are formally or informally exempted from enforcement. Finally, he might advise (although here he would come close to the boundaries of legal ethics) that her risk of being caught for keeping pigs in city streets is low in any event, because so many of her fellow New Yorkers are doing likewise, and because the resources of government are simply inadequate to the task of eradicating the pigs.

Such a perspective on the law of pig keeping in New York City's streets highlights the complexity of the situation. Just to solve what seemed to be an archaic and extraordinarily narrow and sharply defined legal problem, the lawyer would need information of a variety and detail not unlike that used by the modern food and drug or securities lawyer. The law did not embody one coherent policy. It constituted a number of conflicting policies, and the information he could give his client was necessarily uncertain and incomplete. It thus carries us far from the integrated vision of the mayor in *People v. Harriet*.

But does it encompass the point of view of the pig keepers themselves? In part, of course. But in the most important ways, not at all. I do not want to suggest that the common council minutes give me a window into the legal consciousness of the pig keepers, although they do assuredly tell the attentive reader some things. One thing those records clearly announce is the involvement of pig keepers in lawmaking. The Holmesian vision of lawyer and client starts from a premise that law is an external, objective social fact—a complex, perhaps incoherent social fact—but still one outside of the control of the lawyer and client. The law to Holmes was a maze through which the lawyer guided the client in order to help her achieve given ends (like getting to the other side). To the pig keepers, however, the law was a domain of conflict in whose construction they participated. At the heart of the Holmesian lawyer's vision is a kind of passivity towards public power. It is the client who inevitably will have to accommodate herself to "that which is so much stronger than [s]he is." To the pig keepers, however, the law was both an external force imposing itself on them and also, and at the same time, a structure within which they resisted and worked to control their traditional social practices.

All this becomes increasingly speculative, but I remain convinced that when pig keepers thought about the law of pig keeping they thought of themselves as owning a customary right to keep pigs in New York City streets. Assuredly, lawyers and judges could not have formally recognized the existence of such a right. But even they knew the right survived. And the pig keepers themselves knew it survived because they, the pig keepers, worked to make it so.

What were the terms of that right? Presumably, the prolonged conflict between pig keepers and their adversaries should have taught the pig keepers by the 1820s that whatever they held was fragile and easily destroyed. Illegality and expropriation were always just around the corner. Yet those who would destroy the right to keep pigs in the streets also faced uncertainties and conflicts. And the pig keepers knew enough to play on the ambiguous political impulses of their enemies. Recall the 1822 report of the aldermen of the seventh and tenth wards, recommending that those wards be exempted from the operation of the law against swine in the streets.[116] The inhabitants of those wards, according to the aldermen, were nearly unanimously opposed to the present law, "and as the Laws are passed for the benefit of the Citizens their opinions Should be consulted." On what basis could republican political leaders ignore such a claim? The aldermen went on to imply that the residents of those wards were already being treated unequally. Unlike other wards, "the Bell carts do not often come into those wards." Thus, the pigs were serving their customary municipal purpose because of the corporation's failure to provide the preferred alternative.[117]

My point is not that pig keepers could or did insist that their right was absolute and beyond external control. Most rights, even the most conventional of property rights, are held with an awareness of partiality and of our subjection to other claims in particular circumstances. How we hold what we regard as ours changes with time and context. Indeed, it may be that consciousness of the right to keep pigs was ultimately overwhelmed and delegitimated by the 1849 cholera epidemic and the unambiguous identification of street pigs with harm to the public health.

Pig keeping was not a legal right because it met the formal requisites of a legal custom. (It didn't.) Nor was it a legal right because it met the objective functional "needs" of the artisanal community of pig keepers. As suggested earlier, it may be that most street pigs were not held as a cheap and uncommercialized food source by the working poor.[118] Harriet's lawyers and other defenders of pig keepers may have largely fantasized their vision of poor families dependent on hogs. It may well be, if only we could do a census, that we would find that most of the pigs were owned by butchers who imported them from Long Island and New Jersey and then fattened them for a period of time before slaughter. Pig keeping was a practice connected with a particular way of life, but I would be hard put to make it crucial, or to link the end of the practice to the end of the community.

What made the keeping of pigs in the streets of New York City a right had nothing to do with its objective characteristics or functions. It was, rather, the fact that a politically active and insistent community of New Yorkers believed pig keeping to be their right and, also, that those who opposed the social practice were (for a significant period of time) unwilling and unable to do what was necessary to stop it. The legal right to keep pigs in New York City's streets was constituted both by the activities of the right's defenders and by the relative passivity and ineffectuality of its opponents.

If I am right that for thirty years after *People v. Harriet* New Yorkers would have recognized a right to keep pigs in the city, does that mean that throughout that period pig keepers would not have recognized that what they were doing was illegal? The question demands more knowledge than I can have about the consciousness of the pig keepers. But even if one assumes that they knew that what they were doing was in some way illegal, what difference does that assumption necessarily make? We all have engaged in practices—say walking a dog without a leash—which we know to violate some law yet which are also legal within our own better understanding of the legal order. Knowing that what they did subjected them theoretically to prosecution did not transform pig keepers into a criminal subculture (whatever that is), skulking in alleyways. Likewise, the knowledge that they were engaged in criminal conduct certainly did not limit their political participation.[119]

The problem is that our conventional legal theory makes it impossible to account for the legal consciousness of a group like the pig keepers of New York City. In defining law as the command of the sovereign we ordinarily deny the legitimacy of interpretive stances other than those—like the mayor's—which have the benefit of formal authoritativeness. Although the sovereign in American political ideology incorporates the pig keepers, our implicit Federalism restricts their participatory role and empowers others to determine the content of the law, which is expected to become their "civic religion."[120]

That way of thinking allows us to maintain our valued vision of law as a (single) text. But in doing so it represses the existence and the relative autonomy of competing and conflicting socially constituted visions of legal order. It is, as a result, clearly false to our own experience of political life and can only distort our understanding of the conflict over the legal right to keep pigs in the streets.[121]

My point is not, as I hope is obvious, that there are not winners and losers in the law, that repressive laws never are imposed from above, that effective participation in this society never has been restricted and debased, that consciousnesses are never shaped by the content of the law. Those may all be empirical realities of our legal history. They are not, however, a priori deductions from the nature of law. If a legal historian has to define or assume a nature of law, and I am not at all certain that it is necessary to do so,[122] he or she might as well start with a definition of law as an arena of conflict within which alternative social visions contended, bargained, and survived.

Having made such a move, a case like *Harriet* comes to be seen as less about the continued existence of a social practice than it is about the terms under which the practice is going to continue. Assume that it made a difference to all concerned that pigs in the streets were labelled a public nuisance. Once so labelled, an important symbol of power had been transferred to those who opposed pigs in the streets. But, however important that victory was, however important control of that element of public discourse might be, *People v. Harriet* did not affect the continued existence of the practice; or its legality, within the worldview we are here exploring. The case was one episode in an ongoing story of bargaining and conflict between contending normative orders.

Such a perspective depends on a recognition of the implicit pluralism of American law—its implicit acceptance of customs founded on multiple sources of legal authority.[123] A custom, as I am using the term here, is not necessarily a practice confirmed by judicial doctrine or statute. Legal authority may emerge from numbers of governmental and quasi-governmental institutions and practices. Prosecutorial discretion, bureaucratic inertia, fiscal incapacity may all play parts as sources and justifications for the practice, as may the realization that action against the custom might undermine the legitimacy or the effectiveness of the political order. But in the end, the legality of the practice of keeping pigs in the streets rested on its actual possession by a group with some political significance, a group capable of imposing its practices, within limits, on the larger community, a group capable of resisting invasions of its relative autonomy. Until the late 1840s, the artisan pig keepers of New York evidently were such a group. An adequate account of our legal history should be capable of incorporating their values as well as those of the mayor of the city of New York.

Notes

1. The conceptual structure of this paper was worked out with the support of summer fellowships from the National Endowment for the Humanities and the Graduate School at the University of Wisconsin-Madison. A draft was presented at a conference on "The Law in America, 1607–1861," at the New York Historical Society. I have benefited from critical readings by Charles Donahue, Nancy Hartog, Willard Hurst, G. Thomas Johnson, John Kidwell, Warren Lehman, and David Sugarman. I would also like to acknowledge the patience of students in my course in American Legal History, who have heard entirely too much from me about Mr. Harriet and his pigs.

The model of competing interpretive strategies emerged out of discussions with Martha Fineman. An early and incomplete attempt to pose the methodological issues can be found in Fineman and Hartog, *Family Law as Text and as Arena of Conflict*, presented to the 1984 Legal History Program seminar at the University of Wisconsin.

2. It does seem to me, however, that legal history's attachment to the first strategy has left it relatively blind to the social meanings of legal rules.

3. I have been much influenced in this project by recent work in English legal history. *See*, in particular, E.P. Thompson, *Whigs and Hunters: the Origin of the Black Act* (1977); E.P. Thompson, *The Poverty of Theory & Other Essays* (1978); Thompson, "The Grid of Inheritance: a Comment," in J. Goody, J. Thirsk, & E.P. Thompson, *Family and Inheritance: Rural Society in Western Europe* 328 (1976); Ignatieff, "State, Civil Society and Total Institution: a Critique of

Recent Social Histories of Punishment," in *Legality, Ideology and the State* 183 (D. Sugarman ed. 1983), Sugarman, "Law, Economy and the State in England, 1750–1914: Some Major Issues," in *Legality, Ideology and the State* 213 (D. Sugarman ed. 1983); Sugarman & Rubin, "Introduction: Towards a New History of Law and Material Society in England, 1750–1914," in *Law, Economy and Society 1750–1914: Essays in the History of English Law 1* (G.R. Rubin & D. Sugarman eds. 1984).

4. Enemies of the pigs tended to describe them as epidemic in the city. I imagine they exaggerated, if only because the amount of food available to the pigs in the streets must have been limited. *See infra* note 7. It also seems likely that a large number of the pigs found in the streets in the 19th century were owned by butchers who fattened them there for a limited period of time before slaughter. *See infra* notes 25 & 51. Even in those wards of the city where pig keeping was most prevalent, I am uncertain how many individuals owned them as personal property.

5. Much of what we know of the urban American hog is, in fact, largely derived from the descriptions of Europeans, who found our acceptance of his presence curious and a little exotic. *See, e.g.*, "The Journal of Mederic Louis Elie Moreau de Saint-Mery," excerpted in *This Was America: True Accounts of People and Places, Manners and Customs, as Recorded by European Travelers to the Western Shore in the Eighteenth, Nineteenth, and Twentieth Centuries* 92 (O. Handlin ed. 1949) and "The Watercolor of the Baroness Hyde de Neuville," reproduced in J.A. Kouwenhoven, *The Columbia Historical Portrait of New York* 111–12 (1953), which is the source for the description in the previous paragraph. *See also infra* text accompanying notes 81–92.

6. The notion that a city is a place where most animals are not is, of course, a recent invention, and one still occasionally controversial. In Madison just recently, a couple were given some chickens with a modern easy-to-clean chicken coop. When the zoning board objected, the couple went to court on the theory that keeping chickens was part of the customary expectations of single-family home ownership. The Wisconsin Court of Appeals ruled in their favor. *See* Capital Times, February 26, 1985. *See also* M. Gold, *Jews Without Money* 53–54 (1930), for a description of goats in New York City in the early 20th century. I am indebted to Rick Abel for the latter reference.

7. We can imagine such an ecological cycle, and contemporary observers insisted on its existence. I have, however, been informed by reliable sources at the experimental farm of the University of Wisconsin-Madison, confirmed by Professor G. Thomas Johnson, of the University of Western Ontario Law School, that pigs today do not eat excrement. My research assistant, Janis Tabor, formerly a reproductive physiologist and agriculturalist, disagrees, pointing to a modern method of feeding swine by having them follow cattle. She argues that pigs do eat excrement so long as it contains grain. I could play historian and suggest that, whatever pigs do today, pigs then might have been different, but this is as good a place as any for me to reveal my abysmal ignorance of things swinish, even though my grandfather once owned a ham factory.

8. Rock, "A Delicate Balance: the Mechanics and the City in the Age of Jefferson," 63 *N.Y. Hist. Soc'y Q.* 93 (1979). The Webbs mention the laconic

presentment before a Welsh court leet of a town in 1804 in which "all [was] well but the pigs." B. Webb & S. Webb, *The Manor and the Borough* 122 (1906).

9. W. Cronon, *Changes in the Land* (1983) describes some of the ways rural pigs became nuisances in colonial New England; see especially *id.* at 135–37. The standard description of the lean and nasty early American pig, which in rural environs was expected to survive through most of the year in the woods, can be found in P. Bidwell & J. Falconer, *History of Agriculture in the Northern United States, 1620–1820* 31–2 (1941). Bidwell and Falconer describe the swine of New Netherlands as relatively larger and heavier than their New England equivalent, although they too were not penned. I have no idea who were the genetic forebears of the urban pigs of early 19th century New York City.

10. *See* Rock, *supra* note 8 at 93, 101–04; R. Mohl, *Poverty in New York,* 1983–1825 11 (1971). On artisanal politics, *see generally* H. Rock, *Artisans of the New Republic* (1979) and S. Wilentz, *Chants Democratic: New York & the Rise of the American Working Class 1788–1850* (1984).

11. *See* W. Cronon, *supra* note 9, at 201. For a somewhat similar analysis of the post Civil War South, see S. Hahn, *The Roots of Southern Populism: Yeomen Farmers and the Transformation of the Georgia Upcountry, 1850–1890* (1983).

12. *See* 6 Minutes of the Common Council of the City of New York, 1758, at 152 [hereinafter cited as C.C. Min.] 7 C.C. Min. 1770, at 246; 1 C.C. Min. 1788, at 369, 379, 385, 417. In colonial New York there had also been a fair amount of provincial legislation dealing with problems of swine. In 1683, for example, a statute was passed giving any one finding a pig loose off of its owner's property the right to kill or capture it. This statute was premised on the "dayly Experience that Swine are Creatures that occasion trouble and difference among Neighbours and rather prejudiciall than beneficiall to the Province while they have liberty to run att randome in the woods or Townes . . ." 1 Colonial Laws 134. Two years later, however, the legislature came to the opposite conclusion that the earlier statute was itself "prejudiciall and of ill consequence to the Inhabitants of this province." And so it was replaced by a local option statute. 1 Colonial Laws 177. Similar pieces of legislation were passed and repealed over the remainder of the colonial period, always applying only to specified counties. 1 Colonial Laws 616, 811; 2 Colonial Laws 301, 992; 3 Colonial Laws 881; 4 Colonial Laws 40, 393, 844, 872, 1069; 5 Colonial Laws 679, 866. It should be noted that none of these statutes, except possibly the early 1683 statute, applied to the pigs of New York City residents. *See infra* note 63.

13. 5 C.C. Min. 692; *see also id.* at 199, 215, 252, 465, 508.

14. *See also infra* text accompanying note 31. I can find no petitions or complaints in the public records protesting the law requiring rings. On the other hand, the evidence on enforcement is mixed. *See, e.g.*, the successful petition to the common council of Peter Witt, a butcher, who asked it to remit his fine. He had not intended, he said, to let his hogs run at large, and had therefore never put rings in their noses. They had, however, "escaped" from his yard into the street. 8 C.C. Min. 1816, at 710. *See also* the "complaint" of some citizens against hogs in their neighborhood running in the street without rings. 9 C.C. Min. 1818, at 653–64.

15. On change and city government, see H. Hartog, *Public Property and Private Power: the Corporation of the City of New York in American Law, 1730–1870* 69–175 (1983). It is worth noting how little attention was ever devoted to public health in debates over swine prior to the 1840s.

16. 8 C.C. Min. 595, 607, 666, 670.

17. 9 C.C. Min. 129–30, 143, 155, 215, 310

18. *Id.* at 393, 462. *See* Rock, *supra* note 8 at 102–04.

19. 9 C.C. Min. 462.

20. *Id.* at 668, 703.

21. Under the Montgomerie Charter of 1730, which remained in 1818 the fundamental law of the corporation of the city of New York, the mayor of the city was an officer appointed by the state Council of Appointments, rather than one elected by municipal residents. Under the charter also, the mayor retained authority to sit and hear cases both in the Mayor's Court (equivalent to a court of common pleas) and in the quarter sessions court. As far as I can tell, 19th century mayors rarely exercised their right to do so. *See generally*, J. Kent, *The Charter of the City of New York* (1836).

Cadwallader Colden (1769–1834), born into a leading Tory family, was a Federalist appointed by a Federalist-dominated Council of Appointments at a time when the city council was controlled by Jeffersonians. He was one of New York City's leading lawyers of the first quarter of the 19th century. *See* D. Fischer, *The Revolution of American Conservatism* 312–313 (1965) and H. Taft, *A Century and a Half at the New York Bar Being the Annals of a Law Firm and Sketches of Its Members* 23, 29, 39 (1938).

22. Louis Lashine and Christian Harriot's Cases, 4 New York City Hall Recorder 26 (1819).

23. *Id.*

24. *Id.* The best record of the case can be found in the New York Judicial Repository 258–72 (1819). (References will be to the latter source). Commentators at the New-York Historical Society Conference suggested that this case might have been a collusive law suit, constructed to test and settle the issue. I see no evidence that it was, and it seems unlikely to me since the pig keepers had nothing to gain from a suit. They were, after all, in control of the city council.

25. On cross-examination Ames insisted that Harriet's pigs were not a nuisance, since the neighborhood was one inhabited primarily by other butchers. The butchers, Ames explained, kept the pigs for up to two weeks after taking them from the sloops before slaughtering them. Was it necessary, asked the district attorney, to let those pigs run at large during that time? No, answered a very cagey witness, "but it is very well if they find plenty of feed in the street to get fatter." *Id.* at 258–61.

It is worth noting that a large, but undisclosed, number of the city's pig keepers were butchers, undercutting claims that the pigs were necessary to provide minimal protein for the urban poor. *See supra* note 4. As we shall see, though, the right to keep pigs in the city had a symbolic significance that seems to have gone well beyond its dietary and economic significance.

26. Defense attorneys attempted to make the prosecution prove that it was Harriet's hogs specifically that were the nuisance, but the mayor ruled that "the

question is, whether the people, the citizens, generally suffer, or are liable to suffer, from hogs running at large." Risk of harm was all that needed to be demonstrated. New York Judicial Repository 261 (1819).

27. *Id.*at 261–64.

28. Harriet's lawyers conceded that he kept pigs. Implicitly, they also conceded that he kept pigs on the street in front of his place, although they argued the insufficiency of the evidence presented by the prosecutor. *Id.* at 264–67.

29. *See* M. Horwitz, *Transformation of American Law* 9–16 (1977). *See also* R. Ellis *The Jeffersonian Crisis: Courts and Politics in the Young Republic* 176–77 (1971); W. Sampson, "Motion to Quash Indictment," People v. Melvin (The Trial of the Journeymen Cordwainers of the City of New York), Yates Select Cases 611 (1810).

30. People v. Harriet, New York Judicial Repository 265–66 (1819).

31. *Id.* at 266.

32. *Id.* at 267. On the dependence of New York City government on state legislation, see Hartog, *supra* note 15, at 126–42. *See, generally*, Frug, "The City as a Legal Concept," 93 *Harv. L. Rev.* 1059 (1980).

33. On comparative institutional choice, see Komesar, "In Search of a General Approach to Legal Analysis: a Comparative Institutional Alternative," 79 *Mich. L. Rev.* 1350 (1981); Komesar, "Taking Institutions Seriously: Introduction to a Strategy for Constitutional Analysis," 51 U. *Chi. L. Rev.* 366 (1984).

34. People v. Harriet, New York Judicial Repository 267–70 (1819).

35. *Id.*

36. *Id.* at 266.

37. *Id.*

38. *Id.* at 268–69.

39. *Id.* at 270. There is a flourishing literature on private nuisance law during the 19th century, *See*, in particular, the superb recent essay by John McLaren, "Nuisance Law and the Industrial Revolution—Some Lessons from Social History," 3 *Ox. J. Leg. Stud.* 155 (1983). *See also*, Brenner, "Nuisance Law and the Industrial Revolution," 3 *J. Leg. Stud.* 403 (1973); Nedelsky, "Judicial Conservatism in an Age of Innovation: Comparative Perspectives on Canadian Nuisance Law 1880–1930" in *I Essays in the History of Canadian Law* 281 (D. Flaherty ed. 1981) M. Horwitz, *The Transformation of American Law*, 1780–1860 74–78(1977). We know much less about public nuisance doctrine. Horwitz suggests that its main purpose was to divert and block private plaintiffs who might otherwise have forced polluters and other nuisance producers to internalize their costs. *Id.* at 76–77. I am unconvinced.

40. *See* G. Wood, *The Creation of the American Republic*, 1776–1787 (1969).

41. Village of Euclid v. Ambler Realty Co., 272 U.S. 365, 388 (1926).

42. People v. Harriet, New York Judicial Repository 271 (1819).

43. *See* G. Wood, *supra* note 40.

44. *See* H. Hartog, *supra* note 15, at 44–68.

45. People v. Harriet, New York Judicial Repository 272 (1819).

46. *Id.*

47. *See generally*, K. Polanyi, *The Great Transformation* (1944); A Smith, *The Wealth of Nations* (1776). This sense of the dependency of labor on the market is often captured by the Marxist notion of "the reserve army of the unemployed."

48. F. Maitland, *Township and Borough* 9 (1899).

49. I had always thought it was Chesterfield who was responsible for the quip that dirt was "matter in the wrong place." The Oxford English Dictionary, however, simply labels it "modern."

A similar sense of urgent need to separate discordant nature from constructed urban civilization is an important part of the rural cemetery movement of the early 19th century, which sought to remove death from urban life (and which also used nuisance law as a tool for effecting the separation). *See* H. Hartog, *supra* note 15, at 71–81; Story, "Consecration Address at the Opening of Mount Auburn Cemetery," *Miscellaneous Writings* 572 (W.W. Story ed. 1852).

50. People v. Harriet, New York Judicial Repository 272 (1819).

51. David Sugarman reminds me that this urge to separate life from the city is surely connected in complicated ways to the general 19th century transformation and sentimentalization of relations with the "natural" world, and in particular with domestic animals. *See generally*, K. Thomas, *Man and the Natural World: Changing Attitudes in England, 1500–1800* (1983); J. Turner, *Reckoning with the Beast: Animals, Pain and Humanity in the Victorian Mind* (1980).

At the same time it is also important to note that the mayor's dislike of pigs, a dislike which he presumably shared with most of his class, did not mean that there was no place for animals in elite visions of 19th century urban life. *See, e.g.* C. Haswell, *Reminiscences of an Octogenerian of the City of New York* (1897):

> Before the introduction of shop butchers, when a butcher in any of the public markets became possessed of an exceptionally fine beef or a number of sheep, he would parade them through the principal streets, as Broadway, Bowery, Greenwich, and Grand streets, preceded by a band of music and followed by the fellow-butchers of his market, with their aprons and sleeves on, in their wagons . . . the cortege being arrested before the house of the customers of the butcher, when it was expected of the occupants to step out and give an order for such part of the animal paraded as they elected.

For more on butchers' retention of pre-industrial work patterns, see Wilentz, *supra* note 10, at 137–139.

52. *See* S. Wilentz, *supra* note 10, at 267.

53. R. Malcolmson, *Popular Recreations in English Society, 1700–1850* 117 (1973) *quoted in* E. Foner, *Tom Paine and Revolutionary America* 157 (1976). *See also* Thompson, "The Moral Economy of the English Crowd in the Eighteenth Century," 50 *Past and Present* 23 (1971); Thompson, "Eighteenth Century English Society: Class Struggle Without Class?" 3 *Soc. Hist.* 133 (1978); Rock, *supra* note 8; S. Wilentz, *supra* note 10. *See also supra* note 3.

54. People v. Harriet, New York Judicial Repository 264 (1819).

55. *See supra* note 32.

56. *See* H. Hartog, *supra* note 15, at 142 *passim*.

57. This conflict within artisans' political values is sensitively explored in E. Foner, *Tom Paine and Revolutionary America* 145–182 (1976).

Whether English rural inhabitants were at all like the standard sociological model of peasants has been a subject of vigorous debate, particularly since the publication of A. Macfarlane, *The Origins of English Individualism* (1978). *See generally*, Sugarman & Rubin, *supra* note 3, at 23–42. What is important here is not whether "plebian" Englishmen would have defined their rights as peasants would but, rather, that Americans of the early nineteenth century thought in terms of a sharp contrast between an imagined English society, in which rights were defined by status, and the freedom of their own society, where "accidents" of birth and social origin could not determine legal rights. See, of course, A. DeTocqueville, *Democracy in America* (1850); M. Meyers, *The Jacksonian Persuasion: Politics and Belief* (1956); W. Hurst, *Law and the Conditions of Freedom in the Nineteenth Century* (1956).

58. To answer that question we should also ignore the obvious and often voiced question whether any American social practice could ever technically constitute an immemorial usage.

One standard source states that conventional American-legal answer:

> Are there any particular customs in the United States? In the strict sense of the word, probably not. . . . We have in fact no *time out of mind* in which such local customs could originate, and no local divisions which could serve as basis for such particular customs. The subdivisions of our oldest states have very rarely any history which cannot be traced back to the formal action of the state or colonial legislature. If there were particular customs originating in such action they would not comply with the requirements described here, and usages not so particularly located would, as has been shown above, be of entirely different character. It is doubtful also how the existence of local customs could be proved in an American state, even if they could be supposed to exist there. . . . Upon what grounds could any American court say, as a matter of law, that a usage thus proved prevailed within the boundary lines of any particular township, county, or other subdivision of the state, in opposition to the common law prevailing on the other side of that boundary.

Hammond, *Note*, in W. Blackstone, 1 *Commentaries on the Laws of England* 135–36 (W.C. Jones ed. 1915). *See also* Ackerman v. Shelp, 3 Hals. (N.J. Law) 125 (1825); Harris v. Carson, 7 Leigh 632 (Va. 1836); Ocean Beach Assoc. v. Brinley, 34 N.J. Eq. 438 (1881).

Much recent colonial history, on the other hand, has detailed the pervasive reliance on local custom characteristic of 17th and 18th century American governmental and legal practice. *See* D. Allen, *In English Ways: The Movement of Societies and the Transferral of English Local Law and Custom to Massachusetts Bay* (1974); Waters, "Family, Inheritance, and Migration in Colonial New England: the Evidence from Guilford, Connecticut," 39 *Wm. & Mary Q.* 64 (1982); Roeber, "*We Hold These Truths . . .:*" *German and Anglo-American Concepts of Property and Inheritance in the Eighteenth Century* (Prepared for the New York

Historical Society Conference on "The Law in America, 1607–1861."). It may also be, as Willard Hurst suggested in commenting on an early draft of this essay, that the reception clauses of the early state constitutions—which formally made English law our law—might have been regarded as importing at least some customs into American law.

59. *See* W. Blackstone, *supra* note 58, at 74. "And indeed it is one of the characteristic marks of English liberty, that our common law depends upon custom; which carries this internal evidence of freedom along with it, that it probably was introduced by the voluntary consent of the people." *Id. See also* C. Allen, *Law in the Making* (1927); M. Hale, *The History of the Common Law of England* (C. Gray ed. 1971); J. Pocock, *The Ancient Constitution and the Feudal Law* (1957); J. Pocock, *The Machiavellian Moment* (1975); Thompson; *supra* note 3. For a clear statement of the anthropological usage of the term "customary law," and a comparison with common law usage, see I. Hamnett, *Chieftainship and Legitimacy* 9–23 (1975). Throughout this section I have been aided by the research assistance of Victoria List and her memorandum, "Custom in England, 1600–1900."

60. *See* E.P. Thompson, *supra* note 3, for a number of examples.

61. *See* W. Friedmann, *Legal Theory* 251–252 (5th ed. 1967). *See* W. Blackstone, *supra* note 58 and M. Hale, *supra* note 61 for a similar analytic division. Blackstone also added a third analytical category: the custom of incorporating civil and ecclesiastical bodies of law into the common law.

62. Hamnett distinguishes this common law definition of custom from customary law, which to anthropologists refers to any popularly produced binding normative order. *See* I. Hamnett, *supra* note 59, at 9–23.

63. Eben Moglen suggested at the New York Historical Society conference that the practice of keeping pigs on the streets could not have been characterized as a custom because technically a legal custom disappeared as soon as a practice was made the subject of legislation. As note 12 illustrates, there were a number of colonial statutes dealing with the problem of pigs running free. Thus, if Moglin is correct, Harriet's lawyers could not have argued the case for a customary right.

It strikes me us unlikely that anyone in 1819 regarded the issue as foreclosed by the existence of colonial statutes. In the first place, only the first provincial statute dealing with swine (1683) could conceivably be read as having applied to New York City, and I remain uncertain whether it was meant to be read in that way. Moreover, even though one might logically say that subsequent acts cannot recreate an immemorial usage destroyed by legislation, the municipal charter enacted by Governor Dongan in 1686, as well as the Montgomerie Charter of 1730, seemed to give the city an immunity from provincial regulation which might well have extended to past acts. More importantly, nothing in the arguments made in Harriet, indeed nothing in what we know of legal practice in New York City in the second decade of the 19th century, suggests that the lawyers involved in the case had any knowledge of those earlier statutes. In some positivist conceptual heaven, the existence of a statute passed in 1683 might well cut off an otherwise plausible claim to a customary right to run pigs in the streets. In New York City in 1819, however, such a claim, if made, would not have been foreclosed by that earlier exercise of legislative authority.

64. Readers of the previous note may also wonder whether the lawyers in *People v Harriet* would have had any knowledge of English common law doctrine and legal practice regarding particular customs. In fact, much in the case does demonstrate the lawyers' immersion in English legal doctrine—notably the ongoing debates over the relevance of the practices of the corporation of London and the applicability of English nuisance law. Although the legal historical writing of the last few years has gone far to demonstrate the significance of an "Americanization" of legal practice, that body of scholarship should not be read as suggesting that American lawyers did not self-consciously work to identify themselves with an English common law tradition. To be a member of a "learned" profession still meant to be learned in English law.

65. *See supra* note 3.

66. Carleton Kemp Allen follows Bentham in regarding the effect of Blackstone's standards for the recognition of customs by courts as being to "reprobate" many customs on grounds of non-existence. Allen, "The Young Bentham," in *Legal Duties and Other Essays in Jurisprudence* 132 (1931). *See generally* Diamond, "The Rule of Law versus the Order of Custom," in *The Rule of Law* 115 (R. Wolff ed. 1971).

67. *See* W. Blackstone, *supra* note 58, at 75–79. *See also* C.K. Allen, *Law in the Making* (7th ed. 1964); J. Lawson, *The Law of Usages and Customs, with Illustrative Cases* (1881). These standards make it easy to see why John Austin and other legal positivists saw no challenge to their position in the existence of legalized customs:

> The admirers of customary law love to trick out their idol with mysterious and imposing attributes. But to those who can see the difference between positive law and morality, there is nothing of mystery about it. Considered as rules of positive morality, customary laws arise from the consent of the governed, and not from the position or establishment of political superiors. But, considered as moral rules turned into positive laws, customary laws are established by the state: established by the state directly, when the customs are promulgated by its statutes; established by the state circuitously when the customs are adopted by its tribunals.

J. Austin, *The Province of Jurisprudence Determined* 32 (H.L.A. Hart ed. 1954).

68. *See* Anon., 2 Dyer 363a (1579) and Gateward's Case, 6 Co. Rep. 59b (1607). There were many English cases of customs identified with the inhabitants of a particular parish, but it is hard to see how the residents of New York City could be equated with the members of a parish, both because of the demographic uncertainty inherent in New York City's explosive growth and because of the emergence of an American conception of localities as administrative subdivisions of the state. Who "belonged" to the community was both practically undeterminable and legally impossible to establish. In an English parish, by contrast, inhabitants held a property interest in their "settlement" (including a right to poor relief if they became destitute).

69. Identifying the custom with "the poor" would also have failed under English law. In a 1788 trespass case a custom giving "poor householders" the right to cut and carry off rotten boughs and branches was declared too vague and uncertain to warrant recognition. Selby v. Robinson, 2 D & E. 758 (1788).

70. *See* W. Blackstone, *supra* note 58, at 140.

71. *See* cases collected in J. Lawson, *supra* note 67, at 465.

72. S. Carter, *Lex Costumaria, or a Treatise of Copy-Hold Estates* 34 (1701).

73. "Evidence of custom and usage is useful, in may cases, to explain the intent of parties to a contract. But the usage of no class of citizens can be sustained in opposition to principles of law." Homer v. Dorr, 10 Mass. 29 (1813). On the identification of republicanism with a general public good antithetical to local customs, see O. Handlin & M.F. Handlin, *Commonwealth* 94–96 (rev. ed. 1969); G. Wood, *supra* note 40, at 53–65, 344–89, 500.

74. Lawson desperately wanted to retain the notion that it was "no objection to a common-law custom that it was contrary to the common law of the land," since he realized that without such a notion the subject of his treatise would hardly have had much legal significance. *See* J. Lawson, *supra* note 67, at 645.

75. *Id.* at 485–486. *See* C.K. Allen, *supra* note 67, at 614–32.

76. People v. Harriet, New York Judicial Repository 272 (1819).

77. An ambiguous result, as we shall see.

78. I should confess that I find no published cases before 1818 which directly confront the issue either. *But see* Shepherd v. Mees, 12 Johns. 433 (N.Y. 1815), where a town by-law requiring that all hogs be kept penned up became the basis for an action of trespass for damages done by defendant's hogs. The trial verdict for the plaintiff was reversed on appeal. The New York Supreme Court held that the by-law could only be read as intending that no hogs should go at large upon the highways, not as interfering with the "interior management" of every man's farm. The power of towns to make such a more expansive "interior regulation" was considered doubtful. And thus, the by-law had no application, as the pigs entered the plaintiff's farm not through an outer fence, adjoining a highway or commons, but through the partition fence between the two neighbors.

79. Many of these cases turned on the interesting question of whether the city had the power to impound the animals of non-residents. *See* cases collected in West Century Digest under *Animals* (1888), particularly sec. XII: "Animals Running at Large."

80. In view of later emphases on health regulation and on the pig's causative role in cholera epidemics, it is surprising how little attention was paid to the unsanitary and unhealthy nature of the social practice.

81. *See* Raeder, in *This Was America: True Accounts of People and Places, Manners and Customs, as Recorded by European Travelers to the Western Shore in the Eighteenth, Nineteenth, and Twentieth Centuries*, *supra* note 5, at 217.

82. C. Dickens, *Martin Chuzzlewit* 290 (Signet ed. 1844). *See likewise* C. Dickens, *American Notes* 34–35 (1842); F. Trollope, *Domestic Manners of the Americans* 88–89 (1949).

83. American contemporaries usually shared this presumption which historians today think entirely mistaken. *See* McMahon, "A Comfortable Subsistence: the

Changing Composition of Diet in Rural New England, 1620–1840," 42 *Wm. & Mary Q.* 26 (1985); P. Gates, *The Farmer's Age: Agriculture, 1815–1860* 214–21 (1960).

84. C. Rosenberg, *The Cholera Years* 17 (1962).

85. 1 *The Diary of George Templeton Strong* 110 (A. Nevins & M.H. Thomas, eds. 1952). *See also* W. Dodge, *Old New York. A Lecture* 20 (1880): "There were then a special kind of street-cleaners, in the vast number of swine, owned by the poorer classes, that crowded some portions of the city, making travel dangerous. It was by many claimed that they ate up the garbage thrown into the streets in spite of law, and thus were to be tolerated."

86. As we shall see below, such an ordinance was typical of several passed by the city council between 1820 and 1850.

87. Levy v. The Mayor, 1 Sandford 465 (N.Y. Sup. Ct. 1848).

88. *Id.* at 467.

89. It is important also to remember that the second third of the 19th century was a time when New York courts were particularly insistent on imposing liability on the city, whenever the city could be characterized as having "voluntarily" assumed particular duties or responsibilities (as in this case). *See* Hartog, *supra* note 15, at 224–39.

90. *See* Raeder, *supra* note 81 at 217–18.

91. *See* C. Rosenberg, *supra* note 84, at 143–44. *But see* the illustration on the succeeding page entitled *The Police, under the direction of Inspector Downing, clearing the Piggeries of Bernard Riley, New York City*, Leslie's Illustrated Newspaper, Aug. 13, 1859. I am grateful to Susan Levine and the New-York Historical Society for finding this illustration and for permitting its reproduction here.

92. *See* C. Rosenberg, *supra* note 84, at 113, 143–44. While I am confident that New York pig keeping did end in 1849 (as the illustration surely indicates), it is clear that pig owners could no longer assume the tolerance of city officials. In other cities, swine remained an accepted part of public life for a longer period. *See, e.g.*, C. Green, *I Washington. A History of the Capital, 1800–1950* 211 (1962); D. Mollenhoff, *Madison, A History of the Formative Years* 45, 62, 111, 158, 394, 396 (1982).

93. *See* Sarat, "Legal Effectiveness and Social Studies of Law: On the Unfortunate Persistence of a Research Tradition," 9 *Legal Stud. F.* 23 (1985); Gordon, "Critical Legal Histories," 36 *Stan. L. Rev.* 57 (1984); Trubek, "Where the Action Is: Critical Legal Studies and Empiricism," 36 *Stan. L. Rev.* 575 (1984).

94. David Sugarman notes, in commenting on an early draft of this paper, that there may never be a shared consciousness around conceptions of the law as law. We do not really need to posit legitimation or hegemony as structures of belief in the state shared by all groups within a political regime. On the other hand, we do need to think seriously about shared notions of "wrongs"—such as murder, rape, theft, and other forms of mistreatment—from which all might agree we need protection.

I find this an appealing formulation. But at the same time, I still wonder about the seeming pervasiveness of an American commitment to "rights discourse," a discourse founded on a belief in the ability of many groups to confirm and legitimate their identities through public and legal means. Is that a distinctive feature of American political consciousness?

In any event, gap analysis builds from an unquestioning commitment to the positivist assumption that a law, by definition, is an act of state commanding the obedience of a constituency. Given that commitment, legal sociologists then proceed to show the "failure" of the state to achieve actual obedience. As Sarat and others have argued, *see supra* note 93, this commitment makes the method one easily corrupted into advice by experts to lawmakers and enforcers how to make more effective commands which will be more enforceable—how, in other words, to lessen the gap.

95. 11 C.C. Min. 603, 611.

96. 12 C.C. Min. 158.

97. The accepted anonymity of pig keeping in the city does suggest that *People v. Harriet* may have been a test case. *See supra* note 24.

98. As such it was a reform at one with the deepest bureaucratic longings of municipal administrators and political leaders of the early 19th century. *See* H. Hartog, *supra* note 15, at 143–57.

99. 12 C.C. Min. 383, 444–45, 600.

100. In June, 1826 the council resolved that the law ought to be rewritten to recreate a public pound system. The resolution was referred to the police committee which reported against the proposal on the grounds that maintaining a hog pound would cause more trouble and expense without correcting the nuisance. And the proposal was then rejected by the full council. 15 C.C. Min. 484, 515–16.

101. 11 C.C. Min. 722.

102. The petition complained of the pigs which "since the late law restricting their being in the Street to the outer wards infest the Village and praying a law may be passed compelling the owners to put rings in their noses." 12 C.C. Min. 293.

103. 11 C.C. Min. 731–732, 751, 766; 12 C.C. Min. 17, 95–96, 114, 458, 471; 13 C.C. Min. 171; 14 C.C. Min. 694; 15 C.C. Min. 466, 468, 536, 570, 618. These petitions were at least sometimes granted. *See* the accounts listed for 25 September 1826, when three supplicants were each given ten dollars for the taking of their hogs. 15 C.C. Min. 615. Evidently, petitioners played on council members' uncertainties about a law which redistributed wealth from "poor" citizens to poor inmates of the almshouse. Since it was often impossible to identify the true owner of the pig found in the street, one can well imagine that neighborhood widows and others likely to evoke middle-class sympathy would usually play the part of petitioner when the need arose.

104. 12 C.C. Min. 430, 447.

105. *Id.* at 460–61.

106. *See* 13 C.C. Min. 365, 410–11; 14 C.C. Min. 515; 18 C.C. Min. 489.

107. 13 C.C. Min. 365, 410–11; 14 C.C. Min. 674; 15 C.C. Min. 269–70.

108. 18 C.C. Min. 295, 489, 546; 19 C.C. Min. 115.

109. 19 C.C. Min. 168.

110. I am guessing here, since I have not been able to find a report of the case, aside from the record in the council minutes. *Id.* at 465.

111. Any persons finding swine at large in the city could take them to a pound. The pound master would pay such finders one dollar for each animal they brought. The owner of the swine could redeem them within five days by paying a fee of fifty cents a day per animal, plus whatever was paid to the person who brought the swine to the pound. *Laws and Ordinances of the Corporation of the City of New York* tit. vii, at 133–35 (1833).

112. In other situations, particularly when enforcement was founded on ordinances it had drafted, the common council was perfectly willing to enforce nuisance laws. *See, e.g.*, the cemetery cases described in H. Hartog, *supra* note 15, at 71–81.

113. There were, needless to say, problems of enforcement, but these cannot be distinguished from questions about the legal authority of the council and its agencies.

114. The phrase is of course that of Oliver Wendell Holmes, Jr., see O. W. Holmes, "The Path of the Law," in *Collected Legal Papers* 167 (1921).

115. *Id.*

116. *See supra* text accompanying note 104.

117. 12 C.C. Min. 447.

118. *See supra* text accompanying notes 4 & 25.

119. I have been immensely helped here by a paper called "OK Lawbreaking," prepared for my legal history class by Richard Claus in the fall of 1984. *See also* Rule, "Wrecking and Coastal Plunder," in D. Hay, P. Linebaugh, J. Rule, E. Thompson, & E. Winslow, *Albion's Fatal Tree: Crime and Society in Eighteenth Century England* 167 (1975).

120. The classic statement of this legal theory can be found in Lincoln, "Address Before the Young Men's Lyceum of Springfield, Illinois" in A. Lincoln, *The Political Thought of Abraham Lincoln* 11 (R. Current ed. 1967). *See generally* G. Wood, *supra* note 40.

121. Paradoxically, it may also legitimate the emergence of law as the arena of conflict. But that is a subject for another day.

122. For one marvelous attempt to do so, see E.P. Thompson, *The Poverty of Theory & Other Essays* 96 (1978).

123. Here I contradict an argument I made in "Distancing Oneself from the Eighteenth Century; a Commentary on Changing Pictures of American Legal History," in *Law in the American Revolution and the Revolution in the Law* 229 (Hartog ed. 1981). In that essay I argued for the relative truth of legal positivism as a description of the underlying legal theory of the "makers" of the 19th century legal order. In contrast to their 18th century predecessors, those men whom we conventionally label as the founders of our legal order thought of law as an analytically distinct sphere of human activity and as the command of a political sovereign (as opposed to the expression of consensual moral values). In general they would have derived the legitimacy and obligatory character of legal rules from the given institutional processes, rather than from the substantive rightness or morality of the rules themselves. I still believe that I fairly characterized their legal assumptions in that essay (although Robert Gordon and others have recently pointed to the complexities of elite legal thought). However,

that essay wrongly transformed a limited and partial (yet influential) legal consciousness into the dominant feature of the legal order itself.

Folk Law in Conflict

If there are any societies remaining in the world that are totally isolated from all other societies, we might find an instance of a folk law system which is not in conflict with some other legal system. The truth is that legal pluralism of some kind is to be found in virtually all human societies. In Europe, the conflict may involve folk law versus official legislation; In Africa and Asia, the conflict is more typically between folk law and so-called received law, the latter being the imposed law of the original colonizer of the area.

One should also keep in mind that many countries of the world have geo-political boundaries that are the accidents of world history and various wars of conquest. As a result within a particular country there may be literally dozens of individual folk groups, each with its own folk law system. When a member of one folk group marries a member of another folk group, there may be a de facto instance of legal pluralism. Residency is another variable. What happens when a member of one folk group leaves his or her group to settle in another area occupied by another folk group? Does he or she abandon his or her original folk law and accept the folk law of the dominant group in the place of new residence? When colonial imperialists moved to an area of colonization, they took their law with them. When refugees from a culture moved to escape persecution, they were usually required to leave their folk law behind them.

A pressing problem in legal pluralism is what place, if any, should be given to folk law. Should folk law be given precedence? Should it be given any weight at all? Some students of folk law feel that it should be given priority over enacted legislation on the grounds that folk law represents the will of the people, the common people. Other students feel that folk law is an outmoded relic of the past that impedes progress towards a unified legal system in a given community.

The most serious issue surrounding legal pluralism involving folk law concerns individuals caught between the competing demands of two or more legal systems. What is correct or even required by a folk law may be deemed a criminal act by the official legislation in force in the area. This could be the case in what was once colonial Africa or among the minority residents in urban London or New York City. Such instances serve as constant reminders of the continuing importance of folk law in the modern world.

L.C. GREEN

"Civilized" Law and "Primitive" Peoples

Although the distinction, so-called, between civilized and primitive is an unfortunate ethnocentric vestige of nineteenth-century evolutionary dogma, which argued that all peoples were progressing or would progress from initial savagery through an intermediate stage of barbarism before finally arriving at the desired final state of civilization, it continues to haunt us. Even if one puts the terms in quotation marks so as to distance oneself from the concepts, the implicit negative nuances of the term "primitive" as applied to many non-western peoples remain and these nuances remain offensive. The persistence of such terms may remind us that the days of colonialism are not yet completely over. In any event, in the absence of any satisfactory term—even the label "non-western" is insulting insofar as it presumes that "Western" culture is the model or mark from or by which all other peoples are measured—the problem of legal pluralism is still a genuine one.

In the following interesting survey, L.C. Green, Professor of Law at the University of Alberta, tries to place the problem in some historical perspective by citing a variety of specific cases. See also the same author's "The Common Law and Native Systems of Law," in Robert R. Wilson, ed., International and Comparative Law of the Commonwealth *(Durham: Duke University Press, 1968), pp. 81–107, and "Native Law and the Common Law: Conflict or Harmony,"* Malaya Law Review, *12 (1970), 38–59.*

For other general discussions, see Walter S. Johnson, "Usage or Custom in the Conflict of Laws," Canadian Bar Review, *15 (1937), 68–85; Rene R. Gadacz, "Folk Law and Legal Pluralism,"* Legal Studies Forum, *11 (1987), 125–144; and Amado Adip,* Conflicto entre ley y costumbre, *2nd ed. (Buenos Aires: Ediciones Depalma, 1975). Most discussions of folk law in conflict center upon individual countries or peoples. J.A. Todd, Native Offences and European Law in South-West New Britain,"* Oceania, *5 (1935), 437–460; A. Arthur Schiller, "Conflict of Laws in Indonesia,"* The Far Eastern Quarterly, *2 (1942–1943), 31–47; M.B. Hooker, "The Interaction of Legislation and Customary Law in a Malay State,* American Journal of Comparative Law, *16 (1968), 415–430; Kwamena Bentsi-Enchill, "The Colonial Heritage of Legal Pluralism,"* Zambia Law Journal, *1 (1969), 1–30; Joseph J. Westermeyer, "Traditional and Constitutional Law: A Study of Change in Laos,"* Asian Survey, *11 (1971), 562–*

Reprinted from the *Osgoode Hall Law Journal*, 13 (1975), 233–249, with permission.

569; E. Arsenio Manuel, "The Conflict of National and Custom Law in Central Mindanao," Philippine Social Sciences & Humanities Review, *43 (1979), 93–105; Masaji Chiba, ed.,* Asian Indigenous Law in Interaction with Received Law *(London: KPI, 1986); and Mary Fisher & Peter Hennessy, "Aboriginal Customary Laws and the Australian Criminal Law in Conflict,"* Law & Anthropology, *3 (1988), 83–102. These are merely specimens of a voluminous literature.*

On July 16th, 1974, Judge King-Hamilton sitting in the Central Criminal Court, London, found Felicia Foluke Adesanya, a Yoruba, guilty of assaulting her sons, Roufemi, aged 14, and Lanre, aged 9, occasioning bodily harm, having cut their faces with a knife. For Mrs. Adesanya it had been pleaded that the boys had agreed to her actions, which after all only involved tribal scarification during new year celebrations. The learned judge felt he was able to take a lenient view of the case and order her absolute discharge, for "this is a test case, the first of its kind, and . . . I am convinced you did not realize you were breaking the law."[1] This case immediately throws into profile a fundamental issue of anthropological jurisprudence—the conflict and the interplay as between 'civilized' systems and concepts of law and the 'primitive' people to whom such systems seek to apply.

In order to avoid unnecessary semantic disputation as to the meaning of words, it is as well that we define how the terms 'civilization' and 'primitive' are being used in this paper. Civilization is a relative term depending upon the ethos, culture and background of the person using it, and that person's concept of the primitive condition is formed on exactly the same basis. According to Article 36 of the Statute of the International Court of Justice, one of the 'sources' of international law consists of general principles of law recognized by civilized nations[2], although the Court has never found it necessary to decide a case on these alone. This inability is by no means surprising, for it would be well-nigh impossible to decide what constituted general principles of law, other than perhaps that unjustifiable homicide constitutes a punishable offence. Moreover, who is to decide which are the civilized nations? Every member of the United Nations, which is automatically also a party to the Statute of the Court, regards itself as 'civilized' and would contend that if it did not recognize any particular legal principle, that principle could not therefore be a general principle of law for if it were, it would obviously be recognized by the state in question since that state is, as the whole world knows, civilized. All that one can say of this concept is that general principles of law recognized by civilized nations are nothing but those principles of law which are generally recognized by us and those nations which we consider to be civilized. For our purposes, therefore, the term civilization will be used to connote a state which possesses a sophisticated legal system in the common and civil law traditions. It is equally difficult to define 'primitiveness', and we will use the term to connote a people which is not sophisticated in the above sense, which is regarded as primitive by the ordinary lay person, and which has found itself in a special relationship with one of the more sophisticated groups which latter has attempted to impose, graft or adapt its system of law on to such primitive society.[3]

The interplay between a civilized and a primitive people requiring some examination of the legal framework may arise in one of two ways. On the one hand, the sophisticated may arrive and take over the territory inhabited by the primitives, establishing themselves and their own government, making the territory in question their own country, as happened in such places as Australia, New Zealand, North America and South Africa. In other places, the invaders took the territory but did so only as a colony or a protectorate, establishing their alien order, but not intending to make the land their own home, for they sent their children 'home' to school and themselves hoped to 'return home to die'. In the former case, there was no hesitation about imposing their own system of law, especially when the settlers were English, for an Englishman took his law with him: "Colonists carry with them only so much of the English law as is applicable to their own situation and the condition of an infant colony; such, for instance, as the general rules of inheritance and of protection from personal injuries. The artificial refinements and distinctions incident to the property of a great and commercial people, the laws of police and revenue, . . . the jurisdiction of spiritual courts, and a multitude of other provisions, are neither necessary nor convenient for them, and therefore not in force. What shall be admitted and what rejected, at what times, and under what restrictions, must, in case of dispute, be decided in the first instance by their own provincial judicature, subject to revision and control of the king in council"[4].

This comment is only concerned with the rights of the settlers. The reason for this is that, so far as the established states of the time were concerned, newly-discovered territories were considered uninhabited, regardless of the size of the aboriginal population, and therefore there was no existing legal system which could conflict with that known to the settlers and which they took with them. In those cases where there was already an established state which had been conquered or ceded, the newcomers recognised that the already-existing law prevailed until such time as it was amended by the new sovereign. This was a matter of necessity and convenience, for if the existing law were abrogated immediately anarchy would probably ensue. At the same time, it was recognized that the local population would not be any more familiar with the new law being introduced than the conquerors would be with the already existing one. Sometimes this meant that the two systems could, for a time at least, continue to survive side by side, operating independently with each controlling its own community. This is, for example, what happened in the case of the North American Indians in the United States, but not in Canada. As Chief Justice Marshall pointed out[5]:

> America, separated from Europe by a wide ocean, was inhabited by a distinct people, divided into separate nations, independent of each other and of the rest of the world, having institutions of their own, and governing themselves by their own laws.

The importance of this fact became clear some fifty years later, when the Supreme Court held[6] that an Indian who had murdered another Indian on a reservation was not amenable to federal criminal law, but only to tribal law. This situation, however, was terminated by statute two years later.[7]

In some instances attempts have been made not merely for the two systems to exist side by side independently, but for them to work cooperatively, although this may produce the most incongruous results. This is illustrated by the trial of a 'crocodile man' in Nyasaland in 1962.[8] Elland brought an action before a Native authority court seeking payment from one Odrick who had contracted to pay him £4.10s. if he killed a girl suspected of witchcraft. Elland, assuming the guise of a crocodile, carried out his part of the arrangement, but only received 10s. from Odrick, whom he therefore sued for non-payment of debt. The court ordered Odrick to pay £2.10s into court in settlement and issued a receipt. Subsequently, both men were indicted before the Nyasaland criminal court for murder.

This clash between the two systems often becomes evident when an issue affecting the public policy of the ruler is involved. Thus, when England settled abroad the general tendency was not to interfere with local customs unless these were repugnant to English concepts of morality and *ordre public*. Perhaps the most important instances of England's refusal to recognize local ways are the rejection of *suttee* in India, even though this was a country which the settlers recognized as having its own legal system at least in so far as the personal rights of the Native inhabitants were concerned, and the refusal to recognize the validity of polygamous marriages, even though they might be acceptable locally. But on occasion the concept of public policy was carried to much greater extremes, particularly when the judge was a member of a colonial legal service whose natural tendency was to look to the concepts of his own system and proved unwilling to accept anything completely alien thereto. This happened in Tanganyika when Wilson, J. held[9] that

> a Turu custom whereby the property of a father might be seized in compensation for a wrong done by his son was so repugnant to British ideas of justice and morality that it would not be endorsed in the High Court. It would, however, almost certainly have succeeded in a local court, to which such ideas of vicarious liability would not be so difficult to accept.

A somewhat similar approach is to be found in Nigerian judicial practice, even in the field of customary family law. Thus,

> in *Joshua Chawere* v. *Hannah Aihenu*[10] it was held that any native custom to the effect that a wife who committed adultery . . . became the wife of the male adulterer would be repugnant and unenforceable. And in this same field, the English common law concept of "public policy", which would forbid the encouragement of promiscuous intercourse[11], has been suggested[12] as capable of striking down the now well-established[13] customary rule that an originally illegitimate child whose paternity is acknowledged and recognized by its father thereby acquires the same status as a child born legitimate.[14]

This peculiar attitude to 'public policy' has also been described as a rejection of barbarism, although the Judicial Committee of the Privy Council has recognized that 'barbarous' habits may become modified by the impact of 'civilization'[15]:

> . . . the more barbarous customs of earlier days may under the influences of civilization become milder without losing their essential character of custom . . . so as in that form to regulate the relations of the native community *inter se*. In other words, the court cannot itself transform a barbarous custom into a milder one. If it still stands in its barbarous character, it must be rejected as repugnant to "natural justice, equity and good conscience." It is the assent of the native community that gives a custom its validity, and, therefore, barbarous or mild, it must be shown to be recognized by the native community whose conduct it is supposed to regulate.

The importance of the modifying character of the last two sentences is to be seen in a judgment by the Chief Justice of Gambia which makes clear that even a custom which might be rejected by Christian missionaries and would certainly not be tolerated in Europe is not necessarily contrary to 'natural justice'. He held in *Koykoy Jatta* v. *Menna Camara*[16] that female circumcision "is your custom but can only be your custom in your own tribe and applied to your own people".

When dealing with custom and its creation, judges, particularly in English colonial jurisdictions, are likely to apply their own backgrounds rather than have regard for local realities. Thus, the Chief Justice of the Gold Coast held[17] that "according to the principles of English jurisprudence" a local custom must date back to 1189, which is the date at which 'time immemorial' begins at common law, but this view was rejected forty years later[18]. It never applied in Singapore, for "the history of Singapore began in 1819, more than 600 years after 1189, and that in itself concludes the matter"[19]. This problem at least has been avoided in New Guinea, for there custom is regulated by statute, permitting judicial declaration and recognition of recent and altered custom, and since in this case native custom means local custom, it may vary from place to place.[20]

On occasion, a courageous judge has been prepared to disregard the general law and apply local custom. Perhaps the best known practitioner in this field was Sissons, J. in the North West Territories when dealing with the Inuit,[21] although it may well be argued that he was doing nothing but applying the approach of his predecessor Witman, J. when determining whether a marriage between Indians in the Territories, contracted in a form which would have been valid before the introduction of English Law in 1870, was to be recognized. In 1885 the latter asked[22]:

> [A]re the laws of England respecting the solemnization of marriage applicable to these Territories *quoad* the Indian population? I have great doubt if these laws are applicable to the Territories in any respect. According to these laws marriages can be solemnized only at certain times and in certain places or buildings. These times would be in many cases most inconvenient here and the buildings, if they exist at all, are often so remote from the contracting parties that they could not be reached save with the greatest inconvenience. I am satisfied however that these laws are not applicable to the Territories *quoad* the Indians. The Indians are for the most part unchristianed,[23] they yet adhere to their own peculiar marriage customs and usages. It would be monstrous to hold that the law of England respecting the solemnization of marriage is applicable to them. . . . [A] marriage between Indians by mutual consent and according to Indian custom since 15th July 1870, is a valid marriage, providing that neither of the parties had a husband or wife, as the case might be, living at the time . . .

Witman, J. could have reached the same conclusion by holding that a common law marriage had been created by repute, but he preferred to apply the native law, while insisting on monogamy. Some thirty years later a United States court also recognized an Indian customary marriage, although polygamous[24].

In the case before Sissons, J. the issue was not directly that of the validity of a marriage. *Re Noah Estate*[25] turned on the application of the Northwest Territories *Intestate Succession Ordinance* which depended on whether the claimants were in fact the 'widow' and 'issue' of the deceased. To decide this the Inuit marriage in question had to be examined to see whether it satisfied the conditions of a 'Christian' marriage as required by English law. The suggestion that Eskimo cohabitation and marriage in accordance with Inuit custom was mere concubinage was dismissed by the judge as 'fanciful and scandalous', since "marriage according to Eskimo custom is not 'the Eskimo custom of concubinage'." He considered that the Inuit system of trial marriage was as separate from marriage proper as is the Western system of 'engagement' or 'going steady'. He pointed out that the relationship in question complied

> in every respect with the requirements of what was known, according to the old law of England, as a consensual marriage, that is formed or existing by mere consent. The old law of England recognized a consensual marriage. The general law of Europe apparently also recognized a consensual marriage as being in all respects perfect. . . . The *Marriage Ordinance* . . . has no provision stating that a native marriage is invalid and no statement that a marriage carried out on the basis of common law is null and void. . . . This ordinance is misnamed. In spite of its title, this is not a *Marriage Ordinance* but a *Solemnization of Marriage Ordinance*. . . . I think there was considerable solemnization of this marriage, even if tinged with irregularity.
>
> The solemnization of an Eskimo marriage follows pretty well that of the Anglican Church, or rather the Anglican Church's solemnization seems to follow that of the Eskimos. In Christian countries marriage did not become a religious ceremony before the 9th century, when newly-wed couples began coming to the church door to have their union blessed by the priest. The marriage had already taken place and was generally a family and community affair . . .

as was the case with the instant marriage, where everybody knew of the union and accepted it.

> The marriage custom of the Society of Friends (Quakers) seems very much like that of the Eskimos. The Friends marry at a special meeting called for the occasion, the only formality being a public declaration of the marriage by the couple and the signing of a certificate by all present as witnesses. . . . [As for the *Intestate Succession Ordinance*, t]his Ordinance does not apply to Indians. *The Indian Act* . . . has its own provisions for interstate succession. . . . The rights and customs of the Indians have not been completely ignored. They have their treaties and their *Indian Act*, codifying

> some at least of their rights and customs. The Eskimos have no treaty. They have not given the covenant appearing in the Indian treaties, whereby: "They promise and engage that they will, in all respects, obey and abide by the law." They have no *Eskimo Act*. . . . [T]hey have no one to represent them in Parliament. They have no representation on the Territories Council of the Northwest Territories. This Court must guard their rights, when it can, and sometimes must write upon a clean slate. While I think that generally the *Intestate Succession Ordinance* has no application to Eskimos, I think there are times and circumstances when these provisions are applicable to an Eskimo estate . . .

and among such circumstances was the instant case where the deceased had gone to live in white society and had become part of that society and economy.

As an instance of a situation in which colonial judges thought they were applying native customs of marriage and concubinage one might cite the *Six Widows* case[26] in Singapore. Here, English judges introduced into Singapore a concept of Chinese law not previously known and still not recognized in China[27]. The case concerned the status of Chinese 'concubines', and Hyndman Jones, C. J. accepted that

> the evidence is very contradictory, but I am disposed to think that when it is intended to take a woman into a man's household as a concubine for the purpose of securing a succession, or at all events as more than a temporary mistress, there is some sort of ceremonies; although these ceremonies, in some districts and among some classes are of a more or less perfunctory character, and always much less elaborate than those adopted in the case of a *t'sai* [principal wife].

Braddell, J., whose knowledge of Chinese law was no better than that of the Chief Justice, declared

> I entirely adopt the exposition of the Chinese law given in the judgment of the Chief Justice and concur with him in the conclusion to which he has arrived, namely, that concubinage is recognized as a legal institution under the law, conferring upon the *t'sip* [secondary wife] a legal status of a permanent character.

Halfway through the twentieth century, judges were still anxious to uphold domestic arrangements of Singapore citizens if they possibly could. This is clear from the attitude of the Privy Council in upholding a local decision recognizing as a marriage a ceremony conducted by a Chinese between a Chinese Christian woman and a Jewish man in a house before witnesses, with each party offering prayers in his own way[28]:

> [While] it is not suggested that either party to the marriage in question was a Christian [,] . . . the evidence as it stands sufficiently proves a common law monogamous marriage. The wishes expressed by the respondent and her mother for a Church marriage, the reason why a modified Chinese ceremony was substituted, . . . the words spoken by the Chinese gentlemen who performed the ceremony as to a life-long union, the cohabitation as man and wife which followed and continued until the husband's death, and the introduction by the deceased to a Christian pastor of the respondent as his wife, and last, but not least, the baptism of their children as Christians with the approval of their father, all indicate that the spouses intended to contract a common law monogamous marriage.

Although it may be true that the parties did intend to effect a lifelong marriage which was rendered respectable by the introduction of the common law to modify the rigours of the local law, a similar result might have been obtained if the court had adopted the words of Lord Phillimore in an earlier case involving Chinese parties[29]:

> In deciding upon a case where the customs and the laws are so different from British ideas a Court may do well to recollect that it is a possible jural conception that a child may be legitimate, though its parents were not and could not be legitimately married.

The need to recognize potentially strange jural conceptions because of basic deviations from the British way of life is to be seen in the memoirs of Austin Coates, a former Special Magistrate in Hong Kong who never qualified legally and perhaps, therefore, found it comparatively simple to apply rough justice in accordance with local Chinese custom[30]. In fact there may be much to be said for appointing non-home trained personnel or non-lawyers to deal with issues among 'primitive' peoples, for even though the 'case' may appear as a formal legal process, the person hearing it has often to act as a 'Dutch uncle' or a mediator rather than as a judge. Such mediation is likely to be far more successful if the officer is aware of or amenable to native susceptibilities, reactions and habits. Such a case came before a native 'specialist' local court magistrate in Wewak, New Guinea in 1967[31]. Joana claimed that Anton had married her at Rabaul, having paid the required bride-price. She contended that the custom of her people was 'one man one wife', and although a child had been born she sought dissolution on the ground that Anton had become interested in Agnes, whom he regarded as his second wife, and had told Joana to return to Rabaul. Anton complained of Joana's conduct towards him and his relatives, and pointed out that she could not work because of the child, and so he had to get another wife, but

> I have not paid Agnes's bride price yet. However, since she has been in my village for one week, we claim it is a marriage by native custom. I believe her parents would not dispute her marrying me.

The magistrate advised them that in his view

> a valid marriage obtained between Joana and Anton by native customs, bride-price having been paid; the 'marriage' between Agnes and Anton was not a valid marriage according to native custom, no bride-price having been paid to Agnes's parents and no celebrations held by way of recognition of marriage in accordance with the local custom; Joana would be entitled to have her marriage dissolved by native custom since in her community there should be only one woman and one man in a marriage.

Joana thereupon agreed to withdraw her suit, provided Anton would send Agnes away, and to this Anton agreed. We have here, therefore, an instance of a magistrate preserving a marriage when, had there been a formal local, court hearing, he would almost certainly have found it necessary to issue an order for dissolution in accordance with the Local Courts Ordinance, 1963, s. 17.

As long ago as 1919 Lord Sumner recognized the need to acknowledge the existence of native institutions of law and the limitations inherent in seeking to impose 'civilized' law upon 'primitive' people[32]:

> The estimation of the rights of aboriginal tribes is always inherently difficult. Some tribes are so low in the scale of social organization that their usages and conceptions of rights and duties are not to be reconciled with the institutions or the legal ideas of civilized society. Such a gulf cannot be bridged. It would be idle to impute to such people some shadow of the rights known to our law and then to transmute it into the substance of [e.g.] transferable rights of property as we know them. . . . On the other hand, there are indigenous peoples whose legal conceptions, though differently developed are hardly less precise than our own. When once they have been studied and understood they are no less enforceable than rights arising under English law.

Unfortunately, however, judges from the colonial powers or from among settlers who have become the establishment are rarely prepared to study or understand such local legal systems.

On the other hand, recent trends in the recognition by the law of the significance of psychology have often resulted in local judges taking a special—and often more lenient—view of the law when a 'primitive' is involved. Evidence of this is to be found in as widely separate jurisdictions as South Africa, Papua and New Guinea and Australia. In

1951 the Appellate Division of the South African Supreme Court heard the appeal of Mrs. Mkize[33] who had been found guilty of murder, having placed arsenic, which she believed to be a love potion, in her husband's beer. In substituting a finding of culpable homicide for the murder conviction, the court stated:

> The belief which the accused says she had in the results of administering the potion . . . may appear to educated minds to be absurd but it must be borne in mind that the accused is an illiterate native woman living in a native kraal and that it is well known that natives genuinely believe in magic and witchcraft.

The question of native beliefs was equally important in an earlier case in which a murder verdict had been reduced to culpable homicide. Some Native children thought they had seen a *tikoloshe* in a hut, and since it would be fatal for humans to look such an evil spirit in the face they summoned the accused, a Native youth of 18, to deal with it. Like them, he thought it was a *tikoloshe* and struck it with a hatchet. When he dragged the *tikoloshe* from the hut, he found that he had killed his nephew who had been sleeping there. In the course of its judgment, the Appellate Division held[34] that the standard of reasonableness in such a case was "not that of an ordinary 18–year-old Native living at home in his kraal, but that of a reasonable person of his age.[35]

A somewhat more reasonable approach to the ideal of legal reasonableness has been adopted by judges dealing with Papuan Natives and Australian aborigines. It is a well-established rule of 'civilized' law that words alone are not sufficient to ground a defence based on provocation. Brennan, A. J. of the Supreme Court of Papua and New Guinea had to decide whether insulting words could provoke a killing[36]. The words had been spoken by a woman to a man who had himself used a coarse expression to the woman's daughter: she said 'You cannot find a woman to marry, and if you talk like that to a girl child you will die still unmarried.' The judge pointed out that in

> western communities which apply common law principles, the view that words alone cannot be relied upon as a provocation has hardened since the seventeenth century. As a general proposition that thesis is hardly open to dispute, but it does not necessarily follow that the same principle should apply in a native community where sophistication does not approach to that of, say, seventeenth-century England, where a type of insult such as the one here in question is calculated and not infrequently intended to throw a man into an ungovernable rage.

This seems to be a not unusual attitude for judges in that part of the world to adopt and in *R. v. Zariai-Gavene*[37] the judge expressly took into consideration the effect of the words spoken upon a Goilala villager, of whom the accused was one. Equally aware of the realities in that jurisdiction was the comment of Smithers, J.[38] that "for the exemplification of the ordinary man [in the Territory] one must take the ordinary native living the rural life of low standard led by the accused and his relatives and similar lines. . . . The man in the *lap lap* takes the place of the man on the Clapham omnibus."

Perhaps one of the most enlightened judgments in this field is that of Bright, J. of South Australia in *R. v. Gibson.*[39] The accused, an aborigine living on the Yalata reserve, was charged with killing another aborigine, and as soon as the case came for trial the judge was faced with a problem that is more likely to affect 'primitive' rather than 'civilized' defendants. It was argued on behalf of the defendant that the case concerned 'men's secrets' and therefore no woman should be allowed on the jury or in the courtroom, for if any were present witnesses would refuse to give evidence and the defendant would be denied the opportunity of a fair trial. This request was acceded to by the learned judge, and one cannot help but wonder what might have happened in a similar case in Canada affecting an Indian or an Inuit in view of the Bill of Rights and the ban on discrimination against women—although it must be remembered that a Canadian judge has the right to order a hearing in camera if he considers that justice so demands. The killing arose out of a quarrel occasioned by insulting remarks concerning aboriginal circumcision at a time when both the deceased and the accused were somewhat the worse for liquor. During his judgment, Bright, J. soon made it clear that he was aware of the peculiar problems confronting him because aborigines were involved, for one of the preliminary issues related to the accused's statement to the police. It was pleaded that Natives tended to say what they thought the authorities wished them to say, and while the judge agreed

> . . . that there is a distinction to be made between white persons who have been brought up in the concepts of society and ideas (including the idea of independence of authority) prevalent in Europe and Australia on the one hand, and indigenous persons who not only have a limited command of English but whose whole culture differs radically from the white culture [, . . . and] if the accused had been able to express his state of mind he might have said,
>
> "Yes, I know that you have told me that I don't have to answer, but I am an uneducated black man from my tribe and you are white men in authority over me and I am frightened of you; so when you ask me a

> question I answer you because I can't exercise my right to keep silent when people like you ask me questions."
>
> [But i]f I were to exclude the statement on that ground I should be creating a different law for Aborigines from the law applicable to white men. And I should be overlooking the fact that many white accused persons who are cautioned are ignorant, simple minded and scared. . . .

In the course of his address to the jury, Bright, J. constantly indicated his awareness that the accused was an Aborigine:

> The accused, like the deceased, is a member of the Pitjantjajara tribe living in a tribal environment. From the foundation of the Province of South Australia black people and white people have lived under the same laws of the country. The tribesman is more immediately aware of the laws of the tribe which preserve his culture and ensure his survival in the arid conditions of outback Australia. In the same way a nun in a convent may be more aware of the laws of the convent. I must hasten to add that I should regard a nun as being much less remote from the general white culture than a Pitjantjajara tribesman. Perhaps it is unnecessary for me to add that I am in no way talking of relative intelligence. Indeed, I do not know what is the measure of intelligence. If it be an ability to survive and to thrive in the environment in which one finds oneself, and I would think that this is the proper test, then the Pitjantjajara Aboriginal displays an ability to do both, according to his own lights, in his own environment. I am not prepared to say that white persons in general, display a greater ability to thrive according to white concepts in a white environment than black persons, in general, do according to black concepts in theirs. In each case one must apply not absolute standards but standards of achievement capable of attainment in the particular environment.
>
> . . . What the rules of a convent or a tribe may do by way of retribution to a member who broke the criminal law is no concern of ours at present. . . . [A] nun might be shocked more readily and more deeply than many members of the general public by a blaspheming of the Christian faith. And a tribesman would be more shocked, disturbed and aroused by an improper disclosure of the sacred mysteries of tribal lore than you or I would be. The law is not foolish. It takes account of these matters.
>
> . . . We shall often have more difficulty in understanding black men's ways than white men's ways for we are ignorant in these matters. . . .
>
> Your task is to determine whether it is reasonably possible that a tribal Aboriginal who took a reasonable view of the matter—if you like, *a reasonable tribal Aboriginal*—might have been so provoked by the things that the deceased said and did, that when he struck . . . the deceased he was so carried away that he was not the master of his mind but had lost control of himself, that at the most he is guilty of manslaughter. . . .

> ... It is true that the blows were heavy, but we are not dealing with dainty members of society. We are considering tribal Aborigines living in the desert....
>
> ... [H]e had been provoked by violence himself and by the insulting and terrifying use of ritual references. These ritual references, if he heard them without protest might expose him to punishment, and punishment in the tribe might go as far as death.
>
> ... Not every form of provocation is of effect in the criminal law. The provocation is usually said to be such as would cause a reasonable man to lose control of himself. Where tribal lore in a tribal setting is improperly referred to by an initiated tribesman to an uninitiated tribesman *it is useless to think of a reasonable white man. One must think of a reasonable man having the awareness, the timidity, the ordinary reactions of a Pitjantjajara tribesman, viewing the tribe as a social group and the accused as a member of the group....*

In fine, the jury found the accused not guilty of murder or manslaughter.

Even when courts in 'civilized' countries have had to deal with 'primitive' people, not aboriginals or other indigenous groups, but alien persons coming from less sophisticated cultures, they have in recent years adopted a more reasonable attitude than was formerly the case. Marriage is probably as good an example as any to take. The general rule of the common law is that marriage as understood by Christendom is monogamous and *Hyde* v. *Hyde*[40] has been generally accepted as establishing that rule, although in Canada this seems not to have been the case, at least in so far as Indian marriages were concerned, for as was pointed out by Monk, J. in *Jones* v. *Fraser*[41]

> It has been said that polygamy existed among the Indian tribes of the North-West, and that the marriage invoked by the respondent could not therefore be supposed to possess the character required for marriage in all christian countries, that is unity and perpetuity.... [P]olygamy did not exist, as a rule, among those who married Indian women, but only among the Indian tribes. A marriage which took place there according to the local usage was considered as an ordinary marriage.

Today, even jurisdictions which applied *Hyde* rigorously have moved away from so narrow an approach. An example is *Ochochuku* v. *Ochochuku*[42]. The parties, though Christians, had entered into a marriage in accordance with Native custom in 1949 in Nigeria, at which time Nigeria permitted polygamy. While in England they went through a register office marriage and subsequently the wife sued for divorce, which was granted. However,

> [W]hatever might be the effect on the marriage for other purposes and in other courts of the parties being Christians, in this Court and for this

> purpose the Nigerian marriage must be regarded as a polygamous marriage over which this court does not exercise jurisdiction.
>
> I therefore pronounce a decree nisi for the dissolution not of the Nigerian marriage but of the marriage in London. I am told that, in fact, that will be effective by Nigerian law to dissolve the Nigerian marriage; but that forms no part of my judgment. That is for someone else to determine and not for me.

By 1968, in *M.* v. *K.*[43], the English courts were adopting a far more liberal attitude to what were potentially polygamous marriages. Justices had committed a fourteen-year-old Nigerian girl to the care of a local authority as being exposed to moral danger. Some five months earlier she had gone through a potentially polygamous marriage with a Nigerian male of 25 in Nigeria where they were both domiciled. The magistrates in making the order for care, protection and control held, wrongly, that since the marriage was potentially polygamous it could not be recognized in England. The Queen's Bench Divisional Court held, however, that in so far as the girl's status was concerned, the marriage would be recognized and she would be a wife. Lord Parker, C.J. pointed out:

> . . . the question was whether the evidence justified such an order [of protection]. The justices had found that before the marriage the [man] had lived with a woman and had had three illegitimate children, and that after the marriage, at a time when the wife had almost certainly not reached puberty, he had had intercourse with her. After the marriage he had contracted gonorrhea from a prostitute, but he was now cured and intended to resume intercourse with his wife. The justices had found that the continuance of the association between the girl and the appellant would be repugnant to any decent minded English person.
>
> . . . They had misdirected themselves and were considering the reactions of an Englishman regarding an English man and woman in the western way of life. *A decent Englishman realising the way in which the Nigerian man and woman were brought up would not say it was repugnant.* They developed sooner and there was nothing abhorrent in a girl of 13 marrying a man of 25. To say the girl was in moral danger would be *ignoring the way of life in which she and her husband had been brought up.* It had been suggested that every time that the appellant slept with his wife in England, he was committing a criminal offence under the *Sexual Offences Act*, 1956, s. 6 which made it an offence for a man to have unlawful intercourse with a girl between 13 and 16. . . . [The Lord Chief Justice did] not think the police could properly prosecute cases where a foreign marriage was recognized in England. . . . Intercourse between a man and wife was lawful. . . . Where a husband and wife were recognized as validly married according to the laws of England, His Lordship would not say the wife was exposed to moral danger because she carried out her wifely duties.

Within the last ten years or so a new issue as between 'civilized' law and 'primitive' people has arisen in some countries possessing indigenous populations. This concerns the meaning of the relationship established between the original inhabitants and the invaders on the basis of treaties drawn up between them. This is not the place to discuss whether these documents are 'treaties' in the technical sense of that term or what their exact legal significance and import may be[44]. What is important, however, is that these documents were drafted by sophisticated lawyers operating within their own legal *milieu* and that the terms they used were the technical terms known to them and probably impossible of translation into the language of the aboriginals with whom they were negotiating. This is largely true whether the invaders were government spokesmen or the representatives of such trading companies as the British and Dutch East India Companies or the Hudson Bay Company, or whether the Natives with whom they were dealing were North American Indians, Malay or east Indian princes, Australian Aborigines, Javanese or Sumatrans, or New Zealand Maoris. In none of these cases could it be said that the parties were operating on a basis of true equality and it is doubtful whether the Native negotiators were at any time really *ad idem* with the westerners. Problems therefore arise with regard to the interpretation of these documents which were held out to be legally binding arrangements and requiring legal interpretation. Recognition of this fact is to be found in the judgment of the United States Supreme Court at the end of the nineteenth century, when Justice Gray commented[45]:

> In construing any treaty between the United States and an Indian tribe, it must always . . . be borne in mind that the negotiations for the treaty are conducted, on the part of the United States, an enlightened and powerful nation, by representatives skilled in diplomacy, masters of a written language, understanding the modes and forms of creating the various estates known to their law, and assisted by an interpreter employed by themselves; that the treaty is drawn up by them and in their own language; that the Indians, on the other hand, are a weak and dependent people, who have no written language and are unfamiliar with all the forms of legal expression, and whose only knowledge of the terms in which the treaty is framed is that imparted to them by the interpreter employed by the United States; and that the treaty must therefore be construed, not according to the technical meaning of the words to learned lawyers, but in the sense in which they would naturally be understood by the Indians.

When looking at the treaties made with the Canadian Indians, it is equally necessary to bear this comment in mind, particularly in the light of the historical background of the treaties. Thus, in a despatch relating to the North-West Angle Treaty negotiations, 1873, Lieutenant-Governor Morris reported[46] that

> The principal [Indian] spokesman, Mawedopenais, came forward and drew off his gloves, and spoke as follows: "Now you see me stand before you all. What has been done here today, has been done openly before the Great Spirit, and before the nation, and I hope that I may never hear any one say that this treaty has been done secretly. And now, in closing this council, I take off my glove, and in giving you my hand, I deliver over my birthright, and lands, and in taking your hand I hold fast all the promises you have made, and I hope they will last as long as the sun goes round, and the water flows, as you have said." To which I replied as follows: "I accept your hand, and with it the lands, and will keep all my promises, in the firm belief that the treaty now to be signed will bind the red man and the white man together as friends forever".

The Manitoban, in reporting the meeting, stated[47] that Morris also told the Indians:

> . . . you ought to see by what the Queen is offering you that she loves her red subjects as much as her white. . . . [T]hat what I offer you is to be while the water flows and the sun rises. You know that in the United States they only pay the Indians for twenty years. . . . I only ask you to think for yourselves, and for your families, and for your children and children's children . . .

Again, when negotiating with the Cree at Forts Carlton and Pitt[48], Morris gave assurances:

> I told you that what I was promising was not for today or tomorrow only, but should continue as long as the sun shone and the river flowed. My words will pass away and so will yours, so I always write down what I promise, that our children may know what we said and did. Next year I will send copies of what is written in the treaty, printed on skin, so that it cannot run out or be destroyed, and one shall be given to each Chief so that there may be no mistakes.

This was also the understanding of the Indians as is shown by the comment of Chief Mis-tah-wah-sis:

> What we speak of and do now will last as long as the sun shines and the river runs, we are looking forward to our children's children, for we are old and we have but few days to live.

Apparently not all the agreements were made in this way, at least in the case of British Columbia:

> The practice was to pay the Indians the purchase price against their signature by mark on blank paper to be filled in later as a deed. In 1854 the Saalequun tribe so surrendered their lands on Commercial Inlet, 12 miles up the Nanaimo River. For that surrender no deed was made up but the signatures or marks were obtained on blank paper against payment.[49]

Recognizing the disproportionate relationship between the parties and the peculiarities of language used, as well as the need to uphold the dignity of the Crown in whose name these arrangements were made, Canadian judges have, for the main part, accepted the need for an *uberrima fides* interpretation of the rights of the Indians under these treaties. Thus, when holding that the Alberta Game Act did not interfere with the right to hunt embodied in the relevant treaty, McGillavray, J. A. held[50] that the latter must be interpreted:

> with the exactness which honour and good conscience dictate.... It is satisfactory to be able to come to this conclusion and not to have to decide that "the Queen's promises" have not been fulfilled. It is satisfactory to think that the legislators have not so enacted but that the Indians may still be "convinced of our justice and determined resolution to remove all reasonable cause of discontent"

as stipulated in the Royal Proclamation of 1763 guaranteeing their rights against encroachment.

A somewhat similar approach is to be found in a judgment of Patterson, Co. Ct. J.[51]:

> Having called the agreement a treaty, and having perhaps lulled the Indians into believing it to be a treaty with all the sacredness of a treaty attached to it, it may be the Crown should not now be heard to say it is not a treaty.... That is a matter of representations to the proper authorities—representations which ... could hardly fail to be successful.

This view, however, may be regarded as somewhat sanguine, for in 1964 when construing Morris's promises and their interminability, McGillavray, J.A. said that at the time of drafting the legislation being interpreted, and which was alleged to be inconsistent with treaty promises, it appeared "likely that these obligations under the treaties were overlooked"[52].

There can be little doubt that the legislative body of any of the countries alleged to be bound by such treaties is competent to pass legislation abrogating, controverting or disregarding these alleged undertakings. However, it should be borne in mind that equity and morality demand a modicum of good faith even, or perhaps especially, in the relations between 'civilized' and 'primitive' peoples. Moreover, the political framework of the present era suggests that one can no longer ride roughshod over the rights of people and that aborigines have their rights as well as others, and that there are plenty of bodies, some truly altruistic and others perhaps with an ideological axe to grind, who will publicize what they consider to be disregard or abuse of such rights. However, there is a limit to the extent to which modern and newly discovered or invented rights can be used in order to interpret documents and undertakings that were entered into before such concepts were even dreamed of. This is true of, for example, aboriginal rights in the sense of continued ownership or independence and self-determination[53].

It is perhaps inevitable that difficulties and controversies arise when a 'civilized' system of law attempts to deal with the problems, rights and status of 'primitive' peoples, and it may well be that complete elimination of such confrontation is beyond human reach. However, it may be possible to reduce the *contretemps* and effect a more congenial *modus vivendi*. Insofar as arrangements like treaties are concerned, an attempt should be made on both the political and judicial level to recognize the extent to which the 'primitives' were misled into certain beliefs and the 'civilized' took advantage of those beliefs. So far as possible the arrangements should be interpreted in the sense in which the 'primitives' were led to understand them and, in accordance with the principle of normal interpretation, *contra proferentem* the party responsible for putting forward the particular terms or holding out particular promises. When a legislature wishes to abandon its undertakings towards the 'primitives' and effect a state of affairs which appears to be contrary to the anticipations of those 'primitives', care should be taken to ensure that these people are not given the impression that their rights are being disregarded under the guise of 'civilized' legality. Effort should be exercised to ensure that the reason for change is fully explained, some *quid pro quo* extended, and the participation of the representatives of the 'primitives' arranged for.

Insofar as the situation relates to the judicial application of 'civilized' law, it is perhaps time that we start teaching the magistrates who will be called upon to judge such cases some of the folk lore and folkways of the people concerned. It might also be wise to encourage the use of mediators rather than judges. Perhaps, best of all would be to encourage members of the 'primitive' community to make themselves acquainted with the requirements of the 'civilized' system of law and enable them to qualify for judicial office or appointment as mediators, recognizing that they will be called upon to temper this 'black letter' law with an equitable understanding of native needs. There is not really any reason why even a sophisticated society should not be willing to recognize the special needs of a particular group, in much the same way as customs of a particular trade are recognized and accepted. It is all very well to say that the law must be obeyed and its grandeur upheld. To do this, however, sometimes entails injustice and denial of the rule of law. Writing in 1851, John Ruskin said[54]:

> All things are literally better, lovelier, and more beloved for the imperfections which have been divinely appointed, that the law of human life may be Effort, and the law of human judgment, Mercy.

Notes

1. *The Times* (London), 16, 17 July 1974.
2. See, e.g., B. Cheng, *General Principles of Law as Applied by International Courts and Tribunals* (London: Stevens, 1953); G. Herczegh, *General Principles of Law and the International Legal Order* (Budapest: Akademiai Kiado, 1969).
3. See, e.g., L.C. Green, *Native Law and the Common Law: Conflict or Harmony* (1970), 12 Malaya L. Rev. 38.
4. 1 Blackstone, *Commentaries on the Laws of England* 108.
5. *Worcester* v. *Georgia* (1832), 6 Pet. 515 at 542.
6. *Ex parte Crow Dog* (1883), 109 U.S. 556.
7. (1885), 23 Stat. 385; see now 18 U.S.C. s. 1153.
8. *The Times* (London), 25 August 1962.
9. *Gwao bin Kelimo* v. *Kisunda bin Ifuti* (1938), 1 T.L.R. (R.) 403; J.S.R. Cole and W.N. Denison, *Tanganyika, The Development of its Laws and Constitution* (London: Stevens, 1964) at 131.
10. (1935), 12 Nigeria L. R. 4 (Div. Ct.).
11. See 'The Ladies' Directory Case', *Shaw* v. *D.P.P.*, [1962] A.C. 220 (H.L.).
12. *In re Sarah Adadevoh* (1951), 13 W.A.C.A. 304 (W. African C.A., Nigeria) at 310 (*per* Verity, C.J.).
13. *Savage* v. *Macfay*, [1909] Ren. 504; *Re Sapara*, [1911] Ren. 605.
14. F. Ajayi, *The Interaction of English Law with Customary Law in Western Nigeria, II* (1960), 4 J. African Law 98 at 105–05.
15. *Eshugbayi Eleko* v. *Government of Nigeria (Officer Administering)*, [1931] A.C. 662 (P.C.) at 673 (*per* Lord Atkin).
16. (1964), 8 *Journal of African Law* 35.
17. *Welbeck* v. *Brown*, [1882] Sar. F.C.L. 185.
18. *Mensah* v. *Wiaboe* (1925), Div. Ct. Judgments (1921–5, 172; cf. T.O. Elias, *Ghana and Sierra Leone, The Development of their Laws and Constitutions* (London: Stevens, 1963) at 119.
19. *Anguillia* v. *Ong Boon Tat* (1921), 15 S.S.L.R 190 at 193.
20. Native Customs (Recognition) Ordinance 1963), s. 4.

21. J.H. Sissons, *Judge of the Far North* (Toronto: McClelland & Stewart, 1968).
22. *Reg.* v. *Nan-E-Quis-A-Ka* (1889), 1 Terr. L. R. 211 (N.W.T. Sup. Ct.) at 215.
23. It is perhaps worth mentioning that Mrs. Adesanya, the defendant mentioned in n.1, was formerly a Muslim who had become a Christian.
24. *Kobogum* v. *Jackson Iron Co.* (1889), 43 N.W. 602 (Mich. S. Ct.).
25. (1962), 32 D.L.R. (2d) 185 (N.W.T. Terr. Ct.) at 197–99, 202–03; 205–06 (It was in connection with this case that Sissons, J. is alleged to have said: "I am not going to have a lot of bastards in Ottawa tell me that my people here are a lot of bastards.").
26. (1888), 12 S.S.L.R. 120 at 187, 209.
27. Information imparted to the writer by senior Chinese judges in Singapore and Malaysia.
28. *Penhas* v. *Tan Soo Eng*, [1953] A.C. 304 (P.C.) (Singapore) at 318–20.
29. *Khoo Hooi Leong* v. *Khoo Hean Kwee*, [1926] A.C. 529 (P.C.) (Straits Settlements) at 543.
30. A. Coates, *Myself a Mandarin* (London: Muller, 1968), esp. at 22–25, 204–12.
31. *Joana-Vapor* v. *Anton Susami and Agnes-Daporobu* (cf. B.J. Brown, ed., *Fashion of Law in New Guinea* (Sydney: Butterworths, 1969) at 209).
32. *In re Southern Rhodesia*, [1919] A.C. 211 (P.C.) at 223–34.
33. *R* v. *Mkize*, [1951] 3 S. Afr. L. R. 28 (App. Div.) at 33 (*per* Centlivres, C.J.).
34. *R.* v. *Mbombela*, [1933] S. Afr. L. R. (App. Div.) at 271 (*per* de Villiers, J.A.).
35. For consideration of the concept of the 'reasonable man' in relation to the armed forces, see L.C. Green, *Superior Orders and the Reasonable Man* (1970), 8 Can. Y. B. Int. Law 61.
36. *R.* v. *Awaba* (1960) unreported (cf. Hookey, *The "Clapham Omnibus" in New Guinea*, in Brown, *op. cit.*, fn. 31, 117 at 126).
37. [1963] P. & N.G.L.R. 203.
38. *R.* v. *Rumints-Gorok*, [1963] P. & N.G.L.R. 81 at 83.
39. Judgment No. 1810, delivered 12 November 1973. The writer is indebted to Bright, J. for having supplied him with a transcript of the judgment (italics added).
40. (1866), L.R. 1 P. & D. 130.
41. (1886), 12 Q.L.R. 327 (S.Ct.) at 335. See also his decision in *Connolly* v. *Woolrich* (1867), 11 Lower Can. Jur. 197 (Sup.Ct.), and G.W. Bartholomew, *Recognitions of Polygamous Marriages in Canada* (1961), 10 *Int. & Comp. Law Q.* 305. See, also, *Kaur* v. *Ginder* (1958), 13 D.L.R. (2d) 465 (B.C. S.Ct.) in which the court upheld a valid polygamous marriage in India by an East Indian domiciled in B.C. to an Indian woman domiciled in India, as barring a subsequent monogamous marriage.
42. [1960] 1 W.L.R. 183 (P.D.A.) at 185 (*per* Wrangham, J.). See, also, T.C. Hartley, *Polygamy and Social Policy* (1969) 32 *Modern Law Rev.* 155.

43. *The Times* (London), 29 March 1968; reported as *Mohamed* v. *Knott*, [1968] 2. W.L.R. 1446 (Q.B.) at 1456 (italics added).

44 See L.C. Green, *Legal Significance of Treaties Affecting Canada's Indians* (1972), 1 Anglo-American L. Rev. 119.

45. *Jones* v. *Meehan* (1899), 175 U.S. 1 at 10–11.

46. A. Morris, *The Treaties of Canada with the Indians* (Toronto: Belfords, Clarke, 1880) at 51.

47. 18 Oct. 1873 (cf. Morris, *op.cit.* fn. 46 at 61).

48. Morris, *op.cit.* fn. 46 at 208, 213.

49. *R.* v. *White and Bob* (1965), 50 D.L.R. (2d) 613 (B.C.C.A.) at 622 (*per* Sheppard, J.A.).

50. *R.* v. *Wesley*, [1932] 2 W.W.R. 337 (Alta. C.A.) at 351–53.

51. *R.* v. *Syliboy*, [1929] 1 D.L.R. 307 (N.S.Co.Ct.) at 314.

52. *R.* v. *Sikyea* (1964), 46 W.W.R. 65 (N.W.T.C.A.) at 74.

53. See, e.g., L.C. Green, *Canada's Indians and Trusteeship* (1975), 4 Anglo-American Law Review.

54. *The Stones of Venice*, vol. 2, ch. 6, s. 25.

R.D. KOLLEWIJN

Conflicts of Western and Non-Western Law

In the following essay by a distinguished Dutch jurisprudence scholar, we see the question of folk law in conflict from a different perspective. In this instance, the issues are limited to those arising from intermarriage, and we learn that not surprisingly the legalities are handled differently in different countries. From a comparison of Dutch, French, and English data, we get an idea of the variety of complications that exist. Even if some of the legislation pertaining to intermarriage that the author describes is no longer in effect, it was at the time the essay was written.

It should, however, be pointed out that cultural differences in marriage customs continue to present a problem. For example, polygamous marriages are permitted in Islamic societies, but what happens when a polygamous family moves to a country where monogamy is practiced? For a sampling of such a situation in England, see W.E. Beckett, "The Recognition of Polygamous Marriages under English Law," Law Quarterly Review, *48 (1932), 341–373; I.H.C. Morris, "The Recognition of Polygamous Marriages in English Law,"* Harvard Law Review, *66 (1953), 961–1012; Adrian Briggs, "Polygamous Marriages and English Domiciliaries,"* International and Comparative Law Quarterly, *32 (1983), 737–741; and Alec Samuels, "The Polygamous Wife: How Far is She Treated as a Wife in English Law?"* Journal of Social Welfare Law *(1984), 271–276.*

For another essay by Kollewijn who served as Professor of Interracial Private Law at the Faculty of Law (Batavia), see his "Interracial Private Law (The Colonial Conflict of Laws)," in B. Schrieke, ed., The Effect of Western Influence on Native Civilisations in the Malay Archipelago *(Batavia: G. Kolff, 1929), pp. 204–236. In the same volume, see also the essay by B. Ter Haar, who was Professor of Indonesian Customary Law on the same faculty, "Western Influence on the Law for the Native Population," pp. 158–170.*

Reprinted from *The International Law Quarterly*, 4 (1951), 307–325.

I

The subject which I propose to discuss is of necessity but a small part of a vast field, namely the situation which arises when a country whose law is founded in the civilisation of Western Europe, is obliged to consider what degree of recognition it will give to laws practised and obeyed by communities of its subjects, which laws have their origin elsewhere.

Two questions arise: (a) Does the country and its courts acknowledge the non-Western[1] legal order as law? (b) Do they acknowledge the non-Western law as the equal of their own Western system?

We should further bear in mind that the reverse question is also possible: it has happened before and will happen again, that the judges of a non-Western State ask themselves the same question with reference to Western law. For instance the Ottoman Empire in the height of its power allowed Christian and Jewish communities of its subjects to live under their own Christian and Jewish law, but without acknowledging such law as the equal of Muhammadan law. Muhammadan law was always applied in legal relations between Muhammadans and non-Muhammadans and also in the disputes between Christians on one hand and Jews on the other. This aspect of the problem will probably once more become important in the new Asiatic States having an Eastern Family Law.[2]

The earliest attitude of Westerners to this question, an attitude which is not yet wholly extinct, is to regard the rules of social intercourse observed in non-Western communities as not being in any true sense law: according to this view, they may be usages or customs or they may have been imposed by force but they cannot be recognised as law. This conception has been nourished by purely material interests and defended by bombastic theories.

When in the beginning of the sixteenth century the Spaniards conquered Mexico and Peru, and enriched themselves by robbing the treasures of the Aztecs and the Incas, their action was excused by the historians of those times who asserted that these treasures were not owned by anybody since the American Indians, barbaric non-Christians as they were, were devoid of any law. It is one of the great merits of Francisco de Vitoria, professor of Theology and International Law at Salamanca, that in his *Relatio de Indis* (1539) he defended the rights of the Peruvians.[3] Apparently Vitoria's contemporaries had based on their reading of Aristotle an argument that the Indians, being barbarians, were slaves by nature, albeit slaves *a non domino*, and therefore incapable of property. Vitoria replied: 'The Europeans who discovered America could have no better right with respect to the persons and properties of these Indians than the Indians would have had had they been the first to discover the Spaniards or French'.

But although Vitoria in this manner defends the rights of the Indians to their properties and their estates, it is noteworthy that he does not do so on the ground of their law, but by virtue of Roman law, regarded as *ratio scripta* and *jus naturæ* and therefore of universal validity and applicable also to the Indians. Justinian's *Digest* and perhaps also the universal claims of the early Canon law, are the basis of his argument. The Indians, when the Spaniards arrived, were in peaceful possession—*in possessione*—of their goods. Consequently they must be looked upon as proprietors *donec probetur in contrarium.*

This was a great step forward but it was not yet acknowledgment of non-Western law. Before such law can be acknowledged it must be studied and understood; and down to the present day the failure to appreciate non-Western law at its true value is commonly based on ignorance.

Knowledge of American-Indian law was first obtained by the men on the spot, the civil servants and missionaries, Jesuits especially, who lived among the Indians: for instance Josephus de Acosta whose *Natural and Moral History of the Indies* (1590), originally written in Spanish, was published in an excellent English version by the Hakluyt Society (1880). De Acosta points to the misery which arose from a failure of the rulers to acknowledge the law of the people. This, he says, is the reason why the Spaniards were hated even when their measures were well intentioned. He contends that the Indians are entitled to abide by their customs; that no more Spanish law should be introduced than is strictly necessary, since a state of anarchy will arise if the Indians are no longer allowed to observe their own law while they do not understand ours.

'Let them have their own customs', he writes, 'let them keep their own religion as much as possible, leave them in the possession of their temples and idols, but only see to it that no inhumanities occur. Impart to them Christianity in their own language—and, God willing, this people that God seems to have forgotten so long, will be enlightened and will abandon their idolatry.'

Vitoria's conception may perhaps have rested not only on the view that the *corpus juris* contained a principle of universal application, but also perhaps on the principle that in a conquered country the law of the conqueror, in this case Spanish law based on Roman and Canon rules, is to be applied.

One may compare a change in the attitude of the Dutch East Indian Company. In 1619 when J. P. Coen took Djarkarta by force, Dutch law was introduced for the whole population: but in the territories, which were later yielded by treaty by the Javanese and other princes of Middle

Java, the native population continued to enjoy their own law, Dutch law being valid only for the Dutch.

It was by this time out of the question for Indonesian law not to be recognised. Grotius in his early work *Mare Liberum* declares: 'Java, Sumatra, the Moluccas have their own kings, public institutions, laws and rights and they have had them always. One is not entitled to deprive these infidels of their civil and princely power because they do not believe. Indeed it is even heresy to assume that the infidels should not be master of their goods, for it is no less theft and robbery to deprive them of their goods than it would be if a Christian were concerned'. But all these things are different if there should have been a justifiable war (*bellum justum*). In that case the property becomes the property of the conquering state and the latter is qualified to introduce into the conquered country its *own* law.

In England also this doctrine held good in olden times, but at the beginning of the seventeenth century a distinction is made according as the conquered country is Christian or non-Christian.

In *Calvin's Case*[4] appears the following: 'If a king conquers a Christian Kingdom, he may at his pleasure alter the laws of the Kingdom, but until he does so, the ancient law remains. But if a Christian King should conquer the Kingdom of an infidel, and bring them under his subjection, then *ipso facto*, the laws of the infidels are abrogated, for that they are not only against Christianity, but against the law of God and of nature contained in the Décalogue'.

This is the generalisation of ignorance. Without scrutiny of any sort, the laws of a non-Christian State are estimated to be contrary to Christian principles and subject, therefore, to wholesale condemnation. Such sweeping generalisation is, I venture to say, un-English; and it is not surprising therefore that before the end of the seventeenth century in the case of *Blankard* v. *Galdy*[5] Coke's sentence was mitigated as follows: 'Where it is said in *Calvin's Case*, that the laws of a conquered (non-Christian) country, do immediately cease, that may be true of laws for religion, but it seems otherwise for laws touching the government'.

And in 1744 the distinction made in *Calvin's Case* between Christian and non-Christian countries was entirely put aside in *Campbell* v. *Hall* (Co., p. 209) 20 St.Tr. 239, in which Lord Mansfield laid down the rule: '. . . that the laws of a conquered country continue in force until they are altered by the conqueror', and he added, '. . . that the absurd exceptions as to pagans mentioned in *Calvin's Case*, in all probability arose from the mad enthusiasm of the Crusaders'. Indeed, it appears that during the argument Lord Mansfield interrupted counsel for the plaintiff with the words 'Don't quote the distinction [between Christians and non-Christians] for the honour of my Lord Coke'.

A modern example of the conception that non-Western law is no law, is given by German colonial theory. When the imperial German Government, in the wake of private merchants and the trading companies, cast covetous eyes upon African territory, extensive estates were already found there, some simply occupied by the German pioneers, others obtained from African chiefs in exchange for cheap circulating mediums.

What law had been applied in these transactions between Africans and Germans? Could there be a question of any African law? Did the Africans have any *right* to the lands they cultivated, to the goods they considered as their own? One of the best-known German authors in the domain of international private law, Professor Karl Neumeyer, still answered these questions in the negative in an article in *Die Zeitschrift für Völkerrecht und Bundesstaatsrecht* of 1912, that is just before Germany lost her colonies. According to him, there could be no valid local law *before* Germany took possession of these African territories, because those territories were not States, at least they did not belong to the States acknowledged by Germany according to international law. Before their incorporation in the German Imperium 'indigenous laws' says Neumeyer 'could not be acknowledged as such'. Accordingly there could be no question of the application of any but German law to the acquisition of land by the German pioneers since there was no other law in force. Only after incorporation does it appear that there has been a conflict of laws concerning those land transactions: a conflict between the retrospectively acknowledged indigenous African law and the German law. What bearing, if any, Neumeyer's theory was to have on judicial decisions is far from clear: but the acquisitive bias is obvious.

But at the present day it is hardly, if at all, doubted that non-Western law is valid law for the autochthonous population in a country under Western rule. The question then arises what law is to be applied when Westerners enter into legal relations with non-Westerners. In Holland we call this *intergentiel recht*; the French speak of it as *Droit international privé interne*—a contradiction in terms—or of 'le conflit de lois colonial'. English writers have spoken of it as inter-racial, inter-communal or inter-religious private law, for in most cases in which the English have had to deal with it, a difference of religion is involved. The field is further narrowed by the fact that it has been found essential to have uniform law of contracts and other commercial topics, such as bankruptcy, and civil wrongs, and of land ownership and possession common to all persons in the territories concerned. In general such uniform law has been arrived at on models almost entirely Western except in the case of land, where (as for instance in India) a composite of Western and non-Western elements has been evolved. Almost the only field in which acute cases of conflict arise is, therefore, that of family law.[6] As far as my information goes, these conflicts in the field of family law have been more numerous in the French colonies and in Indonesia than in the British possessions, a circumstance which is perhaps due to the much wider social gap in the latter between the European and the autochthonous population. Let us then, compare the Dutch and French conceptions.

II

French legal theory and French case-law start from the postulate of the superiority of the French law to the law of the autochthonous population. Very recently this theory has been modified but so far without any appreciable change in the law. Accordingly French law in such cases is always given primacy since it is the law of the more developed and more highly civilised nation, namely France, whose duty it is felt to be to raise the colonial peoples, by history entrusted to her, to the same level of civilisation which she herself has reached. It is felt that France would be false to this 'mission sacrée' if she allowed French law to be overruled by any other system.

You will note that the French doctrine, like that of Lord Coke in *Calvin's Case*, passes a sweeping judgment on the indigenous law as a whole without going into the examination of separate rules. The system as a whole is regarded as inferior to French law and therefore must give way to the latter.

It follows that if anyone to whom French civil law is applicable enters into a personal relation with another who is subject to the indigenous law, the relationship must be governed by French law. If a French citizen marries an Algerian or Indo-Chinese, this marriage must be celebrated before the French registrar of marriages; it is subject to French law and the children also are *citoyens français de statut français*, governed by the French Code Civil. The citizen to whom the Code Civil is applicable continues to be governed by it in all inter-racial relations, nor will his or her children ever be governed by the indigenous law. Of this a striking instance may be given in a decision of the Court of Justice of Algiers of December 12, 1932.[7] In Tunis an Italian woman married a Tunisian Jew. He repudiated her by *ghett* under Tunisian Jewish law. This she refused to accept and petitioned for divorce. The conflict was not between French law of Civil Code and the Tunisian Jewish law, but between the Italian law of the wife and the law of the French protectorate, regarding a marriage celebrated in Tunisia in Tunisian fashion, between parties living in Tunis, the husband being a Tunisian Jew. Had this been an ordinary case of international private law, either the *lex loci celebrationis* or the law of the matrimonial domicile (according to the system of private international law prevalent in the courts concerned) would have been applied. In either case the result would have been the same, namely, the application of Tunisian law. But the Algerian court held that the rules of private international law presupposed a certain equality between the laws which may be applied and this equality is lacking in a conflict between European and Tunisian Jewish law. The court says that Tunisia is a protectorate and that the *raison d'etre* of the political position is a certain limitation of the sovereignty of the protected State not only in matters of public law but also in matters of private law in order to secure the predominance of the European law, in this case the Italian law of the wife, over the Tunisian law of Oriental origin. Is not this Coke *redivivus*?[8]

So the Minister for the French overseas territories, writing in *The Revue Critique*, 1948, p. 545, says: 'In case of a conflict between the normal legal system of the French common law and a local legal system, it is the former which must necessarily win'. That is to say French law is the norm; indigenous law is abnormal, temporary, transient, '*jurisprudence d'exception*', and limited in its scope.[9]

III

In Indonesia quite a different attitude has been taken alike by the Legislature, the courts and the theoretical jurists. Inter-racial conflict of laws, or as in those old days it was still called 'quasi-international private law', was discussed in detail at a congress of the Dutch East Indian Society of Jurists in Batavia in 1887; and the fundamental equality of Eastern and Western private law was accepted by the majority of those present. The congress was principally concerned to solve the problem of mixed marriages; and it was part of the general legal atmosphere of that period that in matrimony the law of the husband was regarded as more important than the law of the wife. The following proportions were therefore accepted:

(a) in a marriage between a European man and an Indonesian or Chinese woman: (i) the marriage must be solemnised according to the personal law of the man, (ii) it is this law which governs the relations betwen husband and wife, and prohibits polygamy, and (iii) it is again this law which decides whether, and if so, on what grounds, and by what procedure a divorce may be obtained;

(b) *e converso* the personal law of the man must prevail as regards forms of matrimony, incidents of the matrimonial status, including polygamy and dissolution of marriage, in all cases where an Indonesian or a Chinese man marries a European woman.

The conclusions of this congress were embodied in a Royal Decree drawn up in 1896, which has remained the law of Indonesia to this day. Accordingly, where a European man marries an Indonesian woman, the marriage must be celebrated in the presence of a European registrar. But if a European woman marries an Indonesian man, the marriage must be solemnised according to the personal law of the Indonesian man, and if he is a Muslim, according to the Islamic law. Further, as the woman, according to the prevalent system of Islamic law of the *Shafi'i* school, must be given in marriage by a guardian (*wali*) who should normally be a relative and a Muslim, and as the European woman generally speaking will not have such a relative, the requirements of the Muslim law are met by a so-called *Penghoeloe*, who acts as her *wali*. Many such marriages have been contracted by women who, before their marriage, were subject to European law, but there is no doubt that by this marriage they became subject to Muhammadan matrimonial law with its possibilities of polygamy and private divorce by the husband. I am not personally aware of any case in which an Indonesian man, having married a European woman took a second wife, but I do know of a case where a European woman consented to marry an Indonesian, a Balinese prince, who was already married.

Not only in matrimonial law, but also in the law of inheritance and in cases concerning illegitimate children the same postulate of equality of Western and non-Western law prevails in Indonesia, irrespective of whether application of European or Indonesian law will be the result. At this point I must refer to a doctrine which is unknown in English law, but familiar to many Continental systems, the doctrine of recognition of illegitimate children. The child of an Indonesian woman born out of wedlock but recognised by its European father follows its father's status; similarly the child of a European woman born out of wedlock but recognised by its Chinese father, follows the status of the Chinese father and will be a Chinese in the eyes of the law. This would be impossible according to French law in which the status of the child always follows the status of that parent who is governed by the higher esteemed code civil.

Similarly in Indonesia succession, both testate and intestate, is governed by the personal law of the deceased, whether European or Indonesian, and not the law of the heirs. Consequently the Christian wife of a Muslim Indonesian husband will be barred from inheritance by difference of religion, since that is a bar to inheritance in Islamic law; but the Indonesian wife of a European husband will not be barred since in the system of the husband there is no such qualification.

What basic principle underlies this Dutch concept of equality? Surely this, that one can never call one legal system in itself, higher or lower, better or worse, than another, there is no standard by which to measure it (Koschaker). The question whether a legal system is good or not can only be considered in connection with a group of persons to be governed by it. For persons living under other social conditions, having other customs and other moral and religious conceptions than we Westerners have, other legal systems, different from ours, may be appropriate and therefore right. It is not for the judge to try to promote through judicial channels the spread of Western civilisation. To the judge Western and non-Western law must be equal since each applies to a part of the population of one and the same territory, though a Western judge may well believe his own system to be the better and an Eastern judge in his place be of the opposite opinion. But each should realise that his personal preference should not guide him in his judicial decisions. Had the Dutch attitude been different there would have been reason to fear that after the transfer of sovereignty in Indonesia, now that all Dutch judges have been, or are being, replaced by Indonesians the latter would apply in all inter-racial cases the Eastern family law, the Islamic law, Chinese law, Adat law, which (and this is particularly true of the Islamic law) was considered to be of far higher value than the Western. But as the Indonesian judges have absorbed the Dutch doctrine of the equality of our laws, one may reasonably expect that they will continue in inter-racial relations to apply Western law wherever legal grounds for doing so are present.

IV

So far I have spoken about legal conflicts as they presented themselves in overseas territory only, *i.e.*, between Western law, which has penetrated into that territory, and the indigenous law which is still in force there. But similar legal conflicts may present themselves in the European homeland, when Asiatic or African people from the overseas territories come to Europe; as for instance when Indonesians come to the Netherlands, or Hindus and Muhammadans from India and Pakistan come to Britain, or Algerians and Moroccans come to France. In the case of Holland the question is whether to apply the indigenous law of Indonesia or the civil law of Holland to such persons. Obviously in this case we have *not* to do with an inter-racial conflict. The Adat law of Indonesia and the Civil Code of Holland do not apply in such a case in one and the same country, as they are laws of different territories; the conflict between them therefore is a normal international conflict of law, and would be presumably so regarded in England. But in Holland this sort of legal conflict is in a class by itself. We did so, formerly, when Indonesian still formed part of the Netherlands Kingdom, in the first place because these conflicts occurred *within* one State, and accordingly were not international; but, secondly (and this reason is still operative) because we applied to legal conflicts which concern both Indonesia and the Netherlands principles other than those we apply in international private law. In international private law, the Netherlands is one of the countries which applies the principle of nationality to questions of personal status. However, in Dutch-Indonesian conflicts we adhere, like England, to the principle of domicile. Therefore we formerly called this part of the law of conflicts by a separate name: conflicts of inter-regional law, and now that Indonesia is a sovereign State, but united with the Netherlands in a Union, we call them Union-regional conflicts of law.

These conflicts of law, arising from the fact that Asiatics and Africans go to Europe, are of perhaps the greatest practical importance for France.

At the moment there are about 180,000 French Muhammadans in France, in Paris alone there are about 75,000. The number of Algerians in France married to French women is estimated to surpass 5,000 (J. J. Rager—*Rev. de la Mediterranée*, 1950, No. 2, k. 78). Their number has highly increased since 1946 when all French nationals acquired the status of 'citoyens' and the regulations of immigration for French citizens and Algerians were unified. After that date as a consequence of these new laws the social provisions, especially the allowances for the unemployed, apply in France to the Algerians as much as to the French. The wages are higher in France than in Algeria. The Algerian, unemployed, is better off in Paris than the Algerian unskilled labourer at work in his own overpopulated country.

I know of no English statistics concerning immigration from the Asiatic and African parts of the Commonwealth but I believe that at any rate the number is greater than in the Netherlands, though in the Netherlands it is also impossible to give any exact figure of the number of Indonesian settlers. Judging from the census taken in 1947, we can only gather that in May, 1947, 2,227 Netherlands subjects, who were not Netherlanders in the narrow sense of the word, found themselves in the Netherlands. However, not all of them were Indonesians; among them were a thousand Chinese who were Netherlands subjects, possibly from Indonesia. So we may reckon that about one thousand Indonesians live in Holland, even though in the same census of 1847, only 300 persons gave Islam as their religion. This figure is certainly too low. These figures make it clear that the problem of the conflict of Western and non-Western law in the home-country itself is of a far greater importance for France than it is for Holland.

How does France solve this conflict? Since even in the overseas territories French law ranks above Indo-Chinese or African law, it follows that in 'La France Metropôle' only the application of French law can be considered for marriage and divorce. Similarly, though on different grounds as we shall presently see, the Indian or African in London, and the Indonesian in Amsterdam can only contract a valid marriage according to the *lex loci celebrationis*. But what law governs such a marriage contracted in the European country when the married couple make their home in the Asiatic or African country of the husband? The tribunal of Hanoi gave judgment on this question on March 16, 1920.[10] A native of Annam, one of the States of Indo-China, had married a French woman in Paris by French ceremony and the married couple had settled in Annam. Some years later the woman sued for divorce under the French Code Civil on the ground that her husband had taken a concubine, a woman of Annam, concubinage being permitted by the law of his domicile and giving no ground for divorce to the first wife.[11] The court gave judgment for the plaintiff on the ground that the Annamite husband, having married a French woman in France before a French registrar, had broken that marriage which was governed and must continue to be governed by French law. His defense was rejected with the remark that he surely could not have expected that a polygamous relation could result from a ceremony accomplished before the French registrar. The quintessence of the position is not merely that the marriage contracted in France was governed by French law, but that the marriage continued to be governed by French law, even after the couple had made their matrimonial domicile in Annam, and consequently that a French marriage could never be converted into an Asiatic marriage permitting polygamy, no matter how long a married couple may remain in Annam. Yet by contrast, suppose a marriage between a French woman and a Dutch, English or American man, and suppose that the couple after marriage establish their domicile in the country of the man, and that the woman takes the husband's nationality. In such a case the French judge would certainly have not hesitated to hold that the matrimonial status treated by a French ceremony was governed *quoad* divorce by the personal law of the husband.[12] The basic postulate of the Hanoi court's decision is that the law of the husband, being a non-Western law, is inferior to French law and that therefore French law continues to govern the marriage; and this postulate the Hanoi court was in a position to enforce. The consequence of this view would appear to be not only that the marriages of 5,000 Algerians contracted with French women in France would continue to be governed by French law if the married couples should go to Algeria, a view with which we may well sympathise, but also that Algerian men who have married Algerian women in France will find that French law continues to be applicable to the marriage in Algeria in spite of their return to their own homes. Direct legal authority, however, for this extreme but logical result appears to be lacking.

And now for the English view of the question.

After Lord Mansfield's strictures on Coke, questions raising the conflicts, which we are considering, appear to have been mainly questions of marriage, either of the recognition which English law could or could not accord to marriages under polygamous systems, or of mixed marriages between Westerners and non-Westerners. I am not sure that English law is quite settled and I hesitate to express any opinion too positively. It may well be also that the attitude to these problems taken in different jurisdictions of the British Commonwealth differs by reason of local conditions and particularly the constitutional laws of each separate territory. With due diffidence I submit that in the development of English law on these problems during the last 120 years successive phases can be distinguished. The first phase is characterised by a view that British courts can take no cognisance whatever of the non-Western law on these matters unless it is proved to be substantially identical with the English law in regarding marriage as the 'voluntary union for life of one man and one woman to the exclusion of all others'. The earliest judicial pronouncement in this sense appears to be that of Lord Brougham in *Warrender* v. *Warrender*.[13] His Lordship laid down that a marriage good by the laws of one country (namely the country where it is celebrated), is held good in all others where a question of the validity may arise. But afraid of the possible results of applying this doctrine to marriages under non-Western systems he added, 'there may go two different things under one and the same name of marriage in two different countries'; and he proceeds: 'marriage is one and the same thing substantially all the Christian world over, and it is important to observe that we regard it as a wholly different thing, a different status, from Turkish or other marriages among infidel nations'.

This is the first case which marks the line of separation in this field between Western and non-Western law, or Christian and non-Christian law; on which has been built the doctrine that English municipal and also English international private law take cognisance of marriages which may be called Christian and regard all others juridically as a mere nothing. This view was summed up in the well-known sentence of Lord Penzance which I have already quoted.[14] But for many years the definition was given a far wider application than Lord Penzance himself intended. He prefaces it with the words 'for this purpose', *i.e.*, for the purpose of considering the jurisdiction of his court: and he explicitly stated that he was not passing upon questions of the rights of succession, legitimacy, or mutual duties.

In 1887[15] it was decided that the marriage of a domiciled Englishman in Africa with a woman of the Baralong tribe according to the custom of that tribe, although it may there take the name of 'marriage' and the parties to it be designated as 'husband' and 'wife,' cannot be regarded as a marriage according to the law of England because it is not formed on the same basis as marriages throughout Christendom, in as much as it is not in its essence the voluntary union for life of one man and one woman. Consequently the children of this so-called marriage were held to be illegitimate, not being born in wedlock in the Christian sense of the word.

In recent years this judgment has been defended on the ground that Bethell at the time of the marriage was still domiciled in England, and therefore, according to English conceptions, the law governing the essentials of the marriage was still English law and not the native custom. He could have been married to the Baralong woman by the British chaplain at Buluwayo. But this was not the *ratio decidendi*. The decision was based on the postulate that the non-Western, non-Christian marriage which admitted the possibility of polygamy could not find, in any way, acknowledgment in English law. As another judge in *Harvey* v. *Farnie*[16] formulated the rule, a polygamous marriage is 'a union falsely called marriage'.

This opinion has now been abandoned. To have carried it out consistently would have led to much hardship and injustice.[17] The first change of view is marked by the *Sinha Peerage Claim Case*,[18] 1939, in which Lord Maugham L.C. said:

'It cannot, I think, be doubted now that a Hindu marriage between persons domiciled in India is recognised in our courts, that the issue is regarded as legitimate, and that such issue can succeed to property, with a possible exception'.

Following this: In *Srini Vasan* v. *Srini Vasan* [1946] P. 67, an English woman domiciled in England secured a declaration of nullity in respect of her marriage in England with a Hindu, on the ground that he was previously married to a Hindu woman in India. This was followed in *Baindail* v. *Baindail* ([1946] P. 122), but as Dicey, or rather his later editor (p. 25) says: 'There is still remarkably little English authority as to the precise extent to which such (polygamous) unions will be recognised'.

In English legal theory the most important point is always the construction of statutes, where such statutes are to be applied. So it has been suggested that succession to the personal property of a Hindu who died domiciled in England, including the rights of his children born of polygamous marriage celebrated while he was domiciled in India, will depend upon the construction of the Administration of Estates Act, 1925; and in *Baindail's Case* already quoted Lord Greene M.R. expressly left open the question whether a man domiciled in a country where polygamy is permitted can be prosecuted in England for bigamy in respect of a second marriage in England. This, he said, would depend on the construction of the words 'being married' and 'marries', in the Offences against the Person Act, 1861, s. 57.

It would probably be agreed, first and foremost, that when the term 'marriage' occurs in a British statute territorially intended for the homeland only, it must be understood in the English sense. But I venture to suggest that if English municipal law is applied in international relations in accordance with English doctrines of the Conflict of Laws, this does not necessarily mean that the word should have in its international relation exactly the same sense as it has in its internal or municipal aspect; some modification becomes necessary when the Act is applied to a situation which is not in contemplation of Parliament when it was passed. Thus Lord Penzance was right when he said that it would be absurd to divorce a Hindu from one of his women on the ground that he had committed adultery and bigamy by marrying another.[19] But I suggest that if, for the purposes of international private law, it is admitted that a polygamous marriage must be regarded as a marriage, then, if according to the English rule the internal law is applicable to such a union the conception of its rules and terms must be adapted to the new situation which has arisen. Adultery will have to be regarded as sexual intercourse with any woman other than the women to whom the defendant is lawfully married.

Again, if, according to English law, the father is obliged to maintain his legitimate children, then, if this rule is applied to a father who is now domiciled in England, but who, according to the law of his former domicile was married lawfully to two wives at the same time, this father will be obliged to maintain the children of his two marriages. He cannot escape his duty of supporting these children on the pretext that under English law he is only obliged to maintain his legitimate children, and that according to English law it is impossible that children, born at the same time of different women, should all of them be legitimate. And likewise this same husband and father will be obliged to provide the two women with maintenance according to the English law applicable to them, although in English law, as enacted for the English citizen, one never thought of the possibility that a husband would have two legitimate wives.

So, since English international private law accepts as valid a family relationship which is rooted in the domiciliary law of another country, of India for example, English internal law, which becomes applicable when the spouses remove their domicile to England, will have to show understanding for the strange but continuing relation, which is thus brought under its authority.

But in another respect, the old view that English law only recognised the Christian marriage has maintained its influence. According to this idea, it was obvious that a marriage celebrated in England was a Christian marriage, which, as regards the relations between husband and wife, was governed by English law and continued to be governed by English law even if the parties removed their domicile to a polygamous country. For as polygamous law was no law at all according to this train of thought, only English law of marriage could be considered. However, now that in the last few years marriages contracted in India, between Hindus or Muhammadans who live there, have come to be recognised in England as valid marriages, the theory that a marriage contracted in England always continues to be naturally a monogamous marriage becomes more difficult to defend.

A marriage of an Englishman contracted anywhere in the world is to be regarded as an English monogamous marriage because, according to the law of his English domicile, he can only contract a monogamous marriage. *E converso*, assuming that a Hindu, according to the law of his Indian domicile, could not deprive himself of his right to polygamy; should he be deprived of that right by reason of a marriage contract in England during temporary residence here?[20] It will be universally admitted that the non-Western right of polygamy or repudiation cannot be exercised in England in respect of a marriage celebrated in this country, since the exercise of these rights will be against the public policy of English law. But when the young Hindu returns to India his English marriage—if it is still considered as a marriage at all—will not be regarded as an obstacle to the exercise of his polygamous privileges. Difficult as it may be for English law, or indeed any Western law, to accept the conclusion that women of European origin may be bound by the ties of a polygamous marriage through a form of marriage solemnised in England, one should not forget that this would be the conclusion of the law in force in the country where the husband and wife fix their domicile, in the same way as the consequence of the English domicile of the English spouses is that their marriage, celebrated in a polygamous country is a monogamous marriage.

And so Professor Cheshire, who in his brilliant book on Private International Law describes not only the law that is in force, but gives also his opinion on English law as it ought to be, comes to the conclusion that some improvement would be effected if what is believed to be the sound principle were adopted by the courts, namely, that whether a marriage is polygamous or monogamous is to be determined by the law of domicile, which means in the theory of Professor Cheshire, the law of the matrimonial domicile.

The suggestion of Professor Cheshire is substantially the solution already in force in Dutch Indonesian relations. This solution is laid down in an Indonesian statute, namely the Royal Decree of 1848 on the general principles of the law, as it was amended in 1915, where the general principle is that if a Netherlander goes to the Indies (*i.e.*, Indonesia) and settles there, the law of Indonesia will apply to him and if, on the other hand, Netherlands subjects from Indonesia, no matter what their race or religion, settle in Holland the Netherlands Civil Code will be applied to them.

The word 'settle' in this enactment may perhaps be modernised as 'fix their domicile'.[21] The result of this regulation as interpreted in all the legal literature is, first, that the matrimonial status (including questions of polygamy and divorce) is governed by the law of the husband's domicile. Whatever limitations may be imposed on this general principle in Holland by Dutch public policy, it is undoubted that as soon as the husband and wife are in Indonesia, a repudiation (talaq) issued by the man and valid by his personal Muhammadan law will also be held good in Holland. Although I know of no reported judicial decision on this point, it has frequently been held by the Dutch Registrar-General of Marriages on the advice of the department of overseas territories that a wife of Dutch origin who married an Indonesian in Holland, went with him to Indonesia and was repudiated there, was free to marry again in Holland, her first marriage having been validly dissolved by the Muhammadan repudiation. Indeed, even if an Indonesian had fixed his domicile in Holland and thereby become subject to the Netherlands Civil Code, and while so domiciled has married a Dutch woman, nevertheless, if thereafter he returned with his wife to Indonesia and so re-acquired an Indonesian domicile, the Dutch monogamous marriage would be transformed into an Indonesian (and if the husband were a Muslim, a Muhammadan) marriage.

Borderline cases, however, are conceivable where an Indonesian husband in Holland sends a *talaq* by mail to his wife in Indonesia, or where an Indonesian husband in Indonesia sends a *talaq* by mail to his wife who is still in Holland. I speak with diffidence but I am inclined to think that, in the former case at least, a Dutch judge would say: 'While you are in Holland, if you wish to dissolve your marriage, you can only do so by some means which is not in such manifest contradiction with accepted Dutch principles of fair dealing'.

By contrast it is remarkable that in France the right of the Algerian Muhammadan resident in France to repudiate by *talaq* his Algerian wife left behind in Algeria is not only accepted but is even regulated by circulars issued in 1930 and 1931 under the authority of the Ministère de l'Intérieur, the Ministère de Justice and the Procureur-Général de la Republique. Even before that Algerians in Paris had been used to giving powers of attorney to a friend or a member of the family to repudiate their wives in their name. But then the act of repudiation itself took place in Algeria and not in France. However, it seems that many difficulties arose in respect of these delegated divorces so, in 1930, at the instance of the Procureur-Général of Algeria, the authorities in France provided that the repudiation itself could take place in France before a notary and two witnesses, and that the friend in Algeria need only get letters of procuration to serve the deed of repudiation upon the wife. A notary in Paris, le notaire Sabot, was indicated, who practically has a monopoly of these Muhammadan repudiations. I have not complete figures on this subject, but I know that in 1939, 126 of these deeds of repudiation were drawn up in this Parisian notary's office.

The result is certainly odd. French jurists whose cardinal axiom in these matters is the superiority of the French Code Civil to all non-Western law find themselves compelled by circumstances to recognise an act of repudiation in the capital city of France contrary to the principles of that Code. In Holland (and, I submit, in England also) such an act would be regarded as void on grounds of public policy. [And what would the position in France be, if both the Algerian and his wife had taken up permanent residence there?]

For the second question just formulated, judicial authority is equally lacking; and the connection with the public policy of Dutch law is not so obvious. The repudiation is pronounced in Indonesia, the domicile of the husband, where it is valid: but its consequences reach Holland where the wife (though matrimonially domiciled in Indonesia with her husband) is still living. The validity of such a repudiation would probably be accepted by the Dutch Courts, as it would have been if the wife had accompanied her husband to Indonesia, a view in contrast with that taken in England by all the judges in the *Hammersmith Marriage Case*.[22]

Contacts between different civilisations are a fascinating field of study: but even the legal aspects of such contacts which we have now traversed would require, for their adequate survey, a bulky volume. We have traced the history of the topic from a time when non-Westerners were regarded as incapable not merely of a law of their own but even of rights under Western law. This barbarous attitude to alleged barbarians gave way to a more civilised conception when it was realised (under Vitoria's leadership) that at least Roman law doctrines of *jus naturale* must apply to them. But even up to the end of the seventeenth century it was held that if a Christian king conquered a non-Christian country the non-

Christian law as a whole was automatically superseded by the Christian law of the conqueror. Today, the view is universally accepted that non-Western law is law and must be recognised as such: but in France it is regarded, as a whole, as being law of a lower standard than Western law and therefore as bound always to give way when it comes into conflict with Western law.

In Holland and in Great Britain non-Western law is accepted, on the whole, as of equal status with Western law, though in regard to some peculiar institutions, polygamy for example, difficulties still exist, and I am not altogether sure (speaking with diffidence) that in England at least some traces of the old postulate of superiority do not remain. When we are brought face to face with legal relations unknown to our own law, we may well find that we have no rules of conflict appropriate to these unknown institutions. But we ought not therefore to refuse to recognise, or even in appropriate circumstances to give effect to, an institution or status unknown in our Western countries; rather, we should work out new rules applicable to the interplay of these strange institutions with our own. International private law is not merely a static group of fixed rules confined to the legal institutions of a definite number of Christian or Western States, but a dynamic entity which is constantly growing with the progressive integration of what is after all (and more obviously as time proceeds) a single world.

Notes

1. The term 'non-Western' perhaps needs explanation and justification. The alternative 'Oriental' is inapt since some of the laws concerned, *e.g.*, those of Mexico, Peru and of the American Indian tribes of Canada and the United States, are in no sense Oriental. The words 'native' and 'indigenous' have sometimes been used in a derogatory sense and are therefore to be avoided: moreover Islamic law, one of the principal systems to be considered, cannot really be called native or indigenous anywhere but in Arabia. Nor can a clear definition be made on a religious basis since at least one important body of law concerned, namely the Adat law of Indonesia, is not a religious law. By the phrase 'non-Western' therefore is implied all law which is not of European ancestry.

2. As we proceed with our discussion we shall see that the problem narrows down to one of family relations.

3 The book, like Aristotle's *Ethics*, consists of notes of his lectures taken by diligent pupils. *Sit bonis boni exemplar.*

4. (1608) 7 Rep. 17.

5. Comberbatch 228.

6. There are signs that in countries such as India, Pakistan and Indonesia which have recently achieved independence, the new rulers intend far more drastic reforms in their ancient laws than the former foreign rulers would have ventured to contemplate.

7. Clunet 1936, pp. 158 fol.

8. The doctrine found outlined underwent an apparent rather than a real modification (Art. 8 of the Constitution of the same year). For in fact, the difference in personal law remains unaltered, though instead of distinguishing between 'citoyens' and 'sujets français', the terms in use are *'citoyens de statut civil'* and *'citoyens de statut personnel, particulier ou local'*.

9. For further illustration of the French point of view see also p. 785.

10. Dareste 1930–3, 110; Penant 1930–1, 46.

11. For the purposes of this case it is immaterial whether the second woman was a second wife or a concubine. Annamite law, like Chinese law, recognises both these possibilities, and the line between them is sometimes difficult to draw. The point at issue was that the husband's continued *consortium* with the second woman would have been a matrimonial offence in French law, giving grounds for divorce, but would not have been such an offence by Annamite law.

12. The fact that generally speaking Western laws do not recognise extra-judicial divorce is not the ground of distinction in French law.

13. (1835) 2 Cl. and F. 488.

14. *Hyde* v. *Hyde and Woodmansee* (1866) 1 P. & D. 130.

15. *In re Bethell* (1887) 38 Ch.D. 220.

16. (1882) 8 App. Cas. 43.

17. In South Africa, however, it seems to be still accepted, for as late as 1931 it was decided by the Supreme Court of South Africa that an Indian woman, married in India to an Indian Hindu, was an unmarried woman by the law of the Union of South Africa. (Journal of Comparative Legislation 1934, 107.)

18. 1938, 171 Lords Journals 350, S.C.; [1946] 1 All E.R. 348.

19. This, however, is exactly what is contemplated by the India Divorce Act, where the first wife is Christian, although the second union is lawful.

20. Although the view of English law would apparently refuse to recognise that right, the prevailing view of the Indian courts is that an Indian who has contracted marriage in England is not deprived of his polygamous privileges thereby, although an English wife may regard the exercise of them as grounds for divorce.

21. The test of domicile in Dutch law is not quite the same as in English law. In both systems a merely temporary residence, *e.g.*, of a student for purposes of education, does not involve a change of domicile: and it is in respect of such temporary residents that most cases of mixed marriage arise. But a man who goes to another country to earn his livelihood, hoping to retire to his native land only when he has made a fortune or earned a pension, would be held in Dutch law to have acquired a domicile of choice in the country where his working life is being spent, though in English law he has not abandoned his domicile of origin.

22. [1917] 1 K.B. 634.

E.G. UNSWORTH

The Conflict of Laws in Africa

Nowhere in the world are there more instances of folk law in conflict than on the continent of Africa. Several centuries of colonial rule by Belgium, England, France, Germany, Italy, and Portugal have left their indelible legal mark. It was during the colonial period that conflicts of law first came to the attention of law enforcement agencies and courts. Even after colonial rule finally ended and emergent African nation-states came into being, the conflicts of folk law with the old colonial established law framework continued unabated.

The following short essay summarizes the different areas of conflict. Although the data is drawn from particular parts of Africa, the general issues discussed are applicable to most of Africa and elsewhere. It is probably not necessary to remind the reader that there is no longer a British central African protectorate called Northern Rhodesia. In 1964, the area became the independent nation of Zambia.

For samples of the enormous literature devoted to the conflict of laws in Africa, see such essays as Julius Lewin, "The Conflict of Native Law and Common Law in South Africa," The South African Law Journal, *58 (1941), 365–374; A.C.A. Wright, "The Inter-Action of Various Systems of Law and Custom in British Somaliland and their Relation with Social Life,"* Journal of the East Africa Natural History Society and National Museum, *17 (1943), 62–102. J.N.D. Anderson, "Colonial Law in Tropical Africa: The Conflict Between English, Islamic and Customary Law,"* Indiana Law Journal, *35 (1960), 433–442; F.A.Ajayi, "The Interaction of English Law with Customary Law in Western Nigeria,"* Journal of African Law, *4 (1960), 40–50, 98–114; A. Arthur Schiller, "Conflict of Laws in East Africa,"* Nederlands Tijdschrift voor International Recht, *9 (1962), 430–454; W.C. Ekow Daniels, "The Interaction of English Law with Customary Law in West Africa,"* International and Comparative Law Quarterly, *13 (1964), 574–616; I Oluwole Agbede, "Conflict Between Customary and Non-Customary Systems of Law: Preliminary Observations,"* Journal of Islamic and Comparative Law, *4 (1969–1976), 48–58 (the same paper appears in* Verfassung und Recht in Übersee, *5 (1972), 415–422); Kwame Opoku, "Traditional Law under French Colonial Rule,"* Verfassung und Recht in Übersee, 7 *(1974), 139–153; S.N. Nwabara, "The 'Received' Nigerian Law and the Challenge of Legal Independence,"* Journal of

Reprinted from *The Rhodes-Livingstone Journal*, 2 (1944), 49–55, with permission.

Asian and African Studies, *14 (1979), 99–108; and T.W. Bennett, "Conflict of Laws in South Africa: Cases involving Customary Law,"* Tydskrif vir Hedendaagse Romeins-Hollandse Reg, *43 (1980), 27–38.*

Introductory

The subject matter of the Conflict of Laws may be defined as the rules which are adopted by the English Courts for determining whether they will recognise and enforce rights which are conferred by foreign law. In dealing with this branch of the law the English Courts in Africa have to decide the circumstances under which they will enforce the Native customary laws[1] of the African inhabitants of the country. In Northern Rhodesia matters relating to Native law may come before an English Court in three different ways, namely (1) when the Court is sitting as a Court of first instance; (2) when it is reviewing a decision of a Native Court, or (3) when it is hearing an appeal from a Native Court. In the first case the English Courts can apply Native law only in civil matters[2] although Native customs may indirectly become material in criminal cases; for example, in deciding whether there has been provocation in a case of homicide. In the latter two cases an English Court has power to apply Native law not only in civil matters, but also in matters which are criminal in accordance with Native law; for example, on reviewing or hearing an appeal from a conviction for adultery.[3]

Native law most frequently comes into issue when the Courts are dealing with civil causes and matters relating to marriage and to the tenure and inheritance of property. Native law on these matters differs considerably from English law; for example, property descends to an heir or heirs in accordance with rules which differ from tribe to tribe and the power to make a will is not generally recognised. It is true that a Native frequently states in his lifetime that he wishes certain property to be given to a particular person but these directions are not binding on the heir and the Native Court will not interfere with the decision of the heir if he fails to comply with these directions. It is obvious that difficulties may arise in deciding whether the property of a detribalised and educated Native should descend in accordance with English or Native law, and in particular in deciding whether a will made by such a Native should be recognised. It is submitted that the property of a Native must descend in accordance with Native law unless such law is unenforceable for one or other of the reasons which are later set out in this article. In the same way Native law must be applied between Natives in other matters which come before the English Courts unless such laws are unenforceable[4]. In addition Native law may be applied in a dispute between a Native and a non-Native if a strict adhesion to English law would cause injustice.

In Northern Rhodesia[5] and most other British possessions Native law is enforceable unless

(1) it is repugnant to natural justice or morality; or
(2) it is inconsistent with statute law;[6] or
(3) it is inapplicable to the particular circumstance of the case.

Native Laws Which Are Repugnant to Natural Justice or Morality

The question whether any Native law is repugnant to natural justice or morality will be a question of fact to be decided on the facts of each particular case which comes before the Court. A Native law must, however, be manifestly unjust before the Courts will refuse to enforce it. In a Southern Rhodesia case[7] Mr. Justice Tredgold stated that "Native customs should not be interfered with unless they impress us with some abhorrence or are obviously immoral in their incidence". In a Southern Rhodesia case[8] it was held that a Native custom which prevented a married woman from obtaining a divorce without the consent of her husband was contrary to natural justice and unenforceable. In another Southern Rhodesia case[9] it was held that a Native custom which enabled a husband to refuse to accept payment of compensation for adultery and thereby deprive the genitor[10] of the right, according to local Native custom, to the custody of the children was contrary to natural justice and unenforceable.

The author has not been able to discover any reported cases in which the question of morality has been considered. It is submitted, however, that the ordinary English principles would apply and that a contract which is made upon an immoral suggestion or for an immoral purpose would be unenforceable.[11] If this view of the law is correct, certain Native laws which recognise the right of a woman to recover an agreed payment for prostitution are unenforceable.

Native Laws Which Are Inconsistent with Statute Law

Native law is unenforceable if it is inconsistent with statute law. Native law, however, is not inconsistent with statute law unless it comes into direct conflict with it. The provisions of Native law and statute law are not inconsistent if the two laws can stand together and both operate without either interfering with the other. This was the principle applied by the House of Lords in England in deciding whether the provisions of an earlier Act of Parliament were inconsistent with the provisions of a later Act[12] and similar principles have been applied by the Courts in Southern Rhodesia in deciding whether Native law is inconsistent with statute law.[13] An example of the way in which the two laws may stand together is afforded by a Southern Rhodesia case[13] in which two Natives contracted a Christian marriage in accordance with the provisions of the Marriage Ordinance. Bride wealth[14] was paid in accordance with Native law although such a payment forms no part of a marriage under the Marriage Ordinance. One of the parties was later granted a judicial separation and a claim was then brought for the recovery of the bride wealth. The Court held that the claim was enforceable as a contract for the payment of bride wealth could exist side by side with an English marriage under the Marriage Ordinance.

An example of inconsistency and conflict between Native law and statute law is provided by a Kenya case[15] in which a Native Christian male gave notice of marriage under the Marriage Ordinance of his intended marriage to a minor Mohammedan girl aged fifteen years. The girl's father was dead and her mother gave her written consent to the marriage. A caveat was entered by the girl's uncle against the intended marriage on the grounds that his consent was required to the marriage under Mohammedan law and that in any case it was contrary to Mohammedan law for a Mohammedan woman to contract a valid marriage except with a Mohammedan. It was held that the Mohammedan law was inconsistent with the provisions of the Marriage Ordinance and therefore inapplicable; that the uncle's consent was not required and that there was nothing in the Marriage Ordinance to prohibit a marriage between a Mohammedan and a Christian.

In view of the fact that Native law is unenforceable if it is inconsistent with statute law, it is usually unnecessary to repeal Native law. It automatically becomes redundant and unenforceable as soon as a statute is enacted which is inconsistent with it. In a Southern Rhodesia case[16] it was held that a Native law granting hereditary rights of chieftainship became redundant on the passing of the Native Affairs Act, and that the only Chief who could be recognised was the person who had been appointed in accordance with the provisions of that Act. In that case Mr. Justice McIlwaine stated that there was no authority for the contention that Native law and custom obtained until repealed so that an Act of Parliament dealing with Native affairs must be read subject to such law and custom unless expressly repealed. On this principle the Native law regarding wills has become redundant in many British possessions as express legislation has been enacted enabling Natives to dispose of property by will.

Cases in which Native Law Is Inapplicable

The question whether Native law is applicable to the facts of any particular case is often a difficult matter to decide. In a Nigerian case[17] it was laid down that "The Court is not bound to observe Native custom in *every* case where the custom is not repugnant to natural justice, etc., nor incompatible with any local Ordinance. When the Court has before it a matter which is purely "Native", or where all the circumstances to be taken into account are connected with Native life, habit, or custom, then undoubtedly Native law and custom should apply. Where, on the other hand, the matter before the Court contains elements foreign to Native life, habit, and custom, the Court is not bound to observe Native law and custom." The following general principles have been laid down by the Courts in Africa.

1. Native law will not be enforced where Natives have entered into a relationship inconsistent with Native law.

Natives frequently enter into relationships which are inconsistent with Native law and in these cases the English Courts will apply English law and not Native law. In most British possessions, though not in Northern Rhodesia, Natives can contract a Christian marriage under the Marriage Ordinance in the same way as a European and it has been laid down that English law and not Native law is applicable to the incidence of such a marriage; for example, such Natives can only be divorced in accordance with English law;[18] the custody of the children is dealt with in accordance with English law[19] and claims for damage for adultery and semble, criminal actions for adultery in accordance with Native law cannot be sustained.[20]

2. Native law will not be enforced where the Native parties to a contract have expressly or impliedly shown that they intend the contract to be interpreted and enforced in accordance with English law.

In English law a contract is interpreted in accordance with the proper law of contract, that is to say the law which the parties intend, or may reasonably be presumed to have intended, to be applied to the interpretation of the contract.[21] In Northern Rhodesia[22] and most other British possessions it has been expressly provided by legislation that "no party shall be entitled to claim the benefit of any Native customary law, if it shall appear either from express contract or from the nature of the transaction out of which any civil cause matter or question shall have arisen, that such party agreed or must be taken to have agreed that his obligations in connection with all such transactions should be regulated exclusively by some law or laws other than Native customary law." It was held in a Nigerian case[23] that English law applied to a contract between two Natives because a promissory note in the English form had been signed and stamped and the parties had thereby shown that they intended English law to be applied to the interpretation of the contract between them.

3. Native law will not be enforced when the Court is dealing with land which is held under a special title unknown to Native law.

Land which is held and occupied in accordance with Native law should be dealt with in accordance with Native law and it must be used and occupied in accordance with the provisions of that law. It is, however, possible by special conveyancing to convey land to a Native to be held independently of Native law. In a Southern Rhodesia case[24] it was held that certain property which was held under an ordinary English title to land descended in accordance with English law and not in accordance with Native law. It should, however, be noted that it must be perfectly clear from the conveyance that the land has been conferred on the Native to hold personally and independently of Native law, as it was laid down by the Privy Council in an appeal from Nigeria[25] that "although it is possible by special conveyancing to confer a title to land in West Africa on an individual Native, there is a strong presumption that the title of a Native is a usufructuary right held on behalf of the community or family. Consequently, a Native holding land in Lagos under a grant from the Crown is to be presumed to hold on behalf of the family and so unable to acquire by exclusive possession an individual title against other members of the family." The decision in this case would appear to be equally applicable to Northern Rhodesia and other British possessions where Natives hold communal and family land.

4. Native law will not be enforced when the Courts are dealing with Natives who have abandoned their Native mode of living and adopted a European standard of life.

In most British possessions there are Natives who have reached a high standard of education. For example, in Nigeria there are many professional men such as doctors and lawyers who are Natives. It is obvious that primitive Native customs cannot be applied to men who have attained this advanced standard. An advanced and educated Native may bequeath property by will and in the absence of a will it will descend in accordance with the English law of succession.[26] It is sometimes difficult to decide whether a Native has actually abandoned his Native mode of living. In the Union of South Africa the Courts have laid down the following tests which should be applied in order to find the answer to this question:[27]

(a) What is the Native's general mode of life?
(b) Does he acknowledge membership of any Native tribe or admit the authority of any Native Chief over him?
(c) Did he demand bride wealth on the marriage of his daughter?
(d) Did he pay bride wealth on the marriage of his sons?
(e) Did he or his children attend a European or a Native school?
(f) Did he marry according to Christian rights?
(g) Does he associate with Natives who are still living a Native mode of life?

5. Native law will not be enforced if there is evidence to show that such law has been abandoned or modified by the Native community to which the parties belong.

It should be noted that it is the Native law recognised for the time being which is enforced by the English Courts and not necessarily the ancient laws and customs, as Native law is capable of development, expansion and modification in the same way as the English Common Law.[28] It follows from this that Native law will not be enforced if there is evidence to show it has been abandoned or modified. The Courts, however, will require very strong evidence of abandonment before they will give a decision which is contrary to old and well established customs.[29] It should be noted that it is for the Natives themselves and not the English Courts to alter or modify Native customary laws. In an appeal from Nigeria[30] the Privy Council had to decide whether a Native customary punishment of death had been reduced to a milder custom of banishment. Lord Atkin in his judgment stated "Their Lordships entertained no doubt that the more barbarous customs of earlier days may, under the influence of civilization become milder without lessening their essential character or custom. It would, however, appear to be necessary to show that in their milder form they are still recognised in the Native community as custom, so as in that form to regulate the relations of the Native community *inter se*. In other words, the Court cannot itself transform a barbarous custom into a milder one. If it still stands in its barbarous character it must be rejected as repugnant to 'natural justice, equity and good conscience'. It is the assent of the Native community that gives a custom validity, and therefore, barbarous or mild, it must be shown to be recognised by the Native community whose conduct it is supposed to regulate."

Conclusion

In view of the fact that English and Native law can exist side by side conflict between the two laws is in most cases avoided. A study of the various aspects of the civil and criminal law will show how this conflict is avoided and will show also certain cases in which conflict has in fact arisen. The author of this article hopes to publish in the near future a more comprehensive article dealing with these various aspects of the civil and criminal law. He would be grateful if readers would forward information on Native customs and particulars of any practical difficulties which they may have experienced in the application of Native law.

It should be pointed out that this article has been based on experience in Northern Rhodesia and Nigeria. It is submitted, however, that the general principles which have been ennumerated are applicable to other Protectorates and Colonies in which the laws are similar to those in Northern Rhodesia and Nigeria.

Notes

1. Native customary law includes all those native laws and customs which are recognised and enforced in Native Courts and are subsequently referred to in this article as Native laws or Native customs.
2. High Court Ordinances, s. 17 and Subordinate Courts Ordinance s. 16.
3. Native Courts Ordinance ss 31 and 35 which give an English Court the power to make any order which the Native Court could have made.
4. MacCullum vs. Alfred Kumeni (case 9 of 1932 in Selected Decisions of the South African Native Appeal Court). In this case it was held that the discretion to apply Native law is a judicial discretion and that Native law must be applied between Natives in cases in which it is applicable.
5. Native Courts Ordinance s. 12. See also the sections of the Ordinance referred to in note (2) and Article 30 of the Northern Rhodesia Order-in-Council, 1924.
6. Statute law for this purpose includes any Order in Council or Ordinance and any local law made under the authority of any Order in Council or Ordinance.
7. Chiduku vs. Chidano (1922 S.R.L.R. page 55)
8. Chawa vs. Bvuta (1928 S.R.L.R. page 98)
9. Vela vs. Mandinika and Mugusta (1936 S.R.L.R. page 171)
10. Adulterer. In this case he had been living with the woman for ten years and had several children by her.
11. Pearce vs. Brooks (1866 L.R.1 Exch, page 213)
12. Tabernacle Building Society vs. Knight (1892 Appeal Cases page 98)
13. Mchenje vs. Kunaka (1912 S.R.L.R. page 107)
14. The word bride wealth is used in preference to dowry as the use of the word dowry is a misnomer. Dowry is a sum of money brought by a woman

to her husband. The money or other value paid on a native marriage is paid by the husband or his relatives to the relatives of the wife.

15. In the matter of Fanuel Lemama (1941 K.R.L. Vol XIX, page 48)

16. Mutandwa vs. Minister for Native Affairs (1937 S.R.L.R. page 137)

17. Cole vs. Cole (1 N.R.L., page 15)

18. Sikwela vs. Sikwela (1912 S.R.L.R. page 168); Rex vs. Ellen and Jim (1931 S.R.L.R. page 118)

19. Dayimano vs Kgaribaitse (1931 S.R.L.R. page 134)

20. Farrent Montengwa vs Stanford Mafeke (S.A. Native Appeal Court C.&O. F.S. vol 12, 1940, page 196)

21. Dicey's *Conflict of Laws* 4th Ed. page 591.

22. See sections of High Court and Subordinate Courts Ordinance referred to in note (2).

23. Saka Bakare vs. Dudley Coker (12 N.L.R. page 31)

24. Komo vs. Liboho and Holmes (1935 S.R.L.R. page 86)

25. Sunmonu vs. Disu Raphael (1927 A C 881)

26. Cole vs. Cole (1 N.L.R. page 15)

27. James Tarr and others vs. Estate Late James Tarr (N.A.C. N,&T, vol 12, page 75)

28. Oshodi vs. Balogun (all Eng. R. 1936 vol 2, page 1632). In this Privy Council case Lord Maugham stated that the native customary law in Lagos was in a "fluid" state and thereby showed that he considered that such law was capable of development and expansion.

29. Eshugbayi Chief Aloto vs. Dawunda and others (1 N.L.R. p. 58)

30. Eshugbayi Eleko vs. Officer Administering the Government of Nigeria and another (1931 A.C. page 662)

ROBERT B. SEIDMAN

The Inarticulate Premise

When a former colony became a full-fledged independent state, the conflict of law debate often came into greater focus. Was the former colonial legal system still in effect? Did it take precedence over folk or customary law? Should folk law be given priority now that the colonial yoke had at last been thrown off or removed? Should both colonial law and customary law be put aside in favor of new revolutionary law designed especially for the special conditions of emergent statehood?

The following novel essay by Professor Seidman of the Boston University School of Law addresses these questions by constructing a hypothetical case involving witchcraft set in the context of an imaginary new African state. Although the case is hypothetical, it is not at all atypical as the author's documentation of other actual cases attests. What is critical is not so much the conflict of different legal systems including folk law, but the courts' or rather the judges' attitudes towards these competing systems. The striking contrast between the diverse opinions of different judges becomes very clear and, more importantly, it is suggested how these differing opinions result in totally different judgments.

What follows purports to give the opinions of three judges of the highest court of appeal in Newstate, Africa. The title is taken from a pregnant phrase of O. W. Holmes, an American writer on jurisprudence. He held that the result of a case depended upon 'the inarticulate major premise' of the judge (or the unstated assumption which most influenced his judgement), at least in matters of first impression—i.e., cases in which the judges must determine for the first time what is the operative rule ('norm') of law. He urged this proposition in sharp opposition to the popular notion that a judge merely applied to the ascertained facts clear rules of law, which he found in earlier cases or in statutes.

In an appellate court in anglophonic Africa, each judge reads (or recites orally) his opinion. Frequently, these have been circulated beforehand, so that each judge knows what his brethren propose to say. Facts are never at issue in such appellant proceedings. The judges in the appellate

Reprinted from *Journal of Modern African Studies*, 3 (1965), 567–587, with permission of Cambridge University Press.

court are required to accept as true the facts found by the trial judge. The only issues before the appeals court are legal: What is the true rule of law? How does it apply to the facts of the case at hand?

On the day of judgement, counsel are present, all in black gowns and short curled wigs. The court bailiff pounds his mace: everybody stands; the three judges walk solemnly to their high-backed seats behind the raised bench. They are dressed in brilliant crimson robes, with black cuffs and black sashes, and long wigs whose curls brush their shoulders. Solemnly, counsel bow from the waist; solemnly, the judges acknowledge the courtesy. The judges take their seats, and a rustling fills the courtroom as spectators and counsel in turn sit down. Then all is silent. The bailiff calls out the name of the case, and the Chief justice begins to read his opinion.

In the Supreme Court of Newstate: December 1965 the Republic Vs. Kwame s/o Nighihili[1]

MUGHIRI, C. J.: This is a novel case, the first of its sort since our recent independence from the British Crown. It raises the question of the approach to law and to legal problems which will best serve our new country.

My position is quite clear. The basic law of Newstate is still English law.[2] I am sworn to apply the law. I do not see how I can do anything except apply English law. My brother Ekpe says that he too is sworn to uphold the law; that he too wants to apply the common law; but he wants to shape the common law to express our African instead of its British background. How he manages this, I cannot say, although I have read his opinion carefully. And my brother Mensah says that our theories of jurisprudence are destructive of the aims of a socialist independent African state. He claims that he can as a judge warp the law to fit what he conceives to be the demands of the new state.

This is all very interesting, but in the event we are at such loggerheads that we have been unable to agree upon the disposition of a very simple case. In my opinion, this demonstrates what happens when judges start trying to adjust what the law is to fit what they think the law ought to be. At any rate, in our judicial bankruptcy, we end by praying the executive to rescue us from the pit we have dug. This is regrettable, and in my opinion entirely because my brethren have wandered from the tried, tested, and true common law paths.

I turn now to the case at hand. This comes before us on appeal from a conviction for murder before a magistrate sitting with three assessors. Such a situation is, lamentably, all too common despite the remarkable advances made by Newstate since our independence only a few short years ago. The appellant lives in a primitive tribal community not far from the shores of Lake Swahili, in a compound with his three wives and nine children. His is a simple pastoral tribe, who have been tending their herds in conditions of relative peace and penury for centuries. A school has only recently begun to be built in his village; the appellant is, of course, illiterate.

In October last year, one of the wives of the accused's deceased father, a very old woman, named Chichumbi, came to live with the appellant. Chichumbi was apparently a quarrelsome old lady, and friction quickly developed between her and the appellant. In the course of their many quarrels, Chichumbi frequently claimed to possess powers of witchcraft;[3] and she threatened to use these dark powers to injure the appellant and his family.

In January of this year, the accused's eldest son, a promising lad of some 12 years, became ill of a malady that seemed inexplicable to him and to the other members of his family and tribe. His right leg slowly seemed to atrophy, so that in a matter of a few months the boy lost all use of it; shortly thereafter his other leg became paralysed. His speech became thick and confused, and towards the end he had apparently lost all his senses, being little more than a vegetable. He died in a convulsion in July.

After his son lost the use of his legs, appellant took counsel with the elders of his tribe. They advised him to visit a famous seer, whom the magistrate called a 'witch-doctor', some three days distant from appellant's village. This witch-doctor, after performing a complicated customary ritual that lasted two days and a night, told the appellant that Chichumbi was a witch, and that she was causing the death of his son by occult power.

The appellant returned to his village and accused Chichumbi of being a witch. She at first denied the charge. Later, however, in the course of one of the frequent quarrels that marked the unhappy household, she claimed that in fact she was a witch, that she was slowly gnawing away at the boy's legs, and that she would attack each of accused's children and wives in turn.

Shortly after his eldest son died, accused's next eldest son fell ill of what was apparently the same malady, and Chichumbi again gloated over the illness, claiming to be the cause. As the magistrate and the assessors all found as a fact, the appellant genuinely believed that Chichumbi had killed his son by witchcraft, and was now killing his next eldest son as surely as if he had actually seen her attacking the children with spear or panga.[4] In the custom of his tribe, at least formerly, the killing of witches was not only permitted, but considered a meritorious deed. In former times, appellant might have appealed to the Kiama, or tribal council, who would have tried Chichumbi on the charge of witchcraft; but the Kiama has long since ceased to function.[5] The appellant was thus faced with what seemed to him certain destruction from Chichumbi's witchcraft, and could see no institution to which he could appeal for relief.[6] His tribal custom sanctioned self-help in such a case.

His youngest and favourite wife also fell ill of the same mysterious malady in July of this year. Three days later, the appellant returned late to his compound. He went to his hut and remained there for an hour, drinking beer and brooding. Suddenly, he grabbed his panga, ran to Chichumbi's hut where she lay sleeping, and attacked her in a savage frenzy, inflicting upon her wounds from which she died in a few minutes. Afterwards he appeared quite calm, and voluntarily walked to the headman's hut, where he quietly told the headman what had happened. The headman had him confined and reported the matter the next day to the police. In due course appellant was tried and convicted of murder, and sentenced to death.

The Penal Code of Newstate was enacted in 1930, when this Republic was a British colony. It was modelled, like the Penal Codes of Kenya, Tanzania, Uganda, Zambia, Malawi, Nigeria, and the Gambia, upon the Penal Code of Queensland, Australia, which in its main outlines and indeed most of its details restated the common law of crimes.[7] In this respect it does not differ from the penal codes of Ghana, Northern Nigeria, and the Sudan, although these Codes derive from different models than the Queensland Code.[8] Our task is to apply the Penal Code, expressing as it does in the main the common law of crimes, to the facts of this case. My brethren have invoked many large philosophical concepts to obscure this simple task. But I have taken an oath to uphold the law as it is, and there my function begins and ends. My personal philosophy cannot affect this task, because otherwise ours would become a government of men, not of law.

Appellant has advanced four defences before us. In the first place, he claims that under native custom he was entitled to kill Chichumbi as a witch. He tried to prove this native custom at the trial, by calling two of the village elders to testify. It may be that that was indeed the custom some years ago, but the elders could not cite a specific case occurring within the last decade. No doubt, they said, witches had been killed in that period; but because of the threat of penal sanctions such killings nowadays would be concealed. It is always very difficult to discover what is in fact the native custom obtaining at the time of the events in question. Native custom is changing very rapidly in these revolutionary times, as Newstate moves towards the new society which we all want to see. The assessors, who were familiar with appellant's tribe, were divided about the existence of this particular custom, although they all agreed that it had been prevalent in the past.

But even if the custom had been proved, it is an accepted principle of our law that native custom will not be enforced if it is repugnant to justice, equity, and good conscience.[9] This rule was embedded in our law from the earliest days of the British over-rule. That rule, we are now taught, was in its central motivation an avaricious attempt to exploit our people to satisfy the greed of British entrepreneurs. That may well be; but one of its concomitants was a well-meant attempt to rescue our people from the sinks of superstition, ignorance, and paganism in which we then were, and to some extent still are. The British judges in colonial days were quite willing to invoke native custom in civil cases, where it did not violate the standard of justice, equity, and good conscience.[10] But they rarely, if ever, applied it in criminal cases, and, so far as I can discover, never to excuse murder.

Now by what standard ought one to measure justice, equity, and good conscience? To measure a native custom by the standard of indigenous justice would mean that every native custom would have to be sustained. That would deny the civilising mission of the English law. Obviously, therefore, the colonial judges adopted the standard of Englishmen.[11] Since our law today is the same as it was before independence,[12] I conceive that I must apply the same standard.

My brother Ekpe makes a feeble attempt to show that the African personality is expressed in native custom. He claims that justice, equity, and good conscience is to be measured in terms of something he calls the African personality. How he can claim that his personality, educated at a British-run Christian secondary school, at Oxford, and the Inns of Court, bears any relationship to the personality of this appellant, still steeped in the ignorance and superstition of the bush, I find impossible to understand. At any rate, as I have said, our job is to apply the law. The law today with regard to native custom in Newstate, as in all the anglophonic African states, is exactly the same as it was under the British. If there is such a native custom as the killing of witches, it plainly violates every English notion of justice. My brother Ekpe can if he likes, I suppose, disregard the law which he is sworn to uphold. I cannot. I therefore have no hesitation in declaring absolutely void the supposed native custom upon which appellant relies.

Even if I did not, however, I could not allow the defence. Our Penal Code states that defences to charges of criminal harm are to be interpreted in accordance with English law.[13] Even if it did not so state, I should have so to interpret it, in light of the Code's origins, except in the rare case where the Code plainly departs from the common law.[14] What the appellant is really asserting is that he made a mistake of law. He thought that he was entitled by law to kill Chichumbi as a witch. In this he was mistaken. But mistake of law has never been a defence in British law,[15] except in very exceptional cases, of which this is not one. Indeed, our Penal Code says in explicit terms that mistake of law shall not be a defence to a criminal charge.[16] I must, therefore, disallow the defence.

The second principal defence asserted by defendant is that of mistake of fact. He claims that he mistakenly believed Chichumbi to be a witch who was threatening the lives of everybody in his family, so that the only defence was to kill her; and that he killed her in self-defence and in defence of his family.[17] Now it is an accepted principle of the Penal Code, and indeed of the common law, that where a criminal harm is done under mistake of fact, the guilt of the defendant must be measured by the state of affairs which he imagined to be true, not the state of affairs which was in fact true.[18] If a man threatens me with a water pistol which looks like, and which I believe to be, a real pistol, and I kill him because I believe that my life is threatened and there is no other way for me to save my life, I am not guilty of criminal homicide.

But there is a limit to the defence of mistake. The common law and our Penal Code declare that a mistake, to excuse a criminal harm, must be 'reasonable'.[19] If I see my wife's car in front of my home, and I know that she almost never leaves the house unless she drives herself, I may say to myself, 'My wife is at home'. If she is not at home, then my mistake is a reasonable one; it is a mistake which the average person in my shoes would have made. But if I do not see my wife's car, and I still say to myself, 'My wife is at home', then my mistake is unreasonable, for the average man in my shoes would not have made that mistake. If the limitation of reasonableness did not exist in the penal law, then every defendant could claim that he acted under mistake, and nobody would ever be convicted of crime.

It thus falls to be considered whether it was a reasonable mistake for the appellant to believe that Chichumbi so threatened his life and the lives of his family by her witchcraft that his only recourse was to slay her. In interpreting any statute, the primary consideration is to give effect to the intent of the legislature; our job is to apply the law, not to make the law. This Code was enacted in colonial days by a colonial Council, and introduced by the colonial governor on the orders of the British Colonial Office. It was modelled upon the English common law. The legislature must therefore have intended that the test of reasonableness would therefore be that of the English common law—i.e., that of the reasonable Englishman, not the reasonable African. A few years ago the celebrated Chief Justice of the unlamented Federation, Sir Robert Tredgold, said exactly that.

> The test of reasonableness [in assessing mistake of fact as a defence] in itself implies an objective standard. . . . In applying it, the standard is what would appear reasonable to the ordinary man in the street in England. The lives of considerable numbers of people are profoundly influenced by strange beliefs and phobias. But the existence of these peculiarities and the reactions that eventuate from them cannot be taken into account. It is the normal and average that must be the guide . . .
>
> On this basis, and bearing in mind that the law of England is still the law of England even when it is extended to Nyasaland, I do not see how any court, applying the proper test, could hold that a belief in witchcraft was reasonable so as to form the foundation for a defence that the law could recognize.[20]

Applying this standard to the facts of this case, it would seem plain that a belief that one's family is being destroyed by a witch, and that the only recourse in the circumstances is to kill her, is an unreasonable mistake. No doubt, Englishmen believed such nonsense hundreds of years ago.[21] But the law cannot serve its educative and civilising function unless we insist that the norms to be followed are those of civilised people of the twentieth century. Our law enjoins us that the model to be followed to achieve that objective is that of the reasonable Englishman. My brother Ekpe would use a different, African standard. My brother Mensah would not use any standard at all except his own subjective notion of what is beneficial to society. Presumably, if he happened to believe that the slaying of witches was to be desired, he would sanction homicides of this sort. Neither of them, it seems to me, can square their result with the plain fact that the Penal Code was intended by its authors to enforce civilising, *English* standards. Since that was the intent of the legislators, we have no choice but to carry it out.

There is another deep fallacy within the claim of mistake in this case. If we were to try to deal with the appellant on the basis that he thought that he was being threatened by Chichumbi's witchcraft, how ought we decide? English criminal law is based, in the main, upon a rational, scientific world. It deals with real, physical threats. It does not comprehend threats from occult powers. As has been often said in cases of this sort, the threat must be physical, not metaphysical.[22] This is part of the civilising function of the law. If we are ever to lift our people from the slough of superstition in which they now lie, we cannot tolerate a system of law that accommodates witchcraft.

The third defence asserted by appellant is that of insanity. He claims that the very fact that he believed in witchcraft proves that he was insane. After all, he says, you measure my mistake by the reasonable Englishman, and then you say that the mistake is not reasonable. But is there any doubt that any Englishman who believed in witchcraft would be deemed insane?[23] Therefore, he says, the proper verdict here ought to be 'guilty but insane'.

The argument, despite its seeming force, is thoroughly specious. The Penal Code, like the common law, is built upon the assumption that man has free will.[24] In the words of an American court, it imagines that there are, as it were, two little men, labelled 'reason' and 'emotion' or 'instinct', wrestling for control of the individual's will.[25] The defence of insanity, like the defence of infancy, is available only when reason is incapacitated by disease or physical incapacity.[26] Apart from such incapacity, the law insists that the defendant must be judged by objective standards applicable to all reasonable men. This appellant had no mental disease; many normal Africans believe in witchcraft.[27] And this is how it must be. The purpose of the criminal law is to protect society. It protects society in the main by punishing criminals as examples to the rest of the community.[28] Except for a very few defences, like insanity, it disregards the personal idiosyncrasies of the individual defendant. It sets up a norm for all normal men to follow. That norm is expressed by the law which we are sworn to uphold. It may well be that the individual cannot control himself, as apparently this appellant could not. But if he is not severely punished for this crime, we shall be giving the green light to commit murder to everybody with a real or fancied grievance against any old or eccentric man or woman.[29]

Thus the punishment of this appellant will serve as a deterrent to others in his community. His life is available to the state as a means to the greater safety of the whole community. In the words of Mr Justice Holmes, a distinguished American judge upon whom my brother Mensah so heavily relies,

If I were having a philosophical talk with a man I was going to have hanged (or electrocuted), I should say, 'I don't doubt that your act was inevitable for you but to make it more avoidable by others we propose to sacrifice you to the common good. You may regard yourself as a soldier dying for your country if you like. But the law must keep its promises.'[30]

The appellant's final claim is that he is entitled to the protection of the partial defence of provocation. It is our law[31] as it is the common law,[32] that a man who kills as the result of the sort of provocation which would have aroused the passions of a reasonable man from the community from which the defendant comes,[33] who actually kills while under the sway of that passion,[34] before sufficient time has elapsed for a reasonable man's passion to cool,[35] and who uses no more force than appropriate to the provocation,[36] will be guilty not of murder but of manslaughter—a lesser crime, for which there is no death penalty. It is a concession which our law makes to the frailty of the common clay. But that defence must fail here, as there was a very long time indeed between the provocation and the deed; there was ample time for passion to have cooled. The courts have never permitted the defence of provocation in witchcraft cases, save in the very narrow situation where the deceased is surprised in the very act of juju, as a result of which the defendant loses his temper and kills the apparent witch then and there.[37] Since none of these conditions applies to this appellant, I am constrained by authority to deny the defence of provocation.

This is a case of first impression in our recently independent Newstate. Our task as judges is to uphold the law. That law, in this case and in most cases that arise, is either the common law of England, or statutory law with some accommodation to customary law in limited situations. In either case, our job is to look to the language of the legal norm, and apply it to the facts. My brother Mensah urges that we are entitled to make choices based upon our notions of what is best for the community in determining what the law ought to be in cases where it is ambiguous; and so he proposes to change the provocation rule for purposes of this case. But judges do not legislate; yet brother Mensah says that we should act like legislators. Indeed, he does not like any part of the criminal law; he says so. Not liking it, he proposes to change it.

Nor can I blithely overrule precedent as does my brother Mensah. As I have said, I am sworn to uphold the law. The law is expressed by statute and by the cases interpreting it. My oath does not bind me to uphold only statute law; it binds me to uphold all the law. I cannot amend my oath at will; and I fail to see how brother Mensah manages to square his light dismissal of the doctrine of *stare decisis* with this judicial oath.[38] Obviously, if a decision be taken *per incuriam*, that is one thing;[39] but how can the law lay any claim to even-handed justice when one rule will be applied today, and another tomorrow, depending upon what the individual judge conceives to be best for society?

I say that that is nonsense, and dangerous nonsense at that. A prominent Ghanaian writer on legal subjects, Dr Ekow Daniels, has defined the common law as 'unchanging principles distilled from the sayings of sages and wise judges over the centuries'. He says, 'the more the common law changes (or seems to change), the more it remains the same.'[40] I agree. Our job is simply to announce what the law is.[41] When new situations arise, all that we must do is to apply these unchanging principles to them. That does not call for us to determine what the sociological effect of our judgement could be. The law demands stability. We cannot give it stability by manipulating it to match our personal notions of what is 'just' or 'proper' or even what we may personally think desirable for Newstate. We are only jurisprudential slot-machines; insert the facts, and we are supposed to grind out a decision in accordance with the immutable principles of the common law.

We are, no doubt, Africans by heritage. But we are also trained in the English cultural tradition. There is not one of our leaders, nor one of our lawyers or judges, who has not been trained in that tradition. If our new fatherland is ever to advance to the levels of culture and civilisation of the modern, western world, we must adhere to the time-tested, eternal principles of the common law. Dr Daniels concludes his excellent book on *The Common Law in West Africa* by saying, 'Whatever declaration is made in the future [about the content of the law of the West African Anglophonic states], English law will certainly remain its basis.'[42] I fervently hope and trust that that prediction will remain true of Newstate as of West Africa. I would dismiss the appeal.

* * *

EKPE, J.: My learned brother the Chief Justice says that this is a simple case, and then writes twelve pages of philosophy, jurisprudence, penology, and criminology to show us how simple it all is. Obviously the result in this case depends upon one's philosophical approach to the problem.

I refuse to yield one inch to the Chief Justice in my devotion to the common law, nor in my belief that as judges we must apply the law that is, not the law that ought to be. But I disagree with him sharply about the defence of native custom.

Customary law—the law that governed the African people before the advent of colonialism, and that still governs most of the day-to-day legal relationships of most Africans—expresses the spirit of the African people, just as every system of law expresses the spirit of the community from which it springs. Nobody could be more dismayed than I at the chaotic condition of our present law, where every tribe and indeed every clan has its own system of customary law. Some day, we must have a single, unified, state-wide system of law. I would endorse the following statement by the distinguished Professor of African Law at the School of Oriental and African Studies of the University of London:

> If the uniform legal system which I have referred to is to evolve in a satisfactory manner, one which expresses the characteristic ethos and way of life of the people, it is essential that immediate attention be paid to the present customary law, which reflects, *par excellence*, the people's own choice of legal system.[43]

My learned brother disposes of the defence of custom on three different grounds. In the first place, he says that it does not exist; in the second, he says that it violates English notions of justice, equity, and good conscience; and in the third place, he says that it is not a defence under the Penal Code. I disagree on all three counts.

There is no doubt that the custom which appellant claims exists did exist not so many years ago. That custom, therefore, expressed the choice of law made by the people of whom appellant is one. The fact that the British imperial masters in the years before independence did not allow it as a defence is simply another indication of the blind refusal of the British to let Africans be Africans. I take it that the custom was adequately proven by proof of its existence before the British destroyed it.

But then it is urged that the custom denies justice, equity, and good conscience, as measured by British standards. To justify this claim, the Chief Justice insists that he is merely interpreting the intention of the legislature. He says that since the same statute is now in force as in colonial days, the legislature must have intended it to be interpreted in the same way. By what crystal ball my brother peeps into the brains of all our legislators he does not reveal.

We all know, however, that one of the great motivating forces for our African revolution is that expressed by the concept of the African personality. Every people has certain characteristics which are uniquely theirs—their language, their history, their customs, in short their very genius. The phrase 'African personality' sums up all that is distinctively African about us—everything that makes us what we are. Our African personality was submerged during the days of Empire, and today remains submerged in those territories regrettably still under foreign overlordship. If the African revolution has any meaning, it must be a vehicle in which we can express ourselves. It must express, therefore, the African personality.

What better expresses our African personality than the law which, as Professor Allott puts it, we voluntarily chose when we had the choice available? To insist, as does my brother, that we must follow English standards denies the historical meaning of the stirring times through which we have all lived. Is it for this that the martyrs who died before the bullets of the white-supremacist police gave their lives? Did the brave thousands who demonstrated in the face of terror do so in order to be told by this court of an independent African state that their long-standing tribal customs are to be void because the average Englishman thinks them wrong?

My brother reaches his conclusion because he places English law on a higher plane than African.[44] In the light of modern anthropological notions of the relativistic nature of all culture, this is plain nonsense. Our African law is neither better nor worse than that of England; it is only different. It does express our ethos, our *Volksgeist*, in a way that no English law can. I deny that we need the so-called civilising influence of England, either in law or elsewhere.

Our indigenous customs need no defence from me. Witchcraft belief starts from fundamentally different premisses from those of English scientific thought. It assumes that man is divided into three parts: a personality soul, a mystical soul, and a physical shell. A mysterious, other-worldly entity—call it a god, if you will—is believed to seize control of the personality soul of the witch, which can then travel forth from its physical shell to attack the physical shell of its victims.[45] Now I personally do not believe this, but how can I say that one who does believe it is fundamentally wrong? How different is this belief from any mystical belief in another world? And if, in defence against such dread forces as these, African custom deems it proper to take up arms in self-help, I fail to see that the custom denies justice, equity, and good conscience. All our concepts of justice are relative. I for one cannot see that this custom is any more barbarous than the gentle art of modern warfare, for example, or the notion that a policeman may kill a prisoner who is guilty of the most petty offence while attempting to escape. In short, the concept of justice, equity, and good conscience must be measured by African, not English standards.

My brother's assertion that the Penal Code does not admit of the defence of custom is merely a function of his exaggerated deference to the common law. I agree with him that the common law expresses the distilled essence of unchanging principles.[46] But those principles infuse its spirit, not its particular form.

Perhaps the most important of those principles in the criminal law is that no man may be convicted, at least of serious crime, unless he has a guilty mind—a *mens rea*, to use the familiar Latin term.[47] The essence of this doctrine is that every crime demands a sense of guilt on the part of the defendant. Here, this appellant acted according to the custom which he believed to apply to him. He believed that he acted under overwhelming necessity to defend the very lives of his children, his wife, and himself. How can my brother say that he had *mens rea?* And without this, no man ought to be convicted of serious crime.

My brother the Chief Justice keeps insisting that he is only applying the law which he is sworn to uphold. I think that he was sworn to uphold the law of Newstate, not the law of England. That law, like all law, must reflect the ethos of our own people. He denies the whole meaning of African independence by his slavish devotion to the narrowest interpretation of the common law. The function of the African judge is to mould and adapt the received common law, faithful to its basic and unchanging principles, to its new setting. Anything less will be a betrayal of the revolution and of the African personality.

Nor can I agree with my brother Mensah that he has a right to mould the law to meet his own idiosyncratic notions of what is best for society. I agree with the Chief Justice that such a notion changes the law, from the rules by which the game is to be played, to a mere device by which society can be manipulated to reach ends that may be thought desirable. The very essence of justice is predictability. The subjects of the law are treated fairly when the law is applied with absolute, even-handed precision; not for nothing is Justice invariably portrayed as the blind goddess. To adopt the view that law is merely a technique of social engineering, and the judges merely social engineers, negates the whole notion that ours is indeed a government of law, not of men.

I would allow the appeal and discharge the appellant.

* * *

MENSAH, J.: I had thought that I was sitting on a bench with fellow-judges. Instead, I find myself in the company of two mystics. One adheres to the *mystique* of the common law, and the other to the *mystique* of the African personality, and together they try to dispose of a practical, rather simple problem in government. I cannot seem to make my colleagues understand that as judges we participate in the process of government. We participate in a special, indeed a unique way. Our task, however, is not to apply immutable principles, but rather to solve practical problems.

Before I can answer the problems posed by this murder case, I must examine briefly how judges in fact solve problems. A few problems that judges face are simple; the rule of law applicable clearly covers the case. In such a situation, I agree with the Chief Justice that we are merely judicial slot-machines, so to speak. But those situations only come to this court because some lawyer is either too avaricious or too stupid to tell his client that he is wasting his time and money. Every case that comes to an appeals court (where we can consider, of course, only points of law) almost always involves situations where the applicable rule is vague as applied to the facts in question.

So judges are mainly concerned with trying to solve questions where the law is vague or ambiguous. The question that we must always resolve is, by what rule or test are we to resolve the ambiguous? My brethren find the answer in some transcendental principle. The Chief Justice finds it in the immutable principles of the common law.[48] Brother Ekpe find it in the ethos of the African personality, which he holds is expressed in the rule of customary law. Like the Chief Justice, he believes in immutable principles. Why the one chooses the common law as his principle, and the other the African personality, I do not know. I search the stars, but can find no clue which will identify for me the great Immutable Principle which ought to control our decision.

Now it seems to me that the only intelligible way to resolve the pervasive ambiguities in the law is by reference to the social effect of the decision.[49] My brethren charge me with being a sociologist-cum-legislator. But a legislator can select any rule which he wants to solve a problem. Our job is much narrower. We can only select a rule which is tenable within the ambiguities of the authoritative statute. And in deciding what will be the most desirable rule, it seems to me that we should make use of all the material available from the social scientists—the sociologists, the economists, the political scientists. We should make our choice in the light of Newstate's declared national objective of socialism.

No doubt my brethren will charge me, as my brother Ekpe already has, with believing in a government of men and not of law. To a degree, of course, this is true. But it is true of their decisions also. The only difference is that I look for the test in the pragmatic results of the rule upon society. They look for guidance in what they call an immutable principle. I suggest that the real source of any immutable principle lies locked in the personal prejudice of the individual judge. So theirs is a government of men and not of law just as much as mine, except that they will not admit it, nor will they expose their inner processes of reasoning to the light of discussion, as I feel I do.

Law has a dual function. It must give stability to social relationships, and at the same time admit of social change. So long as we abide within the limits set by statute or common law rule, I submit that we are giving the law as much stability as is possible. At the same time, because I would adapt it to new situations as they arise by frankly shaping it to social ends, it is continuously reshaped according to the demands of our emerging, socialist society.

Now all law developed in just this way; as Holmes has said, 'The life of the law has not been logic, but experience'.[50] In every case, judges have interpreted the existing law in light of social demands as they viewed them.[51] Since judges in the past have come mainly from the exploiting classes in society, in general their decisions have tended to reflect their class interests. But not invariably; sometimes judges have given expression to interests far wider and more democratic than their class position might indicate, with the result that there exist in the common law, of both England and the United States, many very democratic elements.

Sometimes a whole area of law which was developed in an earlier period becomes irrelevant in a later one; or sometimes, as here, a foreign import simply does not meet the local situation. The common law of crimes was developed to meet the emergent demands of England, mainly in the nineteenth century. When it is applied to twentieth-century Africa, it creaks at the joints, for it is based upon values and concepts which were apt to meet the demands of nineteenth-century England, but not necessarily apt to meet present-day African requirements.[52] It can be applied here, today, only by wrenching our society, our values, or the law, into weird and unseemly forms. Fundamental reform, of course, is for the legislature, not for us; but where we can reach a more defensible result within the scope of the Code, we ought to feel free to do so.

By the same token, customary law was developed to meet the demands of a subsistence economy, based upon a culture that was mainly pre-scientific. Laws developed for that society are, like the common law, largely irrelevant to the modern, industralised, African society which is our common aim.[53] To impose a rigid system of law, drawn from another society or another time, upon modern Africa is to condemn us to the same system of domestic backwardness and foreign domination as existed in the imperial era. Brother Ekpe's invocation of customary law has an attractive revolutionary air. But it is only pseudo-revolutionary, for it condemns us to stagnation.

Turning now to the facts of this case, what result ought to obtain? In the first place, we are faced with the problem of native custom. Obviously, many native customs are simply inappropriate to a modern, industrialised, socialised economy. One such custom that we can do without is the slaying of supposed witches, not to speak of the whole pre-scientific superstition of witchcraft itself. I suggest that a custom of that sort ought to be outlawed, not because it violates English notions of justice, but because it violates sensible rules for our new country,

We can dispose of the defences of mistake of law, and of insanity, with equal celerity. No country has ever admitted the defence of mistake of law. To do so makes the defendant, and not the judge, the person who determines the applicable law; and that would be an impossible result. The defence of insanity, as my brother has said, is limited to physical infirmities; and this defendant is perfectly sane.

The defence of reasonable mistake is rather more tricky, but on the whole I reach the same conclusion as the Chief Justice. Recently, an African in London was charged with practising medicine without a licence.[54] He had received a bogus certificate as a doctor in 'natureopathy', and supposed that he was entitled to call himself doctor by reason of that certificate. The Court found that it was not unreasonable for him so to believe, considering his recent arrival in England (he had been there but two years). If we stand that case against *Frank*, cited by the Chief Justice, we reach the amazing result that an African in England is judged by the standard of a reasonable African, but in Africa, by that of a reasonable Englishman!

The answer, of course, revolves around the devilish little word 'reasonable'. The Chief Justice says that the reasonable man means the average man. That is not exactly true. Judges decide what is a reasonable man. They determine this not on the basis of a statistical average, but rather on the basis of what they think is a proper standard for the community. They set this standard in terms not of the ideal, but not necessarily of the average either. Rather, it is a statement of what is, in their belief, an attainable standard for the average citizen. Obviously, it must be set a little higher than the statistical average, or else there would never be any improvement in society. When we set a standard as 'reasonable', therefore, we are setting a norm of conduct.[55] The proper way to set a norm of conduct is to look at the results desired.

The Chief Justice does exactly that when he says that, without the limit of reasonableness, every defendant could plead mistake as a defence. I believe that if we do not exclude the defence of witchcraft in cases like this, every rogue who wants to kill an enemy will claim witchcraft as a defence. I would therefore say that mistake of fact in this case fails as a defence, because it is not reasonable.

There remains the defence of provocation. Now I am quite prepared to say that a reasonable man in the defendant's position, with his background and in the circumstances, would have been provoked to kill. The nature of the threat of witchcraft is that the passage of time serves only to inflame the passions, not to cool them, as the facts here demonstrate. The operative result of admitting provocation as a defence here is consonant with the demands of society. The appellant will remain under judicial control, since he will receive an appropriate jail sentence. Realistically, his crime is not that he killed, but that he believed in witches. In jail—assuming that we have a modern penal system, which is probably illusory—he could be educated out of his superstitions, thus saving society the threat of a repetition of his crime.

This seems to me the best practical solution of the problem available within the scope of the Code. To reach this decision requires that we overrule a number of cases in which it has been held that provocation is not available in witchcraft cases unless the act of witchcraft takes place in the immediate presence of the accused. But far better to over-rule authority which no longer accords with present notions of justice, than to do injustice!

I cannot help but point out that if I were free to decide this case as a legislator I would unload as excess baggage the whole conceptual framework of British criminal law. That law is based almost entirely upon the notion of deterrence as the principal objective of punishment, and hence of the criminal law. It assumes that, once a man has committed a crime, he may be used by society as a means of social control. I deny that this postulate is compatible with the African revolution, which ought above all else to base itself on humanitarian considerations. Our President has publicly endorsed the view of President Nkrumah of Ghana, that a central assumption of our Government is that no man shall be a means, but only an end.[56] In the criminal law, that means to me that we may not use him as an instrument of deterrence, but only treat him with a view to reformation. To achieve such a goal would require the complete re-working of our penal codes. That project ought to have high legislative priority throughout Africa.

In the event, I would reduce the crime to manslaughter. The Chief Justice would affirm the conviction for murder; and my brother Ekpe would acquit. Since there is no majority in this court in favour of any course, the conviction below must stand.

I am, however, authorised by my brethren to state that, in the unusual circumstances of this case, we all join in petitioning the President to exercise his powers of clemency to reach a result which accords with justice. What that result may be, he will have to say. Obviously, we judges, who are supposedly experts on the subject, have been unable to agree on this, being unable to find a common jurisprudential basis on which to reach a decision.

Notes

1. The facts of this case are invented; but there are many similar cases which have arisen in the courts of anglophonic Africa. See, e.g. *Konamba*, 14 E.A.C.A. 175 (Uganda, 1951); *Kasale*, [1944–6] R.L.R. 110; *Kajuna s/o Mbake*, 12 E.A.C.A. 104 (Tanganyika, 1945); *Gadam*, 14 W.A.C.A. 442 (Nigeria, 1954); *Philip Muswi s/o Musele*, 23 E.A.C.A. 622 (Kenya, 1956); *Magata s/o Kachenhakana*, [1957] E.A.C.A. 330 (High Court, Uganda); *Fabiano*, 8 E.A.C.A. 96 (Uganda, 1941); *Akebe s/o Karuen*, 14 E.A.C.A. 105 (Kenya, 1947); and *Kekementi Maganga s/o Ochieng*, 10 E.A.C.A. 49 (Uganda, 1942).

Citations to cases in this article are given in the customary form used by lawyers. The *underlined* name, if alone, is the name of the accused; if the prosecutor is not the Government, the names of both parties are given. The first figure in the citation is the volume; next come the initials of the series of law reports, followed by the page reference. In East African cases, the letters 's/o' and 'd/o' mean 'son of' and 'daughter of' respectively.

2. All the anglophonic African states look to English law as the basic law. Several Nigerian statutes, for example, enjoin the courts to apply 'the common law of England'. See, e.g., Law of England (Application) Law, W.R. No. 9 of 1958, sec. 3; and Interpretation Ordinance, Law of the Federation of Nigeria

and Lagos, 1958, cap. 89, sec. 45(1). The Ghanaian Courts Act of 1960 is somewhat broader. It declares that the basic law is the common law, but states explicitly that the courts may look for precedent in any common law jurisdiction: Constitution (1960), sec. 40(e); Interpretation Act, 1960, sec. 19(1); Court Act, 1960, C.A. 9, sec. 154(4). A member of the Supreme Court of Ghana has, however, stated that the relevant clause requires the Court to treat as binding precedent every decision of the Privy Council and the West African Court of Appeals prior to independence; Mr Justice Ollenu, quoted by S. K. Asante, '*Stare Decisis* in the Supreme Court of Ghana', in *University of Ghana Law Journal* (Accra), 1964, p. 52.

3. See *Kasalo*, [1944–6] R.L.R. 110; and *Kajuna s/o Mbake*, 12 E.A.C.A. 104 (Tanganyika, 1945). In *Alice Eriyamremu*, [1959] W.N.L.R. 270 (High Court, Western Nigeria), the accused claimed that she met with other witches in a coven, and participated in ghastly cannibalistic feasts. She was found to be legally sane.

4. See E. Winter, 'The Enemy Within: Amba witchcraft', in J. Middleton and E. Winter (eds.), *Witchcraft and Sorcery in East Africa* (London, 1963), p. 289: Witchcraft beliefs offer an explanation for the misfortunes which afflict people . . . particularly . . . illness and death. . . . The explanatory significance of witchcraft goes even deeper. . . . Witchcraft offers one type of answer to the ultimate question of why. Everywhere and at all times, men have sought to penetrate behind the façade of the observable world and to grasp the meaning of human misfortune. Witchcraft, viewed as a system of thought, offers one solution for this problem and is equivalent to ideas which have been formulated in other societies such as Fate or the will of God.'

Judges in witchcraft cases have frequently affirmed the reality of the defendant's fear of destruction by the witch. See, e.g. *Kanwaka Wa Malumbi & 69 Others*, 14 K.L.R. 137 (1932); *Galikuwa*, 18 E.A.C.A. 175 (Uganda, 1951); and *Konomba*, 14 W.A.C.A. 236 (Gold Coast, 1952).

5. See, e.g. E. S. Haydon, *Law of Justice in Buganda* (London, 1960), p. 283; and Middleton and Winter, op. cit. *passim*.

6. The increased insecurities arising from the rapid change through which Africa has been passing in the past half-century have apparently increased, rather than decreased, the incidence of witchcraft belief. See, e.g., E. G. Parrinder, *Witchcraft: European and African* (London, 1958), p. 205; H. Debrunner, *Witchcraft in Ghana* (Basel, 1959), p. 71; and Middleton and Winter, op. cit. *passim*. A similar increase took place in Europe during the Renaissance. Cf. E. White, 'The Spared Wolves,' in *The Saturday Review* (New York), 13 November 1954. At the same time, the colonial overlords removed from the people the institutionalised defences which they had developed. See, e.g., M. Kingsley, *Travels in West Africa* (London, 1897), p. 489. The result is insecurity compounded.

7. J. Read, 'Criminal Law in the Africa of Today and Tomorrow', in *Journal of African Law* (London), Spring 1963, p. 5.

8. The Penal Code of Ghana was introduced in 1893 and has remained virtually unchanged to the present day. It is modelled upon the St. Lucia Code, which in turn is modelled upon the Jamaica Draft Code. The Northern Nigerian

Penal Code and the Sudanese Penal Code are almost identical. They are both modelled upon Macaulay's Indian Penal Code of 1839. All (including the Queensland Code), except the Northern Nigerian and Sudanese Codes, are ultimately derived from Sir James Stephen's Draft Code of 1878, which was an attempt to codify the existing common law. It was never introduced in England.

9. All the Orders in Council which served as the constitutional basis for the several British Colonies and Protectorates, and successor legislation to this day, preserve native law and custom so far as it does not violate 'natural justice, equity, and good conscience' (or some similar phrase). See, e.g., Law of England (Application) Ordinance (The Gambia), cap. 3; Court Ordinance (Sierra Leone), sec. 38; and High Court Ordinance (Northern Rhodesia), sec. 17.

10. See, e.g., *Balogun v. Amodu Balogun*, 2 W.A.C.A. 290, 306 (Nigeria, 1935); *Cole v. Cole*, I N.L.R. 15, 21 (1898); and *Lukwago v. Bawa Singh*, [1959] E.A.C.A. 282.

11. See, e.g., *Luka Matengula*, 5 L.R.N.R. 148 (1952). Accused were carrying a coffin through the village that it might 'point out' the witch who caused the death. While opposite the deceased, an old lady, the coffin 'jumped forward' and struck her so hard in the chest that she died. The accused sought refuge in native custom. The Court denied the claim, finding all guilty of manslaughter. The applicable repugnancy clause allowed native custom 'not being repugnant to justice'. The Court added, 'not being against justice as we people in England see it'. See Abrahams, 'The Colonial Legal Service and the Administration of Justice in the Colonial Dependencies', in 30 *J. Comp. Leg. I.L.* (3rd Series, 1948, parts 3 and 4), I 8. *Accord; Gimo Bin Lilime v. Kusunda bin Futi*, I T.L.R. 403 (1938).

12. The typical constitution of an independent African state includes a proviso that all the laws in force immediately before the adoption of the constitution remain in force thereafter. See, e.g. Constitution, Ghana (1957), art. 40; and Constitution, Nigeria (1960), art. 154(4)—maintaining in force the Interpretation Act of 1889 (which made English law the rule in the Colony and Protectorates), as in force on October 1960.

13. See, e.g., Penal Code, Tanganyika, sec. 4. This clause appears in all the Codes following the 1930 Colonial Office model.

14. In *Wallace-Johnson*, 5 W.A.C.A. 56 (Gold Coast, 1941), the Privy Council said, in an oft-quoted dictum, that where a Colonial Code is 'exhaustive', it must be read without glosses derived from English or Scots Law. However, African courts almost invariably cite English precedents as authoritative in interpreting the Codes, not infrequently even when the Codes are in terms to the contrary. In *Tene Dagarti* [1961] January-June Judgements (mimeographed) 48, for example, the Supreme Court of Ghana followed *D.P.P. v. Smith*, [1960] 3 All E.R. 161 (House of Lords), in refusing to permit a defendant to advance a claim that although death was the reasonable and probable consequence of his act, he subjectively did not intend death and hence was guilty only of manslaughter. Cf. Criminal Code, 1960 (Ghana), sec. II(3): defendant presumed to intend reasonable and probable consequences of his acts unless he proves to the contrary.

15. *Esop*, 7 C. & P. 456 (Central Criminal Court, England, 1836); *Bailey*, R. & R. I (Court for Crown Cases Reserved, England, 1800). See G. Williams, *Criminal Law: The General Part* (London, 1961 edn.), p. 289.

16. See, e.g., Criminal Code, Nigeria, sec. 22; and Criminal Code, 1960 (Ghana), sec. 29(2).

17. See, e.g., *Rose*, 15 Cox 540 (Court of Crown Cases Reserved, England, 1884). Defendant came downstairs to see his father, who was seemingly threatening his mother with a gun; he shot and killed his father; held, a reasonable mistake and hence not guilty of criminal homicide.

18. See, e.g. (Criminal Code, Nigeria, sec. 25; Penal Code, Tanganyika, sec. II; and Criminal Code, 1960 (Ghana), sec. 29(I). For the Common Law, see *Levett*, Crown Cases 538 (England, 1638). Cf. J. Hall, *General Principles of Criminal Law* (Indianapolis, 1960 edn.), p. 363: 'To understand the rationale of *ignorantia facti excusat*, it is necessary to recognise and take into account the relevant ethical principle, namely, moral obligation is determined not by the actual facts but by the actor's opinion concerning them.'

19. See, e.g., *Wilson v. Inyang*, [1951] 2 All E.R. 237 (King's Bench Division, England); Penal Code, Tanganyika, sec. 11; and Criminal Code, Nigeria, sec. 24. Also J. C. S. Kenny, *Outlines of Criminal Law* (Cambridge, 1962, 18th ed.), p. 54.

20. *Attorney-General of Nyasaland v. Frank*, [1957] R. & N.L.R. 443.

21. Lord Hale is reported to have once charged a jury: 'That there were such creatures as witches he has no doubt at all; for first, the Scriptures affirmed as much; secondly, the wisdom of all nations had provided laws against such persons, which is an argument of their confidence of such a crime. And such hath been the confidence of this Kingdom, as appears by the Act of Parliament which hath provided punishments proportionable to the guilty of the offence'; *A Trial of the Suffolk Witches* (1695), 6 St. Tr. 687, 700–1. See also W. Blackstone, *Commentaries* (London, 1781), vol. IV, pp. 60–1.

22. See, e.g., *Eria Galikuwa*, 18 E.A.C.A. 175 (Uganda, 1951); and *Kajuna s/o Mbake*, 12 E.A.C.A. 104 (Tanganyika, 1945).

23. Kenny, op. cit. p. 54.

24. J. Hale, *Pleas of the Crown* (1736), vol. I, pp. 14–15: 'Man is naturally endowed with these two great faculties, understanding and liberty of will. . . . The liberty or choice of will presupposeth an act of the understanding to know the thing or action chosen by the will'. See also P. Brett, *An Inquiry into Criminal Guilt* (London, 1963), pp. 57–8.

25. *Holloway v. United States*, 148 F. 2nd 665, 667 (App. D.C.[U.S.], 1945).

26. In the M'Naughten Rules, the defect had to be caused by mental disease. *Kemp*, [1957] 1 Q.B. 399 (Queen's Bench, England). Compare *Tadee Oyee s/o Duru*, [1959] E.A.C.A. 407 (Uganda): a high-grade mental defective not suffering from any specific disease of the mind permitted to plead insanity. In *Hotema v. United States*, 186 U.S. 413, 22 S. Ct. 895, 46 L. ed. 1225 (Supreme Court, U.S., 1901), the defendant killed a person he thought to be a witch, believing he was thereby obeying the Biblical injunction. Held, that if the defendant had formed an erroneous opinion regarding witches, although sane, he was liable;

but otherwise, if suffering from mental disease. *Accord: Alice Eriyamremu*, [1959] W.N.L.R. 270.

27. *Muswi s/o Muselo*, 23 E.A.C.A. 622 (Kenya, 1955).

28. Cf. Reverend Sydney Smith, editor of the *Edinburgh Review* in the 1830s; quoted by L. Radzinewicz and J. W. C. Turner, 'A Study of Punishment: introductory essay', in *Canadian Bar Review* (Ottawa), 21, p. 91: 'When a man has been proved to have committed a crime, it is expedient that society should make use of that man for the diminution of crime; he belongs to them for that purpose. Our primary duty, in such a case, is so to treat the culprit that many other persons may be rendered better, or prevented from being worse, by dread of the same treatment.'

29. See *Akope s/o Karven*, 14 E.A.C.A. 105 (Kenya, 1947); *Gadam*, 14 W.A.C.A. 442 (Nigeria, 1954).

30. O. W. Holmes, *Holmes-Laski Letters* (Cambridge, Mass., 1953), p. 806.

31. See, e.g., Criminal Code, 1960 (Ghana), secs. 52–4; Criminal Code, Nigeria, secs. 283, 284; and Penal Code, Tanganyika, secs. 201–2.

32. For the common law, see *Welsh*, 11 Cox C.C. 336 (Central Criminal Court, England, 1869).

33. *Mensah*, [1946] A.C. 83 (Privy Council, England); *Bedder* v. *D.P.P.*, [1954] 2 All E.R. 801 (House of Lords, England); and *El Baleila Balla Baleila*, [1958] S.L.J. & R. 12.

34. *Tembe*, [1944–6] R.L.R. 123; *Holmes* v. *D.P.P.*, [1946] 2 All E.R. 124 (House of Lords, England).

35. *Green*, 15 W.A.C.A. 73 (Nigeria, 1955).

36. *Mulenga Musesa Rieba*, 5 L.R.N.R. 718 (1954).

37. *Fabiana*, 8 E.A.C.A. 96 (Uganda, 1941); and *Akope s/o Karuen*, 14 E.A.C.A. 105 (Kenya 1947).

38. The doctrine of *stare decisis* requires a judge, save in exceptional circumstances, to follow a rule of law established in a precedent case.

39. A decision given *per incuriam* is a decision which inadvertently overlooks controlling case or statutory authority. If the earlier precedent decision was given *per incuriam*, the doctrine of *stare decisis* does not require the judge in the later case to follow it.

40. E. Daniels, *The Common Law in West Africa* (London, 1964), p. 169.

41. In *Edgal* 4 W.A.C.A. 133 (Nigeria, 1948), the defendant was convicted of obtaining a substance intended to be used to procure an unlawful abortion. The relevant Nigerian statute had been drafted in 1916, but the first English case declaring certain abortions unlawful had been *Bourne*, [1939] 1.K.B. 687 (King's Bench, England). The Court held that the draftsmen of the Nigerian statute meant by 'an unlawful abortion' what the common law held to be an unlawful abortion—and then relied upon *Bourne* to define the common law. Presumably the draftsman in 1916 knew what the Court in 1939 would announce was the common law!

42. Daniels, op. cit. p. 396.

43. A. N. Allott, 'The Study of African Law', in *S.J.L.R.*, 1958, p. 257.

44. Cf. B. Nwabueze, *The Machinery of Justice in Nigeria* (London, 1963), p. 126.

45. The details of witchcraft belief vary, of course, throughout Africa. This description is basically that of the Akan of Ghana. See M. Field, *Search for Security: an ethno-psychiatric study of rural Ghana* (London, 1960), pp. 35 ff.

46. Cf. Nwabueze, op. cit. p. 21.

47. *Brend v. Wood*, [1946] 62 L.T.R. 462, 463 (King's Bench Division, England); *Harding v. Price* [1948] 1 K.B. 695, 700 (King's Bench); but query the effect of provisions such as Penal Code, Tanganyika, sec. 10, and Criminal Code, Nigeria, sec. 24—no criminal responsibility 'for an act or omission which occurs independently of the exercise of his will'.

48. Cf. Blackstone, op. cit. *passim.*

49. See, e.g., B. Cardozo, *The Nature of the Judicial Process* (New York, 1921), *passim.*

50. O. W. Holmes, *The Common Law* (Boston, 1881), p. 1.

51. For a detailed exposition of this view with respect to the law of theft, see J. Hall, *Law, Theft and Society* (Indianapolis, 1952).

52. See, e.g., Criminal Code, Nigeria s. 417(e), making it a crime for a person to be found at night 'having his face . . . blackened . . . with intent to commit felony'. Identical clauses appear in all the East African Codes.

53. Cf. A. Park, *The Sources of Nigerian Law* (London, 1964), p. 139: 'It can . . . be predicted that this process [of unification of English and customary law] will be at the expense of customary rather than of English law. For it should be recognised that customary law, despite its remarkable adaptability, is basically not suited to the type of developed and industrialised society which it is the earnest desire of Nigeria to become. It will of course be a pity for the indigenous institution, which has its roots firmly fixed in Nigerian soil, to disappear, but any attempt to preserve customary law merely for its own sake and after it has ceased to perform the valuable function it still performs at present would be useless and potentially harmful antiquarianism.'

54. See *Wilson* v. *Inyang*, [1951] 2 All E.R. 237 (King's Bench).

55. G. Williams, 'Provocation and the Reasonable Man', in [1954] *Criminal Law Review*, pp. 740, 742; 'In the law of contract and tort, and elsewhere in the criminal law, the test of the reasonable man indicates an ethical standard.'

56. Kwame Nkrumah, *Consciencism* (London, 1964), p. 95.

ROY CARLETON HOWELL

The *Otieno* Case: African Customary Law Versus Western Jurisprudence

From a hypothetical case, we move to an important actual case involving burial laws in Kenya in the late 1980s. It turns out that jurisdiction in death can be every bit as complicated as jurisdiction in life as anyone familiar with testamentary law well knows. In this case, the question concerned who had final say over the disposition of the body of a prominent Kenyan attorney, S.M. Otieno, who died in Nairobi on December 20, 1986. His ethnic origins were Luo and his Luo kinsmen claimed the right to bury him on ancestral turf in accordance with Luo folk law. His widow, however, was not Luo, but Kikuyu. She wished to bury her late husband near Nairobi where the family home was located. The legal struggle took on not only ethnic dimensions: Kikuyu versus Luo, but also urban versus rural tensions, not to mention women's rights versus men's rights. All of Kenya took notice of the case as so many critical issues of modern life there were involved.

In the following account of the Otieno case, the author makes no attempt to conceal his bias against folk or customary law. He feels strongly that folk law constitutes a dangerous impediment to the establishment of a coherent rule of law in modern African society. For other accounts of the case, see John W. Van Doren, "Death African Style: The Case of S.M. Otieno," American Journal of Comparative Law, *36 (1988), 329–350; Evans Monari, "Burial Law—Reflections on the S.M. Otieno Case,"* Howard Law Journal, *31 (1988), 667–674. J. B. Ojwang and J.N.K Mugambi (Eds.),* The S.M. Otieno Case: Death and Burial in Modern Kenya *(Nairobi: Nairobi University Press, 1989); Minneh M. Karanja, "Otieno Versus Ougo and Omolo: A Case Study of Conflict in Modern Kenya" (L.L.M. Thesis, Harvard Law School, 1987); Alan Goldfarb, "A Kenyan Wife's Right to Bury Her Husband: Applying the Convention of the Elimination of All Forms of Discrimination Against Women,"* ILSA Journal of International Law *14 (1990), 1–21; Patricia Stamp, "Burying Otieno: The Politics of Gender and Ethnicity in Kenya,"* Signs *16 (1991), 808–845; Ralph Schuhmann, "Interne Kollisionsnorm und traditionelles Recht im Spannungsfeld kulturellen Wandels: "The Case" S.M. Otieno,"* Verfassung und Recht in Übersee *24 (1991), 245–270. For the court decision, see* Virginia Edith

Reprinted from *Southern University Law Review*, 16 (1989), 231–248, with permission.

Wamboi Otieno v. Joash Ochieng Ougo and Omolo Siranga, The Kenyan Appeal Reports Vol. 1 *(London: Butterworths, 1991), 1049–1061. For an earlier monograph surveying Luo folk law, see Gordon Wilson,* Luo Customary Law and Marriage Laws Customs *(Nairobi: Government Printer, 1961).*

The author is an Adjunct Professor of Howard University School of Law and has served as a Lecturer at the University of Nairobi Faculty of Law in Nairobi, Kenya.

I. Introduction

In Black Africa today, there is a conflict between Western Jurisprudence, Islamic Law, and traditional African Customary Law. African Customary Law is dismantling Western institutions left by European colonialists, and it is dominating Islamic traditions left by the Arabs.[1] African Customary Law is not a uniform system which applies to a given Black African nation. Unlike Western Jurisprudence or Islamic Law, African Customary Law lacks uniformity in its application to a multiplicity of rival ethnics. Typically, African Customary Laws for ethnic groups differ from one another. Although African tribes may share a common border, their customs and languages are generally radically different.[2]

As long as conflicts are between rivals of the same ethnic groups, African Customary Law is an effective medium for resolution. But, what happens when the rivals are from different tribes? Which African Customary Laws apply to resolve inter-tribal conflict? This is the problem with African Customary Law in modern day Africa. Perhaps one hundred years ago, when Africans lived out their lives within tribal boundaries, Customary Law was an effective medium for resolution of social conflict. But in modern day Africa, which comprises many ethnic groups in large cities, antiquated rural folk ways of ethnic tradition will not suffice.

The recent Kenyan case of *Virginia Wambui Otieno vs. Joash Ochieng 'Ougo*[3] is an illustration of the conflict between Western Jurisprudence and African Customary Law. The results of the *Otieno* case illustrate the omnipotent reemergence of traditional African Customary Law, and dismantlement of Western Jurisprudence. Through *Otieno*, we find antiquated tribal traditions taking precedent over Western Jurisprudence in modern Kenya. Unfortunately, the message *Otieno* sends to the world community is that Kenya is not moving toward becoming a modern state with a uniform body of laws. Kenya is a loose confederation of rival tribal groups, whose traditional Customary Laws are so radically different until jurisprudence is a quagmire of anomaly. This article will examine *Otieno*, and the conflict between Western Jurisprudence and African Customary Law within the scope of this principal case.

II. Background of the *Otieno* Case

Mr. S.M. Otieno was a thoroughly modern African, who traced his ethnic origins to the Luo Tribe of Western Kenya. S.M. Otieno was a renowned criminal lawyer, who lived in a fashionable Nairobi suburb and sent his children abroad to attend college in the United States. There can be no doubt that he lived the life of a modern urbanite, and he did not practice Luo Tribal customs of his ancestors.[4] S.M. Otieno's lifestyle more appropriately finds its genesis in the histories of the Renaissance and Enlightenment periods, from which modern Europe emerged, rather than Luo Tribal customs. S.M. Otieno frequently recited Shakespeare, and enjoyed watching old Perry Mason videos of American criminal trial dramas.[5] Indeed, he was a product of the modern middle-class. No doubt, if the late founder of Kenya, Jomo Kenyatta, could have invented the type of citizen independent Kenya should have, S.M. Otieno was that model.

The creator of the Kenyan middle class was the late founder of the country, Jomo Kenyatta. The vision of the late founder, Kenyatta, was to transfer Kenya into a modern industrial state with a uniform body of law. Thus, as a modern day man, S.M. Otieno was not Luo—but was Kenyan and believed in the laws of the state and not the rural customs of the Luo.

As a modern Kenyan, S.M. Otieno never practiced or promoted Luo Customary traditions.[6] He married based on individual rights and laws of the modern state.

> "Typical of Mr. Otieno's modernity was his marriage. He married a wealthy woman who was not a member of his tribe, the Luo. That was in 1963, the year of Kenya's independence, a time when intertribal marriages were rare and scandalous. Mr. Otieno's family and tribal elders did not sanction the marriage and they did not like his new wife, a strong-willed, college-educated woman from the rival Kikuyu tribe."[7]

S.M. Otieno's marriage to the educated Kikuyu, Virginia Wambui was an illustration of his sincere belief in individual freedoms and rights guaranteed by a new modern Kenyan state. Moreover, his inter-tribal marriage was an overt testimonial to his resolute rejection of Luo Customary traditions. Not only did S.M. Otieno live the life of an educated modern day Kenyan, he vociferously criticized Luo Customary traditions as primitive.[8]

> "The lawyer did not seem to care what the Luo liked. He changed his last name from that of his father. He went against Luo custom and permitted

> his sons to be circumcised, a rite required by his wife's tribe. He refused to teach his nine children the Luo language, kept them away from their Luo relatives and told them that tribal ways were 'primitive.' Family friends and colleagues say Mr. Otieno saw himself not as a Luo, but as a Kenyan."[9]

S.M. Otieno was a modern Kenyan lawyer who believed in the law of the state and Western Jurisprudence. Although he lived his life as a modern lawyer who saw himself as a Kenyan, in death his views would die with him having no bearing on his estate.[10] On December 20, 1986 at fifty years of age he died of a heart attack.[11] No longer alive and able to protect his family from what he characterized as primitive Luo Customary traditions, the Luo Tribe quickly moved for possession of S.M. Otieno's body and estate. The death of S.M. Otieno began a legal battle between the Kikuyu widow Virginia Wambui Otieno, and the decedent's Luo brother, Joash Ochieng 'Ougo. The decedent's brother, Joash Ochieng 'Ougo pursued the widow Virginia Wambui Otieno for the possession of the body for burial in the tribal homeland pursuant to Luo Customary traditions. The Kikuyu widow, Virginia Wambui Otieno wanted to bury her late husband on their large estate right outside Nairobi.[12]

The legal issue in *Otieno* was whether the Decedent Estate Laws of modern Kenya take precedent over Luo Customary traditions. The factual controversy was whether the widow has a right to bury her deceased husband in Nairobi pursuant to the Kenyan Statutory and Common Law; or whether the African Customary traditions of the decedent's tribal group dictate burial and estate matters.

On December 30, 1986, plaintiff Virginia Wambui Otieno sued for an injunction to enjoin her brother-in-law Joash Ochieng 'Ougo from removing the body of her late husband from the Nairobi City Mortuary. She requested a declaratory judgement from the High Court declaring that as a matter of law she was entitled to her late husband's body. The defendant brother-in-law, Joash Ochieng 'Ougo answered by citing Luo Customary Law, which holds that the body of a deceased Luo must be buried in Luoland in Western Kenya. Mr. Justice Frank J. Shields ruled in favor of the widow Virginia Wambui Otieno[13] citing a precedent set in 1970.[14] Mr. Justice Shields' decision was based upon the Kenyan Common Law of decedent's estates, which traces its origins to the English Common Law. Mr. Justice Shields ended this first round of the tug-of-war, when he granted leave to the widow to collect the body from the Nairobi City Mortuary for burial at the Otieno farm outside Nairobi.

In his decision, Mr. Justice Shields states, *inter-alia*:

> The deceased was an eminent advocate known and respected by the judges of this court and his colleagues in the legal profession. It would be idle of this court to pretend that it didn't know him well.
>
> He was a Luo by tribe, educated in Makerere and India and had a very substantial and varied legal practice in Nairobi. He married the plaintiff, a Kikuyu lady of one of Kenya's leading Kikuyu families and numbered among his clients people of all tribes and races. He was a metropolitan and a cosmopolitan, and though he undoubtedly honoured the traditions of his ancestors, it is hard to envisage such a person as subject to African Customary Law and in particular to the customs of a rural community.[15]

Mr. Justice Shields takes judicial notice of the late S.M. Otieno's lifestyle within the community. The court characterizes the decedent as being "educated" and "cosmopolitan." Next the court distinguishes the known lifestyle of the decedent from those of similar ancestry who live in rural communities. Why does Justice Shields distinguish rural from urban? Here, the court is trying to draw a distinction between the educated urban members of a tribe *vis-á-vis* the uneducated rural members. Moreover, the court concludes that the decedent's well-known lifestyle within the community leads to the rational conclusion that said decedent did not live his life in accordance to Luo Customary Law.

Mr. Justice Shields' factual analysis is sound. Moreover, the court's legal analysis is likewise correct and based on *stare decisis*. Justice Shields' states, *inter-alia*:

> The plaintiff's case is that she is the person entitled to be the deceased's personal representative and—in conformity with the decision of the Court of Appeal at Kisumu in Civil Appeal No. 12 of 1979, James Apoli and Enoka Olari (appellants) versus Prisca Buluku (respondent)—is entitled to the custody and disposal of the body until it is buried. Further, she has the right and duty to bury it. (Tristram & Coote 25th Ed. p. 38 Note M.)[16]

Notice how Justice Shields cites the Kenyan precedent of *James Apoli and Enoka Olari vs. Prisca Buluku*,[17] which was based on the *Judicature Act* of Kenya. Next, he cites the English Common Law provisions from Tristram and Coote,[18] which is the genesis of modern probate practice in Kenya. Undoubtingly, Justice Shields' decision is based on Western Jurisprudence. Based on Western Jurisprudence, Justice Shields' legal analysis is indeed soundly premised on legal precedent.

The defendant Joash Ochieng 'Ougo filed notice of an appeal, and immediately filed a petition before the Kenyan Court of Appeals before a three judge panel. The defendant-petitioner (Joash Ochieng 'Ougo) moved for an injunction to enjoin the widow, Virginia Wambui Otieno from taking possession of the decedent's body until exhaustion of the appeal. On January 5, 1987 the Kenyan Court of Appeals granted defendant's-petitioner's motion, and enjoined the widow from taking possession of the decedent's body.[19]

> Mr. Otieno, whose body has been in cold storage in the city morgue ever since, [is] the most talked-about man in this country. His corpse has forced Kenya's legal system and millions of Kenyans to re-examine their nation to see just how modern it has become. Should a modern African be compelled, in death, it is being asked, to comply with tribal customs that he had renounced when he was alive?[20]

Subsequently, on January 13, 1987 the Kenyan Court of Appeals remanded the *Otieno* case back to the High Court for trial, and Mr. Justice S.E.O. Bosire was assigned to hear the case.[21]

On February 9, 1987, Mr. Justice S.E.O. Bosire ruled in favor of the Luo brother-in-law Joash Ochieng 'Ougo. Mr. Justice Bosire held that Luo Customary tradition of the decedent's ancestors determine burial location. Justice Bosire states, *inter-alia*:

> The decision as to where and how an adult Luo will be buried rests with the clan from which he hails. Even if a man may have, in his lifetime, expressed a wish as to his place of burial, it is in evidence that the wish will be subject to the customs and traditions of his clan. The clan sages are not, necessarily, bound to comply with those wishes if they do not conform with the customs and traditions of that clan.[22]

Justice Bosire's legal analysis is in total contradiction to Mr. Justice Shields' reasoning. Justice Bosire asserts that an African's lifestyle and beliefs are irrelevant. Even though an African may reject his tribal customs during his lifetime, upon death the customs of the tribe determine burial. Justice Bosire resolved the issue in *Otieno* by ruling that African Customary traditions take precedent over Western Jurisprudence standards of decedent estates. Justice Bosire held that the widow does not have the right to bury her husband pursuant to Western Common Law principles in Kenya; for the African Customary traditions of the decedent's tribal group control and dictate burial requirements.

The widow, Virginia Wambui Otieno filed for further appeals—but to no avail. The controlling decision would be the one issued by Justice Bosire.

III. Synopsis of Luo Customary Law

The Luo are a Nilotic people who live in Western Kenya near Lake Victoria. It is believed that the Luo migrated to the Lake Victoria region of Kenya from Southern Sudan. The Luo are the third largest tribe in Kenya. Only the Kikuyu and Luhya have larger populations in Kenya.[23]

Luo Customary traditions are quite interesting. During the *Otieno* trial, Professor Henry Odera Oruku was called by the defendant Joash Ochieng 'Ougo as an expert witness on the rituals and customs of the Luo. Professor Oruka is a professor of philosophy at the University of Nairobi, and a member of the Kenyan National Academy of Sciences. The professor is ethnically a Luo, and at the time of the trial was Chairman of the Department of Philosophy at the University of Nairobi.[24]

Professor Oruka gave expert testimony relative to the issue of Luo Customary burial traditions.[25] According to Luo Customary tradition, a Luo male can have a "house" and a "home." A "house" is merely a dwelling which a Luo male occupies, and as such has no symbolic meaning within the tribe. However, a "home" is blessed by the Luo parents of the man pursuant to tribal ceremonies.[26] Moreover, a Luo man cannot build a "home" unless he has a son and pays his dowry and bride price to his wife's family. The blessing of the "home" of the Luo male is done by his father through various customary procedures.[27] One such procedure is known by Luo custom as *tudo lum*. The English translation is literally "thing of the grass." So important are these tribal traditions, until a Luo male who has not established his "home" in accordance with custom will be buried at his father's "home."[28]

Inasmuch as the late S.M. Otieno's residence (located outside of Luoland near Nairobi) was never blessed by his parents pursuant to Luo Customary tradition, his estate was (pursuant to Luo Customary Law) a "house" and not a "home." Hence, pursuant to Luo Customary tradition, the late S.M. Otieno cannot be buried at his estate near Nairobi; furthermore, under these circumstances he must be buried at his father's "home" in Luo land.

In regard to the *Otieno* case, the cogent rules of Luo Customary traditions are, *inter-alia*:

1. Otieno was born and bred a Luo and as such under Luo Customary Law his wife on marriage became part and parcel of her husband's household as well as a member of her husband's clan. Their children are also Luo as well as members of their deceased father's clan.

2. On the death of a married Luo man the customs are that the clan takes charge of his burial as far as taking into account the wishes of the deceased and his family.

3. But a Luo who has not established his own home in accordance with custom will be buried at his father's home.
4. Under the Luo custom to which as we have said she is bound she has no right to bury her husband and she does not become the head of the family upon the death of her husband.
5. As with other African communities a man cannot change his tribal origin.[29]

Professor Oruka testified further about Luo belief in spirits of the dead. The professor stated that when the body of a deceased male Luo is not buried in compliance with Luo Customary traditions, in turn the family and tribe can be haunted by spirits.[30] In regard, to this issue of spirits, defendant-petitioner Joash Ochieng 'Ougo testified that unless he is allowed to bury his brother's body in the ancestral home, angry spirits will harm him.

> The Luo, like many of Africa's tribes, take their burial customs seriously. Mr. Otieno's brother, Joash Ochieng 'Ougo, testified that unless he was allowed to bury the body on the ancestral farm, the dead man's angry spirit would sabotage his life, pester him in his sleep and make his Luo clansmen spit on him.
>
> The Luo attribute car accidents, birth defects and house fires to the restless ghost of a clansman buried in violation of tribal law.[31]

Among rural Luo, these Customary traditions are very strong. There have been incidents where Luo have died attempting to recover the bodies of tribal members for burial purposes in accordance with Customary traditions. The Luo strongly believe that misfortune will befall them through spirits if the body of a deceased Luo is not buried pursuant to tradition.[32]

> Extraordinary efforts are made by the Luo to ensure that spirits rest easy. Last July, when 13 Luo fishermen drowned in a Lake Victoria storm, tribal elders rushed to their boats to retrieve the bodies, even as the storm raged. Thirty-one Luos died looking for the original 13.
>
> It is a political axiom on Luo land that a man who does not see to the proper burial of his father and his sons has no chance in local or parliamentary elections.[33]

Customary tribal traditions influence modern day elections among the Luo, as well as other rural tribal groups in Kenya. This political situation illustrates the symbolic relationship between traditional African society and the modern Kenyan state. Tribalism is a political reality in Africa in general, and in Kenya in particular. Supporting issues such as the circumcision of females in Africa,[34] is analogous to the Western political gesture of kissing babies during a campaign. Tribal politics to Africa is what the Democratic and Republican parties are to the United States. The vast difference is that the Democratic and Republican parties have their origins in the modern state, and membership is not restricted to birth and race. African Customary traditions predate the modern African state, and is much stronger a political ethnic phenomenon.

> Across Africa, there are traditionalists, middle-aged and older people born in small villages, who believe that birth into a tribe entails privileges and duties that have nothing to do with free will or how one chooses to live one's life. For these Africans—epitomized by Mr. Otieno's brother and Luo clan elders—an African can no more wish away the laws of gravity.
>
> These traditionalists, who include many of the best-educated and most influential people on the continent often live in ranch-style houses in modern cities such as Nairobi or Lagos all their adult lives, but they insist that a small hut in the village of their birth is their only "home". The fundamental decisions of their lives, those concerning marriage and children and death, are governed by the laws of their village and tribe, not of their nation.[35]

To the Luo, Luo Customary tradition is more valid than the laws of the modern Kenyan state. It is important to understand that Luo Customary tradition predates the Republic of Kenya. Thus, Luos are Luo first and Kenyans second.

IV. Women's Rights in Kenya

Kenyan women are, at best, second class citizens, and at worse viewed as chattel property of men.[36] *Otieno* illustrates the lack of rights Kenyan women have. In regard to women's rights, Kenyan tribes typically share the same conviction that women are not equal to men. Thus, relative to women's rights, Luo are no different from any other Kenyan tribe.

Luo Customary tradition provides that women have absolutely no rights equal to that of men. Thus, a widow cannot have any control over her deceased Luo husband's estate.[37]

> "In Luo custom, the widow has no say over the property of her late husband. Its disposition, as well as burial arrangements, are matters for men to decide. One Luo elder testified, 'Women are told what to do!'"[38]

As aforementioned, it is important to note that on the issue of women's rights, Luo Customary traditions are no different than most tribes in Kenya. Kenyan women are to be subservient to men by tribal custom.

> "In most Kenyan tribes, wives are viewed as the property of their husbands. They are expected to work the field[s], prepare food, raise children and obey their husbands."[39]

Luo Customary tradition holds that the family of the deceased husband has a vested right to the property of the decedent. Therefore when a Luo man dies, his blood relatives have been known to raid the house and carry off whatever they want.[40]

> "On the day Mr. Otieno died, his wife took no chances. She ordered her servants to put away the video recorder and roll up the carpet. . . . By the time Mr. Ochieng, the brother who sued for custody of the body, arrived at the widow's house, it was almost bare. 'She even locked the toilets,' he complained in court. . . .
>
> The woman in this instance was not accustomed to being told what do to, nor was she willing to bend to Luo custom."[41]

Members of the Kenyan Parliament typically are more familiar with their particular tribal Customary Laws than the laws of the Republic of Kenya. In 1979 the Kenyan Parliament considered a bill to legalize polygamy.[42] Indeed, polygamy in Kenya today is a common practice. The legislative intent of the bill was to codify polygamous marriage standards. At the time, the Kenyan Attorney General devised an amendment to the bill to protect the interests of wives and children—who often lost their inheritance when a husband died. Many men of the Kenyan Parliament raised strong objection to the Attorney General's proposed amendments.[43]

> "One of them, Kimurai Soi, argued that the corporal punishment section of the bill would deny a man his traditional right to beat his wife. 'It is very African to teach women manners by beating them', *M.P. Kimurai Soi* said on the floor of Parliament. 'If this legislation is passed, even slapping your wife is ruled out.' Another lawmaker . . . contested a clause requiring a man to get permission from his first wife before marrying another. This, he said, was putting the horse before the cart. What was needed instead was to educate women so they would understand the necessity of polygamy. The majority agreed and the bill was scrapped."[44]

In Africa in general and Kenya in particular, typically women inherit nothing from their fathers and can be divorced by their husbands without any property settlement. In 1981 Kenya tried to protect the inheritance rights to widows through a new law passed by Parliament. Unfortunately, this revolutionary "widow inheritance statute" is generally ineffective and ignored.[45] Hence in regard to women's rights, Kenyan women have a very, very long road to travel.

V. Luo Customary Law vs. Kenyan Statutory and Common Law

How does Kenyan statutory and common law coexist with African Customary Law on burials? Section 82 (4)(b) of the Constitution of Kenya allows for the tribal application of burial customs of a decedent.[46] Therefore, tribal burial laws are not unconstitutional for being racially discriminatory in application.[47] Pursuant to Section 51 of the *Kenyan Evidence Act*, the party which asserts African Customary Law has the burden of proving the tribal tradition.[48] Furthermore, pursuant to Section 3 (2) of the *Kenyan Judicature Act*, before African Customary Law is admissible as evidence it must meet a two prong test. First, the African Customary Law must not be repugnant to justice and morality, second it must not be inconsistent with statutory enactments of Parliament.[49] Once the relevant African Customary Law meets these two requirements, it is admissible as evidence and enforceable.[50]

But here, *sub-judice* Luo Customary Law is indeed inconsistent with the written statutes of Kenya. Luo Customary Law on burials violate the *Married Women Property Act* of 1882. This English law has been applied in Kenya as a statute even though consummated before Kenya became an independent state. Therefore, *Kenyan* courts are obligated to take "judicial notice" of the *Married Women Property Act* of 1882.[51] Moreover, Kenyan courts have indeed taken "judicial notice" of this statute.

> "At common law before 1882 the wife would not have been able to take up letters of administration without the consent of her husband. It was after the Married Women Property Act 1882 sections 1 (2), 18, and 24, that a married woman could take up administration without the consent of her husband and to act in all respects in the matter concerning the intestate as if she were a 'feme sole' . . ."[52]

Hence, pursuant to Sections 1 (2), 18 and 24 of the *Married Women Property Act* of 1882 plaintiff-Virginia Wambui Otieno, *sub-judice* has a statutory right as personal representative of her intestate husband's estate to determine burial site. For this reason, Luo Customary Law on burials fail to meet the second prong of the test as set out by Section 3(2)of the *Kenyan Judicature Act*. As aforementioned, Luo Customary Law on burials is inconsistent with the written statutes of Kenya; thus, it may not be enforced by a court of law.

Section 3(1) of the *Kenyan Judicature Act* limits the application of African Customary Law in Kenya. Moreover, pursuant to Section 3(2) of the *Judicature Act*, African Customary Law prevails where there is a conflict between Customary and Common Law.[53] Hence Kenyan Common Law provides plaintiff—Virginia Wambui Otieno, *sub-judice* no remedy against Luo Customary Law on burials. The plaintiff's only relief from Customary Law is statutory and pursuant to the *Married Women Property Act*, thus said plaintiff (Virginia Wambui Otieno) should have prevailed *sub-judice*.

VI. Conclusion

The fight for the body of the late S.M. Otieno has become the most controversial conflict among rival tribes in Kenya.[54] The *Otieno* trial was marked by racial hate and ethnic slurs.

> "One of Mr. Otieno's sons, who is studying economics at Paterson State College in Wayne, New Jersey, denounced the Luo tribe in court. In Africa, it is apostasy for a young man of good family to show disrespect to his elders. But Jairus Outo Otieno, 23, took the witness stand and called Luo people 'lazy' and 'uncivilized.'"
>
> As he said this, he stared coldly at the faces of the Luo clan chairman and his own uncle, the men who sued for custody of his father's body. The courtroom, packed with supporters of the Luo cause, was electric with hatred."[55]

True enough the legal conflict involved modern day urban values against rural ethnic traditions; but, the human drama was filled with racial hate and pitted the Kikuyu against the Luo. During the controversy, plaintiff-Virginia Wambui Otieno scheduled a family burial near Nairobi. Simultaneously, defendant—Joash Ochieng ´Ougo arranged a Luo burial in rural Luoland on the same day.

Each side fought bitterly for the possession of a corpse. Kenyans generally took sides according to tribal loyalty. Kikuyus supported the plaintiff-Virginia Wambui Otieno the Kikuyu widow. Luos supported the defendant —Joash Ochieng 'Ougo the Luo brother of the deceased. The Kenyan press exploited the tense controversy by running daily front page inflammatory stories, which heightened ethnic tensions and sold newspapers in record numbers.[56] Death threats were made against the life of plaintiff—Virginia Wambui Otieno, as thousands of Luos poured into Nairobi from Western Kenya.

> "Hundreds of Luos have gathered daily outside the courthouse; others stand vigil near the city morgue. There is widespread concern that the widow's life may be in danger, if the Luo are not permitted to leave town with the body."[57]

On Friday, January 13, 1987 Mr. Justice Bosire ruled that the defendant—Joash Ochieng 'Ougo would get possession of the deceased for burial in Luoland. The late S.M. Otieno was to be buried at his ancestral home pursuant to Luo Customary Law.

> "The court ruled that the late criminal lawyer was subject to Luo Customary Law, although he had lived a Westernised life-style in the city."[58]

Throughout the entire city of Nairobi, police and standby military units were stationed. Every major street intersection was occupied by riot police. On Friday, January 13, 1987 Nairobi looked like a war zone. Hundreds of police were near the courthouse. Traffic was stopped by large crowds of a sea of Luos marching triumphantly from the courthouse. The Kenyan newspapers had turned a simple family feud into a tribal war of hate. As thousands of Luos marched down Kenyatta Avenue, it was clear the Luos had won. But it is equally clear that Kenya's future as a cohesive multiracial state has lost.

Notes

1. A Mazrui, *The African: A Triple Heritage* at 239–259 and 136–137 (1st ed. 1986 Little Brown and Company).
2. D. Lamb, *The Africans* at p. 14 (1st ed. 1982 Randon House, Inc).
3. *Virginia Wambui Otieno vs. Joash Ochieng Ougo*, Opinion of Mr. Justice J.F. Shields, January 5, 1987, High Court of Kenya, Nairobi. Subsequently, Court of Appeal orders a trial on January 8, 1987. On February 13, 1987, Mr. Justice S.E.O. Bosire of the High Court of Kenya, Nairobi, rules in favor of the defendant. On May 15, 1987, the Court of Appeal affirms Mr. Justice Bosire's trial court opinion. Also, see The Washington Post, February 14, 1987 *Kenyan Judge Awards Corpse of Modern Lawyer To Tribe*, at p. A 25, columns 5 and 6.
4. International Herald Tribune, February 13, 1987, *African Tradition and Modern Values: Tribal Loyalties Are Often At Odds With Nationalism*, at p. 1., by Blaine Harden. Also, see The Washington Post, February 14, 1987, *Kenyan Judge Awards Corpse Of Modern Lawyer To Tribe*, at p. A 25, columns 5 and 6.

5. *Id.*
6. *Id.*
7. *Id.*
8. *Id.*
9. *Id.*
10. *Id.*

"Mr. Otieno died of a heart attack. His wife, children and friends said he had often told them he wanted to be buried in Nairobi. But the day he died, Luo elders began pressing his widow for custody of the body."

11. The front page story said simply: 'A prominent Nairobi advocate, Mr. Silvanus Melea Otieno, has died.' Mrs. Otieno said funeral arrangements would be announced later.

Little did she—or anyone else for that matter—realize how much later. Even less did she realize she was about to write an historic chapter into Kenya's legal history.

It was only 146 days after he had died that S.M. Otieno's burial place was known. It was a record for Kenya, if not for elsewhere.

But the epic court battle over burial rights was not just another family squabble. It raised many issues of wide interest to many people: the role of the law and the family, customary law versus common law, the role of women in the family, different ethnic traditions and their place in Kenya society as a whole.

The whole issue evoked strong feelings, emotions and debate. For newspapers it was a bestseller.

For let there be no mistake about it. The Otieno case may be closed. But the debate it gave rise to about many issues has only just begun." See, *S.M. Otieno: Kenya's Unique Burial Saga*, Nation Newspapers Publication at Preface (1987). The Nation printed all the Court's decisions, and all Nation Newspaper accounts in this one book.

12. *Otieno, supra* note 3.

13. The court order, which clears the way for Mrs. Otieno to bury her husband on Saturday, restrains any other person from removing the body from the mortuary.

Mr. Justice Frank J. Shields ruled in favour of Mrs. Otieno, citing a precedent set in 1979.

He said: "The deceased in this case died intestate (without having made any will). His widow is plainly entitled to his corpse in accordance with Civil Appeal number 12 of 1979. I grant the interlocutory injunction. . . ." Nation, *supra* note 11 at p. 3.

14. *James Apoli and Enoka Olari vs. Prisca Buluku*, civil appeal No. 12 of 1979, The High Court of Kenya.

15. *Otieno, supra* note 3. Also, see Nation, *supra* note 11 at p. 6.

16. *Otieno, supra* note 3. Also, see Nation, *supra* note 11 at p. 6.

17. *Apoli, supra* note 14.

18. Tristram's and Coote's Probate Practice, Thomas H. Tristram and Henry C. Coote, Great Britain-Laws, Statutes.

19. "It is the practice of this court to preserve the status quo until the hearing of the appeal so as to preserve the subject matter (Mr. Otieno's body) and avoid the appeal being rendered nugatory (invalid). See *M.M. Butt versus the Rent Tribunal*, civil application No. 6 of 1979, and *Gheewala and Aruna versus Gheela and others*, civil application No. 127 of 1986."

"In this application, the controversy concerns where the body should be buried. It is feasible for the body to be preserved in the City Mortuary and it is unreasonable and unnecessary to risk exhumation." Nation, *supra* note 11 at p. 9. Also see The Washington Post, February 17, 1987. *Delay Is Ordered In Kenyan Burial*, at p. A 14, column 1.

20. African Tradition, *supra* note 4.

21. *Otieno, supra* note 3.

22. Nation, *supra* note 11 at p. 106.

23. Malkiat Singh, GHC—A Combined Course for Standard 5 (Our Nation) at p. 8–13. Published by the Soma Group Limited. P.O. Box 30162, Nairobi, Kenya.

24. Nation, *supra* note 11 at p. 79–82.

25. *Id.* The specific expert testimony given by Professor Oruku on Luo Customary burial tradition was *inter-alia*:

"When a man dies, his first wife (if he is polygamous) is the first one to cry and wail announcing his death. This goes on for a very long time so that everyone knows what has happened. The day after the death, elders meet at the home of the deceased and they decide the details of the funeral ceremony like who is to speak and who is to do what during the actual ceremony. They also decide on the order of the kids, this is important, especially where the man had several wives and it has to be decided who is the eldest son of the deceased.

The elders also decide where the man is to be buried. This is generally near the hut of the first wife if the man was polygamous, which is not the case here.

The elders also decide who will be the first to dig the grave. This means, the person who will strike the ground first with a hoe at the place where the grave is to be dug.

The man is buried near the hut of his first wife. He is laid to rest on his left side, leaving his right hand (the male hand) free and facing the hut. In the case of a wife, she would be laid to rest on her right side with the left hand (female) free.

The elders also decide who is to enter the grave. The body is lowered into the grave. If it is a husband or wife who has been bereaved, they cannot be insistent as to where the partner is to be buried, that is for the elders to decide.

The deceased's first son is the first to throw earth into the grave and he is followed by the rest of the sons, before the grave is finally covered. After burial a *magenga* is prepared by which people warm themselves.

The women should always weep and wail and should start as early as 4 a.m. in order to wake up people. They also sing songs in praise of the deceased.

The relatives do not sleep for four days. During this period, married people do not sleep together. On the last day, a ceremony known as *yweyo liel* (sweeping the grave or cleaning or purifying it) is done and then the people disperse. A few relatives are left behind to console the bereaved.

After some weeks, months or years, another ceremony, *nindo e liel* is performed. This is a big ceremony and if it is not carried out, the spirit of the dead will haunt the people. Many people come, bringing gifts for the ceremony.

After some days, weeks, months or years, another ceremony *tero tipo* (bring back the shadow) is performed. This is mostly done by the daughters of the deceased and other womenfolk who are married far away from home. They do this to "bring back the shadow" of their dead mother or father." At p. 81.

26. *Id.*

27. *Id.*

28. *Id.*

29. Nation, *supra* note 11, at p. 177.

30. *Supra*, note 25.

31. African Tradition, *supra* note 4.

32. African Tradition, *supra* note 4.

33. African Tradition, *supra* note 4.

34. Luo do not circumcise their females, however, the Kikuyu (Mrs. Virginia Wambui Otieno's tribe) do circumcise their female members. For an interesting insight into female circumcision in Africa, see *Female Circumcision: Challenges to the Practice as a Human Rights Violation*, 8 Harvard Women's Law Journal 155 (1985).

35. African Tradition, *supra* note 4.

36. D. Lamb, *supra* note 2, at p. 36–41. Moreover, this observation is likewise premised on the author's own observations while teaching and living in Kenya.

37. "Invoking Luo custom, Mr. Otieno's brother and a tribal clan leader demanded that the corpse be taken "home." The clan insisted that a prominent Luo such as Mr. Otieno must be buried in Luo land, near Lake Victoria.

The widow, Virginia Wambui, would have none of it. She ordered her husband's brother out of her house. Police were called to the house to keep the clan away. The widow left instructions at the morgue that clan members not be allowed to view the body. She reportedly feared they would steal it." African Tradition, *supra* note 4.

38. African Tradition, *supra* note 4.

39. African Tradition, *supra* note 4.

40. African Tradition, *supra* note 4.

41. Miss Wambui, 50, is a short, stout, stern-looking woman who stated flatly in court, 'I come from a rich family.' Her father was a leading figure in Kenya's struggle for independence from the British. One of her brothers was a foreign minister, another is a high court judge.

In 1969, she was the first woman from the Nairobi suburbs to run for parliament, but she lost. She is a long-time leader in the Kenyan women's movement and was treasurer of the international women's conference held here two years ago. She travels frequently to the United States. . . .

By Kenyan standards, therefore, Mr. Otieno's widow, who goes by her Kikuyu name, Wambui, is an astonishingly bold women." African Tradition, *supra* note 4.

42. D. Lamb, *supra* note 2, at p. 39.

43. D. Lamb, *supra* note 2, at p. 39.

44. D. Lamb, *supra* note 2, at p. 39, *emphasis added.*

45. "Since 1981, Kenya's inheritance laws have given widows, in the absence of a will—which Mr. Otieno never wrote—the right to inherit their husband's property. But according to a 1986 Dutch-funded study of women and land in Kenya, the law is ignored in most rural areas. The study said sons of the deceased or his brothers or tribal elders simply take property from acquiescent women who do not know about the law or who feel powerless to demand its enforcement." African Tradition, *supra* note 4.

46. 82. (1) Subject to subsection (4), (5) and (8), no law shall make any provision that is discriminatory either of itself or in its effect.

(4) Subsection (1) shall not apply to any law so far as that law makes provision—

(b) with respect to adoption, marriage, divorce, burial devaluation of property on death or other matters of personal law;

The clear meaning of this particular Constitutional provision obviously allows for the application of racial discriminatory laws with respect to burial practices. See, the Constitution of the Republic of Kenya. Also see, Nation *supra* note 11 at p. 173–178.

47. *Id.*

48. See, *The Evidence Act of Kenya*, at Section 51. Also, see *Otieno, supra* note 3 (Civil Appeal No. 31 of 1987—In the Court of Appeal at Nairobi).

49. Section 3(2) of the *Kenyan Judicature Act* provides, *inter-alia*: "The High Court, the Court of Appeals and all subordinate Courts shall be guided by African Customary Law in civil cases in which one or more of the parties is subject to it or affected by it, so far as it is applicable and is not repugnant to justice and morality or inconsistent with any written law. . . ."

50. "Kenyan law is ambivalent about who has the right to decide where Mr. Otieno should be buried. It says that courts are "to be guided" by customary law, except where it is "repugnant to justice and morality." The vagueness of this language leaves room for the judge's ruling in the Otieno case to establish an important legal precedent." African Tradition, *supra* note 4.

51. "The general common-law rule that the courts of the forum will not take judicial notice of the law of another state does not apply to the law of a state from which the state of the forum was formed. In such a situation the laws of the mother state which were in existence at the time of the separation will be judicially noticed." See 29 Am Jur 2d, Evidence Section 47 at p. 83.

52. See, *The Married Women Property Act of 1882*. Also, see *Otieno, supra* note 3.

53. The Kenya Appeals Court in *Otieno* stated on this issue, the following language— "Secondly that the proviso to Section 3(1) of the *Judicature Act* limits the application of Common Law to Kenya and thirdly that under Section 3(2) of the *Judicature Act*, it is mandatory to be guided by African Customary

Law and that where . . . there is a conflict between Common Law and African Customary Law, the latter must prevail." Nation, *supra*, note 11 at p. 174.

54. Thousands of Luos kept a constant vigil outside the Courthouse in Nairobi during the controversy. See, Nation, *supra*, note 11 at p. 179.

55. African Tradition, *supra* note 4.

56. "Local newspapers, printing full transcripts of the trial, have made extra press runs to keep up with what has become a national obsession with the case. The dispute, more than any issue in the recent history of this East African country, dominates social conversation at all levels of Kenyan society." African Tradition, *supra* note 4.

57. African Tradition, *supra* note 4.

58. Daily National Newspaper, at p. 1, February 17, 1987, Nairobi, Kenya.

ALEC SAMUELS

Legal Recognition and Protection of Minority Customs in a Plural Society in England

In order to demonstrate that folk law in conflict is not confined to former colonial possessions, we have selected the following essay by Alec Samuels, a Barrister and formerly Reader in Law at the University of Southampton, who surveys the situation as it exists in contemporary England. Many immigrant groups residing in England, especially those who came from countries previously part of the British Empire, continue to live in enclaves wherein to some extent their traditional folk law prevails. Again the critical issue revolves around what happens when the folk law runs counter to English law.

For further consideration of folk law in conflict in England, see Sebastian Poulter, English Law and Ethnic Minority Customs *(London: Butterworth, 1986) and his essay "Ethnic Minority Customs, English Law and Human Rights,"* International and Comparative Law Quarterly, *36 (1987), 589–615. Poulter is one of the leading authorities on this matter. For analogous problems in other societies, see F.O. Shyllon, "Immigration and the Criminal Courts,"* Modern Law Review, *34 (1971), 135–148; and Leon Sheleff, "Tribal Rites and Legal Rights,"* Israel Yearbook on Human Rights, *18 (1988), 153–172. The Law Reform Commission,* The Recognition of Aboriginal Customary Laws, *2 vols. (Canberra: Australian Government Publishing Service, 1986).*

How far does English Law recognize and protect minority customs? How far should it do so? The traditional arguments are that everybody must conform to universal minimum standards in public law, e.g., criminal law, but the law should interfere as little as possible in matters of private concern, e.g., personal and family matters. The ethical and social issue is whether minority groups and individuals should be expected or encouraged or compelled to conform and to integrate, or whether they should be expected or encouraged or permitted to maintain a separate

Reprinted from *Anglo-American Law Review*, 10 (1981), 241–256, with permission.

identity in their own customs. What is meant by the "plural" society and what ethical, social and legal consequences flow from it? In the end the answer must be a value judgment.

It was always said that one of the reasons the English were such good and successful colonial administrators, in comparison with the French, Germans, Belgians, Italians and others, was that the English never interfered with the local people and their customs, except in extreme cases such as suttee.

Criminal Law

In the criminal law a minority custom cannot be a defence to a prosecution: *R. v. Esop* (1836) 7 C. and P. 456; 173 ER. 203, cf. *Wilson v. Inyang* [1951] 2 K.B. 799, unless the legislature expressly says so. Criminal law is public law. It is designed to protect others, the victims, from the defendant, their life, person, integrity and property, and assault and damage may be irreparable, i.e., not really compensatable in terms of damage. The Jehovah's Witness who does not call medical attention or refuses to give consent to a blood transfusion has no defence to manslaughter if the child dies as a result. The assailant inflicting grievious bodily harm upon his Jehovah's Witness victim must take him as he finds him and is rightly convicted of murder if the victim refuses a transfusion and dies: *R. v. Blaue* [1975] 1 W.L.R. 1411, C.A. But a minority custom may be taken into account in sentence, especially for a first offender. The length of time during which the defendant has been in the UK and his level of intelligence and understanding would be factors properly to be taken into account: *R. v. Rapier* [1963] Crim. L.R. 212; *R. v. Singh* [1967] Crim. L.R. 247. Parental chastisement must conform to English standards: *R. v. Derriviere* (1969) 53 Cr. App. R. 637. Making tribal markings on a child is criminal because of the risk to the health and well-being of the child, the unreality of the consent of the child, and the different attitudes of the rising generation: *R. v. Adesanya, The Times* 16 and 17 July 1974 (Poulter). It might well be appropriate to make the child the subject of a care order under the Children and Young Persons Act 1969, s.1. By long convention matters such as ear piercing, tattooing (though not of minors: Tattooing of Minors Act 1969), removal of birth marks, and circumcision, have all been accepted by the law, although they do not represent the custom of any particular identifiable minority group. Sexual intercourse with a girl under 16 is unlawful, even if the West Indian defendant was unaware of the law, the custom is different in the West Indies, and the girl was an encouraging, precocious or promiscuous West Indian. "Whatever the social customs in the West Indies, he must in future comply with English law": *R. v. Byfield* [1964] Crim. L.R. 378; *R. v. Bailey* [1964] Crim. L.R. 671; *R. v. Finley* [1963] Crim. L.R. 299. Kidnapping a woman in the course of a family feud cannot be justified by minority custom: *R. v. Dad and Shafi* [1968] Crim L.R. 46. Duelling is not permitted by English law. The principle is well over a century old, e.g., the famous duelling case: *R. v. Barronet* (1852) Dears C.C. 51, 169 E.R, 633.

Lord Campbell LCJ:

> "These two persons [the defendants] are placed in exactly the same situation as if they were native born subjects of this kingdom, and will have the same justice administered to them as would be administered to native born subjects. Persons who fly to this country as an asylum must obey the laws of the country and be content to place themselves in the same situation as native born subjects."

Coleridge J:

> "[F]oreigners who come to England must in this respect be dealt with in the same way as native subjects. Ignorance of the law cannot, in the case of a native, be received as an excuse for a crime, nor can it any more be urged in favour of a foreigner."

Erle J:

> "To make a difference in the case of foreigners would be most dangerous practice. It is of great importance that the administration of the law should be uniform. It must be administered without respect to persons and it would be dangerous and unjust to introduce into a general rule an exception in favour of foreigners."

The immigrant lacking the right of abode in the UK is deported in addition to any ordinary sentence (Shyllon 142–146).

Colour, ethnic origin and religion are material in determining whether murder can be reduced to manslaughter by reason of provocation, and whether, in the totality of the situation, and the circumstances, and having regard to his personal characteristics, physical or mental, the defendant could and should have exercised self-control and whether he may be excused for not exercising that control: *R. v. Camplin* [1978] A.C. 705, 717D Lord Diplock, 721D Lord Morris and 726C Lord Simon. Such matters may well affect the gravity of taunts or insults. It is not clear whether cultural as well as racial characteristics are material, nor whether sensitivity is sufficient or excitability is necessary, nor whether ordinary characteristics or colour, ethnic origin and religion suffice, or some extraordinary characteristic is necessary. The question is ultimately a jury question depending upon all the facts as they see them, and all these factors are capable of being material in certain situations.

However, the normal reaction of a black man of a particular type, even if different from the normal reaction of a white man, is not an abnormality to justify a finding of diminished responsibility in a particular case: *R. v. King* [1965] 1 Q.B. 443, C.A.

Shyllon (p.148) praised the courts. He wrote of "the admirable and skilful way in which the criminal courts have tackled some of the problems that confront them in a multi-racial and multi-cultural society. Whether it be child marriage or child discipline, racial violence or deportation, the courts have ensured that criminal justice is not biased against but rather, in appropriate cases, biased in favour of the immigrant in England."

In a sentencing case, *R. v. Ford* (1976) 62 Cr. App. R. 303, 306, Scarman LJ said:

> "Colour is an absolute irrelevance in the context of our criminal law . . ."

By custom, convention and comity the diplomat is immune from criminal proceedings, although not from liability, although he is expected to observe the local criminal law: Vienna Convention in Diplomatic Immunity 1961 article 42 (largely ignored in practice in respect of parking and other motoring offences).

Road Safety

An interesting example of religious toleration being accorded a higher value than road safety is to be found in the Motor Cycle Crash Helmets (Religious Exemption) Act 1976, which exempts any follower of the Sikh religion from the duty of wearing a crash helmet while he is wearing a turban. The justification for the measure was that otherwise Sikhs would be unable to take employment in the Post Office, the armed services, the AA and other employments requiring the use of a motor cycle. Sikh bus conductors, building employees and Post Office engineers have reached agreement with the employers about not wearing the customary occupational headgear but adhering to turbans. While not doubting the sincerity of the religious tenets of the Sikhs, it is submitted that safety ought to come before religious sensitivity, the employment disability for Sikhs caused by the safety factor in employment has a narrow scope, and the public as a whole object (and there is "poll" evidence to support this) to this privileged discrimination.

Planning Law

If an application is made for planning permission for a temple or similar building, it must be dealt with on its planning merits in exactly the same way as any other planning application, e.g., as though it were for an English religious building. The applicants for planning permission might have certain requirements, such as windows facing the sunrise or Mecca, a particular design and appearance for the building, the traditional means of summoning the congregation such as sunrise chanting. The local planning authority must apply ordinary planning criteria: access, traffic, parking, appearance, density, compatibility with surrounding buildings and the area generally, and also the impact generally of such a building and its use upon the neighbourhood. It is believed that the Scientologists' temple at East Grinstead and the mosque in Regents Park in London have caused controversy.

Employment

The abuse of the closed shop is widely known. The closed shop is contrary to democratic principle, contrary to the right of association and non-association under the Universal Declaration of Human Rights and the European Convention on Human Rights, and productive of immense ill-will in society. *Taylor v. Co-operative Retail Services, The Times* October 24, 1980, EAT— pre-1980 law. The closed shop has been held to infringe the right not to associate under Article 11 of the European Convention on Human Rights: *Young, Jones and Webster v. United Kingdom*, European Court of Human Rights, August 1981.

Unfortunately English statutory law does not outlaw the closed shop, it merely represents an illogical and largely unintelligible compromise: Employment Protection (Consolidation) Act 1978 s.58; Employment Act 1980 s.7. Dismissal for refusal to belong to a closed shop is fair unless the employee can show genuine objection to trade union membership on grounds of conscience or other deeply held personal conviction, or he was an employee before the closed shop came in, or the closed shop was not approved by at least 80 per cent of those entitled to vote voting in secret ballot.

The Christadelphians have succeeded in establishing unfair dismissal as a result of refusing to join a trade union: *Cave v. British Railways Board* [1976] I.R.L.R. 400. See also *Goodbody v. British Railways* [1977] I.R.L.R. 84—membership of a trade union a fundamental and adverse factor in a religious group. The statutory law against discrimination in employment is contained in the Race Relations Act 1976 Part II s.4–16. Inferences of discrimination may be drawn, but care must be exercised: *Owen and Briggs v. James, The Times* February 26, 1981, Forbes J *Selvarajan v. Inner London Education Authority* [1980] I.R.L.R. 313, EAT, upheld on appeal (1981) 131 N.L.J. 929, July 16, 1981—discovery order. An employer is legally justified in insisting upon no beards in a chocolate factory for hygiene reasons, and thus in refusing to employ a Sikh refusing to remove his beard: *Panesar v. Nestle* [1980] I.C.R. 144, C.A. The European Convention of Human Rights article 9 is expressly subject to limitations prescribed by law and necessary in a democratic society in the interest of public health. Freedom of conscience in the Convention of the Protection of Human Rights and Fundamental Freedoms is subject to municipal legislation: *R. v. Greater London Council, ex parte Burgess* [1978] I.C.R. 991, D.C.

Education

The state education system has caused problems for minority groups. The attitude of non-association and exclusiveness cannot excuse Plymouth Brethren parents from the duty of securing school attendance. Every parent has the right to withdraw his child from the non-denominational religious instruction that still forms the only compulsory part of the curriculum. Roman Catholic parents have failed to establish the right to require the education authority to pay for a place in school of their choice: *Watt v. Kesteven C.C.* [1955] 1 Q.B. 408, C.A. Similarly the decision of the education authority to allocate Roman Catholic children to a Roman Catholic school and other children to another school cannot be challenged in the absence of ultra vires or unreasonableness: *Cummings v. Birkenhead* [1972] Ch. 12, C.A. If the education authority acts properly, i.e., within the law, there is no legal remedy for aggrieved parents: *Smith v. Inner London Education Authority* [1978] 1 All E.R. 411, C.A. But greater attention must now be paid to parental choice: Education Act 1980. Parents of Asian origin have objected to co-education and to some school activities such as mixed swimming. A Moslem father has been convicted for failing to send his daughter to a mixed school even though devout Moslem girls are not permitted by their religion to mix with the opposite sex other than close relatives during puberty: *R. v. Abdullah Patel*, Bradford Crown Court February 1975. The now nearly universal character of the state school, namely comprehensive, large, mixed or co-educational, and non-denominational, has exacerbated the problem by severely limiting if not eliminating choice and variety: *S.* [1978] Q.B. 120, C.A.– care order made in respect of child whose parents refused to send him to a comprehensive school.

Religious Toleration

An important feature of English legal history has been the struggle by religious minorities for the removal of disabilities, for emancipation, and for the recognition and protection of minority customs. Roman Catholics and the spouses of Roman Catholics have achieved equality before the law in every public office except eligibility for the Crown: Act of Settlement 1700 s.2. Lord Chancellor (Tenure of Office and Discharge of Ecclesiastical Functions) Act 1974—a Roman Catholic may be Lord Chancellor. Quakers have had special legislation in respect of the taking of the oath, see Oaths Act 1978 s.5. A number of scattered legislative statutes make special provisions for Jewish people, e.g., marriage laws, burial laws, appearance in court, taking the oath (Old Testament, Oaths Act 1978), and voting (Halsbury's Laws, fourth edition, Vol. 14, pp. 806–810, paras. 1423–1432) employment in factories (Halsbury's Laws, fourth edition, pp. 496–497, para. 759) and Sunday Trading Shops Act 1950 and meat and the slaughter of animals (Slaughterhouses Act 1974 s.40, Halsbury's Laws, third edition, Vol. 17, pp. 207–211, paras, 348–355). The principal feature of the special statutory provisions is the substitution of Saturday for Sunday as the Sabbath (see Fawcett 208). This is to relieve the Jewish trader from double closing, i.e., two days a week instead of one: *Thanet D.C. v. Ninedrive* [1978] 1 All E.R. 703; (1977) 76 L.G.R. 320; [1977] J.P.L. 718, Walton J.

A person whose religious observances prevent attendance at an inquiry on a particular day must inform the Minister before the date is fixed and appropriate arrangements must be made wherever reasonably practicable. If no such information is given, then a refusal on the part of the Minister to alter the date does not constitute a denial of natural justice or a breach of the European Convention on Human Rights: *Ostreicher v. Secretary for Environment* [1978] 1 W.L.R. 810, C.A. See also *Paris v. Council of European Communities* [1976] 2 C.M.L.R. 708; [1977] I.C.R. 284, E.C.J.

But the Moslem teacher is not entitled to time off during ordinary working hours with full pay even if religious observance is strictly enjoined by his religion, despite the Education Act 1944 (s.30) and the European Convention on Human Rights: *Ahmad v. Inner London Education Authority* [1978] Q.B. 36, C.A. See also *Ostreicher* (supra) and (1977) *New Society* 19 May 1977.

Lord Denning and Orr LJ took the view that the teacher was not entitled to break his contract by absenting himself during school hours. There is no statutory authority for such conduct, and the European Convention on Human Rights is not incorporated into municipal law, even if relevant. This teacher was apparently unique in that religious community in being unable to accommodate both his teaching duties and his religious practices. If he had been entitled to be absent, he would have thrown an unreasonable burden on his colleagues, standing in for him and religious toleration which constitutes a preference could arouse discontent and resentment. Either the teacher should not apply for a full time teaching job or he should negotiate a 4 1/2 day job at an appropriately reduced salary.

Scarman LJ dissenting took a very robust view:

> "When the section [Education Act 1944 s.30] was enacted, the negative approach to its interpretation was, no doubt, sufficient. But society has changed since 1944: so also has the legal background. Religions, such as Islam and Buddhism, have substantial followings among our people. Room has to be found for teachers and pupils of the new religions in the educational system, if discrimination is to be avoided. This calls not for a policy of the blind eye but for one of understanding. The system must be made sufficiently flexible to accommodate their beliefs and their observances: otherwise they will suffer discrimination—a consequence contrary to the spirit of s.30, whatever the letter of that law. The change in legal background is no less momentous. Since 1944 the United Kingdom has accepted international obligations designed to protect human rights and freedoms, and has enacted a series of statutes designed for the same purpose in certain critical areas of our society. These major statutes include the Trade Union and Labour Relations Act 1974, the Employment Protection Act 1975, the Sex Discrimination Act 1975, and the race relations legislation.
>
> They were enacted after the United Kingdom had ratified the European Convention on Human Rights . . . and in the light of our obligations under the Charter of the United Nations. Today, therefore, we have to construe and apply s.30 not against the background of the law and society of 1944 but in a multi-racial society which has accepted international obligations and enacted statutes designed to eliminate discrimination on grounds of race, religion, colour or sex. Further, it is no longer possible to argue that because the international treaty obligations of the United Kingdom do not become law unless enacted by Parliament our courts pay no regard to our international obligations. They pay very serious regard to them: in particular, they will interpret statutory language and apply common law principles, wherever possible, so as to reach a conclusion consistent with our international obligations: see *Saloman v. Customs and Excise Commissioners* [1967] 2 Q.B. 116 . . . and *Post Office v. Estuary Radio* [1968] 2 Q.B. 740."

The burden of the judgment of Scarman LJ is that society and the legal system must be flexible and adaptive otherwise discrimination will ensue. If Friday instead of Sunday or Saturday happens to be the religious day of a bona fide religious group then society and the legal system must accommodate them, as teachers or whatever it might be, without disadvantage.

The central policy issue in the case was how to reconcile the disadvantage and discrimination approach with the privilege and preference approach.

Religious discrimination is prohibited by the European Convention on Human Rights article 14. Religious discrimination per se does not fall within the Race Relations Act 1976, although the position is otherwise in Northern Ireland: Fair Employment (Northern Ireland) Act 1976.

The witness in court now has the free choice of the oath or the affirmation and he need give no reason for his choice: Oaths Act 1978.

Blasphemy is still a criminal offence, but limited to an attack upon the Christian religion only: *R. v. Lemon* [1979] A.C. 617. See also *The Times* July 15, 1977, a letter advocating extension by legislation to non-Christian religions.

Lord Scarman (658B-F) advocated extending the law to protect the religious beliefs and feelings of non-Christians. The offence is one of a group designed to safeguard the internal tranquility of the Kingdom. In an increasingly plural society such as that of modern Britain it is necessary not only to respect the differing religious beliefs, feelings and practices of all but also to protect them from scurrility, vilification, ridicule and contempt. When Macaulay was a legislator in India, he saw to it that the law protected the religious feelings of all, e.g., punishing a Christian polluting a mosque. In those days India was a plural society; today the United Kingdom is also.

The Welsh

Welsh may be used in Wales in court proceedings and for statutory documents and forms, and a company may be Welsh: Welsh Court Act 1942, Welsh Language Act 1967; Companies Act 1976 s.30 and Companies Act 1980.

European Convention on Human Rights

The European Convention on Human Rights 1953, Cmnd. 8969, has had a most benign influence. For example, as a result of the Convention in Norway the centuries-old prohibition upon Jesuits was removed. The Convention guarantees a fair trial (articles 5 and 6), freedom of thought, conscience and religion (article 9), non-interference in private and family life, except for reasons of national security, safety, prevention of crime, protection of health and morals (article 8), the right to marry and found a family, though subject to national laws (article 12), and the right to ensure education in conformity with parental religions and philosophical convictions (First Protocol article 2). The language problem in Belgium and sex education in Danish schools have come before the European Court, but no such case has emanated from Britain—the Northern Ireland case is only very indirectly a "minority" problem. In any event the European Convention on Human Rights, though ratified by the UK, has not yet been directly incorporated into municipal law, but it has undoubted repercussions.

The European Convention on Human Rights is not part of the municipal law of England, but it is proper to have regard to it and it is presumed that English municipal law will so far as possible be construed so as not to conflict with the Convention, and rules and regulations are presumed to be made in the context of the Convention. Article 8, respect for private and family life, and article 12, right to marry and to found a family, are frequently referred to, also articles 5 and 6, right to a fair trial, and article 9, religious freedom. *R. v. Secretary of State for Home Affairs, ex parte Phansopkar* [1976] Q.B. 606, C.A. (article 8, Scarman LJ 626); *R. v. Chief Immigration Officer , ex parte Bibi* [1976] 1 W.L.R.; 979, C.A. (article 8); *Malone v. Metropolitan Police Commissioner* (1979) Ch. 344 (article 8, telephone tapping); *Ahmad v. Inner London Education Authority* [1978] Q.B. 36, C.A. (article 9); *R. v. Greater London Council, ex parte Burgess* [1978] I.C.R. 991, D.C. (article 9). *Prais v. Council for the European Communities* [1977] I.C.R. 284, E.C.J. (article 9, Jewish person); *R. v. Secretary of State for Home Affairs, ex parte Bhajan Singh* [1976] Q.B. 198, C.A. (article 5, illegal immigration) and *R. v. Secretary of State for Home Affairs, ex parte Hosenball* [1977] 1. W.L.R. 766, C.A. (article 6).

The human rights movement might have considerable minority repercussions, though it is not principally motivated by such considerations.

Family Law

Marriage

England is exclusively monogamous. The only marriages that may lawfully take place in England are monogamous marriages (Matrimonial Causes Act 1973 s.11) whatever the nationality, domicile, residence, religion and culture of the parties. Persons domiciled in England may not enter into a lawful marriage anywhere unless it be monogamous (Matrimonial Causes Act 1973 s.11 (d)). This had led to one curious result, namely that an unmarried bona fide Moslem domiciled in England who goes to Pakistan or Bangladesh and there marries an unmarried girl, domiciled there, in conformity with local laws so as to be recognized there cannot obtain recognition of that marriage in England because it is potentially polygamous, even though the parties are bona fide monogamous and have every bona fide intention of so remaining. Nor can he bring her into England as his wife, so he will have grave difficulty in getting her in at all, except possibly in order to marry or remarry her in England. It is difficult to see any mischief justifying the rule (Poulter (1976) 25 I.C.L.Q. 503–507). Domicile as the operative and overriding factor is stretched too far. A personal law would be a far superior criterion to apply.

A possible justification may be the wish to strike at the "arranged marriage", still apparently very common in Moslem societies, both in Pakistan and Bangladesh and in England. The Moslem domiciled in England cannot readily marry a Pakistani or Bangladeshi village girl and bring her, or have her brought, into UK, yet one more authorized immigrant: Immigration Rules 1977. However, the Moslem domiciled in England may genuinely have difficulty in finding a wife in England because of sex imbalance in the population, and anyway he may prefer an uncorrupted girl to the girl corrupted by Western life.

Sebastian Poulter sums up the matter ((1976) 25 I.C.L.Q. 475, 507):

> "Polygamy, like divorce, should not be actively encouraged by the law. On the other hand, those who enter into marriages under a polygamous system should not be singled out for especially harsh treatment, particularly where their own individual marriages are in fact monogamous. Gone are the days when the English could be so certain of the moral superiority of their own way of life that it must be imposed on all comers, as a matter of law."

Polygamy

Polygamy is a good example of the ambivalence of English law although Sebastian Poulter has pointed out how the judges fostered a tolerance over the years. A, domiciled, and perhaps resident abroad, marries a lawful second wife, W2, abroad and brings her lawfully to England. He could not lawfully marry her in England, in any circumstances, illogically, even if domiciled and resident abroad: *Hashmi* [1972] Fam. 36. In England W2 is accepted and treated as a lawful wife. Thus A does not commit bigamy. Sexual intercourse by A with W1 and W2 does not constitute adultery nor in itself intolerable behaviour. The children of W2 by A are A's legitimate children. W2 is entitled to ordinary matrimonial relief, such as divorce and financial provision and property adjustment. W2 is a widow for the purposes of the law of succession, presumably sharing the widow's share with W1. Yet she is not recognized as a widow for the purposes of social security, only W1 or a de facto monogamous widow is recognized: National Insurance Act 1971 s.12, repealed Social Security Act 1973 s.100(2), Schedule 28, as being no longer necessary. It is argued that it would be unjust for a deceased who paid the normal social security contributions to derive double benefit by leaving two eligible widows. This argument is specious, because one man may have numerous children, be constantly in the care of the national health service, and live for many years in retirement, whereas another may be childless, never miss a day's work through illness, and die before retirement. That is the insurance principle, contribution according to means, benefit according to need. W2 will probably fall on to supplementary benefit anyway, so there may not be much in it financially.

English law has thus reached the position, subject to a few exceptions, that the actual or potential polygamous wife is recognized for all purposes as a lawful wife and is entitled to all the remedies of a lawful wife.

As it happens, polygamy is rapidly declining in popularity and incidence throughout the world and so the problem is diminishing. In England the social pressures militate against polygamy, the new generation born and brought up in England are absorbing and responding to indigenous monogamous culture, and it is believed though it is not capable of proof, that an actually polygamous applicant for permission to immigrate will not obtain permission: see also Hansard House of Commons Vol. 767, col. 1663, 4 July 1968.

If a person is bona fide polygamous then, it is submitted, he ought to be allowed to take a polygamous wife in England provided that he conforms to the law of the polygamous group to which he belongs, or abroad, provided that he conforms to the local laws. There is no longer any reason, if ever there was, for making English law the personal law of all persons domiciled in England. A personal law based upon personal religion or culture is far more acceptable in a multi-racial society.

The proper stance of English law to adopt is one of tolerance and understanding rather than one of indictment and criticism: Sebastian Poulter (1976) 25 I.C.L.Q. 465, 508.

Child Wife

A child wife (14) lawfully married abroad (Nigeria) may technically be made the subject of a care order in England but her status as a wife will be accepted in England: *Alhaji Mohammed v. Knott* [1969] 1 Q.B. 1 D.C. Logically the age of the child wife ought to be irrelevant, although it has been suggested, illogically, that some sort of arbitrary lower age limit should be drawn (Shyllon 138, Karsten). Marriage ought to constitute an alternative form of attaining majority.

Lord Parker LCJ showed a measure of tolerance:

> "When they say that 'a continuance of such an association, notwithstanding the marriage, would be repugnant to any decent-minded English man or woman', they are, I think, and can only be, considering the view of an English man or woman in relation to an English girl and our Western way of life. I cannot myself think that decent-minded English men or women, realising the way of life in which this girl was brought up, and this man for that matter, would inevitably say that this is repugnant. It is certainly natural for a girl to marry at that age. They develop sooner, and there is nothing abhorrent in their way of life for a girl of 13 to marry a man of 25.
>
> Incidentally it was not until 1929 that in [England] an age limit was put on marriage. Granted that this man may be said to be a bad lot, that he has done things in the past which perhaps nobody would approve of, it does not follow that this girl, happily married to this man, is under any moral danger by associating and living with him. For my part, as it seems to me, it could only be said that she was in moral danger if one was considering somebody brought up in and living in our way of life, and to hold that she is in moral danger in the circumstances of the case can only be arrived at, as it seems to me, by ignoring the way of life in which she was brought up, and her husband was brought up."

If he constantly assaulted her or deserted her or introduced her to drugs that would be different. Nonetheless it is submitted that a girl/woman who is lawfully a married woman ought for all purposes to be recognized as such and ipso facto taken right out of the scope of child legislation.

Divorce

The only divorce that is permitted in the UK is monogamous or indigenous divorce. For example, the talaq divorce purported to be made in UK is not recognized in UK (Matrimonial Causes Act 1973 s.16); *R. v. Registrar General of Births, Deaths and Marriages, ex parte Minhas* (1977) Q.B. 1, D.C. One reason was that it was non-judicial, somewhat ironic in view of the breakdown principle in English law and the special procedure now almost universal in England. The talaq divorce lawfully obtained abroad in the country of domicile, residence or nationality is recognized in the UK.

When personal law provides for talaq divorce, then that should be possible in UK, provided the proper talaq procedure is followed. Unilateral divorce based on breakdown is in conformity with current indigenous law and practice.

A respondent spouse may resist the unilateral five year separation divorce on the grounds of grave financial or other hardship (Matrimonial Causes Act 1973 s.5 (1)) although they are difficult if not impossible to establish. However, theoretically at least, social isolation or degradation in India, *Banik* [1973] 1 W.L.R. 860, or) social stigma or ostracism or ostracization in India or Sicily: *Parghi* (1973) 117 S.J. 582; *Grenfell* [1978] Fam. 128, C.A.; *Rukat* [1975] Fam. 63, may constitute such hardship, whether it be in England or elsewhere.

When it comes to property adjustment orders, it has been submitted (Poulter) that as the court is statutorily required to have regard to all the circumstances (Matrimonial Causes Act 1973 ss.23–25), the cultural, religious and family values of the parties, whether Moslem or Jewish or whatever it might be, should be taken into account, e.g., deferred dower [subject presumably to the overriding residual power of the court to do what it thought right for the wife and children]. This is an attractive submission, although not supported so far by judicial approval.

Custody

In disputed custody cases the court must take the welfare of the child as the first and paramount consideration (Guardianship of Minors Act 1971 s.1; see also Child Care Act 1980 s.18, similar duty upon local authority, and Adoption Act 1976 s.6, similar duty in adoption), so that minority customs are a factor but not an overriding factor. The problems have usually arisen in mixed marriages, using mixed in a very wide sense, each parent seeking custody in order that the child shall be brought up in his or her culture. *J. v. C.* [1970] A.C. 668, Spanish boy (natural parents versus foster parents); *Kernot* [1965] Ch. 217, Italy; *L.* [1974] 1 W.L.R. 250, Germany; *O.* [1977] 3 W.L.R. 725, C.A.; *T.* [1969] 1 W.L.R. 1608, Switzerland; *Nash* [1973] 2 All E.R. 704, South African; *Jussa* [1972] 1 W.L.R. 881, Indian Moslem; *C.(A)* [1966] 1 W.L.R. 415, C.A. Moslem Indian child to stay with local authority; *O.*[1962] 1 W.L.R. 724, C.A.; Sudan; B. [1977] C.L.Y. 1964, African; *M.* [1967] 1 W.L.R. 1479 Catholic versus Protestant; *H.* [1978] 2 W.L.R. 608, C.A. and *Hewison* (1977) 7 Family Law 207, C.A. Exclusive Brethren.

A Jehovah's Witness mother lost custody because the child would be isolated, feel different from other children, not be able to celebrate Christmas, and not have the benefits of inoculation: *Buckley* (1973) 3

Family Law 106, C.A. See also *Hewison* (supra). Finance was also an element as it happened.

In this sensitive area the judges adopt a very pragmatic and cautious approach, deciding each case on its individual merits. Relevant factors likely to be given weight include the age of the child, the wishes of the child, psychological health, past history, parental conduct, expectations, economic factors, and so on: *Hutchinson* (1978) 8 Family Law 140, D.C. Whenever possible the case will not be decided directly upon religion or race or similar matter. The African custom of fostering out children and then claiming them back when they are nearly grown up has not been at all favourably received by the judges, especially if it is proposed to go to Africa. The judges have taken the view that the longer the fostering continues the deeper grow the roots in the foster family and environment, and the child who has lived his childhood in England with foster parents has become more of an Englishman, albeit a black Englishman, than an African who should go to Africa: *B* (1977) C.L.Y. 1964, D.V. *A* (1978) 8 Family Law 247.

For access see *Rashid* (1979) 9 Family Law 118, C.A.

Identification

If the law does permit the citizen to have his own special personal law, then the problem of identification arises, who is and who is not eligible or entitled. If the special personal law is seen as a privilege or advantage, e.g., polygamy or exemption from wearing a crash helmet, then people might claim to belong to the appropriate group or join the appropriate group in order to claim the benefit. Usually identification will not present any difficulties, especially in the case of immigrants and persons, from, or connected with overseas, cultures and their communities. In the event of difficulty no doubt recourse can be made to the court or a tribunal, as with disputed cases of conscientious objectors and ministers of religion in wartime.

However, identification in the sense of marking out a minority person by reference to race or colour or religion is now generally prohibited by law as unlawful discrimination. Advertizement, selection for employment, selection for promotion, all must avoid any element of discrimination. Apparently the student accommodation officer ought not to make a secret mark in his files indicating that a particular landlady would refuse a black student and might humiliate him on the doorstep, a situation to be avoided even though the attitude and conduct of the landlady might be reprehensible or possibly illegal. The 1971 census wanted to know the country of birth of parents and that information plus your name plus your address might give a fair indication, to any interested, about your colour and origin and community. The 1981 census dropped the origins question. The old quota principle in employment has now gone, an employer can no longer say that as he already has a large number or a large proportion of coloured employees he can confine new recruits to whites because he has "done his share": Race Relations Act 1976. At ports and airports it is still the normal practice for UK nationals and aliens to be required to pass through different immigration control doors, though the reason is said to be administrative convenience and not discrimination.

Conclusion

Everybody agrees that the fundamental concepts of the dignity of man and equality before the law require the proscription of discrimination in public matters; although the extent to which criminal law and quasi-criminal law is suitable for this purpose is a matter for argument. The concept of minimum universal standards of public law applicable to everybody seems to be generally accepted. What society has not yet thought through and resolved as a matter of moral and ethical and social policy is whether the pressure, social and legal, is to be towards conformity or diversity. Conformity has many advantages: it represents a single standard, is adhered to by the majority, the indigenous majority, is easily identified and followed and enforced, reduces the feeling of being different, especially amongst young people, cohesive not fragmental, centripetal not centrifugal, reduces any sense of injustice which the majority may feel if the minority enjoys any apparent "privilege", and prevents spurious "conversions" of indigenous persons in order to obtain minority benefits, e.g., polygamy or crash helmet exemption. But there are disadvantages: immigrant cultures have many facets capable of enriching national life generally. Conformity to a new culture comes hard to older people. Respect for the individual and his personal customs is an integral part of human rights. Diversity may appear to many to be a desirable feature of what otherwise might become a dull, drab conformist society. Discrimination (real or imagined) arising from the requirement to conform must be balanced against privilege (real or imagined) arising from being excused from the requirement to conform. But the present policy of drift, of response to random pressures, cannot be right. Society should make up its mind what it wishes to do in respect of the plural dimension.

Note

1. I am most grateful for help from my friend and colleague Sebastian Poulter, expert on these things, although he is not to be identified with the text.

Bibliography

Foreign customs and English criminal law Sebastian Poulter (1975) 24, L.C.L.Q, 136—with sources.
Immigration and the criminal courts, F.O. Shyllon (1971) 34 M.L.R., 135.
Polygamy and social policy, T.C. Hartley (1969) 32 M.L.R., 155—excellent article, but pre-dating the 1972 Act.
Polygamy, Law Commission Law Com. 42, 1970.
Polygamy and matrimonial relief, T.K. Rarnshaw and P.J. Pace (1972) 122, N.L.J., 705.
Immigrants' marriages [Matrimonial Proceedings (Polygamous Marriages) Act 1972], Stephen Cretney (1972) 116 S.J., 654.
Race Relations: The new law, Ian Macdonald, Butterworths, 1977.
The new Race Relations Act 1976, Geoffrey Bindman (1977) 74 L.S.G.,33.
Race Relations Act 1976, Alec Samuels (1977) 121 S.J., 127.
Law and racial discrimination, Geoffrey Bindman (1976) 3 British Journal Law and Society, 110.
Excusable loss of self-control in homicide, Alec Samuels (1971) 34 M.L.R., 163—with bibliography.
What colour is the reasonable man? Colin Howard [1961] Crim. L.R. 41.
The death penalty for provocation? Colin Howard [1978] Crim. L.R., 662–672.
Offences against the person, Fourteenth Report of the Criminal Law Revision Committee, 1980, Cmnd. 7844. Comment by Sidney Prevezer [1980] Crim. L.R. 535–539.
Child marriages, Ian Karsten (1969) 32 M.L.R. 215—note on *Alhaji Mohammed v. Knott* [1969] 1 Q.B., 1 D.C.
The new law of employment, Norman Selwyn, Butterworths, 1976.
European Convention on Human Rights.
Universal Declaration of Human Rights 1948.
Sociology of law, editor Vilhem Auber, Penguin.
The rights of Englishmen: The G.L.C's inverted racism Alfred Sherman (1974) 138 L.G.R., 378.
The explosive silence: Immigration and national identity, Alfred Sherman (1975) 139 L.G.R., 189.
The developing European law of Human Rights, Clovis Morrison, Sijthoff, Leiden, 1967.
The application of the European Convention on Human Rights, J.E.S. Fawcett, Oxford, 1969.
The European Convention on Human Rights, Francis Jacobs, Oxford, 1975.

The European Convention on Human Rights: The text of a British Bill of Rights? J. Jaconelli [1976] P.L., 226.
A Bill of Rights? Michael Zander, Barry Rose, 1975.
Custody: The principles, Alec Samuels (1974) 4 Family Law, 141.
Maintenance and Custody Orders in the Magistrates' Courts, Brian Harris (1976)
Talaq divorces, Sebastian Poulter (1977) 127, N.L.J. 7.
Hyde v. Hyde: A reappraisal, Sebastian Poulter (1976) 25 I.C.L.Q., 475, especially 503–508, most excellent article.
Oaths of Hindu, Sikh and Mohammedan witnesses (1972) 136 J.P.N., 831.
Wardship, Alec Samuels (1978) 8 Family Law, 237.
The closed shop case, P.J.Duffy (1980) 5 Human Rights Review, 205–207.
The closed shop cases before the European Court of Human Rights, P. Duffy (1980) 130 N.L.J., 922.
Employment Act 1980, D. Newell (1980) 124 S.J., 635.
Racial discrimination: Discovery, Ian Macdonald (1979) 129 N.L.J., 1143.
The grounds of discrimination under the Race Relations Act 1976 in the United Kingdom, L. Lustgarten (1979) 28 I.C.L.Q., 221.
Religious considerations: Custody and adoption, R. Terrell (1979) 9 Family Law 198–200.
Transracial adoptions, Alec Samuels (1980) 10, Family Law.
European Convention on Human Rights, Jaconelli, 1980.

ALISON DUNDES RENTELN

Culture and Culpability: A Study of Contrasts

Having considered folk law in conflict in England, we shall now examine similar cases in the United States. In the following essay by one of the editors of this volume, the emphasis is on whether or not the culture of the minority group members should be taken into account in the enforcement of criminal law. In brief, do cultural differences constitute a legitimate defense for an individual accused of committing a crime in the larger society? The so-called "cultural defense" viewpoint has both advocates and critics. The conceptual difficulties of this viewpoint are the subject of the paper.

For other discussions of the "cultural defense," see Bernard L. Diamond, "Social and Cultural Factors as a Diminished Capacity Defense in Criminal Law," Bulletin of the American Academy of Psychiatry and the Law *6 (1978), 195–208; Alan Watson, "The Justice of the U.S. Constitution,"* International Journal of Moral and Social Studies *1 (1986), 21–30; Malek-Mithra Sheybani, "Cultural Defense: One Person's Culture is Another's Crime,"* Loyola of Los Angeles International and Comparative Law Journal *9 (1987), 751–783; Carolyn Choi, "Application of a Cultural Defense in Criminal Proceedings,"* UCLA Pacific Basin Law Journal *8 (1990), 80–90; Anh Lam, "Culture as a Defense: Preventing Judicial Bias against Asians and Pacific Islanders,"* UCLA Asian American & Pacific Islands Law Journal *1 (1993), 49–68; and Paul J. Magnarella, "Justice in a Culturally Pluralistic Society: The Cultural Defense on Trial,"* Journal of Ethnic Studies *19 (1991), 65–84. For an analysis of a highly publicized cultural defense case in the United States, see Deborah Woo, "The People v. Fumiko Kimura: But Which People?* International Journal of the Sociology of Law *17 (1989), 403–428.*

The author is a member of the department of Political Science at the University of Southern California and has written International Human Rights: Universalism Versus Relativism *(Newbury Park, California: Sage Publications, 1990). Renteln has also written: "A Justification of the Cultural Defense as Partial Excuse,"* Southern California Review of Law and Women's Studies

Reprinted from the *Beverly Hills Bar Journal*, 22, no. 1 (Winter 1987–1988), 17–27, with permission.

2 (1993), and "Is the Cultural Defense Detrimental to the Health of Children?" Law and Anthropology 7 *(1994).*

In a pluralistic society it is common to encounter "culture conflict." When new citizens arrive, they bring with them legal standards which may differ significantly from those of their new homeland. The question which inevitably arises is whether or not the new citizens should be held criminally liable for conduct which violates American law. Is it justifiable to punish a person in the United States for engaging in activities which were customary in his or her country of origin? This kind of situation in which multiple legal systems are to be found is called legal pluralism. It is the conflict among the various systems that has given rise to a theory of criminal responsibility known as the cultural defense.

This article concentrates on some of the conceptual problems associated with the cultural defense. In particular I will take the view that: (1) the ideology of cultural pluralism does not require the adoption of the cultural defense, (2) mechanisms already exist within the American legal system which can take culture into account, and (3) the consequences of utilizing the cultural defense would be highly undesirable. The cultural defense will be discussed in the context of the United States and of other countries by examining selected cases. Some analysis of the problems in general will be made, paying attention to the distinction between immigrants and indigenous peoples. Although there are many types of crimes for which the cultural defense might be used, such as polygamy in nations that permit only monogamy, the analysis below will focus primarily on cases involving homicide. While cultural sensitivity is arguably an admirable posture, pluralism (actually relativism) does not require the rejection of one's own legal standards. Ultimately, it appears that the cultural defense is a dangerous and unnecessary doctrine.

United States Cases—Immigrants

Two factors appear to be primarily responsible for the recent (1980s) resurgence of interest in the cultural defense. The first is the unusually large influx of (mainly Southeast) Asians into the United States, especially Southern California. The second is the highly publicized case of *People v. Kimura.*[1] This case illustrates not only the context in which the cultural defense has been considered as a possible device for denying responsibility for criminal action but also the way in which American commentators have misinterpreted cultural differences.

Fumiko Kimura discovered that her husband had deceived her by keeping a mistress and had thus shamed the family. On January 29, 1985, she attempted to commit *oyako-shinju*, the Japanese custom of parent-child suicide. She took her two children, a daughter, Yuri, six months old, and her son Kazutaka, four years old, on a bus ride from their Los Angeles home to the beach in Santa Monica. Then, carrying Yuri and leading Kazutaka by the hand, she walked into the ocean. This was a culturally accepted course of action in the Japanese tradition, not to leave the children behind to bear the shame alone. Although onlookers on the shore managed to rescue Kimura, her two children died.

The district attorney charged Kimura with first degree murder in their deaths. Four thousand members of the Los Angeles Japanese-American community signed a petition stating that her act would not be treated as murder in Japan and urging officials to apply modern Japanese law. This would mean charging her with involuntary manslaughter at most. The district attorney refused the request, however, and left a first degree murder charge in place which could have brought the death penalty. The district attorney rejected the use of Japanese law but indicated that Kimura's background could, in fact, be taken into account in determining her mental state at the time of the incident. The crime itself could not be mitigated by legal or cultural standards from another country.

The issue was whether or not a person from another culture should be judged according to standards other than those in force in the United States. Kimura's attorney evidently considered but chose not to use the cultural defense. Interestingly, he relied instead on testimony from six psychiatrists to show that Kimura was "ill" and "mentally deranged," and therefore lacked the intent necessary for first degree murder because the element of malice was absent. A plea bargain ultimately reduced the charge to voluntary manslaughter, and Kimura received five years probation, intensive psychiatric treatment and one year in the country jail (with credit for time already served). It is hard to say whether it was culture or (attributed) insanity which helped change her fate.

Several observations are in order. First, Kimura's act is not legally acceptable in Japan. It is simply more culturally acceptable. Even in Japan, ritual parent-child suicide is still a crime. The culture conflict here is not based on an act which is entirely legitimate in country A but illegal in country B. Rather, the conflict is over the proportionality, *i.e.*, what is the appropriate punishment which corresponds to the crime. Second, even though the defense attorney did not explicitly invoke the cultural defense, the fact that there was a plea bargain suggests that culture was taken into account to some extent. Third, the legal system, as exemplified in this case, treats the logic of another culture as analogous to insanity. Kimura was ordered to undergo intensive psychiatric counseling. In spite of the absence of a formal cultural defense, Kimura's cultural background was influential in determining the disposition of her case. She was treated with compassion though as if mentally disturbed. Finally, Kimura raises another issue worthy of consideration. For what period of time would a "new" citizen be permitted to avail herself of the cultural defense? Would it be necessary to establish a "presumption" of assimilation after a specified period of time elapsed? Kimura herself had lived in the United States for nine years but had not become fully "Americanized" because she had remained extremely isolated.

United States Cases—Refugees

Refugees arriving in the United States from other countries have had their share of legal problems. In some instances they commit acts that are not considered crimes in their native lands but which violate American law.

In the last several years almost thirty thousand Hmong, a people from Laos, have settled in the area of Fresno, California. Some of their traditions involve activities which are illegal here such as polygamy and the use of opium. The Hmong also have a habit of butchering pigs in their backyards in violation of local ordinances. It seems that, among other things, the pigs' squealing disturbs the neighbors.

A more serious matter concerns a practice called *zij poj niam* which, loosely translated, means marriage by capture. *People v. Moua*[2] centered on the interpretation of the traditional courtship ritual among the Hmong. According to custom, there is an exchange of gifts between the man and the woman who are to be married. It is expected that the man will exercise his right to abduct his chosen bride and then consummate the marriage at his family's home. Custom requires that the woman display resistance by weeping and moaning and declaring that she is not ready. Otherwise, she will not appear virtuous enough. The man is supposed to show force or else he will not appear strong enough. After the event, the woman is viewed as "unmarriageable" by other Hmong men.

In this case Kong Moua followed custom but his "wife," Xeng Xiong, an "Americanized" nineteen year-old, rejected tradition and called the police. Consequently, Moua was charged with kidnapping and rape but these charges were dropped when he agreed to plead guilty to a misdemeanor charge of false imprisonment. After hearing testimony about traditional Laotian marriage rituals and after reviewing a doctoral dissertation on the subject, the judge reduced the sentence for Moua from 180 days to 90 days.[3] Some have claimed that the judge implicitly recognized the cultural defense.[4]

Even though the cultural defense was not officially used, it appears that culture played a role in this case. The rule in American law is that if a reasonable, good faith belief in the woman's consent was evident, the act would not constitute rape. This means that although the conduct may not be excused because it is motivated by cultural tradition, it is possible that the motivation may be relevant in establishing the defendant's state of mind.[5] Culture served not to absolve Moua of responsibility altogether but to mitigate the sentence, as in *Kimura.*

We can see the undeniable influence of acculturation and the power of moral injunction in another case, also called *People v. Moua.*[6] In this case a Hmong man by the name of Tou Moua killed his wife when he learned that she planned to take a job working for another man. Evidently, this is an act tantamount to adultery in Hmong culture. Moua's defense attorney explained that in his culture a wife's adultery is punishable by death and that it was "culturally demanded that he [Moua] execute justice, even if it meant his own personal pain and personal loss to do so.[7] Moua's attorney argued for a mitigation of the sentence because of the cultural circumstances involved. The sentencing judge denied the request, however, and sentenced the defendant to eight years in prison.

Belief/Action Distinction

While the American ideology of cultural tolerance has instructed citizens to respect different ways of life, there is a longstanding commitment in the American legal system to a belief/action distinction. As early as 1879 in *Reynolds v. U.S.*[8] the Supreme Court refused to overturn a conviction for bigamy where this was mandated by the defendant's religious beliefs. The court held that to allow such an excuse of illegal conduct would be:

> . . . to make the professed doctrines of religious belief superior to the law of the land, and in effect to permit every citizen to become a law unto himself. Government could exist only in name under such circumstances.[9]

Not only have Mormons been denied the right to have polygamous marriages, but Jehovah's Witnesses have been compelled by the law to have blood transfusions.[10] In the case of *In re Application of Jamaica Hospital*[11] the court ordered a competent adult woman who was eighteen weeks pregnant and suffering from internal bleeding to accept blood transfusions for the sake of her fetus. Because she was a Jehovah's Witness, a religious group which believes that the Scriptures forbid "drinking blood" and that receiving a blood transfusion is the equivalent of "drinking blood," she refused on religious grounds. But the court held: "The state has a highly significant interest in protecting the life of a mid-term fetus, which outweighs the patient's right to refuse a blood transfusion on religious grounds."[12]

The law will reject or require actions based on beliefs if they lead to harming others. In the case just mentioned the court was willing to intervene when the one at risk was a pre-viable fetus. In another case a court ordered a woman to undergo child-birth by Cesarean section when she refused on religious grounds.[13] The physician had predicted that a vaginal delivery would have a 99% risk of the infant dying and a 50% chance for the mother. After the court order was issued, she fled and gave birth to a healthy child a few days later, uneventfully without intervention.[14]

Snake-handling for religious purposes has also been denied by the courts.[15] In *Swann v. Pack*,[16] for example, the Supreme Court of Tennessee held that the handling of dangerous and poisonous snakes in a crowded church (with virtually no safeguards and with children roaming around unattended and with handlers in trances) meant that the Pastor had, in fact, committed a public nuisance. The Court remanded the case so that the trial court could enter an injunction perpetually enjoining and restraining all parties from handling snakes. Although the Court recognized that the decision would impose stringent limitations on a religious practice, it concluded that "paramount considerations of public policy" precluded less stringent solutions.[17]

The courts have been unwilling to allow drug use for religious rites.[18] The freedom to believe is virtually absolute whereas the freedom to act is not. This distinction is central to the analysis of the cultural defense. Cultural pluralism encourages us to recognize the existence of other value-systems but does not force us to relinquish our own standards for judging action. Even where an action is arguably an integral part of the belief system, the legal system has consistently acted to sustain its own legitimacy.

Ignorance of the Law Is No Excuse

Some of the opponents of the cultural defense base their argument on the traditional maxim—ignorance of the law—the mistaken belief that one's conduct is lawful—is no excuse for criminal behavior. They maintain that the court should not create an exception to this rule because of cultural differences. The notion that the cultural defense depends on ignorance suggests that there is a lack of understanding as to the basic premise of the defense. The cultural defense does not presuppose ignorance of the law. Even if the defendants are aware of American legal standards, their cultural conditioning is so powerful that they cannot discard their own standards in favor of American ones. Enculturation shapes their perceptions to such an extent that they cannot readily embrace those of another culture.

In the cases already discussed, it was apparent that the lawyers were not arguing on the basis of ignorance. The prosecutors and judges were not asked to excuse the defendants because they did not comprehend that their actions were considered criminal in the eyes of Americans. The point of the cultural defense is to recognize that the power of enculturation makes it exceedingly difficult for someone from another culture to make his conduct conform to standards of the dominant American culture. The underlying notion is that a person's criminal behavior should be judged according to the legal standards of his or her culture.

Governmental Responsibility

Since the government arranged to bring refugees to the United States, one could advance the argument that the government is responsible for ensuring that new citizens become familiar with particularly important American laws. When it becomes known that certain communities, *e.g.*, the Hmong engage in activities which are not compatible with American legal standards, then there is all the more reason to expect the government to establish some form of educational programs. Even though the cultural defense does not depend on ignorance, in some instances ignorance may be a factor. Moreover, even where refugees are cognizant of American crimes, they may not be as fully aware of the punishments which they face for violation. When the American government brings a large refugee population within its borders, it bears some measure of responsibility for providing information about American customs and laws.

In some cases the duty to inform may turn out to be problematic. There may not be any words or concepts in the language of the new group which can capture the idea of the American crime. And besides technical difficulties the government has to contend with the negative symbolic dimensions, specifically of having Americans trying to indoctrinate newly arrived citizens. Despite these problems, however, the government can obviate the need for the cultural defense to some extent by ensuring knowledge of both crimes and punishments.

United States Cases—Native Americans

Since immigrants and refugees make a conscious decision to move to a new country, one might argue that they should adhere to the legal standards of the new country. But even if one decides that these groups ought to be bound by American law, this does not necessarily mean that indigenous peoples who controlled the territory first should have to surrender to the colonial or dominant legal regime.

That there are major conceptual differences in traditional Native and modern American legal ideals is known.[19] In fact, Native Americans have experienced an unusual legal status, *i.e.*, semi-sovereign status. Federal law has allowed Native American societies some limited rights of self-government but has retained control insofar as violent crimes are concerned (18 U.S.C. 1153). For the most part state courts have jurisdiction unless a Native American commits a proscribed act on Native American land in which case the federal courts have jurisdiction.

There are numerous cases in which the conduct of Native Americans has been judicially evaluated, and in some of them courts have been willing to take culture into account. For example, the case of *United States v. Whaley*[20] in 1888 makes this clear. The defendants were all Native Americans charged with the murder of Juan Baptista, also a Native American. Baptista was a doctor but not a very good doctor. In fact, he was so unsuccessful that the members of the tribe were convinced that he had been systematically poisoning his patients. All of his patients, approximately twenty, had died.

Finally, Hunter Jim, who was extremely popular within the tribe, fell ill and had to be treated by the doctor. The members of the tribe decided to hold a council at which time they informed the doctor that if Hunter Jim died, they would kill him. Hunter Jim died, and so the four defendants were appointed by the council to carry out its determination. They shot the doctor the following morning.

The court decided that the law did apply to Native Americans (which was somewhat in question) but felt that the defendants had not committed murder because malice was absent, an essential element for the crime of murder. Though the offense if committed by a "white man" would certainly have been murder, the court said that in view of the "Indian nature," customs, superstition, and ignorance, they had not committed murder. The prosecutor did not press for a murder charge but for manslaughter. The judge decided that justice should be tempered with mercy and imposed a sentence of five years of imprisonment for each as well as a one dollar fine.

A 1985 Oregon case raises a slightly different set of issues because the murder did not involve only Native Americans. In *State v. Butler*[21] three members of the Siletz tribe were accused of murdering a man who was caught desecrating Native American burial grounds. It was alleged that when they found him digging up Native American artifacts to sell in local antique shops, they smashed his fingers and cut his throat as punishment. The presumption seems to be that this was the culturally determined proportionality, but this is not made clear in what has been written about the case.

Defense counsel stated that he would not use the cultural defense because he did not think it would be fruitful. Instead he intended to show that they did not commit the act charged. But some of the Native Americans in the area felt that the acts committed against the grave-robber could be regarded as justifiable acts of war or self-defense. In the end it appeared that all three defendants were acquitted based on insufficient evidence, rather than cultural considerations. Although the judge did not want the case to center on the culture conflict, he did allow a member of the Siletz tribe to explain their religious convictions concerning burial traditions.[22]

A Principle

The central question is: what principle should govern culture conflict? There are two choices: (1) Might makes right—meaning that the dominant legal system controls or (2) Who arrived first—meaning that the indigenous peoples ought, at the very least, to be permitted to retain control over their own matters. Since it is admittedly quite unrealistic to expect colonial regimes or their descendants to relinquish control because the second principle is determined to be correct, it is possible that the cultural defense ought to function for indigenous groups. Perhaps there should be some guarantee that culture will be considered to mitigate sentences. Since immigrants have come voluntarily to the United States, they should be educated about American law and expected to abide by it. Indigenous peoples, however, made no such choice and should, in theory, have the right to handle legal matters within their own system. When it is necessary for them to enter American courts, culture should probably be taken into account in mitigating sentences.

The Cultural Defense in Other Countries

Killings based on a belief in the supernatural are found across the globe and have been documented in such places as Colombia, Fiji, Papua New Guinea, South Africa as well as in various countries in Africa.[23] But where defenses are tried in such cases, they generally fail. For example, a number of cases involving sorcery killings have arisen in Papua New Guinea and defenses of all kinds are rejected because the courts take an extremely inflexible view of such killings.[24] In Africa there are also many cases in which the courts rigidly apply common law doctrines in witchcraft, juju, and other supernatural cases despite widespread belief in these practices. One legal scholar attests to the depth of commitment to the beliefs, even among the educated and Westernized. Aremu found in one of his criminal law classes in Nigeria that more than 90% of the students (aged 20 and older) believed strongly in witchcraft. Nevertheless, the (formerly colonial) courts in their administration of criminal justice refuse to recognize the supernatural to the dismay of some African legal scholars:

> This attitude, apart from being patently unjust to the accused who had killed under the influence of such forces, also failed to take into consideration prevailing views on criminal law and culture conflicts . . .[25]

It seems that these scholars favor cultural defense because it represents the only realistic possibility for invoking traditional norms. One wonders whether they would support the reinstitution of traditional courts.

The device which the courts have employed to avoid any consideration of culture is the so-called reasonable man standard. Because they rely on an "objective" version of it, they simply define the state of mind of the person (who killed to defend himself against witchcraft) as unreasonable. For instance, in the Nigerian case of *Gadam v. R.*[26] (1954) the Court held that "though prevalent, such a belief is unreasonable, being fraught as it is with such terrible results." In this case the defendant's wife had a miscarriage and became mortally ill. The man attributed this unhappy turn of events to two women. He struck one of them on the head with a hoe-handle in the belief that by so doing he would destroy the spell cast over his wife. The woman whom he hit died, and he was soon convicted of murder, which was affirmed on appeal. Because the belief was considered to be "unreasonable" by the court in its consequentialist reasoning, he was held responsible.

Although the courts will not entertain a cultural defense, they recognize how pervasive supernatural beliefs are. Oddly enough, this undermines attempts to use the insanity defense as can be seen in the Kenyan case of *Philip Muswi v. R.*[27] (1956). The defendant had been having trouble with his first wife after he took a second one. He believed that his first wife was practicing witchcraft against him. In fact, she was trying to alienate their children from him. When she took away their young son from his home, he became so furious that he killed her.

At the trial he testified that he did not know what he was doing and that it was not even until the next day that he remembered having killed his wife. The insanity defense was not persuasive because a belief in witchcraft does not prove insanity where it is so common:

> Even if the defendant believed he was justified in killing his wife because she was practicing witchcraft, there is again no evidence that such belief arose from any mental defect; it is a belief sometimes held by entirely sane Africans. The question whether the appellant's act was or was not contrary to tribal law is irrelevant.[28]

The defendant in such a court finds himself in a dilemma: there is no cultural defense because a belief in the supernatural is not reasonable; but it is not unreasonable enough to warrant the insanity defense.

In some places courts have been willing to mitigate sentences on the basis of culture in witchcraft cases. For instance, in March 1985 in Oakland, California, an Ethiopian man, Hagos Gebreamlak, was accused of attempting to kill a woman whom he claimed had placed a spell over him.[29] There were suggestions that the shooting had followed a lovers' quarrel. At the trial the public defender relied on the defense that beliefs concerning the bouda, voodoo and spells could arise from the man's background. Over strenuous objections from the prosecution, the judge allowed the defense to call an anthropologist as a witness to testify on Ethiopian customs. A psychologist also testified that the man was depressed and under considerable stress. The jury found the defendant not guilty of attempted murder but convicted him of a lesser charge, assault with a deadly weapon. It may be that the jury was more sympathetic to him because he did not actually kill the woman at whom he fired.

The degree to which cultural beliefs are accepted varies considerably. One way to anticipate whether or not culture will be considered is to ascertain what kind of reasonable man standard is used. Where the standard is an "objective" one, cultural beliefs are treated as irrelevant. But where it is "subjective," culture is taken into account. In the Enga Jury case in Papua New Guinea two village surgeons were charged with manslaughter after they operated on an ailing man with bamboo knives who then died. At first they were acquitted because no local Enga jury would have thought they had acted with reckless disregard for human life. But on appeal the court relied on an "objective" standard:

> It is sufficient, in my opinion, to state that the reasonable man is for the purposes of this case to be presumed to be one whose state of knowledge and prudence is such that appreciates the difference in training and skill

> between the qualified doctor and "the village surgeon" without any medical qualification.[30]

In the case of *R. v. Noboi-Bosai* (1971–1972)[31] a "subjective" reasonable man standard was used. Here the accused were charged with improperly or indecently interfering with a corpse. They cooked and ate parts of the body from another village. The judge explicitly applied a standard which was based on the "reasonable primitive Gabusi villager of Daldalibi and Yulabi in early 1971." He concluded that eating the body of the deceased villager was "neither improper nor indecent behavior on their part, being normal and reasonable behavior on their part." For the most part the "objective" standard convicts whereas the "subjective" one will acquit or at least mitigate the sentence.

Westerners in Asian Courts

Two Australians were convicted of drug trafficking in Malaysia. They received the death penalty and were executed.[32] Since the death penalty was approved in 1975 and made mandatory in 1983, 36 men and women have been hanged in Malaysia for the offense of drug trafficking. Although some foreigners were hanged, all were Asians. More than 70 others have been sentenced to death, some of whom are foreigners including some Westerners.

Capital punishment remains the norm in Asia. Both Thailand and Singapore also provide for the death penalty for drug offenses. These countries are trying to cope with the severe drug problems they experience because they are geographically near the "Golden Triangle," famous for the growth of heroin. One estimate of the number of narcotics addicts in Malaysia was 500,000 of the total 15 million population. Should one expect Malaysian courts to use Australian or Western guidelines in sentencing?

Analysis

Most of the debate about the cultural defense takes place in the language of pluralism.[33] The language tends to obscure the real issues underlying culture conflict, issues which are most appropriately addressed in the framework of relativism. Pluralism simply means that a given society is composed of various groups with different mores. The concept of relativism, on the other hand, focuses less on the structural relationship and more on the psychological disposition of individuals within the group. Relativism holds that each person perceives reality in accordance with inculcated standards that have been uncritically accepted and may be unconscious. It is not simply the existence of different groups which gives rise to culture conflict. Rather, it is the power of acculturation which leads each group to perceive reality according to internal standards.

Many of those who see relativism as the issue fail to understand what acceptance of the theory does and does not require. In particular, many anthropologists, philosophers, and social scientists erroneously believe that relativism logically entails tolerance. They cast the theory of relativism as a value or prescriptive theory, which it is not. Unfortunately, this has caused great difficulty for the theory as a whole and for those who mistakenly believe that, by accepting the theory of relativism, they are automatically committed to endorsing the cultural defense.

Relativism is actually a descriptive theory and not connected to any particular value:

> . . . the two parts of the doctrine are not logically or necessarily interdependent. The first part says that people are brought up to see the value in things that their local experience has suggested. The second part says that we should respect all cultures. But there is no true "therefore" between these two parts. It cannot be proved from the proposition that all values are relative, that we ought to respect all systems of values. We might just as well hate them all.[34]

In essence, relativism asks us to acknowledge that there are different ways of looking at the world: but taking a relativist approach certainly does not require us to surrender our own standards. Because acculturation leads to ethnocentrism, if anything, relativism reinforces our commitment to our own standards. So, the argument advanced by some that pluralism (relativism) compels us to adopt the cultural defense is seen to be a misguided one. Cultural sensitivity does not involve abandoning one's own laws.

Secondly, the cultural defense is not needed because culture is already taken into account at the various stages of charging and sentencing. Prosecutors, for example, often will not press charges against Laotian defendants because members of the community are reluctant to testify against one another and prefer to settle disputes by traditional mechanisms. In a number of cases such as *Whaley*, *Kimura*, and *Moua* (Kong), the sentences were mitigated, most likely because of culture.

One advocate of the cultural defense argues that a formal cultural defense is preferable to the informal use of culture.[35] The allegation is that where discretion exists in the United States legal system, it works most often to the disadvantage of minorities. But the cases show this proposition to be false. Moreover, if there is a problem of having prejudiced judges within the system, that should be remedied. It does not necessarily justify having a cultural defense. Furthermore, if judges are unwilling to consider culture, it remains unclear how a formal cultural defense would force them to take culture into account. Judges need not, for instance, accept the insanity defense.

For immigrants there is no real justification for having a cultural defense. But where individualized justice merits it, judges can use culture to mitigate sentences. In the case of individuals upon whom a system of legal norms has been imposed, the cultural defense may not be feasible. This is because adherence to an "objective" reasonable man standard prevents the consideration of culture. For these societies two solutions are possible: (1) restore traditional courts which follow customary law (unless the traditional system is no longer desired), or (2) modify the Western judicial structure so that it incorporates traditional norms. For example, perhaps self defense ought to be allowed in witchcraft killings if the vast majority of citizens want it. Although some may be uncomfortable with the idea of sanctioning defenses for such crimes as witchcraft killings, using the law to force social change is equally troublesome.[36]

Finally, it is necessary to recognize the negative consequences that would follow the adoption of the cultural defense. Anarchy would reign if each person could claim a different cultural immunity from prosecution. One extreme reaction to the attempted use of the cultural defense in the *Moua* (Tou) case was a claim that acceptance of it would lead to a rash of wife killings. While this may seem far-fetched, it is possible that in the absence of any deterrent whatsoever, immigrants might be less circumspect when continuing their customary ways in the United States. Moreover, those who prefer not to follow the traditional way of life would fall prey to the cultural defense. If the perpetrator is not held responsible, women who seek their rights will have no recourse. Women's rights and children's rights will never be protected if their traditions follow them wherever they go.

Even if we assume for the sake of argument that the cultural defense is desirable because it reflects cultural sensitivity, we must acknowledge the overwhelming negative connotations it has. The cultural defense is often compared to the insanity defense. This seems to suggest that different cultural logics are viewed as being delusional.

The use of the cultural defense also presents dangers of distortion. If Americans mistakenly believe that Japanese women kill their children whenever their husbands takes mistresses. this could trigger intensified racial prejudice. In fact, the inexcusable treatment of Japanese-Americans in the 1940s stemmed from racial stereotypes. Not only is there a possibility that the culture itself will be distorted, but the facts in a particular case may be molded to accommodate the cultural defense. Some argue that the trial of Hagos Gebreamlak illustrates this occurrence. It is possible that his beliefs in the bouda were not genuine, suggested by his failure to apply traditional remedies such as using garlic and wearing amulets to break the spell. The district attorney in that case maintained that the public defender had invented the bouda defense merely to absolve Gebreamlak of responsibility.[37] In the long term the cultural defense would probably have serious and detrimental effects, even upon the individuals it was designed to protect.

Conclusion

Some contend that the cultural defense is necessary if we are a truly pluralistic society. This is erroneous. American law recognizes an important distinction between belief and action; the former is absolute, while the latter is not. A culturally sensitive outlook does not require that we relinquish our standards. Others argue that we must reject the cultural defense because we must force new citizens to become assimilated as soon as possible. This is an example of cultural arrogance because retaining our criminal laws does not mean that we should impose ***all*** of the beliefs in the dominant value-system upon new citizens! While it is true that punishment educates and socializes, there are certainly less repressive ways to achieve the same result.

We can be culturally sensitive and retain our standards. There is no need for a cultural defense because mechanisms already exist which can take culture into account. The negative consequences of the defense such as undercutting the legitimacy of government, undermining women's and children's rights, and treating the logic of other cultures as insane all represent good reasons for rejecting the cultural defense.

Notes

1. *People v. Kimura*, No. A-091133 (Los Angeles Cty. Super. Ct., filed April 24, 1985).

2. *People v. Moua* (Kong), No. 315972–0 (Fresno Cnty. Super. Ct., Feb. 7, 1985); Alan Dershowitz, 'Marriage by Capture' Runs into the Law of Rape, *Wall Street Journal*, June 14, 1985, at 5, col. 1.

3. Julia B. Sams, The Availability of the "Cultural Defense" as an Excuse for Criminal Behavior, 16 *Georgia Journal of International and Comparative Law*, 335, 336–337 (1986).

4. Mark R. Thompson, Immigrants Bring Cultural Defense into U.S. Courts, *Wall Street Journal*, June 6, 1985, p. 28. Mark R. Thompson, Cultural Defense, 14(1) *Student Lawyer* 24, 28 (1985).

5. John C. Lyman, Cultural Defense: Viable Doctrine or Wishful Thinking, 9 *Criminal Justice Journal* 87, 94 (1986).

6. *People v. Moua* (Tou. F-9083403 (Fresno Municipal Court 1985); 328–106–O Fresno County 1985).

7. Anon., Cultural Defense Fails to Mitigate Wife-Slayer's Sentence, *Los Angeles Daily Journal*, Nov. 29, 1985, col. 1, p. 15.

8. *Reynolds v. United States*, U.S. 145 (1879).

9. *Id.*, at 167.

10. Ford, Refusal of Blood Transfusions by Jehovah's Witnesses, 10 *Catholic Lawyer* 232 (1964); Cantor, A Patient's Decision to Decline Life-Saving Medical Treatment: Bodily Integrity Versus the Preservation of Law, 26 *Rutgers Law Review* 228 (1973).

11. In re Application of Jamaica Hospital, 128 Misc. 2d 1006, 491 N.Y.S. 2d 898 (N.Y. Sup. Ct. 1985).

12. *Id.*, at 1008; at 899.

13. *Jefferson v. Griffin Spalding County Hospital Authority*, 247 S.E. 2d 457 (1981).

14. Lawrence Nelson, Brian Buggy, and Carol Weil, Forced Medical Treatment of Pregnant Women: 'Compeling Each to Live as Seems Good to the Rest.' 86 *Hastings Law Journal* 703, 707 (1986), George J. Annas, Forced Cesareans. The Most Unkindest Cut of All, 23 (3) *Hastings Center Report* 16 (1982).

15. *Lawson v. Commonwealth*, 164 S.W.2d 972 (Ky 1942).

16. *Swann v. Pack*, 527 S.W.2d 114 (1975).

17. *Id.* at 114.

18. *U.S. v. Kuch*, 288 S.W.2d 972 (Ky 1942), *U.S. v. Leary*, 383 F.2d 851 (1967).

19. Sandra R. Weber, Native-Americans Before the Bench: The Nature of Contrast and Conflict in Native-American Law Ways and Western Legal Systems. 19 *Social Science Journal* 47 (1982); Laurence French (ed.) *Indians and Criminal Justice*. Totowa, New Jersey; Allanheld, Osmun (1982).

20. *United States v. Whaley*, 37 F. 145 (1888).

21. *State v. Butler*, No. 44496 (Lincoln Cty. Cir. Ct. filed Mar. 11, 1981).

22. Tia Nichols, Belief in the Way: Native Americans in the Western Legal System, 1987, unpublished paper.

23. Bernard M. Narokobi, Adaptation of Western Law in Papua New Guinea, 5 *Melanesian Law Journal* 52 (1977); Kharisu S. Chukkol, Supernatural Beliefs and Criminal Law in Nigeria. 25 *Journal of the Indian Law Institute* 444 (1983); L. O. Aremu, Criminal Responsibility for Homicide in Nigeria and Supernatural Beliefs, 29 *International and Comparative Law Quarterly* 112 (1980); David S. Clark, Witchcraft and Legal Pluralism: The Case of Celimo Miquirucama, 15 *Tulsa Law Journal* 679 (1980). For more general references on the cultural defense in other countries, see Sebastian Poulter, *English Law and Ethnic Minority Customs*. London: Butterworths, 1986, Sebastian Poulter, Hyde v. Hyde—A

Reappraisal. *International and Comparative Law Quarterly* 475 (1976); Sebastian Poulter, Foreign Customs and the English Criminal Law 24 *International and Comparative Law Quarterly* 136 (1975), Alec Samuels. Legal Recognition and Protection of Minority Customs in a Plural Society in England, 10 *Anglo-American Law Review* 241 (1981); Justin Lewis, The Outlook for a Devil in the Colonies. 1958 *Criminal Law Review* 661 (1958); A . Gledhill, The Reception of English Law in India, In William B. Hamilton (ed.), *The Transfer of Institutions* (pp. 165–191). Durham, N.C.: Duke University Press, 1964. David Weisbrot, Note: Law Reform Commission Working Paper No. 6– Criminal Responsibility: Taking Customs, Perceptions and Beliefs into Account. 5 *Melanesian Law Journal* 164 (1977); T.O. Elias, Customary Law: The Limits of Its Validity in Colonial Law, 13 *African Studies* 97 (1954).

24. Narokobi, *Id.* at 60.

25. Aremu, *supra* note 23, at 113.

26. *Gadam v. R.*, 14 W.A.C.A. 442 (1954).

27. *Philip Muswi s/o Musele v. R.* 23, E.A.C.A. 622 (1956).

28. *Id.* at 625.

29. Anon., Profile, *Los Angeles Daily Journal*, Oct. 25, 1985, pp. 1,17.

30. Narokobi, *supra* note 23, at 60.

31. *R. v. Noboi-Bosai* (1971–1972), P. & N.G.L.R., 271; see Narokobi, *supra* note 23 at 58; *see also.*, Howard, What Colour is the "Reasonable Man"? 1961 *Criminal Law Review* 41.

32. Nick B. Williams, Malaysia Standing Firm on Drug Laws, *Los Angeles Times*, July 5, 1986; anon., 2 Australians Hanged by Malaysia for Drug Crimes, *Los Angeles Times*, July 6, 1986, p.4.

33. Milton E. Gordon, Models of Pluralism: The New American Dilemma. 454 *Annals, American Academy of Political and Social Science* 178 (1981), Charles M. Lamb, Legal Foundations of Civil Rights and Pluralism in America, 454 *Annals, American Academy of Political and Social Science* 13 (1981).

34. Robert Redfield, *The Primitive World and Its Transformations.* Ithaca, New York: Cornell University Press, 1962 at 146–47; see also Alison Dundes Renteln. Relativism and the Search for Human Rights. 90 *American Anthropologist* 56 (1988).

35. Anon., The Cultural Defense in the Criminal Law, 99 *Harvard Law Review* 1293 (1986).

36. Studies indicate that it can be disastrous to employ law as a vehicle for social change when the values in the society support the retention of traditional legal norms. See, for example, Gregory Massell, Revolutionary Change in Soviet Central Asia. In D. Black and M. Mileski (eds.), *The Social Organization of Law* (pp. 226–261). New York: Seminar Press. 1973; Haleh Afshar. The Legal, Social, and Political Position of Women in Iran. 13 *International Journal of the Sociology of Law* 47 (1985); F.J.M. Feldbrugge, The Role of Soviet Law in the Integration of Non-Slavic Peoples, 3 *Review of Socialist Law* 3 (1977).

37. Lauren Arenson, *Hagos Gebreamlak v. California*, 1987, unpublished paper.

International Folk Law

Up until this point, we have considered folk law only in the context of individual states or countries. However, it turns out that folk law is quite crucial with respect to international law. The treatment of envoys and diplomats, that is, individuals representing one country while residing in another, has been a matter of concern ever since the rise of nation-states. Questions of diplomatic immunity, asylum, prisoner exchange, not to mention rules for the conduct of war or rules of the road for ships at sea in international waters are also the subject of folk law.

As the world shrinks in size through modern communications and transportation systems, the need for international agreement on a variety of problems and issues becomes ever more acute. From pollution of the shared environment to matters involving the exploration of outer space, from the difficulty in stamping out communicable diseases to efforts to encourage international commerce, there are countless new areas which require international consensus. Bilateral and multilateral treaties constitute one way of creating the order necessary for smooth international functioning, but folk law is another. One advantage of folk law is that it does not always require the years and years often involved in getting all the parties to a treaty to ratify it formally.

Still, international folk law, like national or local folk law, presents certain serious difficulties. How does one ascertain the existence of international folk law? To what extent, if any, can international folk law be enforced in a given national context? Can it indeed be enforced in an international context? Who has the responsibility or the ability to enforce such folk law? These and other vital questions are part of the ongoing debate about the value and importance of international folk law.

PETER E. BENSON

François Gény's Doctrine of Customary Law

The possible relevance of the concept of folk law to international law is not a new idea. In the following essay, the theoretical discussion of the nature of customary law by François Gény (1861–1959) is examined for its implications for international law.

For a sample of the abundant literature devoted to the role of custom in the formation of international law, see S. Séfériadès, "Aperçus sur la Coutume Juridique Internationale et Notamment sur son Fondement," Revue Generale de Droit International Public, *43 (1936), 129–196; Lazare Kopelmanas, "Custom as a Means of the Creation of International Law,"* The British Year Book of International Law, *18 (1937) 127–151; Hans Kelsen, "Théorie du droit international coutumier,"* Revue Internationale de la Théorie du Droit, *1 (1939), 253–274; Helen Silving, "'Customary Law': Continuity in Municipal and International Law,"* Iowa Law Review, *31 (1946), 614–633; Anthony A. D'Amato, "Wanted: A Comprehensive Theory of Custom in International Law,"* Texas International Law Forum, *4 (1968), 28–41; Quincy Wright, "Custom as a Basis for International Law in the Post-War World,"* Texas International Law Forum, *2 (1966), 147–166; H. Bokor-Szegó, "Le rôle du droit coutumier dans le droit international contemporain,"* Acta Juridica, *15 (1973), 299–318, Michael Akehurst, "Custom as a Source of International Law,"* British Year Book of International Law, *47 (1974–1975), 1–53; Rama Rao, "International Custom,"* The Indian Journal of International Law, *19 (1979), 515–521; Brigitte Stern, "La coutume au coeur du droit international: Quelques réflexions," in* Mélanges offerts à Paul Reuter, Le droit international: unité et diversité *(Paris: Editions A. Pedone, 1981) pp. 479–499; Luigi Condorelli, "Custom," in Mohammed Bedjaoui, ed.,* International Law: Achievements and Prospects *(Dordrecht: Martinus Nijhoff, 1991), pp. 197–211; and Jörg Kirchner, "Thoughts About a Methodology of Customary International Law,"* Austrian Journal of Public and International Law *43 (1992), 215–239. This is by no means an exhaustive list of articles, but is meant merely to be representative.*

Reprinted with permission of the publisher from *The Canadian Yearbook of International Law* (Vancouver: UBC Press), 20 (1982), 267–281.

For more about Gény's contributions to jurisprudence, see B.A. Wortley, "François Gény,' in Modern Theories of Law *(London: Oxford University Press, 1933), pp. 139–159; and Jaro Mayda,* Francois Gény and Modern Jurisprudence *(Baton Rouge: Louisiana State University Press, 1978). For biographical and bibliographical details, see pp. 229–233.*

Most students of public international law are of the opinion that coming to terms with the nature of international custom goes to the root of understanding international law itself. It is not surprising, therefore, that the past failure of both the International Court of Justice and scholars to articulate a consistent and comprehensive notion of custom has required and indeed stimulated a fundamental rethinking of the nature of international customary law.[1] This reappraisal of custom has been undertaken with the explicit aim of overcoming serious inadequacies in the notion of custom that was inherited from the writers of the nineteenth century and adopted without change by the scholars and judges of our century. Certainly, for several decades, writers recognized the paradoxical nature of the traditional notion of *opinio juris*, which is that a customary rule can be created only by virtue of states' necessarily erroneous belief that this same rule already exists and binds them.[2] But, at the same time, these writers were unable to resolve the paradox because they did not free themselves from the fundamental perspective that characterized the inherited notion.[3]

The fruits of the most recent reformulations of custom may provide the hoped-for solution, for an examination of these efforts reveals that the approach adopted is fundamentally different from that entailed in the hitherto accepted conception of custom. Custom is now understood in terms of the process of its creation, and this process is explained from the wholly internal and fully autonomous standpoint of the states which themselves bring into existence and recognize as binding, authoritative customary rules.[4] The idea of process has been introduced by breaking up the undifferentiated notion of the *opinio juris* into two or more stages which include a purposive or teleological element.[5] This purposive element, which may be, for example, the belief "that a particular course of action is of such a kind that its recognition as in accordance with law . . . would be socially desirable,"[6] is meant to allow for the temporal dimension of the coming into existence of custom and yet to preserve the specificity of custom as a truly legal phenomenon. Moreover, the introduction of the teleological principle is only the first step. For it is necessary to articulate the concept of custom, which integrates this principle as one of its essential elements.[7]

The aim of this note is strictly limited. In order to understand these more recent developments it is essential that we elucidate a theoretical standard with which to measure the validity and implications of them. One way to further this end is to identify the authoritative formulation of the traditional notion of custom and to discover its fundamental perspective. Understanding the essential limits of this older conception will clarify, if only negatively, the theoretical requirements which a truer notion of custom must satisfy.[8]

Historians single out François Gény as the writer whose work crowned the nineteenth century's analysis of custom and whose ideas were directly incorporated into our approach towards international custom.[9] Gény's doctrine of custom may be found in sections 109–37 of his famous *Méthode d'Interprétation et Sources en Droit Privé Positif* (1899).[10] We propose to present a fairly close reading of these sections so as to bring to the reader's attention elements of that doctrine which have not thus far received sufficient notice

Gény sets out to understand the nature of custom as a source of positive private law in municipal law systems. In a footnote, he states that the consideration of international custom is beyond the horizon of his inquiry.[11] Indeed, the full realization of general customary law might seem, *prima facie*, improbable at the level of the international community as a whole:

> These conditions favourable to customary law can fully materialize only when the community is limited. As soon as the state expands, general custom becomes rare and particular customs appear within autonomous groups placed under the common sovereignty . . . it is hardly possible to conceive how a general custom dealing with an important matter could be formed. For this process presupposes a full community of views between a number of units which are endowed with a greatest freedom of discretion under the sovereign authority of the central authority.[12]

But in fact, Gény observes that custom has found a fertile ground for development in contemporary international law.[13] We might explain this success in terms of the limited number of participants in the international arena, the increasing efficiency and frequency of communications among them, and the urgency of the need to co-ordinate their actions.[14] In short, the fact that Gény examines custom in a municipal law setting need not disqualify *ab initio* the application of his analysis to the international law field.

Gény seeks to understand custom as an original and autonomous source of positive law. Its existence and validity do not presuppose the existence of a legislature or another standard of legal recognition. In fact, custom antedates both statutory law and the centralization of authority. Thus,

Gény's essential and unequivocal aim is to discover the rational foundation of the obligatory force of custom such that, by virtue of its "inherent force which makes it a formal source of law parallel with or subsidiary to written law"[15] it must be considered as able to create positive legal rules.

However, as even the title of the treatise suggests, Gény conceives this aim in the light of the task of interpreting the law.[16] And, in this respect, there arises the possibility of a fundamental ambiguity in his account of the nature and obligatory force of customary law. For the question to be answered is no longer merely. "Why is custom rationally binding upon those who create it and live according to it?" but also, and necessarily, "why and how does the interpreter decide that a custom is binding for him?" The interpreter's perspective need not be identical with the perspective of those who create and are bound by a custom. Sometimes, Gény indicates that the two perspectives are indeed identical. For example, he writes that a custom is binding for the interpreter simply because it is binding on a particular group of persons. The inherent obligatory force of an existing custom compels recognition on the part of the interpreter. Other times, Geny suggests that the two perspectives differ. A custom that is binding upon a group of persons may be deemed to be of no force by the interpreter on the basis of a different standard.[17]

But, even if the two perspectives diverge, the interpreter must fulfil two requirements to accomplish his task of deciding whether or not a custom is truly binding for him. According to Gény, custom is a specific form of law and is therefore radically distinct from mere usage, however ancient and universal it may be. It is therefore essential that the interpreter be able to distinguish between usage and custom. The theorist (i.e., Gény) must be able in turn to provide an account of the conceptual basis of that distinction and consequently of the obligatory force inherent in custom. Moreover, since the interpreter must be able to resolve disputes between parties who disagree whether an alleged custom has actually come into existence and is therefore legally binding upon them, the interpreter must understand the genesis of custom so that he can rationally determine when and in which circumstances a true custom has arisen. The theorist, in turn, must provide an account of the intelligible process whereby binding customary law is born.[18]

The question of perspectives is of particular importance when the object of study is international law. For it is characteristic of the sphere of international customary law that the interpreter (i.e., the judge) who is to determine whether or not a binding custom exists cannot occupy a juridical vantage point outside of the actual process of custom formation. The standard of legal recognition is wholly internal to this process, and the interpreter necessarily shares with the international actors the identical perspective. Ideally, the criteria for the judicial determination of the existence of international custom are the clearest and most rational *expression* of that process.[19]

Therefore, we must be alert to the possibility that Gény's treatment of the nature of custom *qua* law may, in fact, presuppose the existence of a juridical order or standpoint which does not owe its origin to custom itself. If this proves to be the case, Gény's account will have failed to explain the rational inner ground of custom and will be singularly inapplicable to the international community, where there is no authoritative legal ruler but only authoritative legal rules.[20]

In Section 110, Gény offers a preliminary and tentative definition of custom as a complex of facts (usages) that reveals a legal sentiment. Before he examines the constitutive parts of custom, Gény identifies certain permanent social needs which "not only . . . fully justify custom but also . . . define exactly its conditions and determine its effects . . . and makes it a parallel *independent* source which has its own existence and indispensable role to play."[21] Three principal social needs which custom *qua* law fulfils are suggested:

> First, the security of private interests and the necessary stability of individual rights, as well as the need for equality which is the foundation of all justice, require that a rule *which has been recognized through long usage as having the character of a legal obligation* be binding in the same manner as a statute, so as to guide with assurance the actions of all persons. Secondly . . . human nature . . . considers the ancestral customs with a respect mixed with fear and hesitates to change them. Finally . . . [the] essentially voluntary general recognition [of custom] is a decisive evidence of the intrinsic value of the rule and the best guarantee of a balance of the interests involved.[22]

The first social need presupposes that custom is already binding on others and suggests why the interpreter should *also* deem it binding for himself; the original obligatory force of custom is not explained but simply given to the interpreter as a fact. The second reason, respect for the ancestral, applies equally to legal and non-legal (e.g., religious) practices and therefore does not justify the obligatory force and utility of customary *law*. Moreover, the creation of new customary rules that displace older rules cannot thereby be justified. Finally, the third social need derives from the inference that a custom must have some *intrinsic* value because it was assented to by a community, but it does not explain what that value is. In sum, the interpreter should not disturb the established balance of interests and *therefore* he ought to recognize the custom as binding.

The analysis of permanent social needs has not sustained the proposition that "the force of customary law as a source of law is implied in its nature and is *therefore* binding for the interpreter."[23] The original obligatory force is not explained but, on the contrary, given to the interpreter as a fact. The reasons which move the interpreter to recognize this fact as binding are applicable to all legal phenomena. It is therefore difficult to understand how Gény can rightly claim that the essence of custom as a specific legal type is deducible from this analysis.[24]

In section 119, Gény determines the prerequisites that a custom must fulfil to be binding upon the interpreter as a formal source of law. There are "positive elements" which specifically and substantially constitute customary law.[25] Given a fully constituted custom, there are, in addition, certain "higher reasons" which may sometimes intervene, paralyze its force, and prevent it from counting as a law.

Among these higher reasons, one is of particular interest. The irrationality of what in every positive respect is a true customary law may nullify its status as recognized customary law. The standard which determines the rationality of a custom is derived from general morality or from the social and political organization of a society.[27] Thus, the very possibility of higher reasons presupposes the existence of a standpoint external to the process of custom formation.

The positive elements include a "material" element, viz. long and constant usage, and a "psychological" element, "the conviction about a legal sanction which specifies and qualifies a usage as binding custom."[28] The material element is described as a "series of actions (or . . . omissions) of a kind to constitute a well-defined social relationship *susceptible of legal sanction*."[29] It is essential that, during its formation as custom, the relevant material practice not meet serious opposition from those individuals who might have an interest in contesting it. However, it is not necessary that the series of constitutive acts be absolutely uninterrupted by omissions or opposing acts. What is required is a certain regularity of practice. It is noteworthy that Gény repudiates the idea, still espoused by certain contemporary theorists, that the obligatory force of custom derives from a "tacit and common convention."[30]

Gény proceeds to examine the psychological element of custom. Since it is this element, the so-called *opinio juris*, that has played such a momentous role in the development of the jurisprudence of international custom, it is appropriate to quote the crucial passages in the original French:

> la coutume juridique requiert pour son existence positive une condition immatérielle et psychologique . . . que l'on traduit souvent par sa qualification traditionnelle: *opinio juris seu necessitatis* . . . cela signifie que l'usage, *pour engendrer la coutume*, doit avoir chez ceux qui le pratiquent, le caractère d'exercice d'un droit subjectif, qui contient l'expression d'une règle de droit

> objectif... que les actes, composant cet usage, n'ont effet, *pour la création du droit*, que s'ils ont lieu dans la pensée d'une sanction effective... c'est *l'élement spécifiquement caractéristique de la coutume juridique*, le seul qui la distingue de ces habitudes du monde... auxquels on ne saurait, à aucun degré, reconnaître force juridique obligatoire.[31]

In a footnote, Gény agrees with another writer that it is not sufficient that "l'usage fut pratiqué dans la pensée qu'il est convenable que cela soit, ni même que *cela devrait juridiquement être*. Il faut la persuasion *qu'il en est juridiquement ainsi*, que la pratique applique *le droit existant*."[32]

How does this analysis of custom in terms of its material and psychological elements contribute to understanding the specific essence of custom and the reason for its being binding upon the interpreter? Upon examination, the analysis amounts merely to a classification of the types of social practice. There is the genus, "practice." Practices include *all* the "manifestations of society"—from the practice of giving tips and receiving gifts to the practice of conferring upon French women their husbands' names.[33] Next, Gény distinguishes between two species of practice: practices which are part of the positive legal order and practices which remain outside that order. The specific difference which sets off a practice belonging to the positive legal order is the existence of the *opinio juris*, or the belief that the practice is legally obligatory. Since according to Gény, the very essence of positive law is the idea of coercion,[34] the *opinio juris* is the belief in the existence of an effective social sanction that renders obligatory the practice in question. Formally, the meaning of *opinio juris* is simply the belief that a practice is legally obligatory. It is only true by virtue of the additional equation of the essence of positive law with the idea of coercion that the belief is given a content and becomes the belief in the existence of an effective social sanction.

But the form and content of the *opinio juris* must characterize all legal phenomena simply because they are immediately derived from the essence of positive law. How then is custom to be distinguished from other legal practices? Perhaps the material element—long usage—is crucial in this respect. Then the fundamental question is: what is the process whereby certain usages and not others come to be seen as being legally binding on a community, the members of which need not have consented unanimously to be bound? Only an answer to this question can illuminate the specific essence of customary law.

Gény's discussion of the *opinio juris* has established only the tautological proposition that a practice is legal insofar as it is considered to be legally binding by those who regard it as authoritative. It is a restatement of the fact that custom is a legal practice. Gény expressly excludes a teleological element from the notion of *opinio juris*. The reason for this exclusion is that the obligatory force of custom would no longer be simply a fact, given to the interpreter, but rather a mere possibility yet to be realized in the process of custom formation. The reasons why the interpreter should recognize that a custom is binding for him presupposes, we have seen, the fact, itself unaccounted for, that a custom is already legally binding upon a group of persons. The constituent elements of the specific essence of customary law serve merely to differentiate formally a usage that is legally binding from a usage that is not. Thus, the limited significance of the analysis of the essence of custom, which merely classifies it as an unexplained legal *fact*, corresponds exactly to the limited significance of the discussion of the sociological explanation of its obligatory force.

The success of Gény's theoretical endeavour must be evaluated in the light of the limited theoretical import of his analysis of custom. It is relatively clear that his aim encompasses the attempt to provide a coherent account of the genesis of custom. For example, in the crucial passage, quoted above, that deals with the *opinio juris*, Gény describes the conceptual function of the *opinio juris* in terms of its capacity to explain how usage "engenders" or "creates" custom.[35] Or again, Gény writes that "custom presupposes a slowly growing usage, the diagnosis of which is open to much greater errors"[36] than is written law. In an earlier section, Gény requires that the interpreter be able to determine "*when* a custom is legally binding."[37] Indeed, it is precisely when Gény tries to make sense of the *formation* of custom that a host of theoretical difficulties arise and these are the paradoxes which a generation of scholars unsuccessfully sought to resolve. The reason for this failure is that these difficulties are the consequence of a more fundamental inadequacy of the doctrine of custom. The doctrine is grounded upon the juridical perspective or viewpoint of an interpreter who stands wholly outside the actual process of custom formation and who interprets an alleged custom according to a standard wholly underived from that process. Therefore, he is unable to account for the obligatory force of custom as a specific and original mode of legal rule formation. But because the interpreter's task entails understanding the process of custom formation and objectively presupposes the logically prior work accomplished by that process,[38] he is willy-nilly led to speak about the process in terms fundamentally inadequate to its reality as an autonomous creation in time of customary law.

It is both historically and theoretically significant that Gény himself is very much aware of these paradoxical consequences that plagued later writers. Gény attempts to resolve them and he does so, it will be seen, in a manner consistent with his fundamental perspective. Two instances where Gény grapples with difficulties arising from his account of the genesis of custom will be discussed.

Gény concludes that at the source of the formation of custom, there *must* be an erroneous belief on the part of those who are the creators of custom that they are already legally bound by the very rule which they are in the process of creating: "an error seems at least at the beginning of a usage a *sine qua* condition for the conviction that such a usage is binding. [But] to cut off a custom on the ground that it rests on an error practically amounts to a repudiation or sacrifice of this source at a moment when it seems to be securely established."[39] The problem or error is, for Gény, viewed as a problem only for the interpreter, who must decide whether or not to recognize a given custom as binding. As long as the interpreter has before him a custom which fulfils both the material and psychological requirements for the existence of custom, it is irrelevant for him that at some prior time the psychological element was initially tainted with error. What is an error on the part of the makers of custom need not trouble the outside interpreter who understands the social needs served by his not disturbing existing customary rules. The solution therefore does not resolve the paradox but merely displaces it. It must be stressed that Gény believes that the error does in fact characterize the actual formation of custom. In this respect, the characterization transcends the limited viewpoint of the interpreter to whom custom is given as a fact. But because Gény does not abandon this limited viewpoint when making a judgment that is not derived from that same viewpoint, he has not properly established the objective basis of the supposed error. One might say that he has arbitrarily imputed the error to the makers of custom. On the contrary, the introduction of a teleological principle into the subjective element of custom resolves the paradox of error inasmuch as it reveals that there is no error when the process is understood, not from Gény's perspective, but rather from a viewpoint wholly internal to the makers and the making of custom in time.[40]

Between mere usage and true custom lies so-called conventional usage, and Gény set himself the task of explaining the transformation of this middle term into custom. This explanation is the sole instance in the treatise of an account of the actual formation of custom, and it is therefore of special interest.

These conventional usages are practices, "some of them general, but most of them local or professional—which tacitly surround the formation of legal transactions, especially contracts."[41] The usages are presumed in all documents in order to interpret them or to supplement the wills of the parties to the transaction and the intention of the author of the document. Both usages and true custom share in the same material element but differ in that the latter, unlike usage, is constituted by the *opinio juris*. Gény concedes that in the minds of the parties these conventional usages are endowed with legal value. However, he denies to them the quality of objective law because "the parties are considered to have *freely* referred to them. This freedom of choice excludes the possibility of attaching to the usage an *inevitable* sanction."[42] In this respect, conventional usages are more akin to *de facto* habits of daily life; they, along with many other factors, as for example, the personal habits of the contracting parties, help to reveal the true intent of the actors in a legal transaction. On the other hand, if the parties come to refer to those usages because they feel that they must do so or else suffer inevitable sanction, then these usages have become true customary rules.

Gény formulates the task of explaining the metamorphosis of usage into custom in the following terms: "Now I must show *how* in the majority of practical instances the essential differences [between usages and custom] are eliminated *little by little* and finally disappear, so that *in a given moment* a conventional usage can *become* a genuine custom."[43] According to Gény, the underlying cause of this transformation is "a gradual substitution of a common, collective will for the individual will, isolating the conventional rule from the subjective intention of the parties and making it finally into an objective legal provision."[44] In more concrete terms, the process entails that a certain rule becomes increasingly fixed and generally applied, not according to the subjective inclinations of the parties but because of the "general conditions defined by the nature and circumstances of their legal transaction."[45] However, at this point, custom has not yet emerged. One further step is required to "detach it still more from the will of the individual parties"[46] to bring into existence a true customary rule with the requisite *opinio juris*. Gény observes that it is very difficult to say exactly when this moment of transformation has occurred. It is even more difficult to see what this moment is. Gény immediately goes on to say that at a certain moment it will no longer be necessary for a judge to inquire whether the parties did in fact accept the usage or could have known about it at all. He will presume that they voluntarily adopted it.[47]

What does this mean? The critical moment is when an additional step is required to change usage into custom. Until this additional step occurs, the practice is still essentially usage. Many non-legal usages and habits are fixed and homogeneous and certain non-legal practices, such as religious practices, may express a common, collective, and non-legal will. Without explanation, Gény suddenly presents us with a third party, the judge, who presumes that the parties are bound by a rule whether or not they assented to it. In a footnote, Gény agrees that this movement in the "process of evolution" of custom may be described as a transition from tacit agreement to the presumption of a legal rule.[48] However, earlier, Gény expressly repudiates the notion that the obligatory force of custom may be derived from tacit agreement. It now appears that without the judge's crucial act of presuming the existence of a legal rule, the process of customary law formation cannot be completed. In short, the generation of custom is not a wholly autonomous, and, as such, intelligible, process.[49] More particularly, the creation of the necessary *opinio juris* is explained in terms of an act, the judge's presumption, that imposes this subjective element, which fundamentally distinguishes true custom from conventional usage, upon the parties. Gény's resort to a common collective will to explain the autonomous creation of custom only obscures matters even more. Gény has already repudiated as inadequate the historical school's notion of a collective legal consciousness.[50] Since, according to Gény, a common collective will is logically entailed in the very idea of an objective legal provision and an individual will is logically entailed in the very idea of usage,[51] the process of the substitution of the common for the individual will is logically equivalent to the statement that law replaces usage. But this is precisely what must be explained.

The reason for the inadequacy of this account is clear. The birth of the *opinio juris* is necessarily *ex nihilo* and as such unintelligible. Gény seeks to mediate the qualitative difference between fully realized conventional usage and fully realized custom by a series of quantitative rapprochements. This is impossible unless the first term, usage, contains as a real potentiality, the subjective principle of the *opinio juris*, which essentially characterizes custom. In other words, since custom is distinct from conventional usage by virtue of *opinio juris*,[52] this subjective element can never be derived from usage and custom can never be developed out of usage. The introduction of a teleological principle into the formation of the *opinio juris* permits the theorist to develop the subjective element of custom out of a quality which, *ab initio*, differentiates the process of custom formation from mere usage. Gény, on the contrary, cannot account for the birth of the *opinio juris* and therefore has a judge impose it by fiat on the parties thereby bound by the rule.

The outcome of this analysis of Gény's doctrine of custom might be considered simply negative. On the other hand, it is suggested that Gény's doctrine is not merely inadequate in part[53] but rather fundamentally unsuitable as a paradigm to be utilized in understanding international customary law. It is precisely this radical incompatibility that may provide us with positive instruction concerning a more fruitful approach to the study of international custom. Most contemporary conceptions of international custom pre-suppose the very perspective underlying Gény's doctrine. Faced with the theoretical difficulties which, as suggested above, arise from this perspective, writers continue to remedy these defects with what amount to merely verbal reformulations that leave the cause of the ailment intact.[54] No serious advance in our understanding will be made until theoretical efforts are devoted to the clear explication of the juridical possibility of the coming into existence of legal rules which are autonomously made by and therefore rationally bind the members of an international community not endowed with an authoritative ruler. On a practical level, the utility and indeed ultimately the very existence of custom as a mode of creating general international law depend essentially upon a certain degree of clarity and consensus among nations and judicial officers as to the nature and effects of this mode of law-formation. It is difficult enough for a court to determine whether or not this or that practice amounts to international custom. This determination becomes of necessity uncertain, confused and, at worst, arbitrary, if there is disagreement or lack of clarity among the participants of the international community concerning the very nature of custom-formation itself. Undoubtedly, the theoretical and practical tasks to be accomplished are very difficult. Fortunately, the process of rethinking custom has already begun.

Notes

1. The failure of the International Court of Justice is judiciously treated by Professor Skubiszewski in "Elements of Custom and the Hague Court," in 810–54 Z.a.o.Ru. 31 (1971), *The North Sea Continental Shelf* cases ([1969] *I.C.J. Rep.* 1, provides ample proof of the fundamental disagreement among the judges as to the necessity, nature, and effect of the subjective element of *opinio juris*: see opinions of Judge Lachs, 230–31; Judge Tanaka, 176; *Ad Hoc* Judge Sorensen, 247. The fact that, in general, the writers have failed is now commonplace. See, for example, D'Amato, *The Concept of Custom in International Law*, (1971) Part I Israel L.R.; Walden, "The Subjective Element in the Formation of Customary International Law," 12 Israel L.R. 344 (1977). The recent renewal of theorizing about international custom includes, among others, the following books and articles: D'Amato, *The Concept of Custom in International Law* (1971); Thirlway, *International Customary Law and Codification* (1972); Meijers, "How is International Law Made?: The Stages of Growth of International Law and the Use of Its Customary Rules," in 9 Neth. Y.B.Int'l L. 1 (1978); Walden, "Customary International Law: A Jurisprudential Analysis," in 13 Israel L.R. 86 (1978); Finnis, *Natural Law and Natural Rights* (1980).

2. See, for example, Josef Kunz, "The Nature of Customary International Law," in 47 Am. J. Int'l L. 662, at 667.

3. See, for example, Kelsen, *Principles of International Law* 307 (1952).

4. The most systematic and remarkable argument to this effect is found in Finnis's *Natural Law and Natural Rights* 230–45.

5. It is interesting to note that Judge Lachs, in the *Continental Shelf* case, stated that "[states] may also have been convinced that the instrument . . . was intended to become and would in due course become general law (*The teleological element is of no small importance in the formation of law*)" in [1969] *I.C.J. Rep.* at 230–31; quoted in Thirlway, *op. cit. supra* note 1, at 54.

6. Thirlway, *op. cit. supra* note 1, at 55.

7. The outstanding feature of Finnis's account is that it does precisely this.

8. The present renewal of theorizing was preceded by historical as well as critical investigations into the origins of the dominant conception of custom. See, for example, Paul Guggenheim, "Contribution à l'Histoire des Sources du Droit des Gens," in 94 Hague Recueil des Cours 5–82 (1958, II); Walden, "The Subjective Element in the Formation of Customary International Law," *supra* note 1.

9. Guggenheim, *supra* 52–53; D'Amato, *op.cit. supra* note 1, at 48.

10. Hereafter Gény. Quotations in the original French are from the 2d ed., 1954, Librairie Générale de Droit & Jurisprudence. Quotations in English and all references to the work are from Mayda's translation of the 2d ed., Louisiana State Law Institute, 1963.

11. Gény, 225, note 376

12. Gény, 222.

13. *Supra* note 11.

14. See Parry, *The Sources and Evidences of International Law* 59 (1965).

15. Gény, 228.

16. Gény, 239, s. 117; see also, 228–29, s. 114.

17. Gény, 237; see also, 253–55, s. 121.

18. Gény, 218–29, s. 110; see also, 239–40, s. 117.

19. See De Visscher, "Cours Général de Droit International Public," 136 Hague Recueil des Cours 63–64 (1972, II) and Judge Barwick's remarks concerning the scope of the judicial role in the formation of custom in *Nuclear Tests* cases, *I.C.J. Rep.* 253 at 434. See also Gény's account of the role of the judge in the formation of custom at 261–63, s. 123, and Finnis's discussion of the different perspective vis-á-vis authoritative rules, *op. cit. supra* 4, at 233–37.

20. Note that in this case, Gény will have failed to fulfil his own theoretical goal. See Gény. 235

21. Gény, 238.

22. Gény, 236, s. 116 (emphasis added).

23. Gény, 237 (emphasis added).

24. Gény, 243, S. 119.

25. *Ibid.*

26 *Ibid.*

27. Gény, 255.

28. Gény, 243

29. Gény, 244.

30. French edition, 360, S. 119. The English translation seems to be incorrect here (at 246, s. 119). See also, English translation, 229. The idea of tacit consent was central to the tradition of thought associated with the names of Suarez, Rachel, Grotius, Bynkenshoeck, and Vattel. See, for example, Vattel, *The law*

of Nations or the Principles of Natural Law (Scott ed. 1916) preface, 11a. For a contemporary exposition, see Tunkin, *Theory of International Law* 123–33 (1974).

31. Gény, 361, s. 119; English trans., 246 (emphasis added).
32. *Ibid.*
33. Gény, 219, and 223–25, s. 111.
34. Gény, 219, note 345.
35. *Supra*, text at note 31.
36. Gény, 242.
37. Gény, 239, s. 117.
38. *Supra*, text at note 17.
39. Gény, 251–52.
40. For example, see Finnis, *op. cit. supra* note 4, at 239–41.
41. Gény, 285.
42. Gény, 287, s. 131 (author's emphasis).
43. Gény, 292, s. 133 (emphasis added).
44. Gény, 293.
45. Gény, 292, s. 133.
46. *Ibid.*
47. *Ibid.*
48. Gény, 292, note 738.
49. This consequence is fundamentally inconsistent with Gény's view stated at 262–61, s. 133:

> I still want to assert at least that I would not attribute the power of creating genuine customary law to intellectual products proper, whether they are by writers or by courts. For they lack the essential substratum of custom . . . that is the usage of the parties involved. Also, no matter how strong the conviction of the lawyers, we can not consider it the sense of legal necessity *(opinio necessitatis) which should emanate from the very persons among whom the custom is law* (emphasis added).

50. Gény, 235.
51. Gény, 292, s. 133.
52. Gény, 287. s. 131; see also 247.
53. This is D'Amato's view, *op. cit. supra* note 1, at 73–74.
54. See, for example, Akehurst, "Custom as a Source of International Law," 47 Brit. Yb. Int'l L. 1–53 (1974–75).

NIRMALA NAGANATHAN

What Constitutes Custom in International Law?

An earlier section of this volume was devoted to the problem of the ascertainment of folk law. The same difficulty with respect to ascertainment obtains in the case of international folk law. The following essay by Nirmala Naganathan, Lecturer in Law at the University of Ceylon in Colombo, Sri Lanka, reviews the question by considering a number of classic cases, cases which have proved critical in the determination of customary international law.

For additional discussion of this issue, see Maarten Bos, "Prolegomena to the Identification of Custom in International Law," in Essays on International & Comparative Law in Honour of Judge Erades *(The Hague: Martinus Nijhoff, 1983), pp. 1–13. For an updated consideration of the age-old question of sanctuary, see Deborah Perluss and Joan F. Hartman, "Temporary Refuge: Emergence of a Customary Norm,"* The Virginia Journal of International Law, *26 (1986), 551–626.*

It is only by an analysis of the ways in which rules of customary international law evolve, that one can try to separate its different constituent elements. But no attempt is made in this analysis to define customary international law. The aim of this article is to examine the traditional doctrine as to the constitution of customary international law, and its applicability to present day developments in the field of customary international law.

The Traditional Doctrine

Customary international law is generally described as that body of rules which has evolved from the practices and usages of nations and which has by constant repetition, and the conviction that the recurrence is the

Reprinted from *Colombo Law Review*, 2 (1971), 68–82.

result of a compulsory rule, acquired the force of law. Hence it is usual to break up customary international law into two components: (i) the material element which is made up of the practice of states, i.e., conduct which is recurrent, consistent and general, and which therefore often presupposes a considerable lapse of time; and (ii) the psychological element which is constituted by the conviction that the practice is obligatory, i.e., the *opinio juris sive necessitatis*.

Article 38 of the Statute of the International Court of Justice states that in deciding disputes the court is enjoined to apply *inter alia*, "international custom, as evidence of a general practice accepted as law." Here again there is recognition of the two elements referred to above: namely the general practice representing the material element, and the requirement of acceptance as law, recognising the *opinio juris*. The clause is drafted so as to imply that international custom is evidence of a general practice accepted as law, and not that the practice accepted as law constitutes customary international law. However it is submitted that this is merely a question of words, and is of no particular significance.

Some of the judgements of the International Court of Justice which deal with questions of customary international law may now be examined in order to see whether the case law reveals that a general practice and an *opinio juris* are necessary constituents of a rule of customary international law. The *Anglo-Norwegian Fisheries case*[1] is often cited as authority for the proposition that a general practice is a necessary element in the formation of rules of customary international law. A general practice would mean a practice which is followed by a large number of states, but is not necessarily universal. In this case, Britain contended that the baselines from which the territorial waters of a state must be measured was the low-water line, and that such baselines must follow the sinuosities of the coastline; further that in the case of bays these could be treated as internal waters only where the closing line of the mouth of the bay was not more than ten miles, although she conceded that this rule would not apply in the case of bays to which Norway had a historic title. These arguments were based on alleged rules of customary international law. The court however refused to accept either of the above propositions. The court's refusal is generally construed as having been motivated by the numerous exceptions in the application of the rule, and hence to the lack of a generality of practice.[2]

It is submitted however that a closer reading of the case reveals that the court in fact agreed that there had been a general practice supporting the low-water line as the baseline for measuring the breath of the territorial sea.[3] But the court refused to apply it to Norway for the reason that Norway had consistently followed a different practice namely, the drawing of straight baselines from which the breadth of the territorial sea was measured, and further that this practice had been acquiesced in by Britain, and other states.[4] In respect of the ten mile rule for bays the court said that it had not acquired the authority of a rule of general international law, and that in any event it was inapplicable as against Norway inasmuch as she had always opposed any attempts to apply it to the Norwegian coast.[5] Hence in this case the court was in effect, conceding to Norway a right to apply a special customary law, in derogation of the general customary law, based on her own particular practice over a period of time.

It is a generally accepted principle of international law that if a state consistently refuses to follow a rule of customary international law during the period of its evolution, it cannot be binding as against that state. Furthermore, if a state has built up a divergent practice which has been acquiesced in by other states a special custom may evolve. In this situation there need not be a generality of practice, because the practice relates only to the particular state, and hence the practice required to establish the custom would be a consistent practice over a period of time by the state in question, and acquiescence in such practice by other states.

However the court did not treat the Norwegian practice as being an instance of special customary international law, i.e., as a practice divergent from general customary international law. The approach taken by the court was rather to see whether such practice was in conformity with principles of international law. This approach of the court was largely due to the way in which the issues in the case were framed, and to Norway's submission that the court should decide the case on the basis of whether or not her system of delimitation was contrary to international law. The court adjudged that Norway's method of delimitation was not contrary to international law on the grounds that this method was an adaptation of the general customary international law to suit Norway's particular geographical configuration and economic situation. Hence the court said that the drawing of straight baselines by Norway constituted no more than "the application of general international law to a specific case."[6] But the court treated this adaptation as being in itself based on extra legal factors which are universally valid, i.e., certain geographical and economic criteria.[7] It was the view of the court that where there is a particular type of geographical configuration and an economic dependence on the sea areas, straight baselines may be validly drawn. It is submitted that in effect the court was notionally deriving a new principle of general customary international law out of certain extra legal factors and the presence of the special practice before it.

Although extra legal factors are at the basis of all usages and practices, the extra legal factors do not in themselves constitute the stuff out of which custom is constituted. According to the traditional view the usages which arise from these extra legal factors must acquire the force of a general practice and furthermore this practice must be carried out in the conviction that it is binding, before it can be regarded as custom. But in this instance the court regarded these extra legal factors as being of themselves sufficient to validate a departure from an existing rule, and the formation of a new rule of customary international law in the form of an adaptation of the old rule.

Hence it could even be argued that a principle of general customary international law can be notionally derived by the court from extra legal factors of universal validity, for example certain geographical or economic factors and the presence of a special practice; and that once the court has given such a principle its *imprimatur* it would become a rule of general customary international law. In the Santiago Declaration, Peru, Chile and Ecuador made a claim to possess sole sovereignty and jurisdiction over the area of the high seas adjacent to the coasts of their respective states to the extent of 200 nautical miles, on the grounds of certain geographical and economic factors.[8] Can it be said that if a regional practice in terms of this declaration can be shown to exist, and it receives the *imprimatur* of the court, this could lead to a general rule of customary international law being derived from it as an adaptation of the existing rules of customary international law on the law of the sea?

If rules of general customary international law can be constituted in this way, it could mean that generality of practice and the presence of an *opinio juris* are not necessarily essential constituents for the formation of custom. However it is submitted that the case is not authority for such a wide proposition, as it only relates to subsidiary rules which arise as adaptations of existing rules. Today the straight baselines rule, as well as the circumstances in which it is applicable as enunciated in the I.C.J's judgement, has been accepted in the Geneva Convention on the Territorial Sea and Contiguous Zone.[9] Hence we see the creative role played by the court in the formation of general customary international law.

In its advisory opinion on the *Reservations to the Genocide Convention*[10] the court dealt with the requirement of generality of practice. In this case the court had to decide the question whether there was a rule of customary international law to the effect that a reservation to a treaty must get the unanimous consent of all the Signatories to the treaty. The court came to the conclusion that there was no rule of international law embodying the unanimity principle, on the grounds that "examples of objections appear to be too rare in international practice to have given rise to such a rule"; that there was a different practice among American states both of the U. N. and O. A. S; and finally that debates in the 6th committee of the General Assembly on this question had revealed a profound divergence of views.[11] Lauterpacht,[12] however, is of the opinion that there was a general practice in favour of the unanimity rule. The International Law Commission too, in its first report on the Law of Treaties, accepted this rule. Could it therefore be said that the court was in fact requiring a universality rather than a generality of practice?

However an examination of the judgement reveals that it was not the absence of universality that motivated the court in reaching its decision, but rather the consideration that a greater degree of flexibility in the operation of multi-lateral conventions was necessary.[13] Hence the court gave the requirement of generality a strict interpretation. It is therefore submitted that the judgement of the court supports the view that a practice must be widespread before it can give rise to a rule of general customary international law. But as to the degree of generality required there could be divergence of opinion.

We will now turn to the other constituent namely the *opinio juris*. This element was considered by the court in the *Lotus* case.[14] In this case France asserted the existence of a rule of customary international law according to which, criminal proceedings in respect of collision cases came exclusively within the jurisdiction of the state of the ships' flag. The court said that even if there was such a practice, it had arisen because states had merely abstained from instituting criminal proceedings, and not because they recognised themselves as being obliged to do so. In other words, they were not "conscious of having a duty to abstain."

Hence the court decided against the existence of such a rule of customary international law. But subsequently the rule was accepted in the 1958 Geneva Convention on the High Seas.[15] Since the convention in its preamble expressly states that it is declaratory of established principles of international law, we may conclude that either a general rule of customary international law existed at the time of the court's decision, even though there was no *opinio juris* in the sense of a duty to abstain, which would suggest that an *opinio juris* in the above sense is not a necessary constituent of a rule of customary international law, or that subsequent to the I. C. J's judgement a conviction as to the duty to abstain had come into being. If one accepts the first alternative this would suggest that the court's interpretation of what constitutes general customary international law is wrong. However there is still another possibility—that there was in fact an *opinio juris*, but that the court reached the conclusion that it did not exist because the court was going on the premise that a subjective element, i.e., the existence of a conviction, can only be proved by some means other than the conduct of states as evidenced by their acts or omissions.

It is submitted that the conviction as to the obligatory nature of a practice is something that can only be implied from a course of conduct pursued by states, because the recurrence of the acts or omissions comprising the practice, necessarily presupposes the presence of some conviction as to its obligatory nature.

The *opinio juris* must now be analysed. The *opinio juris* is said to be the conviction that the practice is obligatory. If the practice is regarded as obligatory this presupposes that it is looked upon as law. Hence article 38 of the Statute of the I. C. J. refers to a general practice accepted as law. It is this acceptance as law that makes a practice a rule of customary international law, and not a mere usage. But there is a difficulty of analysis here, because this amounts to saying that even before it becomes law, it has been regarded as law. The question arises as to why it is so regarded. The answer is generally that the practice generates the conviction that its recurrence is the result of a rule of law, and the conviction that it is obligatory in turn makes for the recurrence of the practice. This is a circular line of reasoning.

Could it not be argued that where states have followed a certain line of conduct, i.e., a practice over a certain period of time, which practice, it is submitted, is followed for reasons of convenience or comity rather than from any sense of obligation, a consent to be bound by the practice may be implied? Thereafter the practice is binding as a rule of law on the basis that consent is binding. Hence it is submitted that the practice is treated as binding, or is accepted as law, because states have impliedly consented to treat the practice as law, by a course of conduct pursued over a period of time. Once given, the consent cannot be withdrawn. In accordance with this theory of consent, a state which has consistently refused to follow a practice during its period of evolution cannot be deemed to be bound by the rule of customary international law, which may subsequently evolve from such practice.[16] From the practical point of view a state will not violate rules of customary international law for reasons of self interest, because to do so would be to invite reprisals of the same nature from other states. Hence it is submitted that the consciousness of a duty to act or abstain from acting in a particular way is a duty which is based on the notion of consent.

In the *Asylum case*[17] however the court explained the nature of the *opinio juris* in terms of rights and duties. Thus the court said,

> "The party which relies on a custom of this kind must prove that this custom is established in such a manner that it has become binding on the other party. The Columbian Government must prove that the rule invoked by it is in accordance with a constant and uniform usage practised by the

> states in question, and that this usage is the expression of a right appertaining to the state granting Asylum and a duty incumbent on the territorial state."

This formulation is often set out in text books as an exposition of the *opinio juris*. But it is submitted that if the conviction as to the obligatory nature of the practice is based on an acknowledgement by states of the presence of rights and duties, this would seem to imply that rights and duties existed before the customary rule of law came into being. Moreover the above quotation refers to the usage as an expression of a right. But rights and duties can only flow from a rule of law. Hence in order to prove the existence of rights and duties one must initially prove the existence of the custom, i.e., a rule of law which confers such rights and duties.

However it might be argued that the notion of an *opinio juris* in the sense of an acknowledgement of rights and duties is apposite in the case of special or regional custom. A special custom is a derogation from existing customary international law, and the practice from which it is constituted is made up of claims or assertions made by one party and acquiescence or lack of protest in such assertions or claims by the other party. These assertions or claims will come to be accepted as binding on the basis of a conviction or acknowledgement on the part of the state against whom it is asserted, that there is a right in the other party, or to put it in another way the acquiescence by the other party will lead to the conviction that such acquiescence is the consequence of a right in the party asserting it, and a duty in the party against whom it is asserted, not to interfere with the exercise of such a right, and it is this acknowledgement of a right and a duty which makes it binding as a rule of law. So that perhaps in the case of special or regional custom an *opinio juris* in the above sense could be a necessary constituent. In this context the above statement of the court in the *Asylum* case is explainable as in that case the court was dealing with a special or regional custom peculiar to South America.

In the *Rights of Passage case*,[18] the court accepted the presence of a local custom as between India and Portugal, on evidence that Portugal had actually exercised a right of passage over Indian territory in which India had acquiesced. The court said that it saw no reason why "long continued practice between two states accepted by them as regulating their relations should not form the basis of mutual rights and obligations between states."

In the International Court of Justice's most recent judgement in the *North Sea Continental Shelf cases*[19] the court once again referred to a general practice and an *opinio juris* as constituent elements of customary international law. Thus the court said,

> "Not only must the acts concerned amount to a settled practice, but they must also be such, or be carried out in such a way, as to be evidence of a belief that this practice is rendered obligatory by the existence of a rule of law requiring it.'[20]

The court then went on to refer to the *Lotus* case and endorsed the view expressed there.

The context in which the court made this statement is of some interest. Here the court had to determine whether or not a rule of customary international law had evolved from an article in the Geneva Convention on the Continental Shelf, which would thus make it binding on non-parties to the Convention, as a rule of customary international law. Thus the question was whether the conventional rule (article 6 of the Convention) could be treated as a norm-creating provision which had constituted the foundation of, or generated a rule of, customary international law. The court was of the opinion that rules of customary international law can be generated in this way, although this notion is quite different from the traditional conception of customary international law as emerging from usages and practices of states, which have, over a long period of time gained acceptance, and have come to be regarded as binding. Moreover the period of time within which such a customary rule could have evolved was very short. Though the Convention was signed in 1958, it came into force only in 1964, when the requisite number of ratifications were received, and the judgement was given in February 1969. This perhaps explains the stress laid by the court on the *opinio juris* as a necessary constituent.

Although evidence of state practice in accordance with the rule as set out in article 6, was cited, the court took the view that only the practice of non parties to the Convention was relevant as they would not have been acting in the application of the Convention. The court found that the action of such non party states was "problematical" and "speculative" because there was no evidence to show that they were acting in pursuance of what they thought was a mandatory rule of customary international law.[21]

As submitted earlier it is difficult to see how a subjective element can be deduced except from objective criteria, i.e., from a course of conduct pursued by the states in question. But perhaps the court meant that some kind of pronouncement should have been made by the states concerned indicating that the particular method of delimitation[22] was not being applied merely as a matter of convenience, but from a consciousness of its obligatory character.

From the analysis of the cases it is apparent that the traditional doctrine, that customary international law is constituted out of a general practice and an *opinio juris*, is subject to certain qualifications which may be summarised as follows: Firstly a distinction must be drawn between general, and special or local, customary international law. In the case of special or local customary international law (which includes regional custom) the *opinio juris* in the sense of an acknowledgement of rights and duties could be considered a necessary constituent. But generality of practice would not be necessary in such circumstances, although there must be a special practice by the state or states concerned. On the other hand, general customary international law by its very name presupposes some element of generality of practice, although such practice need not be universal. Further an *opinio juris* in the sense of a conviction that the rule is binding is also necessary, but need not be stressed as a separate element in the case of time-honoured customs, as it would be implied from a long continued course of conduct. It is also submitted that this conviction is related to the notion of consent. Conventional rules which are norm creating could be regarded as rules of customary international law, where there is a general practice by non parties to the Convention based on such rule, and such practice is in pursuance of a conviction as to its binding nature. But this conviction or *opinio juris* must be expressed in some way other than that which may be implied from a course of conduct. Finally subsidiary rules of customary international law based on extra legal factors may also develop as adaptations of existing rules, but a general practice and an *opinio juris* are not essential constituents of such rules. In the formation of such rules the I.C.J. has a creative role to play as it is the court which notionally derives the principle.

New Developments in Customary International Law

Present day developments in the field of customary international law may now be considered. Professor Parry[23] puts forward a novel theory: namely that no new general customary international law can evolve today, because the rules of general customary international law form the body of customary law, which after a point has exhausted its creative capacity. Hence he says that the only rules of customary international law which can evolve today are derogations from, or local variations of, that law as in the case of local or special custom. He bases his theory on an analogy drawn from the common law of England which is largely made up of the general customs of the land. Today general custom has ceased to be a source of English Law, although it forms the body of the common law. But local custom is still a subsidiary source of law, and may evolve where there are local variations of the common law, which do not violate general legal principles.

However custom, i.e., general custom, as a source of municipal law, has lost its place because more vigorous and less cumbersome law-making processes namely legislation and judicial activity have supplanted it. But this is not the case in international law. For the international law system has no legislative machinery, unless of course one were to approximate General Assembly resolutions to legislation which they are not. There is also no compulsory method of adjudication, except under the optional clause of the I.C.J. statute, adherence to which clause is itself a matter of state discretion. Hence it is submitted that the analogy between the role of general customary law in a municipal law system and that of general customary law in an international law system cannot be carried too far.

In fact even today rules of general customary international law do evolve though perhaps they do not quite fit into the traditional concept. A topical and important example of a new rule of general customary international law is the law relating to the Continental Shelf. The genesis and evolution of this body of customary international law may be considered in some detail as it affords an example of a divergent pattern of evolution.

Till the United States proclamation on the Continental Shelf in 1945, there was no customary international law governing the question of to whom the bed of the sea and subsoil, adjoining a coastal state belonged. In the *North Sea Continental Shelf* cases[24] the I.C.J. reiterated the view that the genesis of the doctrine was the Truman (U.S.) Proclamation of September 1945. This proclamation declared that the government of the United States regards the natural resources of the subsoil and seabed of the Continental Shelf beneath the high seas, but contiguous to the coast of the U.S. as appertaining to the U.S. subject to its jurisdiction and control. The U.S. Proclamation was followed by a spate of similar and even more extensive proclamations. In October 1945 Mexico made a declaration on the Continental Shelf, in October 1946 Argentina proclaimed sovereignty over the Continental Shelf, as well as the epi-continental sea. In 1947 Chile, Peru and Costa Rica made similar proclamations claiming portions of the high seas as well. In 1949 Saudi Arabia and eight other sheikdoms also made proclamations claiming sovereignty over the Continental Shelf. In subsequent years numerous other states have also done so, including Iraq, Burma and Ceylon in 1957. The proclamations relating to sovereignty or jurisdiction over the Continental Shelf did not meet with any protests, although the more extensive claims of some of the South American states did meet with protests.

In 1951 the International Law Commission was unwilling to state that there was a new body of customary international law on this subject although it recommended the adoption of such rules. By 1958, however, this new body of customary international law had been adopted in the Geneva Convention on the Continental Shelf. In the *North Sea Continental Shelf cases* it was recognized that articles 1–3 of the Convention dealing with the definition of the term and seaward extent of the Continental Shelf, the juridical character of the coastal state's entitlement, the nature of the rights exercisable, the kind of natural resources to which they relate, and the status of the high seas above it, embodied rules of customary international law.[25] Thus between 1945 and 1958 a new body of general customary international law on the Continental Shelf had come into being.

Thus we see here an example of a general custom which has developed from the unilateral act of one country. The Truman Proclamation generated a general practice among states, the practice itself taking the form of unilateral acts. These unilateral acts did not meet with any protests and hence the presence of an *opinio juris* may be inferred. The practice itself when viewed from the point of view of each state seems to be more in the nature of a special custom, because it is made up of a claim and acquiescence in that claim by other states. But since it is not limited to one country, or to some particular region, but is universal, it has the element of generality which is required for the formation of general customary international law.

The *opinio juris* can be said to have been present in the form of a conviction as to the binding nature of the rule that the Continental Shelf is subject to the sovereignty of the coastal state. Hence the proclamations made and the lack of protest or acquiescence by other states is evidence of such an *opinio juris*. As has been submitted above, the presence of an *opinio juris* can only be implied from the conduct of states. Hence the lack of protest or acquiescence must be treated as an acknowledgement by states of the presence of a right in the state making the proclamation.

This view is also borne out by an examination of the proclamations, which show them to be merely declaratory of an already existing right, and not constitutive of a new right, the basis of jurisdiction being deemed to be the inherent sovereignty of a state over its territory, and hence over natural prolongations of its territory under the sea. This principle has been recognised in the Geneva Convention on the Continental Shelf, and also in the recent judgement of the I.C.J. in the *North Sea Continental Shelf cases*.[26]

It must, however, be pointed out that the customary international law on the Continental Shelf, although novel in appearance was not contrary to existing customary international law, and could be reconciled with the fundamental principle of the freedom of the high seas.[27] Furthermore, as pointed out above, jurisdiction or sovereignty could be claimed on the basis of an extension of territorial sovereignty, and not on some entirely new ground. Hence it might even be argued that despite its unusual features, it is not an entirely new rule of customary international law, but an adaptation, or extension of customary international law to meet new requirements and pressures. It is however submitted that to interpret it in this way is merely a casuistry. For, after all, an adaptation of, or departure from, an existing rule can be called a new rule, particularly as in this case it covered a lacuna which existed in the law.

The customary international law relating to the Continental Shelf is also of interest because it shows very clearly the operation of extra legal factors in the development of rules of customary international law. The development of this body of customary international law is clearly a development brought about by present day requirements. Economic pressures caused by the need for new sources of food and natural resources, in the face of a population explosion, as well as the exhaustion of traditional resources has made it vital for coastal states to claim exclusive rights over the use and exploitation of areas of the seabed and subsoil of the high seas. Together with this need there has also been tremendous technological progress, which has made exploitation of the sea depths feasible.[28]

Extra legal factors, of course, exist as the raison d'être for all rules of law. But in this instance the very short time within which the custom has evolved enables us to see at work the economic, political, and technological factors which have given rise to, as well as provided for, the evolution and rapid development of this new body of customary law.

An examination of the evolution of this body of law shows clearly the inter-relation between economic factors and legal rules. The proclamations were originally actuated by the desire of coastal states to appropriate the mineral resources, i.e., petroleum deposits which had been discovered off their shores. Hence portions of the seabed and subsoil adjacent to the coastal states viz. the Continental Shelf, came to be claimed as part of the territory of the state. The Continental Shelf was originally used in its geological sense to mean the platform or base on which the continent rests, portions of which are under the sea, and which gradually slopes down under the sea up to the first drop off, which generally occurs at a depth of 200 metres. However as technological advances make exploitation of greater depths possible, we find the concept of the Continental Shelf too, expanding. Thus in the Geneva Convention on the Continental Shelf, the seaward extent of the Continental Shelf is defined so as to include not only depths up to 200 metres but even *"beyond that limit to where the depth of the superadjacent waters admits of the exploitation of the natural resources of the said areas."*

Further extensions have been made in the proclamations of certain countries which include in the Continental Shelf, the epi-continental platform, and the superadjacent seas, and depths well below the 200 metric depth, and even below the limits of present exploitability.[29] These proclamations may well lead to new extensions of the customary international law on this subject.[30] Some of these proclamations are founded on the desire of certain coastal states to appropriate for themselves exclusive fisheries zones. Governments have shown themselves to be aware of these extra-legal factors. Thus in the Santiago Declaration under which portions of the high seas was claimed by Chile, Peru and Ecuador, it was said:

> "Governments are bound to ensure for their people access to necessary food supplies, and to furnish them with the means of developing their economies."

Some of the other fields in which there has been a growth of new rules of customary international law are air law, and space law. These again are new fields of human activity and hence a new body of custom has come into being, regulating human activity in these spheres, and here too within a comparatively short space of time.

The new rules of customary international law do exhibit a few differences from old established rules of customary law. To begin with, the underlying extra legal factors are more evident than in the case of old established rules. Furthermore the time space within which they have evolved does not quite fit in with the notion of custom as being something which is time hallowed. Finally the 'practice' which constitutes the custom may be somewhat different in form and content from the traditional notion of "practice," as being comprised of usages carried on *between* states. Hence new rules of customary international law do have some differences of form and manner of evolution from the old established rules of customary international law, but the differences are not sufficiently basic to lead to the conclusion that such rules are not rules of general customary international law. Hence it is submitted that rules of general customary international law can and do in fact evolve today.

It is now necessary to look at two new institutions which have come to play a part in the development of general customary international law, namely, the International Law Commission, and the United Nations, and their contribution to the formation of custom. The International Law Commission has been given the task of codifying and progressively developing international law.[31] The work of the International Law Commission takes the form of reports which are submitted to the 6th Committee of the United Nations, and which are then debated upon. If the Committee adopts a report, it may call a diplomatic conference to draft a treaty (generally called a convention) on the basis of the report. If a treaty or convention emerges from such conferences, e.g., the 1958 Geneva Convention on the law of the sea, the convention itself has to pass through a number of stages. After it has been signed, and received the requisite number of ratifications by governments it comes into operation. Thus the work of progressive development and codification takes final shape in a convention.

It is generally conceded today that a distinction cannot be drawn between codification and progressive development, because practically all the rules of customary international law are in need of progressive development.[32] Hence the work of the International Law Commission is in a sense law-making. But the question arises as to the state at which there is law-making. Presumably this would be when an international convention, based on a report of the I. L. C., has come into operation. But it could be argued that the convention is only binding on the parties to it, and hence any changes or "progressive development," which it has brought about in the rules of customary international law, is not a change in the general body of customary international law, but applies only to the parties to the convention and is hence binding only as treaty law. However as one writer remarks,[33] "one knows as a matter of fact that, for instance, the law relating to the Continental Shelf was not the same after 1958 as it was before 1958." Certainly it must be admitted that the reports of the I. L. C., and the outcome of a convention, apart from its being evidence of the existence of rules of customary international law, also clarifies and progressively develops rules of customary international law, giving them a precise formulation and hence has an effect on the general body of customary international law.

In the *North Sea Continental Shelf cases*, one of the arguments put forward by Denmark and the Netherlands was that the emerging customary international law on the Continental Shelf, had been brought to its fruition in the 1958 Geneva Convention on the Continental Shelf. Thus they said:

> "That although prior to the conference Continental Shelf law was only in the formative state, and state practice lacked uniformity, yet the process of definition and consolidation of the emerging customary law took place through the work of the I.L.C., the reaction of governments to that work, and the proceedings of the Geneva Conferences; and this emerging customary law became crystallized in the adoption of the Continental Shelf Convention by the Conference."[34]

The court conceded the validity of this argument as a general proposition although it refused to agree that the article in question (i.e., article 6 which set out the equi-distant method of delimitation) had been adopted in the convention as an emerging rule of customary international law. The court pointed out that this article was one which had been entirely constructed by the I. L. C., on an experimental basis, at most *de lege ferenda*, and not at all *de lege lata* or as an emerging rule of customary international law.[35] Hence one must be cautious in stating that all articles in a convention either embody pre-existing customary law, or are a crystallization of emerging rules of customary international law, and hence binding on non parties to a convention as well. Nevertheless, one might safely conclude that a draft proposal by the I. L. C. and its adoption in a convention could be a constitutive element in the evolution of an emerging rule of customary international law.

Having come to the conclusion that an international convention has a part to play in the formulation of existing, customary international law, and in the process of evolution of emerging rules of customary international law, can we go one step further and say that a convention itself can give rise to a rule of customary international law? This interesting question was discussed in the *North Sea Continental Shelf cases*. One of the arguments put forward by Denmark and the Netherlands was that although at the date of the Geneva Convention on the Continental Shelf, there had been *no* rule of customary international law in favour of the equidistance method of delimitation, nevertheless, subsequent to the convention such a rule had come into being partly on its own impact, and partly on the basis of subsequent practice. Hence the argument was that the convention was the basis of the rule of customary international law. The court commenting on this said:—

> "It clearly involves treating that article as a norm-creating provision which has constituted the foundation of, or has generated a rule which, while only conventional or contractual in its origins has since passed into the general *corpus* of international law, and is now accepted as such by the *opinio juris*, so as to have become binding even for countries which have never and do not, become parties to the Convention."[36]

The court went on to say that such a process is a perfectly possible one, and does from time to time occur, and that it constitutes one of the recognized methods by which new rules of customary international law may be formed.

However the court was unable to agree that the rule in question, (the equi-distance special circumstances rule, as set out in article 6) had evolved into a rule of customary international law. The court came to this conclusion on the ground that the rule was not potentially of a norm-creating character; that evidence of a practice based on this rule by non parties to the convention was insufficient; and finally that even in cases where non party states had followed the rule there was no evidence to show that they so acted because they felt legally compelled to do so.[37] But the important point to note is that the court accepted in principle the proposition that a rule of customary international law can evolve from a convention, subject to the above qualifications.

The other institution which has a role to play in the development of customary international law today is the United Nations.[38] Among the political organs of the United Nations the General Assembly is the organ which reflects the attitudes and views of states, and hence would be evidence of state practice. Thus it has been called a "very clear, very concentrated focal point of state practice."[39]

But apart from this evidentiary role does the General Assembly have a more creative role to play in the formation of customary international law? Even a cursory examination shows that the General Assembly has through its resolutions made pronouncements on aspects of customary international law which have affected the direction of development of that law, and even created new principles of law, for example, the General Assembly resolutions on Colonialism, which has affected the law relating to territorial sovereignty, and the General Assembly resolutions on sovereignty over natural resources, which has affected the law relating to Nationalization, and State Responsibility.[40] The General Assembly resolutions on Outer Space have been creative of space law, while its declarations on Human Rights and Self Determination have been creative of new principles of international law. Of course these resolutions are not legislative. Resolutions of the General Assembly are not *per se* binding except on those voting in favour. Nevertheless, such resolutions passed over a period of time by a majority of states can lead to the acceptance of these resolutions into the general body of customary international law. In this instance these resolutions themselves comprise the general practice which is required for the formation of general customary international law. The element of *opinio juris* would perhaps be the notion that the passing of resolutions on a particular matter continuously over a period of time, by a majority of states, is indicative of a conviction as to the presence of certain underlying and basic obligations or principles of customary international law of which the resolutions themselves are merely an expression.

Thus it must be recognised that in the formation of customary international law, certain international institutions also have a part to play, namely, the International Court of Justice, the International Law Commission, and the General Assembly. As we have seen, the judgements and advisory opinions of the I. C. J. are not only evidence of the existence of rules of customary international law, but may also be creative of customary international law, although as submitted earlier the court cannot create entirely new law, but may derive subsidiary rules from already existing rules of customary international law. The reports of the I. L. C. and the conventions based on them have, as we have seen, an important role to play not only in the crystallization of emerging rules of general customary international law, but even in the formation of entirely new customary international law as was contended in the *North Sea Continental Shelf cases.* Similarly the resolutions of the General Assembly can be regarded as law creating. Hence it would appear today, that the practices and usages of states are not the only stuff out of which customary international law evolves. It is submitted that the judgements of the I. C. J., the reports of the I. L. C., and the conventions based on them, and the resolutions of the General Assembly can be the material out of which custom is fashioned. Furthermore the "practice" required to constitute a custom need not be a practice in the sense of a practice between states, but may consist of unilateral acts, or even General Assembly resolutions. Hence, it is submitted that traditional notions of what constitutes "practice," as well as the nature of the *opinio juris* need reformulation.

Notes

1. I.C.J. Reports, 1951.
2. Sir Hersch. Lauterpacht, *The Development of International Law by the International Court* (Revised Edition 1958, Stevens and Sons Ltd.) pp. 369–370.
3. See *op. cit., supra* n. 1, p. 128.
4. *Ibid* at pp. 134–138.
5. *Ibid* at p. 131.
6. *Ibid.*
7. *Ibid* at p. 133.
8. *Santiago Declaration* of 18th August 1952, later adhered to by Costa Rica.
9. See article 4 of the Convention.
10. I.C.J. Reports, 1951.
11. *Ibid* at p. 25.
12. Lauterpacht, *op. cit., supra* n. 2, p. 372.
13. See *op. cit., supra* n. 10, pp. 21–22.
14. P.C.I.J. (1927) series A, No. 10.
15. See article 11 of the Convention.
16. See the Anglo-Norwegian Fisheries case *op. cit., supra* n. 1, at p. 131.
17. I.C.J. Reports, 1950.
18. I.C.J. Reports, 1960 at p. 39.
19. I.C.J. Reports, 1969.

20. *Ibid* at para 77, p. 44.

21. *Ibid* at para 76.

22. A method of delimitation of the Continental Shelf, between states, according to the equi-distance principle.

23. See Clive Parry, *The Sources and Evidence of International Law* (1965, Manchester University Press), pp. 60–61.

24. I.C.J. Reports, 1969.

25. *Ibid.* at para. 63, p. 39.

26. See article 2(3) of the Convention; and I.C.J. Reports 1969, at para. 43 of the judgement.

27. See Lauterpacht, in 1950 *British Year Book of International Law* p. 376; see also articles 3 and 4 of the Convention on the Continental Shelf.

28. See D. W. Bowett, *The Law of the Sea*, (1967, Manchester University Press), p. 33.

29. See Santiago Declaration of 18 August 1952 and also recent Italian-Yugoslav agreement of 8th January 1968 delimiting between them the whole breadth of the Adriatic sea, which includes depths reaching 1,589 metres. See also recent declaration of Saudi Arabia on the seabed of the Red Sea, 30th October 1968.

30. See dissenting judgement of judge Ammoun in the North Sea Continental Shelf cases, p. 109 para. 8, where he poses the question whether these statements of position particularly those of Peru, Chile and Ecuador were not purely declaratory of an already established custom (the reference to custom here being presumably regional custom).

31. Article 13 of the charter of the United Nations charges the General Assembly with encouraging the "progressive development of international law, and its codification." The General Assembly in its turn has handed over this task to the International Law Commission.

32. See Jennings, in 1964 *International and Comparative Law Quarterly*, p. 385.

33. *Ibid.*

34. See I.C.J. Reports, 1969, at para 61.

35. *Ibid.* at para 62. On the genesis of the equi-distance method of delimitation, see para 48–56.

36. *Ibid.* at para 71.

37. *ibid.* at paras 72–79.

38. See Rosalyn Higgins, *The Development of International Law through the Political Organs of the United Nations* (1963, O.U.P.) at pp. 1–10 of the Introduction.

39. *Ibid.* at p. 2 of the Introduction.

40. See Amerasinghe, *State Responsibility for Injuries to Aliens* (1967, Oxford, Clarendon), pp. 30–31.

RUDOLF BERNHARDT

Unwritten International Law

It is one thing to speak of custom as a source of international law; it is another to speak of international law as customary. Some scholars have sought to differentiate folk or customary law from law created by treaties. In the following lucid essay, we are shown some of the arguments in favor of considering international law as customary and at the same time, how treaties themselves may almost certainly entail some connection with folk law.

For an example of the interrelationship of folk law with treaties, the author, Professor of German and Foreign Public Law and of Public International Law at the University of Heidelberg, Director of the Max Planck Institute for Comparative Public Law and International Law, and Vice-President of the European Court of Human Rights, cites what he calls the principle of pacta sunt servanda. *This Latin maxim or axiom refers to the agreement among the parties to a treaty that the treaty terms will be observed. The treaty itself rarely states specifically that those who sign it are thereby committing themselves to carry out its terms. Rather it is a tacit assumption that signatories consider themselves obliged to honor their signatures and to conform to the contract stipulated in the treaty. The question is whether or not this assumption or understanding known as* pacta sunt servanda *is indeed an example of international folk law. For the view that it is "undoubtedly a positive norm of general international law," see Josef L.Kunz, "The Meaning and Range of the Norm* Pacta Sunt Servanda," American Journal of International Law, *39 (1945), 180–197. For a different opinion suggesting that it is "not, strictly speaking, a rule of customary international law," see Roberto Lavalle, "About the Alleged Customary Law Nature of the Rule* Pacta Sunt Servanda," Österreichische Zeitschrift für Öffentliches Recht und Völkerrecht, *33 (1982), 9–28.*

Reprinted from *Law & State*, 16 (1977), 48–70, with permission of the author.

I

The question of unwritten international law is one of the more comprehensive issues concerning the sources of international law and the discussion is wide ranging and continuing. The development of the international community requires us to maintain a constant review and analysis of the sources of international law. In a short paper such as this one can do no more than draw attention to what seem to the author to be the most important contemporary problems. For more detailed treatment the reader must be referred to the larger works on the sources of international law, such as those of Sørensen[1], Suy[2], Parry[3], D'Amato[4], Verdross[5], Barberis[6] and many others; space also precludes further consideration of the juristic concept of a "source of international law"[7].

I would like to put two propositions at the head of this brief account of unwritten international law, propositions which appear to stand in contradiction to each other and to be irreconcilable, but which are both correct. They are:

> All international law is unwritten law.
> All international law is written law.

International treaties bind the contracting parties with regard to the rights and duties specified in them, thus constituting an example of written law in the proper sense (leaving aside the exceptional case of a treaty concluded orally, which would be unwritten law). The written law of the treaty is, however, inseparably bound up with principles of unwritten law. The principle *pacta sunt servanda*, the rules for the conclusion and terminaction of treaties, the rules of interpretation of treaties, the doctrine of *rebus sic stantibus* and a number of other general rules of the law of treaties have hitherto not been expressly incorporated into treaties themselves; even the entry into force of the Vienna Convention on the Law of Treaties of 1969 would leave some scope for the application of unwritten rules. The interdependence of written law and unwritten principles and ideas is particularly evident in the interpretation of treaties. Whenever the words and expressions in the treaty are not completely clear and unambiguous—and they normally are not—there occurs a process by which something is added to the written law.

These few remarks must suffice for the time being to show that all written international law owes its existence to unwritten law and must be supplemented by unwritten law in order to be applied in practice. It is not possible, or indeed necessary, to go into the distinction between the legal norm as an abstract command and the written formulation of the norm, though the two are not the same. All written law is the expression of particular underlying demands and precepts, even though in the course of time the words of the law often acquire an independent meaning and force.

In the strict sense the only written international law consists of treaties in force. Everything else, however, including all so-called unwritten international law, can only be perceived in lasting form through the medium of language, and that means as a rule language which someone somewhere has written down. The conduct of states, as of men, is linked to a moment of time, or to a short period, and the only evidence which can help one to discover the law in force is almost without exception documentary evidence. Diplomatic notes setting out legal justifications for a particular course of action or protesting at alleged illegalities, and resolutions adopted at international conferences or by international organisations only give a final and lasting picture of the positions taken up by the parties or organs concerned when reduced to writing. It is obvious that the opinions of international legal experts are only accessible in written form. Finally it is unlikely that one could still find a rule of unwritten international law to-day that has not yet been put into writing in some treaty or other. So it is that all unwritten law—international law not laid down by treaty—is in the last resort written, or at any rate recorded in writing.

These brief introductory remarks on the indissoluble connection between unwritten international law and written norms, language and documentary records are important in considering our sources of knowledge of unwritten international law. Treaty law and customary law exert a constant influence on each other. Treaties and other documents are of fundamental importance in determining the current state of customary law, and conversely treaty law needs to be supplemented by unwritten rules of international law in order to be applied in practice.

On closer examination we find that unwritten international law contains three areas of differing weight and importance. First there are the fundamental principles of the international legal order, without which international law is altogether unthinkable and incapable of functioning either at all or at any rate in any given historical epoch. In general these are not principles which lay down clear and detailed rules of conduct for the subjects of international law, but principles from which at all events direct precepts can be derived by means of practical interpretation, and by which the detailed rules are sustained and permeated. The unwritten fundamental principles of international law, in Verdross's words[8], form the "constitution" of the international legal community. In the first number of the journal Viktor Bruns[9], writing on international law as a legal system, drew a distinction between principles of law and legal institutions on the one hand and rules of law on the other. It is my impression that this distinction has been somewhat neglected in more recent discussions of the sources of international law. The fundamental principles[10] differ in many respects from that body of law usually described as customary law; they can be, and usually are of course, regarded as forming part of customary law, but one should not lose sight of their special characteristics. They are generally not concerned with defined rules of conduct, such as can be derived with greater or lesser certainty from the practice of states, but with presuppositions and basic concepts held by the subjects of the international legal order. Secondly, unwritten international law also consists of specific rules and precepts which have developed in the course of time, and a considerable proportion of which could be replaced by other rules and precepts without shaking the contemporary international legal order to its foundations. Let me clarify that by means of an example. The international legal system as we know it is scarcely conceivable without the principle of the sovereign equality of states. On the other hand, the rules as to state and diplomatic immunity can change. The specific rules of unwritten law are for the most part concerned with rights and duties of the subjects of international law which have been developed through customary international law. Both these areas—the "constitution" of the international legal community and the specific rights and duties—penetrate each other in much the same way as the constitution and municipal law of a state do and one can scarcely be separated from the other, but the distinction itself seems to me to be necessary and fruitful.

The third area of unwritten international law consists in my view of the general principles of national laws, to the extent that they are applied to fill gaps in the creation of international rights and duties.

II

Taking first the fundamental principles of the international legal order, here the interaction of written and unwritten law can be seen with particular clarity. The most important principles are contained in one form or another principally in the Charter of the United Nations, thereby attaining the binding force of treaty obligations for the 148 current member states, in other words for the great majority of the natural subjects of international law, the sovereign states. The same principles are, however, to a considerable extent binding also on non-member states in their relations with one another and in relations between members and non-members. This extended application may be derived partly from other treaties—for example, the Kellogg Pact for the prohibition of the use of force—and partly from a general more or less unequivocal consensus of states, or it can be regarded simply as a necessity for contemporary international society. Space does not permit a more detailed discussion of these possible bases for the validity of unwritten international law, except to say that the natural and sociological characteristics of the international community and the consensus of states together form the basis, in my view, of the international legal order and endow it and its particular legal norms with binding force.

As for the importance of the fundamental principles of the international legal order at the present day it can be argued that while there exists agreement on broad principles there are nevertheless profound differences of opinion on their scope and application in particular situations.[11] At times a particular "principle" may be more a matter of a verbal compromise than genuine agreement, but mostly difficulties arise from a clash between different principles, to which the various members of the international community accord differing priorities. This aspect is worth a closer look: the best examples are the Declaration on Principles of International Law concerning Friendly Relations and Cooperation among States in accordance with the Charter of the United Nations adopted by the United Nations General Assembly in 1970[12] and the definition of aggression adopted at the end of 1974[13]. Other relevant material include the various United Nations resolutions on the rights and duties of states in the economic sphere[14], especially in relation to the use of natural resources.

The sovereign equality of states is described in Article 2 (I) of the United Nations Charter as the basis of the organisation, and it is one of the principles which are most vigorously supported and defended, not least by the new states. It is indeed fundamental for the international legal order of the present day that all states should be equal in law in spite of the great differences between them in fact. At the same time, however, the disparity between legal equality and real power is becoming increasingly obvious. This is demonstrated by what happens at votes in the United Nations General Assembly, where the danger exists that a majority may overestimate its position and vote in disregard of other principles of the international community. The disparity between legal equality and real inequality is also demonstrated by the distribution of atomic weapons, in the efforts towards disarmament, in demands for preferential economic treatment of developing countries[15] and in the monopoly enjoyed by the oil-producing countries. Groupings of states are, and are becoming, more important in many cases than the legal equality of individual states seen in isolation. This is a point to which international lawyers should direct more attention than they have done hitherto.

Two other more or less uncontroversial fundamental principles of the international legal system, which we may cite as particularly important examples, demonstrate very clearly how agreement on principles may conceal profound differences of opinion. They are, first, the prohibition of the use of force and, secondly, the rule of non-intervention in matters within the domestic jurisdiction of a state by third states or by the international community.

Contrary to the view held at the beginning of the century, or perhaps even fifty years ago, the principle of sovereignty does not at the present day entitle a state to resort unilaterally to the use of force, not even as a means of enforcing valid legal claims after all other measures have failed. The prohibition of aggression has long been recognised, in word at least, by virtually all states, and after decades of effort the United Nations General Assembly adopted a definition of aggression at the end of 1974. There are, however, enough indications that this step will not be of much assistance and that on the contrary several states follow their own interpretation on the prohibition of force. The Friendly Relations Resolution of 1970 recognised not merely the right of self-determination but also the right of repressed peoples to seek and receive outside support[16]. Article 7 of the resolution on the prohibition of aggression concedes a right to fight against repression and a right to receive outside help to "peoples under colonial or racist regimes or other forms of alien domination"—a wide formulation[17]. If there were agreement on the meaning of foreign domination, and if the opportunities of manipulation of such appeals for outside help and of the exercise of foreign influence were not so numerous, the qualifications on the prohibition of the use of force would not be so difficult to accept as they now are for the sceptical observer. When one considers also how force has been used in the past, and may be used again in future, to counter real or supposed attempts by certain states to detach themselves from a power block, as in the case of Czechoslovakia; how discussion has taken place on the possibility that force might be used in the event of certain measures being taken by the oil-producing countries, and how uncertain China's position is on the use of force, it becomes obvious that the existence of the supposed agreement on the prohibition of the use of force is a matter of some doubt. Another noteworthy feature is the lack of discussion of the legal implications of recent events in and involving Cyprus. Altogether there are numerous indications that the distinction between just and unjust wars still plays a part in the application of the prohibition of the use of force at the present day, though rarely mentioned in so many words, with the concepts of just and unjust taking on a more ideological colour than ever before.

It is thus tempting to cite what Bismarck said 100 years ago about the prohibition of the use of force:

> "The object of international law is to uphold the legal position of each state in relation to other states. However, when a large country is involved in a dispute with another state it only acts in accordance with international law while it considers this course to be to its advantage. If this is not the case, then it has no time for international law and asserts its claims by force. A small country can achieve nothing by force and must therefore always act in accordance with the rules of international law"[18].

We would have to amend that at the present day to take account of the fact that it is precisely the small states which can resort to force, given favourable circumstances, much more readily than major international powers certainly, although the prohibition of the use of force rests on a much firmer legal basis than it did in Bismarck's time.

The principle of non-intervention in matters of domestic jurisdiction was contained in Article 15 (8) of the League of Nations Covenant and now forms Article 2 (7) of the United Nations Charter. It continues without doubt to constitute one of the fundamental general principles of international law and has been recognised on several occasions in resolutions of the United Nations. Again however numerous recent events and a series of government statements have raised doubts as to the real extent of the consensus. The asserted right of self-determination of peoples[19], or at any rate certain expressions of the demand for self-determination, can scarcely be reconciled with the rule of non-intervention in domestic affairs. The progressive recognition of human rights guaranteed by international law also conflicts with state sovereignty and the rule of domestic jurisdiction. The protection of human rights by international law has been welcomed in principle on every side—and we shall return to it in a moment—but it involves the risk of unlawful intervention in matters of domestic jurisdiction as well as the danger of double standards where ideologies conflict.

Thus the sovereign equality of states, the prohibition of the use of force, and the rule of non-intervention in matters of domestic jurisdiction are just as much essential features of the contemporary international legal order as the call for self-determination and demands for the protection of human dignity and the fundamental rights derived therefrom. Since these principles imply value judgments and since it is debatable whether general agreement exists on many points, it means that the fundamental principles of the international legal order, and with them the constitution of the international community, are precarious and endangered.

It is not the primary purpose of this discussion to provide a summary of the law as it stands, but rather to explore tendencies, possibilities and dangers in contemporary developments in unwritten international law. In my opinion the accepted fundamental principles of the international legal order require critical re-examination in the light of two developments in particular: firstly, the greater emphasis on obligation to the community at the expense of state sovereignty and secondly, the recognition at the international level of the existence of fundamental rights limiting the power of the state, with its implications for international law.

The special emphasis on state sovereignty, which began its triumphal progress with the emergence of the absolutist states and has been helped rather than hindered by the rise of democratic internal governments, has left a considerable mark on modern international law. As natural law theories and ideas have lost ground, the state has become both internally and externally virtually without obligations in its capacity as a member of the international community. This has had profound implications for unwritten international law. In the Lotus Case, for example, the Permanent Court of International Justice in 1927 held that state sovereignty was the rule and any qualifications to it must be proved as exceptions[20]. In the interpretation of treaties a constantly recurring argument is that contractual provisions must be construed restrictively in case of doubt, so as to preserve each state's freedom of decision[21].

The rule of non-intervention in matters of domestic jurisdiction also underlines the sovereignty of the individual state and plays down its responsibilities to the international community. All in all one can say that prevailing views on the existence and interpretation of rules and principles of international law have up to now treated freedom from obligation as the rule and the existence of obligation as the exceptional case.

At this point we must raise the question whether responsibility to the community, the legal duty to take account of the interests of the community as a whole, should not be recognised to a greater degree than hitherto as a fundamental principle of the international legal order, thus limiting—but not completely negating—the traditional idea of sovereignty. There are numerous indications for a trend in this direction. The resolution on Friendly Relations cites "the duty of States to co-operate with one another in accordance with the Charter" as a principle of international law[22]. Article 2 (2) of the Geneva Convention on the High Seas of 1958 contains one noteworthy reservation on the use of the high seas, which is capable in my opinion of general application:

it provides that the recognised freedoms in the use of the high seas should be exercised by each state with reasonable regard to the interests of other states in the exercise of their freedoms. Articles 24 and 25 of the same Convention oblige states to take steps to prevent oil pollution and radioactive contamination of the high seas. There are many other points which in my opinion support the argument that responsibility to the international community as a whole can be regarded as an essential part of the international legal order. The linking of states in innumerable international organisations to which unwritten powers are conceded, in ever greater contrast to the classical interpretation of the law, is just as much a feature of contemporary international society as the factual interdependence of all states and peoples. The international legal order cannot remain untouched by facts which are staring states and individuals alike in the face. International lawyers should have more regard for this interrelation of fact and law than they have done in the past. It is just as wrong to ignore the inability of a number of states to support their populations, amounting to thousands of millions of people, without imported foodstuffs, as it is to disregard the dependence of the industrial nations on foreign oil and other imported raw materials and products. The unrestricted use of financial power by states and their nationals can shake the international community to its foundations. The dangers of pollution and destruction of the environment know no frontiers and are there for all to see. The risks of atomic warfare are no less incalculable because they have receded into the background in the minds of many people in view of the deceptive peace currently prevailing. With these cursory and much simplified observations it is hoped to indicate certain points of view which should be taken into account in considering the fundamental principles of international law. The recognition of the idea that states are responsible to the community and are obliged to have regard to the interests of the community as a whole as a fundamental principle of international law can have considerable implications for particular rights and duties of states; we will return to this point when we come to discuss customary law. Furthermore as Jörg P. Müller has impressively demonstrated[23] the upholding of legitimate expectations in international law, also reflected in the Friendly Relations resolution[24], is closely related to the concept of states as responsible members of a community. On the other hand, the oft-cited principle of peaceful co-existence has very little to do with it; on the contrary, ideas of state sovereignty have dominated discussions of peaceful co-existence. Wolfgang Friedmann was, it is suggested, correct to contrast, or at any rate distinguish, the international law of co-existence and the law of co-operation[25].

There is also much to be said for regarding the obligation to respect the dignity of man and fundamental human rights as a fundamental principle of the international legal order. We have already pointed out the conflict between this principle and the rule of non-intervention in matters of domestic jurisdiction. It is certainly right that states in practice condemn some denials of human rights while condoning others, depending upon their point of view, so that even the most blatant violations of human rights are overlooked by the international community when they occur in certain developing countries, while racial segregation practised by a white minority regime is condemned as a threat to international peace. But recognition of human rights as rights protected by international law occurs in so many instances, from the Charter of the United Nations, Universal Declarations and Pacts to regional conventions, and with such intensity that one is justified in describing it as a general principle of the international legal community. This principle also has an effect on particular rules and precepts of international law.

Before turning to customary law in the narrow sense, I would like to emphasise again the nature of the relationship between fundamental principles and particular rules of international law. In municipal law, constitutional law and ordinary statute law interact constantly upon each other, and the same interaction occurs between the "constitution" of the international legal community and particular rules of treaty and customary law. This comparison with municipal law must not be misunderstood, of course: in international law, unlike (German) municipal law, there is no rule that fundamental (constitutional) principles enjoy precedence over particular provisions, so that a provision which conflicts with the fundamental principles is invalid. Nor do the fundamental principles constitute *jus cogens*, at least not entirely—but we cannot explore that point here. It is only the interaction, the mutual permeation, of fundamental principles and particular rules which we seek to emphasise. If more weight is put on state sovereignty, this affects the interpretation of treaty provisions and the practical application of rules of customary law; if greater emphasis is placed upon responsible membership of the international community, particular rights and duties will appear in a different light. One final interaction should be mentioned: uncertainty and differences of opinion on the fundamental principles of a legal system can affect every single rule of law, especially the unwritten rules. If many of the rules of customary international law seem at the present day to be more disputed than was the case in the past, the explanation may well be not least the existence of profound differences of opinion between states on the bases and fundamental principles of international law, in spite of all the outward agreement. This is one of several arguments in favour of progressive codification of the most important areas of international law.

III

When we speak of unwritten international law we are thinking primarily of the rules of customary international law and its criteria and problems, to which I now turn. Once again the uncontroversial aspects will be omitted, or merely touched upon, and greater emphasis put on those questions which seem to me to be most important at the present day, at the risk of a somewhat one-sided presentation.

Here again space does not permit further consideration of one of the fundamental problems of customary international law, namely the basis of its binding force, except to say that in my opinion, as in the case of the fundamental principles of the international legal order discussed earlier, the factual and sociological basis together with the *opinio juris* of states generally forms the source of the binding force of international law. Contrary to the view previously held by many international lawyers, and still espoused by Tunkin[26] among others, the binding force of customary law is not a matter of the consent of each state to submit to it, but depends rather on the collective *opinio juris* of the international community. It is true that a particular state can generally prevent the formation of a rule of customary law by protest and contrary practice, but an outward manifestation of consent is not required, nor can the continued validity of an existing rule depend upon the agreement of a particular state. All attempts to base customary international law on an implied contract and the corresponding implied consent of states[27]lead in the last resort to the dissolution of the international legal order and allow each state to accept only those rules which suit it and to reject the others.

Notwithstanding occasional arguments against the admission of any subjective elements at all in the creation and ascertainment of customary law[28], and subject to further consideration of the nature of the state practice required, the great majority of international lawyers now rightly recognises that customary law consists in principle of two essential elements: the practice of states and the opinion of states that the practice is based upon and required by law (the so-called *opinio juris sive necessitatis*). The International Court of Justice (I. C. J.) expressly emphasised the necessity of the *opinio juris* once more in its judgement in the Continental Shelf Case in 1969[29]. At the same time it has been doubtful from the very beginning exactly what *opinio juris* means in practice. As it certainly does not refer to the opinion of individuals as such, even when discharging the highest functions of state, any subjective emphasis is doubtful and to some extent misplaced; as with all references to the will of states and other communities we are dealing with misleading anthropomorphic analogies. That cannot be avoided, however, and does no harm as long as one remains aware of the real issues which lie behind the concepts and verbal formulae. In my opinion the most convincing explanation of the "subjective" or qualitative element in the creation of customary law is that advanced by Verdross[30] among others, and most forcefully by D'Amato[31] in his study of customary law[32]. D'Amato and Verdross argue that the existence of a rule of international law must first be articulated or asserted and the assertion must be received by the international community more or less without contradiction. The existence of a rule of unwritten, or non-treaty based, international law must have been asserted in one form or another—we will return to the question of form later—so that it has nothing to do with the actual subjective opinions of individual persons or with the unpublished views of state representatives but depends on the express assertion of a rule or principle of law. This articulation of the rule must occur in a manner which brings it to the attention of the international community and must be accepted or recognised by the community without serious opposition. There must in addition in general be evidence of state practice in accordance with the alleged rule.

One might suppose that it would be relatively easy to prove the existence of state practice, but in fact the problems are scarcely less than with the *opinio juris*. This is particularly the case with the interpretation of omissions and their implications. The authoritative definition of customary law in Article 38 of the statute of the I. C. J. does not help much. This has rightly been criticised by most writers[33]; it requires an international practice which is evidence of a general practice accepted as law. Although this formulation brings out the point that the practice must be international, in the interesting and difficult borderline cases the Statute of the World Court largely fails us.

In general the only clear cases are those in which unilateral state conduct, both internal and external, and international acts show an unbroken and uniform practice over a longer period of time, supported by an *opinio juris*. Thus, for a long time the three mile limit was established practically beyond doubt as the extent of territorial waters subject to the exclusive jurisdiction of the coastal state, and formed one of the fundamental rules of the international law of the sea; apart from exceptional cases coastal states claimed no greater territorial waters than this in their own legislation and declarations, and other states accepted and respected the three mile limit and used the waters beyond the three mile limit without challenge as high seas. In the rules of customary law governing state and diplomatic immunity, as well as in the formation of rules of customary law on the continental shelf, one can observe how unilateral state acts and indications of consent on the part of other members of the international community combine to create rules of law.

There are many different kinds of evidence of the necessary state practice and the *opinio juris:* there is no closed list[34]. If customary law is regarded as being in truth a network of implied agreements, it would be logical to confine the evidence exclusively to the conduct of accredited representatives of the state, but this view, argued by Strupp[35] among others, has deservedly found few adherents. Every attempt to draw up a complete list of the admissible evidence for customary international law or to establish indispensable features of such evidence is in my opinion of doubtful value and ought to be rejected. Rules of customary law can apply to all types of situations and spheres of life and the indications of the existence of an undisputed practice supported by the *opinio juris* of states can be correspondingly varied. The fewer the sure and certain criteria for the sources of evidence of customary law, the greater is the possible area of uncertainty in any particular case of course, but this disadvantage is unavoidable.

International acts have without doubt a special importance in the creation of customary law but other transactions and events must not be overlooked. It should be pointed out that treaties[36] and resolutions of international organisations[37], though not themselves direct sources of customary international law, can also be evidence of the existence or creation of rules of customary law. Judicial decisions—whether of national or international courts or of arbitral tribunals—can also be sources of international practice supported by *opinio juris*, independently of Article 38 (I) (d) of the Statute of the I.C. J.[38]. Even transactions in which there is substantial involvement of private individuals and interests can shed light on existing rules of international law. Any given case calls for a most careful appraisal whether the alleged practice has been unopposed, but it can, for example, be quite sufficient that national courts or even private corporations have arrived at consistent decisions or taken consistent measures in several cases of international importance without giving rise to state opposition in any significant degree.

The number of relevant acts and the length of the practice in time are less important for the formation of customary international law than the absence of opposition and of measures which are inconsistent with the alleged rule[39]. Regard must be had to the close connection and interrelation between international practice and the *opinio juris.* The clearer and more consistent the signs of a common view of the legal position, the less the extent of the relevant practice matters. If a single act of a single state, such as, for example, putting a communications, meteorological or observation satellite into space, not merely arouses no protest from other states but is generally recognised as a lawful act under international law, there is no need for the "practice" to continue for a longer period of time.

This brings us to the question of the time element in the creation and continued validity of rules of customary international law. The classical theory of customary international law was based no doubt on the idea of state practice so old that its origins were shrouded in the mists of time. It is not easy to reconcile the creation of rules of customary law through a few acts taking place over a very short period of time with the usual notion of "custom" and the traditional assumption of a slow process of growth for customary rules. The International Court of Justice nevertheless rightly pointed out, in the Continental Shelf case[40], that the length of time required must vary according to the nature of the particular subject-matter and that in some circumstances only a very short time may be required for the formation of rules of customary international law. Writers such as Lauterpacht[441], Fitzmaurice[42] and Tunkin[43] have also accepted that state practice extending over a short period of time may be sufficient for the formation of customary international law, and this is now the generally held view[44]. Even an isolated and sporadic practice can thus give rise to a rule of customary international law if it is universally accepted or recognised.

How and when existing customary international law can be modified or abrogated raises more difficult issues than those involved in the formation of customary law. The present state of the law of the sea and the discussions taking place on it provide plenty of examples of the difficulties. Now that a considerable number of states recognises neither the three mile limit nor the twelve mile limit as the extent of exclusive jurisdiction over territorial waters, has the former rule of customary law been abrogated? Is the law subject to modification by contrary usage? These are clearly issues of the most fundamental kind concerning the nature of law itself. It seems to me that if we are to maintain the proper value and normative force of law—which is important politically as well as from a juristic point of view—neither the fact of contrary usage alone nor the will of individual states can be regarded as having power to abolish a rule of customary law, and the rule remains in force even though disregarded by a considerable number of states. It would scarcely be disputed that a party to a treaty, or indeed a large number of the parties to a multilateral treaty, cannot legally renounce the obligations of the treaty by a unilateral act—apart from the *rebus sic stantibus* doctrine—and the same must apply to customary international law. Treaty and custom have in principle the same force of law and the obligations created by them remain, notwithstanding the failure on the part of some states to respect those obligations. It follows, in my submission, that the extension of state sovereignty far into the high seas is still at the present day contrary to international law and that there is still a general right of passage through international waterways. The ancient dilemma of international law, that it can demand conduct according to law but not enforce it, cannot be solved by saying that the law ceases to apply when it is disregarded to a great extent. On the other hand, a change in practice can lead to a change in the *opinio juris* and customary law is no less changeable than other forms of law. The processes of formation, change and extinction of rules of customary international law depend less on what happens at a particular moment of time than on the existence of continuity in time. There is a large grey area between the continuation in force of a rule of customary law in the face of repeated violations and the abrogation of the rule by reason of a change in state practice and the *opinio juris:* each particular case depends upon its own circumstances. The number of states involved is of little relevance, and other factors must also be considered. Similar problems occur with the breach of treaty obligations and the questions of the "frustration" of treaty obligations by the subsequent formation of inconsistent customary law. Recent developments in international economic law have raised this problem on a number of occasions[45]. It may well be that the requirements for a binding modification of treaty law should be more stringent than those for a change in unwritten international law, but in neither case can individual states or groups of states shake off the obligation unilaterally.

Much of what we have said so far also applies to the much discussed problem whether, and to what extent, newly created states, especially former colonies which have become independent, are bound by previously existing customary international law[46]. If newly independent states were completely free of all obligations under pre-existing customary international law, this would be inconsistent with the existence of a legal order of any kind, and this extreme view appears to lack any serious adherents. It follows that individual states cannot declare themselves free from whatever rules of customary law they find burdensome and inappropriate, though such declarations may produce a change in the *opinio juris* which in turn, normally accompanied by a corresponding change in state practice, leads to the abrogation or modification of the previous rule. On the contrary view, based on the dogma of sovereignty, each state is free to choose at will which of the existing rules of international law it will adhere to[47]; logically this view also leads to the dissolution of the international legal order.

One further problem can only be touched upon briefly, namely the possibility of regional, local or particular customary law[48]. The

International Court of Justice has acknowledged the existence of this possibility[49], and correctly so, but space does not permit an examination of the judgments in detail. Insofar as general international law is *jus dispositivum*—subject to the contrary agreement of the relevant parties—it can be displaced in the relations between two or more states to each other not merely by the conclusion of treaties but also by the formation of customary law applying only to those parties. The criteria for the formation of such particular customary law must in principle be the same as for general customary law, except that greater attention will need to be paid to the consent of the individual states. The reason for the greater importance of the consent of the individual state in the case of particular customary law is of course that one is dealing with obligations which go further than those of general international law, thus involving issues of state sovereignty and the sovereign equality of states.

I would now like to return to some propositions advanced in the first section of this paper, namely that obligations to the community and the duty to respect the interests of the international community are just as much fundamental principles of contemporary international law as the obligation to respect the dignity and essential fundamental rights of the individual person. If these propositions can be sustained—and the writer does not dispute that there are valid counter-arguments—the effect on the formation, content and abrogation of rules of customary international law could be considerable. We must therefore take a closer look at the question in the light of some examples, of which the most useful are those where the dangers of a legal vacuum and the unchecked growth of claims of state sovereignty are obvious.

Does customary international law permit states, through their nationals, to exploit the fishery resources of the sea outside their coastal waters to the extent of exhaustion of the stocks or reduction to an insignificant level? Does international law give a riparian state the right to pollute the waters of an international river, or to change the water temperature, etc., without regard to the interests of the other riparian states? To what extent are other forms of pollution lawful if the effects are felt beyond the boundaries of the originating state? How should the dispute concerning the French nuclear tests in the Pacific, which was submitted to the International Court of Justice without securing a decision on the merits[50], have been decided in fact? Is it essential in all these cases that there should be a uniform practice extending over many years and an undivided *opinio juris* one way or the other?

The answers to these questions will probably differ according to one's fundamental assumptions. If state sovereignty is emphasised, the result will be that no attention will be paid to the interests of the community as a whole in many cases; conversely legal obligations imposed in the interest of the international community and of the living conditions of mankind can only exist at the expense of state sovereignty. In my submission there are good reasons for regarding the duty to respect the interests of the community as legally more important than the claims of sovereignty.

The same considerations apply to the question of the modification and abrogation of rules of customary international law. Unlimited and unhindered use of the high seas is a recognised principle of customary international law. The principle was unobjectionable so long as the oceans appeared to be inexhaustible and the selfishness of individual states created no recognisable danger to the interests of the community. Insofar as such unrestricted use of the high seas conflicts with the interests of the international community at the present day, it seems reasonable to conclude that the legal position can soon change, if it has not changed already.

At this point it is appropriate to emphasise the dependence of international law and international legal theory on the nature of the factual subject-matter. The international lawyer needs to work with scholars in other disciplines more than ever before. This raises difficult issues which can be mentioned only briefly.

From various quarters the international lawyer is asked to look beyond the bare rules of international law—which are generally considered to be unsatisfactory anyway—and to take account of reality and of the conclusions of other branches of learning[51]. I believe that the discussion of this question has been marred by many misunderstandings and ambiguities and that in particular the nature and characteristics of law are frequently misunderstood. The close connection between legal rules and all areas of human and international life is evident enough, and it is very doubtful whether anything can be gained by denying the importance of law as such because of the complexity of life[52]. This is particularly true of unwritten law. The application of the law in a given case, on the other hand, depends in many instances on facts and circumstances about which the law itself cannot necessarily inform us. We argued earlier that obligation to the community should be regarded as an important principle of international law; the practical application of this principle would require knowledge of the interests at stake, the risks involved and all the relevant circumstances. For example: a state's economic difficulties, the extent to which fish stocks are endangered, the possible or probable effects of pollution extending beyond international frontiers and other factors can all be legally relevant and must be taken into account when applying the law in practice. What the Club of Rome said about "the limits of growth" and "mankind at the turning-point" can also be relevant for international law and the international lawyer. To this extent at least it is necessary to have interdisciplinary cooperation, and I would refer to Bruno Simma's important work on this.[53]

IV

As we have said, the number of state acts and the length of time for which a practice has continued are, in the conditions of the modern international community, no longer decisive in the formation of new rules of customary international law. A new rule can come into existence in a very short time and on very sparse evidence of state practice if a widespread and unchallenged *opinio juris* can be established. If there is no practice at all, however, one could not talk of customary law in the accepted sense of the term. Nevertheless it would be unsatisfactory and scarcely adequate if new rules of law could not be created spontaneously to meet new situations as they arise. For example, as soon as a real possibility exists that weapons of mass destruction could be stationed in space or on other celestial bodies or in the sea, or that individual states could exploit the Arctic for military purposes, the existence of a consensus among states should be sufficient to produce new rules of law spontaneously to counter the danger without the need for actual practice. If relevant resolutions of the United Nations General Assembly have been passed unanimously and are regarded not merely as politically desirable but as laying down principles which are legally binding, and there has been no contrary practice, this should give rise to new rules of law. Moreover, resolutions within the framework of the United Nations are only one of several possible means by which new law of this kind can be made. Of course, this kind of "instant" law[54], arising spontaneously, does not fit into the traditional categories of the sources of international law, but the categories are not rigidly defined and must be adapted to changing situations. Article 38 of the Statute of the International Court of Justice should also not be understood in my opinion as laying down the sources of international law in a final and immutable form; room must be left to take account of new developments and changes in the *opinio juris*. Spontaneously created rules of international law can scarcely be regarded as customary law in the strict sense, but they are closely related to it. Their distinguishing mark is the general recognition of a principle as a legally binding rule although there has not been, and could not be, any relevant prior state practice with a corresponding *opinio juris*. The *opinio juris*, or as D'Amato describes the qualitative element of customary international law, the articulation of a principle of international law, occurs spontaneously, while the practice appears not to exist. In the example of the weapons of mass destruction the object is merely to prevent the development of a new practice involving danger for the international community, and the case is not too dissimilar to other prohibitions imposed by rules of customary international law. The existence of such prohibitions can as a rule be seen from the fact that states do not in practice take action which it is within their power to take, and their restraint is based on their conviction that it is required by law. The peculiarity of "instant" international law in our sense lies in the fact that states have previously lacked the power to take the prohibited action and also in the speed with which an *opinio juris* is formed. I cannot see why traditional views could not be developed to the point of embracing recognition of the spontaneous formation of unwritten international law in this manner.

V

In addition to the fundamental principles, or "constitution" of the international legal community, and customary international law, including rules which arise spontaneously, I would cite the general principles of municipal law as an example of unwritten international law. This area of the law gains ever-increasing importance in the changing conditions of modern international law.

The fundamental principles and the rules of customary international law are founded on contact between states and on relations between the subjects of international law. The distinguishing feature of the general principles of law in the terms of Article 38 (I) (c) of the Statute of the International Court of Justice seems to me—space does not permit further discussion of previous attempts to define them or of the different views which have been advanced—to lie in the fact that questions of law can arise at an international level for which there exists no relevant state practice, but for which more or less appropriate solutions have been found in municipal systems of law. The internal Law of international organisations, principles of procedure in international tribunals, lists of human rights for the purposes of international law and so on can and often will reveal ambiguities or loopholes which can not be resolved or filled by recourse to customary international law. In this case it is legitimate and necessary to adopt for international law, rules on which national systems of law are agreed. Written (and unwritten) municipal law is thus converted to unwritten international law.

VI

In conclusion we can say that written and unwritten international law are inseparably connected. The greater the degree of agreement on the fundamental principles of a legal system, the less it needs detailed, written rules; if there is less agreement on fundamental principles, the need for written rules to achieve a minimum of legal protection of rights becomes that much greater. In view of the uncertainties which exist at the present day with regard to the fundamental principles of the international legal order it would seem to be desirable to press ahead with the codification of important areas of international law. Codification does not make unwritten international law irrelevant[55], but it does remove some of the uncertainty. We can be sure that unwritten law will continue to play an important part in the development of international law. It is the task of international legal science to research and expound the areas and rules of unwritten law with precision, and here practice plays an essential part. Research cannot, however, be directed merely at recording international events and making state practice known, but must rather seek, by means of critical evaluation of the facts, to develop the law towards a more just, effective and humane order for peace in the world. This applies particularly in the area of unwritten law, which at the present day contains an especially high degree of uncertainty and doubt, with all that implies for the protection of legal rights. Whether progress can be made towards the peaceful regulation of international relations will depend not least upon the success of efforts towards more extensive agreement on the fundamental principles governing the international community.

Notes

1. M. Sørensen: *Les sources du droit international, Etude sur la jurisprudence de la Cour permanente de Justice internationale* (1946).
2. E. Suy: *Les actes juridiques unilatéraux en droit international public* (1962).
3. C. Parry: *The Sources and Evidences of International Law* (1965).
4. A. A. D'Amato: *The Concept of Custom in International Law* (1971).
5. A. Verdross: *Die Quellen des universellen Völkerrechts* (The Sources of General International Law) (1973).
6. J. A. Barberis: *Fuentes del derecho internacional* (1973).
7. See for example G. G. Fitzmaurice: "Some Problems regarding the Formal Sources of International Law". *Symbolae Verzijl* (1958); pp. 153 to 176: the present writer takes issue with Fitzmaurice on a number of important points, however.

8. A. Verdross: *Die Verfassung der Völkerrechtsgemeinschaft (The Constitution of the International Legal Community)* (1926).

9. V. Bruns: "Völkerrecht als Rechtsordnung (International Law as a Legal System)" (1926). *Zeitschrift für ausländisches öffentliches Recht und Völkerrecht* 1, 3, 10.

10. There are numerous divisions and conceptual distinctions which can be made in the fundamental principles, but which space does not permit us to consider. The expression is rather to be understood broadly as embracing all the maxims which are fundamental to the existence and the contemporary state of the international legal order.

11. It remains to be seen whether the Conference on European Security and Cooperation and the practical results which follow from it will confirm this assessment.

12. Res. 2625 (XXV), 24. 10. 1970.

13. Res. 3314 (XXIX), 14. 12. 1974.

14. See now particularly the controversial Charter of Economic Rights and Duties of States, Res. 3281 (XXIX) of 12. 12. 1974, and the Declaration and Programme of Action on the Establishment of a New International Economic Order, Res. 3201 and 3202 (S-VI) of 1. 5. 1974.

15. See, for example, B. E. David: "Quelques réflexions sur l'égalité économique des Etats" (1974). *10 Revue belge de droit international* 399–424.

16. ". . . such peoples are entitled to seek and to receive support in accordance with the purposes and principles of the Charter." The reference to the purposes and principles of the United Nations Charter and other indications reveal on closer examination (see Frowein, below; p. 159 et seq.) that the right to demand and receive help from other states is subject to important qualifications and limitations, but its actual political effect and scope extend far beyond any such limits.

17. See further, for example, the recurring demand for all states "to provide moral and material assistance to all peoples struggling for their freedom and independence in the colonial territories and to those living under alien domination . . ." (General Assembly Resolutions 2908 [XXVII] and 3163 [XXVIII] inter alia).

18. Conversation with a Japanese delegation on 15. 3. 1873, in O. von Bismarck, *Werke in Auswahl (Selected Works)* edited by A. Milatz, Vol. 5 (1973); p. 311.

19. See K. Doehring: "Das Selbstbestimmungsrecht der Völker als Grundsatz des Völkerrechts (The right of self-determination of peoples as a fundamental principle of international Law)" [*Berichte der Deutschen Gesellschaft für Völkerrecht (Reports of the German International Law Association)* No. 14 (1974)].

20. P.C.I.J. (1927) A. 10.

21. See on this Bernhardt: "Die Auslegung völkerrechtlicher Verträge insbesondere in der neueren Rechtsprechung internationaler Gerichte (The interpretation of treaties in international law with particular reference to recent decisions of international tribunals)" [*(Beiträge zum ausländischen öffentlichen Recht und Völkerrecht, 40) (Papers on Foreign Public Law and International Law, 40)*], 1963; p. 143 et seq.

22. This principle stands on an equal footing with the other six principles in the resolution.

23. J. P. Müller: "Vertrauensschutz in Völkerrecht (The Upholding of Legitimate Expectations in International Law)" *[(Beiträge zum ausländischen öffentlichen Recht und Völkerrecht, 56 (Papers on Foreign Public Law and International Law, 56)]*. 1971.

24. "The principle that states shall fulfill in good faith the obligations assumed by them in accordance with the Charter."

25. W. Friedmann: *The Changing Structure of International Law* (1964) especially p. 60 et seq.; id.: "The Relevance of International Law to the Process of Economic and Social Development." In: R.A. Falk and C. E. Black (Eds.): *The Future of the International Legal Order, Vol. 2: Wealth and Resources* (1970); pp. 3, 8; id.: "Human Welfare and International Law, A Reordering of Priorities," in *Essays in Honor of Ph. C. Jessup* (1972); p. 113. See also B. Simma: "Völkerrecht und Friedensforschung (International Law and Peace Studies)." *Die Friedens-Warte*, Vol. 57 (1974); p. 65 at 71: "Alongside the traditional international law of coexistence, which is essentially a catalogue of duties of abstention, there is a rapidly growing international law of cooperation resting on a well developed organisational base and detaching one economic, technical, social, humanitarian etc. area after another from the once so impregnable *domaine réservé* of states and subjecting them to international regulation."

26. See G. I. Tunkin: "Remarks on the Juridical Nature of Customary Norms of International Law (1961)." 49 *California LR* 419; also Tunkin: *Theory of International Law* (German translation, 1972; p. 153 et seq.).

27. No less questionable are the more recent attempts to divide general rules of international law into a large number of bilateral legal relationships peculiar to each rule, as for example in Z. S. Slonka: *International Custom and the Continental Shelf* (1968). The judgment of the I.C.J. in the Fisheries Jurisdiction Case, I.C.J. Reports 1974; p. 3, also reveals a tendency to approach the matter in this way.

28. See on this P. Guggenheim: "Les deux éléments de la coutume en droit international." In: *Etudes en l'Honneur de Georges Scelles*, Vol. 1 (1950); p. 275 et seq., and also Guggenheim's "Traité de droit international public, Vol. 1" (2nd ed. 1967); p. 101 et seq. For summaries of the arguments for and against see, e.g., Suy, above No. 2; p. 221 et seq.; Monaco: *Manuale de diritto internazionale publico* (2nd ed. 1971); p. 75 et seq.; Günther: *Zur Entstehung von Gewohnheitsrecht (The Creation of Rules of Customary Law)* (1970); p. 37 et seq.

29. *I. C. J. Reports* 1969; p. 43; see also the Asylum Case (*I.C.J. Reports* 1950; p. 276, at 286).

30. A. Verdross: above No. 5; p. 104 et seq., with further references.

31. Above No. 4, especially p. 74 et seq.

32. See also Simma: *Das Reziprozitätselement in der Entstehung des Völkergewohnheitsrechts (Reciprocity and the Creation of Rules of Customary International Law)* (1970) especially p. 25 et seq. where Verdross's arguments are taken further.

33. E. g., K. Wolfke: *Custom in Present International Law* (1964); p. 20 et seq.

34. See, e.g., J. L. Kunz: *The Nature of Customary International Law* (1953), 47 AJIL 662, at 667: "Evidence can be taken from diplomatic correspondence,

instructions and so on, municipal laws and court decisions, treaties, negotiations, international decisions, practice of international organizations." M. Hagemann: Die Gewohnheit als Völkerrechtsquelle in der Rechtsprechung des Internationalen Gerichtshofes (Custom as a source of international law in the decisions of the International Court of Justice) (1953). *10 Schweiz. Jahrbuch für internationales Recht*; p. 61, at 78: "The available material indicates that the Court places no restrictions on the evidence which may be adduced to prove the *opinio juris.*"

35. K. Strupp: "Les règles générales du droit de la paix" (1934). *47 Receuil des Cours* 263 at 313.

36. Cf. A. A. D'Amato: "Treaties as a Source of General Rules of International Law," *The Harvard International Law Club Bulletin*, Vol. 3, No. 2 (1962); p. 1–43; id.: above No. 4; p. 103 et seq.; R. R. Baxter: "Multilateral Treaties as Evidence of Customary International Law" (1965). 41 *BYIL* 275; I. F. I. Shihata: "The Treaty as a Law-declaring and Custom-Making Instrument" (1966). 22 *Revue Egyptienne de Droit International* 51.

37. Among the extensive literature on the subject see T. O. Elias: "Modern Sources of International Law, in Transnational Law in a Changing Society," *Essays in Honor of Ph. C. Jessup* (1972); p. 34 et seq.. 46 et seq.

38. This was forcibly argued as long ago as 1929 by H. Lauterpacht: "Decisions of Municipal Courts as a Source of International Law," 10 *BYIL* 65.

39. Cf. I. C. MacGibbon: "Customary International Law and Acquiescence" (1957). 33 *BYIL* 115.

40. *I.C.J. Reports* 1969; p. 43.

41. Above No. 38, at p. 84.

42. Fitzmaurice: "The Law and Procedure of the International Court of Justice, 1951–54: General Principles and Sources of Law" (1953). 30 *BYIL* 1, at 31; also MacGibbon: above No. 42, at p. 121.

43. Tunkin: above No. 27. On the Soviet approach to this question, see also R. J. Erickson: *International Law and the Revolutionary State, A Case Study of the Soviet Union and Customary Law* (1972); p. 30 et seq.

44. See further, e.g., Wolfke: above No. 33, at p. 67 et seq.

45. Cf. E. U. Petersmann: "Völkerrechtliche Fragen der Weltwährungsreform (International Law and International Monetary Reform)" (1974). *34 Zeitschrift für ausländisches öffentliches Recht und Völkerrecht* 452, at 494 et seq.

46. Cf. M. Schweitzer: "Das Völkergewohnheitsrecht und seine Geltung für neuentstehende Staaten (Customary International Law and its Application to Newly Created States)" (1969), Vol. 5 of *Völkerrecht und Außenpolitik (International Law and Foreign Policy)* with copious references. For a general view of the attitude of developing countries to traditional international law see, e.g., J. Castañeda: "The Underdeveloped Countries and the Development of International Law" (1961), 15 *International Organization* 38; G. Abi-Saab: "The Newly Independent States and the Rules of International Law: An Outline" (1962) 8 *Howard Law Journal* 95; id.: "The Third World and the International Legal Order" (1973) 29 *Revue Egyptienne de Droit International* 29; A. A. Fatouros: "Participation of "New" States in the International Legal Order of the Future." In: *The Future of the International Legal Order, Vol. 1: Trends and Patterns* (ed. R. A. Falk C.

E. Black, 1969) At p. 317 et seq.; R. A. Falk: "The New States and International Legal Order" (1966). 118 *Revue des Cours* 1; A. Al-Erian: "International Law and the Developing Countries." In: *Transnational Law in a Changing Society, Essays in Honor of Ph. C. Jessup* (1972); p. 84.

47. This is the view, e.g., of Tunkin, 49 *California L. R.* 428; Schweitzer, op. cit. 58. Considerable practical limitations are imposed on this theory by the refinement that a new state which establishes official diplomatic relations to other countries without reservations is bound by existing law: Tunkin: *Völkerrechstheorie* (Theory of International Law) 159, 191.

48. Cf. Guggenheim: "Lokales Gewohnheitsrecht (Local Customary International Law)" (1961). 11 *Austrian Journal of Public Law [ÖZÖR]* 327; D'Amato: above No. 4, p. 233 et seq.; Barbaris: above No. 6, p. 85 et seq.

49. *I.C.J. Reports* 1950; p. 276 (Asylum Case); I.C.J. Reports 1960; p. 39, 43 et seq. (Right of Passage).

50. *I.C.J. Reports* 1974; pp. 243, 457.

51. See the survey by R. Yakemtchouk: "L'approche sociologique du droit international" (1974). 78 *Revue générale de droit international public* 5–39.

52. It would not help, in my opinion, to draw up a superficial catalogue of different opinions—a criticism which can be made of the work of W. L. Gould and M. Barkun: *International Law and the Social Sciences* (1970).

53. Simma: "Völkerrecht und Friedensforschung (International Law and Peace" Research (1974). 57 *Die Friedens-Warte* 64–83, with further references. See also the English version of this article, below, p. 85 et seq.

54. Cf. Bin Cheng: "United Nations Resolutions on Outer Space: 'Instant' International Customary Law?" (1965). 5 *Indian Journal of International Law* 23, 36.

55. Cf. H. W. A. Thirlway: *International Customary Law and Codification* (1972).

RICHARD J. ERICKSON

Soviet Theory of the Legal Nature of Customary International Law

Not all nations perceive international folk law the same way. Nor does international folk law impinge the same way on all national legal systems. For an idea of the Soviet view of international folk law we are indebted to Richard J. Erickson, a senior officer in the United States Air Force, who at the time he wrote the following essay served as Deputy Director of the International Law Directorate at the headquarters of United States Air Force Europe. He draws heavily from the writings of Professor Grigorii I. Tunkin, one of the Soviet Union's leading authorities on the subject, e.g., "Remarks on the Juridical Nature of Customary Norms of International Law," California Law Review, *49 (1961) 419–430. For another discussion of Soviet attitudes towards international folk law, see Vincent A. Jordan, "Creation of Customary International Law By Way of Treaty,"* The United States Air Force JAG Law Review, *9(5) (September–October, 1967), 38–56. Readers should, of course, keep in mind that national postures with respect to international folk law may change over time as political conditions in nations change.*

In municipal law[1] custom is an important source of law for the Soviet state, but this fact has not disposed the USSR to embrace it enthusiastically. John Hazard has observed that:

> Customary law was applied under the Imperial regime to relations among the peasants. As had been indicated earlier, more than three quarters of the nation had no occasion, except in the event of serious crime, to appeal to the Codes of the Empire. . . . Some of this heritage remains. Division of property belonging to a peasant household communally and inheritance of such property still is governed by peasant custom. A village "comradely" court of peasants settles such matters, and cases have been reported in which the question at issue was whether a family was a peasant family or a worker's family living in a village. The latter would be subject to the civil

Richard J. Erickson, *Soviet Theory of the Legal Nature of Customary International Law*, 7 Case W. Res. J. Int'l L. 148(1975). Reprinted with permission.

> code's provisions concerning the ownership of property and not to peasant custom. In spite of this situation, Soviet text writers are very cautious in viewing custom as a source of law.[2]

Soviet writers approach customary international law with equal caution. Although traces of customary law were implicit in the actions of the Soviet state from very beginning, Soviet spokesmen at first refused to recognize custom as a primary source of law, placing reliance solely upon treaty law.[3] But ever since Evgenii B. Pashukanis'[4] penetrating question in 1935, "Why should the Soviet Government be deprived of those rights which require no treaty formation and derive from the very fact that normal diplomatic relations exist?", the Soviet Union has openly accepted custom as a primary source of international law.[5]

Today, Soviet scholars are in general accord that treaty and custom are the only primary sources of international law, although treaty is emphasized as the more important source.[6] Grigorii I. Tunkin, Chief Legal Advisor to the Soviet Foreign Ministry, has conceded, "Nobody has ever contested that there are customary norms of international law."[7] He has further stated, "It is also indisputable that many of the rules of international law are rules of custom."[8] Even more revealing is Tunkin's statement, ["D]aily observation manifests the considerable role in international law of customary norms; states constantly refer to them in their inter-state relations."[9]

Notwithstanding Soviet acceptance of customary international law in the 1930s, a clear statement of its actual legal nature was not forthcoming until the post-Stalin period.[10] It was at this time that Tunkin called for less dogmatism and more pragmatism, for a concentrated effort to deal with real world problems rather than ideological generalities. Prior to 1953, books and articles devoted to a legal analysis of custom were virtually unknown. After 1953, such writings began to appear with increasing regularity.[11] Soviet writers began posing such questions as: What is customary international law? How is customary law created? When ought a customary norm cease to be binding? The significance of this development cannot be over-emphasized. It marked a shifting of focus away from ideological analysis of the class nature of customary law. Instead, Soviet scholars would begin to contribute to the body of legal thought concerning international custom.

Custom Versus Treaty in the Soviet View of International Law

The Soviet Union recognizes custom together with treaty as the only primary sources of international law. Yet Soviet writers carefully and consistently stress treaty law as the more important of the two. This valuation of custom may at least partially be explained in terms of the combined influences of Soviet ideology and pragmatic foreign policy considerations.

Soviet ideology attributes to customary international law a "bourgeois character."[12] Insofar as it is perceived as evolving from the practice of capitalist states, ancient custom is suspect as serving primarily capitalist interests. A Soviet law text observes, "Exaggeration of the importance of international custom . . . is in line with the policy of certain imperialist circles, a policy of violating treaty obligations and giving legal form to illegal international practices under the label of 'international custom.'"[13] As long as the Soviet Union continues to view custom as composed chiefly of norms created prior to the Great October Revolution, a certain aloofness from customary international law is to be expected on ideological grounds.

The fact that many international legal customs antedate the creation of the Soviet state may also give rise to dissatisfaction with customary law on the more pragmatic level of policy-making. Legal norms delineate what is proper and what is improper in the interaction of states. There must exist a certain uneasiness among Soviet practitioners at having their conduct circumscribed by a body of customary law which they had no part in developing. This is not a feeling unique to the Soviets. The new nations of the Third World have expressed similar dissatisfactions.

On the other hand, Soviet scholars have come to argue that a series of new and progressive customary norms, such as peaceful coexistence, national self-determination, and disfavor of unequal treaties, have been introduced into international law at Soviet insistence.[14] As a result, Soviet perceptions of the "bourgeois character" of custom may be weakening somewhat, and the USSR may presently feel that customary international law bears a recognizable Soviet imprimatur.

A final reason for Soviet disfavor of custom may lie with the unwritten nature of customary law. In Soviet eyes, unwritten law is uncertain law as to principles and their meaning. Such qualities run counter to the Soviet belief that relations with opposing social systems ought to be developed strictly upon the basis of negotiations and agreements.[15] As the USSR grows in strength and acquires a greater sense of security in dealing with non-communist states, it is possible that Soviets may be willing to accept more uncertainty and make greater use of legal custom.

For the present, Soviets have tended to rely on custom only if a treaty source cannot be located and only if there exists a felt need to cite an authoritative source of law. But although treaties are relied upon in preference to custom, in the absence of a treaty custom serves the valuable function of providing an authoritative legal source. Occasionally, however, Soviet practitioners will refrain from identifying the specific source of a given principle of international law or will obscure the source in ambiguous language. Two forms of such ambiguity are discernible. The first is simply to claim that a norm has acquired binding force because it is a "general principle" of law. Since Soviet lawyers refuse to recognize "general principles" as an independent source of international law, and since they hold that "general principles" can acquire binding force of law only if incorporated through treaty or custom, it is ambiguous merely to identify a source of law as a "general principle" without further specifying whether it was embodied through either treaty or custom. A second sort of ambiguity occurs when Soviet scholars assert that a legal rule has its source in the United Nations Charter. Since the Soviets hold that the UN Charter may give rise to treaty as well as customary law, without further clarification the actual source of the rule remains clouded.[16]

Generally speaking, the task of the Soviet lawyer is to state specifically how a customary norm is created and in what manner it ceases to be binding. By asserting guidelines Soviet attorneys set forth the standard by which they will judge the process of customary law-making. No doubt the interplay of international politics will confine Soviet interpretation of this process within certain limits. Nonetheless, the Soviet lawyer may be expected to claim some latitude for his Foreign Ministry in deciding on the crucial factors necessary for the creation or termination of a customary norm of international law. Tunkin realized the significance of this task when he observed:

> There may hardly be any doubt that the problem of customary international law is one of the most difficult of all the problems of international law. It is also one of the most important. Upon the solution of this problem [how custom is created and terminated] depends to a very great extent the whole concept of international law.[17]

Practice as an Indication of Custom

"Customary norms of international law grow out of international practice," Tunkin told those assembled for his 1958 Hague Academy Lectures.[18] The practice of states may consist of their either taking or abstaining from action in a given situation. "As a rule," Tunkin notes, "it is much easier, of course, to establish the existence of a customary norm of international law in the presence of positive action by states, but there is no reason to deny the possibility of a customary norm of international law being established by the practice of abstinence from action.[19]

Chief among the positive acts of states which have resulted in customary norms of international law are diplomatic practices. Certain prescribed actions are expected to be performed by states with respect to diplomatic officers as a matter of law.[20] The abstinence from action, or rather the negative actions of states undoubtedly may lead to the creation of a rule of conduct that may also become a judicial norm.[21] Tunkin writes:

> It should be pointed out that many principles and norms of international law involve, in one measure or another, commitments on the part of states to refrain from certain actions in their relations with other states. Thus, the respect-of-sovereignty principle commits states to refrain from any action constituting a violation of the sovereignty of another state. In accordance with the principle of non-intervention in the internal affairs of another member of the international community, every state is obliged to abstain from any action constituting interference in the internal affairs of another state. Even the open seas principle, for instance, involves an obligation of a negative character, which is that states must abstain from any action likely to injure the "interests of other states in their exercise of the freedom of the high seas." (Convention on the High Seas, Article 2, A/CONF. 13/ L.35/1958, A/CONF. 13/38, Vol. II). Could these customary norms of international law appear if we were to deny that the practice of abstinence can also lead to the creation of a customary norm of international law?[22]

Western scholars are in general accord with their Soviet counterparts. Wheaton, Brierly, Rousseau, and Kunz agree that "customary international law is the generalization of the practice of states."[23] Several western writers have, however, called attention to an ambiguity of terms and a confusion of logic. Hans Kelsen has forthrightly declared the term "custom" to be equivocal, since it denotes at one and the same time the factual situation creating a rule and the rule itself created by that factual situation, hence the term "customary rule."[24] This confusion notwithstanding, Soviet and western scholars are agreed that practice, whether of a positive or abstaining variety, is an indicator of custom.

The Soviet View of Time, Repetition, and Continuity as Factors in Customary Law

According to the Soviet view, duration, or the time element, is important in the process whereby the positive or negative actions of states are converted into customary law. "However, the element of time does not *in itself* create a presumption in favour of a customary norm of international law."[25] A norm can be created almost instantaneously as in the practice of sending satellites into cosmic space over the territories of other states. Expressing the Soviet viewpoint, Karol Wolfke, a Polish international lawyer, writes, "The fact that the Soviet Union and the United States mutually tolerate such practice and do not raise objections against such flights for peaceful purposes over their territories, and that other states, who do not as yet participate in this practice, have not protested, justifies the conclusion that [a customary principle has evolved, because] states do not consider such flights as infringing their sovereignty and even that sovereignty does not extend into outer space."[26]

Moreover, Tunkin notes, "There is even less ground to think that juridicially it is necessary for a customary rule to be 'old' or of long standing."[27] The description of a rule as "old" may mean one of two things: either that the given rule, having long been observed in international practice, has passed the test of time, or that "this very characteristic may give rise to some doubts as to whether a rule of such an ancient origin corresponds to the present circumstances."[28]

The element of repetition constitutes for the Soviet scholar another factor in the formation of custom; it is the reiterated actions of states with the passage of time. Tunkin believes that "In the majority of cases it is precisely the repetition of certain actions in analogous situations that leads to such practices becoming a rule of conduct."[29] But not every repetition of a particular action creates a customary norm of international law. The "habit of doing certain actions may not result in forming a norm of conduct, and if a norm of conduct has been formed this norm may not necessarily be a legal norm. This may be a norm of international morality or a norm of *comitas gentium* [international comity or courtesy]."[30] In ambassadorial law there are many practices of long standing, repeated daily, which are not norms of international law; for example the exemption of baggage from customs. It is also conceivable, though such instances are rare, for a customary rule to result from a single precedent without repetition.[31]

Continuity is a third element important in the development of custom. Soviet writers reject the view that "international practice leading to the formation of a customary rule must have been continued and repeated without *interruption* of continuity."[32] This view is untenable, for according to Tunkin, "no rule of international law has ever been created by practice without interruption of continuity."[33] This does not mean that an interruption in international practice has no effect upon the formation of a customary rule of conduct. "Discontinuity," Tunkin adds, "may destroy a customary norm which is still in the process of formation; it all depends on what character the discontinuity assumes."[34]

In the Soviet view, the three dimensions of custom discussed above; time, repetition, and continuity, do not play a decisive role in the formation of a norm of international law, either individually or together.[35] Each dimension may be necessary for the creation of a customary norm, but none of them is alone sufficient. It is not possible to speak of agreement between western and Soviet writers as to the importance of time, repetition, and continuity because western writers do not agree among themselves.[36] Western thinking on this subject is in a transitional state. The traditional view seems to have been that the development of customary international law is a very slow process. However, the rapidity with which event follows event in contemporary international relations has led to a reevaluation of this position. For western scholars, then, there exists some confusion over the nature of custom.

Agreement as the Decisive Factor in the Soviet View of Custom

A Soviet law review article states, "Practices, even if long standing, are not in themselves norms of international law. They merely mark some particular state in the process of formation of such a norm."[37] Within the Soviet viewpoint, international practices constitute what might be described as the raw material of custom, but it is the element of acceptance which gives practice the mark of law. The essential element in this process "consists of agreement among states."[38] "It is precisely in this sense, in our opinion," writes Tunkin, "that one must understand subsection (b) of section 1, Article 38 of the Statute of the World Court,[39] under which one of the sources of international law is "international custom as evidence of general practice accepted as law.'"[40] For Soviet writers, there can be no norms of international law without agreement between states. Karol Wolfke has summarized the Soviet position in this way:

> One may risk saying that in present international law there are no precise pre-established conditions for custom-creating practices, except the one general condition that it must give sufficient foundation for the presumption that the state concerned accepted it as binding.[41]

How is "agreement" reached among states? To Tunkin, "agreement, as to the means of creating norms of contemporary international law, is the result of the coordination of wills of different states, which in fact are the wills of their ruling classes."[42] The process of reaching agreement on international norms was described by Tunkin in the following manner:

> First, the process of concluding international treaties. In the modern conditions of the coexistence of states belonging to different social systems, the process of conclusion of general international treaties shows that we have a collision of different positions on problems of international law, a collision of wills of states. Then we witness the process of coordinating those wills by negotiation. The result of this process, fixed by treaty, is usually more or less different from what each particular state has originally suggested. In the process of creating customary norms of international law there are no negotiations as such, but as we have shown previously, the essence of this process consists also in framing an agreement between states on the question of recognizing or accepting this or that norm of international law. This agreement is reached not by way of formal negotiations, but by, figuratively speaking, negotiations conducted in the language of fact and action.[43]

"Coordination of wills" of states does not entail merger into some kind of "common will," "general will," or "single will" in the process of creating customary norms of international law. For Soviet writers, the "wills" of states cannot fuse because the aims of states belonging to diverse socio-economic systems, a reflection of their class interests, are different and even antagonistic. However, the "wills" of socialist and capitalist states can be "coordinated" so as to establish a definite rule of conduct. "A norm of general international law is an expression not of a 'single will' but of 'coordinated wills,' *i.e.*, wills equally directed toward a definite aim—recognition of a given rule as a norm of international law."[44]

How is this "coordination of wills" to be achieved? In the Soviet view, agreements between states promote a mutual conditioning of "wills," the substance of which is the readiness of one state to recognize a particular rule as a norm of international law on the condition that the other state display a like readiness. This "interconditionality" is the thread which links the wills of different states within the process of developing, extending, or annulling the sphere of operation of a norm of international law.[45] Such a conception sounds very similar to mutuality of consideration in American contact law.

The *process* of coordinating wills to reach agreement on the formation of customary norms is only one aspect of the element of agreement. Another is the *content*, that which must substantively be agreed upon in order to create a customary norm. As Soviet writers see it, states of diverse socio-economic systems recognize that a norm which regulates their actions is binding upon them, not because of morality, comity, or courtesy, but rather because it is a rule of law. Norms have the force of law because states accept them "with the intention of being bound by norms of law."[46] This means that either implicitly or explicitly a state must agree to the adoption of a customary norm as law. A state's agreement may be expressed openly, as for example, when it publicly declares its intention to be bound by a certain norm. Professor Tunkin cites as illustrations Soviet declarations on prohibition of aggressive wars, self-determination of nations, and peaceful coexistence.[47] A State may also agree to a norm as law implicitly through its actions. Soviet writers are quick to caution, though, that actions do not always "speak for themselves" and are subject to misinterpretation, a situation calling for the exercise of great care among analysts.[48]

Since Soviet writers hold that customary norms result from agreement among states, they are also led to conclude that a norm's sphere of validity is limited to those states which recognize its legal force. Consequently, customary norms of international law may exist between as few as two states or between all states of the international community. In the latter instance the norm is said to be "universal." It is conceivable, therefore, that in the Soviet view a norm of law may first appear as a norm of legal conduct between a few states and then gradually expand through its acceptance by other states until it finally becomes a universal principle of international law.[49] In this respect Tunkin writes:

> The Soviet State has advanced the principle of banning aggressive wars and treating such wars as crimes, the principle of self-determination of nations, the principle of peaceful coexistence, and a number of other principles of international law. In all these cases, the principles originally proclaimed by a single state were gradually recognized by other states and have become, partly by custom and partly by treaty, generally recognized principles of modern international law.[50]

Tunkin continues, "[o]nly a customary rule which is recognized by the states of both systems can be regarded as a customary norm of international law."[51]

Does this mean that only the great powers in each camp must recognize a particular norm in order for it to become universally binding, or is it necessary for all states, great and small alike, to give their consent? Tunkin suggests, in what he terms the "all states doctrine," that for a given norm to become a universal rule of international law it must be recognized by all states.[52] Over this view, Tunkin has exchanged strong words with Professor Hans Kelsen, a noted western international lawyer. For Kelsen, customary norms are not created by the "common consent of the members of the international community," but rather by "a long established practice of a great number of states, including the states which, with respect to their power, their culture and so on, are of certain importance."[53] In disputing this view Tunkin argues that:

> It does not follow from the concept of agreement that all states should participate in creating every specific customary norm of international law. It is not necessary at all that "practice" should be universal. A customary norm of international law may be created by the practice of a limited number of states, and in fact it may become first a customary norm with a limited sphere of application. But to become a norm of international law of universal application it should be recognized by all the states.[54]

Continuing his argument in favor of the principle of the sovereign equality of all states, Tunkin added:

> This concept [of Kelsen's] is in complete contradiction with the fundamental universally recognized principles of international law, and especially with the principle of equality of states. There is no doubt that the attitude of the majority of states, including states of both social systems, and especially the position of great powers, is of primary importance in the process of creation of universally recognized norms of international law. It is a factual situation. Judicially, wills of different states in the process of creating norms of international law are equal. In international relations the majority of states cannot create norms binding upon other states; this is an immediate consequence of the principle of sovereign equality of states.[55]

Tunkin's approach is legalistic; before the law, all nations, great and small, are equal. Yet such a view must be compared with the facts of international life. Is it in fact possible for the great powers or a majority of the world community to wield such influence as to force a nation to subordinate its will to their own? It is not clear whether Tunkin would recognize such political influence as actually creating a legal obligation binding upon the pressured nation or whether, on the other hand, he would hold no binding obligation by virtue of coercion and duress. It is similarly unclear whether Tunkin's assessment of such a situation would hinge upon the ultimate political question of which nation, or nations, was doing the influencing and which was being influenced. If Tunkin is entirely unwilling to admit some politics into the legal arena, it is difficult to see how he might justify certain cases of Soviet influence, if indeed he would attempt to justify them. On the other hand, if Tunkin's analysis does recognize some role for politics within international law, his position would not appear that different from Kelsen's.[56]

By way of comparison, it is interesting to note that, like their Soviet counterparts, many western scholars also believe that in addition to the practices of nations (the material element) there is a second condition required for the creation of a customary legal norm. While Soviet writers speak of "coordination of wills" and the acceptance of norms by the various nations, western scholars point to the psychological element of *opinio juris sive necessitatis*. *Opinio Juris* may be defined as "a certain conviction of the judicial necessity of the act in question."[57] Brierly speaks of recognition by states of "a certain practice as obligatory."[58] Hudson requires a conception by a nation that a given action was "enjoined by law."[59] For Schwarzenberger, "it is necessary to prove that they [nations] act in such a way because they admit a legal obligation to act or refrain from acting in a certain manner."[60] Oppenheim, Wheaton, Higgins, and Kunz,[61] among others, adhere to the view that it is the psychological element of *opinio juris* which differentiates usage from custom.[62]

New States and Old Norms

Western scholars are in general agreement that the need to maintain an ongoing system of world public order demands that states be bound by rules of international law which were formed prior to their statehood.[63] In the Soviet view, the issue of new states and old norms of law is directly related to the question of the sphere of validity of customary norms. Noting the reservation expressed by Professor Verdross that "although the formation of a general customary norm does not imply its application by all states, no general customary norm can appear that contradicts the legal view of any civilized nation."[64] Professor Tunkin continues:

> But if recognition of a new customary norm of international law as such is required from an existing state, why must a newly emerging state find itself in an inferior position? Why cannot the new state object to any customary norm of international law if [the new state] disagrees with it?
>
> The concept that customary norms of international law, accepted as such by a large number of states, must be binding upon all other states is actually based upon the presumption that the majority of states is able in international relations to dictate norms of international law to all other states.[65]

From the Soviet viewpoint the process of creating a universal norm of international law is never permanently accomplished.[66] All states of the international community may consent to a norm as binding law, and at that moment the norm becomes a universal norm of international law. But as soon as a new state is born, that state acquires the same rights as the original states possessed when they first created the binding universal norm, namely, the new state may review the existing universal norm and decide whether it wishes to be bound or not. To refuse to permit new states the right of review would contradict "the basic generally recognized principles of modern international law, the principle of equality of states in particular."[67]

Soviet lawyers have not, however, espoused an unqualified "right of review." Perhaps realizing the dangers inherent in an unlimited right, Soviet spokesmen have circumscribed the right of review by specifying the procedure to be followed in its exercise:

> As for the newly emerging states, they have the judicial right not to recognize this or that customary norm of international law. However, if a new state enters without reservation into official relations with other states, this means that it recognizes a certain body of principles and norms of existing international law which constitute the basic principles of international relations.[68]

In the Soviet view, then, if a new state has entered into relations with the international community "without reservation," it is assumed that the state has accepted the existing international legal system, or at least its fundamental principles. A new state's ability to review, therefore, is limited to the early period of its existence. What substantive law gives, procedure takes away.

The Soviet View of the United Nations Charter as a Source of Customary Norms

In the Soviet view, the principles and norms of the UN Charter acquire their binding legal force upon the signatories from the fact that those signatories have explicitly manifested their assent through a treaty, the Charter itself. The question then arises as to what legal force these principles and norms have upon non-signatories such as Switzerland, North and South Korea, North and South Vietnam, and East and West Germany. In the case of *The Free Zones of Upper Savoy and the Distinct of Gex*,[69] the Permanent Court of International Justice (PCIJ) stated clearly the long established principle that treaties cannot bind third parties without their consent.[70] Article 2, paragraph 6 of the United Nations Charter reads:

> The Organization shall insure that states which are not members of the United Nations act in accordance with these Principles so far as may be necessary to the maintenance of international peace and security.

This provision of the Charter may express the will of the UN or desires of its members, but the question remains whether such a provision can in fact create binding legal obligations for nonsignatories. If this sort of provision could give rise to legal obligations for third party states, what effect would this have on the principles of consent and state sovereignty to which Soviet writers subscribe?

Soviet scholars take the position that a provision, such as Article 2, paragraph 6 of the Charter, can never, *in and of itself*, create obligations binding upon third parties. However, Soviet writers do believe that the principles and norms expressed in the UN Charter, *taken as a whole*, are so basic to inter-state relations that the Charter occupies a special position and that consequently its provisions and norms do bind non-signatories. "The UN Charter is not the usual treaty. In the first place, it is the legal basis for the formation of a world wide international organization for peace and security. In the second place, states have given it pre-eminence over all other treaties."[71] These traits endow the UN Charter with a special character in the eyes of Soviet scholars. Vladimir M. Koretskii, Soviet representative to the 1949 session of the International Law Commission (ILC) observed. "the Charter of the United Nations . . . which laid down new principles of international law, is *essentially* a treaty which has been signed by all peace-loving nations in San Francisco."[72] But it was also something more than a treaty. In the words of Tunkin, a later Soviet representative to the Commission, it was a source of customary norms, since "the new principles of the United Nations Charter were binding on non-members as an expression of customary law."[73] It was the unique character of the Charter itself, and not the wording of any particular provision (Article 2, paragraph 6, for example) which gave the principles and norms of that document their binding effect upon signatories and non-signatories alike.

All of this is not to say that custom is seen as the source of the principles and norms of the UN Charter which are binding upon the Soviet Union. On the contrary, "the same norm of general international law could be conventional [in origin] for some states and customary for others."[74] For the Soviets, the principles and norms of the Charter are binding upon the USSR by virtue of its being a signatory to the treaty.

Those same principles and norms are held to be binding upon non-signatories as a matter of custom.

Such an analysis is indicative of the Soviet view of the hierarchical importance of the sources of international law. If custom, in the Soviet conception, had ranked higher than treaty as a source of law, then Soviet writers would have concluded that for all states (including the Soviet Union) the principles and norms of the Charter derived their legal force from custom. Instead, Soviet scholars consider the Charter's norms and principles as treaty law for the Soviet Union, in accordance with the higher Soviet valuation of treaty over custom.

Such a viewpoint ought not be construed as implying that custom is of no consequence to the Soviet government so long as a principle is codified in the Charter. On the contrary, custom serves to fill gaps and explain how nonsignatories to a treaty can be bound. This is not an inconsequential function. Moreover, treaties themselves have frequently been instrumental in producing future customs. As Pavel I. Lunkin has noted, "many international customary norms have resulted from international treaties."[75] Treaties constitute a precedent, an element of practice, an expression of "coordinated wills." The daily acts of international organizations and of member-states may contribute to the creation of customary norms. Tunkin has pointed out, "[i]t is obvious that change in the Charter of an international organization by custom, *i.e.*, by practice gaining recognition as a legal norm, is possible only with the general agreement of member-states of the international organization."[76]

Prior to 1945, the Soviet Union had accepted many of the principles and norms presently contained in the UN Charter as binding custom. Among these principles were sovereign equality of states, non-intervention, and self-determination. The subsequent codification of these customary norms into the Charter does not preclude the future evolution of new customs through the accumulated practices of states.[77] The process is a continuous one. Furthermore, it is important to recognize that from 1917 to 1945, custom was the source of many of the international legal principles accepted by the USSR. That period was a crucial one in that nation's relations with the international community, and custom played a prominent role in it.

Summary

"There is a fairly close similarity," write the American international legal scholars Jan F. Triska and Robert M. Slusser, "between Soviet and western views on sources of order in international relations. . . ."[78] Treaties rank first and custom second as the only primary sources of international law. Custom is recognized by Soviet lawyers as an important source of legal norms, notwithstanding its ranking below that of treaty. The principles of international law which are custom-based are fundamental to the international system. With the exception of the emphasis which Soviet writers place on the element of agreements between states, Soviet and western views are remarkably in accord as to the legal nature of the customary norm creation process. One should recognize, of course, that there is wide disagreement among western scholars themselves over some aspects of custom.

The Soviet view of the legal nature of customary law may be summarized in the following graphic form:

SOVIET VIEW OF THE LEGAL NATURE OF CUSTOMARY INTERNATIONAL LAW SUMMARIZED

Element	*Necessary*	*Sufficient*
Practices among states (both positive and negative)	*yes	no
Time	*yes	no
Repetition	*yes	no
Continuity	*yes	no
Agreements between states	yes	yes
Opinio juris	no	no

*Necessary in the usual case

Agreement between states is the essential element for the creation and termination of customary law from the Soviet point of view. First, Soviet lawyers view the element of agreement as adding a measure of certainty to traditional western notions of customary law. A nation which agrees to be bound by a customary norm has some notice of the nature and scope of its obligations. Uncertainty has always been a feature of customary law which Soviet writers have found distasteful. Second, Soviet diplomats view the element of agreement as containing political advantages for the Soviet Union. Soviet policy-makers may choose which norms will bind them and which will not.

It is fair to ask at this juncture whether the element of agreement has, in fact, contributed to the lessening of uncertainty or provided the

Soviet Foreign Ministry with real political benefits. Is customary law today more certain because of the Soviet position? Do the Soviets really obtain political advantages in the world of inter-state relations through their preference for explicitly agreeing or not agreeing to a customary norm? In practice, only little impact has resulted from Soviet and western disagreement on the issue of whether agreement is the essential element for the creation or termination of a customary norm. A measure of uncertainty remains inherent in unwritten customs. Similarly, the Soviet Union has agreed to adhere to the great majority of traditional customary norms. The actual degree to which Soviets have come to accept particular principles of customary international law must be the subject of another article.[79]

Notes

1. The term "municipal law" refers to the domestic or internal law of a nation-state.

2. J. Hazard, "The Future Codification in the USSR," 29 *Tul. L. Rev.* 239, 243–244 (1955).

3. *See* R. Erickson, *International Law and the Revolutionary State* (1972); J. Triska & R. Slusser, *The Theory, Law and Policy of Soviet Treaties* (1962).

4. Evgenii B. Pashukanis, Soviet educator and practitioner of international law, was from 1930 until his disappearance in 1937 editor of the leading official law journal *Sovetskoe Gosudarstvo i Revoliutsiia Pravu* [Soviet State and Revolutionary Law]. In 1936 he was appointed Vice-Commissar of Justice, but shortly thereafter became a target of criticism during the purges. He was labeled an "enemy of the people" and presumably executed.

5. E. Pashukanis, *Ocherki po Mezhdunarodomu Pravu* (Essays on International Law), ch. 2. (Moscow, 1935).

6. *See* F. Kozhevnikov, *U.N. Yearbook of the International Law Commission*, A/CN.4/SR237/46 (August 11, 1953) at 367; S. Krylov, *U.N. Yearbook of the International Law Commission*, A/CN.4/SR378/189 (June 29, 1956) at 278; and Akademiia Nauk SSSR, Institut Prava, *International Law* 12. See western writers on the Soviet position: C. DeVisscher, *Theory and Reality in Public International Law* 163 (1957); and Triska and Slusser, *supra* note 3, at 9–31.

7. G. Tunkin, "Coexistence and International Law," 95 *Recueil des Cours* (Collected Lectures) 9 (1958).

8. G. Tunkin, "Forty Years of Coexistence and International Law," 1958 *Sovetskii Ezhegodnik Mezhdunarodnogo Prava* [Soviet Yearbook of International Law] 42 (1958).

9. G. Tunkin, *Droit International Public* [Public International Law] 76 (Paris 1965). It is doubtful whether Tunkin would go so far as to agree with his Polish colleague Karol Wolfke that, "Premature it seems is the recently expressed opinion that, as a result of the accelerated tempo and growing complexity of

international law, customary law is rapidly losing its importance. Customary law being more elastic and best adaptable to new conditions and needs is evolving with the evolution of international life." K. Wolfke, *Custom in Present International Law* 9–10 (Wroclaw 1964).

10. A discussion of the post-Stalin shift in focus from ideological questions of reconciling Marxism and customary law to pragmatic questions as to the legal nature of custom may be found in Erickson, *supra* note 3, at ch. I.

11. See P. Lunkin, *Istochniki Mezhdunarodnogo Prava* [Sources of International Law] (Moscow 1960); N. Minasian, *Istochniki Sovremenogo Mezhdunarodnogo Prava* [Sources of Contemporary International Law] (Rostov on Don 1960); N. Minasian, *Pravo Mirnogo Sosushghestvovania* [The Law of Peaceful Coexistence] (Rostov on Don 1966); G. Tunkin, *Voprosy Teorii Mezhdunarodnogo Prava* [Theoretical Questions of International Law] (Moscow 1962); and Tunkin, "Remarks on the Judicial Nature of Customary Norms of International Law," 49 *Calif L. Rev.* 419–430 (1961).

12. For a depreciation of custom by Soviet writers, *see*: Tunkin, *Remarks on the Judicial Nature of Customary Norms of International Law*, *supra* note 11, at 428–429; Talalayev and Boyarshinov, "Unequal Treaties as a Form of Subjugation to Colonial Dependency of the New States of Asia," 1961 *Sovetskii Ezhegodnik Mezhdunarodnogo Prava* [Soviet Yearbook of International Law] 156 (1961); and Zakharova, "Bilateral Treaties of Friendship, Collaboration, and Cooperation Among Socialist States," 2 *Sovetskoe Gosudarstvo i Pravo* [Soviet State and Law] 80 (1962).

13. Academiya Nauk SSSR, Institut Prava, *International Law*, *supra* note 6, at 12. The normal predilection of lawyers for precedent becomes a "bourgeois deviation" if it involves reference to bourgeois writers, bourgeois legislation, or bourgeois norms in such a way as to point up their superiority to that of socialist writers, socialist legislation, or socialist norms (an ideological problem).

14. *See* D. Levin, *Osnovnye Problemy Sovremennogo Mezhdunarodnogo Prava* [Basic Problems of Contemporary International Law] 11 (Moscow 1958); and Tunkin, *supra* note 8, at 35.

15. *See* De Visscher, *supra* note 6, at 163.

16. The question of the United Nations Charter as a source of customary law could easily be the subject of another separate and extensive article.

17. Tunkin, *supra* note 7, at 9.

18. *Id. See also* Tunkin, *Remarks on the Judicial Nature of Customary Norms of International Law*, *supra* note 11, at 419.

19. Tunkin, *Remarks on the Judicial Nature of Customary Norms of International Law*, *supra* note 11, at 421.

20. It is recognized that the United Nations Convention on Diplomatic Intercourse and Immunities has weakened this example.

21. Tunkin, *Remarks on the Judicial Nature of Customary Norms of International Law*, *supra* note 11, at 421. *See also* Tunkin, *supra* note 7, at 11–12.

22. Tunkin, *supra* note 11, at 422. Implicit in these words of Tunkin is that sovereignty, non-intervention in the domestic affairs of other states, and freedom of the high seas are, in whole or in part, customary norms.

23. Fisheries Case [1951] I.C.J. 191. *See also* Keith (ed.), 2 *Wheaton's Elements of International Law* 10 (6th ed. 1929); J. Brierly, *The Law of Nations* 59–60 (6th ed. 1964); C. Rousseau, *Droit international Public* 64 (Paris 1953); and Kunz, "The Nature of Customary International Law," 47 *Am. J. Int'l L.* 666 (1953).

24. H. Kelsen, "Théorie du Droit International Coutumier" [The Theory of Customary International Law], 1 *Revue Internationale de la Théorie du Droit* 262 (1939).

25. Tunkin, *Remarks on the Judicial Nature of Customary Norms of International Law*, *supra* note 11, at 419–420 (emphasis supplied).

26. Wolfke, *supra* note 9, at 64. It is recognized that the Outer Space Treaty has weakened this example.

27. Tunkin, *Remarks on the Judicial Nature of Customary Norms of International Law*, *supra* note 11, at 419. It is interesting to note that on this point Tunkin cites in his article, *supra* note 7, at 9–10, two western authorities for his position: Basadevant, "Regles Générales du Droit de la Paix" [General Rules of the Law of Peace], 58 *Recueil des Cours* 518 (1936); and Kunz, *supra* note 23, at 666.

28. Tunkin, *supra* note 7, at 10.

29. Tunkin, *Remarks on the Judicial Nature of Customary Norms of International Law*, *supra* note 11, at 419.

30. Tunkin, *supra* note 7, at 10. Tunkin makes the same distinction between "custom" and "usage" as do his western colleagues. He writes, "but it is generally accepted and with good practice that 'custom in its legal sense means something more than mere habit or usage' (James Brierly, *The Law of Nations*, 1955, p. 60)." *Id.* at 12. Other western writers cited to support his view were: A. Verdross, *Völkerrecht* [International Law] 119 (Wien 1955); and Kunz, *supra* note 23, at 667.

31. This writer was unable to find an example given by a Soviet writer of a customary norm created by a single precedent. It may be presumed that the launching of Sputniki I created a customary norm concerning the passage of satellites over the territory of foreign states in a single act.

32. Tunkin, *supra* note 7, at 10, Among the western scholars who hold this view as cited by Tunkin are: Cavaglieri, "Regles Generales du Droit de Paix" [General Rules of the Law of Peace], 26 *Recueil des Cours* 315, 336–337 (1929); and G. Morelli, *Nozionii di Diritto Internazionale* [Elements of International Law] ¶ 18 (3d ed. 1951).

33. *Id.*

34. Tunkin, *Remarks on the Judicial Nature of Customary Norms of International Law*, *supra* note 11, at 420–421.

35. *Id.* at 421. *See also* Tunkin, *supra* note 7, at 11.

36. *See* Brierly, *supra* note 23, at 62–63; DeVisscher, *supra* note 6, at 149; G. Hackworth, 1 *Digest of International Law* 1 (1940); M. Sørensen, *Les Sources du Droit International* [The Sources of International Law] 98 (Copenhagen 1946); Kunz, *supra* note 23, at 666; Lauterpacht, "Sovereignty Over Submarine Areas," 33 *Brit. Y. B. Int'l L.* 120–121 (1957).

37. Tunkin, "The United Nations 1945–1955 (Problems of International Law)," 4 *Soviet Law and Government* 7 (1966).

38. Tunkin, *Remarks on the Judicial Nature of Customary Norms of International Law*, *supra* note 11, at 423. *See also* N. Minasian, *supra* note 11.

39. The full text of Article 38 of the *Statutes of the International Court of Justice* (also referred to as the Statutes of the World Court) reads as follows:

> 1. The Court, whose function is to decide in accordance with international law such disputes as are submitted to it, shall apply:
>   a. international conventions, whether general or particular, establishing rules expressly recognized by the consenting states;
>   b. international custom, as evidence of a general practice accepted as law;
>   c. the general principles of law recognized by civilized nations;
>   d. subject to the provisions of Article 59, judicial decisions and teachings of the most highly qualified publicists of the various nations, as subsidiary means for the determination of rules of law.
> 2. This provision shall not prejudice the power of the Court to decide a case *ex aequo et bono*, if the parties agree thereto.

40. Tunkin, *supra* note 37, at 7. For a full discussion, *see* Tunkin, *supra* note 11, at 419–430.

41. Wolfke, *supra* note 9, at 51.

42. Tunkin, *Osnovy Sovremennogo Mezhdunarodnogo Prava* [Principles of Contemporary International Law] 4 (Moscow 1956).

43. Tunkin, *supra* note 7, at 34–35.

44. Tunkin, *supra* note 37, at 10. The reader's attention is called to the influence of ideology in Tunkin's legal analysis.

45. Tunkin, *supra* note 7, at 35–36. Professor Tunkin is concerned at this point with both the creation and termination of customary norms.

46. Tunkin, *supra* note 9, at 76. *See also* Tunkin, *supra* note 7, at 13. To support his position, Tunkin cites Strupp, "Regles Generales du Droit de la Paix [General Rules of the Law of Peace]," 47 *Recueil des Cours* 306 (1934)

47. Tunkin, *supra* note 9, at 76.

48. Tunkin, *supra* note 7, at 12–13.

49. Tunkin, *supra* note 7, at 14; and Tunkin, *Remarks on the Judicial Nature of Customary Norms of International Law*, *supra* note 11, at 428.

50. Tunkin, *Remarks on the Judicial Nature of Customary Norms of International Law*, *supra* notes 11, at 428. This view of the evolution of universal norms of international law tends itself well to Soviet claims of direct responsibility for positive developments in international law.

51. *Id.*

52. Tunkin, *supra* note 7, at 19–20.

53. H. Kelsen, *Principles of International Law*, 313 (1952).

54. Tunkin, *supra* note 7, at 17–18.

55. *Id.* at 19.

56. A similar question is raised when considering the issue of the "new" states and "old" norms discussed later in this article.

57. Sørensen, *supra* note 36, at 85.

58. Brierly, *supra* note 23, at 61. Earlier in the same work Brierly states, "Customary rule is observed not because it has been consented to but because it is believed to be binding." *Id.* at 52. This runs counter to the belief expressed by Hackenworth, *supra* note 36, at 1, that "Customary . . . international law is based upon the common consent of nations."

59. Manley O. Hudson as quoted by H. Briggs, *The Law of Nations* 47 (2d ed. 1952).

60. G. Schwarzenberger, *A Manual of International Law* 11 (2d ed. 1950).

61. L. Oppenheim: "International jurists speak of custom when a clear and continuous habit of doing certain actions has grown up under the aegis of the conviction that these actions are, according to international law, obligatory or right," 1 *International Law: A Treatise* 25 (7th ed. 1948); Wheaton: ". . . it is usage developed into a rule which is adhered to in the belief that an obligation so to act exists," *supra* note 23, vol. 1, at 10; Higgins: "Custom is more than mere international usage; it is a widespread practice which states engage in because they believe that the law requires it of them," *supra* note 23, at 141; and Kunz: "These conditions are two: usage and *opinio juris*; they have equal importance," *supra* note 23, at 665.

62. Not all western scholars accept *opinio juris*, however. *See* Kopelmanas, "Custom as a Means of Creation of International Law," 1937 *Brit. Y.B. Int'l L.* 127–151; Kelsen, *supra* note 53, at 262–266; and Guggenheim, "Les Deux Elementes de la Coutume en Droit International [The Two Elements of Customary International Law]," 1 *La Technique et les Principles du Droit Public, Etudes en l'Honneur de George Scelle* 275–284 (Paris 1950).

63. *See* Basdevant, *supra* note 27, at 515: "All agree that a new state is bound by international law formed prior to the emergence of this state,"; Kelsen: "The states are bound by general international law without and even against their will. . . . It may be assumed that international law becomes applicable to a newly established community when the latter is recognized as a state by other states," *supra* note 53, at 154; and Verdross: "International customary law is also binding upon those states which did not exist at the time of its inception," *supra* note 30, at 85.

64. Verdross, *supra* note 30, at 85.

65. Tunkin, *Remarks on the Judicial Nature of Customary Norms of International Law*, *supra* note 11, at 427.

66. This should not be confused with the fact that a particular state's acceptance of a principle is permanent in the sense that unilateral withdrawal of consent is not permissible.

67. Tunkin, *Remarks on the Judicial Nature of Customary Norms of International Law*. *supra* note 11, at 427.

68. *Id.* at 428

69. The Permanent Court of International Justice (PCIJ) was the chief judicial organ of the League of Nations.

70. Free Zones of Upper Savoy and the District of Gex [1932] P.C.I.J., ser. A/B, No. 46 at 96.

71. Tunkin, *supra* note 37, at 8. *See also* Tunkin, *supra* note 7, at 22.

72. Koretskii, *U.N. Y.B. Int'l Comm'n, U.N. Doc.* A/CN. 4/SR32/13 (1949) at 232 (emphasis added).

73. Tunkin, *U.N. Y.B. Int'l Comm'n, U.N. Doc.* A/CN. 4/SR621/46 (1961) at 258.

74. Tunkin, *U.N. Y.B. Int'l Comm'n, U.N. Doc.* A/CN. 4/SR794/47 (1965) at 134.

75. Lunkin, *supra* note 11, at 87.

76. Tunkin, *supra* note 37, at 9.

77. It has been the opinion of western writers that treaties and international conventions may become the basis of a rule of customary law. In 1844, Reddie, whose treatment of the subject was astute, explained that a treaty stipulation may "by subsequent imitation and adoption, without special stipulation . . . have become a rule of common and consuetudinary international law." R. Reddie, 1 *Researches in Maritime International Law* 8 (Edinburgh 1844). In 1913, Alvarez wrote of rules expressed in treaties that were later acknowledged by third states as having "changed their nature, one can no longer consider them as conventional but as customary." A. Alvarez, *La Codification du Droit International [The Codification of International Law]* 148 (Paris 1913). In the same year, Oppenheim wrote of looking forward to the time when the Panama Canal shall have been in use for such a length of time "as to call into existence—under the influence and working of the Hay-Pauncefote Treaty—a customary rule of international law according to which the Canal is permanently neutralized and open to vessels of nations." L. Oppenheim, *Panama Canal Conflict* 46 (2d ed. 1913). In 1917, Roxburgh noted, "In practice, this process of extension of a conventional into a customary rule is not only possible but of very constant occurrence." R. Roxburgh, *International Conventions and Third States* 75 (1917). In 1925, Kosters likewise noted, "Already in the conception of past centuries, the conclusion of a treaty is an act which . . . can contribute to the formation of customary international law." Kosters, "Les Fondments du Droit des Gens [Foundations of International law]" 4 *Bibliotheca Visseriana* 221 (1925). In 1932, Derrying wrote, "Every treaty to some extent . . . contributes to the formation and specification of rules of particular or common law." A. Derring, *The Principal Trends of Development of the Law of Nations in the Light of Decisions of the Permanent Court of International Justice* 39 (Lwow 1932). In 1957, Schwarzenberger described the "widespread process of transforming of treaty law into international customary law." G. Schwarzenberger, 1 *International Law* 563 (London 1957). In 1966, Quincy Wright speaking about the U.N. Charter wrote, "The Charter is more than a treaty . . . it gives the United Nations a universal competence to maintain peace, thus going far toward making the principle of Article 2 universal international law." Wright, "Custom As a Basis for International Law in the Post War Period," 2 *Tex. Int'l L. F.* 143, 149 (1966).

The question of the binding effect of resolutions of the United Nations General Assembly is recognized but not considered in depth in the present article.

78. Triska and Slusser, "Treaties and Other Sources of Order in International Relations: The Soviet View," 52 *Am. J. Int'l L.* 726 (1958).

79. For a discussion of the degree of acceptance of customary principles of international law, *see* Erickson, supra note 3.

N.C.H. DUNBAR

The Myth of Customary International Law

Not everyone is persuaded that there is something called international folk law. Just as Josselin de Jong claimed that customary law was nothing but a confusing fiction, so there are skeptics who object to the term 'customary international law.' In the following essay by N.C.H. Dunbar, Professor of Law at the University of Tasmania, one case in particular is reviewed, a case which was decided in part on the basis of alleged international folk law. The case involved a military government in Nigeria in 1975 cancelling a large order of imported cement, resulting in the Central Bank of Nigeria's failure to honor a letter of credit for more than fourteen million dollars. The letter of credit was held by a Swiss company named Trendtex, which sought to take legal action against the Bank of Nigeria in an English court. When the court decided against Trendtex on the grounds of the sovereign immunity of Nigeria, Trendtex took the case to the Court of Appeal and it is the opinions of the three judges of the Court of Appeal that provide the point of departure for Professor Dunbar's argument.

For further discussion of the question of the validity of the concept of international customary law, see Phillip R. Trimble, "A Revisionist View of Customary International Law," UCLA Law Review, *33 (1986), 665–732.*

Introduction

The *Encyclopedia Britannica* commenced the section on (Public) International Law of its 1969 edition as follows:[1] "International law, or the law of nations, is a body of rules and principles which States consider legally binding upon them." The article pointed out that "[o]bviously, every system of law must have criteria by which one can set about discovering the rule of law on a particular matter at a given time. For international law, those tests of validity have been authoritatively stated in art. 38 of the Statute of the International Court of Justice." According

Reprinted from *The Australian Year Book of International Law*, 8 (1983), 1–19, with permission.

to paragraph 1 of that Article, the Court, "whose function is to decide in accordance with international law such disputes as are submitted to it" is to apply inter alia: "a. international conventions, whether general or particular, establishing rules expressly recognized by the contesting States; b. international custom, as evidence of a general practice accepted as law".

In citing those so-called sources of international law, the author merely conformed to the ritual observed by most writers on the subject. He went on to say that to "establish a rule of customary international law it must be shown that there exists not only a practice or habit among States, but also a recognition that the practice follows a rule legally binding on them. Customary law must accordingly be distinguished from mere usage, however well established; and from the rules of international comity which, however well observed they may be, are recognized by States as being demanded by courtesy rather than by law. Thus, the elements necessary to establish a rule of customary law are, in the words of Judge M.O. Hudson,[2] 'the concordant and recurring action of numerous States in the domain of international relations, the conception in each case that such action was enjoined by law, and the failure of other States to challenge that conception at the time.'"

Students of the subject have, from the cradle so to speak, been brought up to embrace this kind of affirmation as an article of faith. Indeed, to question its veracity might well be regarded as tantamount to a heretical attack on the fundamental beliefs and dogma of the creed, shaking, if not destroying, the very foundations on which international law is built.

But feelings of misgiving and of intellectual dishonesty at our slavish obeisance to orthodoxy could no longer be suppressed after reading the judgement of the Court of Appeal in the *Trendtex* case.[3]

On the other hand, it may be that such doubts and fears are groundless and will quickly be dispelled by a wiser and more knowledgeable legal pundit. Meanwhile, however, I venture as an act of conscience to give some reasons for regarding the concept of customary international law as merely a fiction or myth. Somebody once said that it is always healthy to see a gadfly attacking received ideas.

Sources of International Law

The Survey of International Law, in Relation to the Work of Codification, submitted in 1949 by the Secretary-General of the United Nations to the International Law Commission,[4] stated that "the codification of this aspect of international law has been successfully accomplished by the definition of the sources of international law as given in art. 38 of the Statute of the International Court of Justice. That definition has been repeatedly treated as authoritative by international arbitral tribunals. It is doubtful whether any useful purpose would be served by attempts to make it more specific as, for instance, by defining the conditions of the creation and of the continued validity of international custom or by enumerating, by way of example, some of the general principles of law which art. 38 of the Statute recognizes as one of the three principal sources of the law to be applied by the court."[5] It is believed that the late Sir Hersch Lauterpacht was entrusted with the composition of this valuable Survey. Why, one might ask, did he not consider it expedient to attempt to define "the conditions of the creation and of the continued validity of international custom"?

Almost two years earlier, Professor Brierly, the Rapporteur of the Committee on the Progressive Development of International Law and its Codification, which met at Lake Success from 12 May to 17 June 1947, reported that "in connection with the development of the law through the judicial process, the Committee desired to recommend that the International Law Commission consider ways and means for making the evidence of customary international law more readily available by the compilation of digests of State practice, and by the collection and publication of the decisions of national or international courts on international law questions."[6] The Chairman of the Committee explained that this paragraph did not mean "that there were no other sources of international law, but only that the evidence of customary international law was not easily available in contra-distinction to evidence of scientific international law which was always laid down in books."[7]

It is to be noted that Professor Brierly seems to have intended that a distinction should be made between "the development of customary international law" and "the development of the law (presumably international law) through the judicial process." However, the paragraph in question was amended slightly with a view to greater clarity in Sub-Committee 2 of the Sixth Committee of the General Assembly and became without further change Article 24 of the Statute of the International Law Commission. The English text of that Article provides that "the Commission shall consider ways and means for making the evidence of customary international law more readily available, such as the collection and publication of documents concerning State practice and of the decisions of national and international courts on questions of international law, and shall make a report to the General Assembly on this matter."[8] It would appear that the distinction made by Professor Brierly between two different kinds of law was removed in the text of Article 24, and that customary international law was envisaged as embracing both State practice and the judgements of courts. A jurisprudential question is raised when one begins to consider whether State practice can become law before it has been submitted to judicial examination. It is also difficult to understand what the Chairman had in mind when he said that "the evidence of customary international law was not easily available in contra-distinction to evidence of scientific international law which was always laid down in books." What is the meaning of "scientific" in this connection? How is it possible to reconcile scientific knowledge with the mere subjective opinion of writers?

The memorandum on *Ways and Means* proceeded to survey the existing state of the evidence of customary international law including collections of documents (official and otherwise) relating to something like twenty-five countries, digests of State practice, particularly of the United States—no other country appearing at the time to have any digests comparable to the works of Moore or Hackworth; reports and digests of decisions of international tribunals in general and of specific international tribunals such as the International Court of Justice, the Permanent Court of International Justice, the Permanent Court of Arbitration, the Central American Court of Justice, the Mixed Arbitral Tribunal etc.; reports and digests of decisions of municipal courts on questions of international law relating to eight or ten countries; national legislation relating to international law on which there was said to be "a great scarcity of publications"; collections of decisions and opinions of the League of Nations and United Nations; the Harvard Research in international law; the preparatory work for the First Conference on the Codification of International Law; writers; suggestions of organizations and publicists for the improvement of documentations of customary international law. This unbalanced, incomplete and arbitrary miscellany was said to "reveal that a substantial body of evidence of customary international law is available".[9] One of the alternatives suggested for making "the evidence of customary international law more readily available" was "the undertaking of a completely new *Corpus Juris Gentium*, derived from all the different categories of evidence of customary international law".[10] But even if a "systematic and comprehensive compilation of evidence of customary international law" could be accomplished, what would be its value? To what would the evidence relate? Surely it was not suggested that the multifarious sources listed above all relate to law—even in the unlikely event of their unanimity. Moreover, how can there be evidence of law? Either the law exists or it does not. It is possible to have reports of State practice, the opinions of writers and the like; but they do not constitute law.

The maze of speculation in which we are now wandering characterized the draft Convention, formulated in 1926 under the auspices of the

American Institute of International Law, and entitled *Fundamental Bases of International Law.*[11]

The preamble stated that "it is proper to determine clearly for the future the fundamental bases of international law, and an end should be put to the uncertainty and the diversity of doctrines heretofore existing on this subject." Article 1 provided that "the reciprocal relations of nations forming the international community are governed by the principles, rules, customs, practices, or usages which are recognized as applicable and which taken together constitute international law." It is unlikely that such a statement did much to "end the uncertainty and the diversity of doctrines heretofore existing on this subject." There remains the fundamental question of how and by whom are those principles, rules, etc. to be "recognized as applicable" and, indeed, where they can be found.

The problem is not made more tractable by Article 6 which announced that "international principles, rules, customs, etc. are either *general or particular*. Those followed by all or nearly all nations of the world are *general*. The *particular* principles, rules or usages may be: (a) continental, (b) regional, (c) particular to a school, (d) special, (e) national, or (f) constitute rules of civilization." Nothing is to be gained by setting out here the definition given in the draft Convention of those *particular* principles etc. Article 7 stated that "international rules on the American Continent may also be derived from custom recognized as obligatory by the majority of the American Republics"; but Article 10 added that "in the absence of rules of custom, recourse shall be had to the more or less general practices or usages of the American Republics. Such practices or usages can only be invoked by the Republics observing them."

Article 14 provided that "the general principles of international law are those drawn from the rules in force of that law, especially when they have been recognized by diplomatic acts or arbitral awards"; Article 15 that "the precepts of international justice are those which public opinion recognizes should govern the relations between nations. Those precepts must have been expressed in such acts as *voeux* of international conferences, resolutions of recognized scientific institutions, or opinions of contemporary publicists of authority."

Article 18 stipulated that "diplomatic precedents, arbitral awards, decisions of national courts in international matters, as well as the opinion of publicists of authority, have value only in so far as they throw a light upon existing law or upon the other elements mentioned above to which recourse should be had in the absence of legal rules"; and Article 20 that "the observance of international law rests principally upon the honour of the American Republics, under the sanction of public opinion."

The commendable aims expressed in the preamble cited above must surely invite ridicule by the pretences which followed it, and which seem only to add to "the uncertainty and diversity of doctrines heretofore existing on this subject."

The Trendtex Case: "We must take the current when it serves, or lose our ventures" (Julius Caesar, IV, iii), per Lord Denning MR

For present purposes, the facts of the case[12] can be stated simply. In July 1975, there was a queue of 400 ships outside Nigeria's main port of Lagos. Ships were arriving every day bringing more cement. Until 1975 Nigeria had been importing two million tons of cement annually. At the beginning of 1975 Government orders had raised cement imports by ten times and, not unnaturally, the ports were unable to cope with the situation. The chaos in Lagos harbour swelled the tide of impatience with the existing Government which led to its replacement in July 1975 by a military administration. The subsequent cancellation by the new Government of the cement orders resulted in the dishonouring by the Central Bank of Nigeria of a letter of credit for more than 14 million dollars held by Trendtex, a Swiss company. In November 1975, Trendtex issued a writ in the English High Court claiming demurrage on six ships, the price of cement shipped on two, and damages for non-acceptance. The Central Bank applied to set aside the writ claiming that the Bank was a department of the Federal Republic of Nigeria and therefore immune from suit. Donaldson J set the writ aside on grounds of sovereign immunity and discharged an earlier injunction granted by Mocatta J requiring the Bank to retain sufficient funds in London to meet the claim. The appeal by Trendtex came before Lord Denning MR, Stephenson LJ and Shaw LJ.

The leading judgment was delivered by Lord Denning who declared that "the doctrine of sovereign immunity is based on international law. It is one of the rules of international law that a sovereign State should not be impleaded in the courts of another sovereign State against its will. Like all rules of international law, this rule is said to arise out of the consensus of the civilised nations of the world. To my mind this notion of a consensus is a fiction. The nations are not in the least agreed upon the doctrine of sovereign immunity. The courts of every country differ in their application of it. Some grant absolute immunity. Others grant limited immunity, with each defining the limits differently. There is no consensus whatever."[13]

However, his Lordship then proceeded to make the surprising observation that "this does not mean that there is no rule of international law upon the subject. It only means that we differ as to what that rule is. Each country delimits for itself the bounds of sovereign immunity. Each creates for itself the exceptions from it."[14]

But how can this be? If a rule of international law, in the words of the learned Judge, arises from the consensus of civilised nations, and if there is no consensus among the nations in respect of sovereign immunity, how can it be maintained that "this does not mean that there is no rule of international law upon the subject"?

Lord Denning then said that each country decides for itself what that rule is. Each creates for itself the exceptions from the rule. But, with respect, that is not what takes place in practice. In the absence of legislation on the matter, which until recent times has been almost universally non-existent, it is not the executive but the courts which create or declare the law applicable to the case in hand. Moreover, the courts cannot create or declare a rule of *international law* which does not exist; they must perforce create or declare a rule of *municipal law* applicable solely within the confines of the particular country in question. In fact, Lord Denning seemed instinctively to sense this without being willing to carry the argument through to its logical conclusion. For he immediately went on to say: "It is, I think, for *the courts of this country* to define the rule as best they can, seeking guidance from the decisions of the courts of other countries, from the jurists who have studied the problem, from treaties and conventions and, above all, defining the rule in terms which are consonant with justice rather than adverse to it".[15]

In other words, courts must resort to the subjective criteria discussed in the earlier part of this paper. But the mistake is perpetuated by a constant reference to international law, instead of acknowledging frankly that the court is merely applying or fashioning the law of its own country.

The learned Judge then proceeded to consider the fundamental question of the relationship of international law to municipal law, a matter which is not strictly within the ambit of this paper. However, it again involves the problem of customary international law. Lord Denning did not ask, what is the place of international law in municipal law—meaning thereby the municipal law of all States. He did not look for a rule of international law which prescribes universally the relationship of international law to all systems of municipal law. This was because, presumably, such a universal customary rule does not exist. So he had to pose the question in the form: "What is the place of international law in our English law?"[16] This is a different question altogether for the reason that a court, in attempting to answer it, will not apply a rule of international law—which in fact does not exist—but whatever doctrine or principle of municipal law happens to obtain in that particular country. The court is thereby applying its own municipal law to an international dispute.

The complaint is that courts are not prepared to acknowledge the reality of what they do, but remain content to perpetuate the fiction that it is international law which is being applied. Lord Denning did this by discussing what he called two schools of thought. "One school of thought holds to the doctrine of *incorporation*. It says that the rules of international law are incorporated into English law automatically and considered to be part of English law unless they are in conflict with an Act of Parliament. The other school of thought holds to the doctrine of *transformation*. It says that the rules of international law are not to be considered as part of English law except in so far as they have been already adopted and made part of our law by the decisions of the judges, or by the Act of Parliament, or long-established custom".[17]

Let us pause here to inquire what Lord Denning meant by the phrase "long-established custom". What kind of custom was he referring to? Who creates the custom? Who defines the custom? Who applies it? If the judge formulates the custom—and it would appear that no other person has that authority—then this would be done in a judgment and the phrase is without meaning.

The learned Judge proceeded to point out that the difference between the doctrines of incorporation and transformation "is vital when you are faced with a change in the rules of international law. Under the doctrine of incorporation, when the rules of international law change, our English law changes with them."[18] But how can this be? Who but the judge of the municipal court is to say if a rule of international law has changed? What criteria does he use to consider the question? What authority has he to decide for the rest of the world that a rule of international law has changed? Surely, all that he can do is to change the previous rule of municipal law if he believes the occasion warrants it. "But", continued Lord Denning, "under the doctrine of transformation, the English law does not change. It is bound by precedent. It is bound down to those rules of international law which have been accepted and adopted in the past. It cannot develop as international law develops."[19]

It is respectfully suggested that what Lord Denning should really have been saying was that English courts are bound by precedent. They can apply only municipal law. If they wish to alter the municipal law, not to conform with some imagined change in so-called customary international law but to express a different view of what the municipal law should be, there is difficulty because of the doctrine of precedent. This failure to pursue logically to its conclusion the myth of customary international law is apparent in the judgment, cited by Lord Denning,[20] of Cockburn CJ in *R* v *Keyn*:[21] "For writers on international law, however valuable their labours may be in elucidating and ascertaining the principles and rules of law, cannot make the law. To be binding, the law must have received the assent of the nations who are to be bound by it. . . . Nor, in my opinion, would the clearest proof of unanimous assent on the part of other nations be sufficient to authorise the tribunals of this country to apply, without an Act of Parliament, what would practically amount to a new law. In so doing, we should be unjustifiably usurping the province of the legislature." But in common with Lord Denning, Cockburn CJ failed to acknowledge that only the judge can decide for himself whether he thinks some international practice of States has received the "unanimous assent of other nations". What criteria are to constitute "the clearest proof"? And even if the judge is satisfied that such a universal practice of States exists, that practice does not of itself constitute a rule of law. The rule of law does not come into existence until it is created by the judge in a particular case. It then becomes a rule of municipal law. The myth is in assuming that universal State practice ipso facto creates law. Law can only be created by legislation or by the judgment of a court, or, in the case of international law, by a treaty. The same may be said of the judgment, also cited by Lord Denning[22] of Lord Atkin in Chung Chi Cheung v The King.[23] "So far, at any rate, as the courts of this country are concerned, international law has no validity save in so far as its principles are accepted and adopted by our own domestic law." This statement would be unexceptionable if Lord Atkin had substituted "international practice of States" for "international law".

Lord Denning admitted to having contributed to the confusion by accepting without question the doctrine of transformation in *R v Secretary of State for the Home Department; ex parte Thakrar*.[24] "I now believe that the doctrine of incorporation is correct. Otherwise, I do not see that our courts could ever recognize a change in the rules of international law. It is certain that international law does change . . . and the courts have applied the changes without the aid of any Act of Parliament. Thus, when the rules of international law were changed (by the force of public opinion) so as to condemn slavery, the English courts were justified in applying the modern rules of international law. . . . Again, the extent of territorial waters varies from time to time according to the rule of international law current at the time, and the courts will apply it accordingly. . . . The bounds of sovereign immunity have changed greatly in the last 30 years. The changes have been recognized in many countries, and the courts—of our country and of theirs—have given effect to them, without any legislation for the purpose".[25]

It is respectfully suggested that what Lord Denning should have said is that international State practice changes and that municipal courts have reflected such changes in new rules of municipal law. It was the force of public opinion which altered State practice in respect of slavery. The extent of territorial waters does not vary because of a new rule of international law, but in accordance with the current practice of States, and the same may be said for the bounds of sovereign immunity. Moreover, the learned Judge seemed to have forgotten his earlier pronouncement "that nations are not in the least agreed upon the doctrine of sovereign immunity. The courts of every country differ in their application of it."[26] Why could not Lord Denning have conceded that, in the absence of a treaty, there is no rule of international law in respect of sovereign immunity; and that the courts of each State act differently, not in their application of some supposed universal rule of international law—which would not, in any case, permit such deviation—but because of the divergent rules of municipal law created by national courts in the light of their subjective interpretation of State practice?

Lord Denning concluded: "Seeing that the rules of international law have changed and do change—and that the courts have given effect to the changes without any Act of Parliament, it follows to my mind inexorably that the rules of international law, as existing from time to time, do form part of our English law. It follows, too, that a decision of this court—as to what was the ruling of international law 50 or 60 years ago—is not binding on this court today. International law knows no rule of *stare decisis*. If this court today is satisfied that the rule of international law on a subject has changed from what it was 50 or 60 years ago, it can give effect to that change—and apply the change in our English law—without waiting for the House of Lords to do it."[27]

Even supposing that rules of international law can be created otherwise than by treaty or by a judgment of the International Court of Justice, who is to say when such a rule has changed and what evidence for such change is required? Why did Lord Denning impose a time factor of 50 or 60 years? And what has international law to do with *stare decisis*? The latter is merely a product of the English common law and is alien to most other municipal systems. What authority did Lord Denning have for suddenly declaring that *stare decisis* shall not apply to a particular type of municipal dispute? It is not a question of the court being satisfied that a particular rule of international law has changed from what it was 50 or 60 years ago, but of a change in the international practice of States which should be reflected in a municipal decision.

His Lordship then turned his attention to the doctrines of absolute and restrictive sovereign immunity in the light of "the complete transformation in the functions of a sovereign State. Nearly every country now engages in commercial activities. . . . This transformation has changed the rules of international law relating to sovereign immunity. Many countries have now departed from the rule of absolute immunity. So many have departed from it that it can no longer be considered a rule of international law. It has been replaced by a doctrine of restrictive immunity. This doctrine gives immunity to acts of a governmental nature, described in Latin as *jure imperii*, but no immunity to acts of a commercial nature, *jure gestionis*."[28]

The learned Judge pointed out that in 1951 many European countries had abandoned the doctrine of absolute immunity and adopted that of restrictive immunity. "Since that date there have been important conversions to the same view. Great impetus was given to it in 1952 in the famous 'Tate letter' in the United States. Many countries have now adopted it. We have been given a valuable collection of recent decisions in which the courts of America and others have abandoned absolute immunity and granted only restrictive immunity."[29]

But it may be asked how the transformation in the functions of a sovereign State can change rules of international law? How can "many countries depart from the rule of absolute immunity?" It is the courts of the different States which have changed, in varying and individual ways, their domestic rules of law to suit their own purposes. States themselves have nothing to do with the law. It is only their behaviour or practice which has changed. Secondly, when Lord Denning asserted that "so many have departed from it that it can no longer be considered a rule of international law", how many States did he have in mind? And what was the total number of States a proportion of which had transformed their former functions? How much evidence had he received of what is done by all States? Or did he merely refer to a sample? And was the sample based on any criterion of size, wealth, status and the like—or did it depend upon the accessibility of evidence in English, e.g., reports of cases. Only four countries were mentioned by name. There were many others. How many countries have not abandoned the doctrine of absolute immunity? Further, how is one to distinguish acts of a governmental nature from acts of a commercial nature? It is a most difficult task as the French courts, for example, have discovered.[30] His Lordship said that in 1951 many European countries had abandoned the doctrine of absolute immunity. But he did not say how many, or who they were. He said that since then there had been important conversions to the same view. What States was he referring to, and what did he mean by important? The 'Tate letter' is merely evidence of the practice in one State. A municipal court is entitled to look around the world and receive what evidence it likes, sparse or voluminous, of the practice currently adopted by other States, but such practice cannot amount to law. A municipal court creates the law, and it is not international law, to fulfill what it deems to be the requirements of its own State.

In the same vein, the learned judge continued: "Seeing this great cloud of witnesses, I would ask: is there not here sufficient evidence to show that the rule of international law has changed? What more is needed? Are we to wait until every other country save England recognizes the change? Ought we not to act now? Whenever a change is made, someone some time has to make the first move. One country alone may start the process. Others may follow. At first a trickle, then a stream, last a flood. England should not be left behind on the bank—'We must take the current when it serves, or lose our ventures'—*Julius Caesar*, Act IV, Sc III."[31]

What did Lord Denning mean by a great cloud of witnesses? Did he mean that a large number of States engage in commercial activities, or that the municipal courts of a large number of States have changed their view in the matter of sovereign immunity? Presumably the latter. But how many constitute a great cloud of witnesses? And whatever it is that the courts do, they certainly do not change international law, but merely change their own municipal law. Otherwise, what is happening when, as Lord Denning observed, "Someone some time has to make the first move. One country alone may start the process. Others may follow." Does the country or court making the first move change the law, irrespective of the remaining countries? If not, is it acting illegally? If it changes the law, are the remaining States acting illegally? His Lordship said that "others *may* follow"—there is no apparent obligation on them to do so. How many countries are required to change the law? What did he mean by saying that England should not be left behind on the bank? It may suit her to be left behind. It is entirely a matter for her Government to decide so far as State practice is concerned, and for her courts to decide so far as English municipal law is concerned.

Lord Denning then criticized the timidity of the Privy Council in its partial abandonment of the absolute theory in *The Philippine Admiral*,[32] in which that court took the view that the absolute theory still applied to actions *in personam* until the House of Lords decided otherwise. Lord Denning was of the opinion that the restrictive theory was of general application and he saw "no reason why we should wait for the House of Lords to make the change. After all, we are not considering here the rules of English law in which the House has the final say. We are considering the rules of international law. We can and should state our view as to those rules and apply them as we think best, leaving it to the House to reverse us if we are wrong."[33]

With great respect, this pronouncement must be challenged. The court is applying rules of common law laid down in previous decisions of English courts in cases of sovereign immunity. It is quite open to Lord Denning to create a new rule of English law if he wishes, but he may be acting contrary to precedent in so doing. He is supposed to be bound by previous decisions. The question of justice in relation to the restrictive theory is entirely a subjective matter for each court to determine. If the courts were applying so-called external rules of international law, why should it be necessary for the court to "state its view as to those rules and apply them as we think best"? The rule should be imperative. It should not be open to the court to apply it as it thinks best.

The learned Judge cited [34] several English and United States cases,[35] and the United States Foreign Sovereign Immunities Act 1976, in support of his view. But none of them constitute international law—they are all expressions of municipal law.

His Lordship then made the extraordinary observation that even "if there were no settled rule of international law on the subject, there should at least be one settled rule for the nine countries of the European Economic Community. The Treaty of Rome is part of the law of England. One of the objectives contained in Article 3(h) is to ensure "the approximation of the laws of member-States to the extent required for the proper functioning of the Common Market. . . . In view of those provisions, it seems to me that it is the duty of each of the member-States—and of the national courts in those States—to bring the law as to sovereign immunity into harmony throughout the Community. The rules applied by each member-State on the subject should be the same as the rules applied by the others. There is only one acceptable way of doing it. That is by adopting the doctrine of restrictive immunity on the lines I have suggested."[36]

This passage seems to have no relevance in the present context. Neither Nigeria nor Switzerland, for example, is a member of the European Economic Community. Article 3(h) of the Treaty of Rome is in the first place simply stating an objective; secondly, the approximation of the laws is to assist the proper functioning of the Community—quite alien to the circumstances of the instant case; thirdly it is in any event very doubtful if the proper functioning of the Common Market in any way depends upon the doctrine of sovereign immunity.

However, Lord Denning conceded that it is a domestic question—particularly for municipal courts—how the law as to sovereign immunity shall be harmonized. The international law aspect seems momentarily to have disappeared. But his Lordship neglected to examine the municipal law of the nine member-States in order to discover what doctrine of sovereign immunity is applied by their respective courts.

Lord Denning referred[37] to an almost identical case, then before the German courts, and cited a passage from the judgment of the Commercial Court of Frankfurt which relied on decisions in 1962 and 1963 of the Federal Constitutional Court. The latter Court adopted a restrictive view of sovereign immunity based on the proposition that "no general rule of public international law exists under which the domestic jurisdiction for actions against a foreign State in relation to its non-sovereign activity is *precluded*". In other words, the question of sovereign immunity is one for the municipal court applying its own domestic law.

Although espousing the doctrine of restrictive immunity, his Lordship acknowledged some uncertainty by observing that "if we are still bound to apply the doctrine of absolute immunity there is, even so, an important question arising upon it."[38] This hesitation was tantamount to an admission that there is no unanimity in respect of sovereign immunity and that the court may be bound—presumably by the principle of *stare decisis*—to apply the doctrine of absolute immunity. Such a stance seems incompatible with that adopted in his Lordship's previous discussion about incorporation and transformation.

Lord Denning acknowledged that the "cases on this subject are difficult to follow, even in this country: let alone those in other countries. And yet, we have to find what is the rule of international law *for all of them.* It is particularly difficult because different countries have different ways of arranging internal affairs. . . . Another problem arises because of the internal laws of many countries which grant immunities and privileges to its own organisations. Some organisations can sue, or be sued, in their courts. Others cannot. . . . It cannot be right that international law should grant or refuse absolute immunity according to the immunities granted internally. . . . In these circumstances, I have found it difficult to decide whether or not the the Central Bank of Nigeria should be considered in *international law* a department of the Federation of Nigeria, even though it is a separate legal entity. But, on the whole, I do not think it should be. This conclusion would be enough to decide the case, but I find it so difficult that I prefer to rest my decision on the ground that there is no immunity in respect of commercial transactions, even for a government department."[39]

What Lord Denning appears to have been saying, in the first place, was that no clearly defined doctrine of sovereign immunity exists either in English law or in the jurisprudence of other countries. How is it therefore possible to conclude that "we have to find what is the rule of international law *for all of them*"? In the absence of unanimity in the judgments of the courts, was it being suggested that a different rule of international law applies to each of the conflicting decisions? The learned Judge conceded that even the practice of States and their internal laws are as diverse as the number of countries involved. In those circumstances, how can one speak of a rule of customary international law? Secondly, he said that "it cannot be right that international law should permit or refuse absolute immunity according to the immunities granted internally". That observation must confirm the absence of a rule of customary international law in the matter. The granting or refusal of sovereign immunity is a prerogative of national legislation or of municipal courts applying internal law. How can it be decided "whether or not the Central Bank of Nigeria should be considered in *international law* a department of the Federation of Nigeria"? There is no international law on the subject; neither has the question anything to do with international law. Finally, Lord Denning found the problem so intractable that he chose to rest his decision on the ground that "there is no immunity in respect of commercial transactions, even in respect of a government department". This was clearly a personal judgment having no connection with any so-called rule of customary international law. It was an *ad hoc* municipal decision not even based on a binding precedent.

Stephenson LJ, in his judgment, recognized that the first difficulty in deciding between the rule of absolute or restrictive immunity was "caused by the nature of international law and the manner in which municipal courts ascertain what it is, how the law of nations is made and how proved."[40] His Lordship quoted the famous passage from the *Commentaries* of Blackstone, which has probably been more influential than any other writing in perpetuating the myth of customary international law: "The law of nations . . . is here adopted in its full extent by the common law, and is held to be a part of the law of the land."[41]

Blackstone defined the law of nations as "a system of rules, deducible by natural reason and established by universal consent among the civilised inhabitants of the world" and which "must necessarily result from those principles of natural justice in which all the learned of every nation agree".[42] However, Stephenson LJ pointed out that "the universal consent required by this confident and exacting 18th century definition is, as Lord Denning MR has said, a fiction; if it ever existed, it is not now forthcoming in many spheres of international law, and certainly not, in my judgment, in the area of sovereign immunity. There is, however, ample authority not for the view that each nation can decide what rule suggested by any jurist or body of jurists, or laid down and applied by any foreign court or courts, it can and should itself apply, but for the view that it can and should apply a generally accepted rule."[43] His Lordship cited[44] the opinion of Sir Samuel Evans P in *The Odessa*[45] that the law of nations is "the law which is generally understood and acknowledged to be the existing law applicable between nations by the general body of enlightened international legal opinion."

The learned Lord Justice, for his part, was of the opinion that the difference between the doctrines of incorporation and transformation might be "more apparent than real", for "it is the nature of international law and the special problem of ascertaining it which create the difficulty in the way of adopting, or incorporating, or recognizing as already incorporated, a new rule of international law. I would find less difficulty in accepting restrictive immunity . . . in place of absolute immunity if restrictive immunity were as generally accepted today as absolute immunity was in the past—and that may not have been as universally accepted as I have assumed. But rules of international law, whether they be part of our law or a source of our law, must be in some sense 'proved', and they are not proved in English courts by expert evidence like foreign law: they are 'proved' by taking judicial notice of 'international treaties and conventions, authoritative textbooks, practice and judicial decisions' of other courts in other countries which show that they have 'attained the position of general acceptance of civilised nations': the *Cristina* [1938] A.C. 485, 497, per Lord Macmillan: and those sources come seldom if ever from every civilised nation or agree upon a universal rule; they move from one generally accepted rule towards another. But if none moved, old rules would never die and new rules never come into being. Some move must be made by States, or their tribunals, or jurists, to prevent petrifaction of the living law. When should a court of law accept or adopt or incorporate or assent to what is alleged to be a new rule of international conduct? Can an English court ever make the first move in this country? Or must it wait for a 'Tate letter' from the Government of the United Kingdom? Or for an Act of Parliament? . . . Have civilised States agreed that the doctrine of restrictive immunity shall be binding upon them in their dealings with one another? The answer is doubtful; may have. Is there evidence that Great Britain has ever assented to the doctrine? The answer must be no—until she ratifies the European Convention on State Immunity which she signed at Basle on May 16, 1972, and perhaps also the Brussels Convention of 1926. Has it been proved by satisfactory evidence that the doctrine has been recognized and acted upon by our own country? No. Or that it is of such a nature, and has been so widely and generally accepted, that it can hardly be supposed that any civilised State would repudiate it? . . . Have the opinions of jurists received the express sanction of international agreement, or have they grown to be part of international law by their frequent practical recognition in dealings between various nations? On all the material put before us I could not answer that question in the affirmative. It is clearly difficult if not impossible to prove that governments have acted on the "rule" of restrictive immunity by failing to plead immunity for ordinary commercial transactions. How do you prove that the gestation of a new rule is over and that it has come to birth? Or that an old rule has grown and developed into a new form?"[46]

Stephenson LJ then continued: "It is part of Mr. Bingham's case that a vacuum may have been created in the law of nations by the dissent of many from the old rule, but that the vacuum has not been filled by any agreed new rule. Even if the law of nations does not abhor a vacuum, it is entirely unsatisfactory that the courts of this country should not lift a finger to help fill it by a new rule which is 'consonant with justice'. In my judgment this new rule is consonant with justice. It is in accord with the law merchant which requires that payments on letters of credit should be honoured. It is now so widely and generally accepted that no civilised country which has not yet expressly assented to it should be presumed to repudiate it. It would be repugnant to justice if an English court were to repudiate it in modern conditions and so in effect extend the old rule of immunity to transactions which were never considered subject to it by former judges and jurists because such transactions would never in their time have been carried out by sovereign States or their emanations."[47]

This extract from the judgment of Stephenson LJ has been quoted at length because, although his Lordship appeared to acknowledge the problems, contradictions and illogicalities inherent in the idea of customary international law, he continued to manifest a belief in the existence of such a law and a refusal to accept the reality of the situation. While it is unnecessary to reiterate the criticism levelled at the similar stance adopted by Lord Denning, attention might be drawn to the following ambiguities.

The learned Judge recognized the problems connected with the nature of international law—a system of law supposed to be based on the consent of nations—"the manner in which municipal courts ascertain what it is, how the law of nations is made and how proved". His Lordship admitted that "the universal consent required . . . is a fiction", but refused to accept "that each nation can decide what rule suggested by any jurist or body of jurists, or laid down and applied by any foreign court or courts, it can and should itself apply". Even if it were true that customary international law is created by the consent of States, such consent is not the same thing as the writings of jurists or the decisions of courts. If, therefore, there is no universal consent of States to customary international law, why should a municipal court not refer to the writings of jurists or to the decisions of foreign courts in formulating its own judgment, not based on international law? If the "universal consent" of

States is a fiction how can municipal courts "apply a generally accepted rule"? It is difficult to understand what is meant by the assertion of Sir Samual Evans that the law of nations is "the law which is generally understood and acknowledged to be the existing law applicable between nations by the general body of enlightened international legal opinion". What is signified by the phrases "generally understood and acknowledged", and "general body of enlightened international legal opinion"? How does he define "enlightened"? If there were no such thing as customary international law, there would be no question as to doctrines of incorporation and transformation, or of "the difficulty in the way of adopting, or incorporating, or recognizing as already incorporated, a new rule of international law".

How could Stephenson LJ "find less difficulty in accepting restrictive immunity in place of absolute immunity if restrictive immunity were as generally accepted today as absolute immunity was in the past"—and then go on to say "and that may not have been as universally accepted as I have assumed". Surely, some *evidence* is required that absolute immunity was generally accepted in the past, not merely an *assumption* that it must have been universally accepted. The learned Judge realized that customary international law must "be in some sense 'proved', but not be expert evidence". It is suggested that expert evidence is necessary to "prove" the universal consent of States. How else can it be done? What are "authoritative text-books"? Is it not a purely subjective choice of the judge as to which textbooks he prefers to regard as authoritative? How can he take judicial notice of the "practice and judicial decisions" of courts in other countries, unless they are "proved" by expert evidence? What evidence of practice and judicial decisions is the judge prepared to accept? What evidence is required "to show that they have 'attained the position of general acceptance by civilised nations"?

If "those sources come seldom if ever from every civilised nation or agree upon a universal rule"—what is the definition of customary international law, and how can "they move from one *generally* accepted rule towards another"? What is the meaning of "generally" in this context? What is the import of the phrase "some move must be made by States, or their tribunals, or jurists, to prevent petrifaction of the living law"? How can States, tribunals or jurists " move"? Move in what way? Each has a different way of "moving". Do all the different "ways" constitute different sources of international law? How many of those agencies, i.e., States, courts, or jurists, have to "move" before the law is supposed to change? What is meant by "petrifaction of the living law"? Who is to say that the law is petrifying—States, courts or jurists? If one says that the law is petrifying, there must be some objective criteria, otherwise the normative question is purely subjective. What could possibly be the criteria save the convenience or expediency of the law in the eyes of States? His Lordship asked "When should a court of law accept or adopt or incorporate or assent to what is alleged to be a new rule of international *conduct*?" He was at least in the sphere of reality when he substituted the word "conduct" for "law". Nevertheless, a court does not "accept or adopt", etc., international conduct. It tries to discover, if it so chooses, what the international practice is on a particular matter, and then enunciates a rule of municipal law in harmony with it. His Lordship was not even sure whether "an English court can even make the first move in this country? Or must it wait for a 'Tate letter' from the Government of the United Kingdom? Or for an Act of Parliament?" He asked whether "civilized States have agreed that the doctrine of restrictive immunity shall be binding upon them". How can this be "proved" without "expert evidence"? The same applied to the question, "have the opinions of jurists received the express sanction of international agreement". Moreover, in the words of his Lordship, "how do you prove that the gestation of a new rule is over and that it has come to birth? Or that an old rule has grown and developed into a new form"? How can a vacuum be created in international law? If there were no customary international law, the question would not arise. "What is meant by a new rule which is consonant with justice"? Whose justice? What is the criterion? Should it not be "consonant with State practice"? In this case, his Lordship decided that "the new rule is consonant with justice", and his criterion appeared to be based on some requirement of the law merchant that payments on letters of credit should be honoured.

What is the significance of the passage: "It would be repugnant to justice if an English court were to repudiate it (i.e., the honouring of letters of credit) in modern conditions and so in effect extend the old rule of immunity to transactions which were never considered subject to it by former judges and jurists because such transactions would never in their time have been carried out by sovereign States or their emanations"? If such transactions were never in their time carried out by sovereign States and their emanations, there would be no occasion for "former judges and jurists" to consider extending the "old rule of immunity" to them.

Finally, Shaw LJ, in his judgement, said that "in civilized States that law (municipal law) will derive from those principles of international law which have been generally accepted among such States."[48] His Lordship was satisfied "that the preponderant contemporary rule of international law supports the principle of qualified or restrictive immunity."[49] But again it must be asked what is the meaning and what are the criteria for the word "preponderant", and how is it related to the orthodox view of customary international law? In common with the other judges, he maintained that what "*is* immutable is the principle of English law that the law of nations (not what *was* the law of nations) must be applied in the courts of England".[50] The learned Judge affirmed that "even the law of England changes quite apart from what may be happening to international law. Moreover, changes in rules of international law do not come about abruptly; and changes will not be recognised in an English court without convincing support."[51] It may again be asked at what stage is a rule of customary international law supposed to change if such change does not come about abruptly? And what is the measure of "convincing support"? The ambiguous use of terminology is again exemplified in the following sentence: "Lastly, there must be a greater risk of confusion if *precepts* discarded outside England by a majority (or perhaps all) of civilised States are preserved as effective in the English courts in a sort of judicial aspic."[52] What is meant by the word *precepts*, introduced for the first time? How many constitutes all? What States are uncivilised?

Conclusion

The Statute of the International Court of Justice, as we have seen, provides that one of the sources of international law which the Court shall apply in such disputes as are submitted to it is "international custom, as evidence of a general practice accepted as law". The *Encyclopedia Britannica*, cited at the beginning of this article, explained that the term source was there used to connote "those agencies by which rules of conduct acquire the character of law by becoming objectively definite, uniform and, above all, compulsory"[53]

It will have become clear from this article that the supposed existence of such a thing as customary international law has been seriously questioned. In any event, there is little evidence to support the view that it is "objectively definite, uniform and, above all, compulsory". It seems almost impossible to hazard a realistic and satisfactory definition of customary international law. What, for example, is the meaning of a "general practice" and how is one to know if it is "accepted as law"? The specification of the "conditions of the creation and of the continued validity of international custom" (*Survey of International Law* 1949[54]) has been studiously avoided by international organizations, courts and publicists alike. On the contrary, the last mentioned have been satisfied to express, a belief, almost as an act of faith, in the existence of customary international law without requiring evidence to support that supposition or any general consensus in respect of its essential ingredients.

It is submitted that the foregoing analysis of the judgment of the Court of Appeal in the *Trendtex* case manifestly supports the claim that the idea of customary international law is no more than a legal fiction or myth. Even Lord Denning and Stephenson LJ acknowledged that "this notion of the consensus of the civilised nations is a fiction". It must therefore be a hypocrisy for courts to perpetuate the belief in its existence when they are in fact dispensing their own municipal law. This is so even where a new rule of law is created or an old one modified or displaced under the impulse of developing State practice or the decisions of foreign courts.

It is suggested that the time is more than ripe for courts to abandon the use of the term customary international law in favour of international State practice or custom, qualified perhaps by adjectives such as general, particular, regional, etc. Whether or not a court takes cognizance of such practice or custom in the formulation of its judgment or seeks guidance from the decisions of foreign municipal courts is entirely a matter within its own discretion. In many cases the criterion likely to be applied is based for the most part on notions of justice and expediency. In the result, honesty and candour would at last prevail and some difficult jurisprudential conundrums vanish in consequence from the literature.

Notes

1. Vol. 12, 423 (RYJ). The 1974 edition, Vol. 9, 744 (GSc), adopts a different approach.
2. *The Permanent Court of International Justice*, 609.
3. *Trendtex Trading Corporation v Central Bank of Nigeria* [1978] QB 529.
4. A/CN. 4/1/Rev. 1. 10 February 1949.
5. Ibid. 22.
6. A/AC. 10/40.5 June 1947, cited in *Ways and Means of Making the Evidence of Customary International Law more Readily Available*, A/AC., 4/6, 1949 (hereinafter referred to as *Ways and Means*).
7. A/AC. 10/SR. 27. 20 June 1947, 11: *Ways and Means*, 4.
8. *Ways and Means*, 4.
9. Ibid. 103.
10. Ibid. 108.
11. *Documents from the League of Nations Committee of Experts for the Progressive Codification of International Law*, (1926) 20 AJIL Supp. 304–7.
12. [1978]QB 529.
13. At 552.
14. Ibid.
15. At 552–3 (emphasis added).
16. At 553.
17. Ibid.

18. Ibid.
19. Ibid.
20. At 553–4.
21. (1876) LR 2 Ex D 63, at 202–3.
22. [1977] QB at 554.
23. [1939] AC 160, at 167–8.
24. [1974] QB 684, at 701.
25. [1977] QB at 554.
26. At 552.
27. At 554.
28. At 555.
29. At 555–6.
30. See Dunbar, "Controversial Aspects of Sovereign Immunity in the Case Law of some States". (1971–I) 132 HR 199.
31. [1977] QB at 556.
32. [1977] AC 373.
33. [1977] QB at 557.
34. At 557.
35. *Rahimtoola v Nizam of Hyderabad* [1958] AC 379 at 422: *Thai-Europe Tapioca Service Ltd v Government of Pakistan* [1975] I WLR 1485 at 1491 (both pronouncements of Lord Denning himself): *The Philippine Admiral* [1977] AC 373: *Alfred Dunhill of London Inc v Republic of Cuba* 425 US 682 (1976).
36. [1977] QB at 557–8.
37. At 558–9.
38. At 559.
39. At 559–60 (emphasis supplied).
40. At 567.
41. 15th ed. (1809) Book IV. Ch 5. 67.
42. Ibid. 66.
43. [1977] QB at 567.
44. At 567–8.
45. [1915] P 52 at 61–2.
46. [1977] QB at 569–70.
47. At 570.
48. At 575.
49. At 576.
50. At 579
51. Ibid.
52. Ibid.
53. Allen. *Law in the Making* 6th ed. (1958), 1.
54. Above fn 4.

STEVEN M. SCHNEEBAUM

The Enforceability of Customary Norms of Public International Law

If we assume that there is such a thing as international folk law, the critical question still remains, what, if any, are the obligations of individual states or nations to that law? Are the domestic law enforcement agencies of individual states or nations bound to enforce the dictates of international folk law? This is precisely the issue that is addressed by Steven M. Schneebaum, an attorney with the firm of Patton, Boggs & Blow in Washington, D.C. Schneebaum has also been an Adjunct Lecturer at the Columbus School of Law at The Catholic University of America. The following essay was based on remarks delivered by the author at the Colloquium on International Human Rights Law and Policy held at the State University of New York at Buffalo in October of 1981.

For additional discussion of the same basic issue, see John Dugard, "The Application of Customary International Law Affecting Human Rights by National Tribunals," Proceedings of the American Society of International Law, *76 (1982), 245–251; and in the same journal, Lori Fisler Damrosch, "Application of Customary International Law by U.S. Domestic Tribunals," pp. 251–255. See also Edward M. Morgan, "Internalization of Customary International Law: An Historical Perspective,"* The Yale Journal of International Law, *12 (1987), 63–83; and Harold G. Maier, "The Authoritative Sources of Customary International Law in the United States,"* Michigan Journal of International Law *10 (1989), 450–481.*

Introduction

International law is part of the law of the United States. Treaties signed and ratified according to constitutional procedures are expressly stated by the Constitution itself to be "the supreme law of the land."[1] Since the earliest days of the Republic, customary international law has been recognized as having equal dignity.[2]

Reprinted from *Brooklyn Journal of International Law*, 8 (1982), 289–307, with permission.

The jurisprudential basis for the incorporation of customary international law into the *corpus juris americanum* has been the subject of extensive academic analysis, and no small amount of dispute.[3] In many of the reported cases concerning the determination and application of customary norms, it has not been necessary for the courts to resolve this matter. These cases usually have involved statutes or other instruments referring expressly to the law of nations. In such cases, interpretation of this vexed term was required in order to give meaning to the texts in which it appeared.

For example, in *United States v. Smith*,[4] the Supreme Court rejected the contention that a statute imposing capital punishment for "the crime of piracy as defined by the law of nations" was unconstitutionally vague.[5] The Court explained that given the discernible and determinate content of the international proscription of piracy, a potential defendant had sufficient notice of the elements of the offense.[6] Yet, customary international law, not positive law, provided the missing definition.

Similarly, in *The Paquete Habana*,[7] the Court construed a presidential proclamation which expressly limited the seizure of prize during the Spanish-American War to those vessels which could be taken under "the law of nations."[8] The question presented was whether a coastal fishing vessel could be taken as prize, or whether the proclamation's express reference to international law effectively conferred immunity upon it.[9] Mr. Justice Gray found that the exemption of coastal fighting vessels from capture as prizes of war had matured from a principle of comity[10] into one of law,[11] and that therefore the Habana could not be taken from its owners.[12] As in *Smith*, the Supreme Court relied on international custom for a guide to its understanding of the words "the law of nations."

United States v. Smith and *The Paquete Habana*, however, may be seen primarily as exercises, not in international law, but in statutory construction. International questions arose in those cases because the meaning and content of the term "the law of nations" were expressly implicated.

Mr. Justice Gray wrote in *The Paquete Habana* that "[i]nternational law is part of our law, and must be ascertained and administered by the courts of justice of appropriate jurisdiction, as often as questions of right depending upon it are duly presented for their determination."[13] It therefore follows that the application of customary international law in no way depends upon such express reference by the executive or the legislature as was at issue in *Smith* and *The Paquete Habana*. Surely, determining the content of customary law may often present difficulties of identification which do not arise in the interpretation of domestic law or even of treaties. But the resolution of these difficulties—that is, the determination that a particular practice has risen to a level of a binding customary norm—should not call into question the status of international custom as a source of law. The law of nations is part of the United States law whether or not Congress expressly directs the Court's attention to it.[14]

Recently, several federal courts have been presented with claims of rights based primarily in customary international law.[15] In *Filartiga v. Peña-Irala*,[16] the Court of Appeals for the Second Circuit held that the right to be free from torture is a human right, deriving from customary international law and enforceable in domestic courts. Similarly, in *Rodriguez-Fernandez v. Wilkinson*,[17] the Court of Appeals for the Tenth Circuit found that there is an international right to be free from arbitrary imprisonment. However, in *Hanoch Tel-Oren v. Libyan Arab Republic*,[18] a district court declared that if indeed there is a customary norm condemning terrorism, it is not judicially enforceable in the absence of international agreement that such a norm provides for a private right of action.

These cases have provoked a much-needed reexamination in judicial decisions and academic writings of the role of customary international norms in the law of the United States.[19] Yet some judges and commentators have failed to appreciate the role and meaning of custom as a source of international law and hence of American domestic law. In addition, the procedural distinctions between the interpretation of a treaty and the identification of a customary norm have become confused. This has resulted in the introduction of a new and potentially disruptive barrier to the full implementation of the emerging international law of human rights in United States courts.

The nature of the confusion concerning the application of customary law may be simply stated: treaties must be either self-executing[20] or legislatively implemented before they may be invoked as a basis for individual rights. If a treaty is self-executing, it does not require express legislative or executive action to make it enforceable; it is enforceable by its nature. Failing to appreciate the parallelism between treaty and custom as sources of law, some writers have searched for executive or legislative implementation of customary law, and, not finding it, have concluded that international custom is not enforceable.[21] Others, under a logically equivalent misunderstanding, have sought to locate the express creation of "a private right of action"[22] as an element of customary international norms before acknowledging that they may create or recognize individual rights.[23]

It is the thesis of this article that such an analysis is fundamentally erroneous. The existence of a private right of action alleging violation of customary norms follows from, and is determined by, the content of those norms themselves. A private right of action against the perpetrator of certain conduct is the logical correlative of the right to be free from that conduct, or, in other words, of a legal prohibition against that conduct.

It is the same in the interpretation of treaties. A treaty generates the right to invoke the judicial process when, and only when, it creates binding legal obligations. Modern international law, as reflected in both treaty and custom, has made great strides toward specifying and particularizing the rights and duties of individuals.[24] To that extent international law has become a proper basis of federal court jurisdiction in suits implicating those rights and duties.[25]

There is nothing new in this thesis. Indeed, as will presently be shown, courts have consistently relied on such an analysis to distinguish between those treaties which are self-executing and those which are not.

I. When Is a Treaty Self-Executing?

Much of the academic and judicial writing on the issue of when treaties are self-executing has not moved toward a answer to that question. Rather, it has moved in a circle around it. A classic example of such circular reasoning is the following statement of the United States Court of Appeals for the Third Circuit: "[U]nless a treaty is self-executing, it must be implemented by legislation before it gives rise to a private cause of action."[26] Or, as the Court of Appeals for the Fifth Circuit noted, "treaties affect the municipal law of the United States only when those treaties are given effect by congressional legislation or are, by their nature, self-executing." [27]

Since the term "self-executing treaty" generally means a treaty which generates rights that are directly enforceable,[28] it will be seen that these two judicial formulations are straightforward tautologies. They simply reiterate the definition of the term "self-executing." For the purposes of this analysis, that approach will be set aside. Instead of seeking to establish whether a treaty is self-executing to determine the viability of a private cause of action thereunder, the following is the proper question to pose: Does the treaty purport to recognize or create an individual right to demand, or to be free from, certain conduct, whether public or private?[29]

The question posed is far from simple, but it is one which may be assaulted with the traditional weapons of the judicial armory: statutory construction, recourse to legislative history, reasoning by analogy to other areas of law, and an entire battery of precedents, maxims, and principles. Courts routinely approach cases in this manner, although not often expressly and perhaps not even deliberately. No exhaustive list could conceivably be devised of all indicia pointing to or creating individual rights, but some of the more important indicators which the courts must canvass will be discussed below.

A. What does the treaty actually say?

In some treaties rights are quite expressly acknowledged or created, or conversely, it is clearly said that no rights should be inferred. These are the easy cases, over which judges rarely must tarry long. It should be noted that express recognition in a treaty of a private right of action is a sufficient though not a necessary condition for the holding that such a right exists.

Thus, in *Asakura v. City of Seattle*[30], the Supreme Court found the language of a bilateral agreement between the United States and Japan[31] to be unambiguous in its prohibition of a Seattle licensing ordinance.[32] The ordinance required all pawnbrokers to obtain a license but made United States citizenship a prerequisite to qualification.[33] The international agreement read as follows:

> The citizens or subjects of each of the High Contracting Parties shall have liberty to enter, travel and reside in the territories of the other to carry on trade, wholesale and retail, to own or lease and occupy houses, manufactories, warehouses and shops, to employ agents of their choice, to lease land for residential and commercial purposes, and generally to do anything incident to or necessary for trade upon the same terms as native citizens or subjects, submitting themselves to the laws and regulations there established. . . . The citizens or subjects of each . . . shall receive, in the territories of the other, the most constant protection and security for their persons and property. . . .[34]

The Court said of the Seattle regulation that "[t]he ordinance violates the treaty," and enjoined its enforcement.[35] The treaty, however, was silent on the question of its enforceability by individuals.

On the other hand, a treaty may specifically obligate each party to do something, such as to perform an executive or a legislative act, which will engender consequent rights. Until that act is done, those rights are not created. This was the situation in the landmark decision of Chief Justice Marshall in *Foster v. Neilson*,[36] said to be the *locus classicus* of the notion of self-executing treaties. In *Foster*, the treaty under review contained a commitment by the United States to ratify legislatively certain grants of land by the King of Spain.[37] The United States failed to ratify the grant upon which the plaintiff sought to rely. Chief Justice Marshall held that unless and until the required legislation was enacted, the grant could not be recognized.[38] Since the United States had contracted to perform a particular act, rights flowing from that act were created, not by the treaty, but by its legislative implementation.

B. What obligations, if any, does the treaty impose?

Some treaties require that States or their subjects act, or refrain from acting, in certain ways. Others merely exhort them to meritorious conduct. Since the language of the human rights provisions of the United Nations Charter[39] articles 55 and 56—seems to be hortatory rather than mandatory , many courts have concluded that those provisions are not self-executing.[40] Though the matter is far from clear,[41] it is submitted that this view is correct: as treaty provisions in a historical vacuum, articles 55 and 56 are not sufficiently precise to create or to acknowledge individual rights. But to concede that point is not to desert the human rights banner on the field of battle: for through custom, as will be seen, the normative content of the Charter articles reemerges as independently enforceable.[42]

C. Can the treaty fairly be said to create a "protected class" of individuals?

It is commonplace that whether a statute creates a private right of action—that is, whether an individual plaintiff can maintain an action against an alleged violator—depends to a large extent upon whether the individual who would exercise that right is a member of a class protected by the statute.[43] This is a question normally resolved, by American courts at least,[44] after analysis of the intentions of the legislature which enacted the law, as revealed in the legislative history.[45]

In the case of treaties, this analysis contains two strands. First, there is the genesis of the treaty itself: the *travaux préparatoires* of its drafters and negotiators. Second, there is the legislative process surrounding its ratification by the United States.

Thus even when the actual text of a treaty may leave room for doubt as to whether individual rights are either acknowledged or created, the historical process which gave rise to that text may resolve these doubts. Furthermore, the Senate of the United States, in giving its advice and consent as laid down in the Constitution,[46] may expressly decline to endorse rights provisions.[47] To this, however, two caveats must be sounded: such a reservation must comport with the rules of international law governing reservations generally.[48] Also, even an express reservation with respect to a norm of treaty law may be inadequate to deflect the development of an identical norm through customary international law.[49]

It will be noted, however, that the existence of a "protected class" under a treaty does not require an express textual provision to that effect. A statute incidentally conferring a private cause of action need not so state. This is rather a conclusion for the courts to infer, on the basis of the criteria discussed above, and perhaps of others as well.

D. Have subsequent events materially altered the content of treaty obligations?

In the face of a universal tendency to interpret treaty provisions in certain ways, silence by the legislature may well constitute an endorsement of the emerging interpretation. Like the Constitution itself, treaties may be said to evolve, and that evolution may include the birth and maturation of rights perhaps not thought present before.

Some commentators believe that after thirty years of widespread adoption and endorsement as a guide to the interpretation of the United Nations Charter human rights provisions,[50] the Universal Declaration of Human Rights[51] has supplied the requisite specificity to make those provisions enforceable.[52] Nor is construction of a statutory instrument by reference to subsequent legislative action or inaction a novel technique in difficult cases.[53]

Rights founded in a treaty—once they have been determined through such an analysis as this one—take their place in the panoply of rights vouchsafed by the Constitution. They are fully part of the patrimony of all persons subject to the treaty, and they may be protected through appropriate judicial procedures.

II. When Are Customary International Norms Enforceable?

Strictly speaking, international custom cannot be described as self-executing, since that is a term correctly reserved for textual provisions. But with only minor alterations, the analysis suggested above applies equally to the enforceability of customary norms. This result is not unexpected: as we have seen, customary law and treaty law stand on equal footing as part of the law of the United States.[54]

The analytic technique of searching for rights which may be recognized or guaranteed, rather than concentrating on such formal matters as the presence or absence of legislative implementation, yields the same result for custom as for treaty. When customary norms may be said to have created rights, those rights are enforceable in United States courts, because customary international law is part of the law of the United States.

There is, however, one question that must be asked when a customary norm is asserted which need not be posed in the case of a treaty. Since custom cannot be determined unequivocally by however careful a reading of treaty texts, a court confronted with a case asserting a right under customary law must first ascertain whether, in fact, a relevant customary norm exists at all. For example, if it determines that there is a customary prohibition against certain actions, it must then, conducting the kind of survey proposed herein, decide whether the norm is of the sort that warrants private enforcement.

Determination of the existence and content of a customary international norm is no easy matter. But there do exist techniques, endorsed by both domestic and international tribunals, to aid judges in carrying out that task.

These techniques are the ones set down by Mr. Justice Gray in *The Paquete Habana:* in the absence of a controlling treaty or statute,

> resort must be had to the customs and usages of civilized nations; and, as evidence of these, to the works of jurists and commentators, who by years of labor, research and experience, have made themselves peculiarly well acquainted with the subjects of which they treat. Such works are resorted to by judicial tribunals, not for the speculations of their authors concerning what the law ought to be, but for trustworthy evidence of what the law really is.[55]

The Statute of the International Court of Justice,[56] in article 38, lists three primary sources and one secondary source of international law. First to be consulted are treaties,[57] "international custom, as evidence of a general practice accepted as law,"[58] and "the general principles of law recognized by civilized nations."[59] A "subsidiary means" of determining the law to be applied is the body of judicial and academic writings on the point.[60]

Strict standards must be met before a custom is recognized as having been transmuted into a binding legal norm. Lack of unanimity or universality will normally defeat this metamorphosis, unless it can be explained away. Thus, the United States Supreme Court declined to find an international custom prohibiting uncompensated expropriations in *Banco Nacional de Cuba v. Sabbatino*.[61] The International Court of Justice held without normative force a custom concerning delimitation of the continental shelf in the *North Sea Continental Shelf Cases.*[62] And in the *Nuclear Tests* case,[63] the International Court of Justice declined to hold that France was bound by a custom of which the proffered evidence was express endorsement by over ninety nations.[64]

Once a customary norm is found using traditional techniques, it must still be scrutinized before it may be validly asserted as a source of primary rights.[65] In conducting that operation, however, one should neither seek nor expect to find provision for a private right of action as an express component of the norm. Rather, such a right is to be inferred, established as a correlative of the norm's substantive content.

This is precisely the structure of the decision of the Court of Appeals for the Second Circuit in *Filartiga* v. *Peña-Irala.*[66] The court found sufficient authority to indicate the existence of a customary norm of international law prohibiting official torture.[67] It then found that norm sufficiently precise and explicit to create (or to recognize) the right to be free from torture.[68] Plainly such a norm has as its entire inspiration the protection of a class of persons, to which plaintiffs' decedent in *Filartiga* was alleged to belong.[69]

Given these factors, the court held that there is a right in customary international law, and therefore in the law of the United States, to be free from torture.[70] If there is such a right—as the court emphatically concluded—then there should be no need to continue the search for a private cause of action to enforce it. To be free from torture is a right under United States law. That is enough to enlist the aid of the judiciary in the protection of that right.[71]

Specifically at issue in *Filartiga* was the construction of 28 U.S.C. § 1350,[72] which gives the district courts original jurisdiction over tort suits brought by aliens, alleging "violation of the law of nations or a treaty of the United States."[73] Of the three jurisdictional prerequisites, two—that the suit be one in tort and that the plaintiffs be aliens—were plainly satisfied in *Filartiga*. Judge Kaufman eloquently established the third: that the torture alleged in the complaint was a violation of (customary) international law.

Judge Kaufman went further, however, and showed also that torture is a violation of United States law, since international law is part of the law of the land.[74] If this part of the holding is correct—and it is submitted that it is—then jurisdiction in *Filartiga* would have lain not only under § 1350, but under section 1331[75] as well.[76] As Judge Kaufman noted, it was not necessary for the court to address this point;[77] nevertheless, *Filartiga* amply supports the proposition that customary international law is incorporated in United States Law, and that United States courts possess jurisdiction to decide cases in which it is invoked.[78] Nor is *Filartiga* a case of the *United States* v. *Smith* variety: the invocation of custom as a source of law does not derive its force from the express reference to "the law of nations" in a statute. Judge Kaufman found customary law to be enforceable in United States courts to the extent that it creates or recognizes individual rights.

Similarly, the district court in *Fernandez* v. *Wilkinson*[79] found that an international customary norm condemning arbitrary imprisonment had as its correlative an individual right to be free of that practice.[80] Nor did the United States Court of Appeals for the Tenth Circuit, in sustaining the district court's decision on avowedly different grounds,[81] in any way derogate from the underlying principle enunciated by the district court. The court of appeals did not rely on customary international law as the ultimate source of plaintiff's right, as the district court had, finding a more satisfactory basis in the Constitution.[82] But the court of appeals looked to international law as a gloss upon constitutional guarantees of due process.[83] Moreover, the court found that there is an individual right to be free from arbitrary imprisonment and that such a right has a basis in international law.[84]

That rights may have constitutional as well as customary international law underprinnings is, of course, all to the good. It is, indeed, a great measure of the majesty of our Constitution that, after nearly two centuries, its precepts of human dignity have hardly been overtaken by the law of nations however rapidly developing.

The analysis set out above, however, has not been universally observed by the courts. In *Hanoch Tel-Oren* v. *Libyan Arab Republic*,[85] Judge Joyce Hens Green of the United States District Court for the District of Columbia was confronted with a claim that certain terrorist acts allegedly perpetrated by the Palestine Liberation Organization were in violation of a customary norm which gave individuals the right to be free of such acts.

It would have been sufficient to hold that there is inadequate evidence of an international norm prohibiting such acts,[86] and that even if there were such a norm it is of insufficient precision to establish individual rights.[87] The decision of the district court, however, did not stop there.[88] Judge Green's opinion contains the following language, which, it is respectfully submitted, is most unfortunate:

> [U]nless treaties to which the United States is a party or even the law of nations generally provide a private right of action, no jurisdictional grant, be it § 1331 or § 1350, can aid a plaintiff seeking relief in federal district court.... Absent the clear indication... that nations intend to subject themselves to such worldwide jurisprudential assaults [*i.e.* private lawsuits alleging violation of customary international law], jurisdiction under § 1350 will not vest.[89]

It is most important that *Tel-Oren* not be taken in future cases to stand for the proposition that a private cause of action, to enforce a right derived from customary international law, must be separately provided for. As in the case of treaty norms, enforceability is established by the existence of an individual right such a cause would seek to vindicate. One can reasonably infer from the statements cited above and from other *dicta*[90] that Judge Green did posit the requirement of consensus to remedies.[91] Such too is the implication of a sentence the Judge excerpts from a law review critique of *Filartiga*: "[T]o interpret international human rights law to create a private right of action overstates the level of agreement among nations on remedies for human rights violations."[92]

Customary international law creates individual rights, or recognizes their existence, when the indicia of custom point to the evolution of certain legal norms. Just as a treaty need not expressly provide for private enforcement to be the basis for a claim of rights,[93] there need be no specific consensus as to remedies for violations of customary law. The nations of the world may not have agreed to have the legality of alleged acts of terrorism adjudicated in foreign courts, but this is because they have not yet agreed that those acts are committed in violation of the rights of their victims. Were there to be such an agreement, there would be a concomitant acquiescence to the jurisdiction of any court before whom the perpetrator could be brought to justice.

There need not be international agreement for an international wrong to be remediable in United States courts, whether the offending act violates treaty or custom. It is enough that there be agreement on rights. At present, there may be no such consensus with respect to the legal status of the acts alleged in Tel-Oren. But the existence of consensus, indeed near-unanimity, among nations in the prohibition of torture (Filartiga) and of arbitrary imprisonment (Fernandez) has been clearly established.[94] Until cases or controversies alleging other violations of customary international law are presented to the courts for adjudication, it will not be known in what other areas international custom has fully evolved into a guarantor of rights.[95]

Conclusion

Customary international law shares entirely with treaty law the dignity of forming a part of the law of the United States. Where each is of sufficient precision and of proper content to acknowledge or to generate individual rights, it can stand, without more,[96] as the basis of a claim justiciable in United States courts. It is unnecessary that the existence of a private remedy be somewhere expressly provided for customary law to be enforceable, just as it has never been required that a treaty, to be self-executing, expressly so state.

It is respectfully submitted that judges confronted with claims founded in international custom should search for consensus on rights, not remedies.[97] For it is the genius of our legal system that where the former are vouchsafed, the latter inexorably follow.

Notes

1. *U.S. Const.* art VI, § 2: "This Constitution, and the Laws of the United States which shall be made in Pursuance thereof; and all Treaties made, or which shall be made, under the authority of the United States, shall be the supreme Law of the Land. . . ."

2. *See, e.g.* Respublica v. De Longchamps, 1 U.S. (1 Dall.) 111, 114 (1784). For a classic historical analysis of the role of international law in the legal system of the newly independent colonies *see* Dickinson, "The Law of Nations as Part of the National Law of the United States" (pts. 1 & 2), 101 *U. Pa. L. Rev.* 26, 792 (1952–1953).

3. Customary international law may be part of the laws of the United States because it is part of the federal common law, or because the law of nations generally binds a sovereign acting through its judiciary absent a legislative expression that it does not consent to be bound. Whatever the jurisprudential basis for the proposition, however, it is clear that "the Law of Nations is a part of the law of the land to be ascertained and administered, like any other, in the appropriate case." Dickinson, *supra* note 2, at 26. *See also* the learned discussion of this question in Filartiga v. Peña-Irala, 630 F.2d 876, 885–7 (2d Cir. 1980).

4. 18 U.S. (5 Wheat.) 153 (1820).

5. *Id.* at 160–62. *See* An Act to protect the commerce of the United States, and punish the crime of piracy, ch. 77, § 5, 2 Stat. 510 (1819). This statute, essentially unchanged, is today codified at 18 U.S.C. § 1651 (1976).

6. 18 U.S. (5 Wheat.) at 160–62.

7. 175 U.S. 677 (1900).

8. *Id.* at 712. The proclamation announced that the United States would maintain a blockade of Cuba "in pursuance of the laws of the United States, and the laws of nations applicable to such cases." Presidential Proclamation of April 22, 1898, 30 Stat. 1769 (1898).

9. 175 U.S. at 686.

10. *Id.* at 694. "[R]ules of politeness, convenience, and good will . . . are not rules of law, but of Comity. The Comity of Nations is not a source of International Law. But many a rule which formerly was a rule of International Comity only is nowadays a rule of International Law." 1 L. Oppenheim, *International Law* 32–33 (Lauterpacht ed. 1961).

11. 175 U.S. at 708.

12. *Id.* at 714.

13. *Id.* at 700.

14. The Nereide, 13 U.S. (9 Cranch) 388, 423 (1815). ("[T]he Court is bound by the law of nations, which is part of the law of the land."). *See also* Filartiga v. Peña-Irala, 630 F.2d at 886–7.

15. *See, e.g.*, Fernandez v. Wilkinson, 505 F. Supp. 787 (D. Kan. 1980), *aff'd sub nom.* Rodriguez-Fernandez v. Wilkinson, 654 F.2d 1382 (10th Cir. 1981); Filartiga v. Peña-Irala, 630 F.2d 876 (2d Cir. 1980); Hanoch Tel-Oren v. Libyan Arab Republic, 517 F. Supp. 542 (D.D.C. 1981), *appeal docketed*, No. 81–1870 (D.C. Cir. Aug. 4, 1981). *See also* Lareau v. Manson, 507 F. Supp. 1177, 1188 n.9 (D.Conn. 1980); Sterling v. Cupp, 290 Or. 611, 625 P.2d 123, 131 n.21 (1981) (en banc).

16. 630 F.2d 876 (2d Cir. 1980).

17. 505 F. Supp. 787 (D. Kan. 1980), *aff'd sub nom.* Rodriguez-Fernandez v. Wilkinson, 654 F.2d 1382 (10th Cir. 1981).

18. 517 F. Supp. 542 (D.D.C. 1981), *appeal docketed*, No. 81–1870 (D.C. Cir. Aug. 4, 1981).

19. *See, e.g.*, "Federal Jurisdiction, Human Rights, and the Law of Nations: Essays on Filartiga v. Peña-Irala," 11 *Ga. J. Int'l & Comp. L.* 307 (1982); "Symposium on the Future of Human Rights in the World Order," 9 *Hofstra L. Rev.* 337 (1981); 4 *Hous. J. Int'l L.*—(1982) (symposium issue).

20. A treaty is self-executing when it generates rights that are directly enforceable; a self-executing treaty does not require implementing legislation to be effective as domestic law. Thus, in People of Saipan v. United States Dep't of Interior, 502 F.2d 90, 97 (9th Cir. 1974), *cert. denied*, 420 U.S. 1003 (1975), the court held that the United Nations Trusteeship Agreement with respect to United States administration of the Trust Territories of the Pacific Islands could be invoked absent express congressional authorization, since it "suggests the intention to establish direct, affirmative, and judicially enforceable rights." But nowhere is it stated in terms that "this agreement shall be self-executing."

21. *See, e.g.*, Note, "Torture as a Tort in Violation of International Law: Filartiga v. Peña-Irala," 33 *Stan. L. Rev.* 353 (1981).

22. *See generally* Hazen, "Implied Private Remedies Under Federal Statutes: Neither a Death Knell Nor a Moratorium—Civil Rights, Securities Regulation, and Beyond," 33 *Vand. L. Rev.* 1333 (1980). *See infra* note 43.

23. *See, e.g.*, Hanoch Tel-Oren v. Libyan Arab Republic, 517 F. Supp. 542 (D.D.C. 1981), *appeal docketed*, No. 81–1870 (D.C. Cir. Aug. 4, 1981). *See infra* text accompanying notes 85–88.

24. For a collection of human rights instruments *see Human Rights: A Compilation of International Instruments* (1978), U.N. Doc. ST/HR/1/Rev. 1. For background on the development of international human rights *see United Nations Action in the Field of Human Rights* (1980), U.N. Doc. ST/HR/2/Rev.1; L. Henkin, *The Rights of Man Today* (1978); L. Sohn & T. Buergenthal, *International Protection of Human Rights* (1973); E. Schwelb, *Human Rights and the International Community* (1964); Bilder, "The Status of International Human Rights Law: An Overview," in *International Human Rights: Law and Practice* 1, 8 (Tuttle rev. ed. 1978); Sohn, A "Short History of United Nations Documents on Human Rights," in *The United Nations and Human Rights, 18th Report of the Commission* 71 (Commission to Study the Organization of Peace ed. 1968).

25. *See generally* R. Falk, *The Role of Domestic Courts in the International Legal Order* (1964); Lillich, "The Proper Role of Domestic Courts in the International Legal Order," 11 *Va. J. Int'l L.* 9 (1970). *See also* Nayer, "Human Rights: The United Nations and United States Foreign Policy," 19 *Harv. Int'l L.J.* 813 (1978); Salzberg & Young, "The Parliamentary Role in Implementing International Human Rights: A U.S. Example," 12 *Tex. Int'l L.J.* 251 (1977); Weissbrodt, "Human Rights Legislation and U.S. Foreign Policy," 7 *Ga. J. Int'l & Comp. L.* 231 (1977).

26. Mannington Mills, Inc. v. Congoleum Corp., 595 F.2d 1287, 1298 (3d Cir. 1979) (citations omitted).

27. United States v. Postal, 589 F.2d 862, 875 (5th Cir.), *cert. denied*, 444 U.S. 832 (1979) (citations omitted).

28. *See supra* note 20.

29. This is what H.L.A. Hart called a "primary right," as opposed to a "secondary right," the right of access to a specific legal process or remedy. *See generally* Hart, "Definition and Theory in Jurisprudence," 70 *Law Q Rev.* 37 (1954).

30. 265 U.S. 332 (1924).

31. Treaty of Commerce and Navigation, Feb. 21, 1911, United States—Japan, 37 Stat. 1504, T.S. No. 558 [hereinafter cited as Treaty of Commerce and Navigation].

32. 265 U.S. at 342–43.

33. *Id.* at 339–40.

34. *Id.* at 340, *quoting* Treaty of Commerce and Navigation, *supra* note 31, art. 1.

35. 265 U.S. at 343.

36. 27 U.S. (2 Pet.) 253, 314 (1829). Chief Justice Marshall developed the following contractual analysis to determine if any rights existed under the treaty:

> A treaty is in its nature a contract between two nations, not a legislative act. It does not generally effect, of itself, the object to be accomplished, especially so far as its operation is infra-territorial; but is carried into execution by the sovereign power of the respective parties to the instrument.
>
> In the United States a different principle is established. Our constitution declares a treaty to be the law of the land. It is, consequently, to be regarded in courts of justice as equivalent to an act of the legislature, whenever it operates of itself without the aid of any legislative provision. But when the terms of the stipulation import a contract, when either of the parties engages to perform a particular act, the treaty addresses itself to the political, not the judicial department; and the legislature must execute the contract before it can become a rule for the Court.

37. *Id.* at 310. Treaty of Amity, Settlement, and Limits, Feb. 22, 1819, United States-Spain, arts. 6 & 8, 8 Stat. 252, T.S. No. 327.

38. 27 U.S. (2 Pet.) at 315.

39. *U.N. Charter*, art. 55, 59 Stat. 1033 (1945), T.S. No. 993, states:

> With a view to the creation of conditions of stability and well-being which are necessary for peaceful and friendly relations among nations based on

respect for the principle of equal rights and self-determination of peoples, the United Nations shall promote:

(a) higher standards of living, full employment, and conditions of economic and social progress and development;
(b) solutions of international economic, social, health, and related problems; and international cultural and educational co-operation; and
(c) universal respect for, and observance of, human rights and fundamental freedoms for all without distinction as to race, sex, language, or religion.

Article 56 states: "All members pledge themselves to take joint and separate action in cooperation with the Organization for the achievement of the purposes set forth in Article 55." The U.N. Charter is a treaty of the United States.

40. Hitai v. Immigration and Naturalization Service, 343 F.2d 466, 468 (2d Cir.), *cert. denied*, 382 U.S. 816 (1965); Pauling v. McElroy, 164 F. Supp. 390, 393 (D.D.C. 1958), *aff'd*, 278 F.2d 252 (D.C. Cir.), *cert. denied*, 364 U.S. 835 (1960), Sei Fujii v. State, 38 Cal. 2d 718, 242 P.2d 617, 620–21 (1952).

41. For a statement of the opposing view (although the "opposition" is to the means of the conclusion, not to the conclusion itself), *see* Paust, *Book Review*, 56 N.Y.U. L. REV. 227, 238–42 (1981).

42. *See infra* text accompanying notes 50–52.

43. The seminal case on this point is Cort v. Ash, 422 U.S. 66 (1975). The Supreme Court enunciated a four-part test to determine whether plaintiffs had an implied right of action for damages under a criminal statute:

> First, is the plaintiff 'one of the class for whose *especial* benefit the statute was enacted.' . . . that is, does the statute create a federal right in favor of the plaintiff? Second, is there any indication of legislative intent, explicit or implicit, either to create such a remedy or to deny one? . . . Third, is it consistent with the underlying purposes of the legislative scheme to imply such a remedy for the plaintiff? . . . And finally, is the cause of action one traditionally relegated to state law, in an area basically the concern of the States, so that it would be inappropriate to infer a cause of action based solely on federal law? . . .

Id. at 78 (emphasis in original) (footnotes omitted). For recent Supreme Court cases on implied private right of action *see* Transamerica Mortgage Advisors, Inc. v. Lewis, 444 U.S. 11 (1979) (securities regulation): Davis v. Passman, 442 U.S. 228 (1979) (constitutional rights); Cannon v. University of Chicago, 441 U.S. 677 (1979) (statutory civil rights).

44. It is otherwise in England, for example. The existence or absence of a protected class is determined there without recourse to extrinsic authorities, at least in theory. *See, e.g.*, Sagnata Investments Ltd. v. Norwich Corp., [1971] 2 Q.B. 614.

45. *See* Cort. v. Ash, 422 U.S. at 82–84.

46. *U.S. Const.* art. II, § 2, cl.2.

47. For example, President Carter sent the International Covenant on Civil and Political Rights, *G.A. Res.* 2200A, 21 U.N. GAOR, Supp. (No. 16) 52, U.N. Doc. A/6316 (1966), to the Senate with the request that advice and consent be given to its ratification. The President's accompanying transmittal letter explained that "[w]henever a provision [of the treaties] is in conflict with United States law, a reservation, understanding or declaration has been recommended." Message of the President Transmitting Four Treaties Pertaining to Human Rights, 14 *Weekly Comp. of Pres. Doc.* 395 (Feb. 23, 1978). For the specific recommendations *see* Letters of Submittal from Warren Christopher, Department of State, to President Carter, of the Discrimination Convention, the Economic, Social and Cultural Covenant, and the Civil and Political Covenant (Dec. 17, 1977) *S. Exec. Doc. Nos. C,D,E,F,* 95th Cong., 2d Sess. V–XV (1977). For an analysis of these recommendations *see* Comments, "The International Covenant on Civil and Political Rights and United States Law: Department of State Proposals for Preserving the Status Quo," 19 *Harv. Int'l L.J.* 845) 1978).

48. *See* Vienna Convention on the Law of Treaties, arts. 19–23, *done* May 23, 1969, *U.N. Doc. A/CONF. 39/27, entered into force* Jan. 27, 1980 (procedures regarding reservations).

49. There is tantalizingly little express authority on this point. Judge Rogers of the United States District Court for the District of Kansas appears, however, to uphold customary international norms as binding on the United States even in the face of a refusal by the Senate to ratify treaties codifying them. Fernandez v. Wilkinson, 505 F. Supp. 787, 798–900 (D.Kan. 1980), *aff'd sub nom.* Rodriguez-Fernandez v. Wilkinson, 654 F.2d 1382 (10th Cir. 1981). Later emergence of a binding custom should override a prior legislative act under normal canons of statutory interpretation. But cf. L. Henkin, *Foreign Affairs and the Constitution* 221–22 (1972) ("[I]t has not been decided whether a newly developed principle of customary international law would be applied by the courts in disregard of an earlier statute . . .").

50. *U.N. Charter*, arts. 55 & 56. *See supra* note 39.

51. Universal Declaration of Human Rights, G.A. Res. 217, U.N. Doc. A/1810 at 271 (1948).

52. Although the Universal Declaration of Human Rights is not a treaty and was adopted in the form of a nonbinding resolution, international publicists and many governments today assert that it provides an authoritative definition of the fundamental human rights recognized in the United Nations Charter which States are under an obligation to promote. *See* Filartiga v. Peña-Irala, 630 F.2d 876, 881–83 (2d Cir. 1980); Legal Consequence For States Of The Continued Presence of South Africa In Namibia (South West Africa) Notwithstanding Security Council Resolution 276 (1970), 1971 I.C.J. 16, 76 (Advisory Opinion of June 21) (separate opinion of Judge Ammoun); Proclamation of Teheran, Final Act of the International Conference on Human Rights 3, at 4, para. 2, U.N. Doc. A/CONF. 32/41 (1968); R. Lillich & F. Newman, *International Human Rights: Problems of Law and Policy* 7 (1979); Bilder, "The Status of International Human Rights Law: An Overview," *International Human Rights: Law and Practice* 1, 8 (Tuttle rev. ed. 1978); Sohn, "A Short History of the United Nations Documents on Human Rights," in *United Nations and Human*

Rights, 18th Report of the Commission 71–73 (Commission to Study the Organization of Peace ed. 1968).

53. An interesting illustration of this point may be seen in the disagreement between the Courts of Appeals for the Second and Fifth Circuits in Real v. Simon, 510 F.2d 557 (5th Cir. 1975) and in Richardson v. Simon, 560 F.2d 500 (2d Cir. 1977), *appeal dismissed*, 435 U.S. 939 (1978). *See also* Tagle v. Regan, 643 F.2d 1058 (5th Cir. 1981).

54. *See supra* text accompanying notes 1–14.

55. 175 U.S. at 700.

56. Statute of the International Court of Justice, art. 38, June 26, 1945, 45 Stat. 1055, 1060 (1945). It is part of the United Nations Charter, *see id.* art. 92, and therefore is a treaty of the United States. *See supra* note 39.

57. Statute of the International Court of Justice, art. 38(1)(a).

58. *Id.* art. 38(1)(b).

59. *Id.* art. 38(1)(c).

60. *Id.* art. 38(1)(d). Pursuant to Article 59 of the Statute of the International Court of Justice, judicial decisions do not bind parties in future cases, but serve only as evidence of custom.

61. 376 U.S. 398, 428–430 (1964).

62. North Sea Continental Shelf (W. Ger. v. Den., W. Ger. v. Neth.), 1969 I.C.J. 3, 45, para. 81 (Judgment of Feb. 20). In determining whether a mandatory rule of customary international law had crystallized, the Court developed the following test to analyze the evidence of State practice concerning boundary delimitation:

> [E]ven if these instances of action by non-parties to the Convention were much more numerous than they in fact are, they would not, even in the aggregate, suffice in themselves to constitute the *opinio juris;*— for, in order to achieve this result, two conditions must be fulfilled. Not only must the acts concerned amount to a settled practice, but they must also be such, or be carried out in such a way, as to be evidence of a belief that this practice is rendered obligatory by the existence of a rule requiring it. The need for such a belief, i.e., the existence of a subjective element, is implicit in the very notion of the *opinio juris sive necessitatis.* The States concerned must therefore feel that they are conforming to what amounts to a legal obligation. The frequency, or even habitual character of the acts is not in itself enough. There are many international acts, e.g., in the field of ceremonial and protocol, which are performed almost invariably, but which are motivated only by considerations of courtesy, convenience or tradition, and not by any sense of legal duty.
>
> *Id.* at 44, para. 77.

63. Nuclear Tests (Aust. v. Fr.), 1974 I.C.J. 253 (Judgment of Dec. 20); Nuclear Tests (N.Z. v. Fr.), 1974 I.C.J. 457 (Judgment of Dec. 20).

64. *See, e.g.*, Nuclear Tests (Aust. v. Fr.), 1974 I.C.J. 253, 288 (Judgment of Dec. 20) (Separate opinion of Judge Gros).

65. *See supra* note 29 and accompanying text.

66. 630 F.2d 876 (2d Cir. 1980).

67. *Id.* at 884.

68. *Id.* at 884–85.

69. Since at issue in *Filartiga* was defendant's motion to dismiss, the allegations in the complaint were taken as true. *See, e.g.*, Newport News Shipbuilding & Dry Dock Co. v. Schauffer, 303 U.S. 54, 57 (1938) (allegations of facts, but not conclusions of law, accepted as true on motion to dismiss).

70. "[I]nternational law confers fundamental rights upon all people vis-à-vis their own governments. . . . [W]e hold that the right to be free from torture is now among them." 630 F.2d at 885.

71. The author has explored the Latin maxim *ubi jus, ibi remedium* in "The Legal Rights of Refugees," 3 *Mich. Y.B. Int'l Legal Stud.* 373 (1982).

72. 28 U.S.C. § 1350 (1976). The statute was originally enacted as § 9(b) of the Judiciary Act of 1789, 1 Stat. 73, 77.

73. 28 U.S.C. § 1350 (1976).

74. 630 F.2d at 885–9.

75. 28 U.S.C. § 1331 (1976).

76. Judge Kaufman discusses this question briefly in a footnote: 630 F.2d at 887 n.22.

77. *Id.*

78. 630 F.2d at 880–1. The author has discussed this aspect of the *Filartiga* holding in more detail in his article. *The Legal Rights of Refugees, supra* note 71.

79. 505 F. Supp. 787 (D. Kan. 1980), *aff'd sub nom.* Rodriguez-Fernandez v. Wilkinson 654 F.2d 1382 (10th Cir. 1981).

80. 505 F. Supp. at 798.

81. 654 F.2d at 1389. The court of appeals found that the Immigration and Naturalization Act of 1952, 8 U.S.C. § 1101 *et seq.*, did not permit indefinite detention as an alternative to excluding aliens.

82. *Id.* at 1387. The court of appeals declared that "an excluded alien in physical custody within the United States may not be 'punished' without being accorded the substantive and procedural due process guarantees of the Fifth Amendment."

83. *Id.* at 1388.

84. "No principle of international law is more fundamental than the concept that human beings should be free from arbitrary imprisonment." *Id.* Customary international law has similarly been employed by the United States District Court for the District of Connecticut in Lareau v. Manson, 507 F. Supp. 1177, 1187–89 n.9 & 1193 n.18 (D. Conn. 1980) (citing international human rights principles establishing the right to be free from cruel and inhuman prison conditions).

85. 517 F. Supp. 542 (D.D.C. 1981), *appeal docketed*, No. 81–1870 (D.C. Cir. Aug. 4, 1981).

86. The court listed a number of United Nations declarations and treaties, eight of which the United States has not ratified, but apparently concluded that these instruments were not sufficient evidence for the existence of an international prohibition. 517 F. Supp. at 545–46.

87. The court found that neither treaties nor the law of nations provided plaintiff with a cause of action by which individual rights could be vindicated. *Id.* at 548. But the decision does not expressly address the question whether there is a customary norm which is sufficiently precise to create individual rights.

88. The author believes that, for numerous reasons, the decision of Judge Green dismissing the complaint was ultimately correct. For an explanation of these reasons, *see* Schneebaum, "A Reply to Professor Oliver," 4 *Hous. J. Int'l L.*—(1982).

89. 517 F. Supp. at 549–50. Plaintiffs had alleged jurisdiction under 28 U.S.C. § 1331 (1976) (federal question jurisdiction) and 28 U.S.C. § 1350 (1976) (Alien Tort Claims Act). For an examination of the Alien Tort Claims Act as a basis of jurisdiction *see* Filartiga v. Peña-Irala, 630 F.2d at 880, 885, 887–89; Blum & Steinhardt, "Federal Jurisdiction over International Human Rights Claims: The Alien Tort Claims Act after *Filartiga v. Peña-Irala*," 22 *Harv. Int'l L.J.* 53 (1981).

90. For example, the court declares that the drafters of the Constitution and the Judiciary Act "did not contemplate the use of the federal courts as a substitute for an international tribunal, adjudicating claims arising under international law, when no private right of action was provided." 517 F. Supp. at 551 (footnote omitted). Of course, neither in 1789 nor today would private plaintiffs have standing to bring a complaint before an international tribunal. "International Law is primarily concerned with the rights and duties of States and not those of other persons; . . . States only possess full procedural capacity before international tribunals." 1 L. Oppenheim, *International Law* 20 (Lauterpacht ed. 1961).

91. Elsewhere, however, the Judge declares "that only treaties with a specific provision permitting a private action, or one to be clearly inferred, may suffice as the basis for federal jurisdiction." 517 F. Supp. at 546; *see also id.* at 547, 548 ("private rights of action—express or implied"), 549 and 550.

92. 517 F. Supp. at 549, *citing* Note, "Torture as a Tort in Violation of International Law: *Filartiga v. Peña-Irala*" 33 *Stan. L. Rev.* 353, 357 (1981).

93. *E.g.*, the treaty explicated in *Asakura*, *see supra* text accompanying note 34, or that in *Saipan*, *supra* note 20.

94. None of this is to say that offenses against these norms are not committed with alarming and distressing regularity. *See* Filartiga v. Peña-Irala, 630 F.2d at 884 n.15.

95. For a discussion of what acts, other than torture, may be actionable human rights violations *see* Blum & Steinhardt, "Federal Jurisdiction over International Human Rights Claims: The Alien Tort Claims Act after *Filartiga v. Peña-Irala*," 22 *Harv. Int'l L.J.* 53, 87–97 (1981).

96. This assumes that other jurisdictional prerequisites, such as jurisdiction over the person of the defendant, compliance with relevant statutes of limitations, and so on, have been met.

97. Similarly, advocates concerned with the prosecution of such claims bear responsibility for formulating them in ways that emphasize such an analysis.

VLADLEN S. VERESHCHETIN AND
GENNADY M. DANILENKO

Custom as a Source of International Law of Outer Space

It took centuries for folk law of the sea to develop. The international rules of the road proved essential to prevent collisions between ships. Even the tradition of carrying a red light at night on the port side of a ship and a green light on the starboard side as running lights in the days before radar was a help to all who sailed in international waters.

The rise of modern aviation in the twentieth century required similar international rules to avoid collisions between airplanes. The installation of satellites in space and the various attempts to explore outer space brought about new challenges to the international community of nations. Just how far above a nation's land boundaries did that nation's legal jurisdiction extend? Does one nation have the right to have its spaceship pass over the territory of another nation without official permission from the latter nation to do so? These are the sorts of questions which have created a whole new field of space law. Whereas one might well assume that most of space law is the result of written treaties, the fact is that there may be elements of folk law in contemporary international space law.

Vladlen S. Vereshchetin and Gennady M. Danilenko, Professor of Law/Deputy Director and Research fellow at the Institute of State and Law of the Russian Academy of Sciences, respectively, consider the role of folk law in the generation of international law in the following essay. For a discussion of a related issue, see Joseph Z. Gertler, "Custom in International Air Relations," Annals of Air and Space Law, *10 (1985), 63–82 . For the role of folk law in the establishment of international regulations for outer space, see Carl Q. Christol, "Methodology and the Development of International Space Law," in E.S. Wiradipradja and M.K. Kantaatmadja, eds.,* Hukum Angkasa Dan Perkembangannya *(Djakarta: Remadja Karya, 1990), pp. 19–28. See also R. Jennings, "Customary Law and General Principles of Law as Sources of Space Law," one of several essays on the subject contained in Karl-Heinz Bockstiegel, ed.,* Environmental Aspects of

Reprinted from *Journal of Space Law*, 13 (1985), 22–35, with permission.

Activities in Outer Space: State of the Law and Measures of Protection *(Köln: Carl Heymanns Verlag, 1990), pp. 149–152.*

One of the principal features of the process by which the international law of outer space is formulated is that, in contrast to the formation of the traditional parts of the law of nations, the creation of this new branch of international law, which regulates the relations of states in the exploration and use of outer space, even at the early stages was dominated by the making of treaty law. The advent and rapid development of human activities in the exploration and use of outer space more than a quarter of a century ago has led to the prompt conclusion of a number of important multilateral treaties in this field. The foundation of the international legal order in outer space was established by the 1967 Treaty on Principles Governing the Activities of States in the Exploration and Use of Outer Space, Including the Moon and Other Celestial Bodies[1] which laid down the general principles and rules of the law of outer space. The predominance of treaty over custom in the formation of international space law is the result of the operation of at least three factors which have exerted a particular influence on the norm-creating process in this new field of state activity.

The first factor is the number of states participating in the exploration and use of outer space and in the norm-creating processes that produce legal norms for the regulation of the activities of states in this field. Until recently, only a small number of states have participated in either space activities or the relevant lawmaking activities. Participating states were able to reach a consensus on a number of problems within a very short period of time, and this has led to the conclusion of universal legal documents establishing the existing system of the treaty principles and rules of space law. However, the number of states participating in space activities in one form or another is growing. The expansion of space activity and the development of new uses of space technology increasingly affect the legal rights and interests of almost all members of the international community. Thus, the awareness of the importance of space-related activities and the significance of the legal problems connected with these activities is also growing. Consequently, these problems draw the attention of various states, including those which, as yet, do not possess any capacity to engage in space activities. The active participation of an increasingly large number of states in the process of creating treaty law leads to a situation in which the adoption of new conventional rules of universal acceptance, governing new types of activities or new problems, becomes a more difficult task.

The second factor favoring treaty as a source of international law of outer space is the specific character of the problems which arise in the field of space-related activities. A considerable number of these problems arise in various fields of technical cooperation in the use of outer space and, as a result, require the creation of detailed rules which could clearly spell out the rights and obligations of the states concerned. It is obvious that only international treaties can serve as a source of the specific and detailed legal regulation of the relations of states. In this case, custom remains in the background because, as a source of international law, it can produce only general and broad legal obligations.

The third factor is a tendency to the more rapid development of legal regulation of space activities as compared with the development of the actual practice of states in the exploration, use and exploitation of outer space. This tendency dominated the early stages of the formation of outer space law. During the formation of this branch of international law, a number of treaty rules were being created and became legally binding before the problems governed by these rules could be realized in space activities.

Treaty, as a source of international law, can be used as an instrument of anticipatory legal regulation of future types of activities or future situations which do not exist at the moment of the conclusion of a treaty. Custom, in contrast to treaty, cannot serve as a source of anticipatory creation of legal rights and obligations because it is based on the practice of states. Customary international law, as Judge V. Koretsky put it, "turns its face to the past."[2] Where the formation of the law is influenced to a considerable extent by the tendency toward anticipatory treaty regulation, the role of custom is bound to be reduced to a minimum, at least in the areas in which agreement on such an anticipatory treaty regulation has been achieved.

All these factors, however, could not lead to a complete disappearance of the role of custom as a source of the international law of outer space. First, the importance of customary rules of general international law which establish the basis of the international law of outer space should be mentioned. Second, practice has shown that custom served as a source for the creation of a number of important general rules and still serves as a form of the existence of these rules. It should also be borne in mind that the modern practice of states in the exploration and use of outer space continues to produce new customary rules.

Notwithstanding the peculiarities of the formation of various branches of international law, the role of custom as a source of the creation and as a form of the existence of legal rights and obligations of states is conditioned by the structure of the international community. The absence of international legislation is the reason why international law-making is a very specific process having, among others, the following features: (1) the conventional and customary norms can be created only by the agreement of interested states: (2) the broad agreement leading to the creation of customary norms, which are constituted by the constant and uniform practice of states, can be achieved before these states reach an agreement concerning the specific normative content of relevant conventional norms in the framework of the formal treaty norm-creating procedure; (3) the legal norms laid down in a codifying act do not automatically bind all the members of the international community.

It follows, therefore, that international custom will play a significant role in the following two situations: (1) custom serves as a source of legal rights and obligations of states in those fields of their mutual relations, in which the treaty regulation is absent for one reason or another; (2) custom regulates the relations of states which are non-parties to a codifying convention, the relations of states which are parties to a convention and of states which are non-parties.

The practice of international law of outer space shows that states find it necessary to rely on rules of customary international law of outer space in both of these situations.

Customary Rules of Modern International Law of Outer Space

In the first situation referred to above, international custom leads to the creation of legal rights or obligations of states independently of the existence of any treaty regulation. As a specific norm-creating procedure, international custom is based on the constant and uniform practice of states. The emergence of a constant and uniform state practice in a new field of international relations, which requires legal regulation, leads to the establishment of new rules of customary international law if certain requirements laid down by international law are met. These requirements include those of generality, consistency, uniformity and *opinio juris*.[3]

The practice of states constituting an international custom is the result of the interaction of legal claims put forward, in one form or another, by some states in the domain of interstate relations, and of active or passive reaction to these claims on the part of other states whose interests are affected. The interaction of legal claims, which are the expression of a legal standpoint of a given state with respect to a particular problem, and reaction to these claims, is a specific process of "negotiations" among the state concerned. These "negotiations" are conducted not in the framework of formal procedure, but by way of actions, unilateral and/or multilateral acts and statements. This process gradually leads to the emergence of consensus among interested states as to the recognition of a rule of conduct established by constant and uniform practice as a rule of customary international law.

The analysis of the practice of states before the conclusion of the 1967 Outer Space Treaty shows that historically custom was the first source of the international law of outer space. The state practice in the field of exploration and use of outer space has led to the emergence of a number of important principles and rules of international space law.[4]

Among the fundamental principles and rules which were created by the practice of states before the conclusion of the 1967 Outer Space Treaty, and which were subsequently codified by this Treaty, the most important are the following: outer space is open and free for exploration and use by all states; the sovereignty of states does not extend to outer space; outer space is not subject to national appropriation; and states retain jurisdiction and control over space objects launched into outer space.

These principles have emerged in the practice of states within a very short period of time. The acceleration of the formation of customary principles relating to outer space was brought about not only by the fact that all actions of states in the field of exploration and use of outer space were immediately known all over the world, but also by the adoption of a number of United Nations General Assembly resolutions. These resolutions include the General Assembly Resolution of December 13, 1963,[5] which contained a Declaration of Legal Principles Governing Activities of States in the Exploration and Use of Outer Space.[6]

The passage of only a short period of time after the beginning of the exploration and use of outer space did not prevent the customary norms of the international law of outer space from coming into existence. In contrast to certain systems of municipal law, international law does not require the existence of practice from "times immemorial" for the creation of its customary rules. Furthermore, in modern international law the requirement of a long period of time, which was valid in the traditional law of nations, has gradually lost its importance owing to the rapid development of interstate relations. The International Court of Justice confirmed the generally recognized rule when it stated that "the passage of only a short period of time is not necessarily, or of itself, a bar to the formation of a new rule of customary international law."[7]

During the 1960s, on the doctrinal level there were two different points of view as to the question concerning the role and importance of custom in the formation of the emerging law of outer space. Reflecting the traditional approach to the problem of the sources of international law, some western writers have expressed the view that custom would be the main source of space law. In this connection, Myres McDougal, for example, wrote as early as 1965 that "the implicit communications of customary behavior play a much more important role than agreement or other deliberate formulation."[8] The development of space law has shown that, at least with respect to this branch of international law, this statement does not correspond to reality. It should be noted, that even Myres McDougal had to admit that in the area of law relating to space activities, custom was not an adequate source for the legal regulation of some specific technical problems such as in the field of telecommunications, which called for detailed treaty regulation.[9]

The opposing position was that custom could not be an adequate source of the international law of outer space. For example, P. I. Lukin has stated that the "international law of outer space can find the reliable source of its inception and subsequent development only in international agreements."[10] This extreme point of view did not reflect the practice of international law of outer space because, among other things, it led to the unacceptable conclusion that, before the 1967 space Treaty, states had conducted space activities in a legal vacuum.

In the modern international law of outer space, custom serves as a source of the creation and as a form of the existence of a number of rules governing the relations of states in those areas in which, up to now, there was no treaty regulation.

The expansion of the activities of states in the exploration and use of outer space, and the use of new technologies in outer space, create new situations which require legal regulation. As the result of the influence of a number of factors, however, including the increasingly large number of states participating in the making of treaty law, the progress in the formulation of new conventional rules of space law is not as fast as it was before. In some areas, the formulation of new conventional rules is not keeping pace with the requirement of international practice. In these areas, custom plays an important role and serves as a primary source for the creation of international legal rights and obligations of states.

It should be noted that international custom, as a rule, is the result of the agreement of states on a broad principle which only defines the general outlines of the proper and permissible conduct of states and other subjects of international law in a given sphere. This explains the shortcomings of custom as an instrument of legal regulation because, in certain instances, the application of customary law to specific problems fails to give precise results. Nevertheless, as international practice shows, customary law can be successfully used for resolving controversies in the fields of international law where there is no treaty regulation. If there is an international legal dispute, existing customary rules can give an answer at least to the question of what direction should be taken for resolving this dispute.

Among the problems which are not governed by treaty law, the most important one is the problem relating to the delimitation of air space and outer space. During the negotiations on the 1967 Outer Space Treaty, the participating states were unable to reach agreement on this problem. Thus, the Treaty does not contain any rules defining the sphere of its application. Efforts to establish special treaty regulation of the problem have been unfruitful notwithstanding the fact that the issue of delimitation has been discussed in the United Nations Committee on the Peaceful Uses of Outer Space since 1967.

The practice of states in the exploration and use of outer space by means of artificial satellites, has led to the emergence of a customary rule of space law to the effect that the region at and above the line determined by the lowest perigee of satellites so far placed in orbit (approximately 100 km above sea level) is not subject to the sovereignty of underlying states and therefore is outer space. This rule was expressly or tacitly recognized by all, or almost all, members of the international community. That was the reason the Soviet representative stated, during the discussions in the Legal Subcommittee on the United Nations Committee on the Peaceful Uses of Outer Space, that "it had become an international legal custom to regard the boundary between air space and outer space as passing through the altitude of minimum satellite perigee, i.e., at approximately 100 km above sea level."[11]

The problem of delimitation is closely connected with the problem of a right of peaceful or innocent passage for spacecraft of a state through the territorial air space of another state at altitudes lower than 100 km for the purposes of reaching the orbit and returning from the orbit to Earth. The recognition of the right of free passage for spacecraft through the air space of other states is of particular importance for states having small territories because, for physical reasons, these states can only reach outer space by passing through the air space of adjacent states. Thus, without the right of passage, these states would be unable to enter outer space.

Some authors have expressed the view that at this stage there exists,[12] or at least is emerging,[13] a rule of customary law allowing free passage of space objects through the national air space of the other states.

The analysis of international practice shows, however, that it is hardly possible to talk about the existence of a general customary rule governing the relations of all states in this field notwithstanding the fact that there seems to exist a genuine *opinio juris sive necessitatis* on the part of the international community. Up to now, the practice of passage of space objects through foreign air space did not have the required level of generality. It seems that the passage has been carried out only through the air space of some states adjacent to the major space powers. In some cases, the practice of passage has been continued and repeated. Thus, it can probably be argued that this practice is of a longstanding character.

During the 1960s, some of the Soviet space probes passed through the air space of adjacent states for the purpose of landing in the territory of the Soviet Union. The Soviet probe Zond-6, for example, descended to Earth from the southern part of the hemisphere and, as it was reported in the Soviet press, had landed in the territory of the U.S.S.R. at a point which was "9,000 km distant from the area of the southern part of the Indian Ocean where the station plunged into the atmosphere."[14] It is obvious that, while engaged in landing in the territory of the launching state, a space object of this type requires passage through the air space above the territory of the adjacent and, perhaps, not far distant states at the altitudes below the established boundary between air space and outer space. With regard to the United States, at least one clear precedent was established during the landing of the shuttle orbiter Challenger on October 13, 1984. The shuttle Challenger flew directly over Canada through its territorial air space and crossed the U.S. border at the height of 222,000 feet, i.e., 6,767 kilometers.[15]

The existence of such practice is bound to have legal consequences for the relations of the states concerned. In this connection, it should be emphasized that the passage of space objects through the area which, according to the generally recognized rule, is under the sovereignty of underlying states, can and does affect the legal rights and interests of these states. At the same time, the states concerned did not protest against the passage of space objects through their national air space. According to international law currently in force, the absence of protests on the part of states whose interests are affected, amounts to acquiescence in the practice relating to the passage of space objects. In other words, the failure to protest creates a presumption of a tacit recognition of the right of passage for space objects.[16]

Although the existing practice concerning the passage of space objects through foreign air space is not yet able to create a general rule of customary international law, because of its local nature, it is quite possible that this practice has given rise to a local or particular custom governing the relations of neighboring states.[17] In the course of time, and with the development and consolidation of general, constant and uniform state practice in the field of passage of space objects, this local custom may be gradually transformed into a general rule of customary law that is binding upon all states.

At this stage of the development of the international law of outer space, there are other rules of customary law relating to space activities.

It is generally recognized, for instance, that the widespread and longstanding practice of the remote sensing of the earth and of its natural resources, has given rise to a rule of customary law according to which there is a right to carry out remote sensing programs without the prior consent of the sensed states.[18]

The problem of the legal regulation of space activities connected with the exploration of the natural resources of Earth by means of remote sensing has been discussed in the U.N. Committee on the Peaceful Uses of Outer Space for a long period of time. Initially, some of the developing states expressed the view that remote sensing, without the prior consent of the sensed state should be prohibited.[19] However, at this stage of the negotiations on the principles governing remote sensing, there is a consensus among states with respect to the recognition of a right of all states to freely conduct remote sensing programs in outer space. Thus, the major issue in this field has shifted from the existence of the right to carry out remote sensing without the consent of the sensed state, to the problems relating to the dissemination of data and information acquired by remote sensing.

With respect to these problems, there is great dissension among various groups of states. The practice in this field also shows a lack of consistency and uniformity. Some western states, championing the free dissemination of data, have sought to establish a general customary rule allowing the unlimited freedom of dissemination of data obtained by remote sensing. Such unlimited dissemination and analyzed information based on those data, including data concerning natural resources of foreign states, have met with the considerable opposition of a large number of other states. These states represent the view that data above a certain threshold of resolution should not be disseminated without the consent of the sensed state. The opposition was expressed not only in the official statements of various states which objected to the dissemination of data acquired within their territory without their prior consent, but also in the treaty practice. A very important precedent in this field was established by a group of socialist states which concluded the Convention on the Transfer and Use of Data of the Remote Sensing of the Earth from Outer Space.[20] The Convention restricts the dissemination of the acquired data with a spacial resolution finer than 50 meters.

In regard to the question of the right to carry out the remote sensing, it should be noted that the remote sensing has been conducted by states possessing space capabilities for a long period of time, yet the states conducting remote sensing programs sought no permission. This practice has not encountered protests from the states whose interests were affected, notwithstanding the fact that in the early stages of the discussions on this problem, in the U.N. Committee on the Peaceful Uses of Outer Space, there were differences in opinions among various states.

The existence of general consent to current practice, and to the underlying claim on the part of the space powers to the right to engage in remote sensing activities in outer space without the consent of the sensed state, is not only the result of the active sensing practices of the space powers and the passive attitudes of the sensed states which have acquiesced in the legal standpoint claimed by space powers. A growing number of states lacking space capabilities, actively participate in various forms of international cooperation in the field of remote sensing. Further, these states actively establish, operate or plan to construct groundbased receiving stations, and acquire and use the data obtained by the existing remote sensing programs for their economic development. An active practice of this type is strong evidence of recognition on the part of the community of states of the legality of the remote sensing of foreign territory without the prior consent of the sensed state.

Custom as a source of international law, leads to the recognition of the legality of the existing practice if there is general consent, expressed in one form or another, to the observable rule of conduct on the part of the members of the international community. In this respect, the operation of custom in the field of remote sensing is not an exception. In this connection, an American commentator has observed that "when the National Aeronautics and Space Administration sent the first ERTS (remote sensing satellite) up into outer space it also sent it into a relative legal vacuum as an instrument which may, orbit after orbit, carve out for itself the necessary norm permitting it to do legally what it was sent out to do the first place."[21]

The Relationship Between Treaty and Custom in the Modern International Law of Outer Space

Custom as a source of international law is of great importance even in the areas of law where there is a multilateral convention. In this situation, custom operates alongside of the convention and may extend the sphere of the validity of certain general rules contained in the convention. This is of great significance for various branches of international law, including the international law of outer space, where existing multilateral conventions do not formally bind all members of the international community. Thus, the effectiveness of fundamental legal rules in this field depends on the relationship between treaty and custom aimed at extending the scope of application of general international norms of conduct relating to space activities.

It is generally recognized that treaty and custom interrelate on the following two main levels:

(1) A treaty may incorporate and confirm the existing customary law. The treaty rules reflecting existing customary law are legally binding on all states independently of their participation in the treaty containing these rules. The International Law Commission has stated in this respect that "a principle or rule of customary international law may be embodied in a bipartite or multipartite agreement so as to have, within the stated limits, conventional force for the states parties to the the agreement so long as the agreement is in force; yet it would continue to be binding as a principle or rule of customary international law for other states."[22]

(2) A treaty may also contain new rules which regulate new problems or change the existing norms. New rules of conduct contained in a treaty can become rules of customary law binding on all states, if there is a general, constant and uniform state practice accepted as law. The possibility of the extension of the scope of application of treaty rules via custom is recognized by the Vienna Convention on the Law of Treaties.[23] According to Article 38 of the Convention, a rule set forth in a treaty could become "binding upon a third state as a customary rule of law, recognized as such."

The two main levels of the relationship between treaty and custom are of particular importance for the universal validity of a number of fundamental principles and rules of space law embodied in the 1967 Outer Space Treaty. At present, the 1967 Treaty formally binds a little more than 80 states. The analysis of the practice of states, however, shows that there is ground for the assumption that, notwithstanding the fact that there is no universal formal recognition of the Treaty, all the members of the international community are bound by the fundamental principles and rules contained in it because these principles and rules have acquired the status of general customary law. It follows that, independent of the formal participation in the 1967 Outer Space Treaty, all states should observe the obligations arising from its provisions because these provisions are binding as rules of customary law.

A lucid illustration of the importance of the relationship between treaty and custom is the legal situation created by the claims of the equatorial states to segments of the geostationary orbit.

Some of the equatorial states which are not parties to the 1967 Outer Space Treaty, claimed that they are not bound by the principles embodied in the Treaty. In particular, these states claimed that they are not bound by the principles relating to the freedom of exploration and non-appropriation of outer space contained in Articles 1 and 2 of the Outer Space Treaty independent of a formally agreed to and accepted international agreement.[24]

The overwhelming majority of states have rejected the arguments of the equatorial states on the ground that the provisions of the Outer Space Treaty reflected the existing general customary law which binds all states independently of the Treaty. Thus, in the course of the discussion in the Legal Subcommittee of the U.N. Committee on the Peaceful Uses of Outer Space, the representative of Czechoslovakia stated that the provisions of the 1967 Treaty relating to free and equal exploration of outer space "reflected the fundamental principle of space law, which had been declared prior to the elaboration of the Treaty and had become a customary rule in the practice of states."[25] The representative of Italy pointed out that customary international space law allowing for free and equal use of, and free access to, outer space existed before the conclusion of the 1967 Treaty and was codified in it. In this connection, he stated that the "principles embodied in the 1967 Treaty could not be regarded as binding only upon states which had ratified that Treaty."[26] The representative of Japan expressed the opinion that the principle contained in Article 1 of the 1967 Outer Space Treaty, namely that outer space was free for exploration and use by all states, "had already been established in general international law." The representative of the Soviet Union stated that the principles of freedom of scientific investigation in outer space and of non-appropriation of outer space, embodied in the 1967 Outer Space Treaty, "had now acquired the status of norms of customary international law and were binding even upon states which had not yet signed the Treaty."[27]

It should be noted that the doctrine of international law is unanimous on the question of the universally binding character of the fundamental principles laid down by the 1967 Outer Space Treaty. This point of view is generally recognized by the Soviet and western writers and, what is of particular importance in this case, by the writers from the developing countries. An important point made in the legal literature in this connection is that "the fundamental principles of international space law, confirmed and declared by the Outer Space Treaty, have been formulated and recognized and accepted by express consent or acquiescence by virtually all countries, developed as well as developing."[28]

The International Law Association has taken a similar view with respect to the principle of the freedom of outer space. The resolutions adopted at the 53rd and 58th Annual Conferences declared that "the freedom of outer space for exploration and use is a principle of general international law and thus a principle valid independent of any treaty."[29]

It is generally recognized that in some instances a convention may exert an influence on the general practice of states and the development of customary international law even if that convention is not yet in force. It is also recognized that a particular provision in a convention in force may possess certain precedential value even if this convention has received few ratifications. In this connection it is interesting to inquire into the question of whether the rules contained in the 1979 Agreement Governing the Activities of States on the Moon and Other Celestial Bodies[30] have altered the state of general customary international law. Of particular interest in this respect is the provision of Article 11 of the Agreement which stipulates that "the Moon and its natural resources are the common heritage of mankind."

It has been contended that the principle of the common heritage of mankind is an existing or, at least, an emerging rule of customary international law of outer space.[31] It seems, however, hardly possible to accept such a contention for the following reasons. First, one should take into account that, in its abstract formulation, the principle of the common heritage of mankind does not create any new legal obligations. Hence, in discussing the problem of whether this principle has emerged as a new rule of customary law creating new obligations for the states concerned, one should turn to the specific aspects of the principle constituting that new right or obligations of states. Because the principle of the common heritage of mankind applies to the exploitation of the natural resources of the Moon, the specific aspects of this principle find their expression in the relevant provisions of the 1979 Moon Agreement and, in particular, in the detailed provisions of Article 11. Paragraph 5 of this Article provides that "states parties to this Agreement hereby undertake to establish an international regime, including appropriate procedures, to govern the exploitation of the natural resources of the Moon as such exploitation is about to become feasible."

The meaning, if any, of the principle of the common heritage of mankind can be interpreted in different ways. But, it is quite clear that the future regime of the exploitation of the natural resources of the Moon is of considerable importance for the realization of the objectives of this principle.

The detailed provisions of Article 11 of the 1979 Moon Agreement are the result of the tendency toward the anticipatory regulation of a situation which does not exist at this time but is possible in the future. Because there is no actual state practice indicating that these provisions have been applied and accepted in the relations of the members of the international community, one can hardly maintain that the principle of the common heritage of mankind, as embodied in the 1979 Agreement, has passed or is passing into the general customary law of outer space. In any event, one thing that can be said with certainty is that custom, as a source of international law, cannot create legal obligations concerning the future exploitation of the natural resources of the Moon before such exploitation becomes feasible and the relations of states with respect to this problem acquire the necessary level of consistency and uniformity. A treaty, as an instrument of legal regulation, can create rules aimed at regulating future problems, but the actual influence of such a treaty on the future general practice and the development of customary law can only be ascertained when the expected problems become the real and practical issues of interstate relations.

Conclusion

The practice of the international law of outer space shows that custom, as a source of legal rights and obligations of states, can be established within a short period of time even before the states concerned reach an agreement on the provisions of a treaty aimed at governing their relations in a given area. After the conclusion of a treaty, custom regulates the relations of states which do not participate in the treaty and the mutual relations of both states who are parties to the treaty and states which are not. In both situations, custom plays an important role in the maintenance of the international legal order in outer space.

Notes

1. The Treaty on Principles Governing the Activities of States in the Exploration and Use of Outer Space, Including the Moon and Other Celestial Bodies, was signed on January 27, 1967, and entered into force October 10, 1967, [1967] 18 U.S.T. 2410, T.I.A.S. No. 6347, 610 U.N.T.S. 205.

2. *I.C.J. Reports* 156 (1969).

3. *See* Danilenko, "Customary Rule Formation Process in Contemporary International Law," In *Soviet Y.B. Int'l L.* 151–70 (1983) (in Russian, with English summary).

4. *See* M. Lachs, *The Law of Outer Space: An Experience in Contemporary Law-Making*, 136 (1972); Marcoff, "Sources du droit international de l espace," 568 *Recueil Des Cours* 60–61 (1980).

5. Declaration of Legal Principles Governing Activities of States in the Exploration and Use of Outer Space, *submitted by* Committee on Peaceful Uses of Outer Space, Resolution 1962 (XVIII), *adopted unanimously* by the General Assembly on December 13, 1963 (1280th meeting), as recommended by First Committee A/5656, Draft Resolution 1.

6. This does not mean, however, that the practice of inter-state relations in the field of the exploration of outer space has led to the emergence of "instant" customary international law as some authors believe. *See* B. Cheng, "United Nations Resolutions on Outer Space: "Instant" International Customary Law?", 5 *Indian J. Int'l L.* 36 (1965). Customary international law can not come into being "instantly" because custom is based on constant and uniform practice.

The consolidation and recognition of general, constant and uniform state practice require the existence of a number of precedents. It is obvious, that custom calls for the passage of at least a certain period of time.

7. *I.C.J. Reports* 43 (1969).

8. McDougal, "The Emerging Customary Law of Space," 58 *Nw. U.L. Rev.* 625 (1965).

9. *Id.* at 637, 640.

10. Lukin, "To the Question of the Sources of Space Law," in *Questions of International Law* 141 (1963) (in Russian).

11. U.N. Doc. A/AC.105/C.2/SR.392, at 4 (April 5, 1983). *See* Danielenko, "The boundary between air space and outer space in modern international law" (in Russian with English summary), 9 J. *Soviet State & L.* 71–79 (1984). *See also, inter alia,* Cheng, "The Legal Regime of Airspace and Outer Space: The Boundary Problem, Functionalism Versus Spatialism: The Major Premises," 5 *Annals Air & Space L.* 323–61 (1980); Gorove, "International Space Law in Perspective: Some Major Issues, Trends and Alternatives," 181 *Recueil des Cours* 361–62 (1983); Zhukov, "Delimitation of Outer Space," in *Proc. of the 23rd Colloquium on the Law of Outer Space* 221 (1980).

12. *See,* V. Bordunov, "Space Shuttle Flights and Correlation of Legal Regimes of Air Space and Outer Space," in *Proc. of the 25th Colloquium on the Law of Outer Space* 212 (1982).

13. *See Report of the 59th Conference of the International Law Association* 183 (Belgrade, 1980) (remarks by Mr. Chowdrury).

14. *Izvestia,* April 11, 1969.

15. *See* 122 *Aviation Week & Space Tech.* 24 (1984).

16. For this reason we cannot agree with a different view expressed by W. Schwenk. *See* Schwenk, "Der Durchflug von Weltraumrecht durch den nationalen Luftraum," 31 *Zeitschrift für Luft- und Weltraumrecht* 8 (1982).

17. *See* E. Malenovsky, "To the Problem of the Right of the Passage Through the Airspace of Other States During the Post-Take-Off and Return Phases of Space Flights," in *Proc. of the 25th Colloquium on the Law of Outer Space* 134 (1982).

18. *See* Haraszti, "Outer Space and Sovereignty," in *Internationale Festschrift für St. Verosta* 143 (1980); C. Christol, *The Modern International Law of Outer Space* 757 (1982).

19. See, for example, the proposal for the regulation of remote sensing put forward by Argentina and Brazil. U.N.Doc.A/C.1/1047 (October 15, 1974).

20. U.N.Doc. A/33/162 (June 29, 1978).

21. Z.J. Slouka, "International Law-making: A View from Technology," in *Law-making in the Global Community* 164 (N.G. Onuf ed. 1982).

22. *Y.B. Int'l L. Comm'n* 368 (1950).

23. *U.N. Doc. A/Conf. 39/27* Rev.1 (1970).

24. See, for example, the statement by the representative of Colombia in the U.N. Committee on the Peaceful Uses of Outer Space. U.N. Doc. A/AC.105/PV.173, at 56 et seq. (1977).

25. U.N.Doc. A/AC.105 C.2/SR.297, at 4 (1978).

26. *Id.* at 8.

27. Doc.0 A/AC.105/C.2/SR.373, at 6 (1982). See also the statement by R.B. Owen, Legal Adviser, Department of State, to the U.S. Senate, Mr. Owen stated that certain principles laid down in the 1967 Outer Space Treaty, e.g., that outer space and celestial bodies are not subject to material appropriation, are now accepted as "customary international law." *The Moon Treaty: Hearings before the Subcommittee on Science, Technology and Space, of the Senate Committee on Commerce, Science and Transportation*, 96th Cong., 2d Sess. 21–22 (1980).

28. R.S. Jakhu, "Developing Countries and the Fundamental Principles of International Space Law," in *New Directions in International Law* 362 (1982).

29. *Report of the 58th Conference of the International Law Association* 2 (Manila 1978).

30. U.N.Doc. A/Res.34/68 (1979) (entered into force on July 11, 1984).

31. R.V. Dekanozov, "Forming of the Principle 'Common Heritage of Mankind' and The Rules of Customary International Law of Outer Space," in *Proc. of the 25th Colloquium on the Law of Outer Space* 219 (1982).

ALLAN ROSAS

Customary Law: From "Universal" in a European System to "Regional" in a World System

If folk law is indeed an important component of international law, there is an additional matter which must be considered and that is: whose folk law should be utilized in the creation of international law? As we have seen from the preceding essays, most of the folk law elements of international law come from European folk law. With the increasing number of independent nation-states in Africa and Asia, it may well be that European folk law can no longer be regarded as the sole proper source for international standards. The imposition of European folk law upon new nation states would be just as insidious as the old-fashioned imposition of colonial law by individual nations upon tribal peoples around the world.

In any event, the large number of independent nation-states that make up the global community so-called requires that there be more rather than less consensus on issues affecting the rights and welfare of the peoples of all modern nations. On the other hand, a relativistic ethic combined with the principle of equal sovereignty for all nations requires that local systems of folk law be respected as well. It is the need for a delicate balance of uniformity worldwide in international folk law on the one hand, with respect for the integrity of local, regional, and national systems of folk law on the other, that will require the diligent cooperation of all the nations of the world, either through the agency of the United Nations or some other facilitating international organization.

The difficulties inherent in achieving a workable balance among competing folk law systems is the subject of the final essay in this volume by Allan Rosas, Professor of Law and Director of the Institute for Human Rights at Abo Akademi University.

This essay deals with the status and function of customary international law in the light of the shift from a Europe-centred international law to a global approach which has taken place especially after 1945.

Reprinted from Atle Grahl-Madsen and Jiri Toman, eds., *The Spirit of Uppsala* (Berlin; Walter de Gruyter, 1984), pp. 222–232, with permission.

According to one learned author "custom is at the heart of what we mean by international law".[1] According to another "the problem of customary norms of international law is one of the most important and, at the same time, one of the most complex theoretical problems of international law".[2]

It is not surprising, then, that the purpose of the present paper is a very modest one. We are merely trying to present some sketchy notes and ideas on certain aspects of customary law of relevance for our subject. As it does not seem to be possible to isolate the global/regional dimension from certain other problems related to the question of custom we have included some aspects which are central in general theory of customary international law.

Changes in the International System

Here it is pertinent to ask, what specific problems and perspectives for customary law may have followed from the growth and diversification of the international community? What are the consequences of the fact *that* the number of independent States has quadrupled since the nineteenth century and the number of UN members tripled since 1945, *that* five Asian States were recognized by Europe as forming part of the "civilized" nations at the beginning of this century whereas the African and Asian States today form the majority in the UN, *that* the international community of today consists of States representing manifestly different socio-economic systems, cultures and economic and technological levels of development, *that* the number of international organizations has increased dramatically during this century, etc.?

Without attempting to list all the imaginable consequences of these developments one can mention some obvious repercussions: It is presumably more difficult today than, say, one hundred years ago to reach "consensus" on a given rule. It would also seem to be more difficult today to establish the "practice of States" on a given issue, considering the great number of actors which have to be taken into account (as a factor working in the opposite direction, however, are the improved technological means of registering and tracing instances of State practice). In view of the rapid technological development, and taking into account the tendencies mentioned above, it is also more difficult to "capture" a definite norm when a solution is sought to a concrete dispute. And, of course, the decolonization process has highlighted the question of whether new States are bound by customary law which has emerged before independence.

In view of these and other developments one could easily be inclined to think that general customary law is rapidly losing ground and that custom, at best, can play a role on a regional and local level. It is well-known that treaty law has to a large extent superseded customary law. Still, as we shall argue below, it is not that certain that this development will continue unabated.

The Formation and Validity of Customary Law

Facing the abundance of legal writing on the question of the theoretical basis of customary law and the considerable difficulties involved in arriving at coherent and generally acceptable answers one hesitates to enter into the discussion. However, certain problems cannot be brushed under the carpet if one is to have a meaningful discussion on the present function and relevance of customary law.

One fundamental issue may now be considered as settled: The formation of a customary norm requires both a material (State practice) and a psychological (*opinio juris*) element. This point of departure is recognized by the great majority of learned authors, it finds support in the wording of article 38 of the Statute of the ICJ and it has been articulated by the Court, e. g., in the North Sea Continental Shelf cases.[3] This does not mean that there is complete agreement on how State practice or the *opinio juris* are to be determined, or what relative weight should be given to each of these two elements.

It seems to us that one should avoid making a sharp distinction between the two elements, which may interact and be present in one and the same act. This idea, of course, is connected with the question of what type of behaviour should be considered when trying to establish the practice of States (and of international organizations) on a given question. Here we would undoubtedly agree with those who stress that a broad notion of State practice is required, so that not only omissions (passivity) as well as national laws and judgments but also *statements* made, e.g., in the form of resolutions by the UN General Assembly or other similar organs are included as possible constituent elements.[4] This approach seems to enjoy general acceptance today both among States and learned authors. It has also been pointed out that the acceptance of statements *in abstracto* as evidence of practice diminishes the dilemma of changing customary law: "as an alternative to changing customary law by breaking it, States can change it by repeatedly declaring that the old rule no longer exists—a much more desirable way of changing the law".[5]

Also with respect to the manifestation of an *opinio juris* a flexible approach seems to be in order. Express statements to the effect that a given rule is or should be legally binding are not always necessary; the *opinio juris* may be inferred from other conduct as well,[6] although it is often manifested by the use of normative (legal) language.[7] What matters are not the actual or presumed beliefs of national decision-makers but statements and other manifestations of a normative attitude which can be objectively ascertained.[8]

Traditionally the *opinio juris* is often said to imply that States regard a certain rule as a norm of international law in force *(de lege lata)*. To envisage the creation of a *new* rule would then presuppose that the State which is the first to articulate the new rule has made a mistake or a deliberately false statement as to its binding force. In addition to this possibility, however, one should take into account the possibility of statements *de lege ferenda*. There seems to be no reason why such statements could not evince the necessary *opinio juris*.[9] If they are accompanied by State practice (including perhaps new statements *de lege lata*) which can reasonably be regarded as an application of the proposed rule a new norm of customary international law has emerged. It must be acknowledged, on the other hand, that the relation between statements and acts *de lege late* and *de lege ferenda* in regard to customary law is highly problematical and needs further clarification.

The classical question of the personal sphere of validity of a given customary norm, that is, what States are bound by it and under what circumstances do they become so bound, cannot be entirely disregarded here. Let it be said at the outset that we adhere to the "theory of consent" as a theoretical point of departure. This approach certainly has its shortcomings but it is after all the least dissatisfactory solution. It does not seem possible to state that a State as a general rule may become bound by rules the formation and application of which it firmly opposes. We are not aware of any decisions by international courts which would categorically state such as principle.[10] Probably all or at least most States would deny the possibility of becoming bound by rules they cannot accept. It then seems impossible to conclude that there exists a "secondary" rule of customary law stating that States become bound by "primary" rules of customary law *against* their will, by a kind a majority voting.[11]

The crucial question, however, is what constitutes "consent" and "opposition". It seems pertinent to speak of *presumed* consent, which means that a State can become bound by a rule the creation of which it has not participated in as long as it has not clearly voiced its opposition.[12] Perhaps this is better terminology than the often used expression "tacit agreement", which despite the word "tacit" seems to connote the idea of specific "understandings" between the parties to a customary norm, something which might not correspond to reality.

It must be acknowledged, of course, that the notion of presumed consent in practice comes close to the view of those who start by rejecting the "consensualist doctrine" of customary law but then go on to say that a customary rule does not bind a State which from the outset has consistently and unambiguously opposed the rule.[13] But if a State has the right to "opt out"[14] of a developing customary rule, is it not more correct to say that it has given its consent by not using this right, in the same way as a State gives its consent to decisions of international organizations using the opting out-system by doing nothing?[15]

The foregoing leads to the conclusion that a norm of general (customary) international law need not bind every State in the world.[16] A rule may well be called a rule of general international law if, say, 150 States have accepted it while a few States flatly reject it (the latter States not becoming bound by the rule).

In fact, there seems to be no dramatic difference between "general" customary law on the one hand and "special", "regional", "local", etc. customary law on the other,[17] in the same way as there are no clear-cut legal differences between general multilateral conventions and treaties of a more limited scope. The territorial sphere of validity of a customary rule depends on the nature of the rule and the attitudes and intentions of States participating in its creation. It is also possible to imagine that a usage is "a general practice" for all States but that it is customary *law* in the relations between some States only (the other States opposing the rule as a rule of law).[18] Of course, if a certain rule is followed by a considerable number of States and the rule is by its nature suitable for worldwide application there may be a strong presumption for its development into a general norm, which becomes binding on all States that do not voice their dissent. And as one author puts it, "unless dissenting States are numerous, they seldom maintain their dissent for long."[19]

The "presumed consent" referred to above can only be inferred if the interests of a particular State are in some way affected by the emerging rule.[20] One may argue that a rule intended and suitable for world-wide application should be presumed to affect the interests of all States. Thus, emerging principles of the law of the sea may become binding on land-locked States as well, unless they voice their opposition. If, on the other hand, the rule is clearly intended for regional application only, States outside the region do not have to react. It may also be that States outside a region or some other group of States are not even aware of the development of a specific rule within that group. As to States *within* the group it would appear that the requirements for presuming consent become more stringent the smaller and/or the more heterogenous the group is.[21] With respect to bilateral rules it seems difficult to "presume" any consent at all.

It is submitted that the above considerations theoretically speaking also apply to the question of new States. A State which has not existed when a rule has emerged cannot be presumed to have given its consent, and therefore the rule does not seem to become binding on the new State (except in the case of State succession). We would assume—without having conducted any empirical studies—that this is the view not only of the socialist States but also of the majority of States from the Third World.[22] If this is so one could not assert that there is a secondary rule of general validity stating that new States are bound automatically by *all* rules of customary law in force at the moment of independence. But perhaps there is a secondary rule saying that rules of a *ius cogens* nature are today inherent in statehood, and that an entity which claims to be a State has at same time given its "consent" to these rules? Moreover, the common interests of States compel the new State to accept (that is, not to reject) many other norms of customary law as well.

It is true that speaking of consent in the last-mentioned cases may appear as a fiction. But is it not also a fiction to claim that sovereign and independent States become bound by rules of international law against their will, unless such a principle has been established, e.g., in the statute of an international organization? At any rate this discussion may today appear rather academic as the decolonization process is almost completed.

The complexity of the question of customary law is not diminished by the tension which exists between the application and interpretation of *general* principles and rules vs. the creation and subsequent application of *detailed* rules.[23] A State may have accepted a general principle of customary law without accepting its application by way of interpretation to a specific topic. General principles and rules, too, should be interpreted objectively and not as each State bound by them sees fit. On the other hand the consent to a principle cannot be stretched too far to cover specific rules which the State itself does not consider as binding upon it. The problem, which, of course, arises in treaty law as well, can be illustrated by the delicate question of the legality of the use of nuclear weapons. Some (nuclear) States do not recognize a clear-cut prohibition; on the other hand it can be argued that such a prohibition follows from certain general principles and rules of customary as well as treaty law.[24]

Just to mention some other problems which cannot be elaborated here: It seems clear that inter-governmental organizations as subjects of international law can participate in the creation of customary law.[25] But to what extent do rules which, for instance, the organizations have created in their bilateral relations become binding on the member States?

And to what extent are the organizations bound by the customary law which has been created by the member States?

Reference must also be made to the temporal sphere of validity of customary norms. If a State *has* given its consent to a customary rule it cannot arbitrarily and unilaterally escape that rule, especially in the context of a dispute concerning the legality of past conduct. On the other hand every State has the right to participate in the creation of new customary rules. As we have argued above this does not necessarily presuppose that the rule is broken by physical actions but can take the form of statements *de lege ferenda* and later *de lege lata.* Is there in addition a right to "withdraw" from a customary rule (except a *ius cogens* rule) comparable to the denunciation and withdrawal from treaties? According to article 56 of the 1969 Vienna Convention a treaty which is silent on the matter is under certain circumstances subject to denunciation or withdrawal (time-limit: twelve months).[26] One can argue that a similar right with respect to custom would be dangerous for the stability of the international legal order. The question seems to merit further consideration, however.[27]

The Function and Relevance of Customary Law

It is important to stress at the outset that there exist different traditions concerning the status and relevance of customary international law. The Anglo-American tradition has underlined the importance of customary law whereas, e.g., the socialist countries have regarded treaty law as the primary source of international law.

Today, against the background of the statutes of international organizations and the "law-making" conventions which have been concluded since 1945, there seems to be a certain consensus on the primacy of treaty law. Still, customary law can be viewed quite differently in different countries. For instance, in Finland, a country which has been rather isolated from the mainstreams of international relations and where the discipline of international law does not play a primary role in legal traditions, a lawyer invoking a norm of customary international law in a lower court would probably be regarded as an odd figure. If he succeeded in convincing the judge that such a norm (and customary law in general) really exists, the judge might take refuge in the principle of dualism and refuse to apply the norm on the basis that it has not been transformed into Finnish law.[28]

Speaking on a general level, the function of customary law may be viewed from at least three different angles:

1. The reference to customary law in a concrete dispute. This includes the case when an international dispute-settling organ is called upon to state the content of a customary norm (The "interpretation" of international law).
2. The day-to-day application of customary law by subjects of international law. Innocent passage takes place and diplomats enjoy immunity even if the State in question has not ratified the 1958 Geneva Convention or the 1961 Vienna Convention (The application of international law).
3. The notion of customary law as a "constitutional" law of international relations (particularly customary law of a *ius cogens* nature) and as a bond tying the different components of international law to a coherent system (The systematization of international law).

It is evident that customary law will continue to play an important role on the levels of points (2) and (3). We feel particularly inclined to underline the importance of point (3). One cannot think of the present international system as a legal order without the notion of customary law. In this connection reference should also be made to the importance of customary law for an understanding of the historical development of international law and of the relationship between international law and societal developments.

With respect to points (1) and (2), however, one could, as was indicated earlier, envisage that the relevance of customary law is diminishing. It would seem that many international lawyers were inclined to draw this conclusion in the sixties. The instances when international tribunals had in fact concluded that a customary norm did exist were comparatively rare. The ICJ, for instance, had often decided that the existence of a customary norm could *not* be established (the Lotus, the Asylum, the Continental Shelf, etc. cases).

Today the picture is not that gloomy for the relevance of customary law. It has been noted that the ICJ during the seventies has had to grapple, "practically in every case", with customary law.[29] This seems to be indicative of a more general trend. According to a Dutch author "customary law appears to be growing in importance for the Netherlands no less than for other countries".[30]

What are the reasons for this trend? The last-mentioned author refers to three different factors which favour the formation of customary law. First of all, the creation of customary law may be the more opportune political option for a State, as it can take place without the formal procedures existing in most countries for the acceptance and transformation of treaties and thus also "out of sight of the electorate". Secondly, customary law may more easily than treaty law achieve virtual universality as it does not require express acceptance—"the inactive are carried along by the active". Many international conventions, by contrast, do not achieve universal adherence and the ratification process is at any rate slow, partly due to the lack of administrative resources in poor and small countries. Thirdly, customary law sometimes emerges more rapidly than treaty law.[31]

Even if one (as the present writer is inclined to do) adheres in principle to the requirement of repetition for the formation of customary law it is true that customary law may today emerge during a very short period of time ("instant" customary law[32]).

To the above considerations one can today add a factor which is prompted by the experiences of the Third UN Law of the Sea Conference: It appears increasingly difficult to achieve not only rapid and universal ratification of treaties but also approval of the very text of treaties. If the Conference will not, after almost ten years of work, succeed in adopting a new law of the sea convention by consensus there may be an increasing scepticism as to the possibilities of treaty-making on a global level. Obviously the fate of *détente* in the near future will have a bearing upon these perspectives. It is noteworthy that no general disarmament convention has been adopted after the rather marginal ENMOD Convention of 1977 (prohibiting certain environmental modification techniques).

These trends and perspectives indicate that customary law may have a definitive relevance in the future, and precisely on a global level ("general international law"). The formation and evidence of customary law is facilitated by the impressive amount of treaty law which already exists (and which often can be taken as an indication of State practice), the development of the "quasi-legislative" functions of the UN General Assembly and other similar bodies, and so forth. In analysing contemporary customary law it is useful, as has been done,[33] to distinguish between treaties, etc. having (1) declaratory effect; (2) crystallizing effect, and (3) constitutive or generating effect.

But what about special, regional and local custom? As the formulation of our subject indicates there may be a trend towards "regionalism" in the formation and application of customary law. The ICJ has on different occasions envisaged the possibility of special and even of bilateral custom.[34] As an example of a homogenous group of States where special customary rules have emerged one can mention the European Communities.[35] The socialist,[36] capitalist,[37] Latin American[38] and other groupings of States belonging to the same region can be mentioned as other examples.

As these examples show the question of special custom is not limited to geographical areas.[39] The relevant group of States can range from two neighbouring countries to a large group of States united by a common ideology or plainly a common interest in the regulation of a certain topic. As has already been indicated earlier the distinction between general and special custom is not clear-cut. "Where States are divided into two groups of roughly equal size, with one group following one custom and the other following another custom, who can say which is the general custom and which is the special custom?", asks one author.[40] He goes on to note that the fact that custom may exist among some States only may have been lost sight of during the nineteenth and early twentieth centuries, when the international community was small and homogenous, "but in the more heterogenous international community of today the problem is very much alive". Is there, asks the author further, any *general* custom on such topics as the expropriation of foreign property and about the width of the territorial sea and of exclusive fishing zones, "or are there only separate sub-systems of special custom"?[40]

This approach is up to a certain point realistic and maybe attractive. There has probably been too much emphasis on general custom in conjunction with a false belief that old rules created in the nineteenth century by a handful of States claiming monopoly on the denomination "civilized" continue to form part of general customary law binding on all States even if the majority of States clearly does not accept them. On the other hand there is a clear danger in the "regionalization" and "particularization" of customary law. If this development goes too far certain common denominators belonging to customary law and of vital importance for the global world order may be lost. Should we not as international lawyers strive at maintaining as far as possible the universality of international law, while at the same time trying not to lose sight of reality?

It can be argued that these considerations require the abandonment of the "consensualist" theory of custom and the introduction of a flexible and "sociological" approach[41] to the question of custom-formation. As to the concept and requirement of consent, however, one cannot entirely escape something which does exist. And is it not easier to convince national decision-makers that their State is bound to apply a certain customary norm if they are told that the State has earlier given its consent to the rule compared to the alternative that they are told that they must abide by the rule because other States have created it or because the rule corresponds to some extra-legal values (which the national decision-makers perhaps do not share)?

This leads us finally to the question of the relationship between customary law on the one hand and ethical, religious, etc. considerations on the other. It is self-evident that customary law, as indeed all law, is influenced by (or rather, is based on) common interests and values of States and of mankind. When it comes to legal argumentation in a given situation, however, customary law should be approached as a source *of law* and not as a sociological phenomenon only. Otherwise the juridical and binding force of customary law may weaken. Relying too strongly on extra-legal considerations may also be unwise in that the concrete basis of a customary rule might collapse if it is shown that the values invoked are *not*, in fact, shared by all the potential subjects of a rule (even if there has been general acceptance of the rule itself). This emphasis on legalism should on the other hand in no way be an obstacle to a flexible and dynamic application and interpretation of customary law, prompted by a desire to guard and strengthen the international legal order of our times.

Notes

1. D'Amato, Anthony, *The Concept of Custom in International Law*, Ithaca and London, Cornell University Press, 1971, p. xii.
2. Tunkin, G. I., *Theory of International Law*. London, G. Allen and Unwin, 1974, pp. 113–115.
3. *ICJ Reports 1969*, pp. 41–44.
4. Cf., however, D'Amato, A., *op. cit.*, pp. 87–98.
5. Akehurst, Michael, Custom as a Source of International Law. *British Yearbook of International Law*, 1974–1975, p. 8.
6. Walden, Raphael M., Customary International Law: A Jurisprudential Analysis. *Israel Law Review*, 1978, p. 98–100; Meijers, H., How is International Law made? The Stages of Growth of International Law and the Use of Its Customary Rules. *Netherlands Yearbook of International Law*, 1978, p.7.
7. Walden, R. M., *loc. cit.*, pp. 93–100, speaks (with reference to Hart) about the "internal aspect" of customary norms, i.e., a normative attitude which is usually but not always evinced by the use of normative language.
8. See, e. g. Akehurst, M., *loc. cit.*,pp. 36–37; Walden, R. M., *loc. cit.*, p. 95. Cf. Meijers, H., *loc. cit.*, pp. 5–7, who refers to the development *within* States of "the will to make a rule into law". This terminology may lead to unnecessary speculation as to the "real" intentions and beliefs of national decision-makers.
9. See Thirlway, H. W. A., *International Customary Law and Codification*. Leyden, Sijthoff, 1972, p. 55; Walden, R. M., *loc. cit.*, p. 97.
10. On the contrary, the ICJ stated in the Anglo-Norwegian Fisheries case that a certain rule would appear to be inapplicable against Norway "in as much as she has always opposed any attempt to apply it to the Norwegian coast", *ICJ Reports 1951*, p. 131. See also Akehurst, M., *loc. cit.*, pp. 24–26. Some authors, however, (e.g., D'Amato, A., *op. cit.*, pp. 246–252), claim that this and other similar dicta only relate to special (regional) custom.
11. A distinction between primary and secondary rules (secondary rules regulate the creation of primary rules) of customary law is made by Walden, R. M. *loc. cit.*, pp. 87–92.

12. Wolfke, Karol, *Custom in Present International Law*, Wroclaw, Wroclaw Scientific Society, 1964, pp. 158–168. Meijers, H., *loc. cit.*, p. 18.

13. Akehurst, M., *loc. cit.*, pp. 23–27; Jimenez de Arechaga, Eduardo, International Law in the Past Third of a Century. *Recueil des cours, Académie de droit international*, Vol. 159, I, 1978, p. 30.

14. This expression is used by Akehurst, M., *loc. cit.*, p. 26.

15. See Brownlie, I., *Principles of Public International Law*. Third edition. Oxford, Clarendon Press, 1979, p. 11, who states that "toleration of the persistent objector is explained by the fact that ultimately custom depends on the consent of States".

16. Cf., however, the dictum by the ICJ in the North Sea-Continental Shelf cases, according to which "customary rules . . . by their very nature, must have equal force for all members of the international community". *ICJ Reports 1969*, p. 38.

17. Cf. D'Amato, A., *op. cit.*, pp. 246–263; Jimenez de Aréchaga, E., *loc. cit.*, pp. 28–30, who regard consent by a particular State necessary for special but not for general custom.

18. Meijers, H., *loc. cit.*, p. 21–23.

19. Akehurst, M., *loc. cit.*, p. 27.

20. See, e.g., Tunkin, G. I., *op. cit.*, p. 129.

21. See also Akehurst, M., *loc. cit.*, pp. 29–30; Meijers, H. , *loc. cit.*, pp. 20–33.

22. Cf., however, Waldock, Sir Humphrey, General Course of Public International Law, *Recueil des cours, Académie de droit international*, Vol. 106, II, 1962, p. 52; Walden, Raphael M., The Subjective Element in the Formation of Customary International Law. *Israel Law Review*, 1977, p. 356.

23. See also Geiger, Rudolf, Zur Lehre vom Völkergewohnheitsrecht in der Rechtsprechung des Bundesverfassungsgerichts. *Archiv des öffentlichten Rechts*, 1978, pp. 401–407, who refers to the interpretation of general and uncontested rules of customary law to more specific situations in the praxis of the "Bundesverfassungsgericht" of the FRG.

24. See Rosas, Allan, International Law and the Use of Nuclear Weapons. In *Essays in Honour of Erik Castrén*. Helsinki, Hakapää Editor, 1979, pp. 90–95.

25. Cf. Bökor–Szegö, Hanna, *The Role of the United Nations in International Legislation*. Amsterdam, North Holland Pub. Co. 1978, p. 66, who seems to hold that international organizations cannot through their own conduct create customary norms.

26. On this rule see, e.g., Haraszti, György, *Some Fundamental Problems of the Law of Treaties*, Budapest, Akademiai Kiadó, 1973, pp. 260–279.

27. It should be noted that according to article 43 of the Vienna Convention a withdrawal from a *treaty* shall not impair the duty of a State to fulfill obligations to which it would be subject under international law independently of the treaty.

28. There is a strong dualist tradition in Finland, see, e.g., Castrén, E., *Suomen kansainvälinen oikens*. Porvoo, W. Söderström, 1959, pp. 9–11; Bengt Broms, *Kansainvälinen oikens*. Helsinki, Suomalainen lakimiesyhdistys, 1978, pp.

51–52. Naturally, the judge is supposed to interpret internal law so that it does not conflict with international law.

29. Jimenez de Aréchaga, E., International Law in the Past Third of a Century. *Recueil des cours, Académie de droit international,* Tome 159, I, 1978, p. 9.

30. Meijers, H., *loc. cit.*, pp. 3–4.

31. *Ibid.*, pp. 4–5.

32. This expression has been introduced by Cheng, Bin, United Nations Resolutions on Outer Space: Instant International Customary Law? *Indian Journal of International Law*, No 5, 1965, p. 23. According to Baxter, Richard R., Treaties and Custom. *Recueil des cours, Académie de droit international,* Vol. 129, I 1970, p. 67, "the time factor as a separate element in the proof of custom now seems irrelevant". See also Tunkin, G. I., *op. cit.*, pp. 114–115.

33. Jimenez de Aréchaga, E., *loc. cit.*, p. 14.

34. A bilateral custom was recognized in the Right of Passage case, *ICJ Reports 1960*, pp. 39–40.

35. Joutsamo, Kari, *The Role of Preliminary Rulings in the European Communities*, Helsinki, Suomalainen tiedeakatemia: Annales, Dissertationes humanarum litterarum. 16, 1979, pp. 32–33, refers to several customary rules which have emerged within the Communities. See also Meijers, H., *loc. cit.*, p. 4.

36. See, e. g., Tunkin, G. I., *op. cit.*, pp. 427–447.

37. See, e. g., Akehurst, M., *loc cit.*, p. 28; Bring, Ove, *Det folkrättsliga investeringsskyddet*, Uddevalla, 1979, pp. 254, 287.

38. Asylum case, *ICJ Reports 1950*, pp. 276–278.

39. Akehurst, M., *loc. cit.*, pp. 28–29; Meijers, H. *loc. cit.*, p. 21.

40. Akehurst, M., *loc. cit.*, p. 30. A common denominator for general international law with respect to the nationalisation of foreign property is sought, e.g., by Ove Bring, *op. cit.*, pp. 241–254, 286–287.

41. On the distinction between "positivist", "sociological", etc. theories of custom see, e.g., Rousseau, Charles, *Droit international public*, Tome I. Paris, Sirey, 1970, pp. 311–314; Dinh, Nguyen Quoc, *Droit international public*, Paris, L. G. D. J., 1975, pp. 302–303.

Suggestions for Further Reading in Folk Law

There are literally thousands of articles, monographs and books devoted to the subject of folk law, written in hundreds of different languages. At the moment, there is no one comprehensive bibliography listing all these many sources. But even the limited bibliographies which are available demonstrate the enormity of the published record of folk law. Typical are R.L. Abel, "A Bibliography of the Customary Laws of Kenya," *East African Law Journal*, 6 (1970), 100–151; C.K. Meek, *Colonial Law: A Bibliography* with special reference to native African systems of law and land tenure (London: Oxford University Press, 1948); Th. Gerold-Scheepers, "An Annotated Bibliography on Disparity between Law and Social Reality in Africa," *Kroniek van Afrika*, 4 (1975), 76–84; and Charles Mwalimu, "A Bibliographic Essay of Selected Secondary Sources on the Common Law and Customary Law of English-Speaking Sub-Saharan Africa," *Law Library Journal*, 80 (1988), 241–289.

Not all the bibliographies are concerned with Africa. For example, there is Yoneo Ishii, "A Preliminary Bibliography for the Study of Customary Laws of Southeast Asia and Taiwan," *Bulletin of the National Museum of Ethnology* (Osaka), 3 (1978) 780–833; and the more general essay by Laura Nader, Klaus F. Koch, and Bruce Cox, "The Ethnography of Law: A Bibliographic Survey," *Current Anthropology*, 7 (1966), 267–294.

The following list of articles and books is, in light of the above remarks, a *very* selective sampling of what is available on the subject of folk law. Many of what we consider the most important theoretical writings on folk law we have included in this volume. But large as this volume may be, it was not possible to include all the important essays in it. Some were simply too long; others we felt were too technical. Here, however, we have tried to list some of the many key works concerned with folk law.

Adip, Amado
1975 *Conflicto entre ley y costumbre*, 2nd ed. Buenos Aires: Ediciones Depalma, 168pp.

Angelo, A.H.
1970 "Andorra: Introduction to a Customary Legal System," *The American Journal of Legal History*, 14:95–111.

Anyebe, A.P.
1985 *Customary Law: The War Without Arms.* Enugu, Nigeria: Fourth Dimension Publishers, 159pp.

Assier-Andrieu, Louis
1981 *Coutume et rapports sociaux.* Paris: Editions du C.N.R.S. 215pp.

Ballereau, Denise
1941 *La coutume dans la jurisprudence internationale.* Paris: Recueil Sirey. 231pp.

Balossini, Cajo Enrico
1958 *Consuetudini, usi, pratiche, regole del costume.* Milano: A. Giuffre. 895pp.

Bobbio, Norberto
1942 *La consuetudine come fatto normativo.* Padova: CEDAM. 92pp.

Cameron, J.T.
1964 "Custom as a Source of Law in Scotland," *Modern Law Review*, 27:306–321.

D'Amato, Anthony A.
1971 *The Concept of Custom in International Law.* Ithaca: Cornell University Press. 286pp.

Dawson, John P.
1940 "The Codification of the French Customs," *Michigan Law Review*, 38:765–800.

Diamond, Stanley
1971 The Rule of Law vs. the Order of Custom," *Social Research*, 38:387–418.

El-Awa, Mohamed
1973 "The Place of Custom ('Urf) in Islamic Legal Theory," *The Islamic Quarterly*, 17:177–182.

Fotino, George
1925 *Contribution à l'étude des origines de l'ancien droit coutumier roumain.* Paris: E. Duchemin. 460pp.

Freitag, Hans Otto
1976 *Gewohnheitsrecht und Rechtssystem.* Berlin: Duncker & Humblot. 183pp.

Furnish, Dale Beck
1982 "Custom as a Source of Law," *The American Journal of Comparative Law*, 30 (Supplement): 31–50.

Gianni, Gregoire
1931 *La coutume en droit international.* Paris: A. Pedone, 184pp.

Gilissen, John
1982 *La Coutume.* Turnhout-Belgium: Brepols. 120pp.

Grimm, Jacob
1816 "Von der Poesie im Recht," *Zeitschrift für geschichtliche Rechtwissenschaft* 2:25–99.

Guilfoyle, Merlin Joseph
1937 *Custom: An Historical Synopsis and Commentary*, The Catholic University of American Canon Law Studies, No. 105, Washington, D.C.: The Catholic University of America. 151pp.

Haggenmacher, Peter
1990 Coutume. *Archives de Philosophie du Droit* 35:27–41.

Hasluck, Margaret
1954 *The Unwritten Law in Albania*. Cambridge: Cambridge University Press. 285pp. Reprinted Westport, Connecticut: Hyperion Press, 1981.

James, R.W.
1967 "Judicial Development in Customary Law," *Journal of the Denning Law Society*, 2:41–58.

Jayasekera, M.L.S.
1970 "The Sources of Sinhalese Customary Laws," *Journal of Ceylon Law*, 1:81–103.

Klami, Hannu Tapani
1984 *Gewohnheitsrecht als Rechtsquelle*. Turku: Turun yliopisto. 100pp.

Kovalevsky, Maxime
1891 *Modern Customs and Ancient Laws of Russia*. London: David Nutt. 260pp.

Kramer, Karl-Sigismund
1974 *Grundris Einer Rechtlichen Volkskunde*. Göttingen: Verlag Otto Schwartz & Co. 172pp.

Künssberg, Eberhard von
1925 "Rechtsgeschichte und Volkskunde," *Jahrbuch für historische Volkskunde*, 1:69–125; 314–327.

Lamber, Julia C.
1973 "A Married Woman's Surname: Is Custom Law?" *Washington University Law Quarterly*, pp. 779–819.

Lee, Orlan
1978 *Legal and Moral Systems in Asian Customary Law: The Legacy of the Buddhist Social Ethic and Buddhist Law*. San Francisco: Chinese Materials Center. 456pp.

Lefebvre, Maurice
1906 *Le coutume comme source formelle de droit en droit francais contemporain*. Lille: C. Robbe. 243pp.

Leivestad, T.
1938 "Custom as a Type of Law in Norway," *Law Quarterly Review*, 54:95–115, 266–286.

Lewin, Julius
1971 *Studies in African Law*. Philadelphia: University of Pennsylvania Press. Originally published in 1947.

Maunier, René
1938 *Introduction au folklore juridique*. Paris: Les Éditions d'art et d'histoire. 38pp.

Mokre, Hans
1932 *Theorie des gewohnheitsrechts*. Wien: J. Springer, 197pp. Reprinted Glashutten im Taunus: D. Auvermann, 1972.

Pearson, Richard N.
1975–1976 "The Role of Custom in Medical Malpractice Cases," *Indiana Law Journal*, 51:528–557.

Radin, Max
1934 "La Censure des Coutumes," in *Recueil d'Etudes sur Les Sources du Droit en l'Honneur de Francois Geny*, vol. I Paris: Librairie du Recueil Sirey. Pp. 89–99.

Rumelin, Max Friedrich Gustav von
1929 *Die bindende kraft des gewohnheitsrechts und ihre begrundung*. Tübingen: Mohr 68pp.

Sadler, Gilbert T.
1919 *The Relation of Custom to Law*. London: Sweet & Maxwell. 86pp. Reprinted Littleton, Colorado: F.B. Rothman, 1986.

Salt, H.E.
1926 "The Local Ambit of a Custom," in *Cambridge Legal Essays*. Cambridge: Harvard University Press. Pp. 279–294.

Sevareid, Peter
1983 "The Future of Customary Law," *Africana Journal*, 14:34–47.

Tárkány-Szücs, Ernő
1980 "Collecting Legal Folk Customs in Hungary," *Acta Ethnographica*, 29:194–205.

Tedeschi, G.
1977 "Custom and Modern Law," *University of Western Ontario Law Review*, 15:1–20.

Thirlway, H.W.A.
1972 *International Customary Law and Codification*. Leiden: A.W. Sijthoff. 158pp.

Tunkin, G.I.
1961 "Remarks on the Juridical Nature of Customary Norms of International Law," *California Law Review*, 49:419–430.

Varga, Csaba
1983 "From Legal Customs to Legal Folkways," *Acta Juridica Academiae Scientiarum Hungaricae*, 25:454–459.

Villiser, Mark E.
1985 *Customary International Law and Treaties*. Dordrecht: M. Nijhoff. 432pp.

Vinogradoff, Paul
1928 "The Problem of Customary Law," *Actorum Academiae Universalis Iurispredentiae Comparativae*, 1 (1928), 231–243. Reprinted in *The Collected Papers of Paul Vinogradoff* (Oxford: Clarendon, 1928), Vol. II, pp. 410–422.

Wolfke, Karol
1964. *Custom in Present International Law*. Wroclaw: Zaklad Narodowy. 185pp.

For Product Safety Concerns and Information please contact our EU representative GPSR@taylorandfrancis.com
Taylor & Francis Verlag GmbH, Kaufingerstraße 24, 80331 München, Germany

www.ingramcontent.com/pod-product-compliance
Lightning Source LLC
LaVergne TN
LVHW011104300926
849160LV00008B/274